PERSPECTIVES ON PREDICTIVE CODING

And Other Advanced Search Methods for the Legal Practitioner

Jason R. Baron
Ralph C. Losey
Michael D. Berman
Editors

Cover design by Andrew Alcala/ABA Design

Printed in the United States of America.

20 19 18 17 16   5 4 3 2 1

Library of Congress Cataloging-in-Publication Data

Names: Baron, Jason R., editor. | Losey, Ralph C., editor. | Berman, Michael D., editor.

Title: Perspectives on predictive coding / Edited by Jason R. Baron, Ralph C. Losey, and Michael D. Berman.

Description: Chicago : American Bar Association, 2016. | Includes bibliographical references and index.

Identifiers: LCCN 2016047229 (print) | LCCN 2016047518 (ebook) | ISBN 9781634256575 (text : alk. paper) | ISBN 9781634256582 (epub)

Subjects: LCSH: Electronic discovery (Law)—United States—Data processing. | Discovery (Law)—United States.

Classification: LCC KF8902.E42 P47 2016 (print) | LCC KF8902.E42 (ebook) | DDC 347.73/72—dc23

LC record available at https://lccn.loc.gov/2016047229

Dedication

Jason R. Baron

To my wife, Robin, and my daughter, Rachel,

and to my late father, Judson R. Baron,

who encouraged hard work and creative thinking.

Ralph C. Losey

To my wife, Molly, daughter Eva,

son Adam, and the many other lawyers in my family.

Michael D. Berman

To Patricia, my entire extended family,

and to the soldiers of the

2d Infantry and 1st Cavalry Divisions,

past and present.

Foreword

Judge Andrew Jay Peck

In March 2015, I stated:

> In the three years since [my decision in] *Da Silva Moore* [*v. Publicis Groupe* 287 F.R.D. 182 (S.D.N.Y. 2012) (Peck, M.J.)], the case law has developed to the point that it is now black letter law that where the producing party wants to utilize TAR for document review, courts will permit it.[1]

Issues about the use of TAR—technology-assisted review, a.k.a. predictive coding, a.k.a. computer-assisted review—remain, and are addressed in this book. I believe that historical perspective is helpful to understand how we got to this point.

When I started to practice law in the late 1970s, document review for discovery was purely manual. There was no electronically stored information (ESI); it all was paper. Counsel went to the client and asked what files had documents about the XYZ matter, and you pulled those files. Review then was linear. You reviewed whatever file(s) landed on your desk, while other lawyers also received and reviewed files. There was no way to deduplicate documents, but hopefully you and your colleague coded the document the same way. The first "technological" innovation in document review came in 1980—when 3M® began selling Post-It Notes.

In the days of paper discovery, rarely if ever was there disclosure to opposing counsel of the instructions given to the review team, or

1. Rio Tinto PLC v. Vale S.A., 306 F.R.D. 125, 127 (S.D.N.Y. 2015) (Peck, M.J.).

even the workflow and quality control methods (if any) used. Nor was there any discussion of precision, recall, or other metrics.

As volumes of data increased, law firms turned to paralegals, staff, or contract attorneys, and even offshore review to reduce costs. As paper was supplemented and then largely replaced by e-mail and other forms of ESI, the volume of data became too large and manual review too expensive and time-consuming. Counsel turned to keywords to cull ESI for further manual review. But keyword use has problems.

First, lawyers are bad at deciding what keywords to use. Often, it is like the child's game of Go Fish—the requesting party guesses which keywords might have been used by the responding party without much, if any, knowledge of the terminology used by the responding party.

Second, words have multiple uses. In a hypothetical product liability case by William Coyote against Acme Corp., Coyote's lawyer may suggest that Acme use "Coyote" as a search term, but Acme may have had a coyote problem at its Arizona plant, and thus that search term will hit on irrelevant documents. In addition, people can use many words to describe the same thing—for example, the "accident," the "incident," the "unfortunate event," etc.

Third, e-mail collections are not "clean" databases. Even business e-mails contain abbreviations, acronyms, and code names (e.g., during product development or corporate transactions such as mergers). In addition, misspellings are rampant.[2] In *Seroquel*, for example, an index of all the words in the e-mail collection showed that in the very company that made Seroquel, employees spelled Seroquel numerous different ways. Whether this is the result of poor spelling or the small keyboards on smart phones, a keyword search for "Seroquel" will not find its misspellings.

The object of search is to produce high recall and high precision. Recall is the fraction of relevant documents identified during a review, that is, a measure of completeness. Precision is the fraction of identified documents that are relevant, that is, it is a measure of accuracy or correctness. When keywords return false positives—documents that

2. *See, e.g., In re* Seroquel Prods. Liab. Litig., 244 F.D.R. 650 (M.D. Fla. 2007).

have the keywords but are not relevant—the responding party has to use expensive manual review to find the truly relevant documents. It is not uncommon for a poorly chosen keyword to return more "junk" than responsive documents, that is, low precision. The goal of search is to produce high recall and high precision (in a proportional, cost-effective way).

Important early decisions criticizing poorly done keyword searches came from Judge John Facciola (District of Columbia) and Judge Paul Grimm (Maryland). I followed their lead with *William A. Gross Constr. Assocs., Inc. v. American Mfrs. Mutual Ins. Co.*:

> This Opinion should serve as a wake-up call to the Bar in this District about the need for careful thought, quality control, testing, and cooperation with opposing counsel in designing search terms or "keywords" to be used to produce emails or other electronically stored information ("ESI").[3]

My opinion concluded:

> Electronic discovery requires cooperation between opposing counsel and transparency in all aspects of preservation and production of ESI. Moreover, where counsel are using keyword searches for retrieval of ESI, they at a minimum must carefully craft the appropriate keywords, with input from the ESI's custodians as to the words and abbreviations they use, and the proposed methodology must be quality control tested to assure accuracy in retrieval and elimination of "false positives." It is time that the Bar—even those lawyers who did not come of age in the computer era—understand this.[4]

Despite judicial decisions criticizing poorly designed keyword searches, keywords still remain the search method most used today.

Beginning in 2011, computer-assisted review, a.k.a. TAR, was much discussed in conferences and on blogs, but no judicial decision

3. 256 F.R.D. 134, 134 (S.D.N.Y. 2009) (Peck, M.J.).
4. *Id.* at 136.

had yet addressed TAR. I wrote an article in the October 2011 *Law Technology News* entitled "Search, Forward: Will Manual Document Review and Keyword Searches Be Replaced By Computer-Assisted Coding?" I concluded the article by stating:

> Until there is a judicial opinion approving (or even critiquing) the use of predictive coding, counsel will just have to rely on this article as a sign of judicial approval. In my opinion, computer-assisted coding should be used in those cases where it will help "secure the just, speedy, and inexpensive" (Fed. R. Civ. P. 1) determination of cases in our e-discovery world.[5]

By coincidence, just a few months later a case involving TAR came before me, and I held:

> This Judicial Opinion now recognizes that computer-assisted review is an acceptable way to search for relevant ESI in appropriate cases.[6]

My *Da Silva Moore* Opinion concluded:

> This Opinion appears to be the first in which a Court has approved of the use of computer-assisted review. . . . What the Bar should take away from this Opinion is that computer-assisted review is an available tool and should be seriously considered for use in large-data-volume cases where it may save the producing party (or both parties) significant amounts of legal fees in document review. Counsel no longer have to worry about being the "first" or "guinea pig" for judicial acceptance of computer-assisted review. As with keywords or any other technological solution to ediscovery, counsel must design an appropriate process, including use of available technology, with appropriate quality control testing, to review and

5. Andrew J. Peck, *Search, Forward*, LAW TECH. NEWS (Oct. 2011).

6. Da Silva Moore v. Publicis Groupe, 287 F.R.D. 182, 183 (S.D.N.Y. 2012) (Peck, M.J.).

> produce relevant ESI while adhering to Rule 1 and Rule 26(b)(2)(C) proportionality. Computer-assisted review now can be considered judicially-approved for use in appropriate cases.[7]

In the three years since my *Da Silva Moore* opinion, in every case in which the producing party wanted to use TAR, courts allowed it.[8] Indeed, approval of the use of TAR now has gone international: two decisions from the U.K. High Court and one from the Irish High Court (affirmed by the Irish Court of Appeals) have approved the use of TAR, even over objection.[9] "In contrast, where the requesting party has sought to force the producing party to use TAR, the courts have refused."[10]

The case law leaves open important issues about the use of TAR. These issues are discussed extensively in chapters in this book.

The first and perhaps most important open issue is how transparent a party using TAR must or should be. In light of the meet and confer requirement in federal cases required by Federal Rule of Civil Procedure 26(f), I think it would be hard not to at least disclose that you planned to use TAR. But how much more transparency and cooperation is required? The cases are split.[11]

Second, how should the "seed set" be selected? Random sampling or judgmental? How does the "richness" of the collection affect the seed set?

Third, should there be transparency as to the nonprivileged documents in the seed set? If so, should it encompass only the responsive documents or also the nonresponsive? Or does the seed set constitute

---

7. *Id.* at 193.

8. *See, e.g.*, Rio Tinto PLC v. Vale S.A., 306 F.R.D. at 127 (citing cases); *see also Predictive Coding Case Law Wiki*, The Coalition of Technology Resources for Lawyers, www.ctrlinitiative.com/wiki/resource (last visited July 18, 2016) (comprehensive list of TAR cases).

9. Irish Bank Resol. Corp. v. Quinn, [2015] IEHC 175 (H. Ct.) (Ir.), upheld by Irish Court of Appeals (Feb. 2016); Pyrrho Inv. Ltd. V. MWB Prop. Ltd., [2016] EWHC 256 (Ch.) (Eng.); Brown v. BCA Trading Ltd., [2016] EWHC 1464 (Ch.) (Eng.).

10. Rio Tinto PLC v. Vale S.A., 306 F.R.D. at 127 n.l (citing cases).

11. *See id.* at 127 (citing cases).

work product? Does the concept of seed set largely disappear if continuous active learning TAR processes are employed?

Fourth, is it appropriate to first use keyword searches and then use TAR only on the positive keyword hits? The reason parties use keywords before TAR is one of economics based on current vendor pricing models, but keyword culling means that responsive documents that are missed by the keyword search will not be reviewed in the TAR process.

Fifth, what should be the precision and recall target? Should it be established up front or only as the data is reviewed?

Sixth, does *Daubert* apply?[12]

Seventh, should TAR be used in other situations such as in government investigations or for review of the opposing side's document production?

Eighth, how do we ensure that TAR is not held to a different, stricter standard then keywords or manual review?

The sooner there is consensus or clear decisional guidance on these issues, the more likely it is that parties will make greater use of TAR. TAR is at least as good, and significantly cheaper, than other means of document review. The use of TAR should be encouraged. Hopefully, this book will increase the Bar's understanding of TAR, dispel certain TAR myths that cause parties to not use TAR, and encourage TAR's use in appropriate cases.

12. I explained in *Da Silva Moore* why I believe *Daubert* does not apply. *See* Da Silva Moore v. Publicis Groupe, 287 F.R.D. at 188–89. My friend Magistrate Judge Waxse takes the contrary view. Our positions perhaps are not as starkly contrary as they may seem: while *Daubert* does not apply, it is helpful to the Court to have the parties' e-discovery vendors explain TAR procedures. *See* Da Silva Moore v. Publicis Groupe, 287 F.R.D. at 193.

Table of Contents

Editors' Note

The editors realized that there was and is a need to address the issues presented by predictive coding and other advanced search methods for a number of reasons.

First, education is the surest way to increase acceptance by the Bar and expand acceptance in the courts. The common law and guidance are often scattered among case law and journal articles in varied disciplines. This book gathers them under a single roof.

Second, the appropriate use of these technologies and methodologies in the appropriate case is the best, and often only, way to fulfill the mandate of the 2015 amendment to Federal Rules of Civil Procedure 1,[1] which requires that the Rules be employed "by the court and the parties to secure the just, speedy, and inexpensive determination of every action and proceeding." That requires an understanding of what is an appropriate use and what is an appropriate case. This book defines those parameters.

Third, the technical and statistical aspects of advanced search may be an acquired taste to those schooled in the liberal arts. This book is an effort to advance the ball.

While the book is primarily focused on litigation, it is impossible to be comprehensive without looking at predictive coding in other areas, such as information governance, the regulatory arena, and business transactions. Each discipline can, and must, understand and learn from the others.

Some areas in the field of advanced search are well-settled and have been set forth as such. Many, however, are more art than science and some are open, and subject, to hot debate. We have tried to identify those areas and provide a "big tent" that covers disparate views.

1. Fed. R. Civ. P. 1.

In part for that reason, each chapter represents the personal opinions and views of the author or authors, and not necessarily the organizations with which they are associated, affiliated, or employed, the editors, publishers, or other authors. The members of the Bench, Bar, academia, and information sciences communities who have contributed to this work do so solely in their individual capacity and not on behalf of the courts or any other organization, including the American Bar Association, with which they are associated. The editors and authors are not providing legal advice. Each practitioner should conduct independent, jurisdiction-specific research in addressing each search issue. The editors and authors have not been compensated for their work in connection with this book, and have generously donated all of the proceeds to the American Bar Association. We each thank our colleagues for their contributions.

Introduction

Jason R. Baron

"There [were] 5 exabytes of data created between the dawn of civilization through 2003, but that much information is now created every two days, and the pace is increasing. People aren't ready for the technology revolution."

—Eric Schmidt, CEO of Google[1]

Each of the three editors of this volume graduated law school in 1980, which has meant that we have been firsthand witnesses to the transformation of legal practice and especially discovery practice during the past few decades. There was a time when discovery meant searching only through boxes containing paper files, where the big case simply meant searching through more boxes in the client's warehouse.

Discovery did not yet need an "e" as a prefix, and manual searches for relevant documents sufficed. Judge Andrew J. Peck notes this, as well, in his Foreword to this volume.

Fast forward to the present, and how the world of lawyering has changed. The present "inflationary" period of information exploding has been built on copying machines and personal computers in the 1970s, e-mail beginning widespread use in the late 1980s, and the opening of the desktop to the Internet and especially the World Wide Web in the 1990s. The pace of change has

1. *See* Marshall Kirkpatrick, *Google CEO Schmidt: "People Aren't Ready for the Technology Revolution,"* READWRITE (Aug. 4, 2010), http://readwrite.com/2010/08/04/google_ceo_schmidt_people_arent_ready_for_the_tech/.

only continued to accelerate since the turn of the century, with the emergence of social media and mobile devices in the last decade transforming what it means to conduct business. As this book goes to print, we are on the cusp of the Internet of Things, with smart devices proliferating and generating new data streams and new forms of evidence to search.

Today, every lawyer conducting "discovery" in civil litigation needs to confront the fact that—no matter how large or small the case may be—it is insufficient to simply define the search task as being limited to finding relevant documents in traditional paper files. The legal profession lives and breathes in a world of "electronically stored information" (ESI), a term of art introduced into legal practice by virtue of the 2006 amendments to the Federal Rules of Civil Procedure. But what constitutes our doing a "reasonable" job in finding relevant evidence in a world exploding in data?

The initial approach lawyers took (and still take) to confronting large volumes of ESI is to rely on keyword searching, supplemented by manual searches, to cull out relevant and privileged material before a production is made to opposing counsel. Although these "time-tested" approaches have their defenders, simple reliance on manual and keyword searching increasingly is seen as inadequate to the task at hand, both on grounds of accuracy and efficiency, as compared with more advanced search techniques.

The editors of this book are readily willing to stipulate in advance that they have a strong bias in favor of advancing the cause of computer-assisted review and educating the profession on how more advanced search techniques work. In one way or another, they have spent the better part of the last 15 years engaged in initiating and participating in research projects[2] and academic conferences,[3] joining think tanks,[4] communicating through online media platforms,[5] writing law

2. *See, e.g.*, the TREC Legal Track, http://trec-legal.umiacs.umd.edu/.

3. *See, e.g.*, the DESI (Discovery of ESI) international workshop series, http://www.umiacs.umd.edu/~oard/desi6/.

4. *See, e.g.*, The Sedona Conference, www.thesedonaconference.org.

5. *See, e.g.*, e-Discovery Team blog, www.e-discoveryteam.com.

reviews,[6] authoring e-discovery books,[7] and teaching e-discovery in law and graduate schools, in evangelizing on the topic of how lawyers may conduct "better" searches of electronic evidence using smarter methods than manual and keyword searching. Along the way, we have been fortunate to encounter a number of brilliant lawyers and scholars at the cutting edge of e-discovery and information science, many of whom we are grateful to for their contributions to this volume.

This book is an attempt to catch lightning in a bottle; namely, to provide a set of perspectives on predictive coding and other advanced search techniques, as they are used today by lawyers in pursuit of e-discovery, in investigations, and in other legal contexts, such as information governance. We are painfully aware that the shelflife of publications such as the present work is not long. Nevertheless, we trust that a cross-section of related—and sometimes differing—perspectives on how today's advanced search methods at the cutting-edge of legal practice will prove illuminating to a greater legal audience.

The book is divided into four subparts, under the headings "Searching for ESI: Some Preliminary Perspectives," "Practitioner Perspectives," "Information Retrieval Perspectives; E-Discovery Standards," and "Analytics and the Law." As discussed at more length below, the chapters provide insights into predictive coding and other advanced search methods from the perspectives of the judiciary, from requesting and responding parties in litigation, and from information scientists who have been engaged in intensive study of the field of e-discovery search over the past decade.

The book is meant to appeal both to practitioners who are seeking knowledge of what predictive coding and other advanced search methods are all about, as well as to those members of the legal community who are "inside the bubble" of e-discovery already and wish

6. *See, e.g.*, Ralph C. Losey, *Predictive Coding and the Proportionality Doctrine: A Marriage Made in Big Data*, 26 Regent U. L. Rev. 7 (2013–14), https://ralphlosey.files.wordpress.com/2013/12/law_review_pcandpropor.pdf; Jason R. Baron, *Law in the Age of Exabytes: Some Further Thoughts on "Information Inflation" and Current Issues in Legal Search*, 17 Rich. J.L. & Tech. 9 (2011), http://jolt.richmond.edu/v17i3/article9.pdf.

7. *See, e.g.*, Michael D. Berman, Courtney Ingraffia Barton, & Paul W. Grimm, Managing E-Discovery and ESI From Pre-Litigation Through Trial (ABA 2012).

to be exposed to the latest, cutting-edge techniques. We would like to imagine that the book may also be read by lawyers who do not consider themselves litigators or e-discovery practitioners, but who wish to apply a knowledge of smart analytics in other legal contexts.

The reader should be aware that given the relative novelty of predictive coding and other advanced search methods, there have been and will continue to be disagreements over what constitutes "best practices" in the space, and the editors of course have their own preferences and biases. However, the book attempts to be inclusive of a range of views, not always necessarily our own. What follows is a summary of the contents of this volume, representing an attempt to key the reader into recurrent themes, open issues, and present-day controversies.

Searching for ESI: Some Preliminary Observations

Many of us litigators have been on a journey these past two decades, learning as we go about how difficult it is to find all relevant ESI through existing methods in what are increasingly large data haystacks. In Chapter 1, "The Road to Predictive Coding: Limitations on the Defensibility of Manual and Keyword Searching," Tracy Drynan and I "serve notice to the everyday practitioner of the issues surrounding still widely used manual and keyword search methodologies." The chapter consists of a literature review and a basic tutorial on the subject of keyword searching, as well as an overview of certain electronic tools and processes (e.g., deduplication) often used in connection with all search methods. The authors also discuss notions of defensibility, noting the important point to the practitioner that reasonableness, not perfection, is required when conducting a search for relevant ESI.

Part of the journey has been the recently emergent acceptance of predictive coding in the courts, following a half-decade of research studies, law reviews, and commentaries pointing to the deficiencies of keyword searching and the possibility of parties using more advanced techniques in pursuit of justice. A watershed moment was reached when Magistrate Judge Peck issued his decision in 2012 in *Da Silva Moore v. Publicis Groupe.*[8] In Chapter 2, "The Emerging Acceptance

8. 287 F.R.D. 182 (S.D.N.Y. 2012), *aff'd*, 2012 WL 1446534 (S.D.N.Y. Apr. 26, 2012) (Carter, J.).

of Technology-Assisted Review in Civil Litigation," Alicia L. Shelton and Michael D. Berman discuss *Da Silva Moore* and survey its progeny, including the *In re Actos* and *Global Aerospace* cases, through to Judge Peck's later decision in *Rio Tinto.* The authors discuss the tension inherent in the judiciary permitting liberal discovery in an age of Big Data, while attempting to adhere to the goal of ensuring the "just, speedy, and inexpensive" determination of actions in accordance with Federal Rules of Civil Procedure 1.

Practitioner Perspectives

Maura R. Grossman and Gordon V. Cormack, the authors of Chapter 3, "A Tour of Technology-Assisted Review," have been thought leaders in the area of e-discovery search for a long time, even before publication of their seminal 2011 law review piece *Technology-Assisted Review in E-Discovery Can Be More Effective and More Efficient Than Exhaustive Manual Review*,[9] prominently cited by Judge Peck in *Da Silva Moore.* In their chapter, the authors provide the practitioner with an overview of the distinctions among various automated tools and methods that are legitimately grouped within the "TAR" label, as distinguished from other aspects of search, analysis, and review. In so doing, the authors explain in clear language the differences between passive and active machine-learning techniques, as well as between simple versus continuous machine-learning. One of the hottest topics in e-discovery today is the efficacy of what the authors refer to as "continuous active learning" (CAL), and their article makes the business case for CAL methods being presently superior to all others.

In Chapter 4, Vincent M. Catanzaro, Samantha Green, and Sandra Rampersaud provide useful guidance on "The Mechanics of a Predictive Coding Work Flow." While recognizing that "one size does not fit all" in e-discovery, they argue for "commonalities among the various predictive coding applications that allow the user to begin a customized work flow" by starting at a general level. These include beginning with assessment or evaluation of your case as a good candidate for the use of advanced search methods, followed by training and validation of the tools and methods used.

9. 17 Rich. J.L. & Tech. 11 (2011), http://jolt.richmond.edu/v17i3/article11.pdf.

Chapter 5 consists of Ralph C. Losey's "Reflections on the Cormack and Grossman SIGIR Study: The Folly of Using Random Search for Machine Training." Likening random search to searching only under a spotlight because it is easy to do, Ralph discusses why the justifications that have been offered to date on its continued behalf (most prominently, the introduction of lawyer bias), are found wanting. He goes on to describe the Cormack-Grossman study, which was designed to answer the question "Should training documents be selected at random, or should they be selected using one or more non-random methods, such as keyword search or active learning?" In accord with what the study has found, Ralph believes that employing continuing active learning constitutes a "superior method to quickly find the most relevant documents" in a large collection. Along the way, he observes the benefits of using "multimodal" methods of search to optimize the process even further.

Chapter 6 may be of special interest to the greater community of legal practitioners in state courts as well as federal. In the chapter "TAR for the Small and Medium Case," William F. (Bill) Hamilton makes the argument that in a large variety of smaller, more routine cases, counsel may profit from using forms of technology-assisted review and other automated methods, inexpensively, for such purposes as early case assessment, analyzing the opponent's document production, or even preparing for a deposition. The author makes the case that the "hidden promise" of advanced search methods will increasingly be seen "as a critical tool for the 99 percent, not just the 1 percent" of cases (and litigators).

Chapters 7, 8, and 9 present differing perspectives from the plaintiffs and defendants bar, as well as from the judiciary, on the hot button issue of how much transparency and cooperation and required to faithfully execute and get agreement on a given predictive coding method.

William P. Butterfield and Jeannine M. Kenney contribute a "plaintiffs" perspective in Chapter 7, "Reality Bites: Why TAR's Promises Have Yet to Be Fulfilled." They begin with the question, why, given the advantages of TAR, "has it not been more widely adopted by parties in appropriate cases?" After a survey of relevant case law, including the protocols used in *Da Silva Moore* and *In re Actos*, they make the case that a greater level of transparency and cooperation is necessary to build a requesting party's trust that TAR-like methods have resulted in a better (meaning richer, not just speedier) result in productions. In noting the present-day objections of many in the defense bar to disclosure of details of the process used in conjunction with advanced search technologies, the authors nevertheless remain optimistic that when "lawyers and judges become better educated about the processes needed to employ TAR effectively, agreement about the specifics of TAR protocols should become easier to achieve."

Chapter 8 in turn contains an analysis of "Predictive Coding from a Defense Perspective: Issues and Challenges," authored by Ronni D. Solomon and three of her colleagues, Rose J. Hunter-Jones, Jennifer A. Mencken, and Edward T. Logan. Here, in making the case for more widespread use of predictive coding, the authors focus on the cost-saving potential when corporate defendants are required to produce large volumes of ESI in discovery, drawing from their own use case experiences. They also review what cases are a good fit for predictive coding, as well as the challenges associated with the training process for implementing predictive coding in the workflow. The authors go on to provide a defense bar perspective on the issues of transparency and cooperation, arguing for what they consider to be appropriate limitations on transparency to protect client's interests.

In Chapter 9, "Safeguarding the Seed Set: Why Seed Set Documents May Be Entitled to Work–Product Protection," the Hon. John M. Facciola and Philip J. Favro further weigh in on issues of cooperation and transparency in connection with whether "seed sets," that is, the initial subset of documents selected to train software to recognize and distinguish what constitutes a relevant document from ones that are not, are appropriately shielded from production under the work–product doctrine. As reflected in the tension between the positions advocated in Chapters 7 and 8, *supra*, the authors report on the diversity of opinions regarding disclosure of seed sets and responsiveness decisions, and suggest a nuanced approach. They argue that the common-law, paper-days' work–product doctrine holding that the selection and ordering of documents is work product provides the proper rule to apply, but they note significant limitations on its application in this unique context.

Another open issue in current day e-discovery practice is the judiciary's take on whether the Supreme Court's *Daubert* standard for the use of expert testimony in the courtroom applies in the discovery context, in connection with a court's evaluation of the propriety of using predictive coding or other advanced search methods. In Chapter 10, the Hon. David J. Waxse and Brenda Yoakum-Kriz set out the case in favor of a *Daubert* standard, in "Experts on Computer-Assisted Review: Why Federal Rule of Evidence 702 Should Apply to Their Use." Noting the clear disagreement "about whether electronic searching of ESI should be considered an expert process subject to the requirements of Rule 702 and *Daubert*-style challenges," the authors conclude "the better view is that search methodologies such as computer-assisted review should be treated as an expert process subject to Rule 702 and *Daubert* challenges." We know from Judge Peck's decision in *Da Silva Moore*, as well as his Foreword in this volume, that he has weighed in on the contrary side, finding that *Daubert* is inapplicable. This is an area of the law to watch.

Ralph Losey provides a deeper dive into predictive coding in Chapter 11, "License to Cull: A Two-Filter Document Culling Method That Uses Predictive Coding and Other Search Tools." The author is a leading proponent of what he has coined "multimodal" search and culling techniques, and in this piece he steps the reader through his recommended approaches in filtering documents during the collection and processing phases of e-discovery, as well as in using predictive coding techniques. In his words, "[T]he basic idea behind the two-filter method is to start with a very large pool of documents, reduce the size by a coarse first filter, then reduce it again by a much finer second filter." The author makes the important point that "[t]here is much more to efficient, effective review than just using software with predictive coding features. The methodology of *how* you do the review is critical" (emphasis in original).

Information Retrieval Perspectives; Standards in E-discovery

Preceding chapters have cited to a body of research that began around 2006 with the TREC Legal Track, and continued through later research, that acted to support the claims made that keyword searching has limitations, and that more advanced search methods may in fact be more efficient and effective than either manual review or keyword searching.[10] In these evaluation studies, it has been of paramount importance to be able to measure how well one is doing when performing searches for ESI—something that lawyers historically have shied away from.

In this subpart, we first present leading experts in the burgeoning field of information retrieval (IR) taking on the job of explaining the metrics that we as lawyers need to understand to be able to measure or evaluate how well that predictive coding and other advanced search technologies are in fact doing. This is especially the case where the software algorithms that are at the heart of performing advanced searches are "black box" technologies—not easily or intuitively understood (at least by lawyers and judges). The need or desire for better measurement in turn has led to an increased focus on what the standard for measurement should be, and what kind of quality controls should be put into place. Ultimately, these lines of inquiry lead to a discussion of whether the legal profession can and should arrive at a standard for judging e-discovery search efforts.

In Chapter 12, "Defining and Estimating Effectiveness in Document Review," Dr. David D. Lewis cogently makes the case for seeing the e-discovery search problem through the lens of "text classification"—a well-known approach in which there has been "extraordinary progress in computer science, statistics, and related fields in recent decades." He goes on to explain (we might better say, "demystify") the quantitative, statistical measures that function as important tools in achieving, assuring, and demonstrating a high quality and cost-effective review. They are used to both manage the process and justify the results. He explains, for example, the lawyer's role in making the tradeoff between different measures (e.g., recall and precision) to suit the needs of the case. Along the way, he provides the reader with an in-depth, mini "textbook"-like course in IR.

Continuing with looking through the lens of IR in viewing e-discovery, in Chapter 13 Drs. Douglas W. Oard and William Webber approach the subject of "Metrics in Predictive Coding," by assuming

10. *See* Chapter 3, *supra*, authored by Maura R. Grossman & Gordon V. Cormack (and the research cited therein).

that a "core task of discovery" is "to find the highest proportion of relevant documents in the collection at the least cost." To that end, they set out a practitioner's guide to how to measure what they term the "cost-for-completion tradeoff," that is, "how standard metrics and evaluations help" in guiding lawyers to that goal, and "how a misunderstanding of those metrics" act as an obstacle to achieving that goal. The chapter is filled with practical descriptions of what recall, precision, and more arcane IR metrics mean, and goes on to address the potential pitfalls and shortcomings of predictive coding. The authors point to the system's dependency on the accuracy of the subject-matter expert's decision-making, noting, importantly, that "we don't yet fully understand the consequences" of errors in that process.

In Chapter 14, "On the Place of Measurement in E-Discovery," Dr. Bruce Hedin, Dan Brassil, and Amanda Jones further discuss measurement, in the form of sampling and estimation protocols, as an integral part of an e-discovery quality management regimen. As an initial matter, they discuss other essential building blocks of a sound review process, including the need for advanced planning and thorough topic analysis, the proper use of technology, the appropriate use of expertise, the importance of being adaptable, and the need to provide for clear and complete documentation of one's efforts. They then proceed to provide a comprehensive discussion of what they term "general principles governing the use of measurement in e-discovery," what the benefits are of employing rigor to measurement, and the reasons for continued resistance by the legal profession in doing so.

Gilbert S. Keteltas, Karin S. Jenson, and James A. Sherer, eloquently grapple with questions of standards in Chapter 15, "A Modest Proposal for Preventing e-Discovery Standards from Being a Burden to Petitioners, Clients, the Courts, or Common Sense." The chapter discusses a number of existing and proposed standards, some well-known and others that are novel to most practitioners (e.g., an ISO-based standard for e-discovery), why there are so many competing standards efforts, and what kind of standards operating outside the Federal rules can be fashioned that are acceptable to e-discovery practitioners. Along the way, they tackle such issues as whether standards should be about process or result, and how to build flexibility into any contemplated standards—including acknowledgement of the principle that perfection is not required in practicing e-discovery or performing searches.

Analytics and the Law

With 20-20 hindsight, it seems almost self-evident that the advent of the use of advanced search techniques in the e-discovery context would come into being contemporaneously with the emergence of Big Data and the wholesale adoption of new forms of analytics across a variety of disciplines. In these chapters, we survey how advanced search methods of a similar sort are being integrated into a number of aspects of legal practice closely related to, but distinct from litigation and e-discovery.

A step away from the litigation arena, modern antitrust practice has been undergoing a similar transformation in its embrace of predictive analytics. In Chapter 16, "Algorithms at the Gate: Leveraging Predictive Analytics in Mergers, Acquisitions and Divestitures," Jeffrey C. Sharer and Robert D. Keeling explain how predictive analytics "has applications for both buyers and sellers and in all phases of the deal lifecycle." The authors also focus attention on how predictive analytics is being used when corporations must quickly respond to Hart-Scott-Rodino "second requests." As they point out, "the same technologies and workflows that have gained acceptance in the litigation context can be deployed much earlier in the information lifecycle to improve information governance and drive cost savings and productivity gains across the organization." These would include software being trained to make distinctions as to "whether a document is a contract or not, contains intellectual property or not, is a financial report or not, is a personnel record or not, and so on."

The authors believe that predictive coding "is already delivering significant reductions" in the time and the cost of productions in the antitrust space, without a reduction in quality.

Another application of the software analytics behind predictive coding has been their use in the emerging discipline of "information governance," or "IG." IG has been broadly defined by one entity as "[t]he activities and technologies that organizations employ to maximize the value of their information while minimizing associated risks and costs."[11] The next three chapters describe how corporations, law firms, and legal practitioners can all benefit from incorporating—with appropriate customization—the kind of advanced analytics we have been discussing in the e-discovery arena.

In Chapter 17, Sandra Serkes presents "The Larger Picture: Moving Beyond Predictive Coding for Document Productions to Predictive Analytics for Information Governance." She acknowledges what she terms a "fundamental difference" as between IG and e-discovery, namely, that the latter task is consumed with (or limited to) the "safe" culling of relevant, nonprivileged documents for purposes of production—whereas in her view the "hallmark" of IG's use of predictive analytics is moving "*beyond* simple culling, into areas such as classification, organization, trendlining, and forecasting, and modeling past or future behaviors" (emphasis in original). The author shows how businesses, litigators, and law firms may all harness the power of many of the same forms of analytics used in e-discovery to perform better enterprise searching and internal case management.

Continuing in the same vein, Leigh Isaacs in Chapter 18 discusses "Predictive Analytics for Information Governance in a Law Firm: Mitigating Risks and Optimizing Efficiency." Law firms of course have significant security concerns, but they also experience personnel changes, and frequently must import or export volumes of carefully screened law firm data. In short, all of the questions facing American industry are magnified in the unique context of a law firm with its need to preserve client confidences and other fiduciary duties. The author shows how predictive coding may help supply defensible solutions, and how a business case for "return on investment" may be made for the use of such advanced tools and techniques.

In Chapter 19, "Finding the Signal in the Noise: Information Governance, Analytics, and the Future of Legal Practice," Bennett B. Borden and I set out the case for the legal profession embracing both IG and analytics, across a range of legal practice areas, as a way to "break new ground . . . to solve real-world problems of our clients." Use case examples are provided that demonstrate the power of predictive

11. *See* Information Governance Initiative, *Annual Report 2014: Information Governance Goes to Work*, http://www.iginitiative.com.

coding in the evaluation of large data sets handed over by clients for multiple nonlitigation purposes, including, for example, a law firm's evaluation of whistleblowing allegations, or whether a party received full information on the value of an acquired company in a merger and acquisition context. The authors go on to discuss the possible deployment of software as a form of "early warning system" to guard against the loss of trade secrets or even the filing of discrimination claims. In a new supplement to the original article as published, the continuing trend lines recognizing the importance of IG, data science, and the law are emphasized.

Next, in Chapter 20, "Preparing for the Near Future: Deep Learning and Law," author Kathryn Hume takes us on a journey beyond currently used search methods and algorithms, to a time when even more advanced methods springing from the field of "neural networks" and "deep learning" may yet have a place in e-discovery and the law. Neural networks are a type of machine learning using multiple computing layers designed to better mimic the brain. For our purposes, deep learning using these techniques holds out the promise of lawyers being better able to analyze multiple data feeds, not only from traditional texts, but also from audio and video sources as well. The author challenges us to think about what the "practice of law" may mean in a world of machine learning techniques.

The Grossman-Cormack Glossary of Technology-Assisted Review

As an Appendix to this volume, Maura R. Grossman and Gordon V. Cormack graciously have allowed the reprinting here of their Grossman-Cormack Glossary of TAR with a Foreword by Judge John M. Facciola. Since its publication in the *Federal Courts Law Review* in 2013, this important work has greatly contributed to the understanding by practitioners of the many and varied technical terms used by information retrieval experts and increasingly by the e-discovery community when discussing technology-assisted review methods and protocols.

As this book goes to print, there appear to be voices in the profession questioning whether predictive coding has been oversold or overhyped, and pointing to resistance in some quarters to wholesale embrace of the types of algorithmics and analytics on display throughout this volume. Notwithstanding these critics, the editors of this volume remain serene in their certainty that the chapters in this book represent the future of e-discovery and the legal profession as it will come to be practiced into the foreseeable future, by a larger and larger contingent of lawyers. Of course, for some, the prospect of needing to be technically competent in advanced search techniques may lead to considerations of early retirement. For others, the idea that lawyers may benefit from embracing predictive coding and other advanced technologies is exhilarating. We hope this book inspires the latter feelings on the part of the reader.

SEARCHING FOR ESI: SOME PRELIMINARY PERSPECTIVES

EDITORS' INTRODUCTION TO CHAPTER 1

Michael D. Berman

Tracy D. Drynan and Jason R. Baron recount the journey the legal profession has taken since the 2000s on how to search for electronically stored information. Starting with a thorough description of what manual review is and why it is obsolete in large data cases, they discuss the well-known information retrieval technique of keyword searching, including its advantages and shortcomings. Relying on prior studies, they deflate the notion of "eyes on" manual review as the gold standard, and make the case for computer-assisted review using automated search tools.

The chapter provides an overview of those tools and the processes used to deploy them. It introduces a theme of this book—perfection is not, and never has been, the standard. Instead, defensibility, reasonableness, and proportionality are the benchmarks. A process is defensible when appropriate methodologies that are reasonable for, and appropriate to, the specific case are employed. Making those decisions and being prepared to sustain them in court is part of the litigator's role.

CHAPTER 1

The Road to Predictive Coding: Limitations on the Defensibility of Manual and Keyword Searching

Tracy D. Drynan and Jason R. Baron

Introduction

This chapter introduces the reader to the legal profession's interest in using information retrieval technology as a means to identify, filter, retrieve, and categorize data in an effort to respond to requests for discovery during litigation or investigations. In order to efficiently search through documents in the form of electronically stored information (ESI), lawyers need to be savvy in using human means as well as automated tools and techniques for reducing increasingly vast volumes of data and for identifying and categorizing relevant information. Maintaining the status quo of primary or sole reliance on manual review (i.e., document-by-document or linear review), coupled with only keyword searching, is increasingly seen as a flawed means for carrying out one's discovery obligations for at least a portion of the legal docket. Indeed, sole reliance on such methods in complex cases may in the near future raise questions about competence, including what should pass as due diligence in meeting one's professional obligations.

The modest aim of this chapter is to serve notice to the everyday practitioner of the issues surrounding still widely used manual and keyword search methodologies. A brief discussion of certain automated techniques used in conjunction with search methods is also included. We recognize that e-discovery practice has been transformed over the past decade and a half into a far more technical exercise, incorporating advanced search techniques borrowed from other disciplines. The subject of "information retrieval" is itself a science, and the interested reader will be able to explore in greater depth the mathematical, statistical, and algorithmic aspects of advanced search techniques in subsequent chapters in this volume.

Exhaustive Manual Review Is Increasingly an Outdated Approach

> Like the physical universe, the digital universe is large—by 2020 containing nearly as many digital bits as there are stars in the universe.[1]

Contemplating the number of stars in the universe is an amusing distraction, in the abstract; however, when considering the monumental task faced by legal professionals, where we are expected to make reasonable efforts to identify, aggregate, and categorize data to subsequently derive meaning out of ever increasing volumes of data, the celestial diversion loses its levity. The information retrieval task at hand, which currently necessitates a search through and analysis of very large data sets, increasingly poses all too real a burden.

---

1. IDC iView, *The Digital Universe of Opportunities: Rich Data and the Increasing Value of the Internet of Things Executive Summary*, EMC² (Apr. 2014), http://www.emc.com/leadership/digital-universe/2014iview/executive-summary.htm [hereinafter *Digital Universe*]. *See generally* John Foley, *Extreme Big Data: Beyond Zettabytes and Yottabytes*, Forbes (Oct. 9, 2013), http://www.forbes.com/sites/oracle/2013/10/09/extreme-big-data-beyond-zettabytes-and-yottabytes/.

The volume of global data is doubling in size every two years and is predicted to reach 44 zettabytes[2] by the year 2020.[3] Meaning, by 2020, there will be 5,200 gigabytes of data—equivalent to over 150,000 bankers boxes or 10 million pages of data—for every man, woman, and child on earth.[4] One would not conceive of analyzing 10 million printed pages, one by one, on a manual basis, as a practical or even possible method of identifying relevant and actionable information in any context, much less in a legal dispute with parties footing the bill.

This challenge only increases in magnitude with each passing year as data volume and variation continues to grow, while the cost of storing this data continues to decrease.[5] The result—current and certainly future volumes of data cannot humanly be reviewed, for litigation purposes, via a manual document-by-document process given the limited resources of labor, time, and the financial constraints of any given matter.[6] For this reason, leading e-discovery jurists

---

2. A zettabyte is a very large volume of data equating to one trillion gigabytes; *see Zettabyte*, TECHTERMS, http://techterms.com/definition/zettabyte (last visited Aug. 1, 2016). *See also* Foley, *supra* note 1 ("In the hierarchy of big data, there are petabytes, exabytes, zettabytes, and yottabytes. After that, things get murky. The challenge is only partly one of coming to agreement on the right words to describe what lies beyond a yottabyte, which is septillion bytes.").

3. *Digital Universe, supra* note 1.

4. 1 gigabyte = 70,000 pages = 28 bankers boxes (each with 2,500 pages).
5,200 gigabytes = 150,000 bankers boxes = 10,500,000 pages.

5. The Sedona Conference, *The Sedona Conference® Best Practices Commentary on the Use of Search and Information Retrieval Methods in E-Discovery*, 15 SEDONA CONF. J. 217, 228 (2014) [hereinafter *Sedona Search Commentary*] ("More recently, there has been a similar explosion in the use of instant and text messaging throughout organizations, including increasingly, through the use of mobile devices. In many organizations, the average worker maintains several gigabytes of stored data. At the same time, the costs of storage have plummeted from $20,000 per gigabyte in 1990 to less than 3.5¢ per gigabyte in 2013.").

6. Bennett B. Borden, *The Demise of Linear Review*, DRINKERBIDDLE (Oct. 1, 2010), http://www.drinkerbiddle.com/resources/publications/2010/The-Demise-of-Linear-Review_2010 ("The explosive growth in the volume of data can create a crippling financial and administrative burden on parties responding to discovery requests to identify, collect, review, and produce data."); *see also* Harrison M. Brown, *Searching for an Answer: Defensible EDiscovery Search Techniques in the Absence of Judicial Voice*, 16 CHAP. L. REV. 407, 413 (2013) (citing Jason R. Baron & Michael D. Berman, *Designing a "Reasonable" E-Discovery Search: A Guide*

have questioned the continued viability of manual review as a sole means for identifying relevant information.[7] The Sedona Conference recognized this in its best practices commentary on search and retrieval:

> Particularly (but not exclusively) in large and complex litigation, where discovery is expected to encompass hundreds of thousands to hundreds of millions of potentially responsive electronic records, there is no reasonable possibility of marshalling the human labor required to undertake a document-by-document, manual review of the potential universe of discoverable materials.[8]

The era of "information inflation"[9] has brought into sharp relief the growing conflict between the principle of broad discovery,[10] supported by the current breadth of allowable discovery under the Federal Rules

---

for the Perplexed, in MANAGING E-DISCOVERY AND ESI: FROM PRE-LITIGATION THROUGH TRIAL 479, 481 (Berman et al. eds., 2011)).

7. *See generally* U.S. v. O'Keefe, 537 F. Supp. 2d 14, 23–24 (D.D.C. 2008); Equity Analytics v. Lundin, 248 F.R.D. 331, 332–33 (D.D.C. 2008); Victor Stanley v. Creative Pipe, Inc., 250 F.R.D. 251, 260 (D. Md. 2008); Jason R. Baron, *Law in the Age of Exabytes: Some Further Thoughts on "Information Inflation" and Current Issues in E-Discovery Search*, 17 RICH. J.L. & TECH. 9 (2011), *available at* http://jolt.richmond.edu/v17i3/article9.pdf.

8. *Sedona Search Commentary, supra* note 5, at 243 (Practice Point 1, "[i]n many settings involving electronically stored information, reliance *solely* on a manual search process for the purpose of finding responsive documents may be infeasible or unwarranted. In such cases, the use of automated search methods should be viewed as reasonable, valuable, and even necessary."). *See also* Nicholas M. Pace & Laura Zakaras, *Where the Money Goes: Understanding Litigant Expenditures for Producing Electronic Discovery*, RAND INSTITUTE FOR CIVIL JUSTICE 97, 99 (2012) (indicating that document review accounts for "$0.73 of every dollar spent on electronic production," and "computer categorized review strategy, such as predictive coding, [is] not only a cost-effective choice but perhaps the *only* reasonable way to handle many large-scale productions.") (emphasis in original).

9. *See* George L. Paul & Jason R. Baron, *Information Inflation: Can the Legal System Adapt?*, 13 RICH. J.L. & TECH. 10, ¶¶ 1–2 (2007), *available at* http://law.richmond.edu/jolt/v13i3/article10.pdf.

10. Hickman v. Taylor, 329 U.S. 495, 507 (1947) ("Mutual knowledge of all relevant facts gathered by both parties is essential to proper litigation.").

of Civil Procedure (the Rules),[11] and the Rules' mandate to resolve disputes in a cost and time effective manner.[12] Broad—sometimes unduly broad—discovery requests for "relevant" information have led to the collection of expansive volumes of information, gradually rendering the "venerated process of 'eyes-only' manual review [as] no longer generally workable or economically feasible."[13] The volume and complexity of information, combined with the proven inaccuracy of manual review of this information, has driven the legal community, including clients, counsel, and jurists, to embrace alternative, hybrid methods of search, retrieval, and review of digital documents.[14]

This is not to say that automated technologies as a cost-efficient means to effectively and accurately identify relevant information will completely supplant the need for manual assessment of data. Manual review is still necessary to review seed sets of data used in supervised machine learning technologies, quality control processes, privilege review, and matters or investigations with smaller volumes of data.[15] It is also, a means to interrogate the data and ferret out the most

11. Fed. R. Civ. P. 26(b)(1) (2016). *See infra* note 18 for a discussion of the 2015 Rules amendments.

12. Fed. R. Civ. P. 1 (2016).

13. *Sedona Search Commentary, supra* note 5, at 229.

14. *See* Hon. Craig Shaffer, *Defensible by What Standard?*, 13 Sedona Conf. J. 212 (2012) (discussing the use of automated tools to review data in a more cost effective manner that is superior to manual review); *see also Sedona Search Commentary, supra* note 5, at 220 ("[J]ust as technology has given rise to these new litigation challenges, technology can help to solve them. The emergence of new discovery strategies, best practices, and processes, as well as new search and retrieval technologies are transforming the way lawyers litigate. Collectively, they provide opportunities for huge volumes of information to be reviewed faster, more accurately, and more affordably than ever before."); *id.* at 224 ("Alternative search tools may properly supplement simple keyword searching and Boolean search techniques. These include using various forms of computer- or technology-assisted review, machine learning, relevance ranking, and text mining tools which employ mathematical probabilities, as well as other techniques incorporating supervised and unsupervised document and content classifiers.").

15. *See* Thomas Y. Allman, Jason R. Baron, & Maura R. Grossman, *Preservation, Search Technology, and Rulemaking*, 30 The Computer & Internet Lawyer 2 (2013); *see also Sedona Search Commentary, supra* note 5, at 244 ("Of course, the use of automated search methods is not intended to entirely eliminate the need for manual review; indeed, in many cases, both automated and manual searches will be conducted, with initial automated searches used for culling down a universe of material to

meaningful or actionable content, regardless of relevancy, or in light of an internal investigation. However, the remaining elements of manual review (and the skill sets that go with them) that apply in any of these contexts are now best used with, and, arguably empowered and magnified by, the latest available technologies.

Nevertheless, continued insistence on lawyers relying on historical "tried and true" methods in reviewing ESI creates a disjointed environment wherein the document review "is divorced from its primary purpose, to marshal the facts specific to a matter to prove a party's claims or defenses . . . ."[16] The would-be cost and labor of such a manual undertaking is anathema to the spirit and mandate of the Rules to resolve disputes in a "just, speedy, and inexpensive"[17] manner, as well as to the principle of proportionality now expressly identified in newly amended Rule 26.[18]

Long before the advent of the 'e' in legal discovery, information science, through the Blair and Maron study, debunked the myth that the human review of information has a level of accuracy that is acceptable or as high as imagined.[19] The 1985 study revealed that attorneys and supervising paralegals, employing an iterative process using search terms to identify relevant documents, achieved only a 20 percent

more manageable size (or prioritizing documents), followed by a secondary manual review process.").

16. Bennett B. Borden, et al., *Why Document Review Is Broken*, William Mullens EDIG: E-Discovery and Information Governance 3 (May 2011), *available at* http://www.umiacs.umd.edu/~oard/desi4/papers/borden.pdf.

17. Fed. R. Civ. P. 1 (2016).

18. Amended Rule 26(b)(1), with effective date Dec. 1, 2015, states that "Unless otherwise limited by court order, the scope of discovery is as follows: Parties may obtain discovery regarding any nonprivileged matter that is relevant to any party's claim or defense and proportional to the needs of the case, considering the amount in controversy, the importance of the issues at stake in the action, the parties' resources, the importance of the discovery in resolving the issues, and whether the burden or expense of the proposed discovery outweighs its likely benefit. Information within this scope of discovery need not be admissible in evidence to be discoverable"; *see generally* The Sedona Conference, *The Sedona Conference® Best Practices Commentary on Proportionality in Electronic Discovery*, 14 Sedona Conf. J. 155 (2013) [hereinafter *Sedona Commentary on Proportionality*] (explaining the principle of proportionality).

19. *See generally* David C. Blair & M.E. Maron, *An Evaluation of Retrieval Effectiveness for a Full-Text Retrieval System*, 28 Communications of the ACM (1985).

level of accuracy, or recall, and, yet, assumed that they were achieving a 75 percent level of recall—a wide disparity given the historical assumption that manual/linear review of hardcopy and, subsequently, electronic information was reliable and accurate.[20] A similar analysis of the reliability of human manual or linear review was conducted in studies published as part of the TREC Legal Track (2006–2011).[21] As of at least 2011, scholarly research has demonstrated the ability of technology to assist with the identification and categorization of documents to a degree of accuracy that meets or surpasses the level achieved by human review—and doing so on a scale and speed that surpassed any human ability to make such determinations.[22]

In line with this research, more advanced search and review techniques, as discussed throughout this book, provide an opportunity to leverage limited resources, time, labor, and money, alongside advances in technology, to more accurately, affordably, and quickly identify data both relevant to and informative about a matter or investigation. However, notwithstanding such identifiable advantages, the use of the most advanced automated search techniques has not yet taken hold over discovery, even in clearly advantageous circumstances. Rather, the employment of keyword searches to cull a data set and the subsequent linear manual review of the results remain the most frequently used method of information retrieval.[23] The legal community at large, as well as their clients, appears to have an inherent distrust in newer technology and, yet, a misplaced faith in the accuracy and efficiency of the application of search terms (as well as the use of manual review).

---

20. *See Sedona Search Commentary, supra* note 5, at 230 ("[T]here appears to be a myth that manual review by humans of large amounts of information is as accurate and complete as possible—perhaps even perfect—and constitutes the gold standard by which all searches should be measured. Even assuming that the profession had the time and resources to continue to conduct manual review of massive sets of electronic data sets (which it does not), the relative efficacy of that approach versus utilizing newly developed automated methods of review remains very much open to debate.").

21. Reports of the findings of the TREC Legal Track (2006–2011) are available at http://trec-legal.umiacs.umd.edu/.

22. *See* Maura R. Grossman & Gordon V. Cormack, *Technology-Assisted Review in E-Discovery Can Be More Effective and More Efficient Than Exhaustive Manual Review*, 17 RICH J.L. & TECH. 11 (2011), *available at* http://jolt.richmond.edu/v17i3/article11.pdf. *See also* Maura R. Grossman & Gordon V. Cormack, *A Tour of Technology-Assisted Review*, Chapter 3 of this volume.

23. *See Sedona Search Commentary, supra* note 5, at 229.

There is a fear that any method, other than a document-by-document, "eyes only" review, will fail to capture relevant and informative data.[24] Additionally, there are lingering concerns regarding the lack of scientific validity coupled with the "lack of knowledge or even confusion about the capabilities of automated search tools."[25] This mindset over the use of manual review to identify relevant data, and the belief that advanced information retrieval techniques lack scientific validity, is, in our view, wholly misplaced. This chapter, as well as the subsequent chapters in this volume, is aimed at addressing these misperceptions.

Overview of Electronic Tools and Process

Search and information retrieval, outside of selecting paper documents by hand, invariably involves using some form of technology. Even keyword search leverages the ability of machine programming to identify documents satisfying this type of search—however fallible. Before we discuss keyword searching proper, it may be appropriate to briefly review some of the leading automated means of reducing and organizing data sets, regardless of what automated search method is performed. An exigent need exists for lawyers to quickly and efficiently identify key information potentially relevant to a matter or investigation, beginning within the identification phase, and through to the final analysis and ultimate production phases of discovery.[26]

Identification of Data Sources

The identification of relevant data sources begins prior to the discovery phase, during the period of time in which preservation of data has been triggered.[27] This phase, more often than not, is a complicated

---

24. *Id.*

25. *Id.*

26. *See generally* ELECTRONIC DISCOVERY REFERENCE MODEL, *available at* http://www.edrm.net/resources/guides/edrm-framework-guides) (last visited Aug. 1, 2016) [hereinafter EDRM]. For an alternative schematic workflow worth considering, *see* Ralph C. Losey, www.edbp.com (Electronic Discovery Best Practices Model) (last visited Aug. 1, 2016).

27. *See generally* Paul W. Grimm, Michael D. Berman, Conor R. Crowley, & Leslie Wharton, *Proportionality in the Post-Hoc Analysis of Pre-Litigation Preservation Decisions*, 37 U. BALT. L. REV. 394 (2008).

and detail-oriented process that requires a reasonable understanding of the claims, the defenses, the types of relevant information available, the client's data sources, as well as how information is or may be stored within these data sources. Identification of data sources is not an exhaustive process. As with all phases of discovery, the goal is not perfection; nevertheless, the goal of this identification phase, along with preservation,

> is to implement a discovery plan that identifies and collects relevant and responsive non-privileged materials and data from a larger universe of electronically stored information *using appropriate methodologies that are reasonable to the particular circumstances* of the client and litigation and provide a quality result.[28]

For our purposes, the identification stage "involves finding the information in the diverse information processing ecosystem that must be searched."[29] Identification is a labor-intensive process that is concerned with not only collecting data, but also with identifying individuals and sources of data likely to contain relevant information. Identification starts with a plan that is iterative and used as a means to "validate potentially relevant ESI sources including people and systems."[30]

Following the identification of relevant data sources, custodians, and key players, data is preserved and, subsequently, collected. While data may be preserved broadly, it is, nevertheless, guided by rules of reasonableness and proportionality[31] and is followed by a collection of data that is targeted, methodical, documented, and reasonable based on the circumstances of the case[32] and, thus, defensible.

---

28. *See* Shaffer, *supra* note 14, at 2 (emphasis added).

29. Douglas Oard & William Webber, *Information Retrieval for E-Discovery*, 7 Foundations and Trends® in Information Retrieval 99, 113 (2013), *available at* https://terpconnect.umd.edu/~oard/pdf/fntir13.pdf.

30. *Identification Guide*, EDRM, *available at* http://www.edrm.net/resources/guides/edrm-framework-guides/identification (last visited Aug. 1, 2016).

31. *See Sedona Commentary on Proportionality*, *supra* note 18, at 292; *see also* Fed. R. Civ. P. 26(b)(1) (2016).

32. *See* Shaffer, *supra* note 14, at 4 ("While a defensible e-discovery plan is not held to a standard of perfection, Rule 34 of the Federal Rules of Civil Procedure does

Essentially, the collection phase provides the first opportunity to create a detailed outline that limits the data to be gathered and that operates as early filters or search and retrieval methods to cull the volume of data that will eventually be collected, processed, reviewed, and produced.[33] Early identified filters would include date ranges, key custodians, data types, initial search terms, and relevant document types.[34]

Throughout the identification, preservation, and collection phases of discovery, planning each phase, sampling of data sources, as well as documenting the phases are all part of a well thought-out and defensible process, which travels through into the processing, searching, review, and production stages of discovery. These later stages, processing through to production, heavily rely on the initial information gleaned from the data identification, preservation, and collection phases, all of which must be conducted in a defensible manner and, during which, more accurate search terms are identified.[35]

Processing

In its simplest terms, the processing phase of discovery functions to normalize, reduce, and index data gathered during the identification and collection stages of the discovery lifecycle.[36] Before any search

---

require a party to undertake reasonable efforts to identify and produce responsive, non-privileged material in its possession, custody or control.").

33. *See generally* Pace & Zakaras, *supra* note 8.

34. Not all document types may be relevant to the claims and defenses; *see eDiscovery Identification: Data Scope*, *available at* http://technology.findlaw.com/ediscovery-guide/identification-data-scope.html (last visited Apr. 10, 2016).

35. *See* The Sedona Conference, *The Sedona Conference® Commentary on Achieving Quality in the E-Discovery Process*, 15 SEDONA CONF. J. 265, 273 (2014) [hereinafter *Sedona Commentary on Achieving Quality*] ("Achieving 'consistency across the production' requires sound project planning and oversight, which is often enhanced by integrating measurements of quality within the overall e-discovery process.").

36. Oard & Webber, *supra* note 29, at 114 ("Processing, in this context, refers to operations performed on service copies to prepare the collection for review. In the era of linear review, this involved rendering page images for each file type and formatting appropriate metadata for display with each page image. In the era of technology-assisted review, the Processing function would also involve feature generation and indexing; essentially, processing is whatever needs to be done in advance of Review.").

and review of data can begin, the data must, generally, be (i) organized, with the variegated forms of the data formatted in a standard manner, and (ii) indexed, such that the data term frequency, relationship of terms to one another, co-occurrences, and more are all recognized and ascribed values within an index. Additionally, "noise" programs are removed from the data, such as executable files, which are voluminous and almost never relevant to a matter. These steps then render the data searchable, and further facilitate the efficient review of the data.

As with each step of the litigation, effectuating the processing stage requires planning, coordination, quality control, and assurance to align the processing with e-discovery strategies as well as to ensure a defensible process.[37] An in-depth presentation of the technical nature of the processing phase is beyond the scope of this chapter, however, an overview of the steps and their importance is presented in the following sections.

Normalization

Data gathered during prior stages of discovery will normally arrive in varying formats. These may include back-up tapes, voicemail, email with attachments stored in .pst or .zip files, text messages, instant chat messages, Microsoft Word and Excel documents, and more. Each of these formats presents in a different manner not only visually, but also structurally. Processing reorganizes the smaller pieces of data that comprise these data types into a more homogeneous structure—a normalization of sorts—which then allows a search algorithm to quickly identify terms, term proximity and/or co-occurrences, and other characteristics of a data type in order to provide a resulting set of documents that answer a specific search command—however simple or complex—using Boolean or more sophisticated methods of search and information retrieval.

De-NISTting

Much of the data gathered during the identification and collection phase of discovery includes software executable programs and applications

37. *Processing Guide*, EDRM, *available at* http://www.edrm.net/resources/guides/edrm-framework-guides/processing.

that are not relevant to a matter and generally not created by a user or custodian. The National Institute of Standards and Technology (NIST) maintains a list of executable and program files that include a unique identifier, or hashtag, that is used to search, identify, and cull out these nonrelevant file types.[38] This assists in removing static from a database prior to moving the data into any review platform.

De-duplication, Threading

During the processing stage, the identification and removal of duplicates and near-duplicates of documents, as well as the threading of email is accomplished, all of which further reduces the size of the ultimate data set to be searched and reviewed. While this section presents a simple overview, it must be noted that decisions around near-duplicate and threading processes do involve a degree of sophistication that demand a knowledge of the technical process (including its shortcomings), that can occur during this phase of discovery.

Indexing

Indexing the contents of data is a complex process whereby the individual terms, information, and character of documents are placed into a database or index. This index becomes the backbone of most search technology, though not all, against which searches are conducted. "'[I]ndexing,' [is] a term which places emphasis on the construction of data structures to support rapid responses to queries."[39] The index can identify, depending on the technology used, the relationship between terms, their distance and frequency, or even their association with predefined lists of terms such as dictionaries, thesauri, or ontologies.

Keyword and Boolean Search Methods

Following the identification, preservation, collection, and processing phases, data is, normally, loaded onto software platforms for review in order to determine its relevancy, as well as its privilege status,

38. Craig Ball, *De-NISTing; De-FECTive*, Ball in Your Court: Computer Forensics, E-Discovery (Aug. 31, 2011), *available at* https://ballinyourcourt.wordpress.com/2011/08/31/de-nisting-defective/.

39. Oard & Webber, *supra* note 29, at 129.

or to conduct investigations for a variety of internal and external non-litigation reasons. Prior to the review, various search technologies may be utilized to target relevant data in order to more efficiently reduce and review the body of data.

Keyword search, or search terms, are currently the most employed means of both filtering, or culling, the size of a data set and identifying potentially relevant information.[40] For the purposes of this chapter, "keyword searches" include the use of search terms, Boolean logic, and somewhat more advanced techniques including stemming and fuzzy searches.

The use of search terms entails the identification and use of select terms identified as likely to retrieve documents relative to a matter or investigation.[41] This would include the use of individual terms without any modification or placement within a search phrase. For example, a search for "cat," "dog," "house," or "bank," individually, would return documents with one or all of these terms exactly as they are keyed into a search program. The search technically would look like the following:

> Search 1: cat
>
> Search 2: dog
>
> Search 3: house
>
> Search 4: bank

However, without more, neither "cat*s*," "dog*s*," "house*s*," nor "bank*s*" (plural) would be returned unless these exact terms were also

---

40. *See Sedona Search Commentary, supra* note 5, at 231 ("The most commonly used search methodology today still entails the use of "keyword searches" of full text and metadata as a means of filtering data for producing responsive documents in civil discovery.").

41. *Electronic Discovery/E-Discovery*, EDRM, *available at* http://www.edrm.net/resources/glossaries/glossary/e/electronic-discovery (last visited Apr. 10, 2016) ("Keyword Search: A common search technique that uses query words ("keywords") and looks for them in ESI, using an index. A keyword search is a basic search technique that involves searching for one or more words within a collection of documents and returns only those documents that contain the search terms entered.").

included as searches. Therefore, the more complex a matter is, the more necessary it becomes to develop and/or imagine all permutations of a single term that are critical in retrieving a body of documents containing material potentially relevant to a document request or investigation; otherwise, the search runs the risk of being under-inclusive of relevant information.

An additional limitation of developing simple search terms is the inability of a search to limit the retrieval of documents based on context. In other words, the terms "cat," "dog," "house," and "bank" will retrieve documents without any consideration of context—meaning, a search for the term "bank" may return documents related to finance or a river.[42] Therefore, the return set of documents captured by search terms is not only literal, it is effectively over-inclusive. When considering the number of contextually false hits in a data set that houses millions or billions of documents, the risk of developing an over-inclusive set of search terms grows into the very real liability of added expenses in terms of cost, labor, and time.

Stemming and fuzzy search technologies improve upon the use of search terms used for information retrieval by accounting for misspellings in search terms and variations in the prefixes and suffixes, respectively, and can help reduce the problem of under inclusivity highlighted in the previously described search example. Stemming technology identifies variations of a root or stem of a word and returns documents reflecting this root word along with any additional prefixes or suffixes.[43]

42. *See Sedona Search Commentary, supra* note 5, at 233.

43. *See* Maura R. Grossman & Gordon V. Cormack, *The Grossman-Cormack Glossary of Technology-Assisted Review, with Foreword by John M. Facciola, U.S. Magistrate Judge*, 2013 Fed. Cts. L. Rev. 7, 30 (see Appendix in this volume) (*Stemming*: "In Keyword or Boolean Search, or Feature Engineering, the process of equating all forms of the same root word. For example, the words 'stem,' 'stemming,' 'stemmed,' and 'stemmable' would all be treated as equivalent, and would each yield the same result when used as Search Terms in a Query. In some search systems, stemming is implicit, and in others, it must be made explicit through particular Query syntax.").

For example,

Search 1: view

> Stemming search of the root "view" = viewing, review, preview, viewer

Search 2: house

> Stemming search of root "house" = houses, housing

Applying stemming technology will return documents with the term "view" along with the additional and related terms "viewing," "review," "preview," and so forth. Therefore, even though the specific term "view" may not appear anywhere in a document, stemmed words, such as "viewing" and "review," will appear in documents that are returned and will aid in improving the completeness of a return set of documents.

Stemming search technology will not return documents that misspell the original search term, "view" or account for variations in a root word. Fuzzy search technology will account for such errors and variation in the human language.[44]

For example,

Search 1: man

> Fuzzy search of the word "man" = men, woman,

Search 2: break

> Fuzzy search of the word "break" = brakes, broke, bloke

---

44. *Definition of Fuzzy Search*, WHATIS.COM, *available at* http://whatis.techtarget.com/definition/fuzzy-search (last visited April 10, 2016) ("A fuzzy matching program can compensate for common input typing errors, as well as errors introduced by optical character recognition (OCR) scanning of printed documents. The program can return hits with content that contains a specified base word along with prefixes and suffixes. For example, if 'planet' is entered as a search word, hits occur for sites containing words such as 'protoplanet' or 'planetary.'"); *see also Definition of Fuzzy Search*, EDRM, *available at* http://www.edrm.net/resources/glossaries/glossary/f/fuzzy-search (last visited Apr. 10, 2016) ("A search technique that identifies ESI based on terms close to another term, with closeness defined as a typographical difference and/or change.").

Fuzzy search technology allows for any misspellings and changes in the root of a word and, as with stemming, aids in returning a more complete set of documents likely to hold relevant information, as identified by initial search terms.

However, neither stemming nor fuzzy search technology is capable of describing the relationship of search terms to one another. Boolean search, on the other hand, is a method used to describe a relationship between two or more search terms in an effort to retrieve documents matching this defined relationship. Boolean search uses operators such as "AND" and "OR" as well as distance operators that identify words lying within a defined distance of one another.[45]

For example:

Search 1: cat AND dog

> Boolean search for terms 'cat' and 'dog' = documents having both the term 'cat' and 'dog' (limiting a search set to documents with both of these terms)

Search 2: cat OR dog

> Boolean search for terms 'cat' or 'dog' = documents having either the term 'cat' or 'dog' (increasing a search set to include documents with either of these words)

Search 3: cat within two terms of dog[46]

> Boolean search for terms 'cat' and 'dog' = documents having both the term 'cat' and 'dog' (limiting a search set to documents with both of these terms within two spaces of one another). (Note: one must use caution with differing technologies and confirm that such a proximity search is multi-directional—meaning,

---

45. *See* Grossman & Cormack, *supra* note 43, at 10 ("Boolean Search: A Keyword Search in which the Keywords are combined using operators such as 'AND,' 'OR,' and '[BUT] NOT.' The result of a Boolean Search is precisely determined by the words contained in the Documents.").

46. Technologies use different methods of instructing a proximity search, which can include W/2 or NEAR2 to describe the relationship of two words within two spaces of one another.

"dog" may precede "cat" by two spaces or terms, and "cat" may precede "dog" by two spaces or terms.)

Using search terms in combination with fuzzy, stemming, and Boolean searches contributes to the level of accuracy within a return set of documents, identifying a larger number of documents likely to be relevant, while also reducing and refining the original size of this set.

Advantages

Keyword search, as previously described, provided the first, readily available, and convenient methodology able to meet the onslaught of information explosion, allowing counsel to reduce the original volume of data based on a level of informed judgement. Keyword search is able to reduce the size of a data collection by a significant amount. This methodology is also useful in sampling large volumes of data retained on backup tapes and other repositories in order to test the richness and, therefore, feasibility of restoring the data. Additionally, for small volumes of data, keyword search is a reasonable and affordable means of identifying relevant information.

Ideally, keyword search is best used when parties have an informed and deep understanding of the language used by a client, company, group, and/or custodians who have generated the communications and documentation; have knowledge or possession of the types of documents sought; and concepts do not play a large part in the content of the data.[47] However, when parties are not savvy about special terms or "code" phrases used by a specific company or group, or lack examples of unique "lingo" used by custodians, or when concepts, rather than single or a series of words, are critical in a matter, then keyword searches fall short of delivering document results that are representative. In such cases, arguably counsel may fail to meet its obligation to reasonably identify information relevant to a matter.[48] Aside from identifying what is relevant to a request for discovery, search terms

47. *See Sedona Search Commentary*, *supra* note 5, at 232 ("Keyword searches work best when the legal inquiry is focused on finding particular documents and when the use of language is relatively predictable.").

48. *Id.; see also* Borden, *supra* note 6 (explaining that parties must know, in advance, exactly what they seek and "enumerate" through search terms—yet,

can fail greatly in identifying what is informative or hidden within a data set for other purposes, such as early case assessment, on matters that may be crucial to the representation of the client.

Limitations

Despite the ability of keyword search to reduce the size of a data set, and its use in other areas, keyword search methodologies suffer from significant limitations and have been called into question when used as the sole means of cost effective, efficient, and accurate identification of relevant material. Both expert commentaries and the judiciary have expressed the growing realization that reliance on keyword searching alone is sub-optimal, and, in some contexts, simply not a reasonable search and retrieval methodology.[49]

Accuracy of Human Development of Keywords

The Blair and Maron study, mentioned earlier in the chapter, debunked the myth that humans are able to utilize both keyword searching and manual, linear document review as a means of accurately identifying relevant information.[50] Yet attorney-crafted search terms and manual review and identification of relevance has been, and to a degree still is, held to achieve an accuracy rate that has been dubbed the "gold standard."[51] The fault in using keyword search techniques lies not within computers, but with the human inability to "anticipate all the possible ways that people might refer to the issues in a case."[52] The reliance on both an attorney's ability to draft accurate search terms as well as consistently identify,

---

enumerating every possible use of the term or idea, in order to capture all relevant data, may still not capture all relevant information).

49. Baron, *supra* note 7, at 8 (citing *Victor Stanley*, 250 F.R.D. at 256–61 (discussing the *Sedona Search Commentary*'s practice pointers and stating that "while it is universally acknowledged that keyword searches are useful tools for search and retrieval of ESI, all keyword searches are not created equal; and there is a growing body of literature that highlights the risks associated with conducting an unreliable or inadequate keyword search or relying exclusively on such searches for privilege review")).

50. *See generally* Blair & Maron, *supra* note 19.

51. *See generally Sedona Search Commentary, supra* note 5; Grossman & Cormack, *Exhaustive Manual Review, supra* note 22.

52. *Sedona Search Commentary, supra* note 5, at 240; *see also* William A. Gross Constr. Assoc., Inc. v. Am. Mfrs. Mut. Ins. Co., 256 F.R.D. 134, 134 (S.D.N.Y.

through manual review, relevant information, is misplaced. Blair and Maron effectively highlighted the limitation of keyword search as failing to achieve the perceived level of accuracy when used as the sole means to search, retrieve, and classify documents as relevant.[53]

Drafting an accurate keyword search is a complex undertaking, as alluded to by the Blair and Maron study. More recently, the TREC Legal Track[54] and the various Grossman and Cormack studies[55] on the accuracy of search terms have come to the same conclusion. These studies bring into sharp relief the legal community's misplaced confidence in their ability to craft accurate terms and phrasing that will, in fact, retrieve most, if not all, potentially relevant data.

Parties often draft search terms in a vacuum, without having seen any exemplar documentation that informs the keywords that will be used, or without having conferred not only with the client, but also with individual custodians on their natural language used within a business group. Were parties able to draft accurate keyword searches that mirror words used by custodians, these terms would, nevertheless, fail to capture all relevant data, missing false negatives or documents and/or terms that initially appear to be irrelevant unless analyzed. "Informed" search terms would also identify and capture or group irrelevant documents that hold one of the search terms but are, in context, irrelevant, or false positives.

For example, using the search term "bank" in a financial matter may return documents with the terms "bank" as used in the phrase "river bank," a false positive, and yet fail to return documents with the phrase "financial institution," a false negative. This under- and over-inclusive limitation of keyword searching is due to the inherent flexibility of the human language, which includes the habit of individuals to speak in code, truncate terminology, to develop office, group, and industry specific language.[56] In addition to "code" speak, found in

---

2009) (magistrate judge points out "the latest example of lawyers designing keyword searches in the dark, by the seat of the pants. . . .").

53. *See generally* Blair & Maron, *supra* note 19.

54. *See* TREC Legal Track, *supra* note 21.

55. *See, e.g.*, Grossman & Cormack, *Exhaustive Manual Review, supra* note 22.

56. *Sedona Search Commentary, supra* note 5, at 233 ("Human language is an inherently elastic, ambiguous, 'living' tool of enormous power. Its elasticity allows for jargon, private codes, and discrete vocabularies to exist in different subcultures

many specific business industries, companies, and individual offices, a single term, or keyword, can often be used to describe more than one idea (polysemy)[57] or used for multiple, similar terms to describe a single idea (synonymy).[58] The term "bank" is an example of polysemy, while the terms "cat" and "feline" are examples of synonymy.

While keyword search technology using Boolean techniques attempts to emulate human use of concepts through language, it is, nevertheless, severely limited in its ability to completely capture the concepts that, very often, embody the relevant and informative content of digital communications and documents.[59]

Nevertheless, keyword searches can reduce the volume of data needing attorney review by appreciable percentages.[60] However, considering what has been noted about the volume of data exponentially increasing, keyword samples returning even 1 percent of a universe of documents as potentially relevant will themselves be effectively beyond human ability to review efficiently, accurately, or in a timely manner.[61]

Crafting keyword searches has been compared to a game of go-fish, where the level of knowledge of each party is asymmetrical: the requesting party can only blindly craft search terms for content which the responding party may more intimately understand—meaning, the responding party holds all the cards.[62] Whatever actual level of

---

in any organization, thereby making the identification of search terms much more challenging.").

57. *Definition of Polysemy*, EDRM, http://www.edrm.net/resources/glossaries/edrmsearchglossary/polysemy (last visited Aug. 1, 2016) ("A single word or expression having multiple meanings.").

58. *Definition of Synonymy*, EDRM, http://www.edrm.net/resources/glossaries/edrmsearchglossary/synonymy (last visited Aug. 1, 2016) ("Having the equivalence of meaning; having the same definition without having the same expression.").

59. *Sedona Search Commentary, supra* note 5, at 234.

60. Borden, *supra* note 6 (data reduced by the application of keyword searches remains "a significant burden to bear").

61. *See* Baron, *supra* note 7, at ¶¶ 7–9 (discussing the "one percent" issue wherein "manual searching, *even after automated methods have been used based on keywords*, will become an increasingly resource-intensive endeavor," and one which will result in data sets "still too large a haystack for manual searches") (emphasis added).

62. Ralph Losey, *Child's Game of "Go Fish" Is a Poor Model for eDiscovery Search, available at* http://e-discoveryteam.com/2009/10/04/childs-game-of-go-fish-is-a-poor-model-for-e-discovery-search/ (last visited Aug. 1, 2016). Arguably, however,

asymmetry that exists, it is obvious that neither party can hope to craft keyword searches with any level of accuracy without consulting the client,[63] reviewing sample material, drafting and testing initial terms, and cooperating with the other party.

Due to the limitations just described, the judiciary has repeatedly found itself in a position of arbitrating or, in the more extreme case, crafting search terms and search methodology in order to help, or guide, the parties in limiting the scope of discovery.[64]

Beyond Keyword Searching

The legal sphere has slowly embraced, or begun to embrace and understand, the science of information retrieval (IR), deploying tested and heavily utilized alternatives found among IR methods and technologies. These IR methodologies and technical applications range from the use of categorization, clustering, or concept searching through to true machine learning—all of which utilize varying algorithms to apply a mathematical value to documents. Each of these IR example methods facilitates an empowered review of documents, helping to reduce efforts at performing document-by-document analysis: they help to ensure "a non-linear review on steroids."[65] We leave to the interested reader the comprehensive, in-depth overview of these techniques in Chapter 3, A Tour of Technology-Assisted Review (along with later chapters), which explains at length

---

the responding party also may lack knowledge of its own data, at least initially, and so particularly in complex data environments may not in fact be all that better in crafting fully accurate search terms relevant to its own data than the requesting party. *See* Jason R. Baron & Edward Wolfe, *A Nutshell on Negotiating E-Discovery Search Protocols*, 11 Sedona Conf. J. 229 (2010).

63. *See generally Sedona Search Commentary, supra* note 5.

64. *See* Baron, *supra* note 7, at ¶ 11 n.38; *Victor Stanley*, 250 F.R.D. at 257 ("while it is universally acknowledged that keyword searches are useful tools for search and retrieval of ESI, all keyword searches are not created equal; and there is a growing body of literature that highlights the risks associated with conducting an unreliable or inadequate keyword search or relying exclusively on such searches for privilege review"); *see also William A. Gross Constr. Ass'n*, 256 F.R.D. at 134 ("This Opinion should serve as a wake-up call to the Bar . . . about the need for careful thought, quality control, testing, and cooperation with opposing counsel in designing search terms or 'keywords' to be used to produce emails or other electronically stored information.").

65. Borden, *supra* note 16, at 3.

various automated tools, techniques, and methods that are now readily coming into vogue and being utilized by skilled and knowledgeable legal counsel.

A Word on Defensibility[66]

Out of frustration with the expense and effort expended on discovery issues, which include preservation, identification and collection, review, and production of relevant information, that are exceeding the value of a matter, courts have been weighing in on both the scope and defensible methodology of the discovery process. In fact, failure to establish a defensible discovery process carries the risk of judicial sanctions, or, to another extreme, the loss of attorney–client privilege.[67] Through judicial opinion, scholarly articles written by jurists,[68] and discovery guidelines,[69] the growing consensus within the legal community is that, regardless of which automated technology is used to cull through, identify, and review data sets, it must be used in a defensible manner.

Several courts have issued discovery preservation guidelines, which also inform the identification, collection, and production of relevant information. For example, both the Northern District of California[70] and the Delaware Court of Chancery[71] have developed checklists that outline what a defensible preservation and collection discovery process would look like.[72]

---

66. *Sedona Search Commentary, supra* note 5, at 227.

67. *Victor Stanley*, 250 F.R.D. at 259 (court found the defendants to have waived privilege after failing to establish a reasonable process to identify and withhold privilege documents that were subsequently produced to plaintiffs).

68. *See* Grimm et al., *supra* note 27; *Sedona Search Commentary, supra* note 5.

69. *Sedona Search Commentary, supra* note 5.

70. *E-Discovery (ESI) Guidelines*, United States District Court, Northern District of California, *available at* http://www.cand.uscourts.gov/eDiscoveryGuidelines (last visited Aug. 1, 2016).

71. Delaware Court of Chancery, *Guidelines to Help Lawyers Practicing Before the Court of Chancery, Sample Document Collection Outline, available at* http://courts.state.de.us/Chancery/docs/SampleDocCollectionOutline.pdf (last visited Aug. 1, 2016).

72. In the Delaware Court, the goal is for the parties to develop protocols for the identification, collection, and review of information that the parties are prepared to

More recently, Judge Peck stated, "it is now black letter law that where the producing party wants to utilize TAR for document review, courts will permit it."[73] He also explored the defensibility of using such technology, which included the use of statistical sampling, quality control, and cooperation among the parties.[74] There is, however, no judicial national standard that outlines which automated technology or technologies to use—and none is expected any time soon, given the understandable judicial reluctance to dictate what search methodology parties should use.[75] Nevertheless,

> Maximizing the use of automated technologies in search and document review to achieve a true quality outcome "is consistent with the highest ethical calling of the legal profession."[76]

The practice of solely employing search terms across any data set and, subsequently, manually reviewing or categorizing the information is no longer a feasible option in light of the continued growth, or explosion, and complexity of data volumes. Not only is it humanly impossible to complete the analysis of a body of information within the time constraints of the discovery process using this "tried and true" methodology,[77] it arguably fails to meet the obligations to conduct reasonable searches for relevant and non-privileged information in an effort to openly exchange information necessary to reach the truth of

---

explain and defend. As the Delaware court put it, "Parties are not required to preserve every shred of information. [They are to][a]ct reasonably." *Id.*

73. Rio Tinto PLC v. Vale S.A., 2015 WL 872294, at *1 (S.D.N.Y. Mar. 2, 2015).

74. *Id.*

75. Dynamo Holdings Ltd. P'ship v. Comm'r of Internal Revenue, 143 T.C. 9, 2014 WL 4636526 (T.C. Sept. 17, 2014) ("[T]he Court is not normally in the business of dictating to parties the process that they should use when responding to discovery. If our focus were on paper discovery, we would not (for example) be dictating to a party the manner in which it should review documents for responsiveness or privilege, such as whether that review should be done by a paralegal, a junior attorney, or a senior attorney."); *see also Rio Tinto*, 2015 WL 872294 n.76 favorably citing *Dynamo* regarding the courts' need to allow parties to dictate search process and technology.

76. *See* Baron, *supra* note 7, at 33 (quoting *Sedona Achieving Quality in the E-Discovery Process* (2009 ed.) 10 SEDONA CONF. J. at 302).

77. The Sedona Conference, *The Sedona Conference® Best Practices Commentary on the Use of Search and Information Retrieval Methods in E-Discovery*, 8 SEDONA CONF. J. 189, 203 (2007).

any matter or investigation. It is incumbent upon the legal community to begin utilizing advanced technology to timely, effectively, and reasonably identify the relevant, non-privileged information that is the foundation of the legal process.

However, turning to automated technologies for the search, retrieval, and categorization of information must be accompanied by the proper skill, pre-planning, and robust process.

> Technologically advanced tools, however, "cutting edge" they may be, will not yield a successful outcome unless their use is driven by people who understand the circumstances and requirements of the case as guided by thoughtful and well-defined methods, and unless their results are measured for accuracy. The first step, then, is the development of a well thought-out process in which the applicable review method can be applied.[78]

As previously noted, even a decade after the 2006 amendments to the Federal Rules of Civil Procedure, there remains a reticence within the legal community to employ automated search and retrieval technologies to identify and categorize relevant information. This is due to several factors: unfamiliarity with the technology, a misplaced faith in the accuracy of human manual review, and fear that the technologies have not been endorsed by the courts and, therefore, fail the due diligence obligations under the Federal Rules of Civil Procedure when challenged by an opposing party or the court itself.[79] A discomfort with the advances in information retrieval technology is not

---

78. Shaffer, *supra* note14, at 2 (citing *Sedona Achieving Quality Commentary*, 10 Sedona Conf. J. at 306).

79. *See generally* ipro, *Survey Finds Majority of Lawyers Still Skeptical of TAR Technology* (Feb. 17, 2015), *available at* https://iprotech.com/news/survey-finds-majority-of-lawyers-still-skeptical-of-tar-technology/ (last visited Apr. 10, 2016); *see also Sedona Search Commentary, supra* note 5, at 235 ("Some litigators continue to primarily rely upon manual review of information as part of their review process. Principal rationales are: (1) concerns that computers cannot be trusted to replace the human intelligence required to make complex determinations on relevance and privilege; (2) the perception that there is a lack of scientific validity of search technologies necessary to defend against a court challenge; and (3) widespread lack of knowledge (and confusion) about the capabilities of automated search tools.")

misplaced. It is no small prospect to incorporate automated search and retrieval into the discovery phase of litigation and, to do so effectively, "the legal profession must employ best-in-class thinking from various disciplines (including project management, quality control, statistics, and information retrieval) to optimize efficiency in modern day discovery."[80]

The Federal Rules, recent case law, as well as the most recent amendments to the Model Rules of Professional Responsibility[81] all fairly demand a level of expertise and ability of the legal profession that includes technical competence, that is, knowledge of the character of electronic information as well as the techniques used and available to identify, collect, process, review, and produce this electronic data.

In recognizing the identified inherent shortcomings of undertaking a manual review process, courts have begun to not only endorse, but also in some cases demand consideration of, through mandate, the use of automated technologies.[82] The judiciary has begun to serve notice that parties reconsider the application of "tried and true" methodologies used to search and identify relevant information. Even absent anything like a uniform consensus on the use of particular automated methods (including a favored technology assisted review technique), there is increasingly a strong message to deploy technology via a process that is defensible, transparent, and reasonably designed to identify and produce relevant non-privileged information.[83] Any use of automated technology must "comport with the requirements of the Federal

80. Baron, *supra* note 7, at ¶ 42.

81. *See* Model Rules of Prof'l Conduct, R. 1.1 cmt 8 (2012), ABA Commission on Ethics 20/20, *available at* http://www.americanbar.org/content/dam/aba/administrative/ethics_2020/2012_hod_annual_meeting_105a_filed_may_2012.authcheckdam.pdf ("The proposed amendment, which appears in a Comment, does not impose any new obligations on lawyers. Rather, the amendment is intended to serve as a reminder to lawyers that they should remain aware of technology, including the benefits and risks associated with it, as part of a lawyer's general ethical duty to remain competent."); *see also* The State Bar of California Standing Committee on Professional Responsibility, Formal Opinion 2015-193 (superseding Formal Opinion Interim No. 11-0004), *available at* http://ethics.calbar.ca.gov/Ethics/Opinions.aspx (last visited Aug. 1, 2016).

82. Tonia Hap Murphy, *Mandating Use of Predictive Coding in Electronic Discovery: An Ill-Advised Judicial Intrusion*, 50.3 Am. Bus. L.J. 609–57 (2013).

83. *See generally Sedona Commentary on Achieving Quality*, *supra* note 35.

Rule of Civil Procedure, be proportionate to the claims, defenses, and circumstances of the particular case, be *reasonably* transparent to the court and opposing parties."[84]

Parties responding to requests for information are in the best position to determine which technology and methodology should be applied to their data.[85] "A defensible e-discovery plan should also expedite the discovery process and minimize, if not eliminate completely, the need for judicial intervention."[86]

Nevertheless, parties must be able to defend any challenge to the technology and methodology chosen and, therefore, must create a process capable of withstanding such a challenge, should it arise or not. The chosen technology and methodology used to search and identify relevant information can be challenged under two scenarios: the requesting party directly questions the sufficiency of the data that is produced, or the court, acting *sua sponte*, challenges the process employed by the producing party.[87] When such a challenge occurs, the producing party must be prepared to defend the decisions to use any technology to search and produce relevant information, regardless of the methodology employed (using traditional or advanced technologies).[88] In fact, it is this *process*, not the courts, that will determine whether the use of automated technology is reasonable and defensible. Courts cannot determine whether an advanced search process was "correct"; however, the court can assess whether the decisions around the use of automated methods, such as technology assisted review, satisfy the parties' obligations under the Federal Rules to take reasonable steps toward producing relevant, non-privileged information.[89]

---

84. Shaffer, *supra* note 14, at 3.

85. *Id.* at 14; *but see* Losey, *supra* note 62.

86. *Defensible by What Standard, supra* note 14, at 14.

87. *See Sedona Search Commentary, supra* note 5, at 230; *Victor Stanley*, 250 F.R.D. at 261 n.10 ("Should their selection be challenged by their adversary, and the court be called upon to make a ruling, then they should expect to support their position with affidavits or other equivalent information from persons with the requisite qualifications and experience, based on sufficient facts or data and using reliable principles or methodology.").

88. *Victor Stanley*, 250 F.R.D. at 261.

89. *See generally* Shaffer, *supra* note 14, at 13.

Perfection is not the goal of any search and retrieval effort within the discovery phase of litigation. Perfection is neither achievable[90] nor expected under the Rules.[91] The standard governing the discovery process, despite the application and appeal of technology and its marked accuracy over a human and manual process, *remains* that of reasonableness.[92] "Reasonableness is the defining characteristic of the discovery Rules."[93]

The question then, becomes, what is a reasonable and defensible process with which to search, retrieve, and produce relevant and non-privileged information. Currently, there is no authoritative standard that serves as the default benchmark for measuring the effectiveness of automated technology used to retrieve information.[94] In fact, whether any information retrieval system accurately returns enough relevant information is a subject of opinion and "[h]uman judgment is ultimately the criterion for evaluating whether an IR systems returns relevant information."[95] However, there is ample expert analysis of what this entails, and the bench has referenced a large body of existing scholarship—including works produced by The Sedona Conference, along with individual expert analyses—all commenting on how a reasonable and defensible discovery process that incorporates automated technology would look.[96]

---

90. *See Sedona Search Commentary, supra* note 5, at 247 ("From decades of IR research, it is clear that a 100% rate of recall, i.e., the ability to retrieve all responsive documents from a given universe of electronic data, is an unachievable goal.").

91. Pension Comm. of the Univ. of Montreal Pension Plan v. Banc of America Sec., LLC, 685 F. Supp. 2d 456, 462 (S.D.N.Y. 2010); Da Silva Moore v. Publicis Groupe & MSL Groupe, 287 F.R.D. 181, 192 (S.D.N.Y. 2012) (Peck, Mag. J.) ("While this Court recognizes that computer-assisted review is not perfect, the Federal Rules of Civil Procedure do not require perfection."), *aff'd*, No. 11 Civ. 1279, 2012 WL 1446534 (S.D.N.Y. Apr. 26, 2012) (Carter, J.).

92. Shaffer, *supra* note 14, at 4; Fed. R. Civ. P. 26(b)(2)(B); Fed. R. Civ. P. 45(c).

93. Shaffer, *supra* note 14, at 4.

94. *See Sedona Search Commentary, supra* note 5, at 237; Gil Keteltas, Karin Jenson, James Sherer, *A Modest Proposal for Preventing eDiscovery Standards from Being a Burden to Practitioners, Clients, the Courts, or Common Sense*, Chapter 15 in this volume.

95. *See Sedona Search Commentary, supra* note 5, at 137.

96. *See, e.g., Sedona Search Commentary, supra* note 5, and the *Sedona Commentary on Achieving Quality, supra* note 35; *see generally* Da Silva Moore, 287 F.R.D. 181, 192.

While a party responding to a request for information is in the best position to determine which technology and methodology should be used in conducting a reasonable search to retrieve relevant information, cooperating with opposing counsel can contribute to the defensibility of the process and, arguably, provide a modicum of protection against any accusation that a jointly developed process is inaccurate or unreasonable.[97] Cooperation provides a level of transparency for the parties, as well as the court, and can help a responding party avoid the risk that the court or requesting party challenges any unilaterally chosen technology for not having accurately, completely, or reliably identified relevant information.[98] As Magistrate Judge Andrew Peck stated in *Da Silva Moore*, "the best solution in the entire area of electronic discovery is cooperation among counsel."[99]

Conclusion

The legal profession continues to embrace many of the automated methods associated with modern-day e-discovery. Manual and keyword searching have a place, but increasingly practitioners handling larger volumes of data need to confront the fact that parties and courts alike view these older methods with less favor. Lawyers owe it to the legal profession and themselves to become more familiar with and competent in using the advanced search alternatives available in the e-discovery marketplace, lest they be left behind in fulfilling their professional obligations to their clients and to the tribunals they stand before.

---

97. *See The Sedona Conference© Cooperation Proclamation*, 10 SEDONA CONF. J. 339 (2009 Supp.); *Sedona Search Commentary, supra* note 5, at 236.

98. *Sedona Search Commentary, supra* note 5, at 236.

99. *Da Silva Moore*, 287 F.R.D. at 192 (quoting *William A. Gross Constr. Assoc.*, 256 F.R.D. at 136).

EDITORS' INTRODUCTION TO CHAPTER 2

Michael D. Berman

Litigation is precedent driven. There is an old joke that law is the only learned profession without a Nobel Prize because, in law, you win by proving that someone else thought of your idea first. The use of predictive coding in litigation was virtually unrecognized in reported case law until 2012, when the first decision approving its use was issued. Since then, courts have struggled to adapt the common law to a wholly new, and complex, process that sometimes appears to operate in a "black box."

In a series of decisions, not wholly consistent and on varying fact patterns, courts have generally seemed willing to authorize predictive coding in appropriate situations. Sometimes the premise is that old-fashioned, manual, document-by-document review is too costly, inaccurate, impossible under time constraints, or all of the foregoing. Other times, it is based on acceptance of new technology based on scientific proof that it is superior to human review. Always, it is with the recognition that no system is perfect. It is the advocate's job to spot the issues and present the proof.

In this chapter, Alicia Shelton and I start with the 2012 decision in *Da Silva Moore* and examine how courts have attempted to permit liberal discovery in the context of "Big Data" while securing the sometimes-contradictory goal of the just, speedy, and inexpensive determination of actions before them in accordance with Federal Rule of Civil Procedure 1.

CHAPTER 2

The Emerging Acceptance of Technology-Assisted Review in Civil Litigation

Alicia L. Shelton and Michael D. Berman

This chapter addresses the common law's adaption to technology-assisted review (TAR) in civil litigation.[1] Justice Cardozo wrote: "Nothing is stable. Nothing absolute. All is fluid and changeable. There is an endless 'becoming.'"[2] Thus, "[e]very new case is an experiment."[3]

1. Frequently, the terms "TAR," "predictive coding," and "computer-assisted review," or "CAR," are used interchangeably. *See, e.g., Da Silva Moore v. Publicis Groupe*, 287 F.R.D. 182, 183–84 (S.D.N.Y. 2012), *adopted sub nom. Da Silva Moore v. Publicis Groupe SA*, No. 11-CIV-1279-ALC-AJP, 2012 WL 1446534 (S.D.N.Y. Apr. 26, 2012). For a definition of "predictive coding," see Bennett B. Borden & Jason R. Baron, *Finding the Signal in the Noise: Information Governance, Analytics, and the Future of Legal Practice*, 20 RICH. J.L. & TECH. 1, 7 (2014). Nevertheless, others draw distinctions between the terms. *See, e.g.*, Chapter 3 and the Appendix in this volume.

2. BENJAMIN N. CARDOZO, THE NATURE OF JUDICIAL PROCESS 28 (1921).

3. *Id.* at 23–24. "[T]he common law is not static but adopts itself to changing conditions and increasing knowledge." *E.g.*, Latz v. Latz, 10 Md. App. 720, 731, 272 A.2d 435, 441 (citation omitted), *cert. denied*, 261 Md. 726 (1971). In that regard:

> [r]ules arise from the application of reason to the changing conditions of society. . . . As was said in *Hurtado v. California*, 110 U.S. 516, 530, 4 S. Ct. 292, 28 L. Ed. 232, "Flexibility and capacity for growth and adaptation is the peculiar boast and excellence of the common law. . . ."

Barnes Coal Corp. v. Retail Coal Merchants Ass'n, 128 F.2d 645, 648–49 (4th Cir. 1942).

Justice Cardozo's statement is particularly apt here, because information, itself, has changed due to the revolution in information technology.[4] Litigation is played out in a world where electronically stored information (ESI) is currently measured in gigabytes, terabytes, petabytes, and exabytes, followed soon enough in the future by zettabytes, yottabytes, brontobytes, and geopbytes.[5] It involves .docx, .wpd, .zip, .mpp, .msg, .pdf, .csv, .mp3, .tax2014, .wav, .mid, .jpg, .xlsx, .xlr, and many other file types, some of which are proprietary.[6] As a direct result, the legal landscape, and litigation, have markedly changed and continue to evolve.[7] "Quite simply, a company's data is the digital imprint of the actions and decisions of all of its managers and employees."[8] This presents both challenges and opportunities for attorneys, especially with voluminous collections.[9] That axiom highlights the need for effective search technologies and methodologies to rapidly uncover key facts in a cost-effective manner. At the highest level of abstraction, those searches may be either manual or computer-assisted.

Manual, or document-by-document "linear," review is often impossible, as well as frequently inaccurate:[10]

> Assume a dispute with one billion emails, 25 percent of which have attachments. Reviewed at a rate of 50 messages per hour, it would take 100 reviewers, working 10 hours per day, seven days a week, 52 weeks per year, approximately 54 years to complete the review! At $100 per hour, the cost would be $2 billion. Even if manual review were limited to 1 percent of the total universe, the hypothetical time and cost would

---

4. *See* Jason R. Baron, *Law in the Age of Exabytes: Some Further Thoughts on "Information Inflation" and Current Issues in E-Discovery Search*, 17 RICH J.L. & TECH. 9, ¶ 11 n.38 (2011), http://jolt.richmond.edu/v17i3/article9.pdf. *see also* George L. Paul and Jason R. Baron, *Information Inflation: Can the Legal System Adapt?*, 13 RICH J.L. & TECH. 10 (2007).

5. "What's a Byte?," http://whatsabyte.com/ (last visited July 12, 2015).

6. For a list of common file types, see http://fileinfo.com/filetypes/common.

7. MANAGING E-DISCOVERY AND ESI: FROM PRE-LITIGATION THROUGH TRIAL 1 (M. Berman et al., eds., 2011). ("MANAGING E-DISCOVERY").

8. Borden & Baron, *supra* note 1 at 1, 27 (2014).

9. "Big Data" is defined by its volume, velocity, and complexity. *Id.* at 1, 15.

10. The inaccuracies of manual review have been well documented. Paul & Baron, *supra* note 4.

> still amount to $20 million for a first-pass review by 100 junior or contract attorneys over the course of 28 weeks, prior to privilege review. . . . Recent case law underscores that this isn't an unrealistic scenario—it is rather all too common, and increasingly so.[11]

As such, "[a]utomated methods of search" are the "wave of the future."[12]

The common law system, however, focused on precedent and stare decisis, has often resisted change,[13] and the move from the historical, exclusive reliance on keywords and manual, linear review has been no exception. Nevertheless, the revolution in information technology has compelled change.[14] One such change has been the emerging acceptance of the use of TAR in civil litigation. Although it is clear that "there is no single, 'fail safe' search or search methodology that guarantees that all or even most relevant documents will be found,"[15] courts have recognized the need to deploy new search methodologies in certain circumstances, in order to secure the just, speedy, and inexpensive resolution of civil lawsuits.[16] This chapter describes that evolution. The starting point is the purpose, role, advantages, and costs of civil discovery. It is axiomatic that "[i]n order to fulfill discovery's

---

11. Jason R. Baron & Michael Berman, *Designing a 'Reasonable' E-Discovery Search*, Managing E-Discovery 481, citing G. Paul & J. Baron, *Information Inflation: Can the Legal System Adapt?*, 13 Rich J.L. & Tech. 10, 20 (2007).

12. *Id.* at 482.

13. Hon. John M. Facciola, *A History of Electronic Discovery*, in Managing E-Discovery 13–14 ("In any society, and particularly one whose legal system is predicated on the common law and its emphasis on following precedent, change is a slow process, following the model that there should be no change unless change is necessary.").

14. *Id.* at 14.

15. Baron & Berman, *supra* note 11, at 479–80.

16. Fed. R. Civ. P. 1. It has been suggested that "[t]he most important rule of all is the last sentence of FRCP 1, which provides that the Federal Rules of Civil Procedure 'shall be construed to secure the just, speedy, and inexpensive determination of every action." M. Mazza et al., *In Pursuit of FRCP 1: Creative Approaches to Cutting and Shifting the Costs of Discovery of Electronically Stored Information*, 13 Rich J.L. & Tech. 1, 5 (2007) (citation omitted). Rule 1 was amended, effective Dec. 1, 2015, to state in pertinent part, that the Rules "should be construed, administered, and employed by the court and the parties to secure the just, speedy, and inexpensive determination of every action and proceeding."

purposes of providing both parties with 'information essential to the proper litigation of all relevant facts, to eliminate surprise, and to promote settlement,' the discovery rules mandate a liberality in the scope of discoverable material."[17] Thus:

> The production of a category of documents, or even at times a single document, can add significantly to the burden on all parties to evaluate the documents and to undertake additional discovery as is necessary to meet the issues disclosed in the newly produced documents. Because of the American discovery process, all parties are assumed to be litigating on a level playing field and to be aware of each other's evidence. They can husband and allocate their resources in light of that understanding. With that common understanding, the parties can evaluate the relative strength and weaknesses of their positions, litigate summary judgment practice, and prepare for trial.[18]

On February 24, 2012, in *Da Silva Moore v. Publicis Groupe*,[19] the first published opinion to endorse TAR, Magistrate Judge Andrew J. Peck held that "computer-assisted review is an acceptable way to search for relevant ESI in appropriate cases."[20] Judge Peck described TAR as:

---

17. St. Paul Reinsurance Co. v. Commercial Fin. Corp., 198 F.R.D. 508, 511 (N.D. Iowa 2000), citing *inter alia*, Seattle Times Co. v. Rhinehart, 467 U.S. 20, 34, 104 S. Ct. 2199 (1984) ("Liberal discovery is provided for the sole purpose of assisting in the preparation and trial, or the settlement, of litigated disputes.") and Oppenheimer Fund, Inc. v. Sanders, 437 U.S. 340, 351, 98 S. Ct. 2380 (1978).

18. Fed. Hous. Fin. Agency v. HSBC N. Am. Holdings Inc., No. 11 CIV. 6189 DLC, 2014 WL 584300, at *2 (S.D.N.Y. Feb. 14, 2014).

19. 287 F.R.D. 182, 182 (S.D.N.Y. 2012), *adopted sub nom.* Da Silva Moore v. Publicis Groupe SA, No. 11-CIV-1279-ALC-AJP, 2012 WL 1446534 (S.D.N.Y. Apr. 26, 2012) ("This judicial opinion now recognizes that computer-assisted review is an acceptable way to search for relevant ESI in appropriate cases.").

20. Rio Tinto PLC v. Vale S.A., No. 14-Civ.3042(RMB), 2015 WL 872294, at *1 (S.D.N.Y. Mar. 2, 2015) (footnote omitted). The year 2012 has been called a watershed year for predictive analytics. Borden & Baron, *supra* note 1, at 1, 1, 5, n.9 (2014), citing a number of earlier decisions discussing search methodology and touching on advanced techniques. *See* Victor Stanley v. Creative Pipe, 250 F.R.D. 251, 256–7 (D. Md. 2008) (subsequent history omitted); *see also* United States v. O'Keefe, 537 F. Supp. 2d 14, 23–24 (D.D.C. 2008); William A. Gross Const. Ass'n v Am. Mfrs.

> tools (different vendors use different names) that use sophisticated algorithms to enable the computer to determine relevance, based on interaction with (i.e., training by) a human reviewer.
>
> Unlike manual review, where the review is done by the most junior staff, computer-assisted coding involves a senior partner (or [small] team) who review and code a "seed set" of documents. The computer identifies properties of those documents that it uses to code other documents. As the senior reviewer continues to code more sample documents, the computer predicts the reviewer's coding. (Or, the computer codes some documents and asks the senior reviewer for feedback.)
>
> When the system's predictions and the reviewer's coding sufficiently coincide, the system has learned enough to make confident predictions for the remaining documents. Typically, the senior lawyer (or team) needs to review only a few thousand documents to train the computer.
>
> Some systems produce a simple yes/no as to relevance, while others give a relevance score (say, on a 0 to 100 basis) that counsel can use to prioritize review.[21]

In *Da Silva Moore*, plaintiffs filed suit against Publicis Groupe, for alleged gender discrimination.[22] A discovery dispute arose over the production of ESI. The defendant had identified more than three million documents from agreed-upon custodians and proposed using a predictive coding tool to cull down the volume of ESI.[23] Although the plaintiffs objected to the defendant's offer to produce the top 40,000 responsive documents, the parties ultimately agreed to a methodology. The methodology laid out several steps, which began by developing a

---

Mut. Ins. Co., 256 F.R.D. 134, 135 (S.D.N.Y. 2009); Equity Analytics, LLC v. Lundin, 248 F.R.D. 331, 333 (D.D.C. 2008); *In re Seroquel Prod. Liab. Litig.*, 244 F.R.D. 650, 663 (M.D. Fla. 2007). *See generally* Baron, *supra* note 4 at 9, ¶ 11 n.38.

21. *Da Silva Moore*, 287 F.R.D. at 183–84.
22. *Id.* at 183–85.
23. *Id.* at 184–85.

seed set to train the predictive coding tool based on a sample of 2,399 documents reviewed for relevance. Statistically, that number would provide a 95 percent confidence level, +/– 2 percent.[24] The defendant would then code certain documents through "judgment sampling" and keyword searches with Boolean connectors.[25] After the seed set was developed, the predictive coding software would then go through at least seven iterative rounds of training to improve the tool's results, reviewing at least 500 documents in each round.[26] After the seventh round, the defendant would then review a random sample of the documents that had been coded non-relevant as a cross-check to ensure that no relevant documents had been included.[27] The court accepted the defendant's proposed methodology with the caveat that if after the seventh round the results were not stabilized, the defendant would have to keep performing additional iterative rounds until the results were stabilized.[28]

Judge Peck concluded that TAR can be an appropriate tool for the initial stages of a document review where a portion or all of the following considerations are present: the parties have agreed to use the technology; the anticipated discovery involves a vast amount of ESI; use of the technology is cost effective compared to the available alternatives; the use of the technology aids the parties in achieving the goals of proportionality under Rule 26(b)(2)(C); and, there is transparency between the parties in the process proposed.[29] After *Da Silva Moore*, the use of TAR continued to gain acceptance in several jurisdictions as a method to increase efficiency and effectiveness in complex cases involving large quantities of ESI.[30]

---

24. *Id.* at 186.

25. *Id.* at 186–87. Defendant agreed to allow plaintiffs to review all 2,399 documents for coding new issue tags to incorporate into the system. *Id.* at 186.

26. *Id.* at 187.

27. *Id.*

28. *Id.*

29. *See id.* at 192.

30. *See* Nat'l Day Laborer Org. Network v. U.S. Immigration and Customs Enforcement Agency, 877 F. Supp. 2d 87, 109–10 (S.D.N.Y. 2012) (suggesting that the use of TAR in discovery is among the "emerging best practices" for discovery involving large amounts of ESI). In some instances, courts have upheld attorneys' fees in cases involving predictive coding. *See, e.g.*, Arnett v. Bank of Am., N.A., No. 3:11-CV-1372-SI, 2014 WL 4672458, at *9–10 (D. Or. Sept. 18, 2014) (approving

In 2012 following *Da Silva Moore*, three opinions discussing TAR were issued. The first, *In re Actos (Pioglitazone) Products Liability Litigation*,[31] detailed an extensive protocol for the production of ESI. Judge Rebecca F. Doherty set forth a detailed order of the parties' agreement for production and specified that the review would be performed under a protective order and possible clawback agreements.[32] The parties agreed to "explore the use of advanced analytics as a technique to ensure appropriate responses to discovery requests" and the "[d]efendants retain[ed] the right to review documents after predictive coding but prior to production for relevance, confidentiality, and privilege."[33] Judge Doherty's Order set forth a notable "proof of concept" methodology which allowed the parties to apply the predictive coding tool to a sample population, and then meet and confer before moving forward with the entire ESI pool.[34]

Shortly after *In re Actos*, Magistrate Judge Nan R. Nolan issued *Kleen Products LLC v. Packaging Corp. of America.*[35] *Kleen Products*

---

fees for a class action where defendants "produced more than 1.1 million documents comprising more than 4 million pages [and] Class Counsel coordinated document storage and review efforts, using search terms, predictive coding, and manual review methods" in addition to taking depositions of eighteen witnesses); Gabriel Technologies Corp. v. Qualcomm Inc., No. 08CV1992 AJB MDD, 2013 WL 410103, at *10 (S.D. Cal. Feb. 1, 2013), *appeal dismissed* (Aug. 20, 2013), *aff'd*, 560 F. App'x 966 (Fed. Cir. 2014) (awarding almost $3 million in fees for the use of TAR because it "seemingly reduced the overall fees and attorney hours required by performing electronic document review at the outset").

31. MDL No. 6:11-md-2299, 2012 WL 7861249, at *3-5 (W.D. La. July 27, 2012).

32. *Id.*

33. *Id.* at *3.

34. *Id.* at *3–5.

35. No. 10 C 5711, 2012 WL 4498465 (N.D. Ill. Sept. 28, 2012); *see also* Dynamo Holdings Limited Partnership v. Comm'r of Internal Revenue, Nos. 2685–11, 8393–12, 143 T.C. 183, 184–85 (Sept. 17, 2014) (rejecting argument that predictive coding was an "unproven technology" and permitting its use over objection to screen for privileged and other confidential information). The *Dynamo* court explained:

> We find a potential happy medium in petitioners' proposed use of predictive coding. Predictive coding is an expedited and efficient form of computer-assisted review that allows parties in litigation to avoid the time and costs associated with the traditional, manual review of large volumes of documents. Through the coding of a relatively small sample of documents, computers can predict the relevance of documents to a discovery request and then identify which documents are and are

resulted from the consolidation of several class actions alleging violations of the Sherman Act.[36] The parties began disputing a discovery protocol, which resulted in meet and confer discussions and a stipulated ESI production order.[37] The parties were not able to resolve their dispute over ESI search methods, with the plaintiffs criticizing the defendants' use of Boolean search methodology for identifying responsive documents.[38] Plaintiffs requested "that Defendants use 'content-based advanced analytics (CBAA) technology analytics to conduct natural language, subject matter searches across corporate departments or corporate functions, using content-based search technology rather than keywords.'"[39] The parties engaged in multiple meet and confer discussions, and Judge Nolan emphasized the importance of Federal Rule of Civil Procedure 26(b)(2)(C) and proportionality in the scope of discovery, balancing costs against the value of

---

> not responsive. The parties (typically through their counsel or experts) select a sample of documents from the universe of those documents to be searched by using search criteria that may, for example, consist of keywords, dates, custodians, and document types, and the selected documents become the primary data used to cause the predictive coding software to recognize patterns of relevance in the universe of documents under review. The software distinguishes what is relevant, and each iteration produces a smaller relevant subset and a larger set of irrelevant documents that can be used to verify the integrity of the results. Through the use of predictive coding, a party responding to discovery is left with a smaller set of documents to review for privileged information, resulting in a savings both in time and in expense. The party responding to the discovery request also is able to give the other party a log detailing the records that were withheld and the reasons they were withheld.

Id. at 190. The tax court credited expert testimony that "estimated that 200,000 to 400,000 documents would be subject to review under petitioners' approach at a cost of $80,000 to $85,000, while 3.5 million to 7 million documents would be subject to review under respondent's approach at a cost of $500,000 to $550,000." *Id.* at 194. The *Dynamo* court wrote that, if the recipient believed that the ultimate response obtained after predictive review was incomplete, "he can file another motion to compel at that time." *Id.*

36. Kleen Products LLC v. Packaging Corp. of America, No. 10 C 5711, 2012 WL 4498465, *1 (N.D. Ill. Sept. 28, 2012) *objections overruled*, No. 10 C 5711, 2013 WL 120240 (N.D. Ill. Jan. 9, 2013).

37. *Id.* at *3.

38. *Id.* at *4.

39. *Id.*

the requested information.[40] Ultimately, the plaintiffs withdrew their demand for TAR regarding the previously produced documents and the parties agreed to meet and confer regarding future requests.[41]

In *Global Aerospace Inc. v. Landow Aviation, L.P.*,[42] the first state court case to address TAR, the court allowed the defendants to proceed with the use of predictive coding over the objection of the plaintiffs.[43] The defendants argued that the use of predictive coding was reasonable due to the large size (250 gigabytes, expected to be more than two million documents) of reviewable ESI and estimated that "[a]t average cost and rates of review and effectiveness, linear first-pass review would take 20,000 [reviewer] hours, cost two million dollars, and locate only sixty percent of the potentially relevant documents."[44]

---

40. *Id.* at *7–9, *13. Judge Nolan explained:

> However, "[a]ll discovery, even if otherwise permitted by the Federal Rules of Civil Procedure because it is likely to yield relevant evidence, is subject to the court's obligation to balance its utility against its cost." *U.S. ex rel. McBride v. Halliburton Co.*, 272 F.R.D. 235, 240 (D.D.C.2011) (Facciola, M.J.); *see* Fed. R. Civ. P. 26(b)(2)(C). More specifically, Rule 26(b)(2)(C) requires the court to consider whether "(1) the discovery sought is unreasonably cumulative or duplicative, or obtainable from a cheaper and more convenient source; (2) the party seeking the discovery has had ample opportunity to obtain the sought information by earlier discovery; or (3) the burden of the discovery outweighs its utility." *McBride*, 272 F.R.D. at 240–41; *see Willnerd v. Sybase, Inc.*, No. 09 C 500, 2010 WL 4736295, at *3 (D. Idaho Nov. 16, 2010) ("In employing the proportionality standard of Rule 26(b)(2)(C) . . ., the Court balances [the requesting party's] interest in the documents requested, against the not-inconsequential burden of searching for and producing documents."). The third factor requires the court to consider (a) the needs of the case; (b) the amount in controversy; (c) the parties' resources; (d) the importance of the issues at stake in the action; and (e) the importance of the discovery in resolving the issues. Fed. R. Civ. P. 26(b)(2)(C)(iii). Nevertheless, "[t]he party opposing a motion to compel carries a 'heavy' burden of persuasion." *U.S. v. AT & T Inc.*, No. 11–1560, 2011 WL 5347178, at *5 (D.D.C. Nov. 6, 2011).

Kleen Products, 2012 WL 4498465 at *13.

41. *Id.* at 20.

42. Global Aerospace Inc. v. Landow Aviation, L.P., No. 61040, 2012 WL 1431215 (Va. Cir. Ct. Loudoun County Apr. 23, 2012).

43. *Id.*

44. Global Aerospace Inc. v. Landow Aviation, L.P., No. 61040, Defendants' Memorandum in Support of Motion for Protective Order Approving the Use of

The defendants argued that manual review was cost prohibitive and keyword searching was less effective than predictive coding.[45] Further, the defendants detailed the proposed predictive coding methodology and argued that predictive coding was the best method to achieve the goals of proportionality.[46]

The court took a different approach in *In re Biomet M2A Magnum Hip Implant Prods. Liab. Litg.*,[47] and refused to force the producing party to use TAR. Judge Robert L. Miller, Jr. framed the issue that it was not "whether predictive coding is a better way of doing things than keyword searching prior to predictive coding . . . [but] whether Biomet's procedure satisfies its discovery obligations and, if so, whether it must also do what the Steering Committee seeks."[48] Judge Miller noted that Biomet had produced 2.5 million documents using a combination of keyword culling and de-duplicating, from the original 19.5 million documents in Biomet's database.[49] Biomet then used predictive coding to identify relevant documents from the 2.5 million.[50] The plaintiffs objected to the original use of keyword searches to cull the database and instead wanted predictive coding employed on the entire 19.5 million-document population.[51] Judge Miller determined that:

> What Biomet has done complies fully with the requirements of Federal Rules of Civil Procedure 26(b) and 34(b)(2). I don't see anything inconsistent with the Seventh Circuit Principles Relating to the Discovery of Electronically Stored Information. Principle 1.02 requires cooperation, but I don't read it as requiring counsel from both sides to sit in adjoining seats while rummaging through millions of files that haven't been reviewed for confidentiality or privilege.[52]

Predictive Coding, 2012 WL 1419842 (Va. Cir. Ct. Loudoun County Apr. 9, 2012).

45. *Id.*

46. *Id.*

47. No. 3:12-MD-2391, 2013 WL 1729682 (N.D. Ind. Apr. 18, 2013).

48. *Id.* at *2.

49. *Id.* at *1.

50. *Id.*

51. *Id.* at *2.

52. *Id.*

Despite the reluctance of many courts to order the use of predictive coding over a party's objection, in 2012, the Delaware Court of Chancery ordered the parties to use TAR sua sponte.[53] In its summary judgment order, the Delaware court wrote that "[t]he parties shall confer regarding a case schedule. Absent a modification of this order for good cause shown, the parties shall (i) retain a single discovery vendor to be used by both sides, and (ii) conduct document review with the assistance of predictive coding. If the parties cannot agree on a single discovery vendor with expertise in predictive coding, the parties shall each submit up to two vendor candidates to the Court."[54]

By 2014, most courts presented with the issue generally accepted the use of TAR in circumstances where the parties had agreed to proceed with its use.[55] In *Deutsche Bank National Trust*, for example, the plaintiff sought to compel discovery from the defendant regarding mortgage loans in the trust at issue.[56] The Illinois Circuit Court limited the scope of discovery to the roughly 3,000 mortgage loans in the trust rather than allowing discovery on all residential mortgage loans originated or underwritten by the defendant during the relevant period.[57] The court determined that "the burden of producing

53. *See* EORHB, Inc. v. HOA Holdings, LLC, Civ. No. 7409-VCL, 2012 WL 4896670, at *1 (Del. Ch. Oct. 15, 2012).

54. *Id.*

55. *See* Deutsche Bank Nat. Trust Co. v. Decision One Mortg. Co., LLC, No. 2013L005823, 2014 WL 764707 at *1 (Ill. Cir. Ct. Jan. 28, 2014); *cf. In re Bridgepoint Educ.*, Civ. No. 12-cv-1737-JM, 2014 WL 3867495 (S.D. Cal. Aug. 6, 2014) (declining to order predictive coding to be used on documents that had already been screened). A discovery order issued by the Honorable Paul W. Grimm in Boardley v. Household Finance Corp. III, Case 8:12-cv-03009 PWG, Doc. 27-1 (11/27/2013), is illustrative. It states: "Parties requesting ESI discovery and parties responding to such requests are expected to cooperate in the development of search methodology and criteria to achieve proportionality in ESI discovery, including appropriate use of computer-assisted search methodology, such as Technology Assisted Review, which employs advanced analytical software applications that can screen for relevant, privileged, or protected information in ways that are more accurate than manual review and involve far less expense." The order also states: "The parties also should discuss whether to use computer-assisted search methodology to facilitate pre-production review of ESI to identify information that is beyond the scope of discovery because it is attorney–client privileged or work product protected."

56. *See* Deutsche Bank Nat. Trust Co., 2014 WL 764707 at *1.

57. *Id.*

the requested discovery, when compared with the minimal probative value, favors denying [the plaintiff's] requests."[58] It noted that "the parties are encouraged to satisfy their discovery obligations in a manner and method that is agreeable, efficient and effective. If the parties agree that predictive coding would be appropriate in this case, they are encouraged to employ that tool."[59]

In some instances, courts have permitted the use of TAR over the objection of an opposing party.[60] For example, the discovery dispute in *Fed. Hous. Fin. Agency v. HSBC N. Am. Holdings Inc.*, arose out of a coordination of 17 actions filed by the plaintiff, Federal Housing Finance Agency (FHFA), as conservator of the Federal National Mortgage Association (Fannie Mae) and the Federal Home Loan Mortgage Corporation (Freddie Mac) against several financial institutions from whom Fannie Mae and Freddie Mac purchased residential mortgage-backed securities between 2005 and 2007.[61] The 17 actions were assigned to a single judge, and the court temporarily stayed discovery in all actions during the pendency of a motion to dismiss in the first-filed case.[62] After the stay was lifted, the parties reached an agreement on a substantial portion of the coordinated discovery protocols.[63] In total, the defendant produced 1.54 million documents from 113 custodians.[64] Nonetheless, the parties continued to dispute the appropriate scope of discovery and sought resolution from the court.[65] In discussing the court's duty to "weigh the likely benefit of the requested discovery against its anticipated burden, and limit the scope of discovery, and the burden of litigation, accordingly," Judge

58. *Id.*

59. *Id.*

60. *See, e.g.*, Fed. Hous. Fin. Agency v. HSBC N. Am. Holdings Inc., No. 11 CIV. 6189 DLC, 2014 WL 584300, at *3 (S.D.N.Y. Feb. 14, 2014).

61. Fed. Hous. Fin. Agency v. UBS Americas Inc., No. 11 CIV. 5201 DLC, 2013 WL 3284118, at *1 (S.D.N.Y. June 28, 2013) *reconsideration denied sub nom.* Fed. Hous. Fin. Agency v. JPMorgan Chase & Co., No. 11 CIV. 6188 DLC, 2013 WL 5354212 (S.D.N.Y. Sept. 25, 2013).

62. *Id.*

63. *Id.*

64. *Id.* at *10.

65. *Id.* at *9–10.

Denise Cote supported the recommendations of The Sedona Conference Commentary on Proportionality in Electronic Discovery.[66]

In one particular instance, the defendants argued that the plaintiff's document production was incomplete and sought to introduce documents that they had obtained through discovery in a separate but related action.[67] Judge Cote rejected the defendants' argument and noted that the defendants had been permitted, over the plaintiffs' objections, to use predictive coding for the defendants' initial document production.[68] Judge Cote concluded that to allow the defendants to challenge the plaintiffs' production "would risk re-opening the entirety of the document production in [the] case," and "[a]ll that can be legitimately expected is a good faith, diligent commitment to produce all responsive documents uncovered when following the protocols to which the parties have agreed, or which a court has ordered."[69]

In 2014, several opinions commented on the use of predictive coding as a successful tool in complex litigation to efficiently produce relevant ESI. Judge Sarah N. Singleton commented that counsel's use of "various advanced machine learning tools such as predictive coding, concept grouping, near-duplication detection and e-mail threading . . . which are often referred to as technology assisted review, or TAR, enabled the reviewers on the document analysis teams to work more efficiently with the documents and identify potentially relevant information with greater accuracy than standard linear review."[70]

The use of technology-assisted review has also been discussed as a method to expedite the production of documents when used in conjunction with a Rule 502(d) or clawback order. In *Good v. Am. Water Works Co.*,[71] the plaintiffs and defendants disagreed regarding the method by which they would address the inadvertent disclosure of attorney–client

66. *Id.* at *12 (*citing* The Sedona Conference Commentary on Proportionality in Electronic Discovery, 11 Sedona Conf. J. 289, 300 (2010)).

67. Fed. Hous. Fin. Agency v. HSBC N. Am. Holdings Inc., No. 11 CIV. 6189 DLC, 2014 WL 584300, at *1–3 (S.D.N.Y. Feb. 14, 2014).

68. *Id.* at *3.

69. *Id.* at *2.

70. N.M. State Inv. Council v. Bland, No. D-101-CV-2011-01534, 2014 WL 772860, at *6 (N.M. Dist. Feb. 12, 2014) (noting the efficiency of TAR to review more than two million documents).

71. No. 2:14-01374, 2014 WL 5486827 (S.D.W. Va. Oct. 29, 2014).

and work–product documents.[72] The defendants proposed that the court enter a Rule 502(d) order to "*encourage* the incorporation and employment of time-saving computer-assisted privilege review," to identify potentially privileged documents, which could then be manually reviewed and logged by an attorney as appropriate.[73] The plaintiffs argued that in order to expedite the discovery process, the court should enter a Rule 502(d) order that privilege review should be limited to computer assisted review only and not allow for a subsequent manual review because, according to the plaintiffs, the Rule 502(d) order would eliminate the need for any review prior to production because privileged documents were subject to clawback protection.[74] The court entered the defendants' proposed Rule 502(d) order allowing for both computer-assisted and manual review "with the expectation that the defendants will marshal the resources necessary to assure that the delay occasioned by manual review of portions of designated categories will uniformly be minimized so that disclosure of the entirety of even the most sensitive categories is accomplished quickly."[75] The court left open the possibility that in the event the defendants' approach resulted in undue delay, the plaintiffs could move to have their approach then imposed for the remainder of discovery.[76]

Additionally, predictive coding has been discussed in respect to potential cost benefits when used in modern large-scale document production. In *F.D.I.C. v. Bowden*, Magistrate Judge George R. Smith encouraged, *inter alia*, the use of predictive coding, in a complex discovery dispute focused around the apportionment of costs where the plaintiffs had "already spent $614,000 to digitally scan about 2.01 terabytes of data or 153.6 million pages," and the parties were contemplating significant additional discovery but could not agree on a Joint ESI Protocol.[77] Judge Smith noted that "the case law recognizes that manual search costs can be devastating, so reasonable technological

72. *Id.* at *3.

73. *Id.*

74. *Id.*

75. *Id.* at *3.

76. *Id.*

77. F.D.I.C. v. Bowden, No. CV413-245, 2014 WL 2548137, at *1, 13 (S.D. Ga. June 6, 2014) (encouraging parties to use TAR in a case involving more than 153 million pages of data).

search and production efforts should first be attempted—discovery law for ESI has evolved to require that much."[78] In large-scale ESI cases, cost-sharing or cost-shifting can be appropriate to "strike a balance between allowing the requesting party to take full advantage of the technologies available to it and protecting the producing party from having to pay to leave no stone unturned. Resting all of the costs of electronic discovery on the producing party may create a perverse incentive on the part of the requesting party to dispense with reason and restraint and unleash every new technology under the sun to try and find information that supports the requesting party's claims."[79] Judge Smith, quoting *Thompson v. U.S. Dept. of Housing and Urban Development*,[80] noted that courts have several methods available to ensure proportionality in cost burdens[81] between the parties including: (i) "shift the cost, in whole or in part, of burdensome and expensive Rule 34 discovery to the requesting party"; (ii) "limit the number of hours required by the producing party to search for electronic records"; (iii) "restrict the sources that must be checked"; or (iv) "delay the production of electronic records in response to a Rule 34 request until after the deposition of information and technology personnel of the producing party, who can testify in detail as to the systems in place, as well as to the storage and retention of electronic records, enabling more focused and less costly discovery."[82]

Judge Smith stressed the importance of the parties' duty to cooperate and attempt to agree to an ESI-protocol, and also ordered that in the event of a disagreement regarding discovery, the parties should

---

78. *Id.* at *7.

79. *Id.* at *6 (quoting Covad Communications Co. v. Revonet, Inc., 258 F.R.D. 5, 16 (D.D.C. 2009).

80. 219 F.R.D. 93 (D. Md. 2003).

81. Generally, "the responding party bears the cost of complying with (hence, organizing and physically turning over documents for) each document request. That includes the cost of reviewing and gathering the documents, then making them available for inspection at the time and place requested. . . . 'Conversely, the burden generally is on the requesting party to pay the cost of copying the documents. However, the court may apportion the costs of production depending on the circumstances.'" F.D.I.C. v. Bowden, 2014 WL 2548137, at *10 (citing Oppenheimer Fund, Inc. v. Sanders, 437 U.S. 340, 358, 98 S. Ct. 2380 (1978); quoting S. Gensler, 1 Federal Rules of Civil Procedure, Rules and Commentary Rule 34, (Mar. 2014)).

82. *Id.* at *6 (quoting Thompson v. U.S. Dept. of Housing and Urban Development, 219 F.R.D. 93, 99 (D. Md. 2003)).

meet and confer before bringing the dispute to the court.[83] "To that end, the parties shall consider the use of predictive coding" and "consider the blend of ESI predictive coding and pretrial statements signed by counsel."[84]

Although the use of technology-assisted review is generally considered as a cost-efficient discovery tool, courts may reject a party's request to impose the use of TAR if it unduly burdens the other party. In *In re Bridgepoint Education*, the plaintiffs moved to compel the defendants to produce documents that the defendants claimed were beyond the agreed upon relevant time period of discovery.[85] The defendants argued that, *inter alia*, "the substantial burden and expense of reviewing documents from this additional period outweighs the limited probative value of any responsive documents."[86] The defendants estimated that the increase in production time frame by an additional nineteen months would also increase their review costs by $390,000, or twenty-six percent.[87] The plaintiffs argued that the use of predictive coding instead of manual review would only impose approximately $11,279 in additional expenses and that the cost of manual review for relevance should not be considered.[88] The defendants countered that predictive coding software did not negate the need for manual review and that "attorney review is still required to ensure that the documents produced are both relevant and not privileged."[89] The court agreed with the defendants that the additional production was unduly burdensome and denied the plaintiffs' request for documents from the additional time period.[90]

The plaintiffs also argued that the documents already produced by the defendants should be run through predictive coding software because the defendants had limited their document production by

---

83. *Id.* at *12–13.

84. *Id.* at *13 (citing *In re* Domestic Drywall Antitrust Litigation, 2014 WL 1909260 at *4 (E.D. Pa. May 12, 2014).

85. *In re* Bridgepoint Education Inc., No. 12cv1737 JM, 2014 WL 3867495, at *2 (S.D. Cal. Aug. 6, 2014).

86. *Id.*

87. *Id.*

88. *Id.*

89. *Id.* at *3.

90. *Id.*

running a list of search terms through their documents before the plaintiffs had propounded their discovery requests.[91] The defendants argued that they should not have to now run documents through predictive coding that had already been screened by other methods, but agreed to run additional search terms against those documents.[92] The court approved the defendants' use of search terms and denied the plaintiffs' request to require the use of predictive coding.[93]

Notably, an important factor in the successful use of technology-assisted review for complex discovery matters continues to be cooperation between the parties. In *Progressive Casualty Insurance Co. v. Delaney*, Magistrate Judge Peggy A. Leen addressed the parties' dispute over compelling the production of documents.[94] *Progressive Casualty Ins. Co. v. Delaney* was one of nine declaratory relief actions filed by Progressive in various federal district courts seeking a declaration that its insurance policy issued to those failed banks did not provide coverage for lawsuits by the FDIC receiver against the directors, officers, and employees of the failed banks.[95] During the discovery phase of the litigation, the parties submitted a Joint Proposed ESI Protocol, approved by the court, which resulted in the plaintiff's collection of more than 1.8 million documents.[96] At a conference of the parties, the parties agreed to an ESI Protocol that included the use of certain search terms for review and production of ESI, and contained provisions to address inadvertent disclosure and clawback.[97] The use of search terms reduced the 1.8 million documents to 565,000 potentially responsive documents.[98] Plaintiff's counsel then began manual review of the 565,000 documents, but due to the expense and time required, the plaintiff began exploring alternative methods for a more effective and efficient method of review.[99] Without waiting for agreement by opposing counsel or seeking leave to amend the ESI Order

91. *Id.* at *4.

92. *Id.*

93. *Id.*

94. Progressive Casualty Insurance Co. v. Delaney, No. 2:11-cv-00678, 2014 WL 3563467, at *1 (D. Nev. July 18, 2014).

95. *Id.*

96. *Id.*

97. *Id.* at *6.

98. *Id.* at *2.

99. *Id.*

from the court, the plaintiff unilaterally began using predictive coding to further cull the document population.[100]

The plaintiff then submitted an amended ESI Protocol incorporating its use of predictive coding in place of manual review of the 565,000 documents, which the defendant opposed.[101] The defendant argued that the plaintiff had already manually reviewed 125,000 of the 565,000 documents, but rather than producing those documents on a rolling basis as the parties had agreed, the plaintiff abandoned manual review to employ predictive coding on the remainder of the documents, and according to the defendant, the plaintiff's methods also deviated from the best practices recommended by Equivio for its software system that had been used by the plaintiff.[102] Based on both the deviation from the agreed protocol and the software's best practices, the defendant argued that the plaintiff should produce all 565,000 documents that had been identified using the agreed upon search terms, subject to a clawback agreement for privileged documents.[103]

The court ordered both parties to have their ESI experts and representatives meet-and-confer in an attempt to resolve the outstanding ESI issues, but ultimately the parties were unable to agree.[104] Judge Leen emphasized that "courts which have allowed predictive coding . . . have emphasized the need for cooperation and transparency in adopting predictive coding processes and methods."[105] Here, however, the plaintiff had acted unilaterally. In discussing the parties' arguments, Judge Leen noted that "[p]redictive coding has emerged as a far more accurate means of producing responsive ESI in discovery. Studies show it is far more accurate than human review or keyword searches which have their own limitations."[106] However, Judge Leen cautioned,

---

100. *Id.*

101. *Id.* at *3–4.

102. *Id.* at *5.

103. *Id.*

104. *Id.*

105. *Id.* at *4.

106. *Id.* at *8 (citing, *inter alia*, Maura R. Grossman & Gordon V. Cormack, *Technology-Assisted Review in E-Discovery Can be More Effective and More Efficient Than Exhaustive Manual Review*, XVII RICH. J.L. & TECH. 11 (2011); Nicholas M. Pace & Laura Zakaras, *Where the Money Goes: Understanding Litigant Expenditures for Producing Electric Discovery* 55–8 RAND INST. FOR CIVIL JUSTICE (2012), http://www.rand.org/pubs/monographs/MG1208.html.) The court also cited the 2007

"the quality of its product depends on the quality of the information used to 'train' the software."[107]

On the facts presented, Judge Leen wrote that:

> Had the parties worked with their e-discovery consultants and agreed at the onset of this case to a predictive coding-based ESI protocol, the court would not hesitate to approve a transparent, mutually agreed upon ESI protocol. However, this is not what happened. Progressive agreed to search the universe of documents identified in the stipulated ESI protocol using search terms. Progressive had the option of manually reviewing the "hit" documents for production in discovery as appropriate, subject to proper objections, including privilege objections. Progressive chose the latter and began manually reviewing the ESI using eight contract attorneys. . . . Progressive's proposal would relieve it of the burden of manual review of ESI according to the ESI protocol it stipulated to and allow it to adopt a predictive coding alternative to a small subset of the universe of ESI collected. Its proposal would also give its counsel exclusive responsibility for training the predictive coding software, and it fails to comply with all of the best practices recommended by the Equivio software program. Progressive proposes a "do-over" of its own invention that lacks transparency and cooperation regarding the search methodologies applied.[108]

Judge Leen explained that in cases where the court has approved the use of technology-assisted review for ESI, "the courts have required the producing party to provide the requesting party with full disclosure about the technology used, the process, and the methodology,

---

Sedona Conference "Best Practices Commentary on the Use of Search & Information Retrieval Methods in E-Discovery," which has since been updated. *See* 15 SEDONA CONF. J. 217 (2014).

107. *Id.* at *8 (citing Equivio, *Top Ten Best Practices of Predictive Coding* (2012), www.equivio.com/resources.php?type=product).

108. *Id.* at *9–10.

including the documents to 'train' the computer."[109] Judge Leen granted the defendant's motion to compel, concluding that Progressive had failed to make a showing of the requisite cooperation and transparency needed for its proposed method of predictive coding, and its proposed methods failed to comply with Equivio's best practices.[110]

Recently, in *Rio Tinto*, Judge Peck revisited *Da Silva Moore* and the number of cases addressing technology-assisted review since his 2012 *Da Silva Moore* opinion.[111] Judge Peck held that "it is now black letter law that where the producing party wants to utilize [technology assisted review] for document review, courts will permit it."[112] When evaluating the effectiveness of the technology, Judge Peck stressed that technology-assisted review should not be held "to a higher standard than key words or manual review. Doing so discourages parties from using TAR for fear of spending more in motion practice than the savings from using TAR for review."[113] In *Rio Tinto*, Judge Peck wrote that courts encourage the use of quality assurance testing and collaboration between the parties, as well as manual review for relevance, confidentiality, and privilege after the TAR process but prior to production.[114] Indeed, in *Johnson v. Ford Motor Co.*,[115] the court ordered the parties "to involve their experts and to consider other methods of searching such as predictive coding" as a way for the parties to resolve their disagreements about sufficiency of document production.[116] Nonetheless, questions remain as to the level of transparency that is required between opposing parties regarding the information necessary to prepare for the use of predictive coding.[117] There is no consensus among jurisdictions as to whether sample test sets should be made

109. *Id.* at *10.

110. *Id.* at *10–11.

111. *Rio Tinto*, 2015 WL 872294, at *1.

112. *Id.*

113. *Id.* at *3.

114. *Id.* at *3; *See In re* Actos (Pioglitazone) Products Liability Litigation, MDL No. 6:11-md-2299, 2012 WL 7861249, at *3–5 (W.D. La. July 27, 2012).

115. Johnson v. Ford Motor Co., No. 3:13-cv-06529, 2015 WL 4137707 (S.D. W.Va. July 8, 2015) objections sustained in part and overruled in part by Johnson v. Ford Motor Co., NO. 3:13-6529, 2015 WL 6758234 (S.D. W. Va. Nov. 5, 2015).

116. *Id.* at *11.

117. *Id.* at *2.

accessible to opposing parties, or might be considered protected work product.[118]

Courts, lawyers, and litigants are still "writing the book" on the use of ESI, and rules, guidelines, and case law "cannot fill all of the gaps. . . partly because technology is advancing at a rapid pace."[119] Undoubtedly, there may always be civil lawsuits that are ill suited to TAR; increasingly, however, there are many others where, properly designed and implemented, TAR presents the most optimal and viable approach. The role of the advocate is to differentiate between cases and make the best case on behalf of his or her client for the selected method. Clearly, as Justice Cardozo noted, "[e]very new case is an experiment."[120]

Postscript

Two decisions issued after this chapter was typeset confirm the emerging majority views described in the chapter. In one decision, the court considered and rejected a challenge to the results of predictive coding. In the other, the court held that a party cannot be compelled to use predictive coding over its objection.

In *Dynamo I*,[121] the Tax Court approved the use of predictive coding, but left the door open to later challenge. In *Dynamo II*,[122] the requesting party presented that challenge, asserting that the production was incomplete. The Tax Court commenced its analysis by noting that advancing technology has made traditional document review

---

118. *Cf. Da Silva Moore*, 287 F.D.R. at 184 (noting that parties may need to allow a party challenging production to review the documents that were used to train the computer), with Chapter 9 in this volume, *Safeguarding the Seed Set*. Those supporting disclosure assert that the information gained from the "seed set" may vary with the type of computer-assisted review used. *See, e.g., Rio Tinto*, 2015 WL 872294, at *3 (explaining that when using technology-assisted review methodology with "continuous active learning" rather than "simple passive learning . . . the contents of the seed set is much less significant").

119. Michael Berman, *Postscript*, Managing E-Discovery at 748.

120. *Id.* at 761, quoting Cardozo, *supra* note 2, at 28.

121. *Dynamo I*, described in the chapter, was decided in 2014. Dynamo Holdings Ltd. P'shp. v. Commissioner, 143 T.C. 183 (2014). *Dynamo II* was decided on July 13, 2016. Dynamo Holdings Ltd. P'shp. v. Commissioner, No. 2685-11, 8393-12 (Tax Court July 13, 2016).

122. *Id.*

impracticable.[123] It commended the parties' cooperative efforts and relied in part on their 16 status reports.[124] The court described the predictive coding process in detail and, interestingly, noted that judgmental sampling was not used to select initial seed documents,[125] a methodology criticized elsewhere in this book.[126] At the end of the process, however, the requesting party asserted that out of 1,645 documents that contained selected keywords, 1,353 were not produced. The producing party offered several explanations, such as asserting that many of the withheld documents were not within agreed date parameters for production.

After reviewing several fallacies, the court considered metrics—the recall and precision described in many chapters of this book. First, it noted that faith in human review is a myth: "[I]f two sets of human reviewers review the same set of documents to identify what is responsive, research shows that those reviewers will disagree with each other on more than half of the responsiveness claims."[127] It also noted that keyword searches are often flawed.[128] Second, it considered "the myth of a perfect response."[129] Having determined that both manual and keyword review may be flawed, and, based on a detailed review of the predictive coding protocol applied, the court held that it was "clear" that the producing party had complied with the discovery rules. It was willing to assume that the TAR production was flawed, but held that perfection is not required and flaws do not necessarily lead to relief. In

123. Slip op. at 3 (noting that as a result of "the advent of electronic record keeping, documents no longer number in the mere thousands" so that manual review has become costly, time-consuming, and less effective).

124. *Id.* at 3.

125. *Id.* at 4.

126. See Chapter 11 in this volume.

127. Slip op. at 7–8, quoting N. Pace & L. Zakaras, RAND Corp., *Where the Money Goes: Understanding Litigant Expenditures for Producing Electronic Discovery* (2012), at 58; *accord* J. Tredennick et al., *TAR for Smart People (Catalyst 2016)*, at 27, citing M. Grossman & G. Cormack, *Technology-Assisted Review in E-Discovery Can Be More Effective and More Efficient Than Exhaustive Manual Review*, 17 Rich. J.L. & Tech. 11 (2011), http://jolt.richmond.edu/v17i3.article11.pdf.

128. *Id.* at 8, citing Moore v. Publicis Groupe & MSL Grp., 287 F.R.D. 182, 191 (S.D.N.Y. 2012). Key word searches will implicitly produce documents that are responsive to the word or Boolean phrase searched, but those documents may not be responsive to the discovery request. *Id.*

129. *Id.* at 8.

doing so, it agreed with Judge Peck's conclusion that predictive coding should not be held to a higher standard than keyword or manual review.[130]

Taken together, *Dynamo I* and *Dynamo II* show the benefits of cooperation and judicial management of discovery. Together, they again demonstrate that, with proper protocols, predictive coding is defensible and efficient.

In *Hyles*,[131] Judge Peck resolved an issue left open in *Rio Tinto*.[132] Hyles, a city employee, sued the city for discrimination. She contended that TAR was more efficient and superior to keyword searching, and asked the court to compel the city to use that methodology. The court made clear its belief that "for most cases today, TAR is the best and most efficient search tool."[133] Nevertheless, it declined to order that relief:

> The key issue is whether, at plaintiff Hyles' request, the defendant City (i.e., the responding party) can be forced to use TAR (technology assisted review aka predictive coding) when the City prefers to use keyword searching. The short answer is a decisive "NO."[134]

The court held that it "cannot, and will not, force the City" to use predictive coding.[135] That appears to be the emerging majority rule. Nevertheless, the court indicated that there may come a time when such an order will be possible, but "[w]e are not there yet."[136]

---

130. *Id.* at 9.
131. Hyles v. New York City, 2016 WL 4077114 (S.D.N.Y. 2016).
132. Rio Tinto PLC v. Vale S.A., 306 F.R.D. 125, 127 n.1 (S.D.N.Y. 2015).
133. Hyles, 2016 WL 407714 at *3.
134. *Id.* at *1 (emphasis in original).
135. *Id.* at *4.
136. *Id.*

PRACTITIONER PERSPECTIVES

EDITORS' INTRODUCTION TO CHAPTER 3

Michael D. Berman

Maura R. Grossman and Gordon V. Cormack's chapter, A Tour of Technology-Assisted Review, updates their seminal 2012 law review article, and brings clarity to the diverse tools and inconsistent nomenclature in the e-discovery industry. Beginning with the basics, they explain the differences among search, analysis, and review. Then, they explain the differences among various sophisticated software packages. In a step-by-step process, they take the reader from simple keyword search, through Boolean logic, to relevance ranking, similarity search, and variants of technology-assisted review. At that plateau, they compare and contrast those variants, explaining both the strengths and weaknesses of each based on differences in their protocols. While the chapter is an important overall contribution to the practitioner's use and understanding of TAR, perhaps its greatest value is in placing it in a context that makes it understandable for use in contemporary litigation.

CHAPTER 3

A Tour of Technology-Assisted Review

Maura R. Grossman and Gordon V. Cormack

Introduction

Since the publication of our 2011 article, *Technology-Assisted Review in E-Discovery Can Be More Effective and More Efficient Than Exhaustive Manual Review*, in the Richmond Journal of Law and Technology (JOLT article),[1] the term "technology-assisted review" (TAR)—along with related terms such as "computer-assisted review" (CAR) and "predictive coding" (PC)—has been used extensively in writings, presentations, and legal documents to advance or assail a plethora of tools and methods aimed at decreasing the cost and burden associated with document review in electronic discovery (e-discovery). The conflation of diverse tools and methods under a single label has resulted in confusion in the marketplace, and inapt generalizations regarding the effectiveness (or ineffectiveness) and proper use of such tools and methods. In this chapter, we outline and illustrate—using a running example—the principal distinctions among the various tools and methods that we consider to be variants of TAR, and differentiate them from other tools and methods, such as concept search, clustering, visualization, and social network analysis, which we do not consider to be TAR. While e-discovery tools fall on a continuum in terms of their utility for search, analysis, and review, we describe

1. Maura R. Grossman & Gordon V. Cormack, *Technology-Assisted Review in E-Discovery Can Be More Effective and More Efficient Than Exhaustive Manual Review*, 17 Rich. J.L. & Tech. 11 (2011), http://jolt.richmond.edu/v17i3/article11.pdf.

certain components that, in our opinion, are essential for a tool to be considered "technology-assisted review."

Distinguishing Among Search, Analysis, and Review

Search, analysis, and review are different tasks with different objectives. The objective of search is to find enough documents to satisfy an information need, such as the answer to a question or support for a proposition. The objective of analysis is to gain understanding from available data, so as to support decision-making. The objective of review is to classify all documents in a collection as meeting—or not meeting—certain criteria, such as responsive to a request for production, subject to attorney–client privilege or work–product protection, or available for disposal. Following information retrieval practice, in this chapter, we refer to documents meeting the review criteria as "relevant," and those not meeting the criteria as "nonrelevant," although in the legal domain, this distinction is sometimes referred to as "responsive" and "nonresponsive."

While there is some overlap between the tools and methods used for search and analysis, and those used for review, we apply the term "technology-assisted review" or "TAR" only to tools and methods used specifically for review.

Almost everyone is familiar with Web search engines like Google, Bing, and Yahoo!, and the ease with which they may be used to find a few relevant documents in response to an information need. Search engines, however, are much less amenable to the task of finding all, or nearly all, relevant documents, as required for review.

Analytic tools such as clustering, visualization, and social network analysis may yield insights leading to the discovery of relevant documents, but, like search engines, they are not in and of themselves well-suited to review.

Search, analytic, and review tools are often combined in commercial document review platforms to provide a suite of options to deal with the large collections of data that are commonly encountered in e-discovery in legal and regulatory investigations or proceedings. The components of these offerings are not always susceptible to easy labels because, in reality, tools used for search, analysis, and review can fall on a continuum, and many e-discovery approaches rely on ad-hoc, hybrid methods that move in iterative cycles among search, analysis, and review.

Defining Technology-Assisted Review and Distinguishing Rule-Based from Supervised Machine-Learning Approaches to TAR

Methods used for technology-assisted review may be broadly classified into those employing rule bases and those employing supervised machine learning. A rule base consists of a large set of rules, composed by one or more subject-matter and rules-construction experts, to separate documents meeting the criteria for relevance, from those that do not. These rules may take the form of complex Boolean queries—specifying combinations of words and their order or proximity—that indicate relevance or nonrelevance, exceptions to those rules, exceptions to the exceptions, and so on, until nearly all documents in the collection are correctly classified. Supervised machine learning, on the other hand, infers, from exemplar documents, characteristics that indicate relevance or nonrelevance, and uses the presence or absence of those features to predict the relevance or nonrelevance of other documents.

Our 2011 JOLT article compared the effectiveness of a rule-based TAR method (H5) and a supervised machine-learning TAR method (Waterloo) to that of human review, concluding that both of these TAR methods were able to equal or exceed the effectiveness of human review—as measured by recall, precision, and F_1—with a small fraction of the human review effort. Since its publication, a number of service providers have cited the JOLT article as support for the efficacy of their own tools or methods, under names such as "technology-assisted review," "computer-assisted review," "assisted review," "language-based analytics," and "predictive coding," among others. Many of these approaches, however, bear little resemblance to the two methods studied in our JOLT article.

It is important to note that there is no standards-setting or regulatory body controlling the application of these terms to various tools and methods, and therefore, there is no guarantee that a tool labeled "TAR," or "predictive coding," or "language-based analytics" employs any particular method, or that the method it does employ—whether aptly named or not—is effective for review. Nevertheless, because a common vocabulary is essential to rational discourse, to this end, in 2013, we published a glossary of terms in Federal Courts Law Review (the Glossary),[2] which we will augment in this chapter, to taxonify current methods used for technology-assisted review. (This glossary also appears as the appendix of this book.) The Glossary defines technology-assisted review (TAR) as:

> A process for Prioritizing or Coding a Collection of Documents using a computerized system that harnesses human judgments of one or more Subject Matter Expert(s) on a smaller set of Documents and then extrapolates those judgments to the remaining Document Collection. Some TAR methods use Machine Learning Algorithms to distinguish Relevant from Non-Relevant Documents, based on Training Examples Coded as Relevant or Non-Relevant by the Subject Matter Experts(s), while other TAR methods derive systematic Rules that emulate the expert(s)' decision-making process. TAR processes generally incorporate Statistical Models and/or Sampling techniques to guide the process and to measure overall system effectiveness.

We intended this definition to exclude search and analytic tools per se because they do not extrapolate relevance judgments to the collection. Certainly, one could use a search tool for review, by deeming all nonretrieved documents to be nonrelevant. Similarly, one could use a clustering tool for review by deeming all members of each cluster, as a group, to be either relevant or nonrelevant. However, neither approach has been shown to be effective for review; thus, to label an underlying search engine or clustering method as a "TAR" tool would, in our view, weaken the definition of TAR so as to render it meaningless. We suggest that it would be more fruitful to label methods as "TAR" only if they rank or make affirmative predictions about the relevance or nonrelevance of documents in the collection based on

2. Maura R. Grossman & Gordon V. Cormack, *The Grossman-Cormack Glossary of Technology-Assisted Review*, with Foreword by John M. Facciola, U.S. Magistrate Judge, 7 Fed. Courts. L. Rev. 1, 32 (2013), http://www.fclr.org/articles/html/2010/grossman.pdf.

human judgments that are applied to a subset of the collection. Rule-based and supervised machine-learning methods meet this definition because they generate rules or mathematical models that discriminate between relevant and nonrelevant documents.

The Path from Keyword Search to TAR

When one tries to delineate the precise boundary between what is and is not TAR, it becomes apparent that this distinction is not entirely clear-cut; rather, methods fall on a continuum from those geared more toward search and analysis, to those geared more toward review. Accordingly, it seemed to us that the best way to explain TAR would be to begin with keyword search and to walk through the process of adding additional technological components that start to convert a search method into technology-assisted review. We thought it might also be useful to demonstrate these different components using a common example to illustrate their relative effectiveness, or ineffectiveness, for review.

A Running Example: Fantasy Football

To illustrate the evolution of methods from simple keyword search to TAR, we use as a running example Topic 207 from the TREC 2009 Legal Track, which was reprised in the TREC 2010 Legal Track, and used again, as a practice example, in the TREC 2015 Total Recall Track.[3] Topic 207 requires the identification of,

> [a]ll documents or communications that describe, discuss, refer to, report on, or relate to fantasy football,

3. Bruce Hedin, Stephen Tomlinson, Jason R. Baron, & Douglas W. Oard, *Overview of the TREC* 2009 *Legal Track*, *in* NIST SPECIAL PUBLICATIONS: SP 500-278, THE EIGHTEENTH TEXT RETRIEVAL CONFERENCE (TREC 2009) PROCEEDINGS, 6 (2009), http://trec.nist.gov/pubs/trec18/papers/LEGAL09.OVERVIEW.pdf; Gordon V. Cormack, Maura R. Grossman, Bruce Hedin, & Douglas W. Oard, *Overview of the TREC* 2010 *Legal Track*, *in* NIST SPECIAL PUBLICATION: SP 500-294, THE NINETEENTH TEXT RETRIEVAL CONFERENCE (TREC 2010) PROCEEDINGS 2 (2010), http://trec.nist.gov/pubs/trec19/papers/LEGAL10.OVERVIEW.pdf; Adam Roegiest, Gordon V. Cormack, Maura R. Grossman, & Charles L. A. Clarke, TREC 2015 Total Recall Track, http://trec-total-recall.org. The Text REtrieval Conference (TREC) is an annual workshop sponsored by the National Institute of Standards and Technology (NIST), the purpose of which is to support research in the information retrieval community by providing the infrastructure necessary for large-scale evaluation of text-retrieval methodologies. The Total Recall Track is part of TREC 2015, *see* http://trec.nist.gov.

> gambling on football, and related activities, including but not limited to, football teams, football players, football games, football statistics, and football performance[,]

from a set of documents collected from Enron Corporation by the Federal Energy Regulatory Commission. The particular collections used for TREC 2009 and TREC 2010 are no longer publicly available; for this example, we used the collection supplied to participants with the baseline model implementation (BMI) for the TREC 2015 Total Recall Track.[4] This collection contains 723,386 documents, of which (unbeknownst to our hypothetical searcher) 7,798, or about 1.1 percent, are relevant to Topic 207.

Basic Keywords or Search Terms

To identify documents concerning fantasy football, our hypothetical searcher might simply begin by selecting all documents containing the word "football"—a task that is readily accomplished using the search feature in most document review platforms. Most likely this search would yield a substantial number of documents concerning actual football teams, players, games, and statistics, but it would also be likely to identify documents with metaphorical, humorous, and other uses beyond those specified by Topic 207. In our example, again unbeknownst to our searcher, the term "football" selects 4,319 documents from the corpus, of which 3,480 are relevant, and 839 are not. In other words, a search for "football" has 44.6 percent recall (where "recall" is defined as the fraction of all relevant documents in the collection identified by the search; in this case 3,480/7,798 = 44.6 percent), and 80.6 percent precision (where "precision" is defined as the fraction of the documents identified by the search that are relevant; in this case 3,480/4,319 = 80.6 percent).

Without additional testing or inquiry, our searcher would have no way of knowing what level of recall and precision her search had achieved, and therefore no tool other than her intuition to assess the adequacy of her search.[5] Human intuition concerning the adequacy

---

4. Roegiest et al., *supra* note 3.

5. Blogger Ralph Losey has compared this approach to the child's game of Go Fish. Ralph C. Losey, *Child's Game of "Go Fish" is a Poor Model for*

of keyword search, however, has been shown to be woefully inadequate. In a seminal 1985 study,[6] Blair and Maron asked skilled paralegals, supervised by lawyers, to use search terms to find documents responsive to each of 51 requests. Although the lawyers and paralegals believed they had achieved an adequate result—which they defined to mean having achieved recall of at least 75 percent—they had, in fact, achieved recall of only 20 percent, on average. No more recent study that we are aware of has shown human intuition about search terms to have improved since then.

Control Sets

The first step in the transition from search terms to TAR would involve the addition of a principled mechanism to ensure that a substantial majority of the relevant documents were identified by the process. To this end, many processes rely on statistical sampling to estimate how many relevant documents there are to be found in the collection, how many relevant documents have been identified by a particular search or review strategy, and thus, the recall and precision of that strategy. A common (but not universal) approach is to use a random sample taken at the outset of the process, known as a "control set," to estimate these quantities, and thereafter to guide the process, or to validate its effectiveness.

Each document in the control set is reviewed and coded as relevant or not by a subject-matter expert (SME). The fraction of relevant documents in the control set provides an estimate of the fraction of relevant documents in the collection, with some margin of error. This proportion is referred to as "prevalence."[7] Provided that the control set is independent of the search effort—that is, no information about the search is used in choosing and coding the control set, and no information about the content or coding of the control set is

---

e-Discovery Search, E-DISCOVERY TEAM BLOG (Oct. 4, 2009), http://e-discoveryteam.com/2009/10/04/childs-game-of-go-fish-is-a-poor-model-for-e-discovery-search/.

6. David C. Blair & M.E. Maron, *An Evaluation of Retrieval Effectiveness for a Full-Text Document-Retrieval System*, 28 COMMC'NS ACM 289 (1985).

7. Grossman & Cormack, *supra* note 2, at 26 ("Prevalence: The fraction of Documents in a Population that are Relevant to an Information Need. Also referred to as Richness or Yield.").

used in devising the search strategy—the control set may be used to yield valid estimates of the recall and precision of the search or review process.[8]

For our running example, we chose a control set consisting of 3,000 random documents. We found that 31 of the 3,000 documents (1.03 percent) were relevant to Topic 207, and therefore assume that approximately 1.03 percent of the collection (7,473 documents) is likely to be relevant. This estimate is reasonably close to the true value of 1.08 percent (7,798 documents). Furthermore, 17 of the 20 "hits" for the term "football" in the control set are relevant, yielding a precision estimate of 85.0 percent, and a recall estimate of 64.5 percent. While the recall estimate is considerably higher than the true value of 44.6 percent, it is still within the margin of error one might expect for a sample of this size.

Combining Search Terms

A single search term is rarely sufficient to capture substantially all relevant documents in a collection. For Topic 207, the term "football" identified 44.6 percent of the responsive documents; the problem remains of how to identify the remaining 55.4 percent. Assuming that it is determined—either by intuition, statistics, or otherwise—that it is necessary to find more relevant documents, an obvious choice would be to add additional search terms; a less obvious choice is *which* search terms to use. Table 3.1 contains 120 possible search terms our searcher might incorporate into her keyword search. Which would you pick?

If we knew, for example, that the term "NFL" selected 1,666 documents, of which 1,542 were relevant, we might be inclined to include this term. But 1,261 of these documents were already selected by the term "football," so the net effect is that "NFL"

8. The validity of the repeated use of control sets for the purposes of statistical estimation is beyond the scope of this chapter, but is addressed in William Webber, Mossaab Bagdouri, David D. Lewis, & Douglas W. Oard, *Sequential Testing in Classifier Evaluation Yields Biased Estimates of Effectiveness, in* PROCEEDINGS OF THE 36TH INTERNATIONAL ACM SIGIR CONFERENCE ON RESEARCH AND DEVELOPMENT IN INFORMATION RETRIEVAL (SIGIR '13), 933–36 (2013), http://dl.acm.org/citation.cfm?id=2484159.

TABLE 3.1 120 Candidate Search Terms Related to TREC Topic 207 (Fantasy Football)

football*	game*	pick*	bass	bowl	nfl	agent	week	sport*	miami
superbowl	qb	wager*	ticket*	defens*	ffl	big	sooner*	fan	giant*
cheatsheet*	lenhart	bid*	tease	arnold	watch	team*	rb	bronco*	lsu
season	lamphier	oct	go	ut	texas	dallas	cuilla	bet	bets
trade	trades	tenn	league	espn	texan*	send	pool	raider*	point*
play*	will	tennessee	sportsbook	quarterback	murrel	minn	horn	commission*	boy
taylor	roster	phillip	phily	mike	mail	hiemstra	eric	want	super
harry	dsc	college	win	wins	tb	faulk	dean	brown	yard*
reagan	ram	rams	osu	mnf	mack	longhorn	kansas	coach	brother
brad	block*	sunday	schroeder	schafer	san	saint	ryder*	playoff	place
oklahoma	niner*	nick	michael	margaux	helsinki	height	george	gary	garcia
draft	denver	dawson	constance	colorado	carolina	burg	bledso	aggie	aggies

* Refers to a root extender, which permits the search to identify alternate forms of a root term; for example, a search for "teach*" would identify documents containing the terms "teach," "teaches," "teaching," "teacher," or "teachers."

identifies only 281 new responsive documents, at the expense of 106 new nonresponsive ones. Knowing this, should our searcher still include the term "NFL"?

As more search terms are used, it becomes increasingly difficult to choose additional terms that select many new, relevant documents, and few nonrelevant ones. There are approximately 10^{40} (i.e., 1 followed by 40 zeros) possible combinations of the terms in Table 3.1. The chance of finding the best combination of them, through intuition alone, is remote.

We could use our control set for this purpose, but once we use the control set to aid our search strategy, it is no longer independent, and therefore ceases to be a valid statistical sample for estimating recall and precision for validation purposes. When the selection of search terms is done with the benefit of feedback derived from the control set, terms may be selected that correctly identify the relevant documents in the control set, but not necessarily in the rest of the collection. This phenomenon is known as overfitting.[9]

When a set of documents is coded and used to guide the selection of keywords—or any other aspect of the search or review process—such a set is more properly referred to as a "training set." The systematic use of a training set is a key factor that distinguishes TAR from search.

For the purpose of illustrating a carefully crafted set of keywords, we selected the terms in Table 3.1, and ordered them by their estimated effectiveness (from left to right, by row), using an algorithm and a training set.[10] While we have no empirical evidence to support our claim, we posit that a human reviewer relying solely on her intuition would be hard-pressed to come up with a better list; we therefore

9. *See* Stefan Büttcher, Charles L.A. Clarke, & Gordon V. Cormack, Information Retrieval: Implementing and Evaluating Search Engines (MIT Press 2010), ch. 10, at 338.

10. We applied the TWFS method described in Section 4.2, at p. 4, of D. Sculley & Gordon V. Cormack, *Going Mini: Extreme Lightweight Spam Filters, in* Proceedings of the Sixth Conference on Email and Anti-Spam (CEAS '09) (2009), http://ceas.cc/2009/papers/ceas2009-paper-47.pdf.

use this list to model the best possible result that could be achieved with reasonable effort. But, even given this list of terms, the question still remains: How many of the "best possible" terms should be used for the search?

As we have seen, the term "football," alone, yields 44.6 percent recall and 80.6 percent precision. The terms "football" and "game," together, yield 67.0 percent recall and 28.9 percent precision. In other words, it is necessary to review 18,092 documents—13,773 more than the 4,319 selected by "football" alone—to raise recall from 44.6 percent to 67.0 percent. In the extreme, the 120 search terms combined select 570,466 documents, or about 80 percent of the collection, achieving 99.7 percent recall, but only 1.4 percent precision.

Table 3.2 illustrates the recall-precision trade-off that ensues from using various combinations of search terms. The first column (Search Terms) shows increasingly large sets of the "best possible" search terms selected from Table 3.1. The second column (Hits) shows the number of documents selected by the set of search terms, representing the amount of effort that would be required to review all documents selected by the search terms. The third and fourth

TABLE 3.2 Hit Counts, Recall, and Precision for Various Combinations of High-Quality Search Terms

Search Terms	Hits	Recall	Precision
football	4,319	44.6%	80.6%
football, game	18,092	67.0%	28.9%
football, game, pick	35,444	73.8%	16.2%
football, game, pick, bass*	42,288	82.1%	15.2%
football, game, pick, bass, bowl	42,737	84.3%	15.4%
football, game, pick, bass, bowl, NFL	42,860	85.1%	15.5%
football, game, pick, bass, bowl, NFL, agent	66,194	85.7%	10.1%

* "Bass" refers to the surname of the employee who oversaw the fantasy football league at Enron Corporation.

columns (Recall and Precision, respectively) show the recall and precision of the search.

It is easy to see that using more search terms increases recall at the expense of increased effort (and, correspondingly, decreased precision). No matter how carefully search terms are selected, high recall can be achieved only at the expense of low precision, which translates to greater review effort.[11] It is therefore unlikely that a human, selecting search terms using her intuition alone, could guess a set of search terms that would yield higher recall and higher precision than any of the searches proposed in Table 3.2.

Boolean and Proximity Operators

The search tools incorporated in most document review platforms allow a searcher to combine search terms using Boolean operators, such as "AND," "OR," and "BUT NOT," as well as proximity operators, such as "FBY [followed by] *n*" or "WITHIN *n*." In this chapter, we refer to a combination of one or more search terms using Boolean operators as a "Boolean expression," and a combination of one or more search terms using Boolean and proximity operators as an "extended Boolean expression."

The simplest Boolean expression is a single search term that selects all documents containing it, but Boolean expressions can consist of more than one search term. Two Boolean expressions, E_1 and E_2, may be combined as follows:

- "E_1 OR E_2" selects all documents that contain *either* "E_1" *or* "E_2";
- "E_1 AND E_2" selects all documents that contain *both* "E_1" *and* "E_2";
- "E_1 BUT NOT E_2" selects all documents that contain "E_1," *but only if they do not contain* "E_2."

11. *See* Eero Sormunen, *Extensions to the STAIRS Study—Empirical Evidence for the Hypothesized Ineffectiveness of Boolean Queries in Large Full-Text Databases*, 4 Info. Retrieval J. 257 (2001), http://www.sis.uta.fi/infim/julkaisut/fire/INRT87-JKwithFigs1.pdf.

Boolean expressions may be extended by including pairs of search terms, T_1 and T_2, combined as follows:

- "T_1 FBY *n* T_2" selects all documents containing the term "T_1" followed by the term "T_2," separated by no more than *n* words;
- "T_1 WITHIN *n* T_2" selects all documents containing both terms "T_1" and "T_2," in either order, separated by no more than *n* words.

In the following discussion, we refer to Boolean and extended Boolean expressions collectively as "Boolean expressions," or, when used for searching, as "Boolean queries." The use of Boolean queries to select documents is referred to as "Boolean search."

Boolean queries allow searchers to particularize the documents selected by search terms. For example, if the term "game" selects a large number of documents about video games, as opposed to football, our searcher might use the Boolean query "game BUT NOT video." Constructing a Boolean query to achieve high recall and high precision is a formidable task that requires testing and iteration. A set of Boolean queries that is systematically constructed with the objective of selecting all and only the relevant documents is a form of rule base, discussed later in this chapter.

Relevance Ranking

As defined in our Glossary, relevance ranking is "[a] search method in which the results are ranked from the most likely to the least likely to be Relevant to an Information Need. . . ."[12] A familiar example of relevance ranking is Web search: A user types a few keywords into a search engine such as Google, Bing, or Yahoo! and receives, as a result, the top-ranked documents from millions of possible hits. These top-ranked documents are those that the search engine's relevance-ranking algorithm determines are most likely to contain the information that the user is seeking. Some (but not all) commercial document review platforms include relevance ranking, but, for reasons that are not entirely clear to us, relevance ranking is seldom used in e-discovery.

12. Grossman & Cormack, *supra* note 2, at 28.

Using relevance ranking with a broad set of search terms (such as those in Table 3.1) is an effective alternative to the use of a narrow, carefully selected set of keywords alone (such as those in Table 3.2). To show this, we fed the 120 search terms listed in Table 3.1 to a well-known relevance-ranking algorithm (i.e., BM25, as implemented by the Wumpus Search software[13]) and achieved results—shown in Table 3.3—which are nearly as good as those achieved by our carefully crafted search terms using an automated method.[14] Table 3.3 shows the recall and precision that would be achieved if various numbers of the top-ranked documents were selected from the collection. The first column (# Top-Ranked Documents) reflects review effort, and is directly comparable to the second column (Hits) of Table 3.2. We can see, in our relevance-ranking example, that selecting the top-ranked 18,092 documents achieves 65.3 percent recall and 28.2 percent precision, whereas, in our keyword-search example, selecting 18,092 documents using the search terms "football" and "game" achieves 67.0 percent recall and 28.9 percent precision.

When using relevance ranking, the key decision that needs to be made—beyond identifying a broad set of search terms—is how many of the top-ranked documents should be selected so as to achieve the desired trade-off between recall and precision (i.e., completeness versus review effort). Although the precise recall and precision measures shown in Table 3.3 can be known only with clairvoyance, they could be estimated using a control set.

TABLE 3.3 Relevance Ranking for 120 Search Terms: Recall and Precision at Various Cut-Off Points

# Top-Ranked Documents	Recall	Precision
4,319	41.4%	74.8%
18,092	65.3%	28.2%
35,444	75.1%	16.5%
42,860	77.7%	14.2%
66,194	83.7%	9.9%

13. *See* STEFAN BÜTTCHER ET AL., *supra* note 9, ch. 5, at 138–41 & ch. 8, at 258–81.

14. *See* Sculley & Cormack, *supra* note 10.

Relevance ranking is a fully automated technique that performs about as well as the best combination of keywords that we were able to construct using a combination of technology, knowledge of the collection, and hindsight, and almost certainly better than any combination of keywords whose selection was based solely on human intuition. Nonetheless, the use of relevance ranking remains relatively uncommon in the e-discovery community. Some of the resistance to its use may be due to the fact that the mechanism behind relevance ranking is not as easily understood as the mechanism behind keyword search, a property sometimes referred to as "transparency." It is important to note, however, that familiarity with the nuts and bolts of a method does not confer any information about the *effectiveness* of that method for its intended purpose. The same sense of familiarity may have led the lawyers and paralegals who participated in the Blair and Maron study to believe they had achieved 75 percent recall when they had achieved only 20 percent.

Similarity Search

Moving further down the path from search tools to TAR, there are a number of methods that seek to identify documents that are similar to a given document, or to one of a given set of documents, for some definition of "similar." These tools are often informally referred to as "find [me] more like this." In essence, the document or documents of interest assume the same role as search terms in a keyword search, and the challenge of choosing a good set of documents—often referred to within the context of similarity search as a "seed set"—parallels the challenge of finding a good set of search terms. There is a common misconception that knowledge of the seed set confers information about the effectiveness of the similarity search, much as there is an unfounded belief that knowledge of the search terms conveys information about the effectiveness of the keyword search. In both cases, the searcher does not know what she does not know, and transparency regarding the search mechanism does not change that. Replacing the unprincipled choice of search terms with the unprincipled choice of seed documents is no less a game of Go Fish.[15]

Many notions of "similar" are employed in similarity search tools. Similarity may be expressed in terms of a similarity measure (e.g.,

15. Losey, *supra* note 5.

X percent) that indicates the degree of similarity between two documents. Alternatively, similarity may be expressed as the "distance" between two documents, where a larger distance means less similarity. Similarity search identifies any document that is more similar (or nearer) to a given document than some threshold value. Most similarity search tools allow this threshold to be adjusted, in much the same way that the cut-off for relevance ranking can be adjusted to vary the trade-off between recall and precision.

The most widely used similarity measures include cosine similarity and, more generally, the vector-space model (VSM), which are based on the words that appear in the documents (typically after stemming, stop-word elimination, and tf-idf (term frequency-inverse document frequency) weighting[16]).

Table 3.4 shows the results of a "find similar" search using cosine similarity and tf-idf weighting, using the 31 relevant football-related documents found in our control set as a seed set. It shows the recall and precision achieved when documents similar to one of the 31 seed documents are selected for various threshold values. When compared to Tables 3.2 and 3.3, Table 3.4 shows, for this particular example and this particular similarity measure, somewhat inferior results to those achieved by the well-crafted search terms or relevance ranking. In this example, for a review effort of 18,092 documents, cosine similarity achieves 49.1 percent recall and 21.2 percent precision—substantially

TABLE 3.4 Similarity Search Using 31 Control-Set Seed Documents: Recall and Precision at Various Cut-Off Points

# Top-Ranked Documents	Recall	Precision
4,319	30.2%	54.5%
18,092	49.1%	21.2%
35,444	61.8%	13.6%
42,860	65.8%	11.9%
66,194	74.2%	8.7%
95,545	80.0%	6.5%

16. *See generally* STEFAN BÜTTCHER ET AL., *supra* note 9, ch. 3 & 4, at 84–136.

inferior to the recall and precision results shown for the 18,092 Hits and # Top-Ranked Documents in Tables 3.2 and 3.3, respectively.[17]

Classifiers

According to our Glossary, a classifier is "[a]n Algorithm that Labels items as to whether or not they have a particular property. . . ."[18] Within the context of e-discovery, classifiers are algorithms that yield a determination of relevant or nonrelevant. Classifiers may be constructed either manually or automatically.

A rule base is a manually (but systematically) constructed set of rules that is subsequently applied automatically to rank or classify documents as to their relevance. Thus, a rule base is simply a manually constructed classifier. In contrast to a rule base, a learned classifier is constructed automatically by a supervised machine-learning algorithm. The systematic construction of classifiers from training documents is the key factor that distinguishes TAR from search and analysis.

Whether manually constructed or learned, there are many different kinds of classifiers. A Boolean query could be used to form a simple classifier by deeming the "hits" to be relevant and the "misses" to be nonrelevant, or vice versa. Similarly, a classifier could be derived from a relevance ranking by deeming the top (or bottom) k results to be relevant, and the rest to be nonrelevant, for some cut-off value, k. A classifier might also be derived from a similarity search by deeming all documents with similarity s or greater to a document in the seed set to be relevant, and the rest to be nonrelevant, or vice versa.

A particularly simple but effective type of classifier is a linear classifier, which is simply a score for each term (or more generally, "feature") that may occur in a document, with positive scores indicating relevance, and negative scores indicating nonrelevance. The score of the document is simply the sum of the scores for the terms

17. It is important to note that the results presented in Tables 3.2 through Table 3.6 are illustrative examples, only. While the results are typical of those we have observed, they do not show that any class of methods is superior to, or inferior to, any other class of methods in all circumstances. Such questions are best addressed through controlled scientific studies. *See, e.g.*, Cormack & Grossman *infra* note 23.

18. Grossman & Cormack, *supra* note 2, at 11.

or features it contains, and the document is classified as relevant if its score exceeds some threshold, *c*, and nonrelevant if its score is less than *c*. Linear classifiers may be constructed by hand, in which case they are rule bases, or by supervised machine-learning algorithms, such as support vector machines (SVMs), logistic regression (LR), or naïve Bayes (NB).[19] Some of these classifiers are transparent, in that the mechanics of their operation—but not their effectiveness—is exposed; most are opaque, either because of their complexity, or because they rely on sophisticated pattern matching, parsing, or inference algorithms.

Rule-Based Methods for TAR

The construction of an effective rule-based TAR system is an expert-intensive process, relying on one or more domain experts (also known as subject-matter experts, or SMEs), as well as one or more rules-construction expert(s) (also known as knowledge engineers, and typically persons with expertise in linguistics, statistics, and/or computer science). While it may be easy to understand operationally how simple rule bases—notably flowcharts and decision trees—work, it is not easy to predict their effectiveness at discriminating between relevant and nonrelevant documents.

The rule-based approach determined to be effective in our JOLT article relied on extensive collaboration among a team of subject-matter experts, linguists, statisticians, and document reviewers, to construct and validate a complex set of rules in the form of Boolean expressions. The rules-construction experts formulated a series of Boolean queries, and reviewed examples of hits and misses for each query. Where the hits were found to contain too many nonrelevant documents, supplemental queries were constructed to remove these false-positive documents; where the misses were found to contain too many relevant documents, supplemental queries were constructed to identify the false-negative documents. This process was continued until the overall set of queries yielded acceptable recall and precision, as estimated using a control set.

19. *See generally* Büttcher et al., *supra* note 9, ch. 10 & 11, at 310–404.

There is some debate in the legal field as to whether Boolean search constitutes TAR. As previously illustrated, a classifier can consist of Boolean expressions. This is not to say that any use of a Boolean query is TAR—it may constitute TAR if the method of construction is systematic and is based on the iterative examination of exemplar documents using a control set. In any event, the label "TAR" does not, in itself, imply that the classifier is effective.

A number of do-it-yourself linguistic tools are available in the market for rule-base construction. One simple method relies on the examination of the vocabulary contained in the document collection—an exhaustive index of the words it contains, with stop-words eliminated—and asks the searcher to identify those words that appear most relevant to the subject matter of interest, and those that appear unlikely to be relevant. Another asks the searcher to highlight terms or phrases of interest. Unless followed up by an iterative query-refinement process, and a method to gauge progress by examining its effect on the documents in the collection, such approaches do not fit our definition of TAR.

Other do-it-yourself rule bases employ different kinds of classifiers, such as patterns or grammars. At the time of this writing, we are unaware of any scientific study demonstrating the effectiveness of any of these methods.

Similarity Search for TAR

Some of the most widely adopted TAR tools on the market rely on similarity search. Although commonly associated with supervised machine-learning methods, TAR methods based on similarity search closely resemble rule-based methods. The seed set represents a set of rules that determine which documents to deem relevant (due to their similarity to a relevant seed document) and which documents to deem nonrelevant (due to their dissimilarity to all relevant seed documents and/or their similarity to a nonrelevant seed document). Some TAR systems based on similarity search construct only a partial classifier, which is unable to classify certain gray-area documents as either relevant or nonrelevant.

As with untested search terms in Boolean rule-base construction methods, an initial seed set chosen intuitively (or at random) is unlikely to yield an effective classifier. It is necessary to apply the classifier to example documents, and, where the reviewer disagrees with the classifier's result, amend the seed set, either by adding new documents to the seed set, or by deleting or changing the coding of the seed document(s) responsible for the incorrect classification. This iterative process of sampling and revision continues until the classifier yields sufficient recall and precision.

While the mechanism of these similarity search tools is easily understood, as we have previously stated, the documents in the seed set—just like a list of search terms or Boolean queries—offer little insight as to the classifier's effectiveness.

Supervised Machine Learning for TAR

A number of TAR tools on the market—often referred to as "predictive coding" in e-discovery circles—employ an approach known in the information retrieval community as supervised learning, in which a machine-learning algorithm infers how to distinguish between relevant and nonrelevant documents, based on exemplar documents, each of which has been labeled by a subject-matter expert as relevant or nonrelevant. The entire set of exemplar documents is properly known as the "training set," although it is often incorrectly referred to as the "seed set." Typically, the learning method identifies combinations of features from the documents that distinguish relevance from nonrelevance; in many systems, the features consist of the words contained in the documents; in other systems, the features may include word fragments, phrases, concept clusters, punctuation, emoticons, or metadata.

Many supervised learning algorithms have been proposed. Among the most effective are support vector machines, logistic regression, bagging, boosting, random forests, and k-nearest neighbor (k-NN).[20] Common, but generally less effective, methods include naïve Bayes (colloquially known as "Bayesian"), nearest neighbor (NN, or 1-NN, which is essentially similarity search), and Rocchio's vector-space method.[21]

20. *See generally id.*
21. *See generally id.*

It is important to distinguish *supervised* learning methods from *unsupervised* learning methods. Unsupervised methods do not use a training set, or any other human input as to what constitutes relevance. Such methods, which automatically group documents or document features without human oversight, include clustering, latent semantic indexing or analysis (LSI or LSA), and probabilistic latent semantic indexing or analysis (PLSI or PLSA).[22] These methods are not TAR tools in their own right, but may be used as a component of similarity search, or to derive features (e.g., concept clusters) for use in a supervised machine-learning method.

We have recently taxonified the various supervised machine-learning TAR protocols in use today into three major categories, referred to as "simple passive learning" (SPL), "simple active learning" (SAL), and "continuous active learning" (CAL).[23] SPL represents the most basic application of supervised machine learning. In SPL, all of the training documents are selected either at random, by the human operator of the TAR system, or through a combination of both methods. SAL extends SPL to allow the learning algorithm to identify exemplar documents to be reviewed, coded, and added to the training set. CAL repurposes the role of the classifier in supervised learning, abandoning the objective of creating, once and for all, the best possible classifier, in favor of constructing a series of disposable classifiers—each with the sole purpose of identifying more relevant documents for review—and continuing to construct classifiers—each trained on all documents reviewed to date—until substantially all relevant documents in the collection have been reviewed. These core protocols are compared and contrasted in the following sections and are set forth in Table 3.7.

Active Versus Passive Machine-Learning Methods

In taxonifying supervised machine-learning protocols for TAR, it is important to distinguish between the roles of teacher and learner. The

22. *See* Grossman & Cormack, *supra* note 2, at 11, 22, 26.

23. Gordon V. Cormack & Maura R. Grossman, *Evaluation of Machine-Learning Protocols for Technology-Assisted Review in Electronic Discovery, in* PROCEEDINGS OF THE 37TH INTERNATIONAL ACM SIGIR CONFERENCE ON RESEARCH AND DEVELOPMENT IN INFORMATION RETRIEVAL (SIGIR '14), 153–62 (2014), http://dx.doi.org/10.1145/2600428.2609601.

teacher is the human operator of the TAR system, while the *learner* is the machine-learning algorithm. The term "passive learning" means that the learner (i.e., the algorithm) is passive in the selection of training examples; it plays no part in that selection and uses for training only those exemplar documents selected by the teacher, or through random selection. By contrast, the term "active learning" means that the learner (i.e., the algorithm) actively selects some—usually most—of the documents from which it will learn. These documents are coded by the teacher and then fed back to the algorithm for further training. In other words, *passive versus active learning is assessed from the perspective of the learner*—the algorithm—and its level of involvement in selecting the documents it will be given for training purposes; the algorithm is either an active or a passive participant in the selection process.

Passive learning must be distinguished from passive teaching. In passive teaching, the teacher plays no role in selecting the training examples for the algorithm; instead they are selected either at random, by the learner, or through a combination of both methods. By contrast, the term "active teaching" means that the teacher selects some—or most—of the documents used for training using her judgment, for example, by selecting training examples identified during witness interviews, through ad-hoc search methods, from prior productions, and even through the creation of "synthetic documents" that would be of interest, if they were to be found in the collection.

One principal factor distinguishing different TAR protocols is how the training documents are chosen: by the teacher, by the learner, at random, or through some combination of these approaches. While some controversy persists as to which method of selecting training examples is preferable, the question is amenable to empirical evaluation.[24]

The argument for exclusively randomly selected training examples appears to derive from several sources:

- The fact that much theoretical and empirical research on supervised machine learning assumes that the training set is a random sample of the collection;

24. *See generally id.*

- The conviction—possibly owing to experience with similarity search—that the training documents *must* represent all the different kinds of potentially relevant documents in the collection, and the mistaken assumption that random sampling is likely to achieve this;
- The erroneous belief—derived from the confusion between control and training sets—that using a random training set of a particular size will guarantee a particular level of classifier effectiveness; and,
- Distrust of reliance on the teacher's skill, knowledge, and goodwill in choosing appropriate training examples, and fear that any "bias" in selection will be transferred to, if not amplified by, the learner.

The argument for active teaching (whether or not augmented by random training and/or active learning) derives from the fact that the teacher is familiar with the subject matter, and therefore best positioned to find a set of representative documents from which the learner can deduce the best classifier, so that no obvious category of responsive document will be overlooked. Current research suggests, that such subject-matter expertise may not be necessary for certain active learning methods, for which a single relevant document may be sufficient to kick-start the TAR process.[25]

The argument for active learning (whether or not augmented by random training and/or active teaching) derives from the fact that the learning algorithm is best positioned to identify the documents from which it would learn most, akin to a small child repeatedly pointing and asking, "Is that a relevant document?" "What about this one?" "And, that one?"

Simple Versus Continuous Machine-Learning Methods

The second principal factor distinguishing supervised machine-learning protocols is: When should training stop? For simple passive learning and simple active learning, the answer is, "When the classifier is good enough," for some definition of "good enough," which

25. Gordon V. Cormack & Maura R. Grossman, *Autonomy and Reliability of Continuous Active Learning for Technology-Assisted Review*, arXiv:1504.06868 (2015), http://arxiv.org/abs/1504.06868.

is typically measured in terms of the recall, precision, or F_1 of the classifier, and often referred to as the "stabilization" point. When the stabilization point has been reached, and it is determined that further training will not improve the classifier, the training phase ceases and the review phase begins. The learned classifier does not continue to improve as more documents are reviewed.

For continuous active learning, the answer to the question, "When should training stop?" is, "When enough relevant documents have been found," for some definition of "enough relevant documents," typically measured by a precipitous drop-off in precision, and subsequently, by calculating recall at the end of the review process. For CAL, there is no distinction between the training and review phases. The learned classifier continues to improve as more and more documents are reviewed.

With all TAR protocols, the definition of "enough"—whether measured by a "good-enough" classifier or by identifying "enough" relevant documents—is based on proportionality considerations: How much could the result be improved, in terms of the value of the relevant information in any new documents found, relative to the additional review effort required to find that information? Over and above imprecision in quantifying the value of the information, and the challenge of measuring it with sufficient accuracy, such a determination requires clairvoyance to determine the future consequences of stopping or continuing training. This is currently one of the biggest challenges for all TAR protocols.

While a standard definition of "enough" has yet to be established, some commentary has argued—and some case law has accepted—a statistical recall estimate of at least 75 percent, with a margin of error of ±5 percent, and 95 percent confidence level, as indicating that "enough relevant documents" have been identified.

Core Supervised Machine-Learning Protocols Used for TAR

The machine-learning approach found to be effective in our JOLT article used a combination of active teaching, active learning, and continuous learning. Initial examples for review and training were the top-ranked hits (based on relevance ranking) of hundreds of simple keyword searches, while subsequent examples were those given the highest score by a logistic regression algorithm, or found through supplemental keyword searches. Review and training continued until an insubstantial fraction of the top-scoring documents that had not yet been reviewed were relevant; in other words, the precision of the top-ranked documents was low, suggesting that there were few relevant documents left to be found.

The protocol just described is an example of continuous active learning. The essential characteristic of CAL is that, after the initial seed set, which may be judgmentally selected by the human teacher, throughout the remainder of the review, it is the learning algorithm that repeatedly suggests additional documents for review. These documents are then coded by the teacher and used for training the learning algorithm. Typically, the selected documents are those that the learning algorithm is most confident are likely to be relevant, hence the name "relevance feedback." Review and training continue in iterative cycles until substantially all relevant documents have been identified. Documents never identified by the process are presumed to be non-relevant, following appropriate sampling and other validation procedures. The use of keyword searches to find documents both at the outset and throughout the TAR process (i.e., active teaching), though beneficial, is not an essential aspect of the particular CAL implementation studied in our JOLT article; nor is the use of logistic regression for the learning algorithm, and certain other design choices.

The results of applying CAL to identify the relevant documents in our fantasy football example are shown in Table 3.5. This CAL

TABLE 3.5 Recall as a Function of Review Effort for the CAL Implementation Distributed to the TREC 2015 Total Recall Track Participants

# Documents Reviewed	Recall	Precision
3,210	40.0%	97.2%
4,079	50.0%	95.6%
5,153	60.0%	90.8%
6,186	70.0%	88.3%
7,580	80.0%	82.3%
10,344	90.0%	67.9%
18,092	95.5%	41.2%

implementation[26] uses a single synthetic seed document, consisting only of the request for production for Topic 207, set forth earlier in this chapter; all other training examples were selected by the learner. A comparison of Tables 3.2, 3.3, and 3.4 with Table 3.5 shows that, for any given level of review effort, CAL achieves substantially higher recall and higher precision than the carefully crafted search terms, relevance ranking using these search terms, and similarity search using as a seed set the 31 relevant documents found in the control set. When 18,092 documents are reviewed, CAL achieves 95.5 percent recall and 41.2 percent precision, as compared to 67.0 percent recall and 28.9 percent precision achieved by the best of the other methods previously described in this chapter.

At the time of this writing, CAL has yet to be widely adopted within the e-discovery community, although its use is gradually increasing. Most commercial TAR offerings still employ either simple passive learning or simple active learning.

The defining characteristic of SPL is that the learning algorithm plays no role in selecting the training examples. Examples are selected either at random, through active teaching (i.e., judgmental selection by the teacher), or through a combination of both. Once reviewed and coded, the examples are used to train the learning algorithm. The effectiveness of the training is evaluated with respect to a sample of documents in the collection (typically, the control set), and, if the effectiveness is found to be satisfactory (a point commonly referred to as stabilization), training ceases and the resulting classifier is applied to the entire collection to identify a "review set" of presumed-relevant documents. Documents not in the review set are presumed to be non-relevant after sampling or other validation processes.

Table 3.6 shows the recall and precision achieved for the fantasy football example for SPL using, as a training set, the same 3,000 randomly selected documents that we previously used as a control set, and for identifying seed documents for the similarity search described earlier in the chapter. The SPL review effort (Total, shown in the third column) has two components: first, review of the training set (Training, shown

26. The particular implementation applied was the baseline model implementation (BMI) supplied to TREC 2015 Total Recall participants. *See* Roegiest et al., *supra* note 3.

TABLE 3.6 Review Effort, Precision, and Recall for SPL Using 3,000 Randomly Selected Training Documents

# Documents Reviewed			Recall	Precision
Training	Top-Ranked	Total	Top-Ranked Only	
3,000	210	3,210	2.6%	100%
3,000	1,079	4,079	13.7%	98.8%
3,000	2,153	5,153	26.3%	95.1%
3,000	3,186	6,186	35.6%	87.1%
3,000	4,580	7,580	44.8%	76.3%
3,000	7,344	10,344	57.4%	69.0%
3,000	15,092	18,092	73.2%	37.8%
3,000	33,444	36,444	84.6%	19.7%
3,000	39,288	42,288	86.3%	17.1%

in the first column) and then, the review set (Top Ranked, shown in the second column). For a total review effort of 18,092 documents, SPL achieves 73.2 percent recall and 37.8 percent precision, substantially better than the previously described search methods, but worse than CAL.

SPL achieves high recall with less review effort than a carefully crafted keyword search, keyword-based relevance ranking, and similarity search, but requires considerably greater effort than CAL to achieve the same recall. Notably, very few responsive documents are found during the initial effort to review the 3,000 training documents. This initially unproductive training effort may serve as a disincentive to the use of SPL.

SAL falls somewhere between CAL and SPL. Like CAL, SAL employs an active learning strategy in which, after using some examples supplied either by the teacher or through random selection, the learner then selects the remaining training examples. However, the SAL learner typically employs an "uncertainty sampling" approach, selecting documents about which it is least certain, and from which it can therefore learn the most. Like SPL, SAL employs separate training and review phases, where the classifier is fixed at the end of the training phase. The net effect is that SAL shares with SPL a generally unproductive training phase (in the sense that a low proportion of relevant documents

TABLE 3.7 Comparing CAL, SAL, and SPL Protocols for TAR

CAL Protocol	SAL Protocol	SPL Protocol
STEP 1: Choose a seed set using judgmental sampling (e.g., attorney search, known relevant documents, synthetic documents, etc.). **STEP 2**: Review and code the documents in the seed set. **STEP 3**: Use the machine-learning algorithm to suggest the next most-likely responsive documents for review (i.e., relevance feedback). **STEP 4**: Review and code the newly suggested documents and add them to the training set. **STEP 5**: Repeat steps 3 and 4 above until substantially all relevant documents have been reviewed (i.e., precision drops off precipitously). **STEP 6**: Validate the TAR process.	**STEP 1**: Create a random control set. **STEP 2**: Review and code the documents in the control set. **STEP 3**: Choose a seed set using random sampling, judgmental sampling (e.g., attorney search, known relevant documents, synthetic documents, etc.), or a combination of both. **STEP 4**: Review and code the documents in the seed set. **STEP 5**: Use the machine-learning algorithm to suggest those documents from which the algorithm will learn the most (i.e., uncertainty sampling). **STEP 6**: Review and code the newly suggested documents and add them to the training set. **STEP 7**: Repeat steps 5 and 6 above until training is deemed to be sufficient and "stabilization" occurs. **STEP 8**: Run the machine-learning algorithm for the final time to categorize or rank all documents in the collection. **STEP 9**: Review the documents categorized as "relevant," or ranked above some "cut-off" score. **STEP 10**: Validate the TAR process.	**STEP 1**: Choose a seed set using random sampling, judgmental sampling (e.g., attorney search, known relevant documents, synthetic documents, etc.), or a combination of both. **STEP 2**: Review and code the documents in the seed set. **STEP 3**: Run the machine-learning algorithm and evaluate the effectiveness of training thus far. **STEP 4**: If the result is insufficient, repeat the steps above with an augmented training set. **STEP 5**: When training is deemed to be sufficient, run the machine-learning algorithm for the final time to categorize or rank all documents in the collection. **STEP 6**: Review the documents categorized as "relevant," or ranked above some "cut-off" score. **STEP 7**: Validate the TAR process.

are initially identified) and the need to determine when the classifier is "good enough" (i.e., a stabilization point). When this determination is accurately made, SAL can achieve similar recall and precision to CAL.

Other Aspects of the Electronic Discovery Process That May Impact TAR

Any implementation of TAR will necessarily occasion certain choices regarding the identification, collection, and culling of the documents subject to search and review; staffing and other workflow decisions related to the specific tool and protocol to be applied; and the selection and implementation of quality-control and validation processes. While these activities are ancillary to TAR per se, they are important aspects of the review process, and can exert a significant impact on the quality and success of a TAR effort. Many of these important issues are addressed in other chapters of this book.

EDITORS' INTRODUCTION TO CHAPTER 4

Michael D. Berman

If there is a truism in the world of search, it is that there is no single solution and that process is critical. This chapter by Vincent Catanzaro, Samantha Green, and Sandra Rampersaud points out that a prudent litigator needs to be aware of the workflow. For example, a process well-suited to a merger and acquisition may be a poor fit to an internal investigation or litigation.

The authors point to the threshold question. Is predictive coding appropriate? Does the document set contain text-rich documents or spreadsheets and graphics? The former are well-suited and the latter may not be suited to use of the software. The authors discuss whether certain file types, such as calendar items or meeting invitations, should be excluded, even though they may be textual. Factors such as richness and rolling productions may also impact the decision to use or not use predictive coding.

Choice of the subject-matter expert is central. That person reviews the documents and decides whether they are responsive or not. The authors discuss how to select the subject-matter expert, and the need for consistent decision-making in "training" the software. Because the software extrapolates decisions regarding documents that are manually coded to the entire population, a smooth and controlled workflow is essential.

The chapter also discusses stabilization, that is, the point at which the software has learned all it can from mere mortals, and overturns, that is, the number of times a human reviewer tells the software that it is wrong. The subject-matter expert may also be critical in validation. That process—using a statistically significant sample as a quality control check—is described by the authors.

Litigators should also consider the end game. What will be done with the output? Full linear review? Or some variant? In answering these questions, the authors provide a general template for establishing a predictive coding workflow.

CHAPTER 4

The Mechanics of a Predictive Coding Workflow

Vincent M. Catanzaro, Samantha Green, and Sandra Rampersaud

Introduction

In every litigation, strategies and procedural processes are designed according to the facts and issues of the particular case. During the course of a litigation, those strategies and processes evolve, develop, and change as more facts are learned. This is also the case with the use of technology to assist in the preservation, collection, review, and production of documents in discovery. While there are high-level processes and workflows that will promote repeatability, reliability, and defensibility, each familiar step may need adjusting or changing entirely given a particular set of circumstances.

Likewise, when utilizing "predictive coding," an algorithm-based solution to aid in the review and organization of data, defensible processes and workflows should be designed according to the needs of a particular case. There is no one-size-fits-all approach. There are many applications offered in the legal marketplace, each using any one or combination of a number of information retrieval algorithms operating in its own unique way. Understanding how those models work in the context of your review is critical to designing effective and defensible workflows. Similarly, when designing specific processes and workflows, the prudent litigator should assess the sufficiency of those decisions according to the standard for completeness of discovery governing the particular case. For example, certain workflows may be appropriate in a second request merger context or in an internal investigation that may not satisfy a party's obligations in a litigation governed by the Federal Rules of Civil Procedure.

Nonetheless, there are commonalities among the various predictive coding applications that allow the user to begin a customized workflow by starting from a general, high-level workflow. This chapter outlines that general workflow, beginning with deciding whether predictive coding should be used in a review, outlining the typical steps of a predictive coding application, and describing the types of decisions that follow at the end of a predictive coding process.[1]

How Predictive Coding Works and Is It an Appropriate Solution in Your Case?

Predictive coding applications utilize text-based data to analyze document content, context, and meaning. Thus, if a data set is not text-rich or if the facts in a case are either largely or in part to be found in graphics, images, or numerical information, predictive coding may not be an appropriate solution. Alternatively, predictive coding may be appropriate for a subset of the data collection. Understanding that predictive coding is not a panacea, the first question should be: "Is predictive coding appropriate in this case?"

In simplest terms, the technology works by analyzing the way people convey information utilizing language. There are only so many ways someone can phrase an idea in order to get a message across. For a computer, those ideas are translated in mathematical formulae by, for example, comparing actual characters and their relation to each other in the context of sentence and paragraph structure. The more similar the characters, the more similar the concepts, and so on. When there is little or no "language" to analyze, the software finds it difficult to make the comparison we want. With nothing more than pictures and numbers, the language evaluation and comparison would be difficult

1. Since there are many "predictive coding" applications available using a variety of different algorithms and methodologies (and more developing every day), the predictive coding workflow discussed in this chapter may not be appropriate for some models.

to accomplish. Understanding that, if you know your document collection will be comprised of scanned, handwritten images, many photos, or mostly financial information found in spreadsheets, the value of using predictive coding may be lost. However, if you can cull out those documents that do not contain language and put them into a different workflow, predictive coding may be effective on the text-based data.

Before embarking on a predictive coding workflow, therefore, you should understand certain characteristics of the data collection, including file types, volume, "richness" (which is the extent to which the collection is likely to contain responsive as opposed to nonresponsive data), as well as the collection and production schedules. Another important fact that may impact the predictive coding process is when the data that will be part of the predictive coding workflow will be available. Often the collection phase of discovery occurs iteratively, leading to rolling data imports into a review platform. While it is not necessary to have all data collected before a predictive coding process begins, a continually changing data set—in terms of volume, file types, and/or substantive content—can impact the performance of the algorithms and add to the time it takes the model to adequately stabilize. Similarly, production deadlines should be considered both in terms of deciding whether predictive coding should be used and defining the data set that should be included in the predictive coding process. For example, it may be that an early production deadline of a key custodian's data warrants a linear review of that collection, while the remaining custodians' data can be part of a predictive coding workflow and produced later. In that example, the coding applied to the key custodian's data may even be used later to train the predictive model.

Having decided that predictive coding should be used, you should next understand what the desired outcome is or what the anticipated post-predictive coding review workflow will likely be. There are many ways to use predictive coding as part of a review, each bringing its own value. Predictive coding may be used to organize an entire data collection or a subset of that collection from highly responsive documents to highly nonresponsive documents. From there, numerous workflows are possible: separating documents according to degree of responsiveness to be reviewed by different level of reviewers, eliminating nonresponsive documents from a second level review, prioritizing the review of highly responsive documents, applying the model to aid in the review of an adversary or third party's production, etc.

Understanding the characteristics of the collection and the ultimate review strategy at the outset will aid in designing efficient and defensible review workflows that incorporate a predictive coding component. It also enables you to effectively estimate resource needs and costs. By identifying your data sets at this early stage, appropriate time can be spent organizing review resources and estimating the amount of time required for production of relevant documents.

Put Together the Right Team

In any well-managed project, putting together the right team of people is important. In a predictive coding project, which typically involves a large volume of documents, technological complexities, and many moving parts, selecting people with the necessary expertise is paramount.

The person training the software, the so-called subject-matter expert, needs to be a knowledgeable attorney familiar with the issues in the case so that responsive/nonresponsive decisions will be accurate and can thus be relied upon by the predictive model. The number of subject-matter experts used to train a predictive coding model can vary from application to application. Bear in mind, however, that coding consistency—that is, similar documents are coded similarly—is integral to the effectiveness of the model, and thus the more subject matter expert reviewers used, the greater the risk of inconsistent coding. Remember, predictive coding works by extrapolating decisions—responsive and not responsive—made for a subset of data across a larger population; thus, those decisions need to be reliable. In addition to subject matter experts, it is often extremely helpful to have technological experts, individuals who have familiarity with both the application's user interface and back-end protocols.

Finally, it is worth mentioning that communication among the team members is critical to effective and efficient use of predictive coding applications. Accurate and consistent responsiveness coding decisions will lead to improved model performance and results. Thus, as information about the issues and collection is learned during the custodian and IT personnel interviews, it should be shared among those who will be training the predictive model. For example, if rolling data collections will lead to rolling data imports into the predictive coding model, it will be important for those training the model to understand with each import the relevance and nature of the custodians' data to better anticipate the types of documents that should be presented during the predictive coding process and identify any errors or issues that should be raised. To promote communication and accurate coding, where possible, subject-matter experts (and technological experts) should be in either close physical or communicative proximity so that questions as to whether a document is or is not responsive can be addressed in a timely manner, enabling every subject matter expert to modify his or her coding decisions as necessary and in real time.

Defining the Scope of Data Included in the Predictive Coding Workflow

Careful thought should be given to which data should be included in the predictive coding workflow and which should be excluded. Predictive coding models operate optimally when the "richness" of the data collection is high ("high" being a relative measure). Richness is a term that describes the number of responsive documents that are included in a predictive coding model as a percentage of the overall collection within the model. Most predictive coding applications work best when richness is at 10 percent or above. Thus, defining the scope of data to be included in the model should be driven, to the extent possible, by the goal of improving richness of that data. To that end, date filters can be an effective means to objectively cull nonresponsive data from the collection. It is also advisable to perform a global deduplication across the entire data collection, so that the data that is loaded into the predictive model will contain (as close to possible) only one version of a document.[2] Some processes have even started by culling data using key word searches prior to ingestion by the predictive coding model.[3]

2. "Global" deduplication is contrasted with "custodian" deduplication, both of which are defined in the Appendix in this volume.

3. See Chapter 11 in this volume.

In addition, any file types that are incompatible with the predictive coding application being used should be excluded from the workflow, set aside, and a decision made separately as to how those excluded documents will ultimately be reviewed. Similarly, in any given case, file types that can be identified as objectively nonresponsive, such as for example calendar items or meeting invitations, that may exist in large numbers but bring little substantive value to the collection may also be excluded. Foreign or mixed-language documents may also be identified using automated applications and removed. Again, decisions should be made as to whether, and if so how, any excluded documents should be separately reviewed.

It is important to note that during the predictive coding workflow, documents are coded on a document, not family, level, with decisions as to responsiveness being made according to the four corners of a document without consideration to any related attachments or parents. After the predictive coding process is complete, documents should be re-associated with their related family members, and some documents that may have been excluded as incompatible file types or objectively not responsive may nonetheless receive predictive coding values, such as a relevancy score, to the extent those values are attributed to any family members that were part of the process. Accordingly, it is important to ensure adequate data tracking measures are in place that enable you to know which documents are included in or excluded from the predictive coding process, and, at the end of the process, which excluded documents will be part of a post-predictive coding workflow by virtue of their relationship to included documents and which excluded documents will need to be part of a separate review workflow as "freestanding" excluded documents.

General Predictive Coding Workflow

As mentioned, there are many different predictive coding applications using different and various information retrieval algorithms, and necessarily, therefore, differing workflows. Similarly, each case should be assessed on its own merits, and no one workflow is appropriate for every case. Following is a high-level description of a typical workflow that can serve as a starting point or simply be informational toward designing an entirely different process.[4]

Assessment Phase

In all discovery, one key question is "How well did you do?" or stated differently, "Have you done enough to meet you legal obligations?" Predictive coding applications aim to provide an answer by using statistics. Because the models operate by taking information about a subset of data and extrapolating those results to a large population, statistics provide a means for practitioners—courts, companies, lawyers, and technicians—to make statements regarding the completeness of a production.

A typical workflow begins with an "assessment" phase, which is an evaluative step. Once data has been imported into the predictive coding application, the model aims to understand something about that collection; namely, how many responsive documents do you estimate are contained within the collection? Using statistically significant sample sets of data drawn randomly from the collection, the subject matter expert is presented with documents to code as either responsive or not responsive. At the end of the process, the coding applied to the statistically significant sample is extrapolated and applied across the entire population. For example, in a sample set of 1,500 documents where 500 are coded as responsive and 1,000 are coded as not responsive, the model can then presume to a certain degree of statistical certainty that the collection is 33 percent responsive. Some models will also begin to categorize the collection by content into those that are similar to the 500 responsive documents and those that are similar to the 1,000 not responsive documents. Others will in effect separate the 1,500 so-called control documents from the larger population, so that they are only used to assess richness and representativeness of the larger population. Where additional data is loaded into the predictive model after the process has begun, further assessment rounds may be

4. For simplicity, the workflow described in this chapter considers a binary decision-making workflow for responsive and not responsive documents. Predictive coding models may also enable a user to make multiple, simultaneous coding decisions beyond a simple binary decision such as coding for various issues in a case.

necessary depending on the volume and character (i.e., does the newly loaded data contain the same types of information as have been loaded previously?). During the course of the predictive coding process, the assessment documents may also be used by some models to evaluate progress and how accurately the model can identify responsive and not responsive content.

Training

The training phase comprises multiple rounds of review to improve the model's understanding of what is responsive and what is not responsive. Documents are selected by the predictive coding application[5] from within the collection and presented to the subject-matter expert to code as responsive or nonresponsive. The manner in which documents are selected varies from application to application—random, smart random, targeted—and the selection criteria can be adjusted manually during the course of training to improve results. After all documents within a round have been coded by the subject matter expert, the results are applied to the larger population, results are generated and the system learns what is relevant. Some applications will inform the user when a point is reached where additional information about what is responsive or not responsive will no longer materially improve the model. Other applications will provide results in the form of overturns, that is, the number of documents where a subject matter expert disagreed with (or "overturned") the model's automated categorization of a document as either responsive or not responsive. In those types of applications, the user aims to arrive at a point at which the overturn rate is reasonable. The point at which the model has adequately learned the boundaries of responsiveness and not responsiveness is sometimes referred to as stability or stabilization.

Once the model is stabilized, you are left with a collection of data that is organized according to relevance to issues in the case. Different applications will organize and/or rank each document in the collection differently. Some models will organize the entire collection with scores of 0 to 100 and require the user to determine where the threshold for responsiveness should be drawn, such

5. As noted previously and in Chapter 11 in this volume, documents may be selected by judgmental decisions of the subject-matter expert.

that documents scoring lower than that threshold will be deemed not responsive. Other models will separate the collection into two buckets, one containing documents that are responsive and ranked according to degree of responsiveness and the other containing documents that are not responsive and ranked according to the degree of not responsiveness.

Validation

Once the training phase is complete, the final step is to ensure that the subset of the population that the model deems not responsive does not contain documents that a producing party has an obligation to disclose. Typical validation is performed by reviewing a statistically significant sample set of documents from within the not responsive subset of the collection to determine how many, if any, responsive documents are found, and to what extent those documents should be produced in the case. If the percentage of false negatives falls below a selected target, the process is deemed valid. It may also be possible to validate documents from a targeted range of scores to determine where the line between responsiveness and not responsiveness should be reasonably drawn.

Where an unreasonable number of responsive documents are identified during the validation stage, further training rounds may be warranted. The predictive coding process is typically complete once the validation review has yielded satisfactory results. In some models, however, a final statistically significant, randomly generated sample of documents from across the entire data collection (similar to the assessment phase at the beginning) is reviewed to provide final precision, recall, and F-measure metrics.[6]

The time it takes to complete a typical predictive coding workflow may vary according to a number of factors, such as volume, richness, character of the data, application used, number of subject-matter experts, and whether the data will be imported on a rolling basis. While it is possible to stabilize a predictive model within only a few days, these and other factors can extend that time.

6. Precision, recall, and F-measure are statistical terms that have been defined in the Appendix, and discussed at length in Chapters 13, 14, and 16 in this volume.

Post-Predictive Coding Review Decisions

After the predictive coding workflow has been completed, you have to determine what you are going to do with the data. There are many possibilities. The post-predictive coding review strategy must be designed according to the case at hand, and different cases will permit different review decisions.

Having an organized and ranked data collection, you may decide that a linear review of the entire collection is warranted, beginning from the most responsive data and working your way down until the final non-responsive document. You could stratify the review by sending highly responsive documents to the key legal team, and highly not responsive documents to less expensive contract attorneys. Alternatively, you may decide that having adequately validated the not responsive documents, no further review of that data is necessary, and you can focus instead solely on a manual review of the responsive data. Alternatively still, you may decide that the particular representation reasonably permits a review of only the C-suite custodians before production and that all other responsive documents could just be screened for privileged terms and non-privileged, non-C-suite custodians' responsive documents produced without review.[7] Similarly, it is important to determine to what extent any documents that may have been excluded from the predictive coding workflow, such as incompatible file types like Excel spreadsheets, will need to be reviewed.

Whatever predictive coding and post-predictive coding workflows are chosen, adequate documentation of material decisions should be maintained during the process. That documentation may be used if those processes are later challenged.

Conclusion

With data volumes growing every day, predictive coding will soon reach a level of everyday acceptance for large discovery matters, just as keywords and date filters are today commonplace. It behooves today's litigator to understand how to integrate predictive coding as an efficient and defensible legal service offering.

7. "C-suite" is used to refer to senior management, such as the chief executive officer, chief financial officer, and other similarly titled personnel.

EDITORS' INTRODUCTION TO CHAPTER 5

Michael D. Berman

Ralph Losey's chapter combines a description of the leading study by Gordon Cormack and Maura Grossman and his own vast experience to tackle terminology and discuss how to run a predictive coding project. He presents the issue of whether machines learn better if the first round of training documents, what others call the *seed set*, is chosen at random by the software or by using reviewer judgment and experience. Further, he analyzes that question in high, mid, and low "prevalence" data sets, and in both the first and subsequent rounds of machine training.

The chapter concludes that random selection of training documents is not as effective as multimodal, judgmental selection. The author analyzes whether and when judgmentally selected documents should be those that rank high in relevance or those that are mid- or low-ranked. Further, he discusses the informed use of keywords to perform judgmental selection. After reading this chapter, a generalist attorney will be better prepared to intelligently discuss issues with a service provider prior to contracting for those services, and to evaluate the opponents' decisions in implementing a machine learning protocol, all without reading a single line of code.

CHAPTER 5

Reflections on the Cormack and Grossman SIGIR Study: The Folly of Using Random Search for Machine Training[1]

Ralph C. Losey

This chapter contains my observations on a scholarly study by Gordon Cormack and Maura Grossman, *Evaluation of Machine-Learning Protocols for Technology-Assisted Review in Electronic Discovery*,[2] as presented at the prestigious international conference known as ACM SIGIR '14, held in July 2014 in Gold Coast, Queensland, Australia.[3] The Cormack and Grossman SIGIR study has important insights for

1. This chapter is a revised version of a blog originally published on Aug. 3, 2014. At the time of original publication, I thanked the authors of the study for reviewing and generously giving their time to try to ensure that my explanations were accurate. Still, any mistakes made on that account are solely my own. The opinions expressed in this article are likewise my own.

2. *See* ACM 978-1-4503-2257-7/14/07, http://dl.acm.org/citation.cfm?doid=2600428.2609601 (hereinafter Cormack-Grossman SIGIR Study).

3. ACM is the Association for Computing Machinery, the world's largest educational and scientific computing society. SIGIR is the Special Interest Group on Information Retrieval section of ACM. Hundreds of scientists and academics served on organizing committees for the 2014 SIGIR conference in Australia. They came from universities and large corporate research labs from all over the world, including Google, Yahoo, and IBM. See http://dl.acm.org/citation.cfm?id=2600428&picked=prox.

all attorneys who do legal search, but does not reveal its mysteries easily. That is mainly because it is written in the arcane language of a peer-reviewed scientific report. The present effort is my attempt to make the findings of Cormack and Grossman more accessible to the legal community, with ample personal (and sometimes highly irreverent) commentary on how the findings square with my own prior writings on the subject of, and personal experience in conducting, computer-assisted review. Toward this end I begin with a brief story that lays a predicate for the report itself.

Using Only Random Selection to Find Predictive Coding Training Documents Is Easy, But Foolish

There is a well-known story found in most cultures of the world about a fool looking for something. This anecdote has been told for thousands of years because it illustrates a basic trait of human psychology, now commonly called after the story itself, the streetlight effect.[4] This is a type of observational bias[5] where people only look for whatever they are searching for by looking where it is easiest. This human frailty, when pointed out in the right way, can be funny. One of the oldest known forms of pedagogic humor illustrating the streetlight effect comes from the famous stories of Nasrudin (or Nasreddin), an archetypal wise fool from 13th century Sufi traditions. Here is one version attributed to Nasreddin:

> One late evening Nasreddin found himself walking home. It was only a very short way and upon arrival he can be seen to be upset about something. Alas, just then a young man comes along and sees the Mullah's distress.
>
> "Mullah, pray tell me: what is wrong?"
>
> "Ah, my friend, I seem to have lost my keys. Would you help me search them? I know I had them when I left the tea house."

---

4. *See* https://en.wikipedia.org/wiki/Streetlight_effect (last visited Feb. 26, 2016).

5. *See* https://en.wikipedia.org/wiki/Observation#Observational_bias (last visited Feb. 26, 2016).

> So, he helps Nasreddin with the search for the keys. For quite a while the man is searching here and there but no keys are to be found. He looks over to Nasreddin and finds him searching only a small area around a street lamp.
>
> "Mullah, why are you only searching there?"
>
> "Why would I search where there is no light?"[6]

The easiest way to train documents for predictive coding is simply to use random samples. It may be easy, but, as far as I am concerned, it also defies common sense. The easy way is not necessarily the right way. This is true in search, as it is in many other things. The search for truth is often hard and difficult. You need to follow your own knowledge, what you know, and what you do not. What do you know about where you lost your keys? Think about that and use your analysis to guide your search. You must avoid the easy way, the lazy way. You must not be tempted to only look under the lamppost. To do so is to ignore your own knowledge. It is foolish to the extreme.

It may be easy to simply pick training documents at random, but it is ineffective. It ignores an attorney's knowledge of the case and the documents. It is equivalent to just rolling dice to decide where to look for something, instead of using your own judgment, your own skills and insights. It purports to replace the legal expertise of an attorney with a roll of the dice. It would have you ignore an attorney's knowledge of relevance and evidence, their skills, expertise, and long experience with search. If you know you left your keys near the front door, why let random chance tell you where to search? You should instead let your knowledge guide your search. It defies common sense to ignore what you know. Yet, this is exactly what some methods of predictive coding tell you to do.

These random-only methods are of course tied to software designed to run entirely on random selection of documents to use in training. The method requires no thought, as if lawyers were not capable of thought, as if lawyers have not long been *the* masters of

---

6. *See* Sufism/Nasrudin (WikiBooks) found at https://en.wikibooks.org/wiki/Sufism/Nasrudin#Nasreddin.27s_keys.

discovery of legal evidence. It seems insulting to the intelligence of any lawyer, and yet some continue to prescribe random selection as the *only* way to do predictive coding search.

Notably, such random-only methods have been criticized as predictive coding "junk science" by search expert and attorney Bill Speros, who used the same classic street light analogy: "Pulling a random sample of documents to train the initial seed set . . . is erroneous because it looks for relevance in all the wrong places. It turns a blind eye to what is staring you in the eye."[7] He goes on to make the point that "[s]ome attorneys employ random samples to populate seed sets apparently because they" either "[d]on't know how to form the seed set in a better way, or [w]ant to delegate responsibility to the computer which said so," or "[a]re emboldened by a statistical rationale premised on the claim that no one knows anything so random is a good a place to start as anywhere."[8]

Still, the practice continues, and in spite of many criticisms, even appears in some quarters to be increasing in popularity. I would be more greatly amused at all of this random-only search propaganda, but for the fact that many lawyers do not *get* the streetlight effect story. They are buying software and methods that rely exclusively on random search for training documents. Many are falling for the streetlight-effect gimmicks and marketing. It is not funny because we are talking about truth and justice here, not just a fool's house keys. In terms of what constitutes best practices for predictive coding, the future of legal search is harmed by this naive foolishness. That is why I have reacted before to propaganda promoting random search, and why I spent over 50 hours doing a predictive coding experiment based in part on random search—an approach I call the Random Borg Approach.[9]

---

7. J. William (Bill) Speros, *Predictive Coding's Erroneous Zones Are Emerging Junk Science*, E-DISCOVERY TEAM BLOG, http://e-discoveryteam.com/2013/04/28/predictive-codings-erroneous-zones-are-emerging-junk-science/ (last visited Feb. 26, 2016).

8. *Id.* (internal quotations omitted).

9. *See* R. Losey, *Comparative Efficacy of Two Predictive Coding Reviews of 699,082 Enron Documents* (Part Two), E-DISCOVERY TEAM BLOG, http://e-discoveryteam.com/2013/06/17/comparative-efficacy-of-two-predictive-coding-reviews-of-699082-enron-documents/ (last visited Feb. 26, 2016); R. Losey, *A Modest Contribution to the Science of Search: Report and Analysis of Inconsistent*

Thoughts on Lawyer Bias

To add insult to injury, some try to justify their methods by arguing that random selection avoids the prejudice of *lawyer bias*. It keeps the whole search process open. They seem to think lawyers know nothing, that they dropped their keys and have absolutely no idea where. If the lawyers think they know, they are just biased and should be ignored. They are not to be trusted. This is not only insulting, but ignores the obvious reality that lawyers—not computers, and not software engineers—are always making the final call on relevance. Lawyers say what is relevant and what is not, even with random selection.

Some engineers who design random-only selected training software for predictive coding may justify the limitation on the basis of assumed lawyer dishonesty. They think that if lawyers are allowed to pick samples for training, and not just have them selected for them at random, that lawyers may rig the system and hide the truth by intentionally poor selections. From my experience, this is the way a lot of computer experts really think when it comes to law and lawyers.

If a lawyer is really so dishonest that they will deliberately mistrain a predictive coding system to try to hide the truth, then that lawyer can easily find other, more effective ways to hide the ball than that. Hiding evidence is unethical. It is dishonest. It is not what we are paid to do. Argue what the facts mean? Yes, most definitely. Change the facts? No. Despite what you may think is true about law and lawyers, this is not the kind of thing that 98 percent of lawyers do. It will not be tolerated by courts. Such lawyer misconduct could not only lead to loss of a case, but also loss of a license to practice law. Can you say that about engineering?

Classifications in Two Predictive Coding Reviews of 699,082 Enron Documents (Part One), E-DISCOVERY TEAM BLOG, http://e-discoveryteam.com/2013/06/11/a-modest-contribution-to-the-science-of-search-report-and-analysis-of-inconsistent-classifications-in-two-predictive-coding-reviews-of-699082-enron-documents/ (last visited Feb. 26, 2016). I have also written several articles on this subject to try to debunk this method, and yet this method lives on. *See, e.g.*, R. Losey, *The Many Types of Legal Search Software in the CAR Market Today; Three-Cylinder Multimodal Approach to Predictive Coding*, E-DISCOVERY TEAM BLOG, http://e-discoveryteam.com/2013/03/24/three-cylinder-multimodal-approach-to-predictive-coding/ (last visited Feb. 26, 2016).

My message to professed software experts is simple: leave it to us, to attorneys and the Bar, to police legal search. Do not attempt to do so by software design. That is way beyond your purview. It is also foolish because the people you are insulting with this kind of mistrust are your customers!

I have talked to some of the engineers who believe in random reliance as a way to protect their code from lawyer manipulation. I know perfectly well that this is what some (not all) of them are trying to do. Frankly, the arrogant engineers who think like that do not know what they are talking about. It is just typical "engineer lawyer bias," plain and simple. Get over it and stop trying to sell us tools designed for dishonest children. We need full functionality. The Cormack-Grossman study proves this.

Some software designers with whom I have debated this topic will, at this point, try to placate me with statements about unintentional bias. They will point out that even though a lawyer may be acting in good faith, they may still have an unconscious, subjective bias. They will argue that without even knowing it, without realizing it, a lawyer may pick documents that only favor their clients. The broad application of this so-called "insight" into subjectivity to justify randomness is insulting to the intelligence of all lawyers. We understand better than most professions the inherent limitations of reason.[10] We are really not that dimwitted as to be unable to do legal search without our finger on the scale, and, this is important, *neither is the best predictive coding software*.

---

10. *See* R. Losey, *Scientific Proof of Law's Overreliance On Reason: The "Reasonable Man" Is Dead, Long Live the Whole Man, Part Two*, E-DISCOVERY TEAM BLOG, http://e-discoveryteam.com/2014/01/26/part-two-of-scientific-proof-of-laws-overreliance-on-reason-the-reasonable-man-is-dead-long-live-the-whole-man/ (last visited Feb. 26, 2016). *See also* R. Losey, *The Psychology of Law and Discovery*, E-DISCOVERY TEAM BLOG, http://e-discoveryteam.com/2014/01/12/the-psychology-of-law-and-discovery/ (last visited Feb. 26, 2016); R. Losey, *The Law's "Reasonable Man," Judge Haight, Love, Truth, Justice, "Go Fish" and Why the Legal Profession Is Not Doomed to Be Replaced by Robots*, E-DISCOVERY TEAM BLOG, https://e-discoveryteam.com/2016/06/29/the-laws-reasonable-man-judge-haight-love-truth-justice-go-fish-and-why-the-legal-profession-is-not-doomed-to-be-replaced-by-robots/ (last visited July 16, 2016).

Precautions can be taken against inherent, subjective bias. The solution is not to throw the baby out with the bath water, which is exactly what random-only search amounts to. The solution to bias is better search algorithms, plus quality controls. Code can be made to work so that it is not so sensitive and dependent on lawyer-selected documents. It can tolerate and correct errors. It can reach out and broaden initial search parameters. It is not constrained by the lawyer-selected documents.

Dear software designers: do not try to fix lawyers. We do not need the help of engineers for that. We will fix ourselves, thank you! Fix your code instead. Get real with your methods. Overcome your anti-lawyer bias and read the science.

Many software companies have already fixed their codes. They have succeeded in addressing the inherent limitations in all active machine learning, driven as it must be by inconsistent humans. In their software the lawyer trainers are not the only ones selecting documents for training. The computer selects documents too. Smart computer selection is far different, and far better, than "stupid" random selection.

I know that the software I use is frequently correcting my errors, broadening my initial conception of relevance. It is helping me to find new documents that are relevant, documents that I would never have thought of or found on my own. The computer selects as many documents as I decide are appropriate to enhance the training. Random has only a small place at the beginning to calculate prevalence. Concept searches, similarity searches, keyword, even linear, are far, far better than random alone. When they are all put together in a multimodal predictive coding package, the results can be extremely good.

The notion that you should just turn search over to chance means you should search everywhere and anywhere. That is the essence of random. It means you have no idea of where the relevant documents might be located, and what they might say. That is again completely contrary to what happens in legal discovery. No lawyer is *that* dim-witted. There is always at least some knowledge as to the type or kind of documents that might be relevant. There is always some knowledge as to who is most likely to have them, and when, and what they might say, what names would be used, what metadata, etc.

The Cormack-Grossman SIGIR Study

The continuing success in the marketplace of the random selection of documents approach is, I suspect, one reason that the Cormack-Grossman SIGIR study was designed to answer the question:

> Should training documents be selected at random, or should they be selected using one or more non-random methods, such as keyword search or active learning?[11]

Although the answer may seem common-sensical and obvious, sometimes common sense and history can be wrong. The only way to know for sure is by scientific experiment. That is exactly what Cormack and Grossman have done, in putting the streetlight effect of using random search software to the test, and giving it serious attention. It should come as no surprise, except to some remaining holdouts, that the experiments performed show that it is more effective to select training documents using nonrandom methods and active learning (a process that I have called multimodal search).[12]

The information scientist behind this study is Gordon V. Cormack, a professor at the University of Waterloo. He has a long history as a search expert outside of legal search, including special expertise in spam searches. The lawyer who worked with Gordon on this study is Maura R. Grossman, Esq., formerly at Wachtell, Lipton, Rosen & Katz. In addition to her JD, she has a PhD in psychology, and has been a tireless advocate for effective legal search for many years.

The primary purpose of their study was *not* to test the effectiveness of training based on random samples. That was a secondary issue. Rather, the primary focus of the study was to test the relative effectiveness of three different training approaches to machine learning, namely: *Continuous Active Learning* (CAL), *Simple Active Learning* (SAL), and *Simple Passive Learning* (SPL).

> Our primary experiments evaluated the specific formulations of CAL, SAL, and SPL described in

11. *See* Cormack-Grossman SIGIR Study (Abstract), *supra* note 2.

12. *See* e-discoveryteam.com multimodal search blog citations, http://e-discoveryteam.com/?s=multimodal.

> Section 2; secondary experiments explored the effect of using keyword-selected versus randomly selected documents for the seed and training sets.[13]

Before describing these three approaches in more detail, it should be clear that the three protocols they tested are not the only approaches used in machine learning. There are many more, including the multimodal approach (previously described). Cormack and Grossman used these three fairly simplistic methods in this experiment because they were easy to reproduce in an experimental setting. Moreover, all three protocols tested had some connection with real world legal practice.

The Cormack-Grossman protocol test was a scientific experiment, not a demonstration of the latest and greatest machine-learning protocols. Cormack and Grossman are scientists and educators. They do not sell software or any particular *secret sauce* legal search methods—although they no doubt have such methods.[14]

Cormack and Grossman set up an ingenious experiment to test the effectiveness of three machine-learning protocols. It is ingenious for several reasons, not the least of which is that they created what they call an "evaluation toolkit"[15] to perform the experiment. They have even made this same toolkit, this same software, freely available for use by any other qualified researchers. They invite other scientists to run the experiment for themselves. They invite open testing of their experiment. They invite vendors to do so, too.

---

13. Cormack-Grossman SIGIR Study, *supra* note 2, at 4.

14. Maura Grossman is also an attorney. In that capacity she no doubt privately advocates for some methods over others, and like I do, sells her secret sauce, her methods, as part of her work for her law firm's clients. But that is not what she is doing here in her work with Gordon. They are testing a few of the most basic training protocols used for scientific purposes. I am in essentially the same position as Maura Grossman in some respects. When I sell my time as a lawyer to lead predictive coding projects, I am, in effect, selling my expertise in particular machine-training protocols. I have my own methods, and I often create special methods to suit a particular project. Notwithstanding my past writings, I have only disclosed the basic outlines of the protocols I use—not all of the details. Plus, I continue to learn and invent new methods.

15. *See* http://cormack.uwaterloo.ca/cormack/tar-toolkit/ (last visited Feb. 26, 2016).

That is the true essence of the scientific approach. Find truth from empirical evidence, not dogma. (That is, by the way, also the approach of all enlightened legal systems, where justice is based on facts, on evidence, and not on social opinions or religious dictates.) Cormack and Grossman have opened up their experiment to full public view and re-testing in an extraordinary way. It is my strong desire, and I am sure theirs as well, that other scientists will take them up on this offer and run their tests to get a clearer and bigger view of the facts, and thus a clearer and better view of the truth of the relative efficacy of these three training methods. One information scientist, William Webber, has already tested their study using his own approach. His findings generally confirmed and expanded upon those of Cormack and Grossman as to the relative ineffectiveness of random-only training, especially on low-prevalence data sets (which is what lawyers typically work with in legal search).[16]

I am not a big fan of acronyms, and so I personally do not like how Cormack and Grossman use three acronyms throughout their study to label the three machine-training protocols. But to understand their report you need to learn and remember these acronyms: CAL, SAL, and SPL (Figure 5.1).

CAL: Continuous Active Learning

Continuous active learning (CAL) protocol uses one method for the first round of training and another for all subsequent rounds. In the first round, documents are selected using human judgmental sampling by use of keyword search; in the second and subsequent rounds, a learning algorithm that classifies documents and ranks them according to probability is used. In the first round, 1,000 of the keyword search results are selected at random. In the second and subsequent rounds, the top 1,000 ranked documents are selected, reviewed, and added to the training set. These are the documents in which the machine has the highest confidence, or the highest degree of certainty as to its prediction that the document is relevant. The rankings change as the training

16. *See* W. Webber, *Random vs Active Selection of Training Examples in e-Discovery*, Evaluating e-Discovery Blog (July 14, 2014), https://web.archive.org/web/20150912091843/http://blog.codalism.com/index.php/random-vs-active-selection-of-training-examples-in-e-discovery/#more-2089 (last visited July 16, 2016).

FIGURE 5.1 CAL, SAL, and SPL machine-training protocols

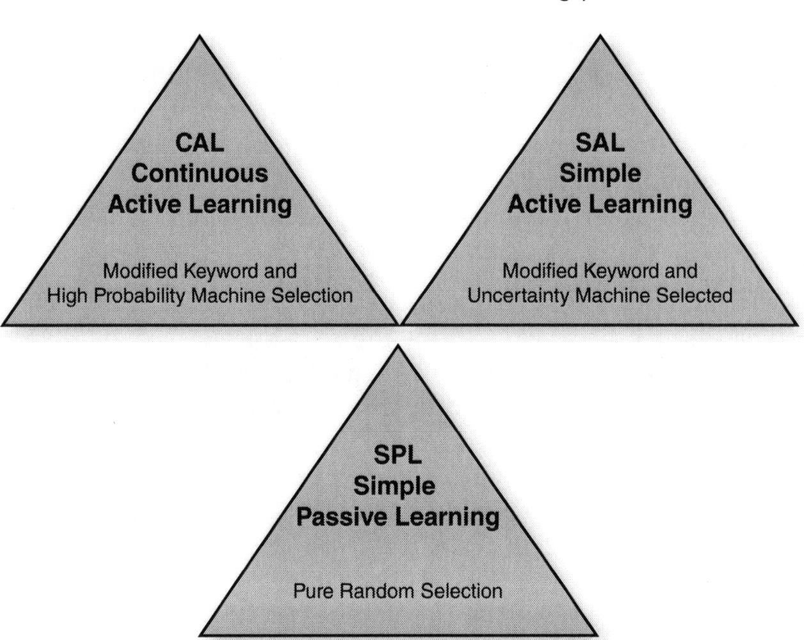

evolves. This process continues until adequate recall is achieved. I call this training protocol a *modified keyword and high probability machine-selected* method.

I call it modified because keyword-selected documents are only used in the first round of training, and thereafter, the keyword search method is dropped. All subsequent training relies exclusively on high probability machine-selected documents for review.

Cormack and Grossman call the first round of machine-training documents the *seed set*. They do so out of tradition and common usage in the legal search community, but frankly, I see no reason to continue to use this dated language. I prefer to call the first round of machine training just that, *the first round*. Otherwise, many people are confused by thinking that the first round of training is somehow special. In fact, machine-training iterations are just like baseball innings. The first inning may be important psychologically, but it is just another inning, like all of the others, and the game is never over until at least the ninth. The score before that is irrelevant.

We do not know from this study the impact of using keyword search in every round. They did not test that exactly; but, in their secondary experiments Cormack and Grossman did explore the effect of adding keyword-selected training documents to the SPL (pure random) methods. They found that adding keywords to the first round of training generally improves performance in SPL, and that keywords for all training sets usually, but not always, improves SPL. They also found that replacing keyword search with random selections harms the performance of the CAL and SAL methods.

In my work I use every possible type of search in every round of training, the first round, second, third, whatever. The only type of search I do *not* use in the first round, the so-called seed set, are machine-selected uncertainty documents. That is because the classification probability ranking has not begun yet. That particular kind of search method can only begin *after* the first round of training. I pick and choose which methods to use in a particular training round depending on the case, the data, and what I see and know from the study as the review progresses. It often depends on what I learned in prior rounds. Maybe I will use 100 machine-selected documents in the second round, maybe more, maybe none. Maybe I will focus on the highest ranking as done here with CAL, or maybe I will focus on the middle rankings, the so-called uncertainty zone used in the next protocol tested here, SAL. I may check out some of the lowest rankings. I may even switch the type of classifications ranked, say move from relevant to irrelevant, or more likely to highly relevant (hot). Maybe I will use some concept search, some similarity search, or more keywords. It all depends on the circumstances and new documents that I may have seen. It all flows, it changes, and is never the same from one project to the next, or even from one round to the next, although the basic parameters remain the same.

From what Grossman and other search experts have told me, they are all doing something similar to this. But they do not share the exact details, the secret sauce, with me, anymore than I do with them. Since we use different software tools, that would anyway be very hard to do. The many types of different things that you can do with legal search in general, and machine training in particular, depend in part on the software tools that you use. The latest software tools available in the marketplace provide tremendous flexibility. However, I almost always follow my own methods, not the default software settings, especially when it comes to the use of random document selections.

SAL: Simple Active Learning

Simple active learning (SAL) protocol again uses one method for the first round of training and another for all subsequent rounds. In SAL, documents for the initial round of training are again selected, the same as in CAL, by random selection of keyword hit documents.

Documents for the following rounds are again selected by a learning algorithm, only this time the highest ranked documents are not the ones used for training. Instead, only the middle ranked documents are reviewed, the ones in which the machine has the highest degree of uncertainty. In my writings I refer to this later type of uncertainty based protocol as machine-selected documents. The machine-selected documents are typically in the 40 to 60 percent probability range. Under this system, after the initial round of training, only documents are reviewed that the machine has the highest degree of uncertainty as to its prediction of coding. Once training is complete, the top-ranked documents are reviewed for production, but not to further train the system, until adequate recall is achieved. So my summary of this training protocol is that this is a *modified keyword and uncertainty machine-selected* method.

Again I say modified because random keyword samples are only used to select documents in the first round of training. In all subsequent rounds, keyword search selected documents are not used; instead, documents are selected solely on the basis of automated uncertainty calculations, what I call machine selection.

Note that in my 50-hour Borg protocol test I used something close to this SAL protocol.[17] I used a totally random sample of 1,183 documents for the first round. In every other round thereafter I used a combination of random and uncertainty machine selected. I called

17. *See* R. Losey, *Borg Challenge: Report of My Experimental Review of 699,082 Enron Documents Using a Semi-Automated Monomodal Methodology* (a five-part written and video series comparing two different kinds of predictive coding search methods), E-DISCOVERY TEAM BLOG, http://e-discoveryteam.com/2013/04/18/borg-challenge-the-complete-report/ (last visited Feb. 26, 2016).

this the Enlightened Borg Approach.[18] In this experiment I used this protocol in 50 rounds of training, plus a final quality assurance round with another random sample. In the 49 rounds after the first, I reviewed 200 documents in each round; 20 percent of the documents, 40 documents, were random selected, and 80 percent, 160 documents, were uncertainty machine selected.

I compared my results with a prior review of the same 699,082 documents for the same issue (employee terminations, excluding voluntary departures). I spent about the same amount of time in the earlier review, 50 hours. But in the earlier review I used a fully multimodal approach, where I used random, machine-selected, and human-judgment-selected documents, primarily keyword. That is what I call the full three-cylinder search engine approach.[19] The first document review experiment is described in *Predictive Coding Narrative: Searching for Relevance in the Ashes of Enron*,[20] plus the blog introducing this 82-page narrative, with a second blog regarding an update.[21]

The random- and machine-selected protocol, which I called monomodal, did surprisingly well in my comparison experiment, but was still surpassed by full multimodal, especially in the all-important search for hot documents. Full multimodal did 57 percent better with that classification.[22]

The SAL protocol tested by Cormack and Grossman uses human input in the form of keyword selection for the first round. Then, in all following rounds of SAL, documents were selected for review based on the machine's uncertainty ranking. The uncertainty rankings change

---

18. *See* R. Losey, *Three-Cylinder Multimodal Approach To Predictive Coding*, E-DISCOVERY TEAM BLOG, http://e-discoveryteam.com/2013/03/24/three-cylinder-multimodal-approach-to-predictive-coding/ (last visited Feb. 26, 2016).

19. *See id.*

20. *See* R. Losey, *Predictive Coding Narrative: Searching for Relevance in the Ashes of Enron (Restatement)*, E-DISCOVERY TEAM BLOG (Mar. 18, 2013), http://e-discoveryteam.com/2013/03/18/predictive-coding-narrative-searching-for-relevance-in-the-ashes-of-enron-restatement/.

21. *See* R. Losey, *Corrections and Refinements to Predictive Coding Narrative*, E-DISCOVERY TEAM BLOG (Mar. 21, 2013), http://e-discoveryteam.com/2013/03/21/corrections-and-refinements-to-predictive-coding-narrative/.

22. *See* Losey, *supra* note 9.

as the training evolves. The exact range of probability uncertainty used in this experiment would depend on the number of documents falling within the 40 to 60 percent zone because the number of training documents used was fixed at 1,000 for each round. As Cormack and Grossman put it, machine-selected documents are those "about which the learning algorithm is least certain."[23]

I advocate for a *three-cylinder* search engine approach because this is part of my multimodal method. I use every known search method as appropriate to the circumstances to try to find the target documents. I use random methods, and human-judgmental methods, including, but certainly not limited to, keyword search; and, I use machine-selected methods, methods that rely on a predictive coding ranking system. The machine-selected-type methods that I use include highest rankings methods, and middle uncertainty rankings, as considered by Cormack and Grossman in this experiment. But in my work I may examine a variety of different ranges of probability ranking. The movement of these rankings can also provide valuable insights. (This may be the most detailed description that I have provided to date as to the finer points of my predictive coding training methods.)

Again, please remember that the few methods selected for study by Cormack and Grossman in this experiment are just a few out of hundreds of different possible search methods. Indeed the combinations possible would reach into the tens of thousands, or higher, depending on duration and complexity of the review. Very few, if any, legal search experts would only use a couple of training protocols, much less just one.

SPL: Simple Passive Learning

The simple passive learning (SPL) protocol uses simple random selection of documents throughout the project, in the initial round and all following rounds. SPL uses no other search methods to find training documents. It does not use machine-selected documents nor human selected documents. Once training is complete, the top-ranked documents are reviewed for production, but not to further train the system,

23. Cormack-Grossman SIGIR Study, *supra* note 2, at 154.

until adequate recall is achieved. My summary of this training protocol is that this is a *pure random* selection method.

In my prior writings on machine training I have called this the Lucky Borg Approach.[24]

Cormack and Grossman used this monomodal *pure random* approach to search the same document sets as the other two protocols. They again used 100 rounds, 1,000 documents per round, and simulated actual human reviewer results by reference to prior TREC studies of the same documents. Aside from the machine-training protocols, the details of how the experimental simulated reviews were conducted were identical for all three processes. That is how they attained comparator information and measured comparative efficacy between the three methods tested.

Findings of Cormack-Grossman Study

Here is how Cormack and Grossman summarized their findings:

> The results presented here do not support the commonly advanced position that seed sets, or entire training sets, must be randomly selected. . . . Our primary implementation of SPL, in which all training documents were randomly selected, yielded dramatically inferior results to our primary implementations of CAL and SAL, in which none of the training documents were randomly selected.[25]

CAL Versus SPL

Now for the details of the results comparing the previously described methods of CAL, SAL, and SPL. First, let us examine the comparison between the CAL and SPL machine-training methods (Figure 5.2).

24. *See* Losey, *supra* note 19 ("Some types of predictive coding software rely entirely on random chance to select documents for machine training. They are, so to speak, a one-cylinder predictive coding search engine. They run on chance alone."), http://e-discoveryteam.com/2013/03/24/three-cylinder-multimodal-approach-to-predictive-coding/.

25. Cormack-Grossman SIGIR Study, *supra* note 2, at 159.

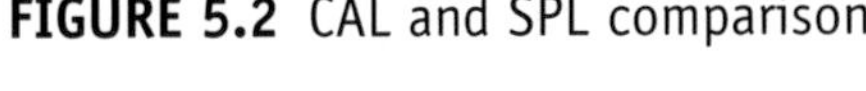

FIGURE 5.2 CAL and SPL comparison

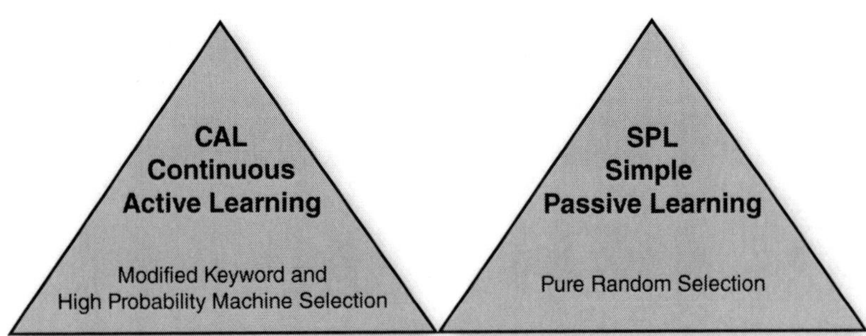

As stated previously, CAL is a simplistic type of multimodal training method wherein two methods are used. Keyword search results are used in the first round of training. In all following rounds, high probability ranked search results are used. SPL is a pure random method, a monomodal method. With SPL, all documents are selected by random sampling for training in all rounds.

Cormack and Grossman found that the "CAL protocol *achieves higher recall than SPL, for less effort*, for all of the representative training-set sizes."[26] This means you can find more relevant documents using CAL than a random method, and you can do so faster and thus with less expense.

To drill down even deeper into their findings it is necessary to look at the graphs in the report that show how the search progressed through all 100 rounds of training, and review for various document collections. This is shown for CAL versus SPL in Figure 1 of the report (see Figure 5.3).[27] The line with circle dots at the top of each graph plots the retrieval rate of CAL, the clear winner on each of the eight search tasks tested. The other three lines show the random approach, SPL, using three different training-set sizes.

26. *Id.* (emphasis added).
27. *Id.* at 157.

FIGURE 5.3 Continuous active learning versus simple passive learning using three different training set sizes of randomly selected documents

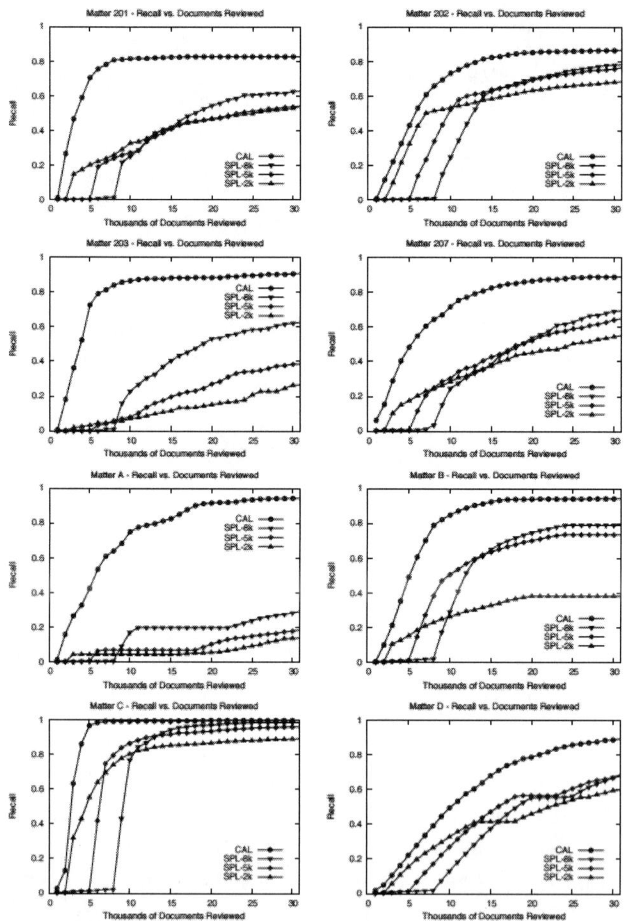

Cormack and Grossman summarize the CAL versus SPL findings as follows:

> After the first 1,000 documents (i.e., the seed set), the CAL curve shows a high slope that is sustained until the majority of relevant documents have been identified. At about 70% recall, the slope begins to

> fall off noticeably, and effectively plateaus between 80% and 100% recall. The SPL curve exhibits a low slope for the training phase, followed by a high slope, falloff, and then a plateau for the review phase. In general, the slope immediately following training is comparable to that of CAL, but the falloff and plateau occur at substantially lower recall levels. While the initial slope of the curve for the SPL review phase is similar for all training-set sizes, the falloff and plateau occur at higher recall levels for larger training sets. This advantage of larger training sets is offset by the greater effort required to review the training set: In general, the curves for different training sets cross, indicating that a larger training set is advantageous when high recall is desired.[28]

CAL Versus SAL

The Cormack-Grossman experiment also compared the CAL and SAL methods (Figure 5.4). As stated above, the SAL method is another simple multimodal method where only two methods are used to select training documents. Keywords are again used in the first round only, just like the CAL protocol. Thereafter, in all subsequent rounds of training machine selected documents are used based on the machine's uncertainty of classification. That means the search is focused on the midrange ranked documents about which the machine is most uncertain.

Cormack and Grossman found that "the CAL protocol generally achieves higher recall than SAL," but the results were closer and more complex.[29] At one point in the training SAL became as good as CAL; it achieved a specific recall value with nearly the same efforts as CAL from that point forward. The authors found that was due to the fact that many *high probability* documents began to be used by the machine as *uncertainty selected* documents. This happened after all of the mid-scoring documents had been used up. In other words,

28. *Id.* at 156.
29. *Id.*

FIGURE 5.4 CAL versus SAL comparison

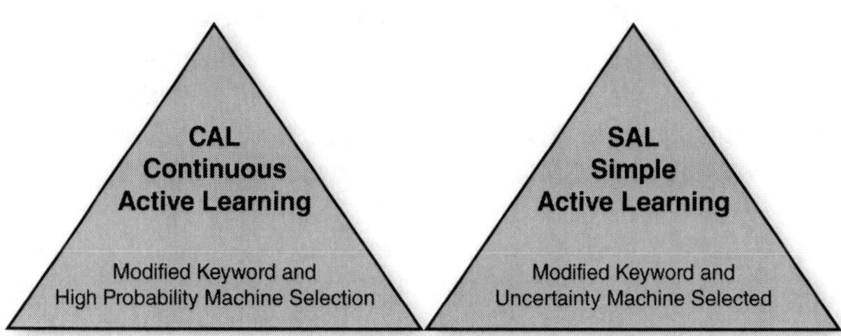

at some point the distinction between the two methods was decreased, and more high probability documents were used in SAL, in almost the same way they were used in CAL. That allowed SAL to catch up with CAL and, in effect, become almost as good.

This catch up point is different in each project. As Cormack and Grossman explain:

> Once stabilization occurs, the review set will include few documents with intermediate scores, because they will have previously been selected for training. Instead, the review set will include primarily high-scoring and low-scoring documents. The high-scoring documents account for the high slope before the inflection point; the low-scoring documents account for the low slope after the inflection point; the absence of documents with intermediate scores accounts for the sharp transition. The net effect is that SAL achieves effort as low as CAL only for a specific recall value, which is easy to see in hindsight, but difficult to predict at the time of stabilization.[30]

This inflection point and other comparisons can be easily seen in Figure 2 of the report (Figure 5.5).[31] Again the line with circle dots

30. *Id.*
31. *Id.* at 158.

FIGURE 5.5 Continuous active learning versus simple active learning using three different training set sizes of uncertainty-sampled documents

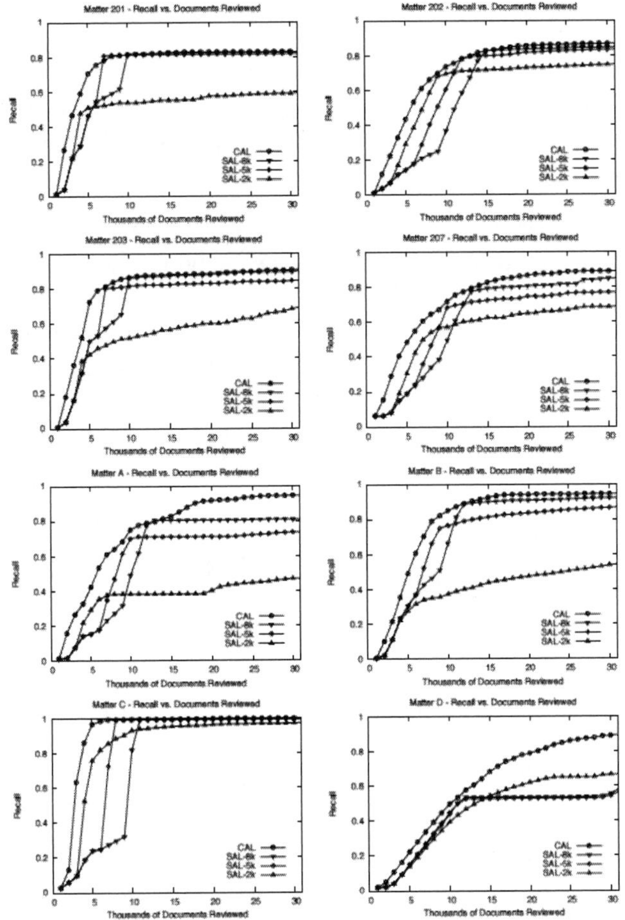

at the top of each graph, the one that always starts off fastest, plots the retrieval rate of CAL. And again, it does better than in each of the eight search tasks tested. The other three lines show the uncertainty approach, SAL, using three different training-set sizes. CAL does better than SAL in all eight of the matters, but the differences are not nearly as great as the comparison between CAL and SPL.

Cormack and Grossman summarize the CAL versus SAL findings as follows:

> Figure 2 shows that the CAL protocol generally achieves higher recall than SAL. However, the SAL gain curves, unlike the SPL gain curves, often touch the CAL curves at one specific inflection point. The strong inflection of the SAL curve at this point is explained by the nature of uncertainty sampling. . . ."[32]

This experiment compared one type of simple, multimodal machine-training method with another. It found that with the data sets tested, and other standard procedures set forth in the experiment, the method that used high-ranking documents for training, what William Webber calls the *relevance* method, performed somewhat better than the method that used mid-ranked documents, what Webber calls the *uncertainty* method.[33]

This does not mean that the uncertainty method should be excluded from a full multimodal approach in real-world applications. It just means that here, in this one experiment, albeit a very complex and multifaceted experiment, the relevance method outperformed the uncertainty method.

I have found that in the real world of very complex (messy even) legal searches, it is good to use both high- and mid-ranked documents for training—what Cormack and Grossman call CAL and SAL, and what Webber calls relevance, and uncertainty, training. I do, however, typically use the uncertainty method sparingly, and place greater reliance on high-ranking documents. The exact mix is an ad hoc process that depends on the circumstances, including the all-important cost component. In the real world you use every method you can think of to help you to find what you are looking for, not just one or two, but dozens.

---

32. *Id.* at 156.
33. *See* Webber, *supra* note 16.

Grossman and Cormack know this very well too, which I know from private conservations with them on this, and also from the conclusion to their report:

> There is no reason to presume that the CAL results described here represent the best that can be achieved. Any number of feature engineering methods, learning algorithms, training protocols, and search strategies might yield substantive improvements in the future. The effect of review order and other human factors on training accuracy, and thus overall review effectiveness, may also be substantial.[34]

My practical takeaway from the Cormack-Grossman experiment is that focusing on high-ranking documents is a powerful search method. It should be given significant weight in any multimodal approach, especially when the goal is to quickly find as many relevant documents as possible. The "continuous" training aspects of the CAL approach are also intriguing, that is, you keep doing machine training throughout the review project and batch reviews accordingly. This could become a project management issue, but, if you can pull it off within proportionality and requesting party constraints, it just makes common sense to do so. You might as well get as much help from the machine as possible and keep getting its probability predictions for as long as you are still doing reviews and can make last minute batch assignments accordingly. That is why most of my projects today utilize a continuous training approach.

I have done predictive coding reviews since 2012 using such a continuous training manner without really thinking about the fact the machine input was continuous, including my first Enron experiment.[35] But this causes me to rethink the flow chart shown in Figure 5.6 that I usually use to explain the predictive coding process. The workflow shown is not a CAL approach, but rather a SAL-type of approach where there is a distinct stop in training after step 5, and the review work in step 7 is based on the last rankings established in step 5.

34. Cormack-Grossman SIGIR Report, *supra* note 2, at 161.
35. *See* Losey, *supra* note 21.

FIGURE 5.6 Ralph Losey's original "pre-CAL" predictive coding workflow

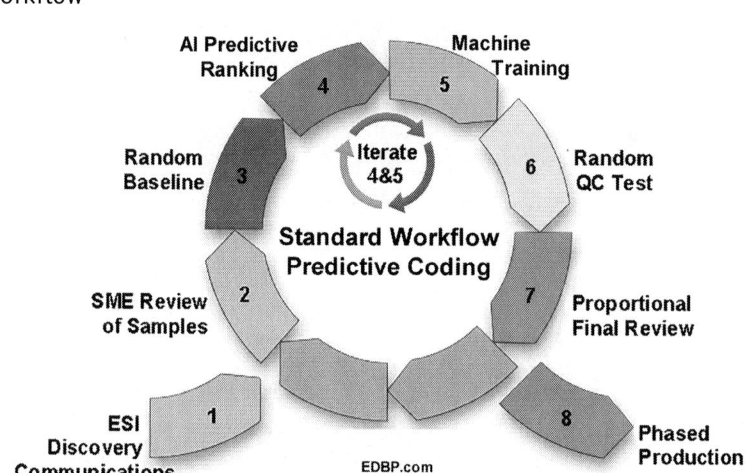

The continuous workflow is slightly more difficult to show in a diagram, and to implement, but it does make good common sense if you are in a position to pull it off. Figure 5.7 illustrates the revised workflow to update the language and show how the training continues throughout the review.

Machine training is still done in steps 4 and 5, but then continues in steps 4, 5, and 7. There are other ways it could be implemented of course, but this is the CAL approach I used in 2014 for review projects. Of course, it is not necessary in any project where the review in steps 4 and 5 effectively finds *all* of the relevant documents required. This is what happened in my Enron experiment.[36] There was no need to do a proportional final review, step 7, because all the relevant documents had already been reviewed as part of the machine-training review in steps 4 and 5. In the Enron experiment I skipped step 7 and went right from step 6 to step 8, production. I have been able to do this in other projects as well.

36. *See id.*

FIGURE 5.7 Ralph Losey's current predictive coding workflow

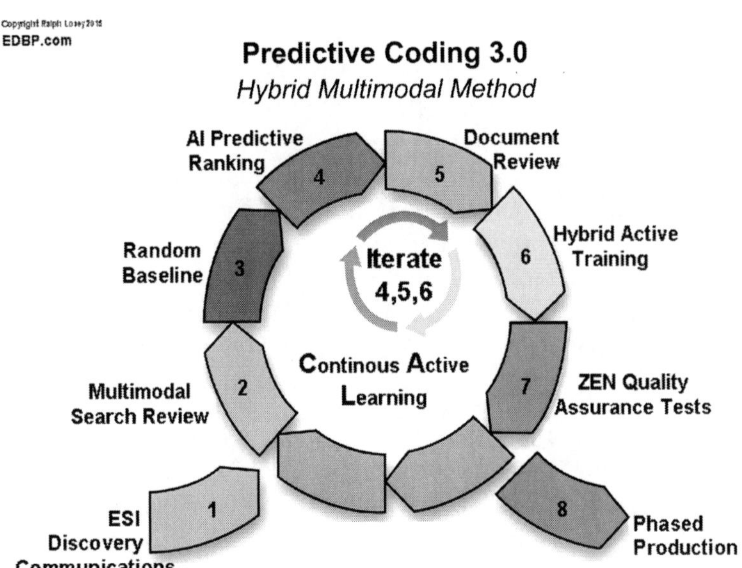

Strengths of a Relevancy-Weighted-Type of CAL

The findings in this experiment as to the strengths of using relevancy training confirm what I have seen in most of my search projects. I usually start with the high-end documents to quickly help me to teach the machine what I am looking for. I find that this is a good way to start training. Again, it just makes common sense to do so. It is somewhat like teaching a human, or a dog for that matter. You teach the machine relevance classification by telling it when it is right (positive reinforcement) and when it is wrong. This kind of feedback is critical in all learning. In most projects this kind of feedback on predictions of highly probable relevance is the fastest way to get to the most important documents. For those reasons I agree with Cormack and Grossman's conclusion that CAL is a superior method to quickly find the most relevant documents:

> CAL also offers the reviewer the opportunity to quickly identify legally significant documents that can guide litigation strategy, and can readily adapt

> when new documents are added to the collection, or new issues or interpretations of relevance arise.[37]

Id.

But then again, I would never rely on just relevancy CAL-type searches alone. It gets results fast, but it could in some cases also lead to a somewhat myopic focus on the high end where you may miss new, different types of relevant documents. At least, that is my concern. I have no proof of that. For that reason, I also use SAL types of searches to include the mid-range documents from the uncertainty method. It can be an important method to help the machine to better understand what documents I am looking for. As Cormack and Grossman put it:

> The underlying objective of CAL is to find and review as many of the responsive documents as possible, as quickly as possible. The underlying objective of SAL, on the other hand, is to induce the best classifier possible, considering the level of training effort. Generally, the classifier is applied to the collection to produce a review set, which is then subject to manual review.[38]

Similarity and other concept-type search methods can also be a good way to quickly find as many responsive documents as possible. So, too, are keyword searches, and not just in the first round, but for any round. Further, this experiment, which is already very complex (to me at least), does not include the important real world component of *highly relevant* versus merely *relevant* documents. I never just train on relevancy alone, but always include a hunt for the hot documents. I want to try to train the machine to understand the difference between the two classifications. Cormack and Grossman do not disagree. As they put it, "any number of feature engineering methods, learning algorithms, training protocols, and search strategies"[39] could improve upon a CAL only approach.

There are many ways to improve the classifier in addition to focus on mid-range probability documents. For instance, sometimes it may

37. Cormack-Grossman SIGIR Study, *supra* note 2, at 161.
38. *Id.* at 160.
39. *Id.* at 161.

be helpful to be sure your training on the low end is also right, meaning review of some of the high probability *irrelevant* documents. Both relevant and irrelevant training are helpful. Personally, I also like to include some judgmental sample and random sample aspects, especially at first, to be sure I did not miss any outlier-type documents, and to be sure I have a good feel for the irrelevant documents of these custodians too. Yes, chance has to place too, so long as it is very small and does not take over and become the whole show.

Supplemental Findings on Random Search

Cormack and Grossman tested this last notion in their experiments. In addition to comparing CAL with SAL and SPL, they experimented with what would happen to the effectiveness of both the CAL and SAL protocols if more random elements were added to the methods. They experimented with a number of different variables, including substituting random selection, instead of keyword, for the initial round of training (seed set). The amount of random selection they inserted was far more than I would ever use.

As you would expect, the general results were to *decrease* the effectiveness of every search method wherein random was substituted, either for keyword, high-ranking relevance, or mid-ranking relevance (uncertainty). The negative impact was strongest in datasets where prevalence was low, which is typical in litigation. Cormack and Grossman tested eight datasets where the prevalence of responsive documents varied from 0.25 to 3.92 percent, which, as they put it: "is typical for the legal matters with which we have been involved."[40] The size of the sets tested ranged 293,000 documents to just over 1.1 million. The random-based search of lowest prevalence dataset tested, matter 203, the one with a 0.25 percent prevalence rate, was, in their words, a "spectacular failure." Conversely, the negative impact was lessened with higher prevalence datasets.[41]

Cormack and Grossman responded to the popular misconception that predictive coding does not work in such low prevalence datasets:

40. *Id.*
41. *Id.*

> Others assert that these are examples of "low-prevalence" or "low-richness" collections, for which TAR is unsuitable. . . .. We suggest that such assertions may presuppose an SPL protocol . . . , which is not as effective on low-prevalence datasets. It may be that SPL methods can achieve better results on higher-prevalence collections (i.e., 10% or more responsive documents).[42]

In fact, information scientists have been working with low-prevalence datasets for decades, which is one reason Professor Cormack had a ready collection of precoded documents by which to measure recall, a so-called gold standard of assessments from prior studies. Cormack and Grossman explain that the lack of pretested datasets with high prevalence is the reason they did not use such collections for testing. They also speculate that if such high prevalence datasets are tested, then the random-only (SPL) method would do much better than it did in the low-prevalence datasets they used in their experiment.

> However, no such collections were included in this study because, for the few matters with which we have been involved where the prevalence exceeded 10%, the necessary training and gold-standard assessments were not available. We conjecture that the comparative advantage of CAL over SPL would be decreased, but not eliminated, for high-prevalence collections.[43]

They are probably right; if the datasets have a higher prevalence, then the chances are that random samples will find more relevant documents for training. But that still does not make the blind draw a better way to find things than looking with your eyes wide open. Plus, the typical way to attain high yield datasets is by keyword filtering out large segments of the raw data before beginning a predictive coding search. When you keyword filter like that before beginning of machine training the chances are you will leave behind a significant portion, if not mt of the relevant documents. Keyword filtering often has low recall, or when broad enough to include most of the

42. *Id.*
43. *Id.*

relevant documents, it is very imprecise. Then you are back to the same low-prevalence situation.

Better to limit any filtering before machine training to obvious irrelevant, or ESI not appropriate for training, such as non-text documents like photos, music, and voice mail. Use other methods to search for those types of ESI. But do not use keyword filtering on text documents simply to create an artificially high prevalence just because the random based software you use will only work that way. That is the tail wagging the dog.

For more analysis and criticism on using keywords to create artificially high prevalence, a practice Cormack and Grossman call collection enrichment, see another excellent article they wrote.[44] This article also contains good explanations of the instant study with CAL, SAL, and SPL.[45] The negative impact of random elements on machine-training protocols is a "no, duh" to experienced searchers.[46] It never helps to turn to luck or random chance to improve search. Once you start relying on dice to decide what to do, you are just spinning your wheels.

Supplemental Findings on Keywords and Random Search

Cormack and Grossman tested what would happen if keywords were used instead of random selections, even when the keywords were not tested first against the actual data. This poor practice of using unverified keywords is what I call the "go fish" approach to keyword

44. M. Grossman & G. Cormack, *Comments on "The Implications of Rule 26(g) on the Use of Technology-Assisted Review*," 7 Fed. Cts. L. Rev. 286, 293–295, 300–301 (2014).

45. *See especially id.* Table 1 at 297.

46. *See, e.g.*, the excellent series of articles by John Tredennick, including his review on the Cormack-Grossman study. J. Tredennick, *Pioneering Cormack/Grossman Study Validates Continuous Learning, Judgmental Seeds and Review Team Training for Technology Assisted Review*, Catalyst E-Discovery Search Blog (May 12, 2014), http://www.catalystsecure.com/blog/2014/05/pioneering-cormackgrossman-study-validates-continuous-learning-judgmental-seeds-and-review-team-training-for-technology-assisted-review/ (last visited Feb. 26, 2016).

search.[47] Under this naive approach attorneys simply guess what keywords might be contained on relevant documents without testing how accurate their guesses are. It is a very simplistic approach to keyword search, yet, nevertheless, is still widely employed in the legal profession. This approach has been criticized by many, including Judge Andrew Peck in his excellent *Gross Construction* opinion, the so-called wake-up call for New York attorneys on search.[48]

Cormack and Grossman also tested what would happen if such naive keyword selections were used instead of the high- or mid-probability methods (CAL and SAL) for machine training. The naive keywords used in these supplemental comparison tests did fairly well. This is consistent with my multimodal approach, where all kinds of search methods are used in all rounds of training.

The success of naive keyword selection for machine training is discussed by Cormack and Grossman as an unexpected finding:

> Perhaps more surprising is the fact that a simple keyword search, *composed without prior knowledge of the collection*, almost always yields a more effective seed set than random selection, whether for CAL, SAL, or SPL. Even when keyword search is used to select all training documents, the result is generally superior to that achieved when random selection is used. That said, even if (random) passive learning is enhanced using a keyword-selected seed or training set, it (passive learning) is still dramatically inferior to active learning. It is possible, in theory, that a party could devise keywords that would render passive learning competitive with active learning, but until a formal protocol for constructing such a search can be established, it is impossible to subject the approach to a controlled scientific evaluation. Pending the

47. R. Losey, *Child's Game of "Go Fish" Is a Poor Model for e-Discovery Search* (Oct. 2009), E-DISCOVERY TEAM BLOG, http://e-discoveryteam.com/2009/10/04/childs-game-of-go-fish-is-a-poor-model-for-e-discovery-search/ (last visited Feb. 26, 2016).

48. William A. Gross Constr. Associates, Inc. v. Am. Mfrs. Mut. Ins. Co., 256 F.R.D. 134 (S.D.N.Y. 2009).

> establishment and scientific validation of such a protocol, reliance on keywords and (random) passive learning remains a questionable practice. On the other hand, the results reported here indicate that it is quite easy for either party (or for the parties together) to construct a keyword search that yields an effective seed set for active learning.[49]

Cormack and Grossman summarize their findings on the impact of keywords in the first round of training (seed set) on CAL, SAL, and SPL:

> In summary, the use of a seed set selected using a simple keyword search, composed prior to the review, contributes to the effectiveness of all of the TAR protocols investigated in this study.[50]

Keywords still have an important place in any multimodal, active, predictive coding protocol. This is, however, completely different from using keywords, especially untested naive keywords, to filter out the raw data in a misguided attempt to create high-prevalence collections.

Cormack and Grossman's Conclusions

In their well-written conclusion, Cormack and Grossman provide a good summary of their findings:

> Because SPL can be ineffective and inefficient, particularly with the low-prevalence collections that are common in ediscovery, disappointment with such tools may lead lawyers to be reluctant to embrace the use of all TAR. Moreover, a number of myths and misconceptions about TAR appear to be closely associated with SPL; notably, that seed and training sets must be randomly selected to avoid "biasing" the learning algorithm.

49. Cormack-Grossman SIGIR Study, *supra* note 2, at 160.
50. *Id.* at 159.

> This study lends no support to the proposition that seed or training sets must be random; to the contrary, keyword seeding, uncertainty sampling, and, in particular, relevance feedback—all non-random methods—improve significantly (P < 0:01) upon random sampling.
>
> While active-learning protocols employing uncertainty sampling are clearly more effective than passive-learning protocols, they tend to focus the reviewer's attention on marginal rather than legally significant documents. In addition, uncertainty sampling shares a fundamental weakness with passive learning: the need to define and detect when stabilization has occurred, so as to know when to stop training. In the legal context, this decision is fraught with risk, as premature stabilization could result in insufficient recall and undermine an attorney's certification of having conducted a reasonable search under (U.S.) Federal Rule of Civil Procedure 26(g)(1)(B).
>
> This study highlights an alternative approach—continuous active learning with relevance feedback—that demonstrates superior performance, while avoiding certain problems associated with uncertainty sampling and passive learning. CAL also offers the reviewer the opportunity to quickly identify legally significant documents that can guide litigation strategy, and can readily adapt when new documents are added to the collection, or new issues or interpretations of relevance arise.[51]

The insights and conclusions of Cormack and Grossman are perfectly in accord with my own experience and practice with predictive coding search efforts, both with messy real-world projects, and the several controlled scientific tests I have done. I agree that a relevancy approach that emphasizes high-ranked documents for training is one

51. *Id.* at 161.

of the most powerful search tools we now have. So, too, is uncertainty training (mid-ranked) when used judiciously, as well as keywords, and a number of other methods. All the many tools we have to find both relevant and irrelevant documents for training should be used, depending on the circumstances, including even some very limited random searches.

In my view, attorneys should never use just one method to select documents for machine training, and ignore the rest, even when it is a good method like Cormack and Grossman have shown CAL to be. When the one method selected is the worst of all possible computer-assisted methods—as random search has now been shown to be—then the monomodal approach is a recipe for ineffective, overpriced review.

Why All the Foolishness with Random Search?

As discussed at the beginning of this chapter, it is only common sense to use what you know to find training documents, and not rely on a so-called *easy way* of rolling dice. A random chance approach is essentially a fool's method of search. *The search for evidence to do justice is too important to leave to chance.* Cormack and Grossman have done the legal profession a favor by taking the time to prove the obvious in their study. They have shown that even very simplistic multimodal search protocols, CAL and SAL, do better at machine training than monomodal random only.

Information scientists already knew this rather obvious truism, that multimodal methods are better: the roulette wheel is not an effective search tool, in other words, random chance just slows things down and is ineffective as a machine-training methodology. Cormack and Grossman took the time to prove the obvious because the legal profession was being led astray. Many are actually using chance as if that were a valid search method, although perhaps not in the way they describe. As Cormack and Grossman explained in their report:

> While it is perhaps no surprise to the information retrieval community that active learning generally outperforms random training. . . , this result has not

> previously been demonstrated for the TAR Problem, and is neither well known nor well accepted within the legal community.[52]

As this quoted comment suggests, many in the information science search community knew this already, that the random-only approach to search is inartful. Most lawyers know this as well, especially the ones with years of hands-on experience in search for relevant ESI. So why in the world is random search *only* still promoted by some software companies and their customers? Is it really to address the so-called problem of "not knowing what you don't know"? That is the alleged inherent bias of using knowledge to program the AI. The total-random approach is also supposed to prevent overt, intentional bias, where lawyers might try to mis-train the AI searcher algorithm on purpose. These may be the stated reasons by vendors, but there are other reasons. There must be, because these excuses do not hold water.

This bias-avoidance claim must just be an excuse because there are many *better* ways to counter the myopic effects of search driven too narrowly. There are many methods and software enhancements that can be used to avoid overlooking important, not yet discovered types of relevant documents. For instance, allow machine selection of uncertain documents, as was done here with the SAL protocol. You can also include keyword searches, similarity searches, concept searches, judgmental and random sampling, even some linear search. That is a multimodal search method.

My preferred solution to the problem of "not knowing what you don't know" is to use a multimodal combination of all those methods, buttressed by a human searcher that is *aware* of the limits of knowledge. The whole premise behind using random as the only way to avoid a self-looping trap of "not knowing what you don't know" assumes that the lawyer searcher is a naive boob or dishonest scoundrel. It assumes lawyers are unaware that they don't know what they don't know. Please, we know that perfectly well. All experienced searchers know that. This "insight" is not just the exclusive knowledge of engineers and scientists. Very few attorneys are that arrogant and self-absorbed, or that naive and simplistic in their approaches to search.

---

52. *Id.* at 8.

No, this whole "you must use random-only search" to avoid prejudice is just a smoke screen to hide what may be the true reasons behind the marketing efforts to sell random-based tools: Arguably, the real reason is that poor software design decisions were *made in a rush* to get predictive coding software to market. Software was designed to only use random search because it was *easy and quick* to build software like that. It allowed for quick implementation of machine training. Such simplistic types of AI software may work better than just using poorly designed keyword searches, but it is still far inferior to more complex machine-training systems, as Cormack and Grossman have now proven. It is inferior to a multimodal approach.

Attorneys want software with the capacity to integrate all search functions, including random, into a multimodal search process. We do not want software with only one type of machine-training ability, be it CAL, SAL, or SPL. We do not want software that can only do one thing, and then have the vendor build a false ideology around their one capacity that says their method is the best and only way. These are legal issues, not software issues.

Attorneys do not just want one search tool; we want a whole tool chest. The marketplace will sort out whose tools are best, so will science. For vendors to remain competitive they need to sell the biggest tool chest possible, and make sure the tools are well built and perform as advertised. Do not just sell us a screwdriver and tell us we do not need a hammer and pliers too.

Leave the legal arguments as to reasonability and rules to lawyers. Just give us the tools and we lawyers will find the evidence we need. We are experts at evidence detection. It is in our blood. It is part of our proud heritage, our tradition. Finding evidence is what lawyers do. The law has been doing this for millennia. Think back to story of the judicial decision of King Solomon. He decided to award the child to the woman he saw cry in response to his sham decision to cut the baby in half. He based his decision on the facts, not ideology. He found the truth in clever ways built around facts, around evidence.

Lawyers always search to find evidence so that justice can be done. The facts matter. It has always been an essential part of what we do. Lawyers always adapt with the times. We always demand and use the best tools available to do our job. Just think of Abraham Lincoln who readily used telegraphs, the great new high-tech invention of his day. When you want to know the truth of what happened in an event that took place in the recent past, you hire a lawyer, not an engineer nor a scientist. That is what we are trained to do. We separate the truth from the lies. With great tools we can and will do an even better job.

Many multimodal-based software vendors already understand all of this. They build software that *empowers* attorneys to leverage their knowledge and skills. That is why we use their tools. Empowerment of attorneys with the latest AI tools empowers our entire system of justice. That is why the Cormack-Grossman study is important. That is why I am so passionate about this. Join with us in this. Demand diversity and many capacities in your search software, not just one.

Conclusion

The overarching message of the Cormack-Grossman study is clear: a *random-only* search method for predictive coding training documents is ineffective. In my view, the same applies to any other training method, if it is applied to the exclusion of all others. Any experienced searcher knows this. Software that relies solely on a random-only method should be enhanced and modified to allow attorneys to search where they know. All types of training techniques should be built into AI-based software, not just random. Random may be easy, but is it foolish to only search under the lamppost. It is foolish to turn a blind eye to what you know. Attorneys, insist on having your own flashlight that empowers you to look wherever you want. Shine your light wherever you think appropriate. Use your knowledge. Equip yourself with a full tool chest that allows you to do just that.

EDITORS' INTRODUCTION TO CHAPTER 6

Michael D. Berman

OK. So, your cases do not involve terabytes of data or millions of dollars. They are, in the view of others, "small." Why should you care about predictive coding? Why should you read this book?

This chapter by William Hamilton notes that the discussion of predictive coding has led attorneys to believe it is expensive and suitable only for "large" cases. The literature seems to indicate that "TAR was for the 1% [of "large" cases], leaving the other 99% [of "small" cases] mired in keyword searches."

> Not only is size and value a perceived problem of applying predictive coding to "small" cases, but counsel has a learning curve. Recall, precision, and error margins are "ancient Greek to the modern litigator . . . .

Further, as the author notes, there may be "pit battles" over experts, methodology for selecting seeds sets, and information sharing. It may be difficult to choose among various service providers. The perceived cost may deter usage of predictive coding in all but the highest-stakes cases.

The author challenges that assumption. The author notes that ruling out predictive coding leaves counsel with only the traditional keyword search, and search scientists have noted the shortcomings of that approach.

Does this leave the litigator between Scylla and Charybdis, that is, having to choose between the two evils of high cost and unreliable searches? The author suggests it does not. TAR, or technology-assisted review, is a big tent. Instead of discussing the small case, Hamilton focuses on the "routine" one. He recommends de-coupling TAR from big document reviews and deploying it for tasks such as early case assessment (ECA). Because ECA does not involve the opposing litigant, Rule 26(g) certifications, and other constraints of litigation, TAR may be used early and inexpensively. Or, he suggests, TAR may be used internally to analyze the opponent's production, or to prepare for a deposition. In short, there are many aspects of the "small," or "routine," case that may benefit from predictive coding.

CHAPTER 6
TAR for the Small and Medium Case

William Hamilton

Technology-assisted review (TAR) is an analytical search methodology. In this chapter we show that TAR incorporates search and analytic tools that are familiar to litigators and that TAR is ready for wholesale adoption in cases that may involve as little as five to ten gigabytes of data. This chapter discusses the hesitancy of attorneys to deploy this analytical tool and debunks some of the mythology surrounding TAR in that context. The early cost, complexity, and challenges of TAR have largely dissipated. TAR should be in every litigator's toolbox. It can now be cost-effective in small- and medium-size cases, while providing analytical assistance that would otherwise be unavailable.

Early Small- and Medium-Case Attorney Perceptions About TAR

The early TAR proponents inadvertently led us to believe that TAR is revolutionary, expensive, suitable only for extremely large cases, and difficult to deploy. Perhaps this impression was unavoidable. After all, it is frequently the large case that provides the fiscal muscle necessary to explore and to drive new technologies that often arrive with a significant price tag. Big cases are big laboratories. Small savings became huge gains when scaled to the larger case. TAR thus found its initial public home in the large case composed of hundreds of gigabytes, if not terabytes, of digital data. TAR was heralded as *the* new e-discovery cause celebre. TAR reduced e-discovery costs by predictively ranking the most likely relevant documents in large collections. TAR was the bellwether—or at least the handmaiden—for the renewed emphasis on proportionality in the 2015 rules amendments.[1] In the early popular imagination, TAR was a magical—yet expensive and highly complex—search and review technology reserved for only a few cases. It was for the 1 percent; keyword searches and manual review were for the other 99 percent.

U.S. Magistrate Judge Andrew Peck's 2012 *Da Silva Moore* decision officially heralded the arrival of TAR.[2] In the background, a TAR buzz had been fermenting for a few years, but Judge Peck's erudite decision—not to mention the creative work of the attorneys who worked on the case—validated TAR in the e-discovery industry and legal community. Unfortunately, *Da Silva Moore* had the unintended consequence of solidifying the perception of TAR's suitability only for high-volume, high-value cases. *Da Silva Moore* was not a routine case—it was a three million-document case. A medium sized "routine" case (at least in 2012) involved perhaps ten gigabytes of electronically stored information (ESI).[3] A gigabyte prints to approximately 20 bankers boxes of paper documents. This amounts to approximately 6,000 documents per gigabyte, assuming each "document" averages ten pages.[4] A ten-gigabyte case thus involves 60,000 documents—far short of *Da Silva Moore*'s three million documents.[5]

Da Silva Moore was also noticed "on the street" for TAR's implementation cost—exclusive of the software acquisition cost. The TAR protocol in *Da Silva Moore* involved curating a seed set approaching

---

1. *See* FED. R. CIV. P. 26(b)(1).

2. Da Silva Moore et al. v. Publicis Groupe & MSL Groupe, 287 F.R.D. 182 (S.D.N.Y 2012).

3. *Study Shows "Traditional Linear Review" Almost Accounts for 73% of e-Discovery Costs*, A.B.A. J., BLOG (Feb. 19, 2013, 4:58 PM), http://www.abajournal.com/advertising/article/reducing_costs_with_advance_review_strategies/.

4. *See also*, John Tredennick, *How Many Documents in a Gigabyte? An Updated Answer to that Vexing Question*, CATALYST E-DISCOVERY SEARCH BLOG, (Jan. 13, 2014, catalystsecure.com/blog/2014/01/how-many-documents-in-a-gigabyte-an-updated-answer-to-that-vexing-question/ (estimating between 4,000 and 5,000 documents per gigabyte).

5. *Id.*

5,000 documents by "expert" attorneys.[6] The initial seed set was then tested through up to seven iterations composed of 500 documents to refine the search algorithm and ensure appropriate recall and precision.[7] *Da Silva Moore* thus presents an up-front cost of hundreds of hours of attorney time to "prime the TAR pump."

Let's assume that keyword searches and other identification methods[8] required TAR review experts to review 5,000 documents to build the seed set. At a not uncommon rate of 50 documents an hour, this volume would require 100 hours of expert attorney review time. One hundred hours of review time at an expert rate of $300 per hour produces a total prime-the-pump investment of $20,000. Put otherwise, it would take a senior attorney nearly one month (working alone) to review documents sufficient to create the seed set. This cost and investment strains the imagination of most attorneys working on small- and medium-size cases. Most litigation attorneys feel comfortable with keyword search, believing it does an adequate job. Why spend $20,000, or even $10,000, to prime the TAR pump when a few hours of attorney work is all that is needed for a serviceable job to cull the data with a few keywords? Of course, the expense of leasing the software is another significant cost component. Loading a terabyte of data could exceed $200,000 assuming a loading cost of a $200 per gigabyte.

The costs in *Da Silva Moore* are not confined to building the seed set. TAR ranks documents as more or less likely to be responsive/relevant. TAR does not eliminate the attorney review of production documents. TAR identifies and ranks documents as more or less likely to be responsive, but leaves the production decision to the attorney review team (unless the "predicted" relevant documents are produced blindly without attorney review). TAR does not do production "review" any more than a keyword search does that "review." Let's assume of the three million documents collected in *Da Silva Moore*, the TAR algorithm ranked 20 percent (600,000) of the documents as highly likely to be responsive. The pre-production review of these 600,000 documents would easily cost $300,000, assuming an optimal rate of

6. *Id.*
7. *Id.*
8. *Id.*

100 documents per hour using contract reviewers at $50 per hour. Few "routine" cases involve expenditures of over a quarter million dollars in document review.[9]

Notwithstanding the lucidity and clarity of *Da Silva Moore*, understanding TAR is a significant challenge for most litigators. Most litigators were not diverted from careers as mathematicians or computer scientists to attend law school. Most law students majored in political science, English, history, philosophy, journalism, and other liberal arts. Unfortunately, even the cursory introduction to TAR in *Da Silva Moore* requires some understanding of sampling, random selection, statistics, precision, confidence levels, error margins, and recall. Smaller firms typically lack the internal resources necessary to negotiate TAR protocols, manage vendors, and defend the TAR process when challenged. Also, many lawyers hesitate hiring external experts on topics that clients (unfairly) may expect their litigators to understand.

Selecting a TAR vendor is no easy task for expert litigation support managers, much less the everyday litigator. The technologies and approaches of vendors differ. Matching oranges to oranges and not apples is a difficult task. Vendors strive for transparency, but costs that disappear at one end, tend to appear in other unexpected places. Per gigabyte changes must be compared. Processing must be understood. Moreover, the cost of promotion to full review is sometimes difficult to estimate without knowledge of the document set richness.[10]

Nor is it the case that in 2012 the TAR legal skirmishes appeared completely resolved to the small- and medium-size case litigator. Counsel worried that deploying TAR technologies inevitably entailed wading into battles involving expert testimony over the seed set selection methodology, the effective results testing, information sharing,

---

9. *See* Nicholas M. Pace & Laura Zakaras, *Where the Money Goes: Understanding Litigant Expenditures for Producing Electronic Discovery*, RAND INST. FOR CIVIL JUSTICE (2012), *available at* http://www.rand.org/content/dam/rand/pubs/monographs/2012/RAND_MG1208.pdf.

10. Vendor costs can include such separate cumulative categories as site setup, monthly hosting per gigabyte, seat licenses, data loading, file processing, threading and analytics, productions and conversions, archiving, and other "professional services." For an explanation of "richness" see *Statistical Sampling Applied to Electronic Discovery, Release 2*, EDRM (Feb. 18, 2015), *available at* http://www.edrm.net/projects/search/statistical-sampling-2.

clawback agreements, and non-responsive document disclosure. Rather than marching to the sound of cannon, cautious litigators were more comfortable staying on the surrounding hills overlooking this alien battleground.[11]

In sum, *Da Silva Moore* strengthened the perception that TAR is for the well-heeled who can afford expert seed set reviewers, significant vendor costs, and sophisticated technologists and computer scientists. Indeed, the likely take-way impression of small- and medium-case attorneys after reading *Da Silva Moore* is a combination of shock, awe, and relief. Shock and awe that any litigation can command such savoir faire and resources, and relief that TAR only inhabits a world populated by litigation giants.

These convening forces resulted in TAR's confinement to the periphery of the small and medium case. Unfortunately, the baby has been thrown out with the bath water. The flip side of the small- and medium-case retreat from TAR has been the dogged entrenchment of flat keyword searching. Of course, the small- and medium-case attorney does not necessarily perceive keyword search as a problem. Blissfully unaware of the Blair and Maron research and other critical, empirical studies, most attorneys have fallen prey to the illusion that keyword searching does an adequate job, is readily understood, and works well.[12] This easy—even cavalier—acceptance of keywords derives from a number of sources.

First, most attorneys are familiar with keyword searching through the use of Google, Bing, and Safari and were trained on—or have become familiar with—Westlaw and LexisNexis. Using keywords is familiar and seems easy. Lawyers in general and litigators in particular are most comfortable with the tried and true. The risks of keyword searching are perceived as low, notwithstanding the contrary evidence.[13]

---

11. *See generally A Visual Representation of Predictive Coding Case Law*, LOGIKCULL BLOG (Sept. 23, 2015), http://logikcull.com/blog/a-visual-representation-of-predictive-coding-case-law/.

12. *See* The Sedona Conference, *Best Practices Commentary on the Use of Search and Information Retrieval Methods in E-Discovery*, 15 SEDONA CONF. J. 239–40 (2014) ("Sedona Search Commentary").

13. *Id., passim.*

Second, most small- and medium-case attorneys do not rigorously test keyword search results for recall and precision. Without valid feedback, keyword searching appears to work just fine. This phenomenon resembles the paradox of "not knowing what you don't know." Recent pedagogical studies have focused on the *illusion* of knowing that often accompanies re-reading materials. Repetitive reading creates a feeling of comfort with the material and an accompanying illusory sense of mastery. The belief that the materials have been mastered suddenly disappears in the objective testing environment or when called upon to explain the materials to another. The best study methodology is continual self-testing and practiced recall. Contrary to the general perception and dread of testing, appropriately spaced testing is a *learning* methodology.[14] Unfortunately, the small- and medium-case attorney spends little time systematically testing the results of keyword searches. At best, the search "hits" may be reviewed and certain keywords added willy-nilly or eliminated. But valid statistical sampling rarely occurs. This failure promotes the grand illusion: flat keyword searches are just fine.[15]

Third, the legal communities in most locales are quite accepting of elementary keyword searching and often consider the exchange or disclosure of search terms as invading work product or impugning character. The financial constraints of most cases are such that harried counsel may simply prefer to exchange documents located with undisclosed keywords rather than challenge opposition to demonstrate the validity of the search results, which, of course, creates the boomerang effect of having to defend against the same challenge.[16]

TAR Knocking on the Door

How can TAR possibly find acceptance in this environment?

---

14. *See generally* Peter C. Brown, Henry L. Roediger III, & Mark A. McDaniel, Make It Stick: The Science of Successful Learning (2014).

15. By a "flat" keyword search, I mean a search that simply consists of one or a string of words as might be used in an elementary Google search.

16. For more on resistance by the legal community, *see* Sedona Search Commentary, Sedona Conference *supra* note 12, at 235–36.

The first step is to understand that the mighty TAR is an extension of—and albeit an advance on—many search and analytical tools utilized in small and medium cases. The name "technology-assisted review" emerged as a vendor neutral alternative to "predictive coding." Other naming conventions appeared, such a "computer-assisted review," or CAR. In fact, the naming game continues to expand as TAR, in various flavors and versions, becomes a feature offered in many e-discovery software applications. Unfortunately, too often, discussions of TAR methodologies are disguised linguistic disputes reflecting branding battles. TAR is really a process involving what the information technology specialists call machine learning.

Let's unpack what is happening in TAR by revisiting computer file structures and search basics. TAR is a chapter in the continuing effort to utilize computers to accelerate the search and review process. The glory of electronically stored information is that it can be searched with computer algorithms. TAR belongs in the pantheon of search technologies and methods and builds on prior techniques. The simple keyword search can be thought of as an elementary form of technology-enhanced review. An elementary keyword search is an algorithm (a set of computer instructions) used to identify in the targeted document set the files that contain the specified bit pattern.

We utilize algorithms (sets of instructions that quickly become habits) to manage the multitude of daily activities. Here, for example, is a simple four-step algorithm for starting a computer:

1. Lift up the laptop cover.
2. Press the Start button for two seconds.
3. When the dialogue box appears requesting a password, type in your password.
4. Hit the Enter key.

Keyword search is a set of computer instructions: the operation of technology assisting in document review. What more does TAR do? Could it be said that our very comfortable "everyday" keyword searching is an early progenitor of technology-enhanced review? But then, if keyword searching is not threatening for the everyday attorney, from whence the emotional anguish about TAR?

A quick technical detour may be helpful to understand "search." Computers are magnificent collections of electrical circuits and switches wired to perform incredible computational feats. Computer devices rely on switching mechanisms—like turning a light switch off and on. A tiny on or off circuit is a *bit* of information. Computers are amazing collections of bits that include data and instructions (the algorithms). A group of eight bits is called a *byte*. These bits and bytes are the foundation of the electronic files that we commonly, albeit sloppily, refer to as documents. These electronically stored bits and bytes ultimately produce the on and off flashing of screen pixels that humans perceive as a document.[17]

English words are typically encoded in a convention called the American Standard Code for Information Interexchange (ASCII).[18] Each character in the alphabet is coded as a byte. For example, a computer memory codes the word "law" in three bytes, or 24 bits. This is what makes search possible. When I type "law" into the search dialogue box on my computer, the computer does not "think" to look for the word "law." There is no such word inside the computer—only streams of on/off values—bits of information. The search for the word "law" is at its most elementary basis an algorithm that spots bit patterns. "Law" is coded into 24 bits and then decoded by the software application to produce on the screen in the pixel pattern we see as "law." "Search" locates these recurring bit patterns. Computers have few operations, but perform those simple steps with awesome speed.

The challenge of electronic discovery is to find relevant documents. Any search is an effort to predict whether a document is relevant. For example, suppose I wish to locate documents about a particular contract authored by a particular person. A keyword search might utilize terms (bit patterns) that the user believes will identify the parties to the contact and terms (bit pattern) that identify the agreement.

A keyword search may produce a number of hits, documents responsive to the search, because they contain the bit pattern.

---

17. *See generally* Roger Young, How Computers Work: Processor and Main Memory (2015), *available at* http://howcomputers.com.

18. *See* the complete table of ASCII characters, letters, codes, symbols, and signs at http://www.theasciicode.com.ar/.

However, the hits are not necessarily relevant documents. The search was designed to predict which documents are relevant, and will bring back any number of false positives. Human review ultimately makes the final decision as to whether the hit is a relevant document. What keywords do is to predict and identify the documents that are likely to be relevant. All keyword searches are not equal. It takes work and skill to compose a good keyword search.

The many steps of the computer's keyword search algorithm are not visible to the user. Not all search applications are equal. Some are elegant, quick, and effective. Others take longer and may not return the intended results.

Keyword search replaces the burden of document-by-document review, that is, manual linear review. The arrival of optical character recognition (OCR) at law firms in the 1980s created a revolution. Paper documents could be converted to electronic files: all of a sudden "search" was possible, replacing a complete reliance on manual review. With search we attempt to construct an algorithm that identifies the documents most likely to be relevant. Reviewing fewer documents generates savings. A search that eliminates one-half the documents requiring review saves approximately one-half the review cost. A perfect search correctly predicts *all* the relevant documents and *only* the relevant documents.[19] However, all keyword searches miss some relevant documents while including some nonrelevant documents. Recall is not perfect, nor is precision. The best search is a balance between these often competing ratios. But ultimately it

19. Precision measures search accuracy. High precision means that a high percentage of the returned documents are relevant documents. Recall measures completeness. A search with high recall means that a high percentage of the relevant documents in the document population being searched were retrieved. Precision and recall are often competing ratios. In some situations, increased recall results in deceased precision. A search that returns every document has perfect recall, but horrible precision. A search that identifies one document and only one document which is a relevant document has perfect precision because no nonrelevant documents were identified. The recall of such a search is likely terrible (unless there is only one relevant document in the document population). The F_1 value is the harmonic mean between the precision and recall ratios. *See* Douglas W. Oard & William Webber, *Information Retrieval for E-Discovery*, FOUNDATIONS AND TRENDS® IN INFORMATION RETRIEVAL (2013), *available at* https://terpconnect.umd.edu/~oard/pdf/fntir13.pdf. *See also* Sedona Search Commentary, *supra* note 12, at 237–38 .

is the human reviewers who make the final decision confirming the predictive search results.

The parallel between keyword search and TAR should be apparent. Both seek patterns: TAR can be thought of as keyword search on steroids: the TAR bit pattern search is more complex, because keywords search for only limited bit patterns. TAR utilizes the bit patterns of an entire document population. But in both a search is conducted that results in the identification of likely relevant documents. Reviewers then finish the job by confirming or rejecting the "predictions."[20] Keyword search and TAR have the same end game.

Notwithstanding these similarities, keyword search and TAR are separated by a huge distance. TAR arrived on the heels of discontent with the quality of manual "linear" review and keyword searches. TAR had the courage not merely to whisper but to shout that the keyword emperor had no clothes. Indeed, keyword searches have a number of drawbacks, notwithstanding the technology's general acceptance by the legal community.

First, language is rich, varied, and ever evolving. Many words have multiple meanings ("bank" may mean a place to deposit money or the edge of a river); similar sounding words can mean different things ("sea" versus "see"); and things and activities can have different names ("lawyer," "attorney," "counselor," and "barrister" all may denote the same or similar persons depending on the context). Moreover, our language is constantly adding new words and changing and modifying "dictionary" meanings. Keyword searches are thus prone to be both over-inclusive and incomplete. To remedy this defect many keyword search technologies come replete with automatic dictionary lookups of synonyms and words in similar categories.[21]

A second keyword search weakness is lack of document ranking. Which documents out of the universe of all the keyword hits are more likely to be relevant to the search and important to the case? That is,

---

20. Of course, the results of any search can be produced without further human review. There may be situations where the risks associated with doing so are outweighed by the benefits or cost and proportionality concerns, but such production is not typical without at least minimal statistically valid sampling.

21. *See generally 6.1. Keyword Search*, EDRM SEARCH GUIDE, VERSION 1.17, *available at* http://www.edrm.net/resources/guides/edrm-search-guide/search-methodologies#6.1.

in its least sophisticated format, keyword searching simply produces a list of "hit" documents. Each document is viewed as a collection of unrelated words, a "bag of words," and the search identifies which bags (documents) contain the keywords. No one document (or bag of words) is more important than another. Those documents most likely to be most relevant are not at the top of the pile.[22]

Various technologies have been developed to rank the documents based on various factors including the keyword frequency and location in any particular document balanced against the frequency of the keyword in the document collection. Intuitively, all other factors being equal, a document with a keyword in the title is likely to be more important than a document that contains the keyword in a footnote on the third page. Similarly, a document is more likely relevant if it contains keywords that are only found in a few documents in the collection. Put otherwise, each document containing a keyword is likely of minimal importance if the majority of documents in the collection contain the keyword. Nonetheless, notwithstanding advances in keyword ranking algorithms, electronic discovery keyword searches typically leave us with the task of reviewing all the document hits.[23]

The natural language characteristics that bedevil keyword searching are not without technological solutions. Keyword search technology has been greatly enhanced from simple word searches used individually clumped together in groups with an implied "AND" connector. For example, stemming is an important enhancement. As discussed earlier, consider a search for "law." Some keyword software allows for the use of stemming. Stemming expands the hits to any word containing the root word, such as "lawyer" and "lawful." Wild cards are also available in many keyword search software technologies. A wild card allows any character to occupy a specified position in the search. A search for "se!" with "!" as a wild card symbol will return both "see" and "sea." Additionally, fuzzy logic expands hits to include common word misspellings. These operations expand keyword recall but often negatively impact precision.[24]

22. *See generally* Oard & Webber, *supra* note 19, ch. 3, at 125–30.

23. Christopher D. Manning, Prabhakar Raghavan, & Hinrich Schütze, *An Introduction to Information Retrieval* ch. 6.2 (2009), *available at* http://nlp.stanford.edu/IR-book/pdf/irbookonlinereading.pdf.

24. *See generally 6.1. supra* note 17.

Keyword searching is an iterative process.[25] Just as a TAR algorithm requires tuning by testing (the correct "process"), so should be the case in using keyword methods. Good search software includes a random sampling tool that can be applied to the population of the "hits" to ensure precision and to the nonresponsive documents to ensure reasonable recall.

Keyword searching and TAR involve attaining a reasonable confidence level. Both require a specified level of confidence that the responsive document population does not contain nonresponsive documents and that the nonresponsive population does contain responsive documents. A 95 percent confidence level plus or minus 3 percent (where the 3 percent is the confidence interval) is an emerging standard. The sampling software should produce a small set of documents to confirm that the confidence level has been reached. It will usually take three or four refinements and iterations to get to the desired level of keyword search confidence.[26]

A thorny keyword searching problem is identifying the right keyword. Cases have context and witnesses. Witness interviews and obviously identifiable relevant documents usually suggest a healthy set of keywords. But what about the secret codes? How do we search for doubly "coded" words? For example, "water" may refer to the drinkable liquid, but it may be used by participants in particular contexts to refer to money need to run a fraudulent operation. A quick e-mail or text message that states "The water has arrived!" may be a highly relevant document. But who would suspect that "water" is a word with a double meaning?

The solution to this problem advances our search technology beyond the search for simple word patterns (albeit refined with wildcards, phrase search, fuzzy search, stemming, and enhancements). Mathematics comes to the rescue. Let's see how this works in a search technology known as latent semantic analysis (LSA). If we think of a document as words bundled together into various patterns, we can create mathematical models of the strength frequency of co-occurrence. One might say these other discovered co-occurrence "keywords" are latent in the document population. The LSA algorithm thus identifies (predicts)

25. Oard & Webber, *supra* note 19, ch. 3 at 135–36.

26. *See* Sedona Search Commentary, The Sedona Conference, *supra* note 12, at 250–52.

relevant documents based on mathematical algorithms that calculate the distances and other variables between words to uncover potentially meaningful co-occurrences. Documents that keywords would not have identified now are identified as potentially meaningful notwithstanding the lack of keywords within the document. Documents are identified as relevant that may contain no attorney-designated keywords! The algorithm appears to be "thinking," but really all that is happening—as in TAR—is that the algorithm is using a complex mathematical analysis to make relevance predictions based on the keywords selected by the attorney *and* how those keywords interact with the document population. A review of the LSA-selected documents may lead to the discovery of hidden "code words" and other relevant documents a simple keyword search would have missed.[27]

The search goal is to identify likely responsive documents. One approach similar to TAR is to deploy a computer algorithm to "Find More Like This." Documents can be said to be composed of vectors of word patterns. A document composed of the words "Dogs have wonderful personalities and can be trained" will have a similar vector (pattern) to a document composed of the words "Dogs' personalities are compliant making training possible." The words in these documents create vectors of different length and at different angles to one another, yet are very close.[28] LSA and other retrieval technologies reveal repetitive word patterns involving keywords and other words. As we discussed earlier in this chapter, every case has context and witnesses. These witnesses can identify key documents.[29] Once these key documents have been identified (what TAR calls the seed set), algorithms can find documents that conceptually resemble the already-identified key documents. In this process, like TAR, the computer is simply asked to "find more documents like the document," or the set, that has been identified.

This "baby TAR" technology is especially helpful in double-checking and quality control to prevent inadvertent disclosure of

27. Thomas K. Landauer, Peter W. Foltz, & Darrell Laham, *An Introduction to Latent Semantic Analysis*, (1998), *available at* http://lsa.colorado.edu/papers/dp1.LSAintro.pdf.

28. Manning, Raghavan, & Schütze, *supra* note 24, ch. 13.

29. Chapter 5 in this volume addresses judgment sampling versus random selection of the seed, or training, set.

privileged documents. Simply running a search for "more like this" of a set of already identified privileged documents against the production population will identify any documents bearing characteristics of the privilege set.

The obverse of searching for responsive documents is the identification of nonresponsive documents. A wonderful near-TAR technology used in this exclusion process is automated clustering. Another name for clustering is concept searching. The professionals in information technology call it unsupervised machine learning. Again, using mathematical models, this search technology very effectively groups documents in categories that respond to particular concepts. Thus instead of searching for words, a conceptual search automatically groups documents according to concepts. For example, clustering technologies would very effectively group documents into separate categories. Suppose for example, a search was initiated for documents about Beatles music. A keyword search for "Apple" (the Beatles record label) would pick up documents related to such categories of Apple Records, but also Apple computers, and the apple fruit. However, a concept search would quickly group the document collection into groups pertaining to music, computers, and fruit. The computers and fruit groups could be quickly tested and discarded.[30]

Another commonly deployed variant of "more like this" is near-duplicate search. A search for actual duplicates uses widely available hash technology, which finds identical documents based on the digital fingerprint. Finding duplicates is critical to reducing review time. Near duplicate location is equally important. One near-duplicate technology deploys a search algorithm called shingling when applied to words.[31] In shingling, documents are broken up into sequential and consecutive word groups. For example, the sentence, "Near duplicate location is equally important" might be shingled (using words) as: "near duplicates, duplicates location, location is, is equally, equally important." The entire document is broken up into shingles and then the shingles of the document are compared to find documents that

30. Oard & Webber, *supra* note 19, ch. 3 at 137–43.

31. *See N-gram Extraction Tools*, http://homepages.inf.ed.ac.uk/lzhang10/ngram.html; *see generally Identifying Similar Documents*, DIGFOR BLOG, (Mar. 27, 2013), http://digfor.blogspot.com/2013/03/fruity-shingles.html.

share a high number of shingles. These documents are "near duplicates." Near duplicates have different hash values, but a high shingles correspondence. Near duplicate search technology, while not full-blown TAR, is critical in the pursuit of the important documents in the case. Near duplicates identification also dramatically improves review. Documents of similar content can be reviewed together, accelerating review speed. Near duplicate technology is also excellent for identifying changes in contract documents and subtle, perhaps nefarious, alterations in other documents.

These technologies are not the only solutions to traditional keyword dilemmas, but each features an important step forward in the continued refined use of mathematical models that increasingly predict relevance from the utilization of samples, which is called supervised machine learning, or autoclassification without samples called unsupervised machine learning. The point for the attorney handling the small and medium case is that these technologies should not appear mysterious: each search technology relies on the binary file structure and some deploy mathematical modeling to assist in the prediction.

The TAR of *Da Silva Moore* should now appear just a bit more accessible. Underneath the hood, TAR deploys a combination of incredibly valuable technologies. TAR did not arrive full-blown from the head of Zeus. It has its own genealogy, and TAR search technologies build on and often incorporate in various flavors, such search technologies as "find more like this," LSA, and near-duplicate identification.

Of course, TAR is a process. The TAR process is elegantly expressed in the Computer Assisted Review Reference Model.[32] Why then the continued hesitancy to use TAR? Why wouldn't the attorney whose initial impulse is to use keyword search to cull data also use the full array of search technologies including TAR? Even ten gigabytes of data—50,000 documents—requires the best processes that identify and rank the collected documents. What are the perceived barriers to adoption?

First, the language of TAR may seem impenetrable. But as we have seen earlier in the chapter, while TAR is an advance, TAR incorporates

32. *Computer Assisted Review Reference Model (CARRM)*, EDRM, *available at* http://www.edrm.net/resources/carrm.

many analytical search features and processes that have been successfully deployed by attorneys and litigation support professionals for some time. TAR is an analytical *process*, and is quite familiar when seen from the perspective of its historical antecedents. Indeed, it is a logical extension of them. We all know TAR, notwithstanding the fact that it is obscured by the fog of terminology. Concepts such as iteration, sampling, confidence level, seed set, and the like are familiar from the early efforts to improve and test keyword searches. The mathematics of TAR that counsel must understand is really just a short step from the mathematics of keyword precision and recall. Untested keyword searches will be sanctioned; that ship left the dock long ago.[33]

Moreover, using contemporary modern TAR technology compared to the world of *Da Silva Moore* feels like moving from DOS to Windows. Current TAR software provides "wizards" to guide the user through the generation of seed sets, provide precision and recall options, and report on whether the algorithm has been sufficiently refined to meet the confidence level goals of the review.

The next perceived concern is cost. Notwithstanding the costs articulated in the *Da Silva Moore* opinion, the use of senior attorneys or experts may not be as critical as earlier perceived. Many TAR technologies are moving to training through a standard review process. In short, the senior attorneys in the case no longer need to be dragged into the review to create seed sets.[34] We have come a long way in four years!

Most importantly, the cost of TAR software has dropped significantly, and at an accelerating rate. Nearly every major e-discovery search and review tool offers a version of TAR. The result of this dramatic competition has been a very significant reduction in cost. Fifteen years ago, the cost of routine processing a gigabyte of information approached $1,000. Today that cost has dropped to less than $100. TAR technology has experienced a similar decrease in four short years since *Da Silva Moore*.

---

33. U.S. v. O'Keefe, 537 F. Supp. 2d 14 (D.D.C. 2008); Equity Analytics v. Lundin, 248 F.R.D. 331 (D.D.C. 2008); William A. Gross. Constr. Assocs., Inc. v. Am. Mfrs. Mut. Ins. Co., 256 F.R.D. 134 (S.D.N.Y. 2009).

34. Gordon V. Cormack & Maura R. Grossman, *Evaluation of Machine-Learning Protocols for Technology-Assisted Review in Electronic Discovery*" (2015), *available at* http://www.wlrk.com/webdocs/wlrknew/AttorneyPubs/WLRK.23339.14.pdf.

Circa 2012 when *Da Silva Moore* was first issued, TAR technology acquisition often presented itself as a choice between purchasing/leasing the software internally with significant investment, maintenance, and operational costs, or accessing the software from third-party providers, often under less than flexible terms. As of 2016, however, newer forms of software as a service (SAAS) have arrived that allow access to the software on a per-gigabyte and other bases. In short, TAR technology acquisition presents more flexible options that can be tailored to the size of medium and small cases. The cloud makes TAR accessible everywhere. With e-discovery managed services pricing depends on the required storage volume and which applications—TAR or otherwise—are appropriate for the case. Technical support is also provided. Attorneys handling medium size cases can pay a fixed-price license fee for the software and for personnel—all wrapped into a convenient monthly invoice that can be billed to clients on a per matter basis. E-discovery managed services are now offered as cloud-based SAAS with realistic profit margins that are not volume-based.

In short, attorneys handling small and medium cases need not purchase or rent in bulk TAR software. The preferred option is now to pay as you go and only buy what you need for as long as you need it at a competitive price.[35]

Moreover, the battle for acceptance of TAR is over. We now have an ecosystem of judicial decisions accepting TAR.[36] TAR, as Judge Peck has noted, is now black letter law[37] and there is now an established body of e-discovery jurisprudence.[38] Any talk about "trying" TAR has the same feel today as would talk about "trying" keyword searches ten year ago.

---

35. Paige Hunt Wojcik, *Managed Services: A Winning Approach to eDiscovery*, Law.com Blog (Aug. 25, 2014), http://www.law.com/sites/paigehuntwojcik/2014/08/25/managed-services-a-winning-approach-to-ediscovery/?slreturn=20160017162844.

36. *See, e.g.*, Chapter 2 in this volume.

37. Rio Tinto PLC v. Vale S.A., 2015 WL 872294 (S.D.N.Y. 2015).

38. Paul Burns & Mindy Morton, *Technology-Assisted Review: The Judicial Pioneers*, The The Sedona Conference (2014), *available at* http://www.americanbar.org/content/dam/aba/administrative/litigation/materials/2014_sac/2014_sac/technology_assisted_review_the_judicial_pioneers.authcheckdam.pdf.

We have entered a new era opening TAR to a wide range of cases heretofore characterized as small or medium. What nontrivial commercial litigation case does not involve ten gigabytes of data? The explosion of data continues unabated. Data remediation and deletion, which resembles building sand castles washed away by each tide, is a challenge for most companies. Considering the explosion of social media, home computers, and the "Internet of things," the volume of data in family law, personal injury, and tort cases will regularly bust the ten gigabyte threshold (50,000 documents). A ten-gigabyte case is clearly TAR-ready! Indeed, TAR will be appropriate for even five gigabyte or less cases. In short, case data volume is not an excuse to avoid TAR.

Counsel handling the small and medium case should also think of TAR as another analytical tool as much as a production tool. The distinction is important. Analytical tools are utilized to understand the story the data will tell. TAR belongs in the pantheon of analytical tools. TAR will quickly bring to the surface documents that are the most likely relevant documents so counsel can begin to understand the case and test and expand the witness interviews. Especially with the more recent utilization of an instant review-feedback loop in continuous active learning, case analysis proceeds on the fly. As documents are reviewed and identified as relevant, TAR moves the highly relevant documents to the front of the review queue meeting time demands. That is something that cannot be done with keywords, and the cost saving can be substantial.

Ranking of documents is often critical in the small-to-medium case. Small cases, in terms of dollar value, can present complicated issues and significant data volumes. TAR is the perfect way to limit discovery costs in these cases because almost all TAR technologies present reasonable review cut-off points that determine when the review has reached its goal. TAR and proportionality are a happy couple. TAR informs us as to the likelihood that continued review will disclose relevant documents. If the likelihood is high, the review continues. But at a critical point, when most of the relevant documents have been identified, it simply is not worth continuing the review when, for example, only one in 20 may be relevant. That continuing review cost is too high for small and medium cases.

Consider a typical small- and medium-size case involving a sale of goods contract breach. The case will require the discovery of documents regarding contract negotiations, purchases, shipments, product quality, and remediation and cure efforts. Past practices are relevant to the course of conduct defense. By the time the data is pulled from email accounts of ten key custodians plus files from associated loose file storage locations and company databases, ten gigabytes of data have been collected that require review—40,000 documents. Let's assume the document richness is 10 percent—that is, one out of every 20 documents collected is relevant. Keyword searching with various weighed ranking technologies might reduce the documents needing review to a jumble of 20,000. However, numerous iterations were required to obtain search precision and recall to reach the negotiated target. Efforts to improve recall dramatically reduced precision. Counsel struggles getting close to a comfort level that even 75 percent of the relevant documents has been identified. The review of the culled 20,000 documents requires 200 hours of review at an estimated cost of $20,000. The amount in dispute is, however, only $100,000. Thus nearly one-fifth of the amount in dispute is expended for e-discovery!

Now let's apply TAR to this hypothetical. The TAR review brings the most likely relevant documents to the surface using continuous active learning, starting from documents the client and key witnesses have identified as highly relevant. After reviewing 3,000 documents, the TAR software reports that 80 percent of the relevant documents have been located. The agreed upon cutoff point has been reached, and going further into the review is not worth the cost. Reviewing 3,000 documents costs approximately $3,000. The TAR software provides a wide variety of metrics confirming the attained confidence levels. Using a managed-services vendor, the bump in the cost of TAR software may modestly exceed the cost of traditional e-discovery software, but the difference is insignificant compared to the cost savings. Applying the principle of proportionality, counsel are comfortable forgoing the search for the remaining relevant (but not likely important) documents. The most relevant documents have likely been located, those which may have been missed by keyword "binary" searching. The decision to use TAR is easy: better results have been obtained at a savings of $17,000.

Conclusion

We have come full circle. TAR has a hidden promise: it is specially suited for implementing proportionality. In the mega case with terabytes of data and billions of dollars at stake, it no longer makes financial sense for reviewers to look at every document. The same is beginning to be true in smaller and medium cases as well: proportionality is demanded and contemporary TAR comes to the rescue. TAR has emerged as a critical tool for the 99 percent, not just the 1 percent.

EDITORS' INTRODUCTION TO CHAPTER 7

Michael D. Berman

The authors, William P. Butterfield and Jeannine M. Kenney, ask: If predictive coding is so good, why has it not been more widely adopted? The answer is that, while the tool itself is well-proven, the lack of understanding of it, combined with the absence of well-defined processes to deploy it, has impeded its use. They note that the cost of negotiating and, perhaps, litigating over the acceptance of analytics prevents some from using it. Further, the concern of deploying a "methodological black box," and the possibility of being ordered to conduct a "do-over," is also a deterrent. In short:

> [N]ot all TAR tools are alike or equally effective . . . . Too much can go wrong: a seed set can be improperly selected, improper judgmental sampling can bias the learning process, coding of the seed set may be inaccurate (and inconsistent, if more than one subject matter expert is used to train the system), the computer learning process may be terminated before it has stabilized, inappropriate relevance thresholds may be adopted, statistical measures to validate the methodology may be improperly selected, and so forth.

Butterfield and Kenney provide a checklist for developing, if not a uniform approach, a mutually agreeable one. The development of standard, or at least agreed, disclosures, they argue, will "eliminate much of the uncertainty and expense associated with negotiating TAR protocols . . . ." By doing so, the use of these valuable tools will be simplified and their cost effectiveness more easily realized.

CHAPTER 7

Reality Bites: Why TAR's Promises Have Yet to Be Fulfilled

William P. Butterfield and Jeannine M. Kenney[1]

Introduction

The complexity and cost associated with discovery of electronically stored information (ESI) have attracted increasing attention in recent years as the volume of ESI that organizations maintain, and thus may be required to preserve and produce in litigation, has ballooned.[2]

1. A previous version of this chapter was presented as a paper at the 14th International Conference on Artificial Intelligence and Law Workshop on Standards for Using Predictive Coding, Machine Learning, and Other Advanced Search and Review Methods in E-Discovery (DESI V workshop) in Rome, Italy. Conor Crowley, a co-author of that paper, is not an author of this chapter and the viewpoints expressed herein should not be attributed to him.

2. For example, Christopher Surdak, author of *Data Crush*, released last year, predicts that the amount of data generated will double each year through the 2010s. *See* Cary J. Calderone, *Review of Data Crush—Sometimes You Can Judge a Book by Its Title*, DATA AND PRIVACY LAW BLOG (Mar. 13, 2014), http://docretention.blogspot.com/2014/03/review-of-data-crush-sometimes-you-can.html (last visited Sept. 26, 2016).Others predict that by 2020, the production of data will have grown by 4,300 percent. Computer Sciences Corp., *Big Data Universe Beginning to Explode*, http://www.csc.com/insights/flxwd/78931-big_data_universe_beginning_to_explode (last visited Jan. 9, 2015). And according to data compiled by IBM from a range of technology sources: 2.3 trillion gigabytes of data are created every day; most companies store at least 100,000 gigabytes of data; 30 billion pieces of content are shared

At the same time, the effectiveness of more traditional tools used to cull nonresponsive from responsive ESI—both manual "eyes-on" review and the use of keyword searching—has been credibly questioned by scientific studies.

It is now well recognized, at least among information retrieval scientists, that human, manual review is not only entirely impractical in the age of ESI, but is also far from the gold standard of review against which other search tools should be judged: inconsistency and errors in human review lead to omission of responsive documents and inclusion of nonresponsive ones compared to other methodologies.[3] And the potential problems with keyword searching using Boolean operators, the accepted methodology to which most attorneys have turned given the volume of ESI and impracticality of manual review, are well-established. Even productions resulting from carefully designed search terms developed through a fully cooperative and iterative process may suffer from both poor precision and poor recall,[4] increasing the costs of pre-production review by the producing party and omitting too many responsive documents, thereby denying the requesting party documents that may be critical to the case. Courts increasingly

---

on Facebook every month; 400 million tweets are sent each day by about 200 million users; and 6 billion people have cell phones. IBM, *The Four V's of Big Data*, http://www.ibmbigdatahub.com/sites/default/files/infographic_file/4-Vs-of-big-data.jpg (last visited Sept. 26, 2016). *See also, e.g.*, John Gantz & David Reinsel, *Extracting Value from Chaos*, IDC (June 2011), http://www.emc.com/collateral/analyst-reports/idc-extracting-value-from-chaos-ar.pdf (discussing growth in the generation of ESI); *The Data Deluge*, THE ECONOMIST (Feb. 25, 2010), *available at* http://www.economist.com/node/15579717?story_id=15579717 (noting information created increased by nearly tenfold between 2005 and 2010).

3. *See generally* Maura R. Grossman & Gordan V. Cormack, *Technology-Assisted Review in E-Discovery Can Be More Effective and More Efficient Than Exhaustive Manual Review*, 17 RICHMOND J. L. & TECH. 11 (2011); *see also* Nicholas M. Pace & Laura Zakaras, *Where the Money Goes: Understanding Litigant Expenditures for Producing Electronic Discovery*, RAND INST. FOR CIVIL JUSTICE, 55–58 (2012), http://www.rand.org/content/dam/rand/pubs/monographs/2012/RAND_MG1208.pdf.

4. *See, e.g.*, The Sedona Conference, *Best Practices Commentary on the Use of Search and Information Retrieval Methods in E-Discovery*, 8 SEDONA CONF. J. 189, 201–02 (2007), *available at* http://www.thesedonaconference.org/; Maura R. Grossman & Terry Sweeney, *What Lawyers Need to Know About Search Tools: The Alternatives to Keyword Searching Include Linguistic and Mathematical Models for Concept Searching*, NAT. L. J., Aug. 23, 2010, *available at* http://www.ned.uscourts.gov/internetDocs/cle/2011-01/National%20Law%20Journal%20(Aug%202010).pdf.

recognize these concerns.[5] In this context, technology-assisted review (TAR)[6] appears to offer a way out of the morass of traditional, but often problematic, legal search methodologies. Appropriately applied, TAR can offer a more accurate and cost-effective means of identifying and producing responsive ESI, at least for larger cases, compared to more traditional tools.[7] Given the availability of TAR, courts may look with skepticism on claims of undue burden resulting from review of keyword search hits.[8]

Why then, given the advantages of this search technology, has it not been more widely adopted by parties in appropriate cases? To a certain extent, that reluctance stems from fear or lack of understanding

---

5. *See, e.g.*, Victor Stanley, Inc. v. Creative Pipe, Inc., 250 F.R.D. 251, 256–57 (D. Md. 2008) (discussing the risks and difficulties of keyword searching); Nat'l Day Laborer Org. Network v. U.S. Immig. & Customs Enforcement Agency, 877 F. Supp. 2d 87, 109 n.112 (S.D.N.Y. 2012) ("There is increasingly strong evidence that '[k]eyword search[ing] is not nearly as effective at identifying relevant information as many lawyers would like to believe.'") (quoting Grossman & Sweeney, *supra* note 4) (alteration in original)). Some have questioned, however, whether keyword searching is necessarily less effective at retrieving responsive documents than more advanced computer-assisted analytics. These commentators suggest that seminal research regarding the effectiveness of search terms has been misinterpreted and that, in the appropriate case and with increasingly sophisticated Boolean search capabilities, the right processes, and appropriate use of precision and recall metrics, keyword searching can yield defensible results. *See generally, e.g.*, Dan Regard & Tom Matzen, *A Re-Examination of Blair & Maron (1985)*, presented at DESI V Workshop, June 14, 2013, *available at* http://www.umiacs.umd.edu/~oard/desi5/additional/Regard-final.pdf.

6. The use of advanced computer learning models in e-discovery is sometimes referred to as predictive coding or computer-assisted review (CAR). While there may be slight differences in the definitions of these terms, when the authors use the term TAR in this chapter, they intend this term to include predictive coding and CAR.

7. *See, e.g.*, John M. Facciola, M.J., *Foreword* to *The Grossman-Cormack Glossary of Technology-Assisted Review*, 7 FED. CT. L. REV. 1, 4 (2013) ("It is now indubitable that technology-assisted review is an appreciably better and more accurate means of searching a set of data."). Estimates of cost savings have varied widely, but all the data suggest the savings are significant. *See, e.g.*, Ann Kershaw & Joe Howie, *Judges' Guide to Cost-Effective E-Discovery* 13–14 (Oct. 1, 2010), *available at* http://www.discoverypilot.com/sites/default/files/JUDGES%20GUIDE-fnl_PDF3v2.pdf (45 percent reduction in review costs); Pace & Zakaras, *supra* note 3, at 66–69 (estimates of reported cost savings ranged from 0 percent up to nearly 80 percent).

8. Chevron Corp. v. Donziger, No. 11-cv-691, 2013 WL 1087236, at *32 (S.D.N.Y. Mar. 15, 2013).

of TAR and a comfort with old patterns.[9] And we have observed that, even in complex cases, some parties, sophisticated and otherwise, still insist that manual or "eyes-on" review is the most effective or preferred form of review, often relying on custodians to identify responsive documents and using search terms only for email or only as a stop-gap measure to capture responsive documents not identified by the lawyers or custodians. Given that perspective, despite the science demonstrating more reliable search methods, it is hardly surprising that TAR has not been more widely embraced. In such cases, it may be only time and judicial skepticism on the defensibility of manual review that may foster greater adoption of TAR.

Others, however, suggest that the lack of judicial endorsement of TAR has fostered concern that litigants using it are vulnerable to post-hoc production challenges that may result in costly do-overs.[10] Some believe that without a judicial imprimatur, few litigants will rely on TAR as the sole means to identify and produce responsive ESI even though the legal basis for defending the use of TAR has been clearly outlined.[11] Finally, some potential TAR users are concerned that the cost of extensive negotiations with the opposing party and ancillary motion practice over the application of a TAR protocol in a given case will outweigh the cost savings otherwise achieved by the tool.[12] Thus,

---

9. *See* Pace & Zakaras, *supra* note 3, at 72–76, 80.

10. *See* Pace & Zakaras, *supra* note 3, at 72–73, 77–80; Henry J. Kelston et al., *Technology Assisted Review from the Plaintiffs' Side*, L. Tech. News, Dec. 10, 2012 (discussing survey results).

11. *See, e.g.*, Conor R. Crowley, *Defending the Use of Analytical Software in Civil Discovery*, 10, No. 16 Digital Discovery & E-Evidence at 3–4, Sept. 16, 2010, *available at* http://www.umiacs.umd.edu/~oard/sire11/papers/crowley.pdf.

12. *See Waiving Work Product with Predictive Coding*, ESI Bytes Podcast (Sept. 17, 2012) *available at* http://www.esibytes.com/waiving-work-product-with-predictive-coding/ (guest Jeff Fowler asserting that the cost of negotiating and litigating a TAR protocol before it is implemented can eliminate cost advantages of TAR); *cf.* Pace & Zakaras, *supra* note 3, at 73 (noting concerns that "costs required to completely eliminate any shortfalls in recall or precision would be out of proportion to any benefit of the additional information"); *id.* at 71 & n.3 (noting that disclosure of TAR may lead to litigation that may negate cost advantages). This concern arose in Progressive Casualty Insurance Co. v. Delaney, discussed in greater depth *infra*, in which the producing party wanted to adopt TAR but the receiving party raised concerns that, *inter alia*, use of the complex TAR protocol would lead to "numerous satellite disputes." No. 11-cv-678, 2014 WL 3563467, at *4 (D. Nev. July 18, 2014).

surveys suggest that TAR has been used chiefly by producing parties for case analysis or to locate documents of interest, not as a substitute for keyword searching in the production process,[13] although some observers suspect producing parties may be using the technology for their productions without disclosure.[14]

Information retrieval scientists and some e-discovery practitioners now herald recent U.S. court decisions endorsing TAR as a sign that technology-assisted review will replace less effective legal search tools.[15] Words like "landmark," "watershed," and "sea change" are not infrequently invoked to describe their significance. Unquestionably, these court decisions provide reason for optimism that TAR will be more widely embraced by litigators. But in two leading cases,

---

13. Kelston et al., *supra* note 10.

14. *See* Pace & Zakaras, *supra* note 3, at 71 & n.3 ("We have been told that computer-categorization techniques have, in fact, been employed in document reviews but that the use was not disclosed to opposing parties or the court."). A 2014 survey of 550 law firms found that 47 percent of responding firms reported using predictive coding in at least one of their matters that year. Kroll Ontrack, *2014 Ediscovery Trends: Industry Survey Results*, 4–5 (2014), http://www.ediscovery.com/cms/pdf/ediscoverytrends_krollontrack2014.pdf. Of those firms, nearly 73 percent reported using predictive coding in discovery productions; other uses were for early case assessment, prelitigation investigation, and defensible deletion and information governance. *Id.* The survey does not reveal whether those firms using TAR in their productions did so to prioritize and expedite review of the documents identified after employing an agreed upon keyword search or other search methodology, or whether TAR was used as the primary means of searching for responsive documents, with or without disclosure to the requesting party.

15. *See, e.g.*, Correy E. Stephenson, *After Breakthrough Year, Predictive Coding Catching On*, New England In-House (Mar. 5, 2013), http://newenglandinhouse.com/2013/03/05/after-breakthrough-year-predictive-coding-catching-on/; Ritter Academy, *Why Court Approval of Computer-based Searches Changes Everything* (commenting on Moore v. Publicis Groupe SA, No. 11-cv-1279, 2012 WL 1446534 (S.D.N.Y. Apr. 26, 2012), which approved the use of predictive coding, and asserting that "the art of discovery is dying. The science of discovery is roaring with the momentum of a shuttle launching itself away from the gravitational pull of the earth."), http://www.ritteracademy.com/blog/why-court-approval-computer-based-searches-changes-everything (last visited Jan. 9, 2015); Patricia Antezana, *E-Discovery: Predictive Coding Decisions May Signal Change in Identifying Relevant Evidence*, Inside Counsel (June 12, 2012) ("The decisions by [courts] approving the use of predictive coding have set the stage for significant change in the legal landscape of court-accepted protocols for identifying relevant and responsive ESI."), http://www.insidecounsel.com/2012/06/12/e-discovery-predictive-coding-decisions-may-signal.

courts endorsed TAR in the context of transparency and cooperation among the parties that is infrequently seen in the litigation trenches. In another, the court endorsed TAR, but rejected a party's unilateral, nontransparent attempts to implement that methodology.[16]

ESI practitioners should not expect, without a dramatic change in the mindset of litigators about the cost-saving benefits of cooperation in discovery, these decisions to alter attorneys' resistance to disclosure of information retrieval methodologies and processes. More commonly, even when traditional search term methodologies are used, requesting parties face a methodological black box, often denied information about both the methodology applied and the basic statistical testing results (assuming any were employed) that provide assurances about the sufficiency of the outcome of the process.

And other recent court decisions suggest that, if parties do not voluntarily agree to a transparent TAR process, there are limits on the degree to which courts will require advance disclosures about the producing party's methodologies. At least one such decision has suggested that some courts may place the cost burdens of TAR on requesting parties if they demand that producing parties use it.[17] Given the often-greater reliability of TAR and the cost savings it can achieve, that viewpoint inexplicably moves away from the presumption that each party bears the costs of its own production.[18]

This chapter posits that, despite growing judicial acceptance of TAR, enthusiasm over the likelihood that TAR will be widely adopted by parties should be tempered with a dose of litigation reality. While information scientists may advocate cooperation and transparency as the way to achieve the best possible results from the use of TAR (and other search methodologies), parties in litigation may have tactical, strategic, or ethical concerns—some warranted, others not—that

16. Progressive Casualty Ins. Co. v. Delaney, No. 11-cv-678, 2014 WL 3563467, at *9, *11–12 (D. Nev. July 18, 2014).

17. *See* Order Regarding Discovery of ESI, *In re Biomet M2A Magnum Hip Implant Prods. Liability Litig.* (*Biomet*), No. 12-md-2391 (N.D. Ind. Apr. 18. 2013) (ECF No. 396).

18. Oppenheimer Fund, Inc. v. Sanders, 437 U.S. 340, 358 (1978) (recognizing the presumption that "the responding party must bear the expense of complying with discovery requests").

limit their willingness to fully cooperate in a transparent manner. Additionally, parties may assert they are not required to achieve the best possible results from TAR, but rather to certify only that they have undertaken a reasonable investigation to identify and produce nonprivileged, responsive information. Whether, given the technical complexity of search methodologies, the reasonableness of which can generally only be demonstrated by statistical testing, courts will accept such certification absent transparency regarding validation procedures and statistical results remains to be seen.

Finally, parties in litigation have been motivated to consider the use of TAR not only because of its promise of greater levels of precision and recall than other review methods, but also because of its promise of significantly reduced review costs. This difference in motivations and objectives may help to explain why such a promising tool has not been as widely adopted as scientists would expect. Producing parties may believe the cost-savings of TAR may be offset by negotiations and disputes associated with it use. Requesting parties may be reluctant to agree to TAR unless they know that the methodology will ensure that its results are not under-inclusive.

Despite these concerns, however, once parties and courts develop a more uniform approach regarding the amount of transparency expected when using TAR, they may be more willing to adopt this approach. The development of standard disclosures expected from producing parties using TAR or pre-production protocols governing its use, developed through a cooperative process and entered by the court, would eliminate much of the uncertainty and expense associated with negotiating TAR protocols, and thereby allow producing parties to realize the cost savings offered by these advanced technologies. Moreover, as courts adopt a more uniform approach to TAR, parties will enjoy increased predictability, and will thus be able to use TAR without the uncertainty and expenses arising from litigation over the tools and protocols associated with these newer technologies. The second part of this chapter offers our suggestions on the types of disclosures that producing parties should make when they plan to use TAR to produce documents and other information to facilitate acceptance by the requesting party and the court.

We begin with a discussion of recent U.S. court decisions generating considerable enthusiasm about the advent of TAR as a mainstream legal search tool, focusing on what they do and do not portend for increased transparency. We then briefly review the doctrines and concerns held by producing parties that impede and discourage the transparency we believe could facilitate wider adoption of TAR. We conclude by offering a checklist of disclosures we believe parties should consider to engender effective and cooperative use of TAR and thus its widespread acceptance, and propose ways to balance competing concerns regarding transparency.

Judicial Acceptance of Technology-Assisted Review

Over the years, as judicial skepticism over the reliability of keyword searching has grown, courts have inched toward acceptance of advanced analytics as a viable information retrieval technology. In 2007, when directing parties to meet and confer to develop a search protocol, Federal Magistrate Judge John Facciola noted "recent scholarship that argues that concept searching, as opposed to keyword searching, is more efficient and more likely to produce the most comprehensive results."[19] Similarly, five years later, Judge Scheindlin, after discussing the shortcomings of keyword searches, concluded that "parties can (and frequently should) rely on latent semantic indexing, statistical probability models, and machine learning tools."[20]

Federal District Court Judge Paul Grimm has likewise pointed to "a growing body of literature that highlights the risks [of] conducting an unreliable or inadequate keyword search or relying exclusively on such searches," and suggested more advanced tools like concept searching may be more appropriate methodologies.[21] Federal Magistrate Judge Peggy Leen concluded that "predictive coding has emerged as a far more accurate means of producing responsive ESI in discovery," citing judicial opinions, scholarly articles, and other commentary

19. Disability Rights Council of Greater Wash. v. Wash. Metro. Transit Auth., 242 F.R.D. 139, 148 (D.D.C. 2007).

20. Nat'l Day Laborer Org. Network v. U.S. Immig. & Customs Enforcement Agency, 877 F. Supp. 2d 87, 109 (S.D.N.Y. 2012).

21. Victor Stanley v. Creative Pipe, Inc., 250 F.R.D. 251, 256–57 (D. Md. 2008) (M.J. Grimm). When *Victor Stanley* was decided, Judge Grimm served as a magistrate judge. He now serves as a district judge for the U.S. District Court for the District of Maryland.

on the effectiveness of TAR (including an earlier draft of this chapter prepared for a conference) over more traditional methodologies.[22]

The U.S. Tax Court, in the first decision of that court to mention (much less discuss) TAR, approved the producing party's request to apply predictive coding to search backup tapes, and discussed the merits and growing acceptance of the technology, citing recent court cases adopting the approach: "[W]e understand that the technology industry now considers predictive coding to be widely accepted for limiting e-discovery to relevant documents and effecting discovery of ESI without an undue burden."[23] And District Court Judge Denise Cote, rejecting a challenge to the completeness of a production, reiterated that court's review of literature indicated that "predictive coding had a better track record in the production of responsive documents than human review . . . ."[24]

Courts have even gone so far as to require parties to at least consider use of TAR in their ESI negotiations.[25] And notably, the Southern District of New York's Pilot Project for Case Management Techniques for Complex Civil Cases requires participants in the project to make a joint ESI submission regarding disclosure of ESI search techniques to be used, and identifies advanced analytical tools, including "machine learning" as appropriate approaches.[26] Similarly, Principle 2.05 of the Seventh Circuit's Electronic Discovery Pilot Program directs that the Rule 26(f)

22. Progressive Casualty Ins. Co. v. Delaney, No. 11-cv-678, 2014 WL 3563467, at *8 (D. Nev. July 18, 2014).

23. Dynamo Holdings LP v. Comm'r, 143 T.C. No. 9, at *5 (T.C. 2014) (citing cases).

24. Fed. Hous. Fin. Agency v. HSBC N. Am. Holdings Inc., No. 11 CIV. 6189 DLC, 2014 WL 584300, at *3 (S.D.N.Y. Feb. 14, 2014) (referencing prior order permitting defendant to use predictive coding over plaintiff's objection and noting that both predictive coding and human review each fell short of identifying all of the documents that parties in litigation may wish to see).

25. *See* FDIC v. Bowden, No. CV413-245, 2014 WL 2548137, at *13 (S.D. Ga. June 6, 2014); *cf.* Chevron Corp. v. Donziger, No. 11 CIV. 0691 LAK, 2013 WL 1087236, at *32 (S.D.N.Y. Mar. 15, 2013) (referencing the court's prior suggestion that, in making their burden arguments, the parties consider "whether and to what extent predictive coding could 'reduce the burden and effort' required to comply with the Subpoena").

26. Standing Order, *In re: Pilot Project Re: Case Mgmt. Techniques for Complex Civil Cases in the S. Dist. of N.Y.*, No. 11-mc-0388 at 21 (S.D.N.Y. Nov. 1, 2011) (ECF No. 1).

conference include discussion of potential methodologies for identifying ESI for production, noting that among the topics for discussion are "use of keyword searching, mathematical or thesaurus-based topic or concept clustering, or other advanced culling technologies."[27]

Finally, Kroll Ontrack reported that, in 2012, 9 percent of federal and state cases addressing e-discovery issues discussed TAR or predictive coding.[28] Then, in 2014, Kroll's case law review reported that 13 percent of federal and state opinions discussed ESI procedural issues, such as search and predictive coding protocols, and that "judges wrote an unprecedented number of opinions about predictive coding and TAR, working to clarify the particularities associated with the process behind using predictive coding, such as its use for [early data assessment], the completeness of production when predictive coding is used, the use of multiple searching methods with predictive coding, and the reasonableness of predictive coding methodologies."[29]

But no court had endorsed use of TAR as a defensible production methodology in a specific case until 2012, when Magistrate Judge Peck broke the ice in *Da Silva Moore v. Publicis Groupe*, formally "recogniz[ing] that computer-assisted review is an acceptable way to search for relevant ESI in appropriate cases."[30] Three years after that decision, Judge Peck concluded that "the case law has developed to the point that it is now black letter law that where the producing party wants to utilize TAR for document review, courts will permit it."[31]

Several subsequent court decisions in the past two years further highlight the growing acceptance of TAR by the court or the parties, or

27. 7th Circuit Electronic Discovery Committee, *Principles Relating to the Discovery of Electronically Stored Information*, at 5 (Aug. 1, 2010), http://www.discoverypilot.com/sites/default/files/Principles8_10.pdf.

28. Julie Beck, *Study Analyzes E-discovery Trends in 2012*, Inside Counsel (Dec. 31, 2012), http://www.insidecounsel.com/2012/12/31/study-analyzes-e-discovery-trends-in-2012.

29. *2014 Ediscovery Case Law: Predictive Coding Takes Center Stage in Key Judicial Opinions*, Kroll Ontrack (Dec. 16, 2014), http://www.ediscovery.com/press-news/press/63614/2014-ediscovery-case-law-predictive-coding-ta/.

30. Da Silva Moore v. Publicis Groupe, 287 F.R.D. 182, 183 (S.D.N.Y. 2012) *adopted* Moore v. Publicis Groupe SA, No. 11 CIV. 1279, 2012 WL 1446534 (S.D.N.Y. Apr. 26, 2012).

31. Rio Tinto PLC v. Vale S.A., No. 14 CIV. 3042, 2015 WL 872294, at *1 (S.D.N.Y. Mar. 2, 2015).

both. More importantly, these decisions suggest a shift in focus away from the acceptability of TAR as a tool and toward the process used to employ it and the results obtained. Much ink has been spilled about *Da Silva Moore* and these subsequent decisions, and thus we limit our discussion here to only those details necessary to distill key issues relevant to our thesis.

Global Aerospace, Kleen Products, and *Biomet*: Court Deference to Producing Parties

Several widely discussed court decisions, which came on the heels of *Da Silva Moore*, have attracted the attention of the information retrieval community. First, in *Global Aerospace, Inc. v. Landow Aviation, LP*,[32] a state court permitted defendants, over plaintiffs' objections, to use a TAR methodology that did not involve seed sets or keywords to search a corpus of some 1.3 million potentially responsive, searchable documents. Importantly, the court did so without prejudice to plaintiffs' right to object, post hoc, to the results obtained and the completeness of the production.[33] During the hearing, the court noted that the producing party ordinarily has the right to select its search and review methodology, subject to the propounding party's right to object if it finds responsive documents have not been produced. Importantly, the court did not specifically endorse the technology or conclude it was better suited than other legal search tools; it merely let defendants proceed as they chose. According to subsequent reports, following application of TAR, defendants presented results showing the methodology produced a precision rate of 80 percent and a recall rate of 81 percent,[34] to which the plaintiffs remaining in the case apparently did not object or respond.[35]

Second, in an interesting twist, in *Kleen Products LLC v. Packaging Corporation of America*, it was plaintiffs, not defendants, who

32. Order Approving the Use of Predictive Coding for Discovery, Global Aerospace, Inc. v. Landow Aviation, LP, No. CL 61040, 2012 WL 1431215 (Va. Cir. Ct., Apr. 23, 2012).

33. *Id.*

34. Joe Palazzola, *How a Computer Did the Work of Many Lawyers*, Wall St. J. Law Blog (Jan. 17, 2013, 4:44 PM), http://blogs.wsj.com/law/2013/01/17/how-a-computer-did-the-work-of-many-lawyers/?mod=WSJBlog.

35. Evan Koblentz, *Predictive Coding Completed in* 'Global Aerospace' *Case*, L. Tech. News, Jan. 16, 2013.

argued that TAR, as applied to the defendant's production, was necessary to ensure that responsive documents were captured and produced, asserting that keyword searching used by defendants was not sufficiently reliable compared to TAR.[36] Defendants balked, at least in part, because they had already applied a keyword search methodology, along with iterative testing and validation procedures, to respond to the first set of production requests. Plaintiffs, on the other hand, were requesting a do-over. In the end, the court conducted two days of evidentiary proceedings to resolve the dispute and required the parties to meet and confer to identify whether refining searches or other steps could provide plaintiffs with assurances that they were receiving a high percentage of responsive documents.[37] Five months and many meet and confers and court conferences later, plaintiffs agreed to withdraw their demand that TAR be applied to existing production requests, but the parties agreed to meet and confer on the appropriate search methodology for any subsequent requests, leaving the door open to using TAR for later productions.[38] The court, in recounting this resolution, noted that "responding parties are best situated to evaluate the procedures, methodologies, and techniques appropriate for preserving and production their own [ESI]."[39]

More recently, in *In re Biomet M2A Magnum Hip Implant Products Liability Litigation* (*Biomet*), the court permitted the producing party to use a hybrid methodology, using search terms to cull a 19.5 million document set to 2.5 million documents, to which TAR was then applied to identify responsive documents.[40] Plaintiffs objected not to the use of TAR per se, but to Biomet defendants' unilateral decision to apply search terms to cull the corpus prior to application of TAR—a process they challenged as too exclusionary—without meeting and

36. No. 10-cv-5711, 2012 WL 4498465, at *4 (N.D. Ill. Sept. 28, 2012).

37. *Id.*

38. *Id.* at *5.

39. *Id.* (citing Principle 6 of the Sedona Principles (Second Ed.): Best Practices Recommendations & Principles for Addressing Electronic Document Production of The Sedona Conference, as discussed in The Sedona Conference, *Best Practices Commentary on the Use of Search and Information Retrieval Methods in E-Discovery*, 8 SEDONA CONF. J. 189, 193 (Fall 2007)). *But see infra* note 82 and accompanying text.

40. Order Regarding Discovery of ESI, *Biomet*, No. 12-md-2391 (N.D. Ind. Apr. 18, 2013).

conferring with plaintiffs. Plaintiffs asked that the TAR process be reapplied without the use of search terms and demanded that they be involved in the computer training process. In response, Biomet defendants offered to produce all 2.5 million documents resulting from the keyword search (responsive or not)—a proposal that did not address plaintiffs' concerns that responsive documents were improperly culled from the original set of 19.5 million documents.

The court's rejection of plaintiffs' proposed do-over was based on both its assessment of the reliability statistics disclosed in the case (which it concluded satisfied Biomet's production obligations) and consideration of the seven-figure cost involved in rerunning the predictive coding process. The court noted that:

> Statistical sampling tests of a random sample [of the unselected documents] projected, with a 99 percent confidence rate, that between .55 and 1.33 percent of the unselected documents would be responsive and (with the same confidence level) that between 1.37 and 2.47 percent of the original 19.5 million documents were responsive. In comparison, [Defendant's] keyword/deduplication approach had identified 16 percent of the original 19.5 million.[41]

Despite plaintiffs' argument that Biomet defendants chose to gamble on the defensibility of its methodology when it unilaterally deployed it, the court concluded that if plaintiffs wanted a do-over, they would have to pay for it.[42] Interestingly, that court had previously adopted, as part of its Case Management Order, the Seventh Circuit's Standing Order Relating to the Discovery of Electronically Stored Information, which required the parties, prior to the first case management conference, to discuss methodologies for culling the relevant and discoverable ESI and documents from the initial subset of ESI sources identified.[43] But it found nothing in its decision inconsistent with the Standing Order.

41. *Id.* at 2.

42. *Id.* at 7.

43. Case Management Order at 3 & Ex. A, *Biomet*, No. 12-md-2391 (N.D. Ind. Feb. 15, 2013) (ECF No. 242).

These cases are important not only because of their outcome, but also because of the deference the courts paid to the producing parties' choice of search methodology and procedures.[44] That deference may lend greater force to objections by producing parties that a mandate for transparency in TAR deviates from Principle 6 of the Sedona Best Practices Recommendations & Principles for Addressing Electronic Document Production—that responding parties are best situated to evaluate the appropriate means of producing ESI.[45] Thus, as discussed in the next section, *Da Silva Moore & Actos*: Transparency and Cooperation Lead to Acceptance, litigants are often reluctant to reveal specifics about their ESI itself and the tools used to search it; and they are even less willing to involve the requesting party in their search process. Yet that lack of transparency and cooperation regarding the nature of the ESI and the search methodologies to be applied may impede the parties' ability to reach agreement on the use of TAR. Consider the following observation by counsel for plaintiffs in *Global Aerospace* explaining their reluctance to grant what they describe as defendants' request for an "advance waiver" on the acceptability of predictive coding absent sufficient disclosures:

> [C]ounsel for the . . . plaintiffs were reluctant to provide any such waiver without first obtaining information showing that the proposed use of predictive coding was the best method for locating responsive documents.
>
> We never received this comfort; many of our questions about the data went unanswered. The [defendants'] counsel refused to state how many emails they had accumulated, how many emails dated from the key time period, how many emails they had collected from the principal officer of the [defendant] entities,

44. In contrast to this deference, Delaware Chancery Court Judge Travis Laster, in addition to ordering parties to select a joint e-discovery vendor to host and review documents, ordered the parties to show cause why predictive coding should not be used in the case although, apparently, neither party had proposed its use. *See* Tr. 66:12-67:13, EORHB, Inc. v. HOA Holdings, LLC, C.A. No. 7409 (Del. Ch. Oct. 19, 2012).

45. *See* David J. Kessler et al., *Search Terms Are More Than Mere Words*, N.Y. L.J. (Mar. 21, 2011), *available at* http://www.nortonrosefulbright.com/files/us/images/publications/20110321SearchTermsAreMoreThanMereWords.pdf.

> or how any of the documents were foldered or organized. The plaintiffs therefore did not consent to the use of predictive coding. The [defendants] then filed a motion for a protective order.
>
> . . . .
>
> As the failed negotiations in *Global Aerospace* demonstrate, it is difficult to gain the comfort necessary to bless a particular search protocol without receiving extensive information about the documents.[46]

Would plaintiffs have provided that waiver with the appropriate disclosures, avoiding the risk that Global might have to rerun its production?

Did the Biomet defendants take an ill-advised gamble by making unilateral decisions on its hybrid search methodology given growing court recognition of the deficiencies (including under-inclusiveness) of search terms, particularly for such a large production? Its statistics on reliability, although accepted by the court, do not seem to support a finding that a reasonable search was conducted. In commentary on the decision, information retrieval experts Maura Grossman and Gordon Cormack noted that these statistics raise concerns about the reliability of the hybrid approach. They concluded that recall for the keyword search itself was just 50 percent; and assuming that predictive coding resulted in about 70 percent recall in the set to which the methodology was applied, the hybrid approach likely identified only 35 percent of the relevant documents from among the 19.5 million.[47] Given those statistics, although Biomet defendants won the short-term gamble, they still risked post-production challenges to the adequacy of its production. As the *Global Aerospace* court noted, its order was "without prejudice to a receiving party raising with the court an issue as to completeness or the contents of the production or the ongoing use of predictive coding."[48]

46. *Predictive Coding—A Dispatch From the Front Lines of E-Discovery*, Jones Day (Sept. 2012), http://www.jonesday.com/predictive_coding/.

47. *In re: Biomet—Doing the Math on Court Approved Multimodal Review*, IT-Lex Tech. Law Blog (Apr. 22, 2013), http://web.archive.org/web/20160508232948/http://it-lex.org/in-re-biomet-doing-the-math-on-court-approved-multimodal-review/.

48. Order Approving the Use of Predictive Coding for Discovery, Global Aerospace, Inc. v. Landow Aviation, LP, No. CL 61040, 2012 WL 1431215 (Va. Cir. Ct., Apr. 23, 2012).

Importantly, for our purposes here, following completion of their document production, the Biomet defendants filed with the court a certification regarding their production and search methodologies.[49] They disclosed not only the general processes used to collect and produce documents (data sources, custodians, volume of the corpus and retrieved documents, etc.), but also the specific procedures used to employ keywords and, subsequently, technology assisted review to further cull the production.[50]

More significantly, the Biomet defendants disclosed the statistical sampling methodologies and resulting statistics to gauge the quality and completeness of its production.[51] They reported, for example, the size of the random samples and the populations from which they were collected (the initial collection and the keyword culled collection), the confidence levels and estimation intervals employed for each, and the recall and precision statistics at the different confidence levels, along with specific disclosures of the number of true and false positives and negatives used to calculate those metrics.[52] This level of disclosure, including statistics and methods, which counsel routinely argue is nondiscoverable as work product, may signal the growing importance of at least post hoc transparency to stave off challenges to production completeness and establish the defensibility of search methodologies. It would not be surprising to see a party argue that a court should require this level of post hoc disclosure to support a Rule 26(g) certification. Counsel reluctant to cooperate with opposing counsel in the development of their search methodologies should consider whether they are willing to risk a do-over should any such required disclosures demonstrate flaws in the application of TAR.

Da Silva Moore and *Actos*: Transparency and Cooperation Lead to Acceptance

The approaches taken by the parties in *Da Silva Moore* and *In re Actos Products Liability Litigation* (*Actos*) strongly suggest that, despite the

49. Biomet Defs.' Certification Pursuant to the Court's Dec. 10, 2013 Order, *Biomet*, No. 12-md-2391 (N.D. Ind. Jan. 3, 2014) (ECF No. 1164).

50. *Id.* ¶¶ 2–5.

51. *Id.* ¶¶ 6–8.

52. *Id.*

deference some courts pay to the producing parties' choices of review tools and procedures noted in the cases previously discussed, transparency and cooperation are more likely to promote both judicial and party acceptance of TAR. In both cases, the courts predicated their approval of TAR on significant transparency—to the court and the requesting party—and on significant involvement of the requesting party in the TAR process.

Importantly, in *Da Silva Moore v. Publicis Group*, Magistrate Judge Peck sent an early signal that he viewed transparency with respect to TAR as a necessary predicate to his endorsement of its use, advising defendants that if they used that methodology they would be required to turn over their seed set to plaintiffs (including documents tagged as nonresponsive in the training rounds) to enable them to determine whether the TAR tool was being appropriately trained.[53] After having agreed to a detailed predictive coding protocol, that cooperation broke down as defendants and plaintiffs ultimately engaged in a heated dispute over how the success of TAR would be measured.

What transpired up to that point, before the process unraveled, is, to us, far more important than the unraveling.[54] Notably, the parties had entered into an extensive TAR protocol replete with plaintiff input into the process, with the parties agreeing: (1) on data sources from which documents could be collected; (2) on the confidence level and interval for sampling, and the sample size for the initial seed set; (3) that plaintiffs would receive all documents in the seed set; (4) that the documents hit by targeted search terms used to populate a portion of the seed set would be disclosed to plaintiffs along with the defendants coding of those documents; (5) that plaintiffs would provide additional search terms to further populate the seed set; (6) that all documents reviewed in the seed set would be turned over to plaintiffs, whether designated as responsive or not; and (7) that after the seventh round, defendants would review a random sample of documents the algorithm deemed to be nonresponsive in

53. Moore v. Publicis Groupe, 287 F.R.D. 182, 185 (S.D.N.Y. 2012).

54. For a discussion of why the subsequent disputes over the predictive coding process in *Da Silva Moore* may have been much ado about nothing, *see* Herbert L. Roitblat, *Da Silva Moore Plaintiffs Slash and Burn Their Way Through eDiscovery*, Information Discovery Blog (Mar. 25, 2012), http://orcatec.blogspot.com/2012/03/da-silva-moore-plaintiffs-slash-and.html.

order to assess recall, and disclose those documents to plaintiffs. The court concluded that resolution of subsequent disputes over the reliability and success of the methodology was premature. Notably, Judge Peck discounted concerns about relevance standards given that the level of transparency would permit plaintiffs to raise concerns with the court as they arose. However, proceeding with the use of TAR without reaching agreement on such a fundamental issue could result in costly, prolonged motion practice that could undercut the savings gained from the use of TAR. Furthermore, requiring the production of nonresponsive documents is facially inconsistent with the language of Rule 26(b) that requires, with limited exceptions, the production of only those documents "relevant to any party's claim or defense."[55]

Transparency was also a critical feature in *Actos*, where the court entered a case management order outlining a "search methodology proof of concept" that provided a set of detailed, step-by-step requirements governing how a specific, identified TAR product would be applied to a subset of a collection to test whether the tool was appropriate for the full ESI collection.[56] The order included not only disclosure requirements, but also obligations for substantial cooperation: (1) the parties agreed to the custodians from whom documents would be collected for the sample collection population; (2) the court set the size of the random "control set"; (3) defendants' experts reviewed documents for privilege first, providing a privilege log; (4) the parties each nominated three experts to review the control set; (5) following review of the control set, using an active-learning approach, the experts coded random sample training sets, permitting the experts to work collaboratively to determine responsiveness, subject to meet and confers when disagreements about coding designations arose; (6) the court required sufficient training rounds until the system stabilized; and (7) the parties were required to meet and confer to agree upon the relevance score above which documents were produced, and below which they were withheld.

55. Fed. R. Civ. P. 26(b).

56. Case Management Order: Protocol Relating to the Production of Electronically Stored Information (ESI) at 6–16, *In re* Actos (Pioglitazone) Prods. Liab. Litig., No. 11-md-2299 (W.D. La. July 27, 2012) (ECF No. 1539).

The levels of transparency in *Da Silva Moore* and *Actos* arguably provided the requesting party with the information and involvement in the document retrieval process necessary to assess whether the process and methodology was sufficiently reliable and thus defensible. Notably, in both cases, the requesting party enjoyed full disclosure about the technology itself, and had full access not only to the sample sets themselves (with the exception of privileged documents) but also to the coding of those sets, permitting them to determine the adequacy of the critical control point of TAR—the human teaching of the tool. Similarly, in *Federal Housing Finance Agency v. HSBC*, Judge Cote "required transparency and cooperation, including giving the plaintiff full access to the seed set's responsive and non-responsive documents (except privileged)."[57]

Transparency was also a factor in the court's decision in *Bridgestone Americas, Inc. v. IBM Corp.* permitting the plaintiff to employ predictive coding to produce responsive documents from the more than two million potentially responsive documents identified *after* search terms agreed to by the parties were used to cull the original document collection.[58] IBM objected to Bridgestone's request, arguing that the methodology was not provided for in the original case management order governing ESI production—providing for search term culling followed by manual review—and that had it known TAR would be applied it would have negotiated different and broader search terms.[59] It further presented evidence that applying TAR after search term screening was technically inappropriate and likely to leave "too much on the cutting room floor."[60] Nonetheless, the court allowed Bridgestone "to switch horses midstream," noting that "openness and transparency in what Plaintiff is doing will be of critical importance," demanding "full openness" on Bridgestone's part, and expecting "the parties to communicate, through their

57. Rio Tinto PLC v. Vale S.A., No. 14 CIV. 3042, 2015 WL 872294, at *1 (S.D.N.Y. Mar. 2, 2015) (discussing bench order in Fed. Hous. Fin. Agency v. HSBC, No. 11 CIV. 6189 (S.D.N.Y. July 24, 2012).

58. Order (Bridgestone Order), Bridgestone Americas, Inc. v. IBM Corp., No. 13-cv-1196 (M.D. Tenn. July 22, 2014) (ECF No. 89).

59. IBM's Resp. to Bridgestone's Request to Add Predictive Coding to the ESI Protocol at 3–4, Bridgestone Americas, Inc. v. IBM Corp., No. 13-cv-1196 (M.D. Tenn. July 14, 2014) (ECF No. 85).

60. *Id.* at 5–6.

attorneys and experts and companies doing the work, on a frequent and open basis."[61] Importantly, Bridgestone agreed to provide the seed documents used to train the system.

The lack of transparency may account for the different outcome on similar facts in *Progressive Casualty Insurance Co. v. Delaney*.[62] There, the ESI protocol provided for the use of only search terms to cull responsive documents from the corpus, followed by either production of the documents hit or manual review, at the producing party's option.[63] Progressive, after determining that manual review of the search term hits would be overly time-consuming and costly, informed the other party that it would propose an alternative approach but declined to be transparent about that alternative.[64] The party opposing use of TAR—the FDIC—explained that it would not have narrowed those terms had it known predictive coding would be used to further screen documents from the production.[65] Although acknowledging the advantages of TAR, the court rejected Progressive's request. Among other reasons for its decision, Progressive's failure to negotiate a transparent predictive coding methodology at the outset and, more importantly its lack of disclosures about the predictive coding methodologies Progressive later proposed appeared to influence the court's decision:

> Progressive's proposal would relieve it of the burden of manual review of ESI according to the ESI protocol it stipulated to and allow it to adopt a predictive coding alternative to a small subset of the universe of ESI collected. Its proposal would also give its counsel exclusive responsibility for training the predictive coding software, and fails to comply with all of the best practices recommended by the Equivio software program. Progressive proposes a "do-over" of its own

61. Bridgestone Order, *supra* note 57, at 2–3.

62. No. 11-cv-678 (D. Nev.).

63. Progressive Casualty Ins. v. Delaney, No. 11-cv-678, 2014 WL 3563467, at *9 (D. Nev. July 18, 2014).

64. *Id.* at *5.

65. *Id.*

> invention that lacks transparency and cooperation regarding the search methodologies applied.[66]

Why are transparency and cooperation deemed so critical to adoption of TAR? *Biomet* notwithstanding, requesting parties and courts increasingly understand that not all TAR tools are alike or equally effective and that none are more reliable than traditional legal search methods if they are not used and applied correctly, with a clearly defined process and sound statistical methodology supporting them. Too much can go wrong; a seed set can be improperly selected, improper judgmental sampling can bias the learning process, coding of the seed set may be inaccurate (and inconsistent, if more than one subject matter expert is used to train the system), the computer learning process may be terminated before it has stabilized, inappropriate relevance thresholds may be adopted, statistical measures to validate the methodology may be improperly selected, and so forth.

Transparency and cooperation at each stage of a TAR process are thus useful to assure the requesting party that the tool as applied is effective. Without those assurances, merely invoking the magic words "predictive coding"—despite its promise of reliability and efficiency—will not guarantee that either requesting parties or courts will endorse the process.

Much has been written about the steps required to achieve a defensible e-discovery process—a process that reflects the producing party's compliance with its discovery obligations to undertake reasonable efforts to identify and produce responsive documents.[67] One way to reduce the susceptibility of the chosen review methodology and process to post hoc challenges is for the parties to reach advance agreement not only on the methodology but also on how it will be applied.[68]

---

66. *Id.* at *10.

67. *See generally, e.g.*, Hon. Craig B. Schaffer, M.J., "*Defensible" By What Standard?*, 13 SEDONA CONF. J. 217 (Fall 2012); Mike Hamilton, *"Defensible E-Discovery": What Does the Phrase Really Mean?*, EXTERRO BLOG (June 28, 2012), http://www.exterro.com/blog/e2-80-9cdefensible-e-discovery-e2-80-9d-what-does-the-phrase-really-mean/.

68. *See* Schaffer, *supra* note 67, at 225 ("The most 'defensible' search methodology is one [that] has been jointly adopted by the parties and endorsed by the court.").

Objections to Transparency: Privilege Doctrines and Litigation Realities

Nonetheless, producing parties are often reluctant to disclose even the most basic information about their search methodologies. The aversion to disclosure of TAR processes is often founded on assertions that (1) revealing methodological decisions reveals protected work product, (2) discovery about discovery is beyond the scope of Rule 26 of the Federal Rules of Civil Procedure, (3) revealing documents that are nonresponsive exposes the producing party to unnecessary litigation risk, and (4) producing parties are bound by the Federal Rules requiring that they conduct a reasonable search for responsive documents, and thus no greater assurances are required or warranted.

The work–product doctrine protects from discovery documents or tangible things that express the mental impressions of an attorney about a particular matter.[69] An attorney is thus protected from being required to disclose his or her written thoughts about relevant versus irrelevant facts, and legal theories and strategies.[70] Likewise, the attorney–client privilege protects from discovery communications between an attorney and his or her client if made for the purpose of providing or obtaining legal advice.[71]

TAR advocates should expect that assertions of work product that have plagued traditional keyword search negotiations will, if asserted as to TAR methodologies, impede adoption and acceptance of technology-assisted review. Even under a keyword search strategy, some attorneys who typically represent producing parties assert that the search terms themselves and related strategies for searching are work product because they "reflect counsel's strategy for the case" and thus courts cannot force, and requesting parties cannot insist on, their disclosure.[72] Additionally, it is not uncommon for produc-

69. Hickman v. Taylor, 329 U.S. 495, 509 (1947); Paul F. Rothstein & Susan W. Crump, FEDERAL TESTIMONIAL PRIVILEGES § 11:1 (2nd ed. 2007–08). *See also* FED. R. CIV. P. 26(b)(3).

70. *Hickman*, 329 U.S. at 510–11.

71. FEDERAL TESTIMONIAL PRIVILEGES, *supra* note 69, § 2:10.

72. *See, e.g.*, Kessler, *supra* note 45 ("What should not become commonplace (and, sadly, is starting to) is the forced disclosure of search terms by courts. Not only are search terms not within the bounds of discovery, but they are windows into

ing parties to refuse to disclose their precision and recall statistics on grounds of work product. Some courts have concluded, however, that details about search methodology are not work product at all, since they merely go to the "underlying facts of what documents are responsive to . . . document requests and [do] not delve into the thought processes of . . . counsel."[73] Rather than reveal an attorney's assessment of what is relevant or even important to the case, disclosures regarding search methodologies merely reveal assessments of what documents are responsive to production requests—a purely factual question.[74]

In the context of TAR, counsel raise similar concerns that work product may be impermissibly disclosed if producing parties are required, for example, to reveal the seed set, particularly if judgmental sampling is used, because it may reveal thought processes about the case.[75] If search terms are used to identify documents used to populate the seed set, as with traditional use of keyword searching, attorneys may express concern that revealing those terms discloses their assessments about the case. Some suggest that even disclosure of sources used to generate random seed set reveals the attorney's strategy on sources to be searched and custodians likely to possess responsive documents.[76] Producing parties' aversion to disclosing reliability statistics for search terms will apply equally to determinations of relevance thresholds and F_1 statistics[77] in the context of TAR. Finally, if,

---

how counsel are considering and evaluating their case . . . . [T]he search terms a party applies in discovery are generally created with the advice of counsel. Thus they represent the work product and mental impressions of the party's counsel."); Graff v. Haverhill N. Coke Co., No. 09-cv-670, 2010 U.S. Dist. LEXIS 142925, at *17 (S.D. Ohio Dec. 22, 2010) (noting "Defendants claim that the search terms and methodology used to obtain all relevant documents from the company's electronic database of documents is protected by the work-product doctrine.").

73. Romero v. Allstate Ins. Co., 271 F.R.D. 96, 110 (E.D. Pa. 2010) (citing cases).

74. *Id.* at 110 n.9.

75. *See generally* Hon. John M. Facciola (Ret.) and Philip Favro, *Safeguarding the Seed Set: Why Seed Set Documents May Be Entitled to Work Product Protection*, 8 Fed. Ct. L. Rev. 1 (2015) (discussing bases on which certain seed sets may be protected and case law regarding seed set disclosure), reprinted and updated as Chapter 9 in this volume.

76. *See Waiving Work Product, supra* note 12.

77. The F_1 statistic is "a measure of the effectiveness of a search or review effort, which accounts for the tradeoff between Recall and Precision. In order to achieve a high F_1 score, a search or review effort must achieve both high Recall and high

as in *Da Silva Moore* and *Actos*, the producing party must not only reveal the seed set, but also the coding decisions of reviewing attorneys, expect claims that doing so requires disclosure of attorneys' work product—their judgments as to relevance.

More serious concerns arise with respect to disclosure of documents in the seed set coded as nonresponsive by producing attorneys. Doing so reveals to the requesting parties documents that are not subject to any production obligation. That might be beyond the scope of discovery obligations, which require production of responsive information.[78] Moreover, producing parties that are the target of repeat litigation by the same set of plaintiffs' attorneys may well be reluctant to turn over documents entirely unrelated to the matter at hand, such as in prescription drug mass torts.[79] Still, there are solutions to even this concern: employing a third-party neutral to review the appropriateness of the coding of the seed set would provide the requesting party the assurance it needs, without disclosing nonresponsive documents.

Finally, some contend that courts and requesting parties should need no greater assurance as to the appropriateness of TAR methodologies than the producing party's obligation to conduct a reasonable inquiry under the federal rules and their certification that they have done so,[80] arguing courts and requesting parties have long had to rely simply on this certification for assurance as to the reasonableness of the investigation conducted to identify responsive documents. A party may insist that as long as it makes that certification, its search methodologies are not open to question absent clear deficiencies in the production. But in an age of ballooning ESI that may render it impossible for a producing party to know the location, volume, and con-

---

Precision." Maura R. Grossman & Gordon V. Cormack, *The Grossman-Cormack Glossary of Technology-Assisted Review*, 7 FED. CT. L. REV. 1, 16 (2013), reprinted in the Appendix in this volume.

78. *See* FED. R. CIV. P. 26(b)(1) ("Unless otherwise limited by court order, the scope of discovery is as follows: Parties may obtain discovery regarding any nonprivileged matter that is relevant to any party's claim or defense—including the existence, description, nature, custody, condition, and location of any documents or other tangible things and the identity and location of person who know of any discoverable matter. . . .").

79. *See Waiving Work Product, supra* note 12.

80. *See* FED. R. CIV. P. 26(g).

tent of responsive ESI, and use of retrieval technologies and statistical validation methodologies beyond the ken of even tech-savvy lawyers, courts may question whether a party's certification of its "reasonable inquiry" under Rule 26(g) amounts to little more than a "trust me" certification without transparency about its ESI search process and validation results.

Another objection to transparency is the principle that a producing party is best positioned to determine the appropriate search methodology for its own documents, embraced by some courts more generally.[81] But given the enormous volume of ESI, varying levels of technical sophistication among litigators, and the technology-centric nature of TAR and other search methodologies, courts may begin to question whether that principle is appropriate as recognition of TAR as a reliable, cost-efficient search methodology grows. Indeed, some court decisions suggest that when it comes to the *technology* to be employed to search ESI, deference may be waning.

For example, one court rejected a third party's attempt to shift production and review costs to the requesting party, noting that the third party could have used predictive coding to reduce its burden.[82] And another, after noting the case was particularly well-suited for TAR, ordered the parties to show cause why TAR *should not* be used.[83] Just as judges may become more comfortable directing

81. See discussion, *infra* section regarding *Global Aerospace, Inc. v. Landow Aviation, LP*, No. CL 61040 (Va. Cir. Ct.) and *Kleen Products LLC v. Packaging Corporation of America*, No. 10-cv-5711 (N.D. Ill.). *See also* The Sedona Principles (2d ed.): Best Practices Recommendations & Principles for Addressing Electronic Document Production ii (June 2007) (Principle No. 6: "Responding parties are best situated to evaluate the procedures, methodologies, and technologies appropriate for preserving and producing their own electronically stored information.").

82. Chevron Corp. v. Donziger, No. 11 CIV. 0691, 2013 WL 1087236, at *32 (S.D.N.Y. Mar. 15, 2013).

83. In EORHB, Inc. v. HOA Holdings, LLC, Delaware Chancery Court Judge Travis Laster, in addition to ordering parties to select a joint e-discovery vendor to host and review documents, ordered the parties to show cause why predictive coding should not be used in the case although, apparently, neither party had proposed its use. *See* Tr. 66:12-67:13, EORHB, Inc. v. HOA Holdings, LLC, C.A. No. 7409-VCL (Del. Ch. Oct. 19, 2012). The court later rescinded the order upon agreement by the parties that, given the small number of documents in the case, predictive coding would not be cost-effective. EORHB, Inc. v. HOA Holdings, LLC, No. 7409-VCL, 2013 WL 1960621 (Del. Ch. May 6, 2013).

search methodologies rather than deferring to the parties' choices, as they develop a greater understanding of when TAR methodologies work and when they do not, courts may likewise be less comfortable deferring to a party's "reasonable inquiry" certification absent disclosures about its methodologies and validation procedures.

In *Biomet*, for example, four months after permitting Biomet defendants to proceed with predictive coding, plaintiffs sought disclosure of seed set documents used to train the predictive coding algorithm, or at least identification of which documents already produced were within the seed set. As a "compromise" in connection with prior order, Biomet defendants "offered to include Plaintiffs' input in the training by adding relevant documents of their choice to the data set and using them to train the predictive coding software going forward."[84] Plaintiffs argued that without knowing *what* documents were already used to train the seed set, their participation in the training process was "illusory and meaningless."[85] Biomet defendants contended that such disclosure required them to reveal work product, tantamount to disclosing instruction manuals used by document reviewers, and that it had no obligation to reveal training methodologies merely to assuage plaintiffs' concerns regarding production adequacy; it nonetheless agreed to disclose which of the documents already produced were among the seed set.[86] The court rejected plaintiffs' request for disclosure of the seed set, concluding that ordering such disclosure would require Biomet defendants to discover "irrelevant or privileged documents used to tell the algorithm what not to find" exceeding the scope of permissible discovery.[87]

Proponents of the view that disclosure is unnecessary further assert that the producing party has a strong incentive to implement an accurate and effective methodology, given the risk that opposing counsel will discover through depositions or other means responsive

84. Pls.' Mot. for Relief from Defs.' Refusal to Disclose Relevant Docs. Used in Predictive Coding Process, *Biomet*, No. 12-md-2391 (N.D. Ind. Aug. 5, 2013) (ECF No. 723).

85. *Id.* at 2–3.

86. Defs.' Resp. to Pls.' Demand for Defs.' Predictive Coding Seed Set, *Biomet*, No. 12-md-2391 (N.D. Ind. Aug. 5, 2013) (ECF No. 722).

87. Mem. and Order at 2, *Biomet*, No. 12-md-2391 (N.D. Ind. Aug. 21, 2013) (ECF No. 763).

documents that were withheld. All of this, though, may be insufficient to allay the legitimate concerns of requesting parties who may acknowledge the theoretical superiority of TAR, but understand that given its complexity, even attorneys acting in good faith can improperly implement an otherwise effective search tool, excluding from production large amounts of responsive documents. Moreover, some courts have rejected the argument that disclosure is unnecessary, concluding that "discovery about discovery"—which arguably encompasses disclosures about search and retrieval methodologies—is well within the parameters of discovery under Rule 26.[88] If such disclosures can be compelled as part of discovery, early transparency and cooperation can be a resource-saving tool for both the parties and the court.

But support for transparency and cooperation, not just in discovery in general, but in the application of TAR, is growing. In 2008, The Sedona Conference issued a *Cooperation Proclamation*, which "urges parties to work in a cooperative rather than an adversarial manner to resolve discovery issues in order to stem the monetary costs of discovery disputes."[89] Numerous courts have now cited to the proclamation, some noting that "the best solution in the entire area of electronic discovery is cooperation among counsel."[90] And one court compelled responses to interrogatories about ESI search methods, noting that had voluntary disclosures been cooperatively made, the process could have been "collaborative rather than contrarian."[91] Even the *Biomet* court questioned Biomet's refusal to voluntarily disclose which documents among those produced were used in the initial seed set. It noted

88. *See, e.g.*, Ruiz-Bueno v. Scott, No. 12-cv-0809, 2013 WL 6055402, at *1–5 (S.D. Ohio, Nov. 15, 2013) (granting motion to compel responses to interrogatories regarding methods used to search for responsive ESI where producing party was less than forthcoming about its methods, and citing case law regarding appropriateness of discovery about discovery).

89. The Sedona Conference, *The Case for Cooperation*, 10 Sedona Conf. J. 339, 348–49 (2009).

90. SEC v. Collins & Aikman Corp., 256 F.R.D. 403, 406–07 (S.D.N.Y. 2009); *see also, e.g., Kleen Prods.*, 2012 WL 4498465, at *6; Cartel Asset Mgmt. v. Ocwen Fin. Corp., No. 01-cv-01644, 2010 U.S. Dist. LEXIS 17857, at *40 (D. Colo. Feb. 8, 2010); DeGeer v. Gillis, 755 F. Supp. 2d 909, 918 (N.D. Ill. 2010); William A. Gross Constr. Assocs. v. Am. Mfrs. Mut. Ins. Co., 256 F.R.D. 134, 136 (S.D.N.Y. 2009); Capitol Records, Inc., v. MP3tunes, LLC, 261 F.R.D. 44, 47 (S.D.N.Y. 2009).

91. *Ruiz-Bueno*, 2013 WL 6055402, at *1–5.

that Biomet's "cooperation [fell] below what the Sedona Conference endorses," and cautioned that "[a]n unexplained lack of cooperation in discovery can lead a court to question why the uncooperative party is hiding something, and [that] such questions can affect the exercise of discretion," and urged Biomet defendants to rethink their position.[92]

Even if parties are inclined to provide the transparency and cooperation envisioned in *Da Silva Moore* and *Actos*, some fear the cost of doing so might outweigh any savings achieved by employing TAR. In *Da Silva Moore*, even though the parties agreed on the use of TAR, the process of reaching agreement on the specifics of the protocol to be employed required days of hearings and testimony from competing experts. In *Actos*, where the parties agreed to use TAR and adopted a joint protocol for its implementation, the costs associated with having six experts review the control set and training sets, and the costs resulting from the need to resolve their disagreements whether by negotiation or by seeking a judicial ruling, could significantly reduce the savings that the parties expected to gain from employing TAR. Still, without empirical studies comparing the costs of TAR protocol negotiation and ancillary motion practice to the costs for more traditional search methodologies and the frequency of challenges to those methodologies, whether such concerns have a basis in fact remains unclear.

Regardless of the relative merits of the arguments against transparency and cooperation in designing and implementing TAR, there is reason for concern that mandating the disclosures and the level of cooperation present in *Da Silva Moore* and *Actos* will have a chilling effect, steering producing parties back to less robust methodologies where less must be revealed.[93] As a consequence, those advocating for TAR as a viable and preferable legal search tool in appropriate cases

92. Mem. & Order at 2, *Biomet*, No. 12-md-2391 (N.D. Ind. Aug. 21, 2013) (ECF No. 763). As noted *supra*, the *Biomet* court had previously adopted, as part of its Case Management Order, the Seventh Circuit's Standing Order Relating to the Discovery of Electronically Stored Information, which incorporates the principle of cooperation and provides that if a party fails to "cooperate and participate in good faith in the meet and confer process or is impeding the purpose of these Principles, the court may require additional discussions prior to the commencement of discovery and may impose sanctions" Case Management Order at 3 & Ex. A, *Biomet*, 12-md-2391 (N.D. Ind. Feb. 15, 2013) (ECF No. 242).

93. *See Waiving Work Product, supra* note 12.

face a difficult task: they must find a way to balance the conflicting concerns of producing parties resisting disclosure with requesting parties demanding it.

Transparency and Cooperation

For all the reasons discussed, enthusiasm over the promise of TAR should be tempered by a strong dose of litigation reality; its widespread adoption likely depends as much on how and whether the parties agree to cooperate and what the producing party discloses as on the technology itself and judicial acceptance of the idea of predictive coding. We offer here a checklist of the information that the parties should consider disclosing to facilitate a cooperative and defensible information-retrieval process using TAR. To information retrieval scientists, the importance of these disclosures may be clear. However, as discussed earlier, in the world of litigation where parties have traditionally not been required to disclose such information and have reasonable concerns about the appropriateness of such disclosures, the disclosures are controversial.

The Tool and the Provider: Not all TAR tools are the same. Knowing what tool from which vendor is proposed aids understanding of the strengths and weaknesses of the tool. Does it use feature engineering, such as latent semantic analysis, to prepare the feature set for classification? What classifier design/machine learning does the tool use? Nearest neighbor? Language modeling? Bayesian?[94] What methodologies are used to categorize documents? Supervised learning? Active learning? Both? Some experts suggest that any tool should include an

94. For a helpful discussion on the different features of search protocols (feature construction, feature transformation, classifier design, and methods), as well as types of legal search algorithms, *see* Ralph Losey, *The Many Types of Legal Search Software in the CAR Market Today*, E-DISCOVERY TEAM BLOG (Mar. 3, 2013), http://e-discoveryteam.com/2013/03/03/the-many-types-of-legal-search-software-in-the-car-market-today/ (crediting Doug Oard for the description of the layers of search algorithms, and Herb Roitblat for the description of search algorithms). Losey advises that good TAR design requires all four features of search protocols must work well together.

active learning component,[95] a process in which the system identifies documents most likely to be misclassified.

The more information disclosed about the tool, the more comfortable a requesting party can be in the appropriateness of that tool for the task. Importantly, disclosure of these facts should provide producing parties with no discomfort.

The Nature of the Documents and the Size of the Corpus: What types of documents will be included in the corpus from which samples will be drawn? E-mail and text documents? Paper scans with unsearchable text? Image files? Spreadsheets with limited text? If the underlying tool relies on semantic analysis, these disclosures inform the appropriateness of the tool's application.

And what is the overall volume? These disclosures aid in understanding whether certain documents are appropriate for machine learning or should be excluded and searched using an alternative methodology.

Culling the Corpus: Will culling techniques be used? If so, which and how? Will date, file type, domain, or custodian filters be applied? Disclosure of date filtering should not be controversial, as the relevant date range is one likely to be resolved through negotiations over the production requests themselves. Similarly, disclosures of associated custodians and sources of ESI are routine in modern litigation, and often mandated at the outset of litigation in a preservation order. Disclosing that certain data stores will be included or excluded should not therefore trouble the producing party, and indeed, physical and human sources of discoverable documents are among the type of discoverable information under Rule 26(b)(1).

If keywords are used to cull the corpus, what are the search terms? As with traditional keyword searching, producing parties may object to revealing search terms, but if used to cull documents, their disclosure will be important not only to gain the requesting party's agreement, but also to defend the methodology if it is later challenged. Concerns about revealing work product or confidential information

95. *Id.* ("If software does not have [active learning] built in as a planned method of use, then, in my opinion, it is not a *bona fide* predictive coding, machine learning, type of CAR (TAR).").

in disclosing search terms can be addressed through protective orders. One such order, in the context of keyword searching, provided that such disclosure does not constitute waiver of work–product protection or attorney–client privilege, the terms will be treated as highly confidential information, and if necessary to file search terms with the court, they shall be filed under seal.[96] And under Federal Rule of Evidence 502, a federal court may order that privilege or work-product protection is not waived by disclosure connected to the litigation, and the parties' agreement on the effect of disclosure is binding.[97]

Control Sets, Sampling Techniques to Seed the Training Set: Does the system provide for a control set against which the tool's performance can be judged (i.e., to assess the prevalence of responsive documents in the corpus)? If so, how large is the control set and what confidence level and interval was used to derive it?

How will documents be selected for the training set? Purely randomly machine-selected? Through the use of judgmental sampling? Or both? If judgmental sampling is used, what tool is being used to select that sample? If keywords are used to do so, what are they? As noted, disclosure of keywords can facilitate significant agreement between the parties.

What is the size of the training set, and how was that sample size established? What confidence level and interval was selected? Was the sample pulled from the entire corpus of documents to be predictively coded?

Workflow Considerations: All TAR tools use some procedure for iterative refinements after the initial training session, whether done sequentially or automatically. What approach does the tool use? How many training rounds are generally necessary to reach stability? If the tool uses active learning, how many documents in total must generally be reviewed before stability is achieved?

Coding the Training Set: Who will be coding the training sets? Experienced attorneys? Relatively junior attorneys with less litigation

---

96. *See In re* CV Therapeutics, Inc. Sec. Litig., 2006 U.S. Dist. LEXIS 38909, at *31–32 (N.D. Cal. Apr. 3, 2006).

97. Fed. R. Evid. 502(d) & (e).

experience? Contract attorneys less familiar with the case? How many coders will be training the system?

With TAR, the effectiveness of the methodology is only as good as the coding used to train the system. Requesting parties will want assurances that experienced attorneys that are intimately familiar with the issues in the case are training the tool and that as few coders as possible are used to minimize the inconsistent relevance determinations that are inherent in human review.

As in *Da Silva Moore* and *Actos*, requesting parties may also want not only to know how documents were coded during the training rounds, but also to play an active role in that coding. As noted, this degree of disclosure and cooperation justifiably generates significant concern among producing parties about not only disclosure of work product but also of nonresponsive documents outside of the scope of discovery.

However, there are tools to minimize those concerns. First, as in *Actos*, the producing party may first cull out potentially privileged documents from the training set. Second, to address both the producing party's concern that nonresponsive documents will be disclosed and work product revealed, and the requesting party's concern that documents will be improperly coded, parties can consider employing a third-party neutral, schooled in the facts of the case, to either conduct the training herself, or to evaluate the accuracy of the producing party's coding.

Relevance Thresholds and Reliability Statistics: What confidence level and interval will be used to determine sample sizes and precision and recall? What level of precision and recall will be deemed acceptable? How will the responsiveness cutoff be determined? This determination is necessarily dependent on determinations of acceptable precision and recall rates (or F_1 statistics). The producing party will want high precision and possibly high recall (depending on its risk aversion); the requesting party will want both. Reaching agreement on the appropriate balance inures to the benefit of the producing party should the production later be challenged.

Conclusion

Although information retrieval scientists have developed wonderful and exciting tools that can provide improved accuracy while reducing the cost of document review, practical considerations specific to litigation have resulted in less widespread adoption than would have been expected in the abstract. The processes employed to maximize the efficacy of these tools must be adapted for use by lawyers and their clients, who face limits on the degree of transparency and must decide how much machine training is enough to achieve defensibility rather than perfection. As lawyers and judges become better educated about the processes needed to employ TAR effectively, agreement about the specifics of TAR protocols should become easier to achieve. This should reduce the costs associated with reaching agreement on TAR protocols and encourage wider adoption of TAR in civil discovery.

EDITORS' INTRODUCTION TO CHAPTER 8

Michael D. Berman

Ronni D. Solomon, Rose J. Hunter-Jones, Jennifer A. Mencken, and Edward T. Logan address the issue of why, given its innumerable advantages and cost-saving potential, predictive coding is not more widely deployed by defendants, who typically have large volumes of data. The authors "make the case" for more widespread usage.

As a starting point, they look at the many uses of predictive coding, such as relevancy screening, privilege review, and confidentiality analysis. They then review studies quantifying the costs savings in actual cases.

The primary focus of the chapter, however, is to examine the barriers to the use of predictive coding. Starting with the premise that "not every case is a good candidate for predictive coding," they identify the factors that would reasonably militate against its usage in certain types of cases.

Having defined where predictive coding is not appropriate, the authors then review and rebut the many arguments offered against its use in *appropriate* cases. For example, they explain how building a successful training process and being transparent can be consistent with cost savings. They also show how reasonable metrics can be negotiated to achieve, rather than frustrate, the goals of predictive coding.

The chapter provides a road map to determine when predictive coding "fits" the case, when it may not, and how to support its utilization to achieve cost reduction.

CHAPTER 8

Predictive Coding from the Defense Perspective: Issues and Challenges

Ronni D. Solomon, Rose J. Hunter-Jones, Jennifer A. Mencken, and Edward T. Logan*

Experts estimate that document review costs $0.73 of every dollar spent on electronically stored information (ESI) production.[1] Given this high cost of document review, producing parties are always exploring alternative techniques to reduce the number of hours dedicated to human review by boosting review speeds and decreasing the total number of preproduction documents to review for relevance, responsiveness, and privilege. For many corporate defendants, predictive coding is one of the tools that can be used to achieve cost savings when producing large volumes of ESI in discovery. As discussed in detail in the following sections, although there has not been universal

*The authors gratefully acknowledge the valuable contributions of Susan Clare, John Buzbee, and Alexandra Royal.

1. Nicholas M. Pace & Laura Zakaras, *Where the Money Goes: Understanding Litigant Expenditures for Producing Electronic Discovery*, RAND INST. FOR CIVIL JUSTICE, xiii–xvi (2012), http://www.rand.org/pubs/monographs/MG1208.html (A 2012 study of discovery costs related to 57 cases conducted by the RAND Institute for Civil Justice concluded that the major cost component of discovery—typically about 73 percent—was the review of documents for relevance, responsiveness, and privilege. Document collection accounted for 8 percent of expenditures and data processing consumed about 19 percent of an ordinary case budget.).

adoption of predictive coding in all complex cases, cost savings can be substantial and have been documented by service providers, practitioners, and producing parties. The cost savings reported by these groups strongly suggests that producing parties should add predictive coding to their arsenal of e-discovery tools, and consider utilizing it at the outset of medium-to-large litigation matters. At the same time, producing parties should know that cost savings may vary from case to case and may not be realized at all depending on the nature of the collected documents, the subject matter of a given case, and the challenges inherent in negotiating predictive coding with the opponent and defending it in court, if challenged. To aid defense practitioners and corporations in determining whether to utilize predictive coding in a given matter, this chapter highlights the cost savings corporate[2] defendants can expect to obtain using predictive coding, as well as the challenges regularly faced by corporate defendants in attempting to use predictive coding technology.

Cost Savings with Predictive Coding

The societal shift from paper documents to ESI has led to sharp increases in discovery costs and overall costs of litigation.[3] Although discovery costs are known to be highly variable depending upon factors such as the number of documents to review, predictive coding technologies can mitigate expenses in a variety of ways. For example, predictive coding can be used to exclude likely irrelevant documents from a population of documents to be reviewed for responsiveness, privilege, confidentiality, etc.[4] Alternatively, a defendant may achieve

2. The term "corporate" as used in this chapter refers generally to businesses.

3. *See* Pension Comm. of the Univ. of Montreal Pension Plan v. Banc of Am. Sec., LLC, 685 F. Supp. 2d 456, 461 (S.D.N.Y. 2010) ("In an era where vast amounts of electronic information is [sic] available for review, discovery in certain cases has become increasingly complex and expensive."); Norton Rose Fulbright, 2015 *Litigation Trends Annual Survey* 19 (May 2015), http://www.nortonrosefulbright.com/files/20150514-2015-litigation-trends-survey_v24-128746.pdf (2014 survey of 803 companies indicates that U.S. litigation budgets exceeding $1 million have been increasing since 2012).

4. *See* Sarah Simmons, *Predictive Coding: The Future of E-Discovery, But Is It the Future of Your Case?*, Global Constr. & Infrastructure Legal Alliance (2012), http://www.gcila.org/publications/files/pub_en_41.pdf ("Predictive coding is a form of document review that combines attorney analysis with a computer program

discovery efficiencies by utilizing predictive coding to automate the prioritization of document subsets for review, allowing important, more relevant information to surface before it otherwise would.[5] These functions, particularly the ability to sort and prioritize documents, also have a myriad of applications in other client contexts such as internal investigations, information governance, and quality control.[6]

---

that runs complicated algorithms to sample and predict relevance across large collections of ESI . . . Ultimately, the program leaves the attorney with the entire data collection automatically segregated into 'relevant' and 'irrelevant' buckets . . . the attorney circumvents reviewing the 'irrelevant' files that are now segregated from the data pool. Thus, the population of documents requiring attorney review is drastically reduced.); Andrew John Sutton, Note, *Discovering Discovery Technology! A Model Order and Pilot Program for Implementing Predictive Coding and Other New Technologies in Document Review*, 42 AIPLA Q.J. 459, 470 (2014) ("The key to the cost savings is the number of documents that can be quickly deemed non-responsive, which are documents that can then safely be assumed to be non-relevant and thus not have to be reviewed by attorneys.").

5. *See Predictive Coding as a Means to Prioritize Review and Reduce Discovery Costs* 3 Equivio (2012), http://www.equivio.com/files/files/White%20Paper%20-%20Predictive%20Coding%20as%20a%20Means%20to%20Prioritize%20Review%20and%20Reduce%20Discovery%20Costs.pdf ("[U]sing a computer-driven analytical solution . . . that takes a legal team's understanding of the case and applies it to an entire document collection, creating a hierarchy of documents from most to least relevant . . .The prioritization of the material gives the review team a better chance of finding the information it is looking for, without having to review the entire collection."); *Most Important Documents Get Looked at First: Using Predictive Coding to Prioritize & Expedite Review*, Consilio (2016) http://www.consilio.com/wp-content/uploads/2016/01/Using-Predictive-Coding-to-Expedite-Review.pdf ("In this case, predictive coding workflows and technology helped attorneys look at the documents most likely to be relevant to the core issues of the case quickly . . . and with minimal wasted time or effort.").

6. *See, e.g.*, Alison Nadel, Daniel McGuire, & Erica Wenninger, *E-Discovery: The Values of Predictive Coding in Internal Investigations*, InsideCounsel (Aug. 13, 2013),http://www.insidecounsel.com/2013/08/13/e-discovery-the-value-of-predictive-coding-in-inte ("Proper use of predictive coding significantly lowers overall costs and increases accuracy. Moreover, it can be a particularly powerful tool in the context of internal investigations, where a high value is placed on swiftly and efficiently identifying only the most significant documents."); Rudy Moliere, Leigh Isaacs, & Samantha Lofton, *Predictive Coding for Information Governance*, Law Firm Information Governance Symposium, Iron Mountain (July 2013), http://www.ironmountain.com/~/media/Files/Iron%20Mountain/Knowledge%20Center/Reference%20Library/White%20Paper/P/Predictive%20Coding%20for%20Information%20Governance.pdf?dmc=1&ts=20160107T1241432595 ("Predictive coding and tools that aid in auto-classification provide opportunities to automate fundamental

Through the use of a properly strategized and implemented predictive coding protocol, many producing parties have realized a significant decrease in discovery expenses.[7] For example, in several case studies, practitioners have reported reviewing 64 to 93 percent fewer documents with predictive coding due to the defensible identification and exclusion of nonresponsive materials, which is confirmed through quality control sampling.[8] Reviewing less documents means producing parties can expect to save that percentage in review costs.

[records and information management] functions"); Edward Sohn, *The Four Pillars of an Effective Predictive Coding Workflow* 6 (Pangea3/Thomson Reuters White Paper, Apr. 17, 2013), *available at* http://www.pangea3.com/effective-predictive-coding-workflow.html ("The ability to sort and prioritize documents also has myriad applications in auditing and quality control processes.").

7. *See* Scott M. Cohen, Elizabeth T. Timkovich, & John J. Rosenthal, *The Tested Effectiveness of Equivio>Relevance in Technology Assisted Review* (Winston & Strawn, eDiscovery and Info. Mgmt. White Paper, Feb. 2014), http://www.winston.com/images/content/7/8/78010.pdf; *Predictive Coding = Great E-Discovery Cost and Time Savings* (interview with David J. Laing), METRO. CORP. COUNS. 17 (Dec. 2011), http://www.metrocorpcounsel.com/pdf/2011/December/17.pdf; John J. Jablonski & Drew Lewis, *E-Discovery-Getting a Handle on Predictive Coding*, EMPLOYMENT & LABOR LAW COURSE MATERIALS 139, 142 (DRI May 2013), http://www.dri.org/DRI/course-materials/2013-Employment/pdfs/07_Jablonski.pdf; Dominic Lacey, Jamie Tanner, & James Moeskops, *Predicting the Future of Disclosure*, LEGAL IT INSIDER (Nov. 23, 2011, 11:38 AM), http://www.legaltechnology.com/latest-news/guest-article-predicting-the-future-of-disclosure; *Advice from Counsel—Can Predictive Coding Deliver on Its Promise?* (FTI Technology White Paper, Aug. 12, 2012) http://www.ftitechnology.com/resources/white-papers/advice-counsel-can-predictive-coding-deliver-its-promise.

8. *See*, Cohen, Timkovich, & Rosenthal, *supra* note 7 at 2, 8 (implementing predictive coding process including training and quality control resulted in 69.5 percent reduction of review volume compared to manual review of the entire 293,185 document set); Jablonski & Lewis, *supra* note 7, (implementing predictive coding process resulted in 75 percent reduction in review volume compared to manual review of the entire 679,349 document set); Cliff Nichols & Tony Reichenberger, *Predictive Coding in Action: A Case Study*, Kroll Ontrack (May 21, 2014), http://www.ediscovery.com/cms/pdf/predictive-coding-in-action-a-case-study-webinar-slides.pdf (implementing predictive coding process resulted in 93 percent reduction in review volume compared to manual review of the entire 280,000 document set); Lacey, Tanner, & Moeskops, *supra* note 7 (implementing predictive coding process resulted in 77 percent reduction in review volume compared with manual review of the entire 250,000 document set); *Predictive Coding Case Study Using Predictive Coding to Reduce Attorney Review Costs*, DSICOVERY (www.DSi.com, undated), http://cdn2.hubspot.net/hub/252640/file-70087736-pdf/DSi_predictive_coding_case-study.pdf

Additionally, vendors are reporting that their clients have reduced their document review costs.[9] In a survey of 11 predictive coding vendors, four reported an average cost reduction of 45 percent, while seven of the vendors reported savings as high as 70 percent.[10] Similarly, another study found that the time and cost it takes attorneys to conduct document review could be cut by 80 percent.[11]

Producing parties may also achieve cost savings by employing predictive coding to organize the documents for review as opposed to using it to exclude documents from the review.[12] Utilizing the tool in this

---

(implementing predictive coding process resulted in 64 percent reduction in review volume compared with manual review of the entire 50,000 document set.).

9. *See* Barclay T. Blair, *Predictive Coding in Practice: Success Stories from Three Years of Predictive Coding*, Metro. Corp. Couns. 22–23 (June 2014), http://www.metrocorpcounsel.com/pdf/2014/June/22.pdf (analysis of four case studies indicates significant savings compared with manual review as a result of using predictive coding on large data sets); Joseph H. Looby, *E-discovery—Taking Predictive Coding Out of the Black Box*, FTI Journal (Nov. 2012) http://ftijournal.com/article/taking-predictive-coding-out-of-the-black-box-deleted (Vendor reported savings of one million dollars to review 5.4 million documents using predictive coding compared to keyword searches and manual review.); Press Release, QDiscovery LLC, *Quantum Discovery's Predictive Coding Expertise Saves Client over* $1 *million in Attorney Review Fees*, (June 20, 2012), http://qdiscovery.com/qd-news/news/10-quantum-discovery-s-predictive-coding-expertise-saves-client-over-1-million-in-attorney-review-fees ("The cost savings involved in avoiding a linear review was staggering.").

10. *See* Anne Kershaw & Joseph Howie, *eDiscovery Institute Survey on Predictive Coding* 14 (eDiscovery Institute Oct. 1, 2010), http://ediscoveryinstitute.org/images/uploaded/272.pdf.

11. *Am Law 100 Firm Uses Equivio>Relevance™ to Find More Relevant Documents and to Find Them Faster*, (Equivio 2009), http://www.equivio.com/files/files/Case%20Study%20-%20Am%20Law%20100%20Firm%20Uses%20Equivio%20Relevance%20to%20Find%20More%20Relevant%20Documents%20and%20to%20Find%20Them%20Faster.pdf ("[T]he first 20% of the document collection as organized by . . . relevance scores would have presented the reviewers with 75% of the total number of responsive documents identified within the collection.").

12. Brochure, *Meet Aggressive Discovery Deadlines and Reduce Costs: Leveraging Predictive Coding to Prioritize and Segment Documents for Review*, (Deloitte 2014), http://www2.deloitte.com/content/dam/Deloitte/us/Documents/finance/us-fas-dynamic-review-case-study-06192014.pdf [hereinafter Deloitte brochure] (savings of 60 percent by prioritizing documents and allocating lower cost resources for review of less relevant documents).

manner allows a party to increase review speeds.[13] In one case study, attorneys were able to review documents 37 percent faster when a predictive coding process was first used to rank and sort the ESI population for responsiveness.[14] Some practitioners have also reported that this use of predictive coding technology has allowed them to meet difficult deadlines.[15]

Barriers to the Use of Predictive Coding

With such potential to reduce the costs of document review, why is it that predictive coding is not being universally embraced by litigants?[16] The following section provides some insight on some of the barriers that presently hinder the widespread adoption of predictive coding by corporate defendants. We also provide suggestions for overcoming these barriers when appropriate.

Is the Case a Good Fit for Predictive Coding?

Producing parties should recognize that not every case is a good candidate for predictive coding. Certain types of litigation may involve documents with little to no text and may not be appropriate for predictive coding.[17] For instance, intellectual property litigation often involves documents that may not be well suited for predictive coding due to the

13. Brochure, *UBIC's CJK TAR (Advanced Predictive Coding Technology) Enables Significant Cost-Savings in Cross-Border IP Case in a U.S. District Court*, (UBIC N. Am., Inc., undated) http://ubicna.com/en/lit_i_view/PDF/CJKTAR_CaseStudy_2.pdf ("low scoring documents were reviewed, at a much higher speed than the higher scoring documents").

14. *Id.* ("37% increase in review speed of non-responsive over responsive documents").

15. Deloitte brochure, *supra* note 12 (predictive coding used to expedite attorney review of 780,000 documents in six weeks to meet a discovery deadline).

16. David R. Cohen & Marcin M. Krieger, *Seven Barriers to the Use of Predictive Coding*, The Legal Intelligencer (Jan. 27, 2015), http://www.thelegalintelligencer.com/id=1202715812509/Seven-Barriers-to-the-Use-of-Predictive-Coding?slreturn=20160210140408 [*subscription required*] (discussing seven practical barriers that have slowed adoption of predictive coding including small document volumes, lack of partner time, absence of adverse party consent, error rate quantification, need for subsequent human review for privilege, training expense and multi-district litigation).

17. Cohen, Timkovich, & Rosenthal, *supra* note 7, at 2 (describing the population of documents subject to predictive coding: "The remaining 8,115 documents

lack of embedded text in the files, such as audio files, photographs, technical documents or drawings, source code information, and patent prosecution files.[18] Likewise, some document sets gathered in the commercial litigation context often contain large amounts of financial data or statistical information and, therefore, are unlikely to benefit from predictive algorithms as schematics, charts, or graphs contained in non-standardized templates may be miscategorized during predictive coding training.[19]

Studies have also proven that while predictive coding can be highly accurate in connecting themes and grouping data within a set of clear parameters, the technology is less accurate in distinguishing between multiple or overlapping legal issues that have fuzzy lines.[20] Similarly, some users have indicated that predictive coding is not as reliable in determining whether documents are likely to be privileged or subject to work–product protection, or not reliable enough to prevent inadvertent production.[21]

---

were excluded because they did not contain any extracted text—a requirement for the Equivio system to import and analyze the data." (footnote omitted)).

18. Herbert L. Roitblat, *Introduction to Predictive Coding* 9 (Org. of Legal Professionals White Paper 2013), http://www.theolp.org/Resources/Documents/Introduction%20to%20Predictive%20Coding%20-%20Herb%20Roitblat.pdf ("Predictive coding generally does not work on non-text documents such as blueprints, CAD drawings, photographs, videos, audio recordings, and so forth, unless they are converted first to text."); John Martin, *The Emperor Has No Clothes—and PC Can't See Image-Only Documents*, BEYONDRECOGNITION.NET (May 8, 2014), http://beyondrecognition.net/predictive-coding-and-the-naked-emperor ("in some industries… half or more of some collections will be engineering drawings and schematics.").

19. Andrew Strickler, *5 Predictive Coding Pitfalls to Avoid*, LAW360 BLOG (Feb. 17, 2015, 2:43 PM), http://www.law360.com/articles/616861 ("But the power of predictive coding . . . breaks down when the algorithm tries to 'read' schematics, charts and graphs, photos and videos and nonsearchable PDFs. Spreadsheets, financial documents, and other number-heavy data can also cause breakdowns.").

20. *Id.* (While predictive coding can be highly accurate "in evaluating and connecting themes and grouping data . . . the technology is less certain in distinguishing among multiple or overlapping legal issues.").

21. *See* Wallis M. Hampton, *Predictive Coding: It's Here to Stay*, PRACTICAL LAW (THE JOURNAL) 30 (June–July 2014) (stating that "predictive coding has not proven particularly reliable at privilege calls" but noting that it can be used to rank the likelihood that particular documents are privileged); Manfred Gabriel, Chris Paskach, & David Sharpe, *The Challenge and Promise of Predictive Coding for Privilege*, ICAIL 2013 Workshop on Standards for Using Predictive Coding, Machine

The facts or circumstances surrounding a particular matter may also impair the technology's ability to achieve cost savings or time efficiencies. For instance, predictive coding may be impracticable in mass tort litigation where new adversaries with new counsel and judges join a matter in which the document review protocol has already been finalized.[22] New litigants may object to the way prior productions were culled and reviewed using predictive coding, necessitating costly duplication of review efforts.[23] Renegotiating discovery protocols or side agreements with each new counsel can be time consuming and often counterproductive.

Cases with small document volumes may also not be good candidates for predictive coding because vendor, machine training, and quality control costs cannot be spread across the population like they can with cases with larger document volumes.[24] The primary bene-

---

Learning and Other Advanced Search and Review Methods in E-Discovery (DESI V Workshop, June 14, 2013), at 1–2, http://www.umiacs.umd.edu/~oard/desi5/research/Gabriel-final2.pdf (stating that in a published test of predictive-coding technology to identify privileged information, the levels of recall that the technology achieved, 63.3 to 71.5 percent recall, would be "insufficient in practice to protect against inadvertent disclosure"); Alaap B. Shah, *Use of "Predictive Coding" to Limit Cost and Improve Efficiency in Healthcare E-discovery: The Light Is Green, But Proceed with Caution*, A.H.L.A Healthcare Liab. & Litig., 9, 10 (Jan. 2012), *available at* http://www.ebglaw.com/content/uploads/2014/06/48548_Shah-AHLA-Use-of-Predictive-Coding-1-2012.pdf (stating that "it remains unclear to what extent predictive coding is a viable substitute for an experienced attorney when it comes to making privilege determinations"). *But see* John C. Eustice, *Evaluating TAR: Can We Trust Technology?*, Legaltech News (Oct. 6, 2015), http://www.legaltechnews.com/id=1202739053260/Evaluating-TAR-Can-We-Trust-Technology?slreturn=20160007130228 (using TAR to review potentially privileged material).

22. Cohen & Krieger, *supra* note 16 ("Sometimes companies find themselves as defendants or investigation targets, about the same products or practices, in multiple jurisdictions. Facing decision makers in multiple jurisdictions compounds the risks of using predictive coding. For example, a company that is sued by a variety of plaintiffs in 15 different jurisdictions knows that, even in the un-likely event that it could get 14 sets of plaintiffs or 14 different judges to approve or condone the use of predictive coding, if there is no approval in the 15th jurisdiction, the company still may be faced with costly motions practice or re-viewing virtually all of the same documents manually, thereby eliminating any cost savings from using predictive coding in the first 14 jurisdictions. Thus, the potential use of predictive coding may be a nonstarter.").

23. *Id.*

24. *See* Simmons, *supra* note 4 ("Predictive coding does come at its own steep price. Some vendors charge $150–$250/GB just to run the predictive coding technology on

fit of using predictive coding is reduced attorney review time, and large document volumes provide the best opportunity to achieve the greatest reduction.[25] Practitioners and vendors estimate that the benefits of predictive coding in achieving cost savings will outweigh the costs at minimum document volumes ranging from 25,000 to 150,000.[26]

In order to determine whether a case is a good fit for predictive coding or not, producing parties should at the outset of the case obtain as much information as possible about the scope and parameters of the data likely to be involved, including likely sources, file formats, volume, and content. Producing parties should also give consideration on a case-by-case basis as to how and when predictive coding will be useful in a particular matter. For example, will predictive coding be used as an exclusionary tool that primarily focuses on culling likely nonresponsive documents from further review and production? Or will it be used as an organizational tool grouping related documents during review to increase review efficiency? Additionally, producing parties must make preliminary determinations regarding the timing or the point in the production sequence at which predictive coding will

---

a data collection."); Roitblat, *supra* note 18 (The value of predictive coding "tends to grow disproportionately as the size of the document collection grows, because the effort typically required to train a system does not grow or does not grow as quickly as the size of the document collection increases. Small collections can require almost the same level of training effort as large collections do.").

25. *See* Simmons, *supra* note 4 ("Attorneys and clients must conduct a cost-benefit analysis of their case to determine whether the high price tag of predictive coding will yield even greater savings by reducing the number of hours necessary for attorney privilege review.").

26. *See id.* ("Small cases . . . less than 150,000 documents . . . are not appropriate for predictive coding."); Chad Jones, *5 Discovery Analytics Workflows for Small Cases*, D4DISCOVERY.COM (June 2, 2015), http://d4discovery.com/discover-more/2015/6/5-discovery-analytics-workflows-for-small-cases#sthash.ZM7fbHmb.dpbs. ("predictive coding and technology assisted review are better suited for cases with more than 100,000 document records"); *Predictive Coding Case Study, supra* note 8 (implementing predictive coding process and achieving cost savings on a document population of 50,000); Ralph Losey, *My Basic Plan for Document Reviews: The "Bottom Line Driven" Approach*, E-DISCOVERYTEAM.COM (Oct. 1, 2013), http://e-discoveryteam.com/2013/10/01/my-basic-plan-for-document-reviews-the-bottom-line-driven-approach ("When you are working with a volume of approximately 25,000 or more documents, as in this example, then the AI enhanced SME type of review is usually a financially viable approach.").

be applied. For example, will predictive coding be used as a final quality control mechanism at the pre-production stage? Or, will predictive coding be used to analyze and organize the documents provided to the plaintiff at the post-production phase? Or both? Answering these and other similar questions early in the process will clearly define the parameters of the project and also help avoid costly mistakes down the road.

It is also important to note that producing parties do not have to use an all or nothing approach with predictive coding. Alternative workflows can be constructed to address challenges that may hinder predictive coding functionality on certain data types.[27] For example, one workflow may include utilizing predictive coding for unstructured text-based data like e-mail but utilizing other methods for reviewing structured data from complaint databases, technical files, and nonstandard media files.[28] Other workflow options might include potential segregation of some or all OCR documents from the predictive coding process to account for poor text quality, and potential classification for complex issue coding.[29]

27. *See* Edward Sohn, *supra* note 6 ("Once the idiosyncrasies of a predictive coding tool are fully investigated, workflows can be constructed to mitigate the limitations or capitalize on the strengths."); Jianlin Cheng & Amanda Jones, *Variability in Technology Assisted Review and Implications for Standards* 1 (Univ. of Md. Inst. for Advanced Computer Studies 2013), http://www.umiacs.umd.edu/~oard/desi5/additional/Cheng-position-final.pdf ("We contend there are numerous matter-specific factors that impact TAR performance and these factors, along with observed TAR performance itself, should play roles in shaping the specific process details adopted for any given TAR implementation.").

28. Strickler, *supra* note 19 ("Documents primarily comprised of numbers without a lot of context in words describing them are going to be problematic, so you're going to want to identify them in the pre-predictive coding process and make allowances for other workflows.").

29. *See* Edward Sohn, *supra* note 6 ("a prudent workflow segregated OCR documents for closer inspection . . . and employs a hybrid approach for identifying issue codes depending on the tool's capabilities.").

Challenges Associated with the Training Time Needed to Build a Successful Predictive Coding Process

The training process that takes place as part of the predictive coding process can be time consuming and lengthy, which must be taken into consideration when planning discovery workflows and determining whether predictive coding is appropriate for a particular case.[30] The richness of the population of documents, for example, is one factor that can affect the length of time it can take to conduct training.[31] Richness measures the prevalence of responsive documents in a population compared to nonresponsive documents.[32] Generally, it takes less time to train predictive coding tools in cases with document populations that have high richness. In contrast, populations with low richness typically require additional iterations of review and consequently more time to train many predictive coding tools.[33] Another factor that can lengthen the training process

30. Sonya L. Sigler, *5 Factors to Consider Before Using Technology Assisted Review,* DISCOVIA.COM, http://www.discovia.com/archive/docs/5factors.pdf ("Training a TAR tool can take a few days or a couple of weeks . . . The training period along with the period of time expected for review or sampling of the documents needs to be considered when deciding to use TAR tools on your case."); Cohen & Krieger, *supra* note 16 ("Depending on the document population and software used, this training can take anywhere from a few days to a few weeks.").

31. Macyl A. Burke, *A Cost-Effective Approach to Quality* 8 (Univ. of Md. Inst. for Advanced Computer Studies Feb. 2012), http://www.umiacs.umd.edu/~oard/desi5/additional/Burke.pdf ("These processes are dependent on the nature and complexity of the case. One of the deciding factors is the richness of the population, which is the percentage of useful documents present. Large populations with low richness are problematic."); Sutton, *supra* note 4, at 479 ("[I]f only a few documents in the entire data set may be relevant, there would likely be too few documents to train the computer. In that case, attorneys would have to review so many documents that they would lose cost efficiency.").

32. *In re* Actos (Pioglitazone) Prods. Liab. Litig., MDL No. 6:11-md-2299, 2012 WL 7861249, at *5 (W.D. La. July 27, 2012) (defining richness as the "percentage of relevant documents in a population").

33. *See* Cheng & Jones, *supra* note 27 ("The importance of richness for TAR may seem obvious. It stands to reason that, when there is a very low concentration of positive exemplars available for algorithms to learn from and generalize, the algorithms will be less successful at comprehensively recognizing or accurately classifying the material of interest."); Gabriel, Paskach, & Sharpe, *supra* note 21 ("Such low

is the use of experts to train the predictive coding platform. Many producing parties employ case team subject matter experts that are knowledgeable on the substantive issues in the case for the machine training and quality control steps of the predictive coding process.[34] In many cases, however, these experts simply do not have the time to spend training the system because it can distract them from their regular tasks and case responsibilities and thereby delay the predictive coding process.[35] These experts may then push the work down to young associates or staff attorneys, who may not have the same grasp as the experts on the facts of the case and who must frequently confer with more senior attorneys, which delays the process.[36] The training time can be further extended because the experts must

richness has implications for predictive coding workflows. Sample sizes will need to be increased, potentially significantly, to . . . train a classifier.").

34. Da Silva Moore v. Publicis Groupe, 287 F.R.D. 182, 186–87 (S.D.N.Y. 2012) (describing the training and quality control process for a predictive coding protocol including senior attorney review of several thousand documents to create a seed set, review of 3,500 documents from relevant concept clusters to stabilize the training, and review of 2,399 documents from the nonrelevant population for quality control); Strickler, *supra* note 19 ("The keystone of predictive coding is the sample set—a selection of documents marked for relevancy that the software uses as the basis for a [sic] complex judgments on relevancy across all the data . . . experts agree that the lawyers reviewing those documents have to be the most knowledgeable about the matter and the legal issues at stake."); *see* Ralph Losey, *Less Is More: When It Comes to Predictive Coding Training, the "Fewer Reviewers the Better"—Part One*, E-DiscoveryTeam.com (Nov. 24, 2013), http://e-discoveryteam.com/2013/11/24/less-is-more-when-it-comes-to-predictive-coding-training-the-fewer-reviewers-the-better-part-one/ ("[P]roper use of predictive coding technology requires the machine to be trained by bona fide SMEs, real experts with years of experience . . . the computer bases its analysis on the input provided. The computer has no innate knowledge or expertise of the issues in the case.").

35. Cohen & Krieger, *supra* note 16 ("Depending on the document population and software used, this training can take anywhere from a few days to a few weeks. Many case team leaders—usually very busy litigation partners—simply don't have that much concentrated time to devote to the software training.").

36. John Tredennick, *Subject Matter Experts: What Role Should They Play in TAR 2.0 Training?*, Catalyst E-Discovery Search Blog (Nov. 2013), at 2, http://www.catalystsecure.com/blog/2013/11/subject-matter-experts-what-role-should-they-play-in-tar-2-0-training ("New uploads are held hostage until the reluctant expert can come back to the table to review . . . [R]eview managers find it difficult to keep their teams waiting while a senior person finds time to look at 3,000 or more documents necessary for TAR training.").

typically educate the attorneys leading the review to understand the makeup of the seed set so that they can confirm the accuracy of the predictive model across the larger dataset.[37]

Additional factors that can impact machine training time are the underlying predictive coding algorithms and complexity of the categorization.[38] Some predictive coding algorithms continuously learn from each document reviewed, which blurs the line between machine training and review of the documents predicted to be responsive.[39] For some algorithms, a process goal is to strike the proper balance between training and review to minimize the total documents reviewed.[40]

One step producing parties can take to try to gauge the likely training time that will be required for a given case and to help determine whether and what type of predictive coding technology is appropriate for a given matter is to sample the document population to determine the level of richness. Sampling may not be practical, however, where there are short production deadlines and substantial pressure to begin the document review.

---

37. Edward Sohn, *supra* note 6, at 8 ("Without insight as to how the seed set calls are being made, there will be limitations in building an appropriate workflow and no institutional knowledge to evaluate the prediction on a document outside of the seed set.").

38. Bill Dimm, *Predictive Coding Confusion*, CLUSTER-TEXT.COM (July 12, 2014), http://blog.cluster-text.com/2014/07/12/predictive-coding-confusion ("The number of documents required for training depends on the algorithm used and the difficulty of the categorization task."); Roitblat, *supra* note 18 ("There are at least nine technologies in common use today to support predictive coding. Different service providers offer varying combinations of these technologies . . . The accuracy of these systems will depend on the specifics of the implementation and on the quality of the training set used. They may also differ in the amount and type of training that must be conducted, including the level of effort.").

39. Bill Dimm, *TAR 3.0 Performance*, CLUSTER-TEXT.COM (Jan. 28, 2016), http://blog.cluster-text.com/2016/01/28/tar-3-0-performance ("TAR 2.0 uses an approach called Continuous Active Learning (CAL), meaning that there is no separation between training and review–the system continues to learn throughout.").

40. *Id.* ("TAR 1.0 involves a training phase followed by a review phase with a control set being used to determine the optimal point when you should switch from training to review.").

Transparency Required to Use Predictive Coding Can Be a Barrier

It is well accepted that producing parties should be afforded broad discretion in deciding which review technology to employ for document collection and review.[41] Sedona Principle 6 recognizes that "[r]esponding parties are best situated to evaluate the procedures, methodologies, and technologies appropriate for preserving and producing their own electronically stored information."[42] This principle holds equally true in the predictive coding context—the producing party is better positioned to make appropriate decisions regarding the use and manner of predictive coding in the review process because it is the party most familiar with the universe of potentially relevant and responsive information.[43] As one court has recognized, "although it is a proper role of the Court to supervise the discovery process and intervene when it is abused by the parties, the Court is not normally in the business of dictating to parties the process that they should use when responding to discovery."[44]

Similarly, a requesting party does not have the right to test the sufficiency of the producing party's discovery processes, including

41. *See* Ford Motor Co. v. Edgewood Props., Inc., 257 F.R.D. 418, 427–28 (D.N.J. 2009) (ESI collection and production "is clearly within the producing party's sound discretion.").

42. Working Grp. on Elec. Document Retention & Prod., The Sedona Conference, The Sedona Principles: Best Practices Recommendations & Principles for Addressing Electronic Document Production 38, (2d ed. 2007).

43. Kleen Prods., LLC v. Packaging Corp. of Am., No. 10 C 5711, 2012 U.S. Dist. LEXIS 139632, at *18 (N.D. Ill. Sept. 28, 2012) (citing Principle 6 of the *Sedona Best Practices Recommendations & Principles for Addressing Electronic Document Production* in noting that "responding parties are best situated to evaluate the procedures, methodologies, and techniques appropriate for preserving and production their own electronically stored information"); *see also* William P. Butterfield, Conor R. Crowley, & Jeannine Kenney, *Reality Bites: Why TAR's Promises Have Yet to be Fulfilled*, U. of Maryland Inst. for Advanced Computer Stud. 5–7 (2013), http://www.umiacs.umd.edu/~oard/desi5/additional/Butterfield.pdf (highlighting the latitude courts give to "producing parties' choice of search methodology and procedures").

44. Dynamo Holdings Ltd. P'ship v. Comm'r of Internal Revenue, Nos. 2685-11, 9393-12 (T.C. Sept. 17, 2014) at 10 (citing Judge Peck and *Da Silva Moore*, court determined that predictive coding was acceptable search methodology and allowed responding party to use predictive coding over the objections of the requesting party).

predictive coding, or obtain discovery about discovery concerning a producing party's predictive coding process unless there is some specific evidence of misconduct as opposed to mere speculation.[45]

---

45. *See, e.g.*, Memry Corp. v. Ky. Oil Tech., No. C04-03843 RMW, 2007 WL 832937, at *3–4 (N.D. Cal. Mar. 19, 2007) (denying motion to compel defendant to produce its computers and storage media for forensic inspection by a third party consultant based upon allegations of "selective and incomplete document production," because "[plaintiff] can only point to two missing emails out of thousands of documents produced in this discovery-intensive case. While [defendant's] document production may not have been absolutely perfect, the flaws do not rise to the level of necessitating production of hard drives."); *In re* Ford Motor Co., 345 F.3d 1315, 1317 (11th Cir. 2003) (vacating order allowing discovery of certain databases where there was no factual finding of "some non-compliance with discovery rules by Ford"); Miller v. York Risk Servs. Grp., No. 2:13-cv-1419, 2014 WL 1456349, at *2 (D. Ariz. Apr. 15, 2014) (denying deposition pursuant to Rule 30(b)(6) concerning manner and methods to store ESI and commenting that the parties should first pursue the merits); Koninklijke Philips N.V. v. Hunt Control Sys., Inc., No. 11-3684, 2014 WL 1494517, at *4 (D.N.J. Apr. 16, 2014) (granting motion for protective order against deposition of IT witness where the moving party failed to show a "material deficiency" in the responding party's e-discovery process, noting that the party's "alleged dissatisfaction with the result of [the] production" was at best "speculative and suggestive"); Little Hocking Water Ass'n, Inc. v. E.I. Du Pont Nemours & Co., No. 2:09-cv-1081, 2013 WL 608154, at *54–55 (S.D. Ohio Feb. 19, 2013) (denying plaintiff's motion for an order compelling defendant to produce a Rule 30(b)(6) deponent to testify to defendant's search of electronic databases; the court found this request was "not well-taken" given that the court had required defendant to supplement its interrogatory responses and to specify whether production was complete); Orillaneda v. French Culinary Inst., No. 07 Civ. 3206, 2011 U.S. Dist. LEXIS 105793, at *18, *24 (S.D.N.Y. Sept. 19, 2011) (finding plaintiff was not entitled to conduct discovery about defendant's document production "without [Plaintiff] first identifying facts suggesting that the production is deficient," and requiring Plaintiff provide "specific statements" to prove deficiency instead of relying on "generalities"); In re Exxon Corp., 208 S.W.3d 70, 76–77 (Tex. App.—Beaumont 2006, orig. proceeding) (granting writ of mandamus overturning trial court's order to compel testimony on document search efforts because plaintiffs failed to establish any evidence of document withholding, "discovery abuse" or "necessity for the inquiry"); Hubbard v. Potter, 247 F.R.D. 27, 31 (D.D.C. 2008) (denying further depositions aimed squarely at discovery on discovery because of only a "theoretical possibility" that additional electronic documents may exist); Am. Home Assurance Co. v. Greater Omaha Packing Co., No. 8:11CV270, 2013 WL 4875997, at *6 (D. Neb. Sept. 11, 2013) (requiring disclosure of sources searched and terms used, but withholding additional relief because plaintiff did not provide specific information that had been withheld or sources not searched); Hanan v. Corso, No. 98-0292, 1998 U.S. Dist. LEXIS 11877, at *23–24 (D.D.C. Apr. 24, 1998) (declaring that it would be "foolhardy" to order discovery about discovery without any clear showing

Despite these well accepted principles, there are many instances where requesting parties have attempted to infiltrate the predictive coding process and dictate the manner of review or have demanded some heightened transparency because of the planned use of predictive coding.[46] Some courts have even indicated that they will likely not authorize the use of predictive coding without cooperation and transparency.[47] While cooperation and transparency in the predictive coding process can be a benefit to the producing party because it can

---

that the additional discovery would lead to relevant evidence and noting there is "no authority for the proposition that the Federal Rules of Civil Procedure contemplate that discovery is itself a fit subject for discovery"); Larsen v. Coldwell Banker Real Estate Corp., No. SACV 10–00401–AG, 2012 WL 359466, at *7 (C.D. Cal. Feb. 2, 2012) (denying a request for a witness to answer questions under oath regarding its ESI preservation, collection, and processing because plaintiff had not shown any bad faith in defendant's production and the "isolated examples cited" of alleged inadequacies in production "fail[ed] to demonstrate that Defendants have not reasonably and in good faith produced the documents required"); Freedman v. Weatherford Int'l, No. 12 Civ. 2121, 2014 WL 4547039, at *1 (S.D.N.Y. Sept. 12, 2014) (plaintiff's request for "discovery on discovery" denied for failure to provide adequate factual basis for finding original production had been deficient); *In re* Honeywell Int'l, Inc. Sec. Litig., 230 F.R.D. 293, 302 (S.D.N.Y. 2003) (denying motion to compel seeking information concerning document retention, preservation, search and collection procedures); Steuben Foods, Inc. v. Country Gourmet Foods, LLC, No. 08-CV-561S(F), 2011 U.S. Dist. LEXIS 43145, at *19 (W.D.N.Y. Apr. 21, 2011) (denying request for discovery of party's document preservation actions).

46. *See, e.g., Kleen Prods.*, 2012 U.S. Dist. LEXIS 139632, at *19 (requesting party sought to impose their predictive coding based search methodology on responding party); *In re* Biomet M2A Magnum Hip Implant Prods. Liab. Litig., No. 3:12-MD-2391, 2013 WL 1729682, at *3 (N.D. Ind. Apr. 18, 2013) (requesting party sought whole seed set used for predictive coding algorithm training, including privileged and irrelevant documents); Gordon v. Kaleida Health, No. 08-CV-378S, 2013 WL 2250506 (W.D.N.Y. May 21, 2013) (plaintiffs' sought involvement of their ESI consultants in establishing a predictive coding protocol); Indep. Living Ctr. v. City of Los Angeles, 2:12-cv-00551 slip op., (C.D. Cal. June 26, 2014) (requesting party sought to require quality assurance testing of court ordered predictive coding methodology).

47. *See Da Silva Moore*, 287 F.R.D. at 192 ("[T]ransparency allows the opposing counsel (and the Court) to be more comfortable with computer assisted review, reducing fears about the so-called 'black box' of the technology."); *In re Actos*, 2012 WL 7861249, at *1 (adopting a case management order requiring full disclosure and cooperation between parties in implementing a predictive coding process to search for and produce ESI); *see also* Working Grp on Elec Document Retention & Prod., The Sedona Conference, The Sedona Conference Cooperation Proclamation 2–3, (2008) (receiving 201 judicial endorsements).

enable cost savings and at the same time decrease the risk that the discovery process will be attacked in the future, the level of sharing that has been accepted and endorsed in many published opinions has made some producing parties gun shy about using predictive coding.[48]

This heightened transparency can include the sharing of the seed set methodology and corresponding responsiveness coding that was utilized to train and stabilize the predictive coding system, including the sharing of documents coded as nonresponsive.[49] This can be problematic for many producing parties because it implicates work–product and privilege concerns.[50] Producing parties may also worry that sharing the seed set with the requesting party, including those documents coded nonresponsive, carries the risk of revealing

48. *See, e.g.*, Progressive Cas. Ins. Co. v. Delaney, No. 2:11-cv-00678-LRH-PAL, 2014 WL 3563467, at *30–31 (D. Nev. July 18, 2014) [hereinafter *Delaney*] ("Progressive is unwilling to engage in the type of cooperation and transparency that its own e-discovery consultant has so comprehensibly and persuasively explained is needed for a predictive coding protocol to be accepted by the court or opposing counsel as a reasonable method to search for and produce responsive ESI.").

49. *See generally Da Silva Moore*, 287 F.R.D. at 184 (Judge Peck noted that if predictive coding was used, the producing party would be required to disclose the seed set documents including those tagged as nonresponsive during the training rounds); *In re Actos*, 2012 WL 7861249, at *3 (court ordered disclosure of seed set as well as outlining multiple disclosure requirements as part of the ESI "search methodology proof of concept"); Bridgestone Americas, Inc. v. Int'l Bus. Mach. Corp., No. 3:13-1196, 2014 WL 4923014 (M.D. Tenn. July 22, 2014) (producing party agreed to provide seed set documents); *but see*, Conn. Gen. Life Ins. Co. v. Health Diagnostic Lab, Inc., No. 3:14-cv-01519, 2015 WL 471720 (D. Conn. Jan. 28, 2015) (ESI stipulation declined to require producing party to "share the intricacies" of search methodology absent a Rule 26 violation); *Gordon*, 2013 WL 2250506 (court declined to require disclosure of seed set documents).

50. Hon. John M. Facciola & Phillip J. Favro, *Safeguarding the Seed Set: Why Seed Set Documents May be Entitled to Work Product Protection*, 2015 Fed. Cts. L. Rev. 1, 16 (2015) (reprinted herein as Chapter 9 in this volume) ("it seems like a fairly straightforward proposition that a seed set derived exclusively from random sampling methods would not quality as work product . . . . On the other hand, seed sets that incorporate elements of judgmental sampling may be entitled to some form of work product protection."); *see also*, H. Christopher Boehning & Daniel J. Toal, *No Disclosure: Why Search Terms Are Worthy of Court's Protection*, Law Tech News (Dec. 3, 2013), http://www.paulweiss.com/media/2209977/5dec13edisc.pdf ("Forced cooperation, in the form of directing a party to turn over . . . search terms or information related to predictive coding seeding [] is . . . a dangerous dance on the edge of violating work product protection.").

otherwise nondiscoverable, irrelevant information that could harm the defendant.[51] Indeed, it is universally understood that the requesting party has no right to obtain documents that are not within the scope of discovery.[52] Pursuant to Rule 26(b)(1), parties routinely object to producing irrelevant documents, and go to great lengths and costs to avoid inadvertently doing so to avoid spawning new litigation, adding to existing claims, or exposing confidential or trade secret information. These concerns over transparency can result in a producing party refusing to use predictive coding altogether or attempting to use predictive coding "behind the scenes without coordination with plaintiffs' counsel in much the same way that some corporations for the past several years have on their own, without plaintiffs' involvement, selected and applied search terms to reduce the volume of documents to be reviewed."[53]

Challenges Negotiating Predictive Coding Protocols

Authorities have recognized that the discovery process has become contentious, expensive, and time consuming with parties using broad ESI requests and discovery about discovery to attempt to force settlement.[54] This is prevalent in asymmetrical litigation where only one

51. *See In re Biomet*, 2013 WL 1729682, at *3 ("The Steering Committee has no right to discover irrelevant or privileged documents seems self-evident.").

52. *See id.*, at *5 (finding no "authority to compel discovery of information not made discoverable by the Federal Rules"); *see, e.g.*, Gen. Elec. Co. v. United States, No. 3:14 cv 00190, 2015 WL 4478294, at *2–3 (D. Conn. July 22, 2015) (finding that the receiving party "has no right to over-production of materials beyond the scope of its subpoenas," and noting that a low percentage of documents produced out of the total documents collected was not sufficient evidence to infer that defendants "failed to produce responsive documents"); Fed, Deposit Ins. Corp. v. Bowden, No. CV413-245, 2014 WL 2548137, at *8 (noting that "[w]hile [plaintiff] must respond to defendants' discovery and inspect its own records to do so, it need produce only those documents that are responsive to the opposing party's requests.").

53. *See* Ronni Solomon, *Are Corporations Ready To Be Transparent and Share Irrelevant Documents with Opposing Counsel To Obtain Substantial Cost Savings Through the Use of Predictive Coding?*, Metro. Corp. Couns. 26 (Nov. 2012), http://www.metrocorpcounsel.com/pdf/2012/November/26.pdf.

54. *See* Final Report on the Joint Project of the Am. College of Trial Lawyers Task Force of Discovery and The Inst. for the Advancement of the Am. Legal Sys., at 8 (Mar. 11, 2009; rev. Apr. 15, 2009), http://www.uscourts.gov/file/document/final-report-actl-iaals-joint-project, (noting that "discovery is very expensive and time

party has significant ESI to collect, review, and produce.[55] In the predictive coding context, these litigation strategies have continued with producing and requesting parties battling over every facet of the predictive coding protocol, including disclosure, scope, implementation, quality control, and cost issues.[56] These battles can span additional months and add significant additional expense relating to non-substantive, peripheral litigation, not the merits of the case.[57] Many producing parties worry that this additional expense will outweigh any cost savings that are able to be achieved with predictive coding.[58]

A related problem is where requesting parties attempt to use predictive coding protocols from prior published opinions as the starting place for negotiation. Many of the protocols contained in the first wave of cases involving predictive coding should not be standard or the starting place for negotiation because they are already the product of substantial negotiation and they are some of the first protocols to be written without the benefit of experience.

---

consuming and easily permits substantial abuse."); Moody v. Turner Corp., No. 1:07-cv-692 (S.D. Ohio Sept. 21, 2010) ("[T]he mere availability of such vast amounts of electronic information can lead to a situation of the ESI-discovery-tail wagging the poor old merits-of-the-dispute dog.").

55. *See* Boeynaems v. LA Fitness Int'l, LLC, 285 F.R.D. 331, 341 (E.D. Pa. 2012) (commenting on the imbalance when one party has very few documents and the other has millions of documents and items of ESI).

56. *See In re Biomet*, 2013 WL 1729682, at *5 (disagreement regarding identification of seed set documents); *Da Silva Moore*, 287 F.R.D., at 185–86 (disagreements regarding inclusion of e-mails from seven custodians in the predictive coding process and incorporating two issue tags into the predictive coding process); *Bridgestone*, 2014 WL 4923014, at *1 (disagreement regarding using keyword searches prior to predictive coding); *Indep. Living Ctr.*, slip op. (disagreement regarding necessity of quality control process); *Delaney*, 2014 WL 3563467, at *7 (disagreement regarding cost sharing).

57. *See* Butterfield, Crowley, & Kenney, *supra* note 43, at 2–3 ("[P]otential TAR users are concerned that the cost of extensive negotiations with the opposing party and ancillary litigation over the application of a TAR protocol in a given case will outweigh the cost-savings otherwise achieved by the tool.").

58. *See* Rio Tinto PLC v. Vale S.A., 306 F.R.D. 125, 129 (S.D.N.Y. 2015) (Judge Peck stated "it is inappropriate to hold [predictive coding] to a higher standard than keywords or manual review. Doing so discourages parties from using [predictive coding] for fear of spending more in motion practice than the savings from using [predictive coding].").

Difficulties Inherent in Measuring the Effectiveness of Predictive Coding

Recall and precision rates are the typical methods to evaluate the effectiveness of predictive coding.[59] Some requesting parties have demanded unreasonable target recall rates.[60] Others have insisted on unreasonably high statistically valid sample sizes to confirm effectiveness.[61] Insistence on unreasonable standards of perfection can frustrate the process—the parties' goal should not be "perfect" discovery, but rather "reasonable" discovery.[62] A responding party is only required to

---

59. *See Da Silva Moore*, 287 F.R.D., at 189–90 (The objective of review in e-discovery is to identify as many relevant documents as possible, while reviewing as few nonrelevant documents as possible. Recall is the fraction of relevant documents identified during a review; precision is the fraction of identified documents that are relevant . . . The goal is for the review method to result in higher recall and higher precision than another review method, at a cost proportionate to the "value" of the case.); *see generally* The Sedona Conference Working Group, *Best Practices Commentary on the Use of Search and Information Retrieval Methods in E-Discovery*, 8 SEDONA CONF. J. 189, 205 (2007) [hereinafter *Sedona Conference Commentary*] (defining recall as "the fraction of known relevant documents which were effectively retrieved" and precision as "the fraction of retrieved documents which are known to be relevant.").

60. Defendants' Memorandum in Support of Motion for Protective Order Approving the Use of Predictive Coding, Global Aerospace Inc. v. Landlow Aviation, L.P., No. CL 61040, (Va. Cir. Ct. filed Apr. 9, 2012), *available at* http://www.ediscoverylaw.com/files/2013/11/memosupportpredictivecoding.pdf (Plaintiff objected to Defendant's use of predictive coding with a target of 75% recall rate); *Delaney*, 2014 WL 3563467 at *3 (Plaintiff objected to defendant's use of predictive coding with a target 70.8 percent recall rate); Maura R. Grossman & Gordon V. Cormack, *Technology-Assisted Review in E-Discovery Can Be More Effective and More Efficient Than Exhaustive Manual Review*, XVII RICH. J.L. & TECH. 11, 23 (2011), http://jolt.richmond.edu/v17i3/article11.pdf (TREC analysis achieved an average recall of 76.7%).

61. *See* Declaration of Paul J. Neale in Support of Plaintiffs' Reply in Support of Rule 72(a) Objections to Magistrate Judge Peck's Feb. 8, 2012 Discovery Rulings, Da Silva Moore v. Publicis Groupe, No. 11 Civ. 1279 (S.D.N.Y. Mar. 19, 2012) (ECF No. 125) (Plaintiff's expert objected to proposed quality control sample size of 2,399 to measure estimated recall and argued that a sample size of at least 16,555 documents was necessary given the low estimated richness (1.5 percent) of relevant documents.).

62. *Sedona Conference Commentary, supra* note 59, at 204; *Larsen*, 2012 WL 359466, at *7–8 (noting a party's obligation to act "reasonably and in good faith" to produce requested documents and rejecting plaintiff's request that defendant redo production due to "a few alleged discrepancies").

"use reasonable measures to validate that production is complete and accurate."[63]

Issues and Challenges Involving Combining Search Terms with Predictive Coding

Applying search terms prior to utilizing predictive coding can narrow the universe of potentially responsive information to a more manageable data set and thereby reduce the costs of discovery.[64] Despite the significant benefits that may be conferred by the combined use of such technologies, requesting parties have argued against this method, insisting instead on a "pristine" data set. The concept of a "pristine" set is inherently flawed, however, because a data set will always have some level of filtering—including custodian, date-range, or file-type filtering.[65] Insistence on a pristine data set may not be practical or proportional in a given case given the cost associated with preserving and collecting such a set and then applying predictive coding technology to all collected data.

Conclusion

It is well documented from various stakeholders in the litigation process that corporations can achieve significant cost savings in connection with the document review process by utilizing predictive coding technology. Based on these cost savings, defense practitioners and

---

63. *See* Chen-Oster v. Goldman, Sachs & Co., 285 F.R.D. 294, 306 (S.D.N.Y. 2012) (quoting the Sedona principle that "the standard for the production of ESI is not perfection").

64. *See Bridgestone*, 2014 WL 4923014 (using keyword searches, Bridgestone culled 16.6 million records down to 2.3 million before it applied predictive coding technology to finalize its production set of documents).

65. Sutton, *supra* note 4, at 471 ("Practitioners should, if possible, begin the process with an initial "culling" of the junk, i.e. removing data and documents that are clearly not responsive or privileged before implementing Predictive Coding in order to reduce cost, ensure accuracy, and prevent inadvertent disclosure of privileged information."); MATTHEW D. NELSON, PREDICTIVE CODING FOR DUMMIES (Symantec Special ed. 2012) ("Keyword search, concept search, domain filtering, and discussion threading are only a few of the other important tools in the litigator's toolbelt that can and should be used together with a predictive coding tool.").

corporations should seriously consider utilizing predictive coding technology to reduce costs in conducting document review. At the same time, defense practitioners and corporations should be aware of the potential barriers to the use of predictive coding technology so that they can make informed, practical decisions as to when and when not to use predictive coding technology in a given case.

EDITORS' INTRODUCTION TO CHAPTER 9

Michael D. Berman

Judge Facciola and Philip Favro wade bravely into a thicket that reflects one of the key tensions of electronic discovery. On the one hand, The Sedona Conference Cooperation Proclamation persuasively calls for cooperation and transparency. On the other hand, compelled disclosure of seed sets, the documents and decisions used to "train" a predictive coding engine, may run afoul of traditional notions protecting work product in document-intensive cases.

To appreciate the tension, it is necessary to understand the predictive coding process in the context of seed sets. Typically, a selection of documents, often called the seed set, is presented to a carefully selected reviewer (subject matter expert), who determines whether they are responsive or not. Additional sets are selected,[1] presented to the reviewer, and iteratively coded. Eventually, the system "learns" sufficiently and when the metrics[2] reflect that fact, the documents are ranked for further review.

The identity of the documents selected, and the decisions made on each of them, train the system. Opponents seeking to test or challenge the validity of the output may argue GIGO, or "garbage in, garbage out"[3] as a basis for seeking discovery of seed sets and decisions made on individual documents in those sets. On the other hand, the common law has long held that, at least in certain instances, the selection and

---

1. For a discussion of various selection methodologies and their impact, see Chapters 5 in this volume.

2. For a discussion of metrics, see Chapter 14 in this volume.

3. GIGO "refers to the fact that computers, since they operate by logical processes, will unquestioningly process unintended, even nonsensical, input data ('garbage in') and produce undesired, often nonsensical, output ('garbage out')." Wikipedia, https://en.wikipedia.org/wiki/Garbage_in,_garbage_out.

ordering of documents is trial strategy that is protected from discovery under the work-product doctrine.

The authors report on the diversity of opinions regarding disclosure of seed sets and responsiveness decisions, and suggest a nuanced approach. They argue that the common-law, paper-days' work-product doctrine, holding that the selection and ordering of documents is work product, provides the proper rule to apply, but they note significant limitations on its application in this unique context. For example, as noted elsewhere in this book, some practitioners suggest that seed sets be selected by random sampling, while others recommend selection using an attorney's judgment, or a combination thereof.[4] This chapter suggests that the former not be protected from discovery because the selection of seed documents does not fit within the definition of work product in that it does not reflect an attorney's mental processes. The chapter suggests, however, that the latter generally should be protected because they reflect counsel's decisions. The authors also suggest that the coding process, that is the reviewer or subject-matter expert's decision on the relevance of individual documents, should fall in the protected category. Finally, they point to the conflicting case law.

In his song "The Gambler," Kenny Rogers sang "[y]ou've got to know when to hold 'em, [k]now when to fold 'em."[5] This chapter provides some answers to questions concerning application of the age-old work-product doctrine to this new technology.

4. For a discussion of random versus judgmental selection, see Chapter 5.
5. Copyright Sony/ATV Cross Keys Publishing (1978).

CHAPTER 9

Safeguarding the Seed Set: Why Seed Set Documents May Be Entitled to Work-Product Protection

Hon. John M. Facciola and Philip J. Favro[1]

Introduction

The civil discovery process is difficult and complex.[2] Between the challenges of locating key evidence to the problem of dealing with truculent adversaries, lawyers have frequently struggled with this

This chapter was first published in 8 Fed. Courts L. Rev. 1 (2015), http://www.fclr.org/fclr/articles/pdf/safegaurding-final-publication.pdf. It is reprinted here with modification and permission.

1. The authors wish to recognize the insightful work of Adam Kuhn, JD/MBA, University of San Francisco, 2013, in connection with the preparation of this chapter. An earlier version of this chapter appeared in the Federal Courts Law Review, and the authors thank the Review for granting permission to reprint substantial sections of it here. The authors' biographies have been updated since the original publishing of this article and are among the other author biographies in this volume.

2. *See* Philip J. Favro & Derek P. Pullan, *New Utah Rule 26: A Blueprint for Proportionality Under the Federal Rules of Civil Procedure*, 2012 Mich. St. L. Rev. 933, 936–38 (2012) (commenting on the increasing costs and related challenges plaguing the discovery process).

all-important yet seldom enjoyable aspect of litigation.[3] The quest to address these difficulties and simplify discovery has been ongoing now for over 75 years.[4] Since the advent of the Federal Rules of Civil Procedure ("Rules" or "Rule") in 1938 and their declared intent to resolve matters in a "just, speedy, and inexpensive" manner,[5] federal rule makers have labored to help counsel, clients, and courts simplify the discovery process.[6]

Nevertheless, with each Rule change that was designed to tackle a problem, other issues—sometimes more complex than those just addressed—began to surface.[7] That was certainly the case after the amendment cycles that ended in 1993[8] and 2006.[9] In each instance, the sheer growth of electronically stored information (ESI), among many other things, threatened to overwhelm the legal system with potentially discoverable materials.[10]

---

3. John S. Beckerman, *Confronting Civil Discovery's Fatal Flaws*, 84 MINN. L. REV. 505, 517 (2000) (observing that it was "naive to expect 'that adversarial tigers would behave like accommodating pussycats throughout the discovery period, saving their combative energies for trial.'").

4. *See generally* Martin H. Redish, *Electronic Discovery and the Discovery Matrix*, 51 DUKE L.J. 561, 600–03 (2001) (discussing generally the achievements and failures of the Federal Rules of Civil Procedure since their implementation in 1938).

5. FED. R. CIV. P. 1.

6. W. Bradley Wendel, *Regulation of Lawyers Without the Code, the Rules, or the Restatement: Or, What Do Honor and Shame Have to Do with Civil Discovery Practice?*, 71 FORDHAM L. REV. 1567, 1573–75 (2003) (explaining generally the "great deal of attention" that rules makers have dedicated to ameliorating challenges associated with discovery practice).

7. *See* Beckerman, *supra* note 8, at 518–20, 530–40.

8. *See* JUDICIAL CONFERENCE OF THE UNITED STATES, REPORT OF ADVISORY COMMITTEE ON CIVIL RULES 83–84 (May 2, 2014) (Report) (discussing the impact of the "information explosion" on the 1993 changes to Rule 26).

9. *See generally* Philip J. Favro, *A New Frontier in Electronic Discovery: Preserving and Obtaining Metadata*, 13 B.U. J. SCI. & TECH. L. 1 (2007) (describing the impact and challenges of data growth on discovery practice and the role of the 2006 amendments in addressing the issues).

10. Report, *supra* note 13, at 84 ("The 1993 Committee Note further observed that '[t]he information explosion of recent decades has greatly increased both the potential cost of wide-ranging discovery and the potential for discovery to be used as an instrument for delay or oppression.' What seemed an explosion in 1993 has been exacerbated by the advent of e-discovery."); Richard L. Marcus, *Confronting the Future: Coping with Discovery of Electronic Material*, 64 LAW & CONTEMP. PROBS. 253, 281 (2001) (observing that "sensible behavior by lawyers and judges may be much more

The latest round of Rule amendments is similarly designed to address issues associated with data growth.[11] The Rule changes emphasize proportionality, cooperation, increased judicial involvement in case management, and a streamlined sanctions analysis for ESI preservation failures as solutions to those issues. These amendments are designed to simplify discovery by making it more efficient and cost effective, thereby allowing matters to be litigated on the merits instead of in costly satellite litigation.[12]

While it remains to be seen whether these changes can simplify discovery and tackle data growth,[13] the recent introduction of predictive coding has the potential to do so. Predictive coding—a computerized process for selecting and ranking a collection of documents[14]—has found welcome recipients in clients, counsel, and the courts.[15] All parties to the litigation process have generally been drawn to predictive coding given its potential to expedite the ESI search and review process.[16] Lawyers and litigants have additionally gravitated toward

useful" than additional changes to the Rules in addressing the problems associated with ESI).

11. *See* Craig B. Shaffer & Ryan T. Shaffer, *Looking Past The Debate: Proposed Revisions to the Federal Rules of Civil Procedure*, 7 FED. CTS. L. REV. 178 (2013).

12. Philip J. Favro, *Getting Serious: Why Companies Must Adopt Information Governance Measures to Prepare for the Upcoming Changes to the Federal Rules of Civil Procedure*, 20 RICH. J.L. & TECH. 5, ¶ 1 (2014).

13. If approved by the Supreme Court before May 1, 2015, and unless Congress acts to modify or reject them, the proposed Rules would be enacted on December 1, 2015. Thomas Y. Allman, *The Civil Rules Package As Approved By the Judicial Conference* (Sept. 2014), http://www.theediscoveryblog.com/wp-content/uploads/2014/10/2014CommentsonRulePackage.pdf.

14. *See* Maura R. Grossman & Gordon V. Cormack, *The Grossman-Cormack Glossary of Technology-Assisted Review*, with a Foreword by John M. Facciola, U.S. Magistrate Judge, 7 FED. CTS. L. REV. 1, 26 (2013); Bennett Borden & Jason R. Baron, *Finding the Signal in the Noise: Information Governance, Analytics, and the Future of Legal Practice*, 20 RICH. J.L. & TECH. 7, ¶ 10 (2014).

15. *See* Andrew Peck, *Search, Forward: Will Manual Document Review and Keyword Searches Be Replaced by Computer-Assisted Coding?*, L. TECH. NEWS (Oct. 2011) (generally discussing the benefits of predictive coding), *available at* https://law.duke.edu/sites/default/files/centers/judicialstudies/TAR_conference/Panel_1-Background_Paper.pdf.

16. *See* Nat'l Day Laborer Org. Network v. U.S. Immigration & Customs Enforcement Agency, 877 F. Supp. 2d 87, 109 (S.D.N.Y. 2012) ("[P]arties can (and frequently should) rely on . . . machine learning tools to find responsive documents.");

predictive coding due to its utility in identifying the key documents required to establish their claims or defenses.[17] These by-products of predictive coding—simplifying the process and identifying strategic information—make this methodology a particularly attractive option for conducting discovery.[18]

Despite the potential that predictive coding holds,[19] its introduction to the discovery process has not been universally embraced or free from controversy.[20] There have been disagreements regarding what is predictive coding,[21] when it should be used,[22] and the process for how to successfully implement it into a discovery workflow.[23] Moreover, the few judicial opinions on predictive coding are based on specific fact patterns that make general application for practitioners difficult.[24] These factors have led to uncertainty regarding the manner

---

Hon. Patrick J. Walsh, *Rethinking Civil Litigation in Federal District Court*, 40 LITIG. 6, 7 (2013) (urging lawyers to use "21st-century computer technology" including predictive coding to address digital age discovery issues and to stop relying on legacy discovery technologies and methods).

17. Walsh, *supra* note 22, at 7 ("Their goal should be to have the computer sift through the millions of documents and distill and organize the hundreds or thousands of documents that are critical to the case . . . ."); Charles Yablon & Nick Landsman-Roos, *Predictive Coding: Emerging Questions and Concerns*, 64 S.C. L. REV. 633, 644 (2013) (describing seed set development and its impact on the need "to identify those documents that are most relevant").

18. *In re* Domestic Drywall Antitrust Litig., 300 F.R.D. 228, 233 (E.D. Pa. 2014) (touting the benefits of predictive coding as a new and "sophisticated" discovery search methodology).

19. *Id.*

20. *See, e.g.*, Dana Remus, *The Uncertain Promise of Predictive Coding*, 99 IOWA L. REV. 1691, 1695 (2014) (suggesting that lawyers "proceed with deliberate care in the use and adoption of predictive-coding technologies").

21. *Id.* at 1706–07 (observing disapprovingly that "the litigation community is uncritically embracing predictive coding as if its definition is unitary and clear, its accuracy and efficacy well-established").

22. Borden & Baron, *supra* note 20, at ¶ 17 ("[W]e bow to the reality that in a large class of cases the use of predictive coding is currently infeasible or unwarranted, especially as a matter of cost.").

23. Maura R. Grossman & Gordon V. Cormack, *Comments on "The Implications of Rule 26(g) on the Use of Technology-Assisted Review,"* 7 FED. CTS. L. REV. 285 (2014) (discussing various disagreements between the authors and other thought leaders on the proper use of and objectives surrounding predictive coding).

24. *Compare* Progressive Cas. Ins. Co. v. Delaney, No. 2:11-cv-00678-LRH-PAL, 2014 U.S. Dist. LEXIS 69166, at *27–33 (D. Nev. July 18, 2014) (interpreting case

in which predictive coding may be used and threaten to impede its proliferation.[25]

Nowhere is this uncertainty more apparent than in the debate over the application of the attorney work–product doctrine to the documents that counsel selects to train the predictive coding process.[26] There is little dispute over the significance that those documents—commonly referred to as training or seed sets—play in a properly functioning predictive coding workflow.[27] Seed set documents are essential for training a predictive coding algorithm to identify the documents that "are the most relevant to the case and most representative of those for which each side is looking."[28]

Cognoscenti and courts disagree whether the identification of seed set documents is work product and entitled to protection from discovery.[29] Some courts and commentators assert that counsel should identify seed documents for its litigation adversaries[30] despite the potential for disclosing work product. Those who support the disclosure of seed information justify their position on the need for greater certainty in the predictive coding process.[31] Disclosure, they argue, will reduce

---

management order provision to prevent the use of predictive coding) *with* Bridgestone Americas, Inc. v. Int'l Bus. Mach. Corp. (*Bridgestone*), No. 3:13-1196, 2014 U.S. Dist. LEXIS 142525, at *3 (M.D. Tenn. July 22, 2014) (allowing the use of predictive coding despite an arguably contrary case management order).

25. *See generally* Remus, *supra* note 26.

26. Richard H. Lowe, James G. Welch, & Kimberly G. Lippman, *Disclosure of Seed Sets: Required to Cooperate or Protected as Attorney Work Product?*, The Legal Intelligencer (Feb. 18, 2014), *available at* http://www.duanemorris.com/articles/disclosure_seed_sets_required_cooperate_protected_attorney_work_product_5140.html (describing how the uncertainty surrounding the issue of whether the work–product doctrine applies to seed sets "may serve to stymie the use of predictive coding").

27. Yablon & Landsman-Roos, *supra* note 23, at 638–39, 642–44 (describing generally the role of seed set documents in training a predictive coding algorithm).

28. *Id.* at 644.

29. Lowe, *supra* note 32; Karl Schieneman & Thomas Gricks, *The Implications of Rule 26(g) on the Use of Technology-Assisted Review*, 7 Fed. Cts. L. Rev. 239, 262 n.92 (2013) (questioning whether seed sets are entitled to work-product protection).

30. *See* discussion *infra* Cases Favoring Disclosure of Seed Sets.

31. *See, e.g.*, Elle Byram, *The Collision of the Courts and Predictive Coding: Defining Best Practices and Guidelines in Predictive Coding for Electronic Discovery*, 29 Santa Clara Computer & High Tech. L.J. 675, 699 ("Courts will look

motion practice over the process the party used to search for, review, and produce responsive information.[32]

Indeed, sharing seed set documents is seen as an important convenience so that "opposing counsel (and the Court) [are] more comfortable with" predictive coding.[33] Courts following this line of analysis have observed that such a step is necessary to alleviate "fears about the so-called 'black box' of [predictive coding] technology."[34] Moreover, by insisting on the cooperative development of seed sets, courts are seeking to ensure that discovery is reasonable, proportional, and proceeds in an orderly fashion.[35] Eliminating the possibility of collateral litigation should make discovery less costly and more focused on disclosing information so matters can be resolved on the merits.[36]

The allure of this position, however, fails to recognize that a seed set may reflect a lawyer's perceptions of relevance, litigation tactics, or even its trial strategy.[37] These conclusions regarding key strategic issues—memorialized in counsel's selection of documents—have frequently been protected in analogous circumstances[38] as work product

---

more favorably upon a party who discloses its key custodians and how it will [search] for the requested documents. Where a party is transparent, 'opposing counsel and the Court are more apt to agree to your approach . . . .'").

32. *Id.* at 698–99; Schieneman & Gricks, *supra* note 35, at 261–63 (advocating that seed documents be identified without waiving any applicable work-product protection).

33. Da Silva Moore v. Publicis Groupe, 287 F.R.D. 182, 192 (S.D.N.Y. 2012).

34. *Id.*

35. *Id. See also* Transcript of Record at 13-15, Fed. Hous. Fin. Agency v. J.P. Morgan Chase & Co., Inc., 11-cv-06188-DLC (S.D.N.Y. July 24, 2012) ECF No. 128 (insisting the parties jointly develop the predictive coding workflow, including seed documents).

36. *See id.*

37. Remus, *supra* note 26, at 1716 ("requiring seed-set transparency threatens core protections for attorney work product"); Yablon & Landsman-Roos, *supra* note 23, at 644 ("If . . . the seed set is made up of documents selected or coded by a producing party as relevant, production of that seed set has a much higher probability of disclosing attorney impressions of the case.").

38. *See* discussion *infra* Application of *Sporck* in Factual Scenarios Involving Selections of Documents.

since they may reveal counsel's "mental impressions, conclusions, opinions, or legal theories."[39]

For example, the specific documents that a lawyer segregated and used to prepare a witness for deposition often merits work-product protection.[40] The work-product doctrine has also protected the subset of materials that a lawyer identifies during a document inspection.[41] In addition, litigants have enjoyed immunity from interrogatories that seek the identity of documents supporting their legal theories.[42] Underlying each of these lines of authority are two key policies derived from *Hickman v. Taylor*, the Supreme Court's seminal opinion on the work-product doctrine.[43] The first is that counsel is entitled to a zone of privacy to prepare its case for trial.[44] The second is a logical corollary to the first: that a litigation adversary should not receive "a free ride on the effort and investment of [] counsel in reviewing and selecting documents and in preparing [its claims] or defense[s]."[45]

---

39. Fed. R. Civ. P. 26(b)(3)(B); United States, *ex rel.* Bagley v. TRW, Inc. (*Bagley II*), 212 F.R.D. 554 (C.D. Cal. 2003) (holding that the relator's disclosure statement reflecting its counsel's compilation of documents was opinion work product).

40. Sporck v. Peil, 759 F.2d 312 (3d Cir. 1985) (holding that counsel's selection of certain documents to prepare a client for deposition was protected as opinion work product). *See* discussion *infra* Document Selections Protected as Opinion Work Product under *Sporck*.

41. Disability Rights Council of Greater Wash. v. Wash. Metro. Transit Auth., 242 F.R.D. 139, 141–44 (D.D.C. 2007) (protecting counsel's selection of materials from a third-party document inspection as fact work product); United States, *ex rel.* Bagley v. TRW, Inc. (*Bagley I*), No. CV94-7755-RAP(AJWx), 1998 U.S. Dist. LEXIS 23585 (C.D. Cal. Dec. 11, 1998) (protecting a lawyer's selection of documents from an opposing party's production as opinion work product). *See* discussion *infra* Application of *Sporck* in Factual Scenarios Involving Selections of Documents.

42. *See, e.g.*, Kodak Graphic Commc'ns. Can. Co. v. E. I. du Pont de Nemours & Co., 08-CV-6553T, 2012 U.S. Dist. LEXIS 15752 (W.D.N.Y. Feb. 8, 2012). *See* discussion *infra* Application of *Sporck* in Factual Scenarios Involving Selections of Documents.

43. Hickman v. Taylor, 329 U.S. 495 (1947). *See* discussion *infra* The Purposes and Policy of the Work-Product Doctrine.

44. *Id.* at 510–11 ("[I]t is essential that a lawyer work with a certain degree of privacy, free from unnecessary intrusion by opposing parties and their counsel.").

45. *Bagley I*, at *4; *Hickman*, 329 U.S. at 516 (Jackson, J., concurring) ("Discovery was hardly intended to enable a learned profession to perform its functions either without wits or on wits borrowed from the adversary.").

In this chapter, we assert that this rationale is equally applicable to seed set protection.[46] Counsel should be provided with a "quiet and secluded corner"[47] to determine which documents are pertinent to the predictive coding process.[48] This is particularly the case for those lawyers who employ predictive coding to identify and isolate highly relevant data.[49] Because those documents could very well reflect the manner in which counsel is pursing discovery and how counsel is establishing what is relevant to the client's claim or defense, the seed set will disclose counsel's thought processes, certain conclusions made on the claims and defenses at issue, and/or its strategy for seeking to dispose of the case.[50]

Where seed sets actually reflect such information, opposing counsel should not be given a "free ride"[51] "on wits borrowed from the adversary."[52] Allowing the opposition to understand counsel's selection process regarding its predictive coding seeds could provide it with access to counsel's "legal strategy, his intended lines of proof, his evaluation of the strengths and weaknesses of his case," and prepare its case accordingly.[53] Under these cases and other authorities,[54] the identity of those selected documents should merit fact or even opinion work-product protection.[55]

---

46. *See* discussion *infra* The Work-Product Doctrine Would Likely Apply Only to Judgmental Samples and Application of the *Sporck* Rule to Predictive Coding Seed Sets.

47. *In re* San Juan Dupont Plaza Hotel Fire Litig., 859 F.2d 1007, 1018–19 (1st Cir. 1988) (finding that counsel's deposition exhibit list was fact work product, but nonetheless ordered its production).

48. *See In re* Biomet M2a Magnum Hip Implant Products Liability Litig. (*Biomet II*), No. 3:12-MD-2391, 2013 U.S. Dist. LEXIS 172570, at *4 (N.D. Ind. Aug. 21, 2013) ("The Steering Committee wants to know, not whether a document exists or where it is, but rather how Biomet used certain documents before disclosing them. Rule 26(b)(1) doesn't make such information disclosable.").

49. Yablon & Landsman-Roos, *supra* note 23, at 643–44.

50. *See* discussion *infra* The Role of Seed Sets in Predictive Coding.

51. *Bagley I*, at *4.

52. Hickman v. Taylor, 329 U.S. 495, 516 (1947) (Jackson, J., concurring).

53. Sporck v. Peil, 759 F.2d 312, 316 (3d Cir. 1985).

54. *See* discussion *infra* Protecting Seed Set Documents as Work Product Under Analogous Scenarios Involving Selections of Documents.

55. *Id.*

While there are limitations to this rule[56] and though there are obvious potential benefits to disclosure,[57] we contend that the convenience created by cooperation should not be used to coerce a lawyer into revealing counsel's work product as reflected in the development of a predictive coding seed set.[58] Instead, where warranted by the circumstances, courts should find that counsel's identification of seed documents are safeguarded as work product.[59]

This chapter will consider these subjects. We first provide a general overview of the law on attorney work product. We next discuss the importance of the seed set to establishing a defensible predictive coding process and the steps counsel typically undertakes to develop that set. This includes a discussion of the differences between judgmental sampling and random sampling and why only those seed sets developed through judgmental sampling should merit consideration for work-product protection. We also analyze the unsettled state of predictive coding jurisprudence regarding the protection of seed documents. Next, we describe the general requirements that parties must satisfy for work-product protection to apply to a lawyer's selection of documents. We then delineate the circumstances when seed set documents would warrant that protection. We conclude by discussing a few of the instances when fact work product might have to yield in the face of compelling litigation interests.

The Attorney Work-Product Doctrine

Before delving into the details regarding the character and development of predictive coding seed sets, it is essential that we examine the basic notions of the work-product doctrine to help frame the

56. *See* discussion *infra* Refining the Scope of the *Sporck* Rule.

57. *Guidelines Regarding the Use of Predictive Coding*, Coalition of Technology Resources for Lawyers 8–10, 14–15 (2014), http://www.ctrlinitiative.com/home/protocol/ (describing some benefits to disclosing seed set documents and other aspects of a predictive coding workflow).

58. *Biomet II*, at *5 ("Biomet, the Steering Committee says, isn't proceeding in the cooperative spirit endorsed by the Sedona Conference and the corresponding Seventh Circuit project. But neither the Sedona Conference nor the Seventh Circuit project expands a federal district court's powers, so they can't provide me with authority to compel discovery of information not made discoverable by the Federal Rules.").

59. *See* discussion *infra* The Work-Product Doctrine Would Likely Apply Only to Judgmental Samples and Application of the *Sporck* Rule to Predictive Coding Seed Sets.

discussion. In this section, we analyze the purposes, policy, and scope of the work-product doctrine. This includes a discussion of the elements required to establish a bona fide work-product claim and the differences between fact and opinion work product.

The Purposes and Policy of the Work-Product Doctrine

The work-product doctrine is one of the cornerstones of modern litigation practice in the United States.[60] Though perhaps lacking the glamour and prominence of the lawyer–client privilege,[61] work product plays an important role in ensuring a properly balanced and functioning adversary system.[62] This fact was established in 1947 when the Supreme Court issued its celebrated opinion in *Hickman v. Taylor*, which formally recognized the concept of attorney work product.[63]

The work-product doctrine is designed to provide a lawyer with the professional space needed to prepare a client's case for trial.[64] As the Supreme Court observed in *Hickman*, counsel must have "a certain degree of privacy, free from unnecessary intrusion by opposing parties and their counsel."[65] The work-product umbrella does so by enabling counsel to "assemble information, sift what he considers to be the relevant from the irrelevant facts, prepare his legal theories and plan his strategy without undue and needless interference."[66] The *Hickman* case is particularly instructive on this issue.

In *Hickman*, the court frowned on a party's obtaining through discovery witness statements or legal memoranda reflecting witness discussions prepared by its adversary. The information they possessed was equally accessible to both parties[67] because the witnesses in

60. United States v. Nobles, 422 U.S. 225, 238 (1975) (discussing the essential nature of the work-product doctrine to a properly functioning adversarial system).

61. Philip Favro, *Inviting Scrutiny: How Technologies are Eroding the Attorney-Client Privilege*, 20 RICH. J.L. & TECH. 2, ¶ 16 (2014) (observing how the lawyer–client privilege has been glamorized in popular culture).

62. *Nobles*, 422 U.S. at 238.

63. Hickman v. Taylor, 329 U.S. 495, 510–12 (1947).

64. *Id.* at 511–12.

65. *Id.* at 510.

66. *Id.* at 511.

67. *Id.* at 508, 513–14.

question were available for interview by either party.[68] Given this circumstance, the court reasoned that a litigant should not be permitted to develop its case "on wits borrowed from the adversary."[69] A contrary result would be "demoralizing" to lawyers,[70] ultimately leading to "[i]nefficiency, unfairness and sharp practices."[71] The work-product doctrine, as envisioned by the Supreme Court, was critical to preventing such developments and "essential to an orderly working of our system of legal procedure."[72]

The Scope of the Work-Product Doctrine

Since the Supreme Court's decision in *Hickman*, the basic thrust of the work-product doctrine has been codified in Rule 26(b)(3)[73] and is also reflected as well established in other rules[74] and cases.[75] Those authorities memorialize the notion that a party generally cannot discover documents, other tangible items, or intangible materials "that are prepared in anticipation of litigation or for trial by or for another party or its representative."[76] Significant to the issue of predictive coding seed

---

68. *Id.* at 513.

69. *Id.* at 516 (Jackson, J., concurring).

70. *Id.* at 511 ("The effect on the legal profession would be demoralizing. And the interests of the clients and the cause of justice would be poorly served."). The concurrence, authored by Associate Justice Robert Jackson——an accomplished trial lawyer, a former Solicitor General and Attorney General of the United States, and the lead prosecutor for the United States at the Nuremburg war trials, also anticipated this same effect. *Id.* at 516 (Jackson, J., concurring); Gail Jarrow, Robert H. Jackson: New Deal lawyer, Supreme Court Justice, Nuremberg prosecutor (2008). Justice Jackson observed: "I can conceive of no practice more demoralizing to the Bar than to require a lawyer to write out and deliver to his adversary an account of what witnesses have told him." *Hickman*, 329 U.S. at 516 (Jackson, J., concurring).

71. *Id.* at 511.

72. *Id.* at 512.

73. Fed. R. Civ. P. 26(b)(3).

74. *See, e.g.*, Fed. R. Evid. 502(g).

75. *See, e.g.*, Upjohn Co. v. United States, 449 U.S. 383, 397–98 (1981) (reaffirming *Hickman* and the nature of the work-product doctrine).

76. Fed. R. Civ. P. 26(b)(3)(A); Fed. R. Evid. 502(g). This includes written witness statements, legal memoranda, letters, and "oral expressions of an attorney's mental impressions, legal theories and subjective evaluations." Lockheed Martin Corp. v. L-3 Commc'ns Corp., No. 6:05-cv-1580-Orl-31KRS, 2007 U.S. Dist. LEXIS 54606, at *26 (M.D. Fla. Jul. 29, 2007).

sets, the work-product doctrine may also safeguard selections or compilations of documents made by counsel.[77]

Notwithstanding the importance that the work-product doctrine plays in fostering a zone of privacy for lawyers to prepare their cases, the privilege that it affords is often only a qualified one.[78] The Supreme Court noted as much in *Hickman*, explaining that signed witness statements might nonetheless be subject to discovery for purposes of impeachment when witnesses are unavailable, uncooperative, or where the interests of justice so require.[79] Consistent with *Hickman*, Rule 26(b)(3) provides that a party may obtain an adversary's work product if it establishes that the materials "are otherwise discoverable under Rule 26(b)(1)," demonstrates a "substantial need" for their production, and shows that they cannot otherwise be obtained "without undue hardship."[80]

On the other hand, "opinion work product"—those materials that reflect a lawyer's "legal strategy, his intended lines of proof, his evaluation of the strengths and weaknesses of his case"—enjoy near absolute immunity from discovery.[81] *Hickman* recognized the primacy of opinion work product, reasoning that "not even the most liberal of discovery theories can justify unwarranted inquiries into the files and the mental impressions of an attorney."[82] Rule 26(b)(3) has captured the importance that *Hickman* placed on safeguarding opinion work product, directing courts to "protect against disclosure of the mental impressions, conclusions, opinions, or legal theories of a party's

---

77. *See* discussion *infra* Protecting Seed Set Documents as Work Product Under Analogous Scenarios Involving Selections of Documents.

78. Fed. R. Civ. P. 26(b)(3)(A).

79. Hickman v. Taylor, 329 U.S. 495, 519 (1947) (Jackson, J., concurring).

80. Fed. R. Civ. P. 26(b)(3)(A). *See In re* San Juan Dupont Plaza Hotel Fire Litig., 859 F.2d 1007 (1st Cir. 1988) (permitting the discovery of a deposition exhibit list that was fact work product).

81. Kodak Graphic Commc'ns. Can. Co. v. E. I. du Pont de Nemours & Co., No. 08-CV-6553T, 2012 U.S. Dist. LEXIS 15752, at *13 (W.D.N.Y. Feb. 8, 2012) (quoting Sporck v. Peil, 759 F.2d 312, 316 (1985)).

82. *Hickman*, 329 U.S. at 513 (observing that it would indeed be "a rare situation justifying production of these matters."). The Supreme Court has confirmed this precedent multiple times, most notably in *Upjohn*. Upjohn Co. v. United States, 449 U.S. 383, 397–98 (1981).

attorney or other representative concerning the litigation"[83] even when they find it discoverable under the Rule 26(b)(3) exception.

In many of the cases involving opinion work product, the mental processes of counsel that courts have sought to protect have been reflected in their selections of documents.[84] In those matters, courts have proscribed the identification of the selected documents from discovery since they could reveal counsel's mental processes, conclusions regarding the merits of claims or defenses, or even its strategy for pursuing the litigation.[85] As set forth in the next section, whether those protections should apply to predictive coding seed sets depends in large part on the underlying process used to compile the seed documents.

Predictive Coding and Seed Sets

To grasp why seed set documents may merit work-product protection, it is important to understand the role they play in developing an effective predictive coding process. Without seed set documents, it would be difficult to train the predictive coding algorithm.[86] Indeed, seed documents are essential for teaching the algorithm what materials it should search for across the universe of potentially responsive information.[87]

Although there is little dispute about the indispensable nature of seed sets, there are different schools of thought regarding how they should be developed.[88] Some have taken the position that a seed set should be created through a random sampling of the entire universe

83. Fed. R. Civ. P. 26(b)(3)(B). Various courts have embraced and even extended the protections from *Hickman* and Rule 26(b)(3), declaring that opinion work product is "absolutely privileged." Caremark, Inc. v. Affiliated Computer Servs., Inc., 195 F.R.D. 610, 616 (N.D. Ill. 2000). Those courts that have not done so have nonetheless held that production of this category of work product should be limited to "rare and extraordinary circumstances." *Upjohn*, 449 U.S. at 399–402; *Bagley II*, at 559.

84. Sporck v. Peil, 759 F.2d 312, 316 (3d Cir. 1985).

85. *Id.*; *see* discussion *infra* Protecting Seed Set Documents as Work Product Under Analogous Scenarios Involving Selections of Documents.

86. Yablon & Landsman-Roos, *supra* note 23, at 638–39.

87. *Id.*

88. *Id.* at 642–44.

of potentially responsive information.[89] Others assert that seed sets should instead be customized with documents that lawyers specifically identify through judgment calls on the relevance and importance of a particular record.[90] Still others maintain that a seed set could include a hybrid approach, incorporating elements from both the sampling and judgmental schools.[91]

While courts have not mandated that one specific approach be used in lieu of the others, the nature of how a seed set is created will certainly impact the application of the work-product doctrine.[92] In this section, we delineate the general differences between judgmental and random sampling and consider why only those seed sets that incorporate a lawyer's specific judgment calls on documents merit consideration for work-product protection. We also discuss the body of case law that exists regarding the protection of seed set documents. That discussion is critical since the jurisprudence on this issue is far from settled and has yet to directly address the application of the work-product doctrine to seed set development.

The Role of Seed Sets in Predictive Coding

There are various issues that must be considered to establish a properly functioning and defensible predictive coding process.[93] Issues such as accurately determining the prevalence of responsive information within the universe of documents, engaging in an iterative training process, and validating the final production results through

---

89. Schieneman & Gricks, *supra* note 35, at 259–61 (arguing that random sampling is preferable to judgmental sampling).

90. Grossman & Cormack, *supra* note 29, at 288, 298 (touting certain benefits of judgmental sampling over pure random sampling).

91. *Id.*; Ralph Losey, *Predictive Coding and the Proportionality Doctrine: A Marriage Made in Big Data*, 26 Regent U. L. Rev. 7, 22 (2013) (describing different sampling methods and the author's preference for using a combined approach).

92. Yablon & Landsman-Roos, *supra* note 23, at 644.

93. *See* Nicholas Barry, Note, *Man Versus Machine Review: The Showdown Between Hordes of Discovery Lawyers and a Computer-Utilizing Predictive-Coding Technology*, 15 Vand. J. Ent. & Tech. L. 343, 354–55 (2013) (describing a predictive coding workflow and related issues associated with its implementation).

different forms of testing are all essential to the process.[94] Despite the magnitude of these issues, the step that is perhaps the most crucial in this process is the proper development of a seed set.[95] Indeed, the effectiveness of a predictive coding workflow and its ability to satisfy the traditional discovery touchstones of relevance, proportionality, and reasonableness[96] will likely turn on what documents counsel uses to train the algorithm.[97]

Simply put, a seed set is a proportionately small subset of data that contains examples of the categories of information being sought.[98] The predictive coding algorithms use the characteristics of the seed set to find similar documents.[99] Those seed documents are then run through the predictive coding process to train the algorithm to obtain documents for production.[100]

Judgmental Sampling

There are two general approaches for developing a seed set.[101] The first is typically referred to as judgmental sampling.[102] Judgmental

94. *Guidelines Regarding the Use of Predictive Coding*, Coalition of Technology Resources for Lawyers 5–7 (2014), http://524.ada.myftpupload.com/wp-content/uploads/2014/07/Guidelines-Regarding-the-Use-of-Predictive-Coding.docx.

95. *See* Daniel Martin Katz, *Quantitative Legal Prediction—Or—How I Learned to Stop Worrying and Start Preparing for the Data-Driven Future of the Legal Services Industry*, 62 Emory L.J. 909, 946 (2013) (explaining that predictive coding "approaches are inductive and typically involve the seeding of the algorithm with training (or labeled) data from which the machine infers the 'true' function for assigning a document to a particular group (i.e., relevant versus not relevant).").

96. *Bridgestone*, at *2–3 ("In the final analysis, the uses of predictive coding is [sic] a judgment call, hopefully keeping in mind the exhortation of Rule 26 that discovery be tailored by the court to be as efficient and cost-effective as possible.").

97. *See* Katz, *supra* note 101, at 946.

98. Grossman & Cormack, *supra* note 29, at 29.

99. Yablon, *supra* note 18, at 638–39, 643–44.

100. Transcript of Record at 114, Fed. Hous. Fin. Agency v. UBS Americas, 11-cv-06188 (S.D.N.Y. July 31, 2012) ECF No. 134; Yablon, *supra* note 18, at 639; *see generally* In re Biomet M2a Magnum Hip Implant Products Liability Litig. (*Biomet I*), No. 3:12-MD-2391, 2013 U.S. Dist. LEXIS 84440, *3 (N.D. Ind. Apr. 18, 2013) (describing the inextricably intertwined process used for seeding and training the predictive coding workflow).

101. Grossman, *supra* note 15, at 29.

102. *Id.*

sampling involves customizing a seed set with specific documents or classes of information that, when submitted into a predictive coding workflow, are targeted to uncover additional documents whose content is similar to that of the seed materials.[103] Such a seed set could be comprised of highly relevant information, marginally responsive materials, privileged communications, nonresponsive data, or a combination of these or even other items.[104] The specific compilation of a seed set, the number of documents in a seed set, and the number of seed sets created will depend on the facts and circumstances of a particular matter.[105]

Judgmental seed documents could be identified through any number of methods. They could include e-mails, contracts, memoranda, tweets, or other records that a client first isolated and then provided to its counsel.[106] A lawyer might also uncover seed documents by searching through client information or an adversary's production with the use of keywords, concept search, data clustering, manual review, or other search methodologies.[107]

Random Sampling

In contrast to judgmental sampling, seed set documents obtained through random sampling do not generally involve the exercise of independent legal judgment.[108] Instead, as the term suggests, the seed set is generated by taking a statistically valid sample from the universe of potentially responsive information.[109] That sample, typically created through the functionality of a particular predictive coding technology, is designed to ensure that the seed set reflects the characteristics of the entire document population.[110]

103. Yablon & Landsman-Roos, *supra* note 23, at 639, 642–43.

104. Nicholas M. Pace & Laura Zakaras, *Where the Money Goes: Understanding Litigant Expenditures for Producing Electronic Discovery*, RAND INST. FOR CIVIL JUSTICE 59 (2012), *available at* http://www.rand.org/pubs/monographs/MG1208.html.

105. Losey, *supra* note 97, at 22.

106. *See id.*

107. Pace & Zakaras, *supra* note 110, at 60; Losey, *supra* note 97, at 22; Da Silva Moore v. Publicis Groupe, 287 F.R.D. 182, 200–01 (S.D.N.Y. 2012).

108. Grossman & Cormack, *supra* note 20, at 27; Losey, *supra* note 97, at 22.

109. Yablon & Landsman-Roos, *supra* note 23, at 639, 643.

110. Schieneman, *supra* note 35, 260–61.

Once the randomly comprised seed set is reviewed and coded for responsiveness, the remaining subset of information is run against the universe of documents.[111] That subset may or may not be increased with additional samples to ensure that it is truly representative of the overall percentage of responsive information within the universe of documents.[112] The additional samples could be derived from further rounds of random sampling or from judgmental samples that a lawyer obtained through its exercise of legal reasoning.[113]

The Work-Product Doctrine Would Likely Apply Only to Judgmental Samples

Whether the work-product doctrine applies to seed documents would depend on a variety of factors.[114] However, it seems like a fairly straightforward proposition that a seed set derived exclusively from random sampling methods would not qualify as work product. This is because the grouping of documents would have been generated through computer software and not by counsel's exercise of skill, judgment, and reasoning.[115] Indeed, it seems counterintuitive that a seed set created through a mere keystroke of computer functionality would implicate the policy concerns articulated in *Hickman* and its progeny.[116] Such functionality does not encompass a lawyer's legal strategy, its intended lines of proof, or its evaluation of the strengths and weaknesses of the case,[117] much less the need for a "quiet and

111. Yablon & Landsman-Roos, *supra* note 23, at 639–40.

112. *Id.* at 643.

113. Losey, *supra* note 97, at 22.

114. *See* discussion *infra* Protecting Seed Set Documents as Work Product Under Analogous Scenarios Involving Selections of Documents.

115. Yablon & Landsman-Roos, *supra* note 23, at 644 ("[i]f the seed set is merely a random sample of the entire document population and is produced without coding as to whether documents are deemed responsive or not, the production is unlikely to concern a producing party."). While a randomly generated seed set generally lacks the indicia that would warrant work-product protection, that may not be the case if counsel subsequently codes the randomly selected documents. Pace & Zakaras, *supra* note 110, at 60. The coding process would likely entail the same exercise of legal reasoning and acumen involved in creating judgmental samples.

116. *See* discussion *infra* The Attorney Work-Product Doctrine.

117. Hickman v. Taylor, 329 U.S. 495, 510 (1947); Sporck v. Peil, 759 F.2d 312, 316 (3d Cir. 1985).

secluded corner" to prepare for discovery.[118] The plain language of Rule 26(b)(3) and the underlying policy from *Hickman* do not permit such a finding.[119]

On the other hand, seed sets that incorporate elements of judgmental sampling may be entitled to some form of work-product protection. While the methods may vary for identifying judgmental seeds, the distinct and overriding characteristic of judgmental seeds is that a lawyer meticulously segregated those materials based on the exercise of legal judgment.[120] At some level, counsel made a determination that a specific seed document was pertinent to the exercise of discovery and the overall direction of the litigation.[121] For those attorneys who specifically use predictive coding to segregate highly relevant data, judgmental seeds may reflect information beyond mere perceptions of relevance.[122] It could memorialize their thought processes, certain conclusions they have made on the claims and defenses at issue, and/or their strategy for seeking to dispose of the case.[123]

Given that judgmental samples are prepared by a lawyer, either in preparation for or in connection with litigation, and that the identity of those samples potentially reflects its "mental impressions, conclusions, opinions, or legal theories," the identity of those documents could merit work-product protection.[124] The courts, however, have yet to issue a holding that directly addresses this question.[125] Contrary to the notion that seed documents may be protected from discovery, some of the courts that have focused on seed set development have urged litigants to disclose or cooperatively develop the seeds.[126] Such decisions seem to gloss over the possibility that the responding party's seed set could constitute work product.

---

118. *In re* San Juan Dupont Plaza Hotel Fire Litig., 859 F.2d 1007, 1018–19 (1st Cir. 1988).

119. Fed. R. Civ. P. 26(b)(3); *Hickman*, 329 U.S. 495.

120. Yablon & Landsman-Roos, *supra* note 23, at 643–44.

121. Losey, *supra* note 95, at 22.

122. Remus, *supra* note 26, at 1716.

123. *See id.*; Yablon & Landsman-Roos, *supra* note 23, at 644.

124. *See* discussion *infra* Application of the *Sporck* Rule to Predictive Coding Seed Sets

125. *See* discussion *infra* Jurisprudence Regarding the Protection of Seed Set Documents.

126. *Id.*

Jurisprudence Regarding the Protection of Seed Set Documents

Nearly three years have transpired since the issuance of the first predictive coding related opinion.[127] While no court has directly applied the work-product doctrine to seed set documents, there are several cases that address issues relating to seed set development.[128] In most of these cases, seed documents have been identified to litigation adversaries.[129] In contrast, only the court in *Biomet II* has unequivocally protected the identity of seed documents from discovery.[130] In this section, we discuss the key jurisprudence on this issue to demonstrate that courts typically favor identification of seed sets to advance the notions of cooperation and transparency.

Cases Favoring Disclosure of Seed Sets

The cases involving disclosure of seed sets are generally divided between those instances where the parties voluntarily shared seed documents with the opposition and others where courts ordered the identification of such information.[131] In either scenario, disclosure occurred to further the cognate aims of cooperation and transparency in discovery.[132] Courts strongly believe that adversarial cooperation and openness can decrease discovery costs and delays.[133] Indeed, even the *Biomet II* decision—which declined to order the production of seed information, touted the "significant, salutary, and persuasive impact on federal discovery practice" of cooperative advocacy.[134] Thus, in the

127. Da Silva Moore v. Publicis Groupe, 287 F.R.D. 182 (S.D.N.Y. 2012).

128. *See, e.g.*, *Bridgestone*; Fed. Hous. Fin. Agency v. HSBC N. Am. Holdings Inc., 11-cv-6189, 2014 U.S. Dist. LEXIS 19156 (S.D.N.Y. Feb. 14, 2014); *Biomet II*.

129. *Da Silva Moore*, 287 F.R.D. at 200–01; *Bridgestone*, at *2.

130. *Biomet II*, at *4–5.

131. *Compare In re* Actos (Pioglitazone) Products Liab. Litig., 6:11-MD-2299, 2012 U.S. Dist. LEXIS 187519 (W.D. La. July 27, 2012) (reflecting the parties' agreement to jointly develop the predictive coding seed set) *with Bridgestone*, at *2 (ordering the plaintiff to share its seed set with the defendant).

132. *See, e.g.*, *In re* Actos (Pioglitazone) Products Liab. Litig., 6:11-MD-2299 (W.D. La. July 13, 2012) ECF No. 1413 (noting the "impressive levels of cooperation, coordination, and negotiation that have taken place among counsel for the plaintiffs and the defense").

133. *See e.g., Biomet II*, at *5; *Da Silva Moore*, 287 F.R.D. at 192.

134. *Biomet II*, at *5.

name of cooperation, courts have encouraged the disclosure or joint creation of seed sets.[135]

Perhaps the most noteworthy example of this occurred in *Da Silva Moore v. Publicis Groupe*, the first predictive coding related opinion.[136] In that case, the parties entered into a stipulated protocol to use predictive coding.[137] According to the terms of the protocol, the defendant agreed to provide the plaintiffs with all of the non-privileged seed documents used to train the predictive coding process, together with the defendant's document coding designations.[138] In approving this arrangement, the court observed that such "transparency" with respect to seed sets was proper and important.[139] Given the convenience that disclosure provided, the court recommended that this practice should generally be adopted:

> Such transparency allows the opposing counsel (and the Court) to be more comfortable with computer-assisted review, reducing fears about the so-called "black box" of the technology. This Court highly recommends that counsel in future cases be willing to at least discuss, if not agree to, such transparency in the computer-assisted review process.[140]

Other decisions have also picked up on the convenience theme from *Da Silva Moore* and insisted that parties who wish to use

135. *Da Silva Moore*, 287 F.R.D. at 192; Transcript of Record, at 9, 13–15, 24, Fed. Hous. Fin. Agency v. JPMorgan Chase & Co., 11-cv-05201 (S.D.N.Y. July 24, 2012) ECF No. 128.

136. *Da Silva Moore*, 287 F.R.D. 182.

137. *Id.* at 193.

138. *Id.* at 186–87.

139. *Id.* at 192.

140. *Id.* Despite the parties' agreement to use predictive coding, there is considerable debate regarding whether the defendant's cooperation and transparency in this regard achieved lower discovery costs. The parties only reached a stipulated protocol after substantial prodding from the court and with the plaintiffs taking the unusual step of "objecting" to the agreement. *Id.* at 187, n.6. The relationship between the parties subsequently deteriorated into protracted motion practice over minor issues of relevance on individual documents. *See, e.g.*, Plaintiffs' Rule 72(a) Objection to the Magistrate's April 25, 2012 Discovery Rulings, Da Silva Moore v. Publicis Groupe, No. 11-cv-1279 (S.D.N.Y. May 9, 2012), ECF No. 190 (seeking reconsideration of various court rulings on discovery issues relating to the defendant's use of predictive coding).

predictive coding should identify their seed set documents.[141] In *Federal Housing Finance Agency v. UBS Americas*, defendant JPMorgan Chase obtained a court order approving its use of predictive coding over the objections of the plaintiff.[142] Faced with a universe of over 2.5 million potentially relevant documents, a production deadline approaching within approximately two months, and a skeptical plaintiff who was throwing up roadblocks to the use of predictive coding, JPMorgan felt compelled to seek a court order approving its predictive coding process.[143]

While the court approved the use of predictive coding, it required JPMorgan to involve the plaintiff in every step of the predictive coding workflow.[144] This included joint development and full disclosure of the seed set.[145] Drawing on the dicta from *Da Silva Moore*, the court observed that such "transparency and cooperation" was necessary for the overall success of the predictive coding process.[146]

A third example of this trend is found in *Bridgestone Americas v. International Business Machines*.[147] In *Bridgestone*, the court approved the plaintiff's use of predictive coding over the defendant's objection.[148] The defendant had argued that predictive coding was not appropriate since the parties had previously agreed to a case management order requiring "attorney review."[149] The court rejected the defendant's argument and allowed the plaintiff to modify its choice

141. Fed. Hous. Fin. Agency v. HSBC N. Am. Holdings Inc., 11-cv-6189, 2014 U.S. Dist. LEXIS 19156 (S.D.N.Y. Feb. 14, 2014).

142. *Id.* at *3.

143. Transcript of Record at 10–15, Fed. Hous. Fin. Agency v. JPMorgan Chase & Co., No. 11-cv-05201 (S.D.N.Y. July 24, 2012) ECF No. 128.

144. *Id.* at 9, 13–15, 24.

145. *Id.* at 24 (excepting privileged materials, the court expected "that the plaintiff will be given full access to . . . . documents within the seed set").

146. *Id.* at 9 ("And for this entire process to work, I think it needs transparency and cooperation of counsel.").

147. *Bridgestone.*

148. *Id.* at *2–3.

149. *See* Case Management Order, Bridgestone Americas, Inc. v. Int'l Bus. Mach. Corp., No. 3:13-cv-1196 (M.D. Tenn. May 20, 2014) ECF No. 76; *see also* IBM's Response to Bridgestone's Request to Add Predictive Coding to the ESI Protocol, Bridgestone Americas, Inc. v. Int'l Bus. Mach. Corp., No. 3:13-cv-1196 (M.D. Tenn. July 14, 2014) ECF No. 85.

of search methodologies.[150] However, because the court permitted the plaintiff to "switch horses in midstream," it insisted on "openness and transparency" in the predictive coding process.[151] Indeed, in response to the plaintiff's offer to share its seed documents with the defendant, the court essentially incorporated that proposal into its order, reiterating its expectation of "full openness" between the litigants and their lawyers.[152]

Da Silva Moore, *Federal Housing*, *Bridgestone*, and other cases[153] exemplify the judiciary's general expectation that parties identify their seed set documents for convenience and expediency in discovery. That trend, though, has not been universally followed by the courts.

Cases Favoring Protection of Seed Sets

In contrast to the decisions favoring disclosure stand those instances where courts have protected seed sets from discovery.[154] The most notable decision in this regard and the lone opinion to directly address this issue is *Biomet II*.[155] The *Biomet II* court denied the plaintiffs' request that the defendant pharmaceutical company identify the seed set documents that were used to train its predictive coding algorithm.[156] The plaintiffs were seeking to develop search terms to run against the subset of documents that the defendant's predictive coding process excluded from its production.[157] The plaintiffs asserted that

150. *Bridgestone*, at *2.

151. *Id.*

152. *Id.* at *3.

153. *See, e.g.*, Indep. Living Ctr. of S. Cal. v. City of L.A., 2:12-cv-00551-FMO-PJW, at *1 (C.D. Cal. June 13, 2014) ECF No. 371 (ordering the defendant "to use a predictive coding system for identifying the 10,000 most relevant documents in its databases and, after reviewing them for privilege, etc., produc[e] them to Plaintiffs.").

154. *Biomet II*; Gordon v. Kaleida Health, No. 08-CV-378S(F), 2013 U.S. Dist. LEXIS 73330, *6–7 (W.D.N.Y. May 21, 2013) (rejecting plaintiffs' motion to compel the production of "important information regarding Defendants' selection of so-called 'seed set documents' which are used to 'train the computer' in the predictive coding search method."); Hinterberger v. Catholic Health Sys., 08-CV-380S(F), 2013 U.S. Dist. LEXIS 73141 (W.D.N.Y. May 21, 2013) (reaching the same holding as in the related *Gordon* case).

155. *Biomet II*.

156. *Id.* at *3–5.

157. *Id.* at *2

identification of the seed documents[158] was necessary so they could prepare their own search terms.[159] Unless they were given an understanding of the defendant's seed documents, argued the plaintiffs, they could not effectively prepare search terms.[160]

The court rejected that argument and held that the plaintiffs' request for seed information was beyond the scope of permissible discovery.[161] Because the defendant had already produced all of the responsive seed set documents to the plaintiffs, the court reasoned that the plaintiffs were not seeking to ascertain "whether a document exists or where it is, but rather *how Biomet used certain documents before disclosing them*."[162] That type of information, the court explained, was not within the permissible scope of discovery.[163]

Lastly, the court sympathized with but ultimately disregarded the plaintiffs' complaints that the company was not being cooperative.[164] While touting the virtues of cooperation enshrined in both the Seventh Circuit Pilot Program[165] and The Sedona Conference Cooperation Proclamation,[166] the court observed that "neither the Sedona Conference nor the Seventh Circuit project expands a federal district court's powers, so they can't provide me with authority to compel discovery of information not made discoverable by the Federal Rules."[167] Moreover, even though the company's lack of cooperation was "troubling" and could possibly lead the court to later conclude it was "hiding something," the court took no action since it had no "discretion" to order the identification of the seed information.[168]

158. It appears that the defendant resorted to a form of judgmental sampling to prepare its seed set. *Biomet I*, at *3.

159. *Biomet II*, at *3.

160. *Id.*

161. *Id.* at *3–5.

162. *Id.* at *4 (emphasis added).

163. *Id.*

164. *Id.* at *5.

165. 7th Cir. Elec. Discovery Comm., Principles Relating To The Discovery Of Electronically Stored Information, at princs. 1.01–.03 (2010), *available at* http://www.discoverypilot.com/sites/default/files/Principles8_10.pdf.

166. The Sedona Conference, *The Sedona Conference Cooperation Proclamation,* 10 Sedona Conf. J. 331 (2009).

167. *Biomet II*, at *5.

168. *Id.* at *5–6.

Biomet II stands for the proposition that Rule 26(b)(1) may protect the identity of seed set documents from discovery.[169] While notions of cooperation and transparency are significant to advancing the tripartite aims of Rule 1 in litigation, they cannot supersede the strictures from Rule 26(b)(1). Absent some showing of relevance or a stipulation between the parties, *Biomet II* teaches that the identification seed set documents should generally be proscribed from discovery.

It is also significant that the court specifically forbade the plaintiffs from discovering the seeds because they sought to understand how the company used those documents in the discovery process.[170] Probing the manner in which a party and its counsel selected documents for purposes of satisfying discovery obligations could very well reflect their deliberations on claims and defenses, along with related tactical choices. These items thus fall squarely within the ambit of Rule 26(b)(3)'s qualified prohibition on the discovery of fact work product and its admonition against disclosing opinion work product.[171] Absent a showing of a substantial or compelling need for such information—let alone a basic demonstration of relevance, the *Biomet II* court properly precluded the plaintiffs' inquiry. Its reasoning supports the conclusion that a judgmental seed set must be protected as work product.

Despite what we believe to be the implicit inference from *Biomet II* that seed sets are nondiscoverable and work product, the fact remains that no court has specifically analyzed whether the work-product doctrine applies to seed sets. Juxtaposed against this absence of authority are *Da Silva Moore* and its progeny, whose holdings in favor of seed set identification sharply contrast with *Biomet II*. Given the conflict in these authorities and the absence of predictive coding decisions on this issue, other case law must be explored for guidance. The jurisprudence that provides the most logical analogue on this issue involves decisions that have addressed the merits of work-product protection over a lawyer's selection of documents in other less technical scenarios.

169. *Id.* at *3–5.

170. *Id.* at *4.

171. *See* discussion *infra* The Attorney Work-Product Doctrine.

Protecting Seed Set Documents as Work Product: Courts and Documents

The question of whether work-product protection should ultimately apply to judgmental seed sets turns on the line of analogous cases that have protected selections of documents as either opinion or fact work product. In this section, we detail the circumstances under which a lawyer's selection of documents would qualify as work product. This includes a discussion of *Sporck v. Peil*, the foundational case on this issue.[172] We then analyze how the rule from *Sporck* has been clarified, refined, and played out in specific case scenarios. Finally, we consider the circumstances when seed documents should be protected in light of those authorities and the circumstances of a case.

Selections of Documents: When Are They Protected as Work Product?

An enduring question over the past 30 years of work-product jurisprudence is whether courts should protect the identity of certain documents that counsel compiles or selects in connection with its case preparations.[173] Since the issuance of *Sporck v. Peil* by the U.S. Court of Appeals for the Third Circuit in 1985,[174] the answer has been a definite yes.[175] *Sporck* unequivocally held that selections of documents could be protected as opinion work product.[176] Since that time, however, the *Sporck* rule has been refined as subsequent opinions delineated the circumstances under which *Sporck* would apply.[177] In this section, we review the development of the selection of documents rule and what parties must generally show to satisfy its present requirements.

---

172. Sporck v. Peil, 759 F.2d 312 (3d Cir. 1985).

173. Charleswell v. Chase Manhattan Bank, N.A., 277 F.R.D. 277, 282–83 (D.V.I. 2011) (confirming that a lawyer's compilation of documents may be protected as work product).

174. *Sporck*, 759 F.2d at 312.

175. *See, e.g.*, Shapiro v. United States Dep't of Justice, 969 F. Supp. 2d 18, 31–32 (D.D.C. 2013) (citing *Hickman* and holding that "there is a clear policy rationale for protecting the compilation of records" as work product).

176. *Sporck*, 759 F.2d at 315.

177. *See* discussion *infra* Refining the Scope of the *Sporck* Rule.

Document Selections Protected as Opinion Work Product Under *Sporck*

The seminal case on the work-product status of documents chosen from a larger population is the Third Circuit's *Sporck* decision.[178] In *Sporck*, the court held that a lawyer's selection of a "few documents out of thousands" constitutes protected work product.[179] The issue arose in the context of a deposition of the defendant.[180] During the deposition, plaintiff's counsel asked the deponent whether he had reviewed any documents in preparation for the deposition.[181] After answering yes, the defendant declined to identify the documents he had reviewed.[182] Explaining that the documents in question had all been produced in discovery, the defendant's lawyer asserted that their particular selection in this context—to prepare the client for deposition—was protected as work product.[183] While the lower court agreed with this assertion, it nonetheless ordered the selected documents identified since they did not constitute opinion work product.[184]

The Third Circuit reversed this finding and instead held that counsel's compilation of documents was opinion work product and protected from discovery.[185] The court reasoned that disclosure of this information could "reveal important aspects of [counsel's] understanding of the case" and thereby divulge his mental impressions.[186] Foreshadowing the need for such work-product protection in today's ESI-driven discovery process, the court declared that safeguarding such document compilations was particularly important in cases "involving extensive document discovery."[187] Citing *Hickman*, the court also observed that the document selection process was an essential aspect

---

178. *Sporck*, 759 F.2d 312.

179. *Id.* at 316 (quoting James Julian, Inc. v. Raytheon Co., 93 F.R.D. 138, 144 (D. Del. 1982)).

180. *Id.* at 314.

181. *Id.* at 313–14.

182. *Id.* at 314.

183. *Id.*

184. *Id.*

185. *Id.* at 316.

186. *Id.* (quoting James Julian, Inc. v. Raytheon Co., 93 F.R.D. 138, 144 (D. Del 1982)).

187. *Id.*

of case preparation.[188] Counsel's assembling of information, sifting "the relevant from the irrelevant facts," preparing "legal theories," and developing "strategy without undue and needless interference" were inherent in this process.[189] Disclosing counsel's document selection would inappropriately reveal these mental processes to a litigation adversary.[190]

Refining the Scope of the *Sporck* Rule

Sporck stands for the proposition that a lawyer's selection of documents may qualify as opinion work product.[191] While many courts have followed *Sporck*,[192] other opinions have refined the scope of its holding to delineate more precisely when work-product protection should apply. That jurisprudence has generally resulted in four clarifying principles to the application of the work-product doctrine to a lawyer's selection of documents.

The most significant of these principles is that the party asserting a claim of work product must show that the identification of the selected documents raises a genuine threat of disclosure of counsel's mental impressions.[193] The purpose of this principle is to distinguish meritorious work-product claims from those that are specious.[194]

188. *Id.* at 316–17 (citing Hickman v. Taylor, 329 U.S. 495 (1947)).

189. *Id.* at 316.

190. *Id.* at 317.

191. *Id.*; *accord* Disability Rights Council of Greater Wash. v. Wash. Metro. Transit Auth., 242 F.R.D. 139, 142 (D.D.C. 2007).

192. *See, e.g.*, Shelton v. American Motors Corp., 805 F.2d 1323, 1328 (8th Cir. 1986) (holding that a lawyer's document selection should be protected as work product since she "identified, selected, and compiled documents that were significant to her client's defenses in this case."); *In re* Allen, 106 F.3d 582, 608 (4th Cir. 1997) (determining that counsel's choice and arrangement of certain materials constituted opinion work product).

193. Gould v. Mitsui Mining & Smelting Co., Ltd., 825 F.2d 676, 680 (2d Cir. 1987) ("the selection and compilation of documents by counsel for litigation purposes is protected opinion work product . . . . but its application depends upon the existence of a real, rather than speculative, concern that the thought processes of [] counsel in relation to pending or anticipated litigation would be exposed.").

194. *See In re* San Juan Dupont Plaza Hotel Fire Litig., 859 F.2d 1007, 1015–16 (1st Cir. 1988).

Memorialized in various cases,[195] this principle has become a standard limitation on the application of the *Sporck* rule.[196]

The second clarifying principle is that the *Sporck* rule generally applies to the identification of relevant documents and typically does not prevent the documents themselves from being produced in litigation.[197] The basis for this principle is that withholding relevant, non-privileged documents from discovery generally does not promote the policies supporting the work-product doctrine.[198] Only in exceptional circumstances could a party justify keeping the selected documents from discovery.[199]

The next refining principle is that a lawyer's compilation of documents may only constitute fact work product in certain instances.[200] Such a restriction on the *Sporck* rule was necessary since "not every item which may reveal some inkling of a lawyer's mental impressions, conclusions, opinions, or legal theories is protected as opinion work product."[201] This is particularly the case where counsel has "no justifiable expectation that the mental impressions revealed by the materials will remain private."[202] This principle is exemplified in *In re San Juan Dupont Plaza Hotel Fire Litigation*, which ordered that a lawyer's exhibit list be produced in advance of a deposition.[203] Although the list was fact work product, it could not attain opinion work-product

195. *See, e.g., Gould*, 825 F.2d 676 (articulating the principle, but declining to rule on the matter and remanding for determination by the lower court); Mercator Corp. v. United States (*In re* Grand Jury Subpoenas Dated Mar. 19, 2002 & Aug. 2, 2002), 318 F.3d 379, 386–87 (2d Cir. 2002) (holding that the movant did not satisfy its burden on the issue since it neglect to disclose ex parte to the court the "defense strategy" that the selected documents would allegedly reveal).

196. *See, e.g., In re* Trasylol Prods. Liab. Litig., No. 08-MD-1928, 2009 U.S. Dist. LEXIS 85553 (S.D. Fla., Aug. 12, 2009) (reasoning that "a party asserting an attorney opinion privilege claim must come forward with some evidence that disclosure of the requested documents creates a real, nonspeculative danger of revealing counsel's thoughts."); *Disability Rights*, 242 F.R.D. at 143 (noting the limitation of the *Gould* holding on *Sporck*).

197. *See, e.g., Mercator*, 318 F.3d 379.

198. *Id.* at 384–85.

199. *See Gould*, 825 F.2d at 680.

200. *San Juan*, 859 F.2d 1007.

201. *Id.* at 1015.

202. *Id.* at 1016.

203. *Id.* at 1018–19.

status because the identified documents would be shared with opposing counsel.[204]

The fourth and final clarifying principle is that courts will only safeguard as fact work-product document compilations that are considerable in size.[205] This is because courts find it unlikely that an adversary can glean a lawyer's mental processes when a voluminous number of documents comprise the selection.[206] While the meaning of "voluminous" will vary depending on the circumstances of a particular matter, various cases have found that selections that number in the tens of thousands will typically only merit fact work-product status.[207]

Despite this clarification, caution should be taken to ensure the rule is applied in a proportional fashion to ensure the achievement of *Sporck*'s overarching objective: protecting counsel's mental impressions in cases involving "extensive document discovery."[208] As *Sporck* observed, "the process of selection and distillation [of documents] is often more critical than pure legal research" in cases involving large volumes of documents.[209] All of which suggests that a seed set numbering in the thousands or more could warrant opinion work-product status since today's cases frequently involve millions—not thousands—of documents.[210]

---

204. *Id.* at 1017–19 ("[t]he exhibits are integral to the taking of the deposition and will, by definition, have to be revealed during the session."). As the *San Juan* court acknowledged, however, such a scenario is distinguishable from *Sporck* where the documents used to prepare a witness for a deposition "were never meant to be placed on public display." *Id.* at 1018.

205. Disability Rights Council of Greater Wash. v. Wash. Metro. Transit Auth., 242 F.R.D. 139, 141–44 (D.D.C. 2007).

206. Wollam v. Wright Med. Group, Inc., No. 10-cv-03104-DME-BNB, 2011 U.S. Dist. LEXIS 106768, *5–6 (D. Colo. Sept. 20, 2011) (granting work-product protection to the compilation of documents at issue).

207. *Disability Rights*, 242 F.R.D. at 144 (citing various cases).

208. Sporck v. Peil, 759 F.2d 312, 316 (3d Cir. 1985).

209. *Id.*; *accord* Shelton v. American Motors Corp., 805 F.2d 1323, 1329 (8th Cir. 1986) ("[i]n cases that involve reams of documents and extensive document discovery, the selection and compilation of documents is often more crucial than legal research.").

210. Such a rule seems logical, particularly given that *Sporck* sought to protect the disclosure of "a few documents out of thousands." *Sporck*, 759 F.2d at 316.

Application of *Sporck* in Factual Scenarios Involving Selections of Documents

The foregoing principles confirm the continuing vitality of the *Sporck* rule, that is, that a lawyer's selection of documents can merit work-product protection. So long as a party demonstrates an actual threat of disclosure of its counsel's mental processes and only seeks to withhold the identity of the compiled documents, the selection could warrant fact or even opinion work-product protection. The context in which courts have applied the *Sporck* rule in specific factual scenarios is instructive on how it should apply to predictive coding seed sets.

Preparing Witnesses for Deposition

One such scenario is the identification and selection of documents in connection with preparing a witness for deposition.[211] A selection of documents is safeguarded as opinion work product where the documents counsel selects have been produced in litigation and where their disclosure would likely divulge counsel's mental processes.[212] This is precisely the fact pattern considered in *Sporck* and which the Third Circuit found to merit opinion work-product protection.[213] Various courts have followed the specific *Sporck* holding,[214] including those cases that found *Sporck* factually inapposite.[215]

---

211. *Sporck*, 759 F.2d at 312; Briese Lichttechnik Vertriebs GmbH v. Langton, 272 F.R.D. 369, 376 (S.D.N.Y. 2011) ("the attorney's decision to select specific documents to show the witness embodies the lawyer's mental processes, specifically, her evaluation of the significance of those documents, and hence is presumptively protected work-product.").

212. *See, e.g.*, *In re* Yasmin & Yaz (Drospirenone) Mktg., Sales Practices & Prods. Liab. Litig., No. 3:09-md-02100, 2011 U.S. Dist. LEXIS 69711 (S.D. Ill. June 29, 2011) ("Forcing Bayer to disclose the compilation would implicitly reveal the thought processes of the attorney who selected the documents and would allow plaintiffs to glean which documents, out of the millions already produced, opposing counsel believes are legally significant."). *Contra* New Jersey v. Sprint Corp., 258 F.R.D. 421, 436 (D. Kan. 2009) ("Having prepared literally hundreds of witnesses for deposition and trial while in private practice, the undersigned simply believes it is too big a leap to suggest that the mere identification of documents a witness reviews at the direction of counsel improperly provides a roadmap of the attorney's strategies and opinions.").

213. *Sporck*, 759 F.2d at 316.

214. *See, e.g.*, *Briese*, 272 F.R.D. at 376; *Yasmin*, at *6–7.

215. Mercator Corp. v. United States (*In re* Grand Jury Subpoenas Dated Mar. 19, 2002 & Aug. 2, 2002), 318 F.3d 379, 385 (2d Cir. 2002) (holding that *Sporck* could safeguard the identity of certain information when the objective of a request was to

Document Inspections

Another protected scenario that has significance for seed sets involves the subset of information that a lawyer identifies during a document inspection.[216] Courts have frequently forbidden adversaries from learning the precise documents that a lawyer picked during an inspection.[217] A contrary result would enable opposing counsel to receive a "free ride" on the lawyer's work in choosing documents that pertain to its claims or defenses.[218] The *Bagley I* and *Disability Rights* cases are particularly instructive on this issue.[219]

In *Bagley I*, the court proscribed the government from learning the identity of the documents the defendant manufacturer selected during an inspection of the government's records.[220] The government had argued that for the sake of efficiency and convenience, the manufacturer should identify the documents its counsel had selected.[221] While the court sympathized with the government,[222] it found that the manufacturer's selection of documents would divulge information regarding its lawyer's "mental impressions or strategy" and "therefore constitutes opinion work product."[223]

Similarly, the court in *Disability Rights* protected as fact work product the documents that were selected from certain records made

---

obtain "the opposing attorney's thinking or strategy"); *In re* San Juan Dupont Plaza Hotel Fire Litig., 859 F.2d 1007, 1018 (1st Cir. 1988) (confirming the viability of *Sporck* in the context of preparing a witness for deposition).

216. Disability Rights Council of Greater Wash. v. Wash. Metro. Transit Auth., 242 F.R.D. 139, 141–44 (D.D.C. 2007).

217. *Id.* at 144. *Contra In re* Shell Oil Refinery, 125 F.R.D. 132, 134 (E.D. La. 1989) (ordering the production of documents over the plaintiffs' work-product objection as it was unlikely that counsel's "theory of the case" could be revealed by "the 65,000 documents out of 660,000 documents . . . . selected for copying.").

218. *Bagley I*, at *4; *Bagley II*, at 564.

219. *Bagley I*; *Disability Rights*, 242 F.R.D. 139.

220. *Bagley I*, at *4–5.

221. *Id.* at *4.

222. *Id.* ("[v]iewed strictly from the standpoint of efficiency, the procedure proposed by the government probably is superior to any of the alternatives . . . . The Court is sympathetic with the general philosophy expressed in some of the cases cited by the government, namely, that full disclosure, conservation of resources, and judicial efficiency usually should predominate over tactical partisan concerns.").

223. *Id.* at *3–5. *See Bagley II*, at 564.

available to the litigants during a third party document inspection.[224] The court found the existence of an actual threat that counsel's thought processes could be divulged if the documents were identified.[225] Nevertheless, opinion work-product protection could not apply since the documents in the compilation numbered in the tens of thousands.[226]

Bagley I and *Disability Rights* demonstrate that counsel's mental processes would be improperly revealed if the precise nature of the documents selected during a document inspection were identified. Whether the selection of documents should attain fact or opinion work-product status, however, depends on whether the compiled materials are proportionately voluminous in relation to the overall production set.[227]

Responses to Contention Interrogatories

Another document selections analogy instructive on the seed set front involves the immunity that litigants often receive from preparing responses to contention interrogatories that seek the identity of documents supporting their claims or defenses.[228] The purpose for this immunity is to protect litigants from a "thinly-veiled effort" by their adversaries to learn about how counsel "intends to marshall [sic] the facts, documents and testimony" in support of its positions.[229] The need for such protection is exemplified in the *Kodak Graphic*

224. *Disability Rights*, 242 F.R.D. at 144–45.

225. *Id.* at 142–44.

226. *Id.* at 143–44 (explained that "it would be difficult to conceive that Plaintiffs' trial strategy could be gleaned solely by virtue of Plaintiffs' disclosure of the documents selected."). The defendants had argued that the compilation of documents at issue would not expose counsel's mental process since "the number of documents totals over 40,000 pages." *Id.* at 142.

227. *See* discussion *infra* Refining the Scope of the *Sporck* Rule.

228. *See* Johnson v. Ocean Ships, Inc., No. C05-5615RJB, 2006 U.S. Dist. LEXIS 52281 (W.D. Wash. July 31, 2006) (relying on *Sporck* and finding that "the exact documents and witnesses [the defendant] intends to use for each affirmative defense reveals defense counsel's mental impressions, is work product and so is privileged.").

229. Kodak Graphic Commc'ns. Can. Co. v. E. I. du Pont de Nemours & Co., 08-CV-6553T, 2012 U.S. Dist. LEXIS 15752, *13 (W.D.N.Y. Feb. 8, 2012).

Communications Canada Company v. E. I. du Pont de Nemours and Co. case.[230]

In *Kodak*, the court proscribed the defendant from discovering the precise documents supporting one of the plaintiff's legal theories.[231] Such an inquiry was calculated to obtain the plaintiff's counsel's mental processes as reflected by the requested compilation of documents.[232] This was all the more apparent since all of the relevant documents had been produced in discovery and the requested compilation would be principally populated from materials derived from the defendant's production.[233] Since the plaintiff agreed to disclose the facts supporting its theory, the defendant could simply review the productions to find the supporting documents.[234]

Kodak teaches that selections of documents should not be disclosed to provide an adversary with a shortcut to completing its own trial preparations.[235] While convenient for opposing counsel, such a result would run contrary to the policies underlying the work-product doctrine articulated in *Hickman* and *Sporck*.[236]

230. *Id.* at *13–18.

231. *Id.* at *17–18.

232. *Id.* at *17.

233. *Id.* at *9, *18.

234. *Id.* at *18.

235. *Id.* at *13; *accord* FDIC v. Brudnicki, 291 F.R.D. 669, 679 (N.D. Fla. 2014) (citing *Sporck* and declining on work-product grounds to order the defendant to categorize documents in response to "contention requests"). *But see* SEC v. Collins & Aikman Corp., 256 F.R.D. 403 (S.D.N.Y. 2009) (distinguishing the *Sporck* rule and ordering the plaintiff to produce documents that supported allegations from its complaint). We appreciate that in *SEC v. Collins & Aikman Corp.*, the court compelled over the plaintiff's work-product objection the disclosure of "approximately 175 file folders" that its counsel created to categorize materials supporting the factual allegations in its complaint. We see a marked difference between being compelled to provide one's evidentiary support for an allegation and demanding that counsel identify what documents it deemed relevant to a legal theory advanced by the client. The former seeks a fact——what documents support the allegation in paragraph 1——while the latter probes improperly into how counsel has constructed the legal theory it is advancing on behalf of the client. *See* Hickman v. Taylor, 329 U.S. 495, 510–11 (1947).

236. *Kodak*, at *9–10 ("The purpose of the attorney work product doctrine is 'to preserve a zone of privacy in which a lawyer can prepare and develop legal theories and strategy . . . free from unnecessary intrusion by his adversaries.'") (quoting United States v. Adlman, 134 F.3d 1194, 1196 (2d Cir. 1998)).

Application of the *Sporck* Rule to Predictive Coding Seed Sets

The analogous factual scenarios previously detailed, taken together with *Sporck* and its four clarifying principles, demonstrate that seed sets prepared using judgmental sampling methods should be protected either as opinion or fact work product. For example, the rationale from the "witness preparation" line of cases—beginning with *Sporck*—that protects document compilations as opinion work product is equally applicable to judgmental seed documents.

Like the documents that counsel segregates for preparing a witness for deposition, the judgmental seeds that counsel identifies represent a proportionately limited number of documents.[237] In addition, those seed documents—as evidenced by *Biomet II*—are not intended for public dissemination.[238] Instead, counsel prepares judgmental seeds to sift "relevant from the irrelevant facts," isolate the most relevant information, and thereby "prepare his legal theories and plan his strategy."[239] These factors regarding the purpose and preparation of judgmental seeds demonstrate that disclosure of the seeds raises a genuine threat that counsel's mental processes would be exposed to its litigation adversaries.

Moreover, protecting judgmental seeds from disclosure also implicates the policy concerns from *Sporck* regarding cases that involve "extensive document discovery."[240] While such large-scale cases in the 1980s may have involved productions numbering in the tens or hundreds of thousands of pages, discovery now routinely

---

237. Edwards v. Nat'l Milk Producers Fed'n, No. 3:11-CV-04766-JSW, 3 (N.D. Cal. Apr. 17, 2013), ECF No. 155 (specifically identifying the composition of the seed set as initially including approximately 1,400 documents); Jason Lichter, *Transparency in Predictive Coding: How Much Is Too Much?*, N.Y. L.J. (Mar. 17, 2014), *available at* http://www.pepperlaw.com/publications_article.aspx?ArticleKey=2887 (explaining that a seed set could range from hundreds to "tens of thousands of documents," depending on their development).

238. *Biomet II*, at *2.

239. Hickman v. Taylor, 329 U.S. 495, 510–11 (1947); *see Biomet II*, at *2–4.

240. *Sporck*, 759 F.2d at 316 (quoting James Julian, Inc. v. Raytheon Co., 93 F.R.D. 138, 144 (D. Del. 1982)).

involves millions of documents and petabytes of information.[241] Measured proportionately under *Sporck*, seed sets involving thousands of documents are properly protected as opinion work product. And should the number of judgmental seeds be deemed too large to reveal counsel's mental processes,[242] a court should nonetheless protect the seed set as fact work product and require the movant to demonstrate "substantial need" and "undue hardship" under Rule 26(b)(3).[243]

The "document inspections" and "contention interrogatories" jurisprudence also justify the protection of judgmental seeds as opinion or fact work product. Just as the courts reasoned in *Bagley I* and *Kodak*,[244] disclosing judgmental seeds could advance the efficiency of litigation and make the pursuit of discovery more convenient for opposing counsel and perhaps the court. However important those objectives are, they cannot supersede the policies that *Hickman* articulated and that are now codified in Rule 26(b)(3).[245] Lawyers and their clients must be given a zone of privacy to prepare a properly functioning predictive coding workflow without "needless interference" from their adversaries.[246]

Nor should the opposition be given "a free ride on the effort and investment" of counsel in meticulously preparing its judgmental seeds.[247] A contrary result would make the court a party to an adversary's "thinly-veiled effort" to discover a lawyer's litigation and trial strategy as reflected in that compilation of documents.[248] As *Biomet II*

241. *See generally* Philip J. Favro, *Sea Change or Status Quo: Has The Rule 37(e) Safe Harbor Advanced Best Practices for Records Management?*, 11 Minn. J.L. Sci. & Tech. 317 (2010) (detailing the data governance challenges that organizations face from the information explosion).

242. *See* Disability Rights Council of Greater Wash. v. Wash. Metro. Transit Auth., 242 F.R.D. 139, 142–44 (D.D.C. 2007).

243. *Id.*; Fed. R. Civ. P. 26(b)(3)(A).

244. *Bagley I*, at *3–5; Kodak Graphic Commc'ns Can. Co. v. E. I. du Pont de Nemours & Co., 08-CV-6553T, 2012 U.S. Dist. LEXIS 15752, *13–18 (W.D.N.Y. Feb. 8, 2012).

245. Hickman v. Taylor, 329 U.S. 495, 510–11 (1947); Fed. R. Civ. P. 26(b)(3)(B).

246. *Hickman*, 329 U.S. at 511.

247. *Bagley I*, at *4. *See also Hickman*, 329 U.S. at 516 (Jackson, J., concurring).

248. *Kodak*, at *13.

confirmed, it is generally improper for opposing counsel to learn how judgmental seeds were used before producing them in discovery.[249]

In summary, judgmental seeds should generally be protected as opinion work product when they satisfy the *Sporck* rule and its refining principles. Nevertheless, as *San Juan* and its progeny have held, not every seed set will merit this type of protection.[250] There will be instances when the quantity of judgmental seeds is simply too large in proportion to the overall production set and will not require opinion or perhaps even fact work-product protection.[251] Legitimate case management considerations could also warrant the disclosure of seed documents.[252] Discovery of seed information might also be ordered when reasonable questions are raised regarding the quality and nature of a production or the structure of a predictive coding workflow.[253] Finally, courts will likely veto a party's attempt to withhold the production of relevant documents in lieu of their identification under *Hickman* and *Sporck*.[254]

While the foregoing circumstances are foreseeable, they are exceptions and should not swallow the general rule that judgmental seeds deserve work-product status. Requiring litigants to routinely disclose such seed information runs contrary to the well-reasoned policies supporting the work-product doctrine and its protection of a lawyer's selection of documents.

---

249. *Biomet II*, at *3–4.

250. *In re* San Juan Dupont Plaza Hotel Fire Litig., 859 F.2d 1007, 1015 (1st Cir. 1988); Northern Natural Gas Co. v. Approximately 9117.53 Acres, 289 F.R.D. 644, 647–50 (D. Kan. 2013) (rejecting the assertion of work product where the plaintiff failed to establish an actual threat that its lawyers' mental processes would be revealed).

251. *See In re* Shell Oil Refinery, 125 F.R.D. 132, 134 (E.D. La. 1989).

252. *See San Juan*, 859 F.2d at 1015, 1018–19.

253. *See* Formfactor, Inc. v. Micro-Probe, Inc., No. C-10-03095 PJH (JCS), 2012 U.S. Dist. LEXIS 62233, at *7, n.4 (N.D. Cal. May 3, 2012) (ordering the production of search terms over the plaintiff's work-product objection so as to ascertain whether an adequate search was performed for responsive information).

254. *See* Mercator Corp. v. United States (*In re* Grand Jury Subpoenas Dated Mar. 19, 2002 & Aug. 2, 2002), 318 F.3d 379, 386–87 (2d Cir. 2002).

Conclusion

Predictive coding represents a wave of innovations that are revolutionizing the discovery process.[255] When properly implemented under the careful and painstaking supervision of counsel, predictive coding has the potential to simplify some of discovery's troubling complexities. To ensure the continued proliferation of this technology, we assert that courts must take the lead in creating certainty surrounding the predictive coding process. In particular, this requires courts to protect judgmental seeds as work product. While parties remain free to enter into a predictive coding protocol that involves the joint development of a seed set, orders that force the parties into such a process are not generally desirable. It is impossible to argue against transparency and cooperation in the discovery process and we certainly make no such arguments. Nevertheless, parties must retain a zone of privacy in which to prepare for trial and marshal the evidence in discovery to do so. Protecting their seed sets as work product is a significant step forward in accomplishing this objective.

Epilogue: 2016 Update

After the Federal Courts Law Review published an earlier version of this chapter as an article in February 2015, certain courts have issued opinions on questions relating to the use of predictive coding.[256] None of these decisions has addressed the issue we considered: that predictive coding seed sets in certain instances should be considered work product. Nevertheless, one case from 2015—*Rio Tinto v. Vale*—implicitly suggested that disputes over seed sets might decrease if parties adopted the continuous active learning training approach in predictive coding.[257] Regardless of whether this happens, we maintain

255. Gareth Evans & David Grant, *Tools Let Attorneys Follow the Breadcrumbs: Analytics applications can help litigators identify surface patterns that point to the key evidence*, NAT'L L.J. (Sept. 1, 2014), *available at* http://www.gibsondunn.com/publications/Documents/Evans-ToolsLetAttorneysFollowTheBreadcrumbs.pdf.

256. *See, e.g.*, Rio Tinto PLC v. Vale S.A., 306 F.R.D. 125 (S.D.N.Y. 2015) (considering issues surrounding the disclosure of seed set information); Boardley v. Household Fin. Corp. III, No. 12-cv-03009-PWG (D. Md. June 1, 2015) (emphasizing the need for cooperation among litigants when using predictive coding).

257. *Rio Tinto v. Vale*, 306 F.R.D. at 128.

that the need for work-product protection over predictive coding seed sets will remain significant, irrespective of the training approach used. A brief discussion of *Rio Tinto* and the nature of continuous active learning is instructive on this issue.

In *Rio Tinto*, the court entered an order approving the parties' stipulation to use predictive coding during the discovery process.[258] In connection with its order, the court discussed the unsettled and highly contentious state of the law regarding whether responding parties should cooperatively develop or transparently disclose their predictive coding seed sets.[259] While acknowledging that "the decisions [on the issue] are split and the debate in the discovery literature is robust," the court mentioned that seed set content is "much less significant" if a party uses a continuous active learning method to train its predictive coding algorithm.[260] While the court did not elaborate further, the clear inference from its assertion is that parties will have fewer disputes over seed sets if they use continuous active learning.[261]

The basis for this position is that the final seed set developed under a continuous active learning environment is generally synonymous with the production set.[262] This is due to the iterative training process typically used with continuous active learning.[263] Under that process, counsel develops a preliminary seed set of documents.[264] Those documents are used to conduct the initial training of the predictive coding algorithm, which then identifies new responsive documents.[265] Those documents are subsequently added to the seed set and the algorithm is retrained

258. *Id.* at 129.

259. *Id.* at 128.

260. *Id.*

261. Bill Dimm, *The Single Seed Hypothesis*, CLUSTIFY CLUSTER-TEXT.COM BLOG (Apr. 25, 2015), http://blog.cluster-text.com/2015/04/25/the-single-seed-hypothesis/.

262. Bill Dimm, *Disclosing Seed Sets and the Illusion of Transparency*, CLUSTIFY CLUSTER-TEXT.COM BLOG (Nov. 2, 2015), http://blog.cluster-text.com/2015/11/02/disclosing-seed-sets-and-the-illusion-of-transparency/.

263. Grossman & Cormack, *supra* note 20, at 8 (defining continuous active learning as "An Iterative Training regimen in which the Training Set is repeatedly augmented by additional Documents chosen by the Machine Learning Algorithm, and coded by one or more Subject Matter Expert(s)."); *see also* Grossman, *supra* note 24, at 289–90.

264. Grossman & Cormack, *supra* note 29, at 289.

265. *Id.* at 289–90.

with the newly expanded seed documents.[266] Unlike simple training methods,[267] this process is iteratively repeated until it fails to yield new, materially responsive results.[268] The final subset of documents that the algorithm identifies and that human reviewers code as responsive—that is, the expanded seed set—is then produced in discovery.[269]

Since the nonprivileged documents from the seed set are produced in discovery, arguments over seed set transparency might be eliminated,[270] thereby lessening the importance of work-product protection. However, even assuming arguendo that continuous active learning could reduce wrangling over seed sets,[271] such a training approach—like simple learning training methods—requires an initial set of documents to begin the training process.[272] If that initial seed set is comprised of judgmental samples,[273] it should implicate the same supporting policies that weigh in favor of protecting judgmental seeds used in simple training approaches.[274] Regardless of the training approach adopted, the work-product doctrine should provide counsel with a zone of privacy in which to develop its seed set for the predictive coding process.[275]

---

266. Gareth Evans & Jennifer Rearden, *Practical Considerations in Using Predictive Coding*, N.Y. L.J. (Oct. 5, 2015), http://www.gibsondunn.com/publications/Documents/Evans-Rearden-Practical-Considerations-In-Using-Predictive-Coding-NYLJ-10-05-2015.pdf.

267. Simple training methods generally end the training process once sufficient information has been obtained to accurately estimate the probability that other unreviewed documents within the document population are relevant to the matter. That subset of unreviewed documents is then reviewed, coded for responsiveness, and (depending on its content) separated for production. *See* Grossman & Cormack, *supra* note 29, at 291–92.

268. *Id.* at 290.

269. *See* Evans & Rearden, *supra* note 272.

270. *See* Dimm, *supra* note 267.

271. While fewer disputes over seed sets would certainly be a welcome development, such a possibility is speculative until continuous active learning is more widely adopted.

272. Grossman & Cormack, *infra* note 29, at 289–90.

273. *Id.* at 298; *see* discussion *infra* The Role of Seed Sets in Predictive Coding.

274. *See* discussion *infra* Application of the *Sporck* Rule to Predictive Coding Seed Sets.

275. *Id.*

EDITORS' INTRODUCTION TO CHAPTER 10

Michael D. Berman

The Hon. Paul W. Grimm has written that "it makes little sense to go to all the bother and expense to get electronic information only to have it excluded from evidence or rejected from consideration during summary judgment because the proponent cannot lay a sufficient foundation to get it admitted. The process is complicated by the fact that ESI comes in multiple evidentiary 'flavors,' including e-mail, website ESI, internet postings, digital photographs, and computer-generated documents and data files."[1]

That observation has particular import in the context of this book. If a technology-assisted review protocol cannot be defended in court, all of the effort may go to naught.

In this chapter, the Hon. David J. Waxse and Brenda Yoakum-Kriz analyze two competing schools of thought in an area with no dispositive solution. After discussing traditional search methods, such as keywords, they define and address computer-assisted review, and a subset, predictive coding.

But the key contribution of the chapter is to address "the role of experts and whether experts who offer opinions on search methodologies are subject to Federal Rule of Evidence 702 and *Daubert* challenges." In this chapter, they correctly pose the issue as follows:

> Although the expert testimony would most likely be presented in a discovery dispute hearing before the court—rather than at trial—should the party offering testimony or affidavits by an expert addressing challenges to the ESI search methods be required to comply with Rule 702 and the Daubert standard? Does

1. Lorraine v. Markel Am. Ins. Co., 241 F.R.D. 534, 538 (D. Md. 2007).

> this mean that a party will need a "qualified" expert witness to defend its search for relevant ESI? If so, how does that advance the goals of a "just, speedy and inexpensive" determination of ESI discovery disputes?

The authors discuss the sparse case law on the topic and related topics, such as *Da Silva Moore*, *O'Keefe*, *Equity Analytics*, and *Victor Stanley*, as well as scholarly writing.

Noting the clear disagreement "about whether electronic searching of ESI should be considered an expert process subject to the requirements of Rule 702 and *Daubert*-style challenges," the authors conclude "the better view is that search methodologies such as computer-assisted review should be treated as an expert process subject to Rule 702 and *Daubert* challenges." They marshal strong arguments in support of their position.

The authors also discuss the "valid arguments for why discovery costs need not be further increased by requiring experts, who provide scientific or technical information to the court in a contested discovery matter, to be 'qualified' under Rule 702." While the editors of this book find those arguments more persuasive, and others have posited other views,[2] absent binding authority all practitioners should be aware of the issue. This chapter represents an important part of the dialog and it presents the issues clearly, fairly, and thoroughly.

2. For example, see the Foreword to this volume.

CHAPTER 10

Experts on Computer-Assisted Review: Why Federal Rule of Evidence 702 Should Apply to Their Use

David J. Waxse and Brenda Yoakum-Kriz

Introduction

Currently, judges and lawyers in federal court are struggling to provide a "just, speedy, and inexpensive determination" of litigation as required by Rule 1 of the Federal Rules of Civil Procedure.[1] A major source of the struggle is the vast volume of electronically stored information (ESI) and the need to preserve and search the discoverable portion of that data. The judicial system must determine if technology can help in that process and, if so, what legal standards apply to its use.

The increasing acceptance of technology in search methodologies, such as computer-assisted review, raises a host of new and complex issues in the e-discovery realm. One of those emerging issues is whether the standards set forth in Federal Rule of Evidence 702 and in *Daubert v. Merrell Dow Pharmaceuticals, Inc.*[2] should be applied

This chapter was first published in 57 WASHBURN L.J. 207 (2013). It is reprinted here, in modified format, with permission.

1. FED. R. CIV. P. 1.
2. Daubert v. Merrell Dow Pharm., Inc., 509 U.S. 579 (1993).

to expert witnesses who either testify before the court or otherwise provide evidence regarding a party's e-discovery search and review methodologies. This chapter examines Rule 702 and concludes that it and the *Daubert* standard should be applied to experts who testify or otherwise provide evidence before the court on discovery disputes involving these ESI search methods.

The Impact of ESI on the Discovery Obligation to Perform a Reasonable Search for Relevant Information

The defining challenge for the e-discovery age is the fact that the amount of information that can be collected, preserved, and stored—and therefore potentially available for discovery—has grown exponentially. This dramatic increase in the volume of ESI has presented new discovery challenges in preserving, managing, collecting, sorting, searching, and retrieving information. One of the most significant challenges to litigants is the skyrocketing costs associated with searching and retrieving relevant ESI.[3] As many commentators have noted, search and review of ESI are the most costly of the steps in the e-discovery process.[4] There is no dispute that the current process is failing to reach Federal Rule of Civil Procedure 1's goal of a "just, speedy, and inexpensive determination of every action and proceeding."[5] While the system seems to do fairly well in providing a

3. The Sedona Conference, *Best Practices Commentary on the Use of Search and Information Retrieval Methods in E-Discovery*, 8 Sedona Conf. J. 189, 192 (2007) [hereinafter Sedona Best Practices on Search & Information Retrieval]. The article states,

> Discovery of the relevant information gathered about a topic in dispute is at the core of the litigation process. However, the advent of 'e-discovery' is causing a rapid transformation in how that information is gathered. While discovery disputes are not new, the huge volume of available electronically stored information poses unique challenges.

Id.

4. *See generally* Nicholas M. Pace & Laura Zakaras, *Where the Money Goes: Understanding Litigant Expenditures for Producing Electronic Discovery*, RAND Corp. (2012), http://www.rand.org/content/dam/rand/pubs/monographs/2012/RAND_MG1208.pdf.

5. Fed. R. Civ. P. 1.

"just" determination, cost and delay in litigation in the United States are major problems.

Numerous conferences and articles have addressed these issues in the past few years. In 2010, the Federal Courts convened a conference at Duke University School of Law to examine these issues.[6] The consensus emanating from that conference was that cost and delay are serious problems and that the ESI discovery process is among the worst contributors to the problems.

Problems with Traditional Search and Review Processes

A number of different processes guide the search for ESI and its review for relevance and privilege. As would be expected, numerous problems are associated with some of the commonly used processes for searching and reviewing ESI.

Historically, the most commonly used discovery search process involves human reviewers looking at each item of ESI to determine whether it is relevant and, if so, whether it is privileged. One of the common misconceptions about this process is that a human "eyeballs-on" review of each and every document in a massive collection of ESI will identify essentially all responsive and privileged documents.[7] Another misconception is that computers are less reliable than humans in identifying responsive and privileged documents. The reality, in fact, is that human reviewers miss a substantial number of responsive documents and fail to determine whether the documents they find are privileged.[8] Research studies have found that computers directed and aided by humans find at least as many responsive documents as humans alone. In many cases, computers find more responsive documents, make fewer errors on responsiveness and privilege determinations, and are

---

6. 2010 Civil Litigation Conference, USCOURTS.GOV, http://www.uscourts.gov/rules-policies/records-and-archives-rules-committees/special-projects-rules-committees/2010-civil (last visited July 19, 2016).

7. Maura R. Grossman & Gordon V. Cormack, *Technology-Assisted Review in E-Discovery Can Be More Effective and More Efficient than Exhaustive Manual Review*, 17 RICH. J.L. & TECH. 11 (2011).

8. *Id.*

far more efficient than humans.[9] In addition to having questionable accuracy, human review of ESI is usually more time-consuming and expensive.

Another process widely used in searching for relevant ESI is keyword-based searches. Under this method, a computer program uses certain keywords or terms, Boolean connectors (such as "&," "or," "w/in," "but not"), or combinations of these methods to locate relevant information. Because of the sheer volume of ESI, keyword searches are frequently used to search for relevant ESI and to pare down results to a more manageable volume for further manual review. One problem with keyword searches is that they are only as good as the keywords or search terms and connectors used. As Ralph C. Losey observes in his article, *Child's Game of 'Go Fish' Is a Poor Model for E-Discovery Search*, the way lawyers often choose keywords appears to be the equivalent of the child's game of Go Fish.[10] The requesting party guesses which keywords might produce evidence to support its case without having much, if any, knowledge of the responding party's "cards" (i.e., the terminology used by the responding party's custodians). Indeed, the responding party's counsel often does not know what is in its own client's "cards."[11]

Another drawback with keyword-based searches is that they are often over-inclusive, finding responsive documents but also large proportions of irrelevant documents.[12] In other words, "keyword searches tend to produce a large proportion of false positives (i.e., documents

---

9. *Id.*

10. Ralph C. Losey, *Child's Game of "Go Fish" Is a Poor Model for E-Discovery Search*, in ADVENTURES IN ELECTRONIC DISCOVERY 204, 204 (West 2011).

11. *See id.* at 209–10.

12. Sedona Best Practices on Search & Information Retrieval, *supra* note 4, at 194. The article states,

> [A]lthough basic keyword searching techniques have been widely accepted both by courts and parties as sufficient to define the scope of their obligation to perform a search for responsive documents, the experience of many litigators is that simple keyword searching alone is inadequate in at least some discovery contexts. This is because simple keyword searches end up being both over- and under-inclusive in light of the inherent malleability and ambiguity of spoken and written English (as well as all other languages).

Id. at 201.

that are identified as potentially relevant that really are not)."[13] As a result, potentially relevant documents identified through keyword searching must usually be reviewed manually, which increases the expense and time involved to find relevant documents.

Keyword searches are also not very effective or accurate in finding relevant ESI. In a landmark 1985 study, David C. Blair and M.E. Maron found a disconnect between the legal profession's perception of its ability to find relevant documents using search terms and its actual ability to do so.[14] In Blair and Maron's study involving 40,000 documents (350,000 pages), expert paralegal searchers estimated that their manual searches had identified 75 percent of relevant documents, when in fact the results showed that only about 20 percent were found.[15] These findings were replicated at the Text Retrieval Conferences (TREC) in 2006 through 2008.[16]

Judicial decisions have often criticized manual linear review and keyword searches.[17] The Sedona Conference has also recognized the problems with these search and review processes and has a specific best-practices commentary devoted specifically to the use of search and information retrieval methods in e-discovery.[18]

---

13. Michael N. Ungar & Christopher P. Fisher, *E-Discovery Strategies and Issues in a Rapidly Changing Technology Environment, in* Ethics in E-Discovery: Leading Lawyers on Navigating Rules and Regulations and Effectively Handling Privacy Issues in the E-Discovery Process *3, (2012), *available at* WL 3058134.

14. David C. Blair & M.E. Maron, *An Evaluation of Retrieval Effectiveness for a Full-Text Document-Retrieval System*, 28 Communications of the ACM 289, 297–98 (1985).

15. *Id.*

16. TREC Legal Track, http://trec.nist.gov/overview.html (July 19, 2016), TREC is an international, interdisciplinary research project sponsored by the National Institute of Standards and Technology and U.S. Department of Defense. *Id.* The project is aimed at studying the e-discovery review process in order to evaluate the effectiveness of a wide array of search methodologies. *Id.*

17. *See generally* Da Silva Moore v. Publicis Groupe, No. 11 Civ. 1279(ALC) (AJP), 2012 WL 607412 (S.D.N.Y. Feb. 24, 2012), *aff'd.* WL 1446534 (S.D.N.Y. Apr. 26, 2012); *see also* United States v. O'Keefe, 537 F. Supp. 2d 14, 23–24 (D.D.C. 2008); Equity Analytics, LLC v. Lundin, 248 F.R.D. 331, 332, 333 (D.D.C. 2008); Victor Stanley, Inc. v. Creative Pipe, Inc., 250 F.R.D. 251, 260, 262 (D. Md. 2008).

18. Sedona Best Practices on Search & Information Retrieval, *supra* note 4, at 192.

Recognizing the numerous problems with keyword-based searches and human review—and the risk of sanctions for failing to produce relevant ESI—software vendors and e-discovery companies have developed more sophisticated technologies to automate and improve the ESI search and review process. A new search and review method that has attracted the attention of the e-discovery community is computer-assisted review, which uses computer technology to categorize an entire collection of documents as responsive or nonresponsive based on human review of only a subset of the document collection. This process or method has several different names, including computer-assisted or -aided review (CAR), technology-assisted or -aided review (TAR), intelligent review technology (IRT), predictive coding, content-based advanced analytics (CBAA), machine-aided review (MAR), and supervised or active machine learning. No name has yet emerged as the standard, most widely accepted term for the process; however, CAR will be used in this chapter.[19]

What Is Computer-Assisted Review?

Computer-assisted review is a generic term for the process of using computers and software—assisted or trained by human reviewers—to search and retrieve relevant ESI or to identify documents that should be withheld on the basis of privilege. One type of CAR is "predictive coding," which uses a computer "trained" to perform the task of searching for relevant and/or privileged ESI. The computer's software uses mathematical algorithms, issue tags, and keyword searches to predict which data is relevant and which is not.[20] The computer-automated process is guided by human reviewers and consists of "coding, organiz[ing], and prioritiz[ing] of entire sets of electronically stored information . . . according to their relation to discovery responsiveness, privilege, and designated issues before and during the legal discovery process."[21] CAR generally involves four steps:

19. For a more in-depth discussion of this issue, see generally Maura R. Grossman & Gordon V. Cormack, *The Grossman-Cormack Glossary of Technology-Assisted Review*, 7 FED. CTS. L. REV. 1 (2013).

20. UNGAR & FISHER, *supra* note 14, at *3.

21. Ben Kerschberg, *E-Discovery and the Rise of Predictive Coding*, FORBES BLOG (Mar. 23, 2011, 10:04 AM), http://www.forbes.com/sites/benkerschberg/2011/03/23/e-discovery-and-the-rise-of-predictive-coding/.

1. Coding a seed set of documents,
2. Using the seed set to train the computer to accurately identify relevant documents,
3. Using the predictive coding software to search an entire document set for relevant documents, and
4. Conducting a quality check of the results.[22]

The first step is for a group of lawyers to manually review a small sample seed set of electronic documents—such as e-mails—from a large set and to identify those within the sample that are relevant so that they can be coded. Generally, experienced and competent lawyers create the seed set because it is used to train the predictive coding software to identify other relevant ESI.[23] The computer then uses the seed set of ESI to generate another small set of potentially relevant ESI, which is then manually reviewed.[24] The result of this second manual review is fed back into the computer, which generates yet another small sample. In practice, each sample should contain a higher proportion of relevant ESI than the prior sample. After several iterations of this process, the system is "trained" to identify relevant ESI, much as a spam filter is trained to recognize spam emails. Once the seed set is complete and the computer is trained, the predictive coding software performs the remainder of the review run against the entire body of data to identify relevant ESI. The various software programs use different methods for determining relevance in order to prioritize review and for quality-control testing purposes. Some software designates relevance using a "yes" or "no," while other software programs assign numerical relevance scores.[25]

While CAR is being used as a generic term that encompasses different types of technology, substantial differences exist among vendors in how the "training set" is constructed. Some use the predictive coding approach previously discussed, while others use Knowledge Engineering (a.k.a. "Rules- Based" Approaches). These approaches seek to incorporate human knowledge into a computer system by using (1) "fuzzy

22. Adam M. Acosta, *Predictive Coding: The Beginning of a New E-Discovery Era*, 56 Res Gestae 8, Oct. 2012, *available at* Westlaw 56-OCT RESG 8.

23. A current issue in CAR is whether these lawyers should be so-called senior lawyers, as experienced and competent lawyers may or may not be "senior lawyers."

24. Acosta, *supra* note 23, at *8.

25. *Id.*

logic" to capture variations on words; (2) conceptual searching, which makes use of taxonomies and ontologies assembled by linguists; and (3) other machine learning and text mining tools that employ mathematical probabilities.[26] Artificial intelligence (AI) methods, in order to find relevant documents, then seek to construct linguistic and other models that replicate the way humans think about complex problems. Other technologies are being developed using similar concepts.

Judicial Acceptance of Computer-Assisted Review

Although there are numerous vendors willing to provide these automated search and review technologies, only a couple of courts have reported decisions approving the use of computer-assisted review.[27] The most often-cited case approving the use of predictive coding, as opposed to keyword searching for initial searches of ESI, is *Da Silva Moore v. Publicis Groupe*.[28] In *Da Silva Moore*, the parties had agreed to allow CAR but had disagreed about how best to implement the process. In his opinion, Magistrate Judge Andrew Peck explained CAR in depth and described some of the problems with other types of searches, such as linear manual searches and keyword searches.[29] He noted that, in the e-discovery area, those traditional search methods are expensive and not very effective or accurate.[30] Judge Peck concluded that:

26. Sedona Best Practices on Search & Information Retrieval, *supra* note 5, at 194.

27. *See generally In re* Actos (Pioglitazone) Prods. Liab. Litig., No. 6:11-md-2299, 2012 WL 6061973 (W.D. La. July 27, 2012); Da Silva Moore v. Publicis Groupe, No. 11 Civ. 1279 (ALC)(AJP), 2012 WL 607412 (S.D.N.Y. Feb. 24, 2012), *aff'd*, 2012 WL 1446534 (S.D.N.Y. Apr. 26, 2012); Order Granting Partial Summary Judgment, EORHB, Inc. v. HOA Holdings, LLC, No. 7409-VCL, 2012 WL 4896670 (Del. Ch. Ct. Oct. 15, 2012) [hereinafter EORHB Order]; Order Approving the Use of Predictive Coding for Discovery, Global Aerospace, Inc. v. Landow Aviation, L.P., No. CL 61040, 2012 WL 1431215 (Va. Cir. Ct. Apr. 23, 2012) [hereinafter Global Aerospace Order].

28. No. 11 Civ. 1279(ALC)(AJP), 2012 WL 607412 (S.D.N.Y. Feb. 24, 2012).

29. *Id.*

30. *Id.* at *9. Judge Peck noted,

> [l]inear manual review is simply too expensive where, as here, there are over three million emails to review. Moreover, while some lawyers still consider manual review to be the 'gold standard,' that is a myth as statistics clearly show that computerized searches are at least as accurate, if not more so, than manual review.

Id.

> [C]omputer-assisted review is an available tool and should be seriously considered for use in large-data-volume cases where it may save the producing party (or both parties) significant amounts of legal fees in document review. Counsel no longer have to worry about being the "first" or "guinea pig" for judicial acceptance of computer-assisted review. As with keywords or any other technological solution to ediscovery, counsel must design an appropriate process, including use of available technology, with appropriate quality control testing, to review and produce relevant ESI while adhering to Rule 1 and Rule 26(b)(2)(C) proportionality. Computer-assisted review now can be considered judicially-approved for use in appropriate cases.[31]

Another federal court approving the use of CAR is In re *Actos (Pioglitazone) Products Liability Litigation*.[32] In this case, the court entered a case management order entitled "Procedures and Protocols Governing the Production of Electronically Stored Information ("ESI") by the Parties."[33] That order contained a search methodology governing the parties' usage of computer- or technology-assisted review during the search and review of ESI.[34]

The only other reported decisions to date approving the use of CAR occurred in *Global Aerospace, Inc. v. Landow Aviation, L.P.*[35] and *EORHB, Inc. v. HOA Holdings, LLC*.[36] In *Global Aerospace*, CAR was used over a party's objection. Loudoun County, Virginia Circuit

31. *Id.* at *12.

32. Case Management Order: Protocol Relating to the Production of Electronically Stored Information (ESI), *In re* Actos, No. 6:11-md-2299, 2012 WL 6061973 (W.D. La. July 27, 2012), *available at* http://www.lawd.uscourts.gov/sites/default/files/UPLOADS/11-md-2299.esi.pdf. [hereinafter Actos Order].

33. *Id.*

34. *Id.*

35. Order Approving the Use of Predictive Coding for Discovery, Global Aerospace, Inc. v. Landow Aviation, L.P., No. CL 61040, 2012 WL 1431215 (Va. Cir. Ct. Apr. 23, 2012) .

36. Order Granting Partial Summary Judgment, EORHB, Inc. v. HOA Holdings, LLC, No. 7409-VCL, 2012 WL 4896670 (Del. Ch. Ct. Oct. 15, 2012).

Court Judge James H. Chamblin entered an order allowing the defendants to proceed with a form of CAR:

> [P]ursuant to Virginia Rules of Supreme Court 4:1(b) and (c) and 4:15, it is hereby ordered Defendants shall be allowed to proceed with the use of predictive coding for purposes of the processing and production of electronically stored information, with processing to be completed with[in] 60 days and production to follow as soon as practicable and in no more than 60 days.

This is without prejudice to a receiving party raising with the court an issue as to completeness or the contents of the [production] or the ongoing use of predictive coding.[37]

In *EORHB*, Vice Chancellor J. Travis Laster in Delaware Chancery Court verbally ordered both sides to use predictive coding and to use the same vendor.[38] This order is interesting because apparently neither side had requested predictive coding.[39]

As lawyers and their clients become more familiar with CAR, more courts are likely to be faced with and asked to resolve parties' disputes regarding these increasingly sophisticated search and review methodologies. Resolving these disputes will likely require the use of experts to help the court understand the technology involved in order to make informed decisions on CAR and other sophisticated e-discovery search methodologies.

Ramifications of Increased Usage of Computer-Assisted Review and Other Technologically Complex Search Methodologies

One issue that arises with the increasing usage and growing judicial acceptance of computer-assisted review and other technologically advanced search methodologies is the role of experts and whether experts who offer opinions on search methodologies are subject to Federal Rule of Evidence 702 and *Daubert* challenges. Although the expert testimony

37. Global Aerospace Order, *supra* note 29.
38. EORHB Order, *supra* note 29.
39. *Id.*

would most likely be presented in a discovery dispute hearing before the court—rather than at trial—should the party offering testimony or affidavits by an expert addressing challenges to the ESI search methods be required to comply with Rule 702 and the *Daubert* standard? Does this mean that a party will need a "qualified" expert witness to defend its search for relevant ESI? If so, how does that advance the goals of a "just, speedy and inexpensive" determination of ESI discovery disputes?

In *Daubert v. Merrell Dow Pharmaceuticals, Inc.*,[40] the U.S. Supreme Court imposed a special obligation on trial judges to "ensure that any and all scientific testimony . . . is not only relevant, but reliable."[41] Along with the responsibility of acting as gatekeepers to exclude unreliable expert testimony, the Court in *Kumho Tire Co. v. Carmichael*[42] clarified that this gatekeeper function applies to all expert testimony, not just testimony based in science.[43] This gatekeeper function is embodied in Rule 702.

Rule 702 permits a witness—who is qualified as an expert by knowledge, skill, experience, training, or education—to testify in the form of an opinion or otherwise if:

(a) the expert's scientific, technical, or other specialized knowledge will help the trier of fact to understand the evidence or to determine a fact in issue;
(b) the testimony is based on sufficient facts or data;
(c) the testimony is the product of reliable principles and methods; and
(d) the expert has reliably applied the principles and methods to the facts of the case.[44]

In addition to the requirements of Rule 702, *Daubert* sets forth other factors for a trial court to use in assessing the reliability of scientific expert testimony. The specific factors include:

1. Whether the expert's technique or theory can be or has been tested—that is, whether the expert's theory can be challenged

40. Daubert v. Merrell Dow Pharm., Inc., 509 U.S. 579 (1993).
41. *Id.* at 589.
42. Kumho Tire Co. v. Carmichael, 526 U.S. 137 (1999).
43. *Id.* at 147.
44. Fed. R. Evid. 702.

in some objective sense, or whether it is instead simply a subjective, conclusory approach that cannot reasonably be assessed for reliability;

2. Whether the technique or theory has been subject to peer review and publication;
3. The known or potential rate of error of the technique or theory when applied;
4. The existence and maintenance of standards and controls; and
5. Whether the technique or theory has been generally accepted in the scientific community.[45]

Only a few cases have mentioned—and even fewer have comprehensively addressed—the standards that should govern the court's evaluation of scientific or technical information provided to resolve a contested discovery matter. In *Da Silva Moore*, the first judicial opinion recognizing that CAR is an acceptable way to search for relevant ESI in appropriate cases, the plaintiffs argued that acceptance of predictive coding protocol "is contrary to Federal Rule of Evidence 702" and "violates the gatekeeping function underlying Rule 702."[46] Judge Peck concluded that Rule 702 and *Daubert* are rules for admissibility of evidence at trial and therefore are not applicable to discovery search methods.

Federal Rule of Evidence 702 and the Supreme Court's *Daubert* decision deal with the trial court's role as gatekeeper to exclude unreliable expert testimony from being submitted to the jury at trial. It is a rule for admissibility of evidence at trial.

If [defendant] sought to have its expert testify at trial and introduce the results of its ESI protocol into evidence, *Daubert* and Rule 702 would apply. Here, in contrast, the tens of thousands of emails that will be produced in discovery are not being offered into evidence at trial as the result of a scientific process or otherwise. The admissibility of specific emails at trial will depend upon each email itself (for example, whether it is hearsay, or a business record or party admission), not how it was found during discovery.[47]

45. *Daubert*, 509 U.S. at 593–94.

46. Da Silva Moore v. Publicis Groupe, No. 11 Civ. 1279(ALC)(AJP), 2012 WL 607412 (S.D.N.Y. Feb. 24, 2012), *aff'd*, 2012 WL 1446534 *7 (S.D.N.Y. Apr. 26, 2012).

47. *Id.* (internal citations omitted).

Although Judge Peck concluded in his *Da Silva Moore* opinion that "Rule 702 and Daubert simply are not applicable to how documents are searched for and found in discovery,"[48] other federal courts have required evidence on keyword-based search methodologies to satisfy the requirements of Rule 702.

In *United States v. O'Keefe*,[49] for example, the defendant challenged the electronic search protocols used by the government to locate all information in its possession, custody, or control related to the indictment charging that he expedited visa requests in exchange for gifts.[50] Magistrate Judge John M. Facciola began by observing that whether search terms or keywords used to locate relevant information will yield the information sought is a "complicated question involving the interplay, at least, of the sciences of computer technology, statistics and linguistics."[51] Given this complexity, Judge Facciola reasoned that analyzing whether a certain search term or terms would be more likely to produce information than the terms that were used is "truly to go where angels fear to tread."[52] Judge Facciola ruled that if the defendants were going to contend that the search terms used by the government were insufficient, they would have to specifically so contend in a motion to compel and "their contention must be based on evidence that meets the requirements of Rule 702 of the Federal Rules of Evidence."[53]

Furthermore, in a civil case raising similar challenges to the adequacy of keyword searches, *Equity Analytics, LLC v. Lundin*,[54] Judge Facciola expanded his prior *O'Keefe* opinion in commenting that "determining whether a particular search methodology, such as keywords, will or will not be effective certainly requires knowledge beyond the ken of a lay person (and a lay lawyer) and requires expert testimony that meets the requirements of Rule 702 of the Federal

48. *Id.*

49. 537 F. Supp. 2d 14 (D.D.C. 2008).

50. *Id.* at 22.

51. *Id.* at 24.

52. *Id.* Judge Facciola noted that "[t]his topic is clearly beyond the ken of a layman and requires that any such conclusion be based on evidence that, for example, meets the criteria of Rule 702 of the Federal Rules of Evidence." *Id.*

53. *Id.*

54. 248 F.R.D. 331 (D.D.C. 2008).

Rules of Evidence."[55] Thus, Judge Facciola required the plaintiff to submit an affidavit from its expert explaining why the limitations proposed were unlikely to capture all the information sought; the impact, if any, of the loading of the new operating system upon defendant's computer; and the data that was on it before the new operating system was loaded.[56] The expert's affidavit was also to describe in detail how the search would be conducted.[57]

In his 2011 article *Search, Forward: Will Manual Document Review and Keyword Searches Be Replaced by Computer-Assisted Coding?,* Judge Peck distinguishes Judge Facciola's *O'Keefe* and *Equity Analytics* opinions as involving keyword searches and explains his opinion that Rule 702 and *Daubert* would not apply to experts offered to provide testimony on CAR.

> In addition to reluctance to be the guinea pig for a decision on predictive coding, lawyers perhaps are concerned that they will have to go through a *Daubert* hearing as to the "admissibility" of the results of predictive coding. Perhaps this fear comes from *O'Keefe*, where Judge Facciola said that opining on what keyword is better "is truly to go where angels fear to tread," and is a topic "beyond the ken of a layman and requires that any such conclusion be based on evidence that, for example, meets the criteria of Rule 702 of the Federal Rules of Evidence," dealing with expert opinions.
>
> Lawyers' fears in this regard seem largely misplaced. First, Facciola's comments were directed at keywords, but everyone is using keywords, and I know of no decision after *O'Keefe* requiring expert testimony as to the use of keywords.
>
> Second, with due respect to Facciola, I do not think *Daubert* applies—it applies when an expert will testify at trial in order to admit into evidence opinions

55. *Id.* at 333.
56. *Id.*
57. *Id.* at 334–35.

> or results (e.g., the result of DNA testing reveals a match).
>
> Here, the hundreds of thousands of e-mails produced are not being offered into evidence at trial as the result of a scientific process. Rather, whether the handful of e-mails offered as trial exhibits is admissible is dependent on the document itself (e.g., whether it is a party admission or a business record), not how it was found during discovery.
>
> That said, if the use of predictive coding is challenged in a case before me, I will want to know what was done and why that produced defensible results. I may be less interested in the science behind the "black box" of the vendor's software than in whether it produced responsive documents with reasonably high recall and high precision.
>
> That may mean allowing the requesting party to see the documents that were used to train the computer-assisted coding system. (Counsel would not be required to explain why they coded documents as responsive or non-responsive, just what the coding was.) Proof of a valid "process," including quality control testing, also will be important.[58]

In *Victor Stanley, Inc. v. Creative Pipe, Inc.*,[59] Judge Paul Grimm weighed in with his view on the issue.[60] In a lengthy footnote, he made it clear that he agreed with Judge Facciola's "self-evident observation" that challenges to search and review methods, such as keyword-based searches, involve technical and scientific subjects. And a lawyer's ipse dixit pronouncements about the party's search and review method—without any supporting affidavit or without any other showing that the search method was effective for its intended purpose—are of little

58. Andrew Peck, *Search, Forward: Will Manual Document Review and Keyword Searches Be Replaced by Computer-Assisted Coding?*, L. Tech. News (ALM Media Props., New York, N.Y.), Oct. 2011, at 2.

59. 250 F.R.D. 251 (D. Md. 2008).

60. *Id.* at 260–61 n.10. Judge Grimm was a magistrate judge at the time of this decision but on December 3, 2012, was confirmed as a district judge.

value to a court ruling upon a discovery dispute where one party is seeking to compel or prevent a more comprehensive ESI search.[61]

Judge Grimm also responded to critics of Judge Facciola's *O'Keefe* and *Equity Analytics* opinions who expressed concerns that these opinions engrafted Rule 702 into discovery with unintended consequences.

> Certainly those concerned about the *O'Keefe* and *Equity Analytics* opinions would not argue that trial judges are not required to make fact determinations during discovery practice. Indeed, such fact determinations inundate them. For example, deciding whether ESI discovery is not reasonably accessible because of undue burden or cost (Fed. R. Civ. P. 26(b)(2)(B)) involves factual determinations, as does determining whether discovery sought is too expensive or burdensome under Fed. R. Civ. P. 26(b)(2)(C); determining whether sanctions should be imposed for failing to preserve ESI or if the loss was a result of the routine, good faith operation of an electronic information system under Fed. R. Civ. P. 37(e); or determining whether documents withheld from disclosure are privileged or protected. Certainly the court is entitled to reliable factual information on which to make such rulings. It cannot credibly be denied that resolving contested issues of whether a particular search and information retrieval method was appropriate—in the context of a motion to compel or motion for protective order—involves scientific, technical or specialized information. If so, then the trial judge must decide a method's appropriateness with the benefit of information from some reliable source—whether an affidavit from a qualified expert, a learned treatise, or, if appropriate, from information judicially noticed. To suggest otherwise is to condemn the trial court

61. *Id.*

> to making difficult decisions on inadequate information, which cannot be an outcome that anyone would advocate.
>
> . . . .
>
> Viewed in its proper context, all that O'Keefe and Equity Analytics required was that the parties be prepared to back up their positions with respect to a dispute involving the appropriateness of ESI search and information retrieval methodology—obviously an area of science or technology—with reliable information from someone with the qualifications to provide helpful opinions, not conclusory argument by counsel.[62]

Judge Grimm rationalized in *Victor Stanley* that requiring expert witness testimony on ESI discovery search methodologies to be "qualified" under Rule 702 served the goal of the Rule to "set standards to determine whether information is 'helpful' to those who must make factual determinations involving disputed areas of science, technology or other specialized information."[63] Because Rule 702 is one of common sense and reason, he argued, "opinions regarding specialized, scientific or technical matters are not 'helpful' unless someone with proper qualifications and adequate supporting facts provided such an opinion after following reliable methodology."[64] He did not find the common sense criteria contained in rules of evidence rather than the rules of civil procedure to be off-limits for consideration during discovery.[65] He referred to summary judgment practice in Federal Rule of Civil Procedure 56(e), which requires that the parties support their motions with "such facts as would be admissible in evidence," as an example where courts look to the Federal Rules of Evidence for assistance when resolving fact disputes in civil cases.[66]

The message Judge Grimm wanted lawyers to take away from *O'Keefe*, *Equity Analytics*, and *Victor Stanley* was that when parties

62. *Id.*
63. *Id.*
64. *Id.*
65. *Id.*
66. *Id.*

decide to use a particular ESI search and review methodology, they need to be aware of literature describing the strengths and weaknesses of various methodologies and select the one that they believe is most appropriate for its intended task. If this selection is challenged and brought before the court, then parties advocating a particular ESI search or retrieval methodology "should expect to support their position with affidavits or other equivalent information from persons with the requisite qualifications and experience, based on sufficient facts or data and using reliable principles or methodology."[67]

The *O'Keefe, Equity Analytics*, and *Victor Stanley* decisions are not alone in characterizing a party's ESI search and review method as a process that must be defended as an expert process.[68] The Sedona Conference's Practice Point 7 related to Search and Information Retrieval Methods advises that a party be prepared to describe and to defend its specific ESI search and review method. Practice Point 7 provides that "[p]arties should expect that their choice of search methodology will need to be explained, either formally or informally, in subsequent legal contexts (including in depositions, evidentiary proceedings, and trials)."[69] It further advises that:

> Counsel should be prepared to explain what keywords, search protocols, and alternative search methods were used to generate a set of documents, including ones made subject to subsequent manual searches for responsiveness and privilege. This explanation may best come from a technical "IT" expert, a statistician, or an expert in search and retrieval technology. Counsel must be prepared to answer questions, and indeed, to prove the reasonableness and good faith of their methods.[70]

Commentators have also argued that lawyers should be prepared to explain what keywords, search protocols, and alternative search methods were used to generate a set of documents. Donald Wochna,

67. *Id.*

68. Donald Wochna, *Electronic Data, Electronic Searching, Inadvertent Production of Privileged Data: A Perfect Storm*, 43 AKRON L. REV. 847, 865 (2010).

69. Sedona Best Practices on Search & Information Retrieval, *supra* note 5, at 195.

70. *Id.* at 212.

in his article *Electronic Data, Electronic Searching, Inadvertent Production of Privileged Data: A Perfect Storm*, suggests that this explanation should come from a technical "IT" expert, a statistician, or an expert in search and review technology and that lawyers should be prepared to answer questions and prove the reasonableness and good faith of their ESI search methods.[71] He additionally comments that "[c]haracterizing electronic searching as an expert process subjects the search to analysis and challenges, requires the search process be defended, and triggers significant implications for attorney issues related to malpractice."[72]

Why Federal Rule of Evidence 702 and the *Daubert* Standard Should Be Applied to Experts Presenting Evidence on ESI Search and Review Methodologies

Clearly there is disagreement about whether electronic searching of ESI should be considered an expert process subject to the requirements of Rule 702 and *Daubert*-style challenges. Based upon the various arguments in support or against each position, the better view is that search methodologies such as computer-assisted review should be treated as an expert process subject to Rule 702 and *Daubert* challenges.

First, the Federal Rules of Evidence are clear that they apply to civil proceedings held before a magistrate judge, such as a contested discovery hearing, and that there is no exception for discovery hearings.[73] Furthermore, Federal Rule of Evidence 1101(a) provides that the Federal Rules of Evidence apply to proceedings before U.S. district courts, as well as U.S. bankruptcy and magistrate judges. They also apply in "civil cases and proceedings."[74] Federal Rule of Evidence 1101(d), however, also sets out the specific proceedings in which the Federal Rules of Evidence do not apply. Discovery hearings are not on the list of exempted proceedings. Nor does any language in Rule 702

71. Wochna, *supra* note 70, at 865.

72. *Id.*

73. Fed. R. Evid. 1101.

74. *Id.* R. 1101(b).

limit its applicability to trial testimony by experts or exempt testimony by expert witnesses offered for discovery-related purposes.[75]

Second, multiple policies are best served by treating search methodologies, such as CAR, as an expert process subject to Rule 702 and *Daubert* challenges. It advances the purpose of the Federal Rules of Evidence to "administer every proceeding fairly, eliminate unjustifiable expense and delay, and promote the development of evidence law, to the end of ascertaining the truth and securing a just determination."[76] In addition, it will help the court understand the scientific or technical evidence being presented to resolve the e-discovery dispute. Thus, it will facilitate more educated decisions by the court, as well as promote confidence in those decisions as being based upon qualified experts. As Judge Grimm noted in *Victor Stanley*, the court should not ignore a purported ESI expert's lack of qualifications if the party opposing his opinion demonstrates that shortcoming.[77] Nor should the court accept expert opinions shown to be unsupported by sufficient facts or based on demonstrably unreliable methodology. Requiring parties to demonstrate that their experts, who are testifying or providing affidavits, are qualified to make the opinions offered provides a standard for scientific and technical evidence presented at discovery hearings on disputed ESI search and review issues. This requirement will ultimately give courts a mechanism to evaluate the reliability of the expert testimony being offered.

One fear associated with requiring experts who provide scientific or technical information to the court in a contested discovery matter to comply with Rule 702 is that the costs of discovery will increase. In *Victor Stanley*, Judge Grimm responded to critics who expressed these concerns.[78] He pointed out that the cost-benefit factors of Federal Rule of Civil Procedure 26(b)(2)(C) apply to all aspects of discovery.[79] Judge Grimm noted that parties worried about the cost of employing properly designed search and information retrieval methods have an incentive to keep the costs of this phase of discovery as

---

75. *See id.* R. 702.

76. *Id.* R. 102.

77. Victor Stanley, Inc. v. Creative Pipe, Inc., 250 F.R.D. 251, 260–61 n.10 (D. Md. 2008).

78. *Id.*

79. *Id.*

low as possible, including attempting to confer with their opposing party in an effort to identify a mutually agreeable search and review method. In addition, Judge Grimm was optimistic that the study and testing of search and information retrieval methodologies will result in identifying those that are most effective and least expensive to employ for a variety of ESI discovery tasks.[80]

Judge Grimm makes valid arguments for why discovery costs need not be further increased by requiring experts, who provide scientific or technical information to the court in a contested discovery matter, to be "qualified" under Rule 702. Requiring ESI search and review methodologies to be an expert process subject to the requirements of Rule 702 and *Daubert*-style challenges does not necessarily mean that every party with ESI will be required to hire a "qualified" expert. Rather, Rule 702-qualified experts will only be needed when the parties cannot work out their ESI search disputes cooperatively and need the court to decide the dispute. Even if there are additional costs for "qualified" experts, these costs may be offset by switching to CAR and other more automated search and review methodologies. Ultimately, the cost savings will result from fewer discovery battles because the parties and their counsel will have more confidence and trust—built and fostered by "qualified" experts—that the ESI search and review processes utilized will find the relevant ESI within a degree of reasonable certainty.

Importance of Cooperation in E-Discovery

The importance of cooperation in the age of e-discovery cannot be overstated, especially given the increasing technical knowledge needed to understand ESI search and review methodology. The parties can realize significant benefits in terms of cost savings and satisfaction resulting from a case being resolved on the merits—either by the court, a mediator, or the parties. As Practice Point 6 of The Sedona Conference's *Best Practices Commentary on the Use of Search & Information Retrieval Methods in E-Discovery* suggests, the parties should make "a good faith attempt to collaborate on the use of particular search

80. *See id.* at 261 n.10.

and information retrieval methods, tools and protocols (including as to keywords, concepts, and other types of search parameters)."[81]

Courts are recognizing the importance of a cooperative discovery approach in computer-assisted review. In *Kleen Products LLC v. Packaging Corp. of America*,[82] the plaintiff criticized the defendants' use of a Boolean method to identify responsive documents.[83] The plaintiff requested that the defendants use "content-based advanced analytics (CBAA) technology analytics to conduct natural language, subject matter searches across corporate departments or corporate functions, using content-based search technology rather than keywords."[84] Magistrate Judge Nan Nolan, after two days of evidentiary hearings on the ESI search dispute issue, as well as 11 status hearings and Rule 16 conferences, convinced the parties that cooperation was a better approach to resolving those issues.

> In pursuing a collaborative approach, some lessons have been learned. First, the approach should be started early in the case. It is difficult or impossible to unwind procedures that have already been implemented. Second, in multiple party cases represented by separate counsel, it may be beneficial for liaisons to be assigned to each party. Finally, to the extent possible, discovery phases should be discussed and agreed to at the onset of discovery.[85]

Her opinion outlined the agreements that had been reached and what efforts had been undertaken to reach those agreements. In the Stipulation and Order Relating to ESI Search that was entered, the plaintiffs ultimately withdrew their demand that the defendants apply CBAA to certain documents.[86] The plaintiffs also agreed to not argue or contend that the defendants should be required to use the types of

---

81. Sedona Best Practices on Search & Information Retrieval, *supra* note 5, at 195 (emphasis added).

82. No. 10 C 5711, 2012 WL 4498465 (N.D. Ill. Sept. 28, 2012).

83. *Id.* at *4.

84. *Id.* (internal quotations omitted).

85. *Id.* at *19.

86. *Id.* at *20.

CBAA or "predictive coding" methodology and technology that were proposed by the plaintiffs with respect to certain discovery requests.[87]

The ESI protocol case management order entered by the court in the case *In re Actos (Pioglitazone) Products Liability Litigation* is also filled with instructions to the parties to cooperate.[88] The governance order repeatedly emphasized that the parties were to collaborate throughout the technology-assisted (TAR) process and required them to meet and confer prior to contacting the court for a resolution.[89] It specifically ordered the parties to "agree to meet and confer regarding the use of advanced analytics" as a "document identification mechanism for the review and production of . . . data."[90] The parties were also ordered to meet and confer in order to select four key custodians whose e-mail would be used to create an initial sample set, after which three experts would train the TAR system to score every document based on relevance.[91] To quell the fears of computer-assisted review skeptics, the court's order required both parties to collaborate for purposes of training the system.[92]

As the courts wisely recognized in both *Kleen* and *Actos*, cooperation plays an important role in e-discovery and specifically in CAR procedures. Cooperation will help the parties gain confidence in both their own and the opposing party's process and ability to identify all—or an acceptable percentage—of the relevant ESI. It will also reduce expenses by preventing costly and time-consuming discovery disputes around e-discovery.

Conclusion

One of the emerging issues of increasingly sophisticated ESI search methodologies such as CAR is what standards apply to determine if an expert witness provides evidence on disputed issues. The best way to resolve this issue is to cooperate with your adversary and reach

87. *Id.*
88. Actos Order, *supra* note 33.
89. *Id.*
90. *Id.*
91. *Id.*
92. *Id.*

an agreement on which search methodology to use. However, when cooperation efforts fail and a discovery dispute is brought before the court for resolution, should the court require these expert witnesses to comply with the standards set forth in Federal Rule of Evidence 702 and *Daubert*?

This chapter argues that Rule 702 and the *Daubert* standard should be applied to experts with technical expertise or knowledge pertinent to a party's ESI search and review methodologies and who provide the court with evidence on discovery disputes involving these methods. Making sure courts can rely on appropriately-qualified experts in making informed decisions on CAR and other ESI search and review methodologies will ultimately advance the goals of a "just, speedy, and inexpensive determination of every action and proceeding."[93]

93. FED. R. CIV. P. 1.

EDITORS' INTRODUCTION TO CHAPTER 11

Michael D. Berman

Ralph Losey provides a two-step process to cull irrelevant data prior to expensive linear review. His basic thesis is that Big Data provides "an opportunity for lawyers" because "the truth is almost always out there." He then notes that "[y]ou just have to find it," and provides a sound methodology for doing so, using a two-filter approach. "Think of the first filter as a rough, coarse filter, and the second filter as fine-grained."

The first filter occurs in connection with collection. At the outset, the author addresses when the use of keywords at this stage may be appropriate—and when it is not. "The obvious danger of keyword filtering is that important documents may not have the keywords. Since they will not even be placed in the review platform, you will never know that the relevant ESI was missed."

As an alternative, the author suggests multimodal culling. "Use your own judgment to mix and match the right kind of culling tools for the particular case and data encountered." This may involve custodian selection, date range delimiters, and many other tools, such as similarity searches, and file size and file type analysis.

The second filter is predictive coding, although the author also provides alternatives, using keyword, concept, and similarity searches. "[T]he basic idea behind the two-filter method is to start with a very large pool of documents, reduce the size by a coarse first filter, then reduce it again by a much finer second filter."

The author describes an actual case in which review speed was 35,000 files per hour at a cost of $0.07 per document. The author notes: "There is much more to efficient, effective review than just using software with predictive coding features. The methodology of how you do the review is critical." This chapter describes that methodology in detail.

CHAPTER 11

License to Cull: Two-Filter Document Culling Method That Uses Predictive Coding and Other Search Tools[1]

Ralph C. Losey

Every attorney has a James Bond-like "license to cull" irrelevant data before beginning expensive linear review. It is part of their proportionality duties to protect their clients and our justice system from waste and abuse. This chapter describes the two-filter culling method that relies heavily on predictive coding for the second filter.[2] The method is designed for use *before* commencing a detailed document-by-document attorney review. In my experience, any large-scale document review project can be enhanced by this double-cull method. It not only helps to reduce costs, it also maximizes recall, allowing an attorney to quickly and efficiently find virtually all of the documents proportionally needed for a case. You can of course use the second

1. This chapter is a revised and updated version of an article originally published on the e-Discovery Team blog on February 1, 2015.

2. For related articles, see R. Losey, *Introducing "ei-Recall"—A New Gold Standard for Recall Calculations in Legal Search—Part Three* (e-DiscoveryTeam, 2015), https://e-discoveryteam.com/2015/01/18/introducing-ei-recall-a-new-gold-standard-for-recall-calculations-in-legal-search-part-three/ (last visited July 17, 2016).

I also describe this process at R. Losey, *Electronic Discovery Best Practices* website, EDBP.com, which outlines my views on the best practices for lawyers doing e-discovery.

filter, predictive coding, without first cleaning out obvious irrelevant files in the first filter, but the predictive coding does not work as well. Or in the case of non-text graphic files, does not work at all, since predictive coding is a text analytics system. Careful use of a first filter based on multimodal search can increase the efficacy of your predictive coding efforts.

FIGURE 11.1 Two-filter culling

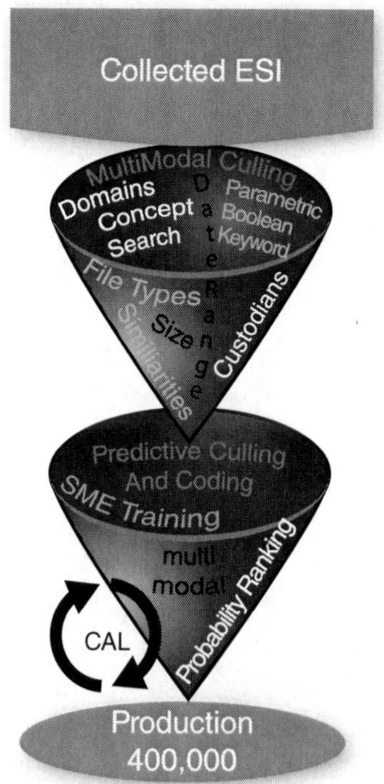

Introduction

The two-filter culling method includes the well-known technology processes of "deduplication" and "deNisting" in the first filter. (Note: I always do full *horizontal* deduplication across all custodians.) Deduplication and deNisting are, however, just technical engineering filters, not based on legal analysis or judgment. They are well-established industry standards.[3]

Many lawyers new to the e-discovery space think that deNisting and deduplication are the end-all of ESI culling, but that is far from true. They are just the beginning. The other methods described here all require legal judgment, and so you cannot just hire an e-discovery vendor to do it, as you can with deduplication and deNisting. Legal judgment is critical to all effective document review, including culling of obvious and highly probable irrelevant documents before lawyers spend their valuable time in review. In my opinion, all legal review teams should employ some type of two-filter culling component.

My 35-plus years of experience as a practicing lawyer have shown me that the most reliable way for the "magic of justice" to happen is by finding the key documents. You find "the truth, the whole truth, and nothing but the truth," when you find the key documents needed to complete the picture of what happened and keep witnesses honest. In today's information-flooded world, that can only happen if you use technology in a strategic manner to find relevant evidence quickly and inexpensively. The two-filter method makes it easier to do that.

This chapter contains a lengthy description of document culling, but still is not complete. Methods vary to adapt to the data and changing technologies. I share these methods to try to help all attorneys control the costs of document review and find the information needed to do justice. All too often these costs spiral out of control, or the review is done so poorly that key documents are not found. Both scenarios are obviously bad for our system of justice. We need cases to be decided on the merits, on the facts.[4]

---

3. For further information on deduplication, see EDRM definition found at http://www.edrm.net/resources/glossaries/glossary/d/de-duplication (last visited Mar. 3, 2016). For further information on deNisting, see *What Does DeNIST Mean and Why Should You Care?, available at* https://percipient.co/denist-mean-care/ (last visited Mar. 3, 2016).

4. Hopefully a more tech-savvy Bar can stem the tide of over-settlement that we have seen in the profession since the explosion of data began in the 1990s. In my view, all too often cases are now decided on the basis of settlement value, not the merits. Also in my view, as it now stands, way too many questionable cases are filed hoping

Many times it turns out that judges and juries are never given the chance to do their job. The cases all settle out instead. As a result *only 1 percent* of federal civil cases actually go to trial. This is a big loss for society, and for the "trial lawyers" in our profession, a group I once prided myself to be a part. Now I just focus on getting the facts from big data, to help keep the witnesses honest, and cases decided on the true facts, the evidence. Then I turn it over to the trial lawyers in my firm. They are then armed with the truth, the key documents, good or bad. The trial lawyers then put the best face possible on these facts, which hopefully is handsome to begin with. They argue how the law applies to these facts to seek a fair and just result for our clients. The disputed issues of fact are also argued, but based on the evaluation of the meaning of the key documents and the witness testimony.

That is, in my opinion, how our system of justice is supposed to operate. It is certainly the way our legal system functioned when I learned to practice law and had my first trials back in 1980. Back then we only had a few thousand files to cull through to find the key documents, perhaps tens of thousands in a big case. Now we have hundreds of thousands of documents to cull through, millions in a big case. Still, even though the data volumes are far greater today, with the two-filter method described here, the few key documents needed to decide a case can be found.

The Promise of Big Data

Big data today presents an opportunity for lawyers. There are electronic writings everywhere and data can be hard to destroy. The large amount of ESI floating in cyberspace means that the truth is almost always out there. You just have to find it. There is so much data that it is much more likely for key documents to exist than ever before. The *digital trails* that people leave today are much bigger than the *paper trails* of old.

The fact that more truth is out there than ever before gives tech-savvy lawyers a great advantage. They have a much better chance than lawyers in the past ever did to find the documents needed to keep witnesses honest, or put more politely, to help refresh their memory. The

---

there will be some kind of payout. These cases tend to drown out the few with merit. Judges are overwhelmed and often do not have the time needed to get down to the nitty-gritty details of the truth.

flood of information can in this way improve the quality of justice. It all depends on our ability to find the truth from the massive quantities of irrelevant information available.

The more advanced culling methods described here, primarily the ones in the second filter that use predictive coding and artificial intelligence (AI)-enhanced document ranking methods, are especially effective in culling the chaff from the wheat in big data cases. I expect this kind of predictive analytics software to keep on improving. For that reason I am confident that we will continue to be able to find the core kernels of truth needed to do justice, no matter how much data we generate and save.

Some Software Is Far Better than Others

One word of warning, although these culling methods are software agnostic, in order to emulate the two-filter method, your document review software must have certain basic capabilities. They include effective, and easy, bulk coding features for the first filter. This is the multimodal broad-based culling. Some of the multiple methods do not require software features, just attorney judgment, such as excluding custodians, but others do require software features, like domain searches or similarity searches. If your software does not have the features that will be discussed here for the first filter, then you probably should switch right away, but, for most, that will not be a problem. The multimodal culling methods used in the first filter are, for the most part, pretty basic.

Some of the software features needed to implement the second filter, are, however, more advanced. The second filter works best when using predictive coding and probability ranking. You review the various strata of the ranked documents. The second filter can still be used with other, less advanced multimodal methods, that is, keywords. Moreover, even when you use bona fide active machine learning software features, you continue to use a smattering of other multimodal search methods in the second filter. But now you do so not to cull, but to help find relevant and highly relevant documents to improve training. I do not rely on probability searches alone, although sometimes in the second filter I rely almost entirely on predictive coding based searches to continue the training.

If you are using software without AI-enhanced active learning features, then you are forced to only use other multimodal methods, such as keywords, in the second filter. Warning, true active learning features are *not* present in most review software, or are very weak. That is true even with software that claims to have predictive coding features, but really just has dressed-up *passive learning*, that is, concept searches with latent semantic indexing. You handicap yourself, and your client, by continuing to use such less expensive programs. Good software, like everything else, does not come cheap, but should pay for itself many times over if used correctly. The same comment goes for lawyers too.

First Filter—Keyword Collection Culling

Some first stage filtering takes place as part of the ESI collection process. The documents are preserved, but not collected nor ingested into the review database. The most popular collection filter as of 2016 is still keyword, even though this is very risky in some cases and inappropriate in many. Typically such keyword filtering is driven by vendor costs to avoid processing and hosting charges.

Some types of collection filtering are appropriate and necessary, for instance, in the case of custodian filters, where you broadly preserve the ESI of many custodians, just in case, but only collect and review a few of them. It is, however, often *inappropriate* to use keywords to filter out the collection of ESI from admittedly key custodians. This is a situation where an attorney determines that a custodian's data needs to be reviewed for relevant evidence, but does not want to incur the expense to have all of their ESI ingested into the review database. For that reason they decide to only review data that contains certain keywords.

I am not a fan of keyword filtered collections. The obvious danger of keyword filtering is that important documents may not have the keywords. Since they will not even be placed in the review platform, you will never know that the relevant ESI was missed. You have no chance of finding them. This is discussed in William Webber's analysis of the *Biomet* case where this kind of keyword filtering was used before predictive coding began.[5] Webber shows that in *Biomet* this method first

5. W. Webber, *What Is the Maximum Recall in Re Biomet?*, EVALUATING E-DISCOVERY BLOG (Apr. 24, 2013), http://blog.codalism.com/index.php/what-is-the

FIGURE 11.2 First filter—Multimodal culling

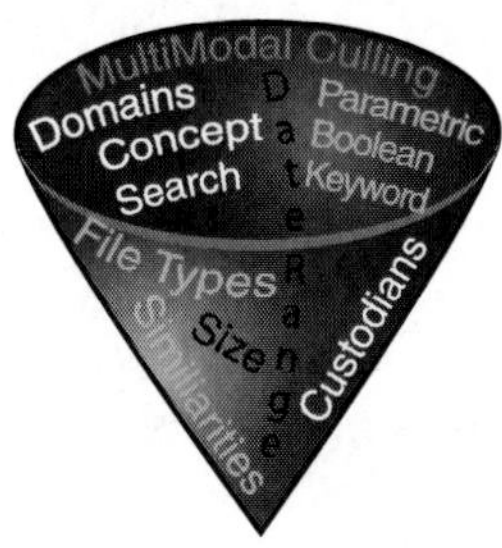

filtered out over 40 percent of the relevant documents. This doomed the second filter predictive coding review to a maximum possible recall of 60 percent, even if was perfect, meaning it would otherwise have attained 100 percent recall, which never happens. The *Biomet* case very clearly shows the dangers of over-reliance on keyword filtering.

Nevertheless, *sometimes* keyword collection may work, and may be appropriate. In some simple disputes, and with some data collections, obvious keywords may work just fine to unlock the truth. For instance, sometimes the use of names is an effective method to identify all, or almost all, documents that may be relevant. This is especially true in smaller and simpler cases. This method can, for instance, often work in employment cases, especially where unusual names are involved. It becomes an even more effective method when the keywords have been tested. I just love it, for instance, when the plaintiff's name is something like the famous Mister Mxyzptlk in Superman comics.

In some cases keyword collections may be as risky as in the complex *Biomet* case, but may still be necessary because of the proportionality constraints of the case. The law does not require unreasonably excessive search and review, and what is reasonable in a particular case depends on the facts of the case, including its value.[6] Sometimes you have to try for rough justice with the facts that you can afford to find given the budgetary constraints of the case.

The danger of missing evidence is magnified when the keywords are selected on the basis of educated guesses or just limited research.

-maximum-recall-in-re-biomet/ (last visited Feb. 26, 2016).

6. *See* R. Losey, *Predictive Coding and Proportionality: A Marriage Made in Heaven,* 26 Regent U. L. Rev. 1 (2013–14).

This "technique," if you can call it that, is, sadly, still the dominant method used by lawyers today to come up with keywords. I have long thought it is equivalent to a child's game of Go Fish.[7] If keywords are dreamed up like that, as mere educated guesses, then keyword filtering is a high-risk method of culling out irrelevant data. There is a significant danger that it will exclude many important documents that do not happen to contain the selected keywords. No matter how good your predictive coding may be after that, you will never find these key documents.

If the keywords are not based on a mere guessing, but are instead *tested,* then it becomes a real technique that is less risky for culling. But how do you test possible keywords without first collecting and ingesting all of the documents to determine which are effective? It is the cart before the horse problem.

One partial answer is that you could ask the witnesses, and do some *partial reviews* before collection. Testing and witness interviews are required by Judge Andrew Peck's famous "wake-up call" case.[8] I recommend that opinion often, as many attorneys still need to *wake up* about how to do e-discovery. They need to add ESI use, storage, and keyword questions to their usual new case witness interviews.

Interviews do help, but there is nothing better than actual hands on reading and testing of the documents. This is what I like to call *getting your hands dirty in the digital mud* of the actual ESI collected. Only then will you know for sure the best way to mass-filter out documents. For that reason my strong preference in all significant size cases is to collect in bulk, and *not* filter out by keywords. Once you have documents in the database, *then* you can then effectively screen them *out* by using parametric Boolean keyword techniques.

By the way, "parametric" is just a reference to the various parameters of a computer file that all good software allows you to search. You could search the text and all metadata fields, the entire document. Or you could limit your search to various metadata fields,

---

7. R. Losey, *Child's Game of "Go Fish" Is a Poor Model for e-Discovery Search*, E-Discovery Team Blog, http://e-discoveryteam.com/2009/10/04/childs-game-of-go-fish-is-a-poor-model-for-e-discovery-search/ (last visited Feb. 26, 2016).

8. William A. Gross Constr. Assocs., Inc. v. Am. Mfrs. Mut. Ins. Co., 256 F.R.D. 134, 134, 136 (S.D.N.Y. 2009).

such as date, prepared by, or the *to and from* in an e-mail. Everyone knows what Boolean means, but you may not know all of the many variations that your particular software offers to create highly customized searches. While predictive coding may be beyond the grasp of most vendors and case managers, the intricacies of keyword search are not. They can be a good source of information on keyword methods.

First Filter—Date Range and Custodian Culling

Even when you collect in bulk, and do not keyword filter before you put custodian ESI in the review database, in most cases you should filter for date range and custodian. It is often possible for an attorney to know, for instance, that no e-mails before or after a certain date could possibly be relevant. That is often not a highly speculative guessing game. It is reasonable to filter on this time-line basis before the ESI goes in the database. Whenever possible, try to get agreement on date range screening from the requesting party. You may have to widen it a little, but it is worth the effort to establish a line of communication and begin a cooperative dialogue.

The second thing to talk about is *which custodians* you are going to include in the database. You may put 50 custodians on hold, and actually collect the ESI of 25, but that does not mean you have to load all 25 into the database for review. Here your interviews and knowledge of the case should allow you to know who the key, key custodians are. You rank them by your evaluation of the likely importance of the data they hold to the facts disputed in the case. Maybe, for instance, in your evaluation you only need to review the mailboxes of ten of the 25 collected.

Again, disclose and try to work that out. The requesting party can reserve rights to ask for more; that is fine. They rarely do after production has been made, especially if you were careful and picked the right ten to start with, and if you were careful during review to drop and add custodians based on what you see. If you are using predictive coding in the second-filter stage, the addition or deletion of data mid-course is still possible with most software. It should be robust enough to handle such mid-course corrections. It may just slow down the ranking for a few iterations, that's all.

First Filter—Other Multimodal Culling

There are many other bulk coding techniques that can be used in the first-filter stage. This is not intended to be an exhaustive search. Like all complex tasks in the law, simple "black letter" rules are for amateurs. The law, which mirrors the real world, does not work like that. The same holds true for legal search. There may be many *Gilbert's* for search books and articles, but they are just 1L types guides. For true legal search professionals they are mere starting points. Use my culling advice here in the same manner. Use your own judgment to mix and match the right kind of culling tools for the particular case and data encountered. Every project is slightly different, even in the world of repeat litigation, like employment law disputes where I currently spend much of my time.

High-quality legal search is at core a heuristic activity, but one that should be informed by science and technology. Although e-discovery teams should be led by attorneys skilled in evidence discovery, in appropriate cases they should include scientists and engineers in some way. Effective team leaders should be able to understand and communicate with technology experts and information scientists. That does not mean all e-discovery lawyers need to become engineers and scientists too. That effort would likely diminish your legal skills based on the time demands involved. It just means you should know enough to work with these experts. That includes the ability to see through the vendor sales propaganda, and to incorporate the knowledge of the bona fide experts into your legal work.

One culling method that many overlook is file size. Some collections have thousands of very small files, just a few bits, that are nothing but backgrounds, tiny images, or just plain empty space. They are too small to have any relevant information. Still, you need to be cautious and look out for very small e-mails, for instance, ones that just say "yes." Depending on context it could be relevant and important. But for most other types of very small files, there is little risk. You can go ahead and bulk code them irrelevant and filter them out.

Even more subtle is filtering out files based on their being very large. Sort your files by size, and then look at both ends, small and big. They may reveal certain files and file types that could not possibly be relevant. There is one more characteristic of big files that you should consider. Many of them have millions of lines of text. Big files can be confusing to machine learning, especially when, as typical, only a few lines of the text are relevant, and the rest are just noise. That is another reason to filter them out, perhaps not entirely, but for special treatment and review outside of predictive coding. In other projects where you have many large files like that, and you need the help of AI ranking, you may want to hold them in reserve. You may only want to throw them into the ranking mix *after* your AI algorithms have acquired a pretty good idea of what you are looking for. A maturely trained system is better able to handle big noisy files.

File type is a well-known and often highly effective method to exclude large numbers of files of a same type after only looking at a few of them. For instance, there may be database files automatically generated, all of the same type. You look at a few to verify these databases could not possibly be relevant to your case, and then you bulk code them all irrelevant. There are many types of files like that in some data sets. The first filter is all about being a smart gatekeeper.

File type is also used to eliminate, or at least divert, non-text files, such as audio files or most graphics. Since most second filter culling is going to be based on text analytics of some kind, there is no point for anything other than files with text to go into that filter. In some cases, and some datasets, this may mean bulk coding them all irrelevant. This might happen, for instance, where you know that no music or other audio files, including voice messages, could possibly be relevant. We also see this commonly where we know that photographs and other images could not possibly be relevant. Exclude them from the review database.

You must, however, be careful with all such gatekeeper activities, and never do bulk coding without some judgmental sampling first. Large unknown data collections can always contain a few unexpected surprises, no matter how many document reviews you have done before. Be cautious. Look before you leap. Skim a few of the ESI file types you are about to bulk code as irrelevant.

This directive applies to all first-filter activities. Never do it blind on just logic or principle alone. Get your hands in the digital mud. Do not over-delegate all of the dirty work to others. Do not rely too much on your contract review lawyers and vendors, especially when it comes to search. Look at the documents yourself and do not just rely on high-level summaries. Every real trial lawyer knows the importance of that. *The devil is always in the details.* This is especially true when you are doing judgmental search. The client wants your judgment, not that of a less qualified associate, paralegal, or contract review lawyer. Good lawyers remain hands-on, to some extent. They know the details, but are also comfortable with appropriate delegation to trained team members.

There is a constant danger of too much delegation in big data review. The lawyer signing the Rule 26(g) statement has a legal and ethical duty to closely supervise document review done in response to a request for production. That means you cannot just hire a vendor to do that, although you can hire outside counsel with special expertise in the field.

Some non-text file types will need to be diverted for different treatment than the rest of your text-based dataset. For instance, some of the best review software allows you to keyword search audio files. It is based on phonetics and wave forms. Kroll Ontrack, has, for instance, had that feature since 2007. In some cases you will have to carefully review the image files, or at least certain kinds of them. Sorting based on file size and custodian can often speed up that exercise.

Remember the goal is always efficiency, and caution, but not over cautious. The more experienced you get the better you become at evaluating risks and knowing where you can safely take chances to bulk code, and where you cannot. Another thing to remember is that many image files have text in them too, such as in the metadata, or in ASCII transmissions. They are usually not important and do not provide good training for second stage predictive coding.

Text can also be hidden in dead Tiff files, which are just images, if they have not been OCR'ed. Scanned document Tiffs, for instance, may very well be relevant and deserve special treatment, including full manual review, but they may not show in your review tool as text, because they have never been OCR text recognized.

Concept searches have only rarely been of great value to me, but should still be tried out. Some software has better capacities with concepts and latent semantic indexing than others. You may find it to be a helpful way to find groupings of obviously irrelevant, or relevant documents. If nothing else, you can always learn something about your dataset from these kinds of searches.

Similarity searches of all kinds are among my favorite. If you find some files groups that cannot be relevant, find more like that. They are probably bulk irrelevant (or relevant) too. A similarity search, such as find every document that is 90 percent or more the same as this one, is often a good way to enlarge your carve outs and thus safely improve your efficiency.

Another favorite of mine is "domain culling" of e-mail. It is kind of like a spam filter. That is a great way to catch the junk mail, newsletters, and other purveyors of general mail that cannot possibly be relevant to your case. I have never seen a mail collection that did not have dozens of domains that could be eliminated. You can sometimes cull-out as much as 10 percent of your collection that way, sometimes more when you start diving down into senders with otherwise safe domains. A good example of this is the IT department with their constant mass mailings, reminders, and warnings. Many departments are guilty of this, and after examining a few, it is usually safe to bulk code them all irrelevant.

Second Filter—Predictive Culling and Coding

The second filter begins where the first leaves off. The ESI has already been purged of unwanted custodians, date ranges, spam, and other obvious irrelevant files and file types. Think of the first filter as a rough, coarse filter, and the second filter as fine-grained. The second filter requires a much deeper dive into file contents to cull out

FIGURE 11.3 Second-filter culling methods

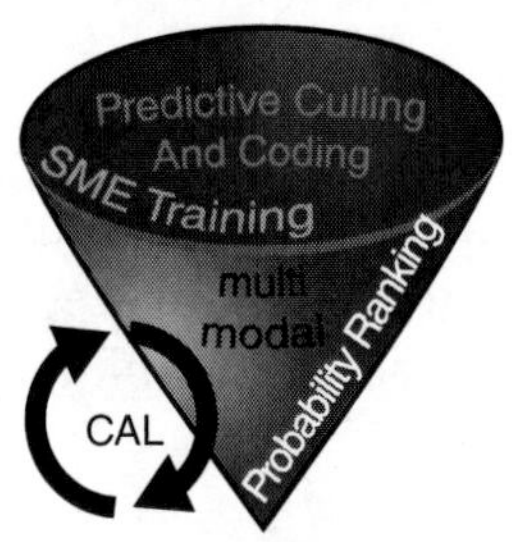

irrelevance. The most effective way to do that is to use predictive coding, by which I mean active machine learning, supplemented somewhat by using a variety of methods to find good training documents. That is what I call a multimodal approach that places primary reliance on the Artificial Intelligence at the top of the search pyramid. If you do not have an active machine learning type of predictive coding with ranking abilities, you can still do fine-grained second-level filtering, but it will be harder, and probably less effective and more expensive.

All kinds of second-filter search methods should be used to find highly relevant and relevant documents for AI training. Stay away from any process that uses just one search method, even if the one method is predictive ranking. Stay *far away* if the *one method* is rolling dice. Reliance on random chance alone has been proven to be an inefficient and ineffective way to select training documents.[9]

The first round of training begins with the documents reviewed and coded relevant incidental to the first-filter coding. You may also want to defer the first round until you have done more active searches for relevant and highly relevant from the pool remaining *after* first-filter culling. In that case you also include *irrelevant* in the first training round, which is also important. Note that even though the first round of training is the only round of training that has a special name—seed set—there is nothing all that important or special about it. All rounds of training are important.

There is so much misunderstanding about that, and seed sets, that I no longer like to even use the term. The only thing special in my mind about the first round of training is that it is sometimes a very *large* training set. That happens when the first filter turns up a large amount of relevant files, or they are otherwise known and coded before the second filter training begins. The sheer volume of training documents in many first rounds thus makes it special, not the fact that it came first.

No good predictive coding software is going to give special significance to a training document just because it came first in time. The software I use has no trouble at all disregarding any early training if it later finds that it is inconsistent with the total training input. It

9. See Chapter 5 in this volume.

is, admittedly, somewhat aggravating to have a machine tell you that your earlier coding was wrong. But I would rather have an emotionless machine tell me that, than another gloating attorney (or judge), especially when the computer is correct, which is often (not always) the case.

That is, after all, the whole point of using good software with artificial intelligence. You do that to *enhance* your own abilities. There is no way I could attain the level of recall I have been able to manage lately in large document review projects by reliance on my own, limited intelligence alone. That is another one of my search and review secrets. Get help from a higher intelligence, even if you have to create it yourself by following proper training protocols.

Irrelevant Training Documents Are Important Too

In the second filter you are on a search for the gold, the highly relevant, and, to a lesser extent, the strong and merely relevant. As part of this second-filter search you will naturally come upon many irrelevant documents too. Some of these documents should also be added to the training. If you judge a document, then go ahead and code it and let the computer know your judgment. That is how it learns. There are some documents that you judge that you may not want to train on—such as the very large, or very odd—but they are few and far between.

Of course, if you have culled out a document altogether in the first filter, you do not need to code it, because these documents will not be part of the documents included in the second filter. In other words, they will not be among the documents ranked in predictive coding. The will either be excluded from possible production altogether as irrelevant, or will be diverted to a nonpredictive coding track for final determinations. The latter is the case for non-text-file types like graphics and audio in cases where they might have relevant information.

How to Do Second-Filter Culling Without Predictive Ranking

When you have software with active machine learning features that allow you to do predictive ranking, then you find documents for training, and from that point forward you incorporate ranking searches into your review. If you do not have such features, you still sort out documents in the second filter for manual review, you just do not use ranking with SAL and CAL to do so. Instead, you rely on keyword selections, enhanced with concept searches and similarity searches, including e-mail string and family searches.

When you find an effective parametric Boolean keyword combination, which is often done by a process of party negotiation, then testing, educated guessing, trial and error, and judgmental sampling, then you submit the documents containing proven hits to full manual review. Ranking by keywords can also be tried for document batching, but be careful of large files having many keyword hits just on the basis of file size, not relevance. Some software compensates for that, but most do not. So ranking by keywords can be a risky process.

I am not going to go into detail on the old fashioned ways of batching out documents for manual review. Most e-discovery lawyers already have a good idea of how to do that. So, too, do most vendors. Just one word of advice: when you start the manual review based on keyword or other nonpredictive coding processes, check in daily with the contract reviewer work and calculate what kind of precision the various keyword and other assignment folders are creating. If it is terrible, which I would say is less than 50 percent precision, then I suggest you try to improve the selection matrix. Change the Boolean, or keywords, or something. Do not just keep plodding ahead and wasting client money.

I once took over a review project that was using negotiated, then tested and modified, keywords. After two days of manual review we realized that only 2 percent of the documents selected for review by this method were relevant. After I came in and spent three days with training to add predictive ranking we were able to increase that to over 80 percent precision. If you use these multimodal methods, you can expect similar results.

Review of Basic Idea of Two-Filter Search and Review

Whether you use predictive ranking or not, the basic idea behind the two-filter method is to start with a very large pool of documents, reduce the size by a coarse first filter, then reduce it again by a much finer second filter. The result should be a much, much smaller pool that is human-reviewed, and an even smaller pool that is actually produced or logged. Of course, some of the documents subject to the final human review may be overturned, that is, found to be irrelevant, false positives. That means they will not make it to the very bottom production pool after manual review in the diagram right.

In multimodal projects where predictive coding is used the precision rates can often be very high. Lately I have been seeing that the second pool of documents, subject to the manual review has precision rates of at least 80 percent, sometimes even as high as 95 percent near the end of a continuous active learning, or CAL, project. That means the final pool of documents produced is almost as large as the pool after the second filter.

Please remember that almost every document that is manually reviewed and coded after the second filter gets recycled back into the machine-training process. This is known as continuous active learning, or CAL, and in my version of it at least, is multimodal and not limited to only high probability ranking searches.[10] In some projects you may just train for multiple iterations and then stop training and transition to pure manual review, but in most you will want to continue training as you do manual review. Thus you set up a CAL constant feedback loop until you are done, or nearly done, with manual review.

As mentioned, active machine learning trains on both relevance and irrelevance. Although, in my opinion, the documents found that are Highly Relevant, the hot documents, are the most important of all for training purposes. The idea is to use predictive coding to segregate your data into two separate camps, relevant and irrelevant. You not only separate them, but you also rank them according to probable relevance. The software I normally use has a percentage system from 0.01 to 99.9 percent probable relevant and visa versa. A very good segregation-ranking project should end up looking like an upside down champagne glass.

A near perfect segregation-ranking project will end up looking like an upside down T with even fewer documents in the unsure middle

10. See Chapter 5 in this volume.

FIGURE 11.4 Document ranking—Vertical

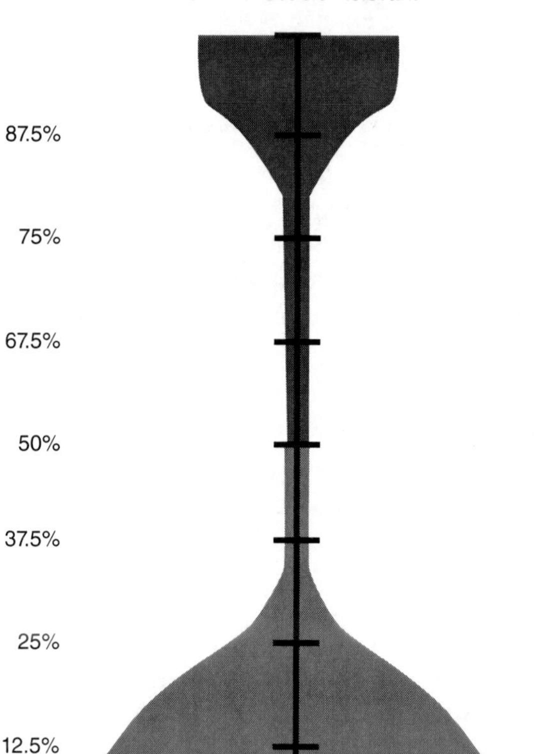

section. If you turn the graphic so that the lowest probability relevant ranked documents are on the left, and the highest probable relevant on the right, a near perfect project ranking looks like this standard bar graph.

Figure 11.5 is a screen shot from a recent project I did using Kroll Ontrack's *EDR* software after training was complete. This project had about a 4 percent prevalence of relevant documents, so it made sense for the relevant half to be far smaller. But what is striking about the data stratification is how polarized the groupings are. This means the ranking distribution separation, relevant and irrelevant, is very well formed.

FIGURE 11.5 EDR screen shot—Document ranking horizontal

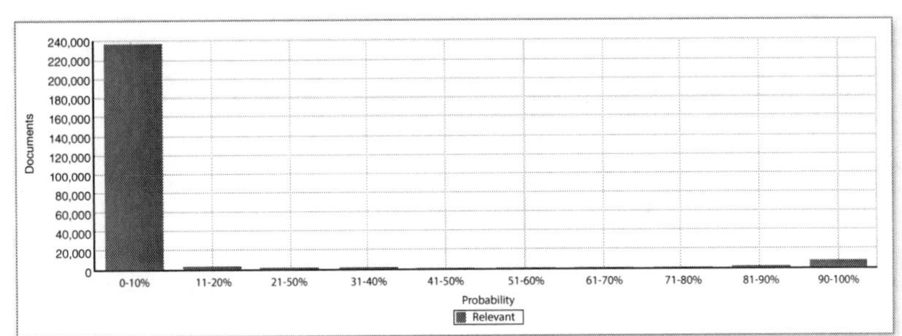

There are an extremely small number of documents where the AI is unsure of classification. The slow curving shape of irrelevant probability on the left (or the bottom of my upside down champagne glass) is gone.

The visualization shows a much clearer and complete ranking at work. The AI is much more certain about what documents are irrelevant. Figure 11.6 is a screenshot of the table form display in EDR of this same project in 5 percent increments. It shows the exact *numerics* of the probability distribution in place when the machine training was completed. This is one of the most pronounced polar separations I have ever seen, which shows that my training on relevancy was well understood by the machine.

After you have segregated the document collection into two groups, and gone as far as you can, or as far as your budget allows, then you cull out the probable irrelevant and review the rest. The most

FIGURE 11.6 EDR screen shot—Document ranking

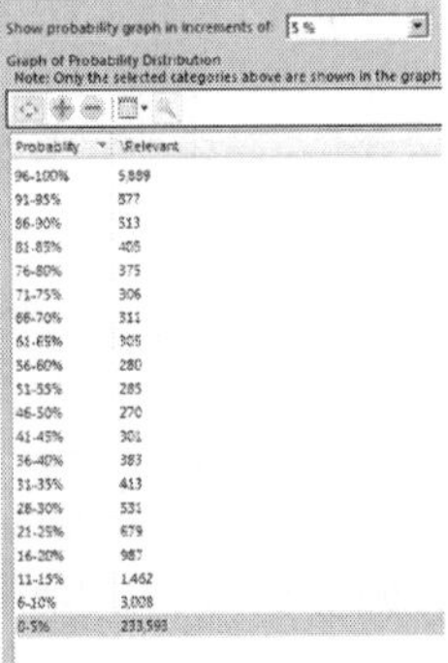
Show probability graph in increments of: 5 %

Graph of Probability Distribution
Note: Only the selected categories above are shown in the graph

Probability	Relevant
96-100%	5,899
91-95%	577
86-90%	513
81-85%	405
76-80%	375
71-75%	306
66-70%	311
61-65%	305
56-60%	280
51-55%	285
46-50%	270
41-45%	301
36-40%	383
31-35%	413
26-30%	531
21-25%	679
16-20%	987
11-15%	1,462
6-10%	3,008
0-5%	233,593

logical place for the second-filter cut-off point in most projects in the 49.9 percent, and less, probable relevant. They are the documents that are more likely than not to be irrelevant. But do not take the 50 percent plus dividing line as an absolute rule in every case. There are no hard and fast rules to predictive culling. In some cases you may have to cut off at 90 percent probable relevant. Much depends on the overall distribution of the rankings and the proportionality constraints of the case. Like I said before, if you are looking for *Gilbert's* black-letter law solutions to legal search, you are in the wrong type of law.

Almost all of the documents in the production set will typically be reviewed by a lawyer or paralegal. Of course, there are shortcuts to that too, like duplicate and near-duplicate syncing. Some of the documents in the irrelevant low ranked documents will have been reviewed too. That is all part of the CAL process where both relevant and irrelevant documents are used in training. If all goes well, however, only a very small number of the low percentage probable relevant documents will be reviewed.

Limiting Final Manual Review

In some cases you can, with client permission (often *insistence*), dispense with attorney review of *all or near all* of the documents in the upper half. You might, for instance, stop after the manual review has attained a well-defined and stable ranking structure. You might, for instance, only have reviewed 10 percent of the probable relevant documents, but decide to produce the other 90 percent of the probable relevant documents without attorney eyes ever looking at them. There are, of course, obvious problems with privilege and confidentiality to such a strategy. Still, in some cases, where appropriate clawback and other confidentiality orders are in place, the client may want to risk disclosure of secrets to save the costs of final manual review.

In such productions there are also dangers of imprecision where a significant percentage of irrelevant documents are included. This in turn raises concerns that an adversarial view of the other documents could engender other suits, even if there is some agreement for return of irrelevant documents. Once the bell has been rung, privileged or not, it cannot be un-rung.

For these reasons the practice of production without review is rarely, if ever, done today in litigated matters.

Case Example of Production with No Final Manual Review

In spite of the dangers of the un-ringable bell, the allure of extreme cost savings can be strong to some clients in some cases. For instance, I did one experiment using multimodal CAL with no final review at all, where I still attained fairly high recall, and the cost per document was only $0.07, using a billable hour rate of $500. I did all of the review myself acting as the sole subject-matter expert (SME). The visualization of this project would look like Figure 11.7.

FIGURE 11.7 Project example of culling

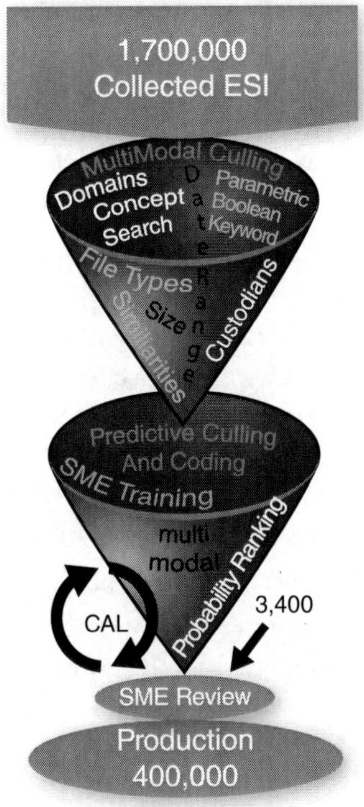

Note that if the SME review pool were drawn to scale according to number of documents read, then, in most cases, it would be much smaller than shown. In the review where I brought the cost down to $0.07 per document I started with a document pool of about 1.7 million, and ended with a production of about 400,000. The SME review pool in the middle was only 3,400 documents.

As far as legal search projects go it was an unusually high prevalence, and thus the production of 400,000 documents was very large. Four hundred thousand was the number of documents ranked with a 50 percent or higher probable prevalence when I stopped the training. I only personally reviewed about 3,400 documents during the SME review. I then went on to review another 1,745 documents after I decided to stop training, but did so only for quality assurance purposes by using a random sample. To be clear, I worked alone, and no one other than me reviewed any documents. This was a rare army-of-one-type project.

Although I only personally reviewed 3,400 documents for training, I actually instructed the machine to train on many more documents than that. I just selected them for training without actually reviewing them first. I did so on the basis of ranking and judgmental sampling of the ranked categories. It was somewhat risky, but it did speed up the process considerably, and in the end worked out very well.

My goal in this project was recall, not precision, nor even F_1, and I was careful not to over-train on irrelevance.[11] The requesting party was much more concerned with recall than precision, especially since the relevancy standard here was so loose. (Precision was still important, and was attained too. Indeed, there were no complaints about that.) In situations like that the slight over-inclusion of relevant training documents is not terribly risky, especially if you check out your decisions with careful judgmental sampling, and quasi-random sampling.

I accomplished this review in two weeks, spending 65 hours on the project. Interestingly, my time broke down into 46 hours of actual document review time, plus another 19 hours of analysis. Yes, about

11. For an explanation of the terms "recall," "precision," and "F_1," see Chapters 12, 13, and the Appendix.

one hour of *thinking and measuring* for every two and a half hours of review. If you want a simple *secret* of my success, that is it.

I stopped after 65 hours, and two weeks of calendar time, primarily because I ran out of time. I had a deadline to meet and I met it. I am not sure how much longer I would have had to continue the training before the training fully stabilized in the traditional sense. I doubt it would have been more than another two or three rounds; four or five more rounds at most.

Typically I have the luxury to keep training in a large project like this until I no longer find any significant new relevant document types, and do not see any significant changes in document rankings. I did not think at the time that my culling out of irrelevant documents had been ideal, but I was confident it was good, and certainly reasonable I saw a slow down in probability shifts, and thought I was *close* to the end.

I had completed a total of 16 rounds of training by that time. I think I could have improved the recall somewhat had I done a few more rounds of training, and spent more time looking at the mid-ranked documents (40 to 60 percent probable relevant). The precision would have improved somewhat too, but I did not have the time. I am also sure I could have improved the identification of privileged documents, as I had only trained for that in the last three rounds. (It would have been a partial waste of time to do that training from the beginning.)

The sampling I did after the decision to stop suggested that I had exceeded my recall goals, but still, the project was much more rushed than I would have liked. I was also comforted by the fact that the elusion sample test at the end passed my "accept on zero error" quality assurance test.[12] I did not find any hot documents. For those reasons (plus great weariness with the whole project), I decided *not* to pull some all-nighters to run a few more rounds of training. Instead, I went ahead and completed my report, added more analysis, and made my production with a few hours to spare.

A scientist hired after the production did some post hoc testing that confirmed an approximate 95 percent confidence level recall achievement of between 83 to 94 percent. My army-of-one work also

12. See my essays on *ei-Recall* for further elaboration this test, which can be found on my education website, https://zeroerrornumerics.com.

did very well in all subsequent challenges. I am not at liberty to disclose further details.

In post hoc analysis I found that the probability distribution was close to the ideal shape that I now know to look for. Figure 11.8 represents an approximate depiction of the ranking distribution of the 1.7 million documents at the end of the project.

The 400,000 documents produced (obviously I am rounding off all these numbers) were 50 percent plus, and 1,300,000 not produced were less than 50 percent. Of the 1,300,000 negatives, 480,000 documents were ranked with only 1 percent or less probable relevance. On the other end, the high side, 245,000 documents had a probable relevance ranking of 99 percent or more. There were another 155,000 documents with a ranking between 99 and 50 percent probable relevant. Finally, there were 820,000 documents ranked between 49 and 01 percent probable relevant.

FIGURE 11.8 Project example of culling with detailed document counts

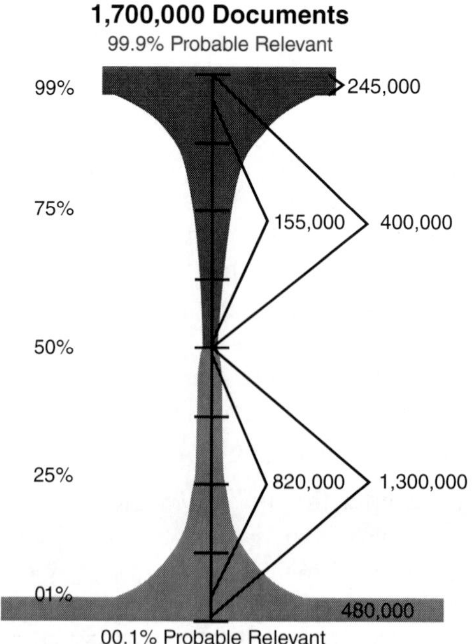

The file review speed here realized of about 35,000 files per hour, and extremely low cost of about $0.07 per document, would not have been possible without the client's agreement to forego full document review of the 400,000 documents produced. A group of contract lawyers could have been brought in for second pass review, but that would have greatly increased the cost, even assuming a billing rate for them of only $50 per hour, which was one-tenth my rate at the time.

The client here was comfortable with reliance on confidentiality agreements for reasons that I cannot disclose. In most cases litigants are not, and insist on "eyes-on review" of every document produced. I well understand this, and in today's harsh world of hard ball litigation it is usually prudent to do so, clawback or no.

Another reason the review was so cheap and fast in this project is because there were very little opposing counsel transactional costs involved, and everyone was hands off. I just did my thing, on my own, and with no interference. I did not have to talk to anybody; just read a few guidance memorandums. My task was to find the relevant documents, make the production, and prepare a detailed report—41 pages—that described my review. Someone else prepared a privilege log for the 2,500 documents withheld on the basis of privilege.

I am proud of what I was able to accomplish with the two-filter multimodal methods, especially as it was subject to the mentioned post-review analysis and recall validation. But, as mentioned, I would not want to do it again. Working alone like that was very challenging and demanding. I prefer teamwork. Further, it was only possible at all because I happened to be a subject-matter expert (SME) of the type of legal dispute involved. There are only a few fields where I am competent to act alone as a SME. In most matters, the SME assigned to a case is not also an experienced ESI searcher and software power user. In fact, most legal SMEs are technophobes.

Even if I have adequate SME abilities on a legal dispute, I now prefer to do a small team approach, rather than a solo approach. I prefer to have one of two attorneys assisting me on the document reading, and a couple more assisting me as SMEs. There is no reason for me to be involved as a SME at all. I can also lead the project with delegation to others as to what is relevant. That is not uncommon. I just work as the software and methodology expert.

Recently I worked on a project where I did not even speak the language used in most of the documents. I could not read most of them, even if I tried. I just worked on procedure and numbers alone. Others on the team got their "hands in the digital mud" and reported to me and the SMEs. This works fine if you have good bilingual SMEs and contract reviewers doing most of the hands-on work.

Conclusion

There is much more to efficient, effective review than just using software with predictive coding features. The methodology of *how* you do the review is critical. The two-filter method described here has been used for years to cull away irrelevant documents before manual review, but it has typically just been used with keywords. This method can now be employed in a multimodal manner that includes predictive coding in the second filter.

Keywords can be an effective method to both cull out presumptively irrelevant files, and cull in presumptively relevant, but keywords are only one method among many. In most projects it is not even the most effective method. AI-enhanced review with predictive coding is usually a much more powerful method to cull out the irrelevant and cull in the relevant and highly relevant.

If you are using a one-filter method, where you just do a rough cut and filter out by keywords, date, and custodians, and then manually review the rest, you are reviewing *too much*. It is especially ineffective when you collect based on keywords. As shown in *Biomet*, that can doom you to low recall, no matter how good your later predictive coding may be.

If you are using a two-filter method, but are not using predictive coding in the second filter, you are still reviewing too much. The two-filter method is far more effective when you use relevance probability ranking to cull out documents from final manual review.

INFORMATION RETRIEVAL PERSPECTIVES; E-DISCOVERY STANDARDS

EDITORS' INTRODUCTION TO CHAPTER 12

Michael D. Berman

H. G. Wells wrote: "Statistical thinking will one day be as necessary for efficient citizenship as the ability to read and write."[1] The American Statistical Association defines "statistics" as "the science of learning from data, and of measuring, controlling, and communicating uncertainty; and it thereby provides the navigation essential for controlling the course of scientific and societal advances."[2] We have all heard a weather forecast that the probability of rain is 40 percent. Does that mean it will rain 40 percent of the time? Or over 40 percent of the area?[3] In fact, it is the product of a pretty complex formula.

> [M]ost of the time, the forecaster is expressing a combination of degree of confidence and areal coverage. If the forecaster is only 50% sure that precipitation will occur, and expects that, if it does occur, it will produce measurable rain over about 80 percent of the area, the PoP (chance of rain) is 40%. (PoP = .5 × .8 which equals .4 or 40%.)[4]

What does that have to do with predictive coding and e-discovery? David Lewis explains that quantitative, statistical measures are important tools in achieving, ensuring, and demonstrating a high-quality and cost-effective review. They are used to both manage the process and justify the results. He explains, for example, the lawyer's role in

---

1. D. Huff, How to Lie with Statistics (1954).

2. American Statistical Association, http://www.amstat.org/careers/whatisstatistics.cfm (last visited Sept. 19, 2015), citing (M. Davidian & T. A. Louis, *available* at 10.1126/science.1218685).

3. *See* National Weather Service Forecast Office, *Explaining "Probability of Precipitation*," http://www.srh.noaa.gov/ffc/?n = pop (last visited Sept. 19, 2015).

4. *Id.*

making the tradeoff between different measures to suit the needs of the case.

While litigation counsel likely will never calculate recall, precision, a false positive rate, elusion, or the harmonic mean, Lewis demystifies those measures and other calculations with simple examples. He also applies them to the tensions in the litigation process. For example, a producing party may have less interest in the level of recall than in high precision, in order to reduce its review costs. While a requesting party may desire high recall because it has the tools to mitigate low precision. Lewis also points to the fact that pre-screening of the corpus or the treatment of e-mail threads may skew the statistics. Because, as Lewis notes, classification decisions are evaluated differently if based on the individual messages versus at the level of threads; an attorney negotiating a discovery protocol may want to be aware of that. These are concepts that litigation counsel needs to know in a Rule 26(f) conference of the parties.

Lewis also states that statistics cannot be the only tool: "[S]tatistical evaluation is just one tool among many, including good judgment and a watchful eye."

CHAPTER 12
Defining and Estimating Effectiveness in Document Review

David D. Lewis, PhD

Introduction

The ability to evaluate how well a review process is finding documents of interest is valuable in both managing that process and justifying its results to potentially skeptical parties and courts. Both the review as a whole, as well as its components or stages, can be evaluated. This chapter discusses techniques that provide quantitative, statistical measures of the effectiveness of the results of a review process.

"Quantitative" here means simply that the techniques associate numbers with some aspect of the review process. "Statistical" refers to the fact that one typically cannot afford to determine the exact values of the desired measures, but must estimate those values from samples. "Effectiveness" refers to how well the process has found documents of interest as opposed to, for instance, what the cost of the process was. Finally, the techniques discussed in this chapter focus on the *results* of a review process at a particular point in time rather than, say, whether a particular protocol was followed in generating those results. The techniques discussed in this chapter are, therefore, only one of several tools that a team might use in achieving, and assuring themselves of, a high quality review. Chapter 14 in this volume, by Hedin, Brassil, and Jones, provides a helpful overview of the broader range of such tools.[1]

Statistical estimation of effectiveness in e-discovery has gained attention through its use as part of technology-assisted review (TAR) processes, and in particular in processes that use supervised machine learning. In supervised learning, often referred to as "predictive coding" in e-discovery, experts train software by providing examples of particular types of documents (e.g., responsive and nonresponsive documents). The software in turn builds a statistical model that enables it to detect responsive documents to some degree.

Effectiveness estimates can aid in making a variety of decisions during the predictive coding process. These include how much and what kinds of training to do, where a cutoff should be chosen on document scores or ranks, and whether the quality of the final results is acceptable. Chapter 13 by Webber and Oard considers at length the role of effectiveness estimates in predictive coding processes.[2]

The close linking of statistical evaluation with predictive coding is, however, a historical accident. The same evaluation techniques can and have been used as part of all types of document reviews, including purely manual ones and ones using Boolean queries on text content (so-called keyword queries). Indeed, estimation of effectiveness is ubiquitous in all areas of information retrieval. One of the great lessons of information retrieval research has been the striking variability of effectiveness found when applying the same method to superficially similar tasks. This variation in difficulty at finding documents for different information needs (even on the same collection of documents) is often far greater than the variation in effectiveness among different information retrieval algorithms.[3]

---

1. Bruce Hedin, Dan Brassil, & Amanda Jones, Chapter 14, *On the Place of Measurement in E-Discovery.*

2. William Webber & Douglas W. Oard, Chapter 13, *Metrics in Predictive Coding.*

3. Jean Tague-Sutcliffe & James Blustein, *A Statistical Analysis of the TREC-3 Data, in* NIST SPECIAL PUBLICATION 500-225: OVERVIEW OF THE THIRD TEXT RETRIEVAL CONFERENCE (TREC-3), pp. 385–98 (1995).

Thus while the performance of various review tools and processes on past projects may help in choosing among alternatives, such historical information provides at best a crude hint at the achieved effectiveness on any particular task at hand. The ongoing need for evaluation is part of why estimation of effectiveness has become an issue of such prominence and controversy in e-discovery.

Classification

A useful perspective on both review as a whole, and on components of review, is classification. Classification simply means sorting objects into two or more groups or classes. For the purposes of this chapter, the assumption is that the objects are documents, that the set of classes is fixed in advance, and that each document must belong to exactly one of those classes. In binary classification, the focus here, there are exactly two allowed classes. In polytomous classification, there are three or more allowed classes.

In the binary case, typically one of the two classes is more interesting (and usually less common) than the other. This will be referred to here as the target class. Depending on the review task, the target class might be responsive documents, privileged documents, or documents about some particular topic.

A review process where each document must be put in one of two classes (e.g., **Responsive** vs. **Nonresponsive**, **Privileged** vs. **Nonprivileged**, **Topic X** vs. **NOT Topic X**) can be viewed as a binary classification task. Any component of the review that sorts documents into those classes, whether that component consists of software or a manual process, is a classifier. A classifier takes a document as input and produces as output a predicted label or class prediction.

If the two classes of interest are, say, **Privileged** and **Nonprivileged**, one can view a classifier for this task as outputting one of two labels, **PRIVILEGED** or **NONPRIVILEGED**. Equivalently, by defining one of the classes to be the target class (say **Privileged**), one can view a classifier as outputting **Yes** (predict the document is in the target class) or **No** (predict the document is not in the target class). When presenting labels in a **Yes/No** fashion, it is important to distinguish the predicted label (e.g., **Yes**, a document is privileged) from the action a process might take based on that label (e.g., no, the document is not produced to another party).

The Classification Perspective

Classification may seem an impoverished perspective in comparison to the subtle judgments that an attorney makes in considering the role of a document in a legal matter. That simplicity, however, brings at least two great advantages.

The first advantage is that technologies for automated classification, particularly machine learning approaches, have seen extraordinary progress in computer science, statistics, and related fields in recent decades. Much of the recent attention to "big data" reflects the penetration of classifiers and other predictive models into a wide range of everyday decision-making processes. The ads seen on a web page, the outcome of a credit application, the mail one receives from political candidates, and the music streamed to a user all may be guided by classifier predictions.

Of particular relevance to e-discovery are technologies for text classification, that is, the classification of objects that consist largely or wholly of human language.[4] Viewing document review as classification allows bringing to bear machine learning methods widely used for text classification. Some commercial predictive coding products incorporate open source machine learning software, and many purported innovations in predictive coding are rebrandings, rediscoveries, or minor tweaks of well-known techniques from information retrieval, machine learning, and statistics.

The second advantage of viewing document review as classification is that this provides a common perspective for evaluating the review process at different stages and levels of detail. Viewed as binary

4. For overviews of text classification, see Fabrizio Sebastiani, *Machine Learning in Automated Text Categorization*, 34 ACM Computing Surveys 1–47 (2002), and Peter Jackson & Isabelle Moulinier, Natural Language Processing for Online Applications: Text Retrieval, Extraction and Categorization (2007).

classification, all of the following have the same input (documents) and output (a **Yes** or **No** label for each document):

- A list of custodians from whom to review documents.
- A rule for culling collected documents based on date, file type, and other metadata.
- A Boolean text query used to select documents for input to a review platform.
- A predictive model trained by machine learning and used to select documents for production or for manual review.
- An attorney reviewing a document to decide whether it is responsive.
- An attorney reviewing a document to decide whether it is privileged.
- A team of such reviewers making such decisions.
- An end-to-end review workflow combining many such actions and leading to the production of some of an organization's documents.

For instance, a list of custodians can be viewed as a binary classifier that output **Yes** for any document whose custodian is on the list, and **No** for any other document. A Boolean text query retrieves all documents containing particular combinations of search terms. The retrieved documents become the **Yes** documents, and the nonretrieved ones are the **No** documents.

Predictive models produced by supervised learning often internally produce numbers rather than **Yes/No** decisions. That is, the predictive model is given a document as input, and produces a numeric score as output, with a higher score being a stronger indication that the input document belongs to the target class. Such a predictive model can be converted into a binary classifier by comparing the output score with a cutoff or threshold score. The classifier is defined to make a **Yes** prediction if and only if the predictive model gives the document a score greater than a specified cutoff. A cutoff may be defined directly as a number or, indirectly, by sorting documents by score and specifying that some fraction of top-ranked documents get a **Yes** label.

Different review approaches and components vary greatly in their implementation, speed, cost, consistency, management complexity, and other properties. From the binary classification perspective, however, all can be evaluated the same way: by how well they assign **Yes/No** labels to documents.

Contingency Tables

Suppose that one can determine unambiguously the class to which any document should be assigned. (In practice, this can be the most fraught aspect of evaluation.) One can refer to some record of the desired class for the document as a gold label for the document.[5] A binary classifier can produce a predicted label for the same document. There are then four possible outcomes for any classification decision, based on the four combinations of gold label and predicted label:

- *True Positive*: classifier predicts **Yes** (the document is predicted to belong to the target class), and **Yes** is the gold label (the document actually does belong to the target class)
- *False Positive*: classifier predicts **Yes**, but **No** is the gold label
- *False Negative*: classifier predicts **No**, but **Yes** is the gold label
- *True Negative*: classifier predicts **No**, and **No** is the gold label

Given n documents where both the gold labels and predicted labels are known, one can count the number of times each outcome occurs. These counts form the entries of a *contingency table* as shown in Figure 12.1, where:

TP = the number of true positives,
FP = the number of false positives,
FN = the number of false negatives,
TN = the number of true negatives, and
$TP + FP + FN + TN = n$

5. Terminology varies widely here, with *gold standard*, *correct*, *authoritative*, *expert*, *true*, and *ground truth* being some of the alternatives to "gold" labels. Alternatives to "label" include *class, category, code, decision, annotation,* and *relevance judgment.*

FIGURE 12.1 A contingency table for binary classification

		Gold Label	
		Yes	No
Predicted Label	Yes	TP: True Positives	FP: False Positives
	No	FN: False Negatives	TN: True Negatives

A contingency table can be defined for any set of documents. If the set of documents is the full collection to be classified, one calls the table a collection contingency table or population contingency table.

As a concrete example, consider a collection containing 1,000,000 documents. Assume a classifier that makes 100,000 **Yes** predictions, of which 70,000 are true positives and 30,000 are false positives. Assume also that there are a total of 90,000 documents actually belonging to the target class, so that there are 20,000 false negatives. This leaves, as is typical, a large number (880,000) of true negatives. Figure 12.2 displays the collection contingency table for this situation.

Since these counts are for a particular collection of documents, one refers to them as collection values or, to use sampling terminology, the population values. One could also refer to these as being the true, correct, or actual values for the counts, recognizing that "truth" here refers to a hypothetical gold labeling of the entire collection by some person or persons, combined with application of some classifier to the entire collection. It is important to distinguish the (typically unknown) collection values of contingency table entries from the corresponding entries for a sample, as will be discussed later.

Most classifiers can be adjusted (directly, or through how they are produced) to be more or less apt to predict that a document

FIGURE 12.2 A collection contingency table for a binary classification of one million documents

		Gold Label	
		Yes	No
Predicted Label	Yes	70,000	30,000
	No	20,000	880,000

belongs to the target class. As discussed previously, a predictive model outputting numeric scores can be converted to a binary classifier by comparing those scores to a cutoff. By changing that cutoff, one may vary how often the binary classifier will make **Yes** predictions. One would ideally like a classifier that makes only correct **Yes** and **No** predictions. This would minimize both false positives and false negatives, or, equivalently, maximize both true positives and true negatives.

Uncertainty, however, is inevitable in text classification. If a classifier always favors a **Yes** prediction for documents of unclear status, it will have fewer false negatives, but more false positives. Conversely, always favoring **No** when the classifier is uncertain will have the opposite effect. Different contexts will call for different tradeoffs, and thus one goal in defining effectiveness measures is to characterize what tradeoff a particular classifier has achieved.

Effectiveness Measures for Binary Classification

An effectiveness measure for binary classification is a formula that combines the counts in a contingency table to produce a numeric value capturing some aspect of classification quality. Several effectiveness measures for binary classification have been used in e-discovery. Most were originally developed in other areas of science and engineering, and several have been reinvented many times under a variety of names. These are the most widely discussed binary classification effectiveness measures in e-discovery:

Recall: This is $TP/(TP + FN)$, the proportion of target class items that the classifier found, that is, for which it predicted **Yes**. For our example in Figure 12.2, the collection recall is 70000/90000 = 0.778. Recall is maximized by using a very low cutoff, in other words, predicting **Yes** for all documents.

Precision: This is $TP/(TP + FP)$, the proportion of **Yes** predictions that were correct. For Figure 12.2, the collection precision is 70000/100000 = 0.700. Precision is typically maximized by using a high cutoff, that is, predicting **No** for most documents.

Fallout or *false positive rate*: This is $FP/(FP + TN)$, or the proportion of nontarget documents for which the classifier predicts **Yes**. For

Figure 12.2, the collection fallout is 30000/910000 = 0.033. Fallout is minimized by using a very high cutoff, that is, predicting **No** for all documents.

Accuracy: This is $(TP + TN)/(TP + FP + FN + TN)$, or simply $(TP + TN)/n$, the proportion of all predicted labels that were correct.[6] For Figure 12.2, the collection accuracy is 950000/1000000 = 0.950. Accuracy is typically maximized by some intermediate cutoff.[7]

Error rate: This is $(FP + FN)/n$, or 1.0 minus accuracy: the proportion of all predicted labels that were not correct. For Figure 12.2, the collection error rate is 50000/1000000 = 0.050. Minimizing error rate is equivalent to maximizing accuracy.

Elusion: This is $FN/(FN + TN)$, the proportion of **No** predictions that were wrong. Elusion was defined by Roitblat for use in e-discovery.[8] It is equal to 1.0 minus the negative predictive value, $TN/(FN + TN)$, a measure used in biomedicine.[9] For Figure 12.2, the collection elusion is 20000/900000 = 0.022. Elusion is typically minimized by using a very low cutoff, that is, predicting **Yes** for almost all documents.

F_1: This is $(2 \times TP)/(FP + FN + 2 \times TP)$, and is equal to the harmonic mean of recall and precision. The value of F_1 is always between the values of recall and precision. The F_1 measure is used in academic research on information retrieval, as well as in some e-discovery software. It is part of a family of measures that strike different tradeoffs between recall and precision.[10] For Figure 12.2, the collection F_1 is 140000/190000 = 0.737. F_1 is maximized by an

6. The term "accuracy" is sometimes used in a looser sense to refer to any measure of effectiveness, but this ambiguous usage is avoided here.

7. If a classifier could perfectly determine its own certainty, it could maximize its expected accuracy (and minimize its expected error rate) by using a cutoff of 0.50 on a probability scale.

8. Herbert L. Roitblat, *Search and Information Retrieval Science*, 8 SEDONA CONF. J. 225–38 (2007).

9. JAMES F. JEKEL, DAVID L. KATZ, & JOANN G. ELMORE, EPIDEMIOLOGY, BIOSTATISTICS, AND PREVENTITIVE MEDICINE (2d ed. 2001).

10. CORNELIS J. VAN RIJSBERGEN, INFORMATION RETRIEVAL (1979).

intermediate cutoff that depends on the details of the classifier and collection.[11]

Note that different effectiveness measures are defined on different subpopulations of the collection. Accuracy, for instance, is a measure based on all documents in the collection, while recall is based only on target documents. This has implications for estimating these measures, as discussed later.

Other population quantities that are not effectiveness measures can also be defined in terms of the contingency table entries. Two quantities of particular interest are:

Prevalence: The prevalence of target documents is $(TP + FN)/n$, that is, the proportion of target documents in the collection. When the target documents are responsive documents, prevalence is sometimes referred to as richness. Prevalence is independent of classifier predictions, and so is not an effectiveness measure. One can define prevalence without reference to a contingency table as k/n, where k is the number of target documents in the collection. For Figure 12.2, the collection prevalence is 90000/1000000 = 0.090.

Positive rate: The positive rate is the proportion of documents on which the classifier makes a positive prediction, that is, $(TP + FP)/n$. If each document receiving a positive prediction requires some cost to handle, then the positive rate is one measure of the cost of using a classifier. Positive rate is independent of which documents belong to the target class, and so is not an effectiveness measure. One can define positive rate without reference to a contingency table as g/n, where g is the number of documents in the collection on which the classifier makes a **Yes** prediction. For Figure 12.2, the collection positive rate is 100000/1000000 = 0.100.

For a classifier that compares numeric scores to a cutoff, the tendency to make false positive versus false negative decisions can be adjusted by changing the cutoff. Some effectiveness measures

11. David D. Lewis, *Evaluating and Optimizing Autonomous Text Classification Systems*, in Proceedings of the 18th Annual International ACM SIGIR Conference on Research and Development in Information Retrieval, ACM, 246–54 (1995).

take on their best achievable value for a given predictive model only when a cutoff is chosen to balance false positives and false negatives to some degree. Accuracy, error rate, and F_1 have this property. In contrast, other measures, if used alone, favor one extreme or another. If recall were the only measure used, for instance, it could be optimized by minimizing false negatives while ignoring false positives (i.e., always predicting **Yes**). Conversely, fallout could be minimized by always predicting **No**. Precision is a more complex case, but typically could be maximized by almost always predicting **No**.

There is, therefore, a mismatch between the goals of review (which require balancing many concerns) and the use of certain single effectiveness measures. One step toward addressing this mismatch is to use pairs of the measures, or of measures and population quantities. Examples of such composite criteria include:

- Maximizing *precision* while keeping *recall* greater than some minimum value.
- Minimizing *false positive rate* while keeping *recall* greater than some minimum value.
- Maximizing *recall* while keeping the *positive rate* below a specified level.
- Requiring that *elusion* be at least a specified factor lower than the *prevalence* of target documents.[12]

Many other composite criteria are possible.

Different measures capture different real world preferences for classifier behavior. Here are three examples of how the measures might be used.

Example 1*:* An entire review for responsiveness that results in a production set can be viewed as a binary classifier. For each document in the collection, that "classifier" either decided **Yes** (the document was put in the production set) or **No** (the document was not put in the production set). The party producing documents has

12. In the author's experience, however, rigorous attempts to compare elusion to prevalence simply lead back to the use of recall and some measure of cost.

some interest in the recall of the production set, to the extent that is indicative of meeting its obligation to produce responsive documents. However, the producing party may be more concerned with high precision, in order to reduce both their costs (e.g., of privilege review) and their risk of including documents they are not required to produce.

Example 2: Conversely, a party making a request for production may desire high recall for the production set (as one measure of how much important information they will receive), but have little interest in precision. Requesting parties increasingly have access to search and predictive coding tools similar to those used in review, and these tools mitigate problems with receiving a low precision production.

Example 3: A predictive coding software vendor may need to choose default settings for a machine learning algorithm. The vendor could use F_1 or other measures that balance false positives versus false negatives as a way to summarize effectiveness of the algorithm at different settings. In contrast to the preceding two examples, the vendor is concerned not with effectiveness on one task, but rather on many tasks to which the software may be applied in the future. The vendor might look, therefore, at effectiveness on many collections when choosing the default settings.

Estimation and Sampling

The collection value of an effectiveness measure for a classifier is usually unknown, since computing it would require knowing the gold labels for most or all documents in the collection. Since labeling a document typically requires reading it, gold labeling every document in a collection is typically too expensive to be practical. (Indeed, that is the rationale for technology-assisted review.)

One must therefore *estimate* effectiveness. This can be done by drawing a random sample of documents from the collection, finding both the gold and predicted label for each document in the sample, and using a statistical procedure called an estimator to produce an estimate of the collection value of the effectiveness measure. Estimation, as opposed to guessing or the use of ad hoc methods, provides not just a plausible value for the effectiveness, but also a characterization of how certain one can be about that value.[13]

The most straightforward type of random sample is a simple random sample. A simple random sample is one drawn in a fashion such that all samples of the same size from the population have the same probability of being chosen.[14] Generating a simple random sample from a collection is usually easy, as this capability is built into most predictive coding and review platforms. Keeping a simple random sample up-to-date as documents are added to or removed from the collection is also possible, but platforms vary in their support for this.

In order to use a random sample to estimate effectiveness, one must know for each document in the sample both its predicted label and its gold label. Gold labels are obtained by having knowledgeable reviewers assess the sample documents. How one obtains the predicted class label for a document varies with the type of classifier. Examples include:

- For a Boolean query or a predictive model, run the classifier on the sample and record its decision for each document in the sample.
- For a human reviewer or human review team, review the documents in the sample.
- For an entire review for responsiveness process, check whether or not each document in the sample is in the current version of the production set.

Before discussing estimation, it is important to note that there is another and very different use of random samples in TAR. Some (but not all) predictive coding approaches also use random sampling to choose documents to be labeled for training the system. Much unnecessary confusion has arisen in e-discovery from failing to distinguish

13. Paul H. Garthwaite, Ian T. Jolliffe, & Byron Jones, Statistical Inference (1995).

14. For a sample to be a simple random sample it is necessary, but not sufficient, that each individual document in the population have the same probability of being included in the sample.

these two uses. This chapter solely considers the use of labeled random samples in estimation, not training.

Point Estimates

Returning to the previous example, suppose one chooses a simple random sample of 2,000 documents from the collection of 1,000,000 documents. The sample can be manually reviewed and a gold label assessment made of whether each document belongs to the target class. The predicted label for each document can be found as well. The contingency table for the sample might then look like Figure 12.3.

The *sample values* of effectiveness measures, and other population quantities, can be computed in the same way as their collection values:

Recall: $TP/(TP + FN) = 135/(135 + 42) = 0.763$
Precision: $TP/(TP + FP) = 135/(135 + 68) = 0.665$
Fallout (false positive rate): $FP/(FP + TN) = 68/(68 + 1755) = 0.037$
Accuracy: $(TP + TN)/n = (135 + 1755)/2000 = 0.945$
Error rate: $(FP + FN)/n = (68 + 42)/2000 = 0.055$
Elusion: $FN/(FN + TN) = 42/(42 + 1755) = 0.023$
F_1: $(2 \times TP)/(2 \times TP + FP + FN) = (2 \times 135)/(2 \times 135 + 68 + 42) = 0.711$
Prevalence: $(TP + FN)/n = (135 + 42)/2000 = 0.089$
Positive rate: $(TP + FP)/n = (135 + 68)/2000 = 0.102$

The sample values are typically not identical to the collection values. For instance, the sample recall is 0.763 while the collection recall is 0.778 (when both are rounded to three decimal places). Effectiveness values and other population quantities computed from a sample

FIGURE 12.3 A sample contingency table for a simple random sample of 2,000 documents

		Gold Label	
		Yes	No
Predicted Label	Yes	135	68
	No	42	1,755

are only estimates of the corresponding (and usually unknown) collection values. In particular, they are point estimates, that is, estimates that consist of a single value.[15]

Confidence Intervals

All else being equal, one should have more confidence in an estimate based on a sample of 500 documents, say, than one based on a sample of five documents. A form of estimate that captures this notion of certainty is a confidence interval. A confidence interval takes the form of a range of values for the quantity being estimated, and is accompanied by a confidence level that measure the certainty of the estimate.

There are two equivalent ways of writing a confidence interval. One is to specify the lower and upper values of the interval directly, for example, [0.751, 0.837]. The other is to specify a point estimate and a margin of error to be added to or subtracted from the point estimate, for example, 0.794 +/- 0.043. The second notation, when applicable, has the advantage that the margin of error provides a concise expression of uncertainty about the point estimate. However, some confidence interval estimation methods do not produce a point estimate. Other methods produce a point estimate that does not lie in the center of the interval, requiring a different notation, for example, $0.800^{-0.049}/_{+0.037}$.

The technical definition of "confidence level" is, unfortunately, counterintuitive. The confidence level is a property of the estimation technique that produced the confidence interval estimate, not a property of any particular estimate produced by that technique. To say that one has a "95 percent confidence interval" means that one produced the interval by a technique that, if applied many times to different random samples, would produce intervals containing the true value of the population quantity at least 95 percent of the time. However, once that technique has been applied to a particular random sample, there is no longer any probability involved. The confidence interval produced from that sample either contains the true value or does not. (Typically one does not know which.)

15. Using the sample value of a quantity as the point estimate of the true value of that quantity is the most common point estimation method, but other methods exist.

Suppose that one draws a random sample and produces a confidence interval for recall of [0.751, 0.837] at the 95 percent confidence level. The following are appropriate ways to describe that estimate:

- CORRECT: A 95 percent confidence interval for recall based on the sample is [0.751, 0.837].
- CORRECT: We are 95 percent confident that recall is between 0.751 and 0.837.
- CORRECT: We estimate with 95 percent confidence that recall is between 0.751 and 0.837.
- CORRECT: If we drew many random samples in the same fashion, and produced a confidence interval from each, then at least 95 percent of the confidence intervals produced in this fashion would contain the true value of recall.

The following are not appropriate statements about this confidence interval:

- INCORRECT: Recall is between 0.751 and 0.837.
- INCORRECT: There is a 95 percent probability that recall is between 0.751 and 0.837.[16]
- INCORRECT: If we drew many random samples in the same fashion, and produced a confidence interval from each, then at least 95 percent of the estimated recall values would be between 0.751 and 0.837.

It is also important to note that "confidence" here refers to how certain the estimate of effectiveness is, not how confident one can be that the classifier did a good job. One can have high confidence, for instance, that a classifier is performing poorly. Conversely, a classifier might be very effective but, due to the small random sample used, one might have low confidence in the estimate of the classifier's effectiveness.

Statisticians must trade off a number of factors in defining confidence interval estimators, and the research literature contains many

16. Bayesian statistics provides an alternative approach to confidence intervals that does allow making such statements, at the cost of introducing subjective probability assumptions.

such estimators. Practitioners will typically use existing software or web calculators rather than working out estimates by hand.

To produce a confidence interval estimate of a particular effectiveness measure from a simple random sample, one typically needs to specify two of the following three quantities:

1. The confidence level.
2. The maximum acceptable width for the confidence interval (i.e., the maximum tolerable difference between the upper and lower values of the confidence interval). Equivalently, one can specify a maximum value for the margin of error when using a method based on a point estimate and margin of error.
3. The size of the simple random sample from the subpopulation on which the effectiveness measure is defined.

The confidence level is typically chosen to be one of a few commonly used values: 90 percent, 95 percent, or 99 percent. One might then decide on a maximum acceptable margin of error, and derive the necessary sample size to ensure, or perhaps just make likely, obtaining a confidence interval with no more than that margin of error. (The actual margin of error will depend on both the population value and on the particular sample drawn, not just the sample size.) In other situations, the sample size may be fixed by cost constraints, and one must simply accept whatever margin of error results.

The data in a sample contingency table, along with the population size, can be used to compute confidence interval estimates for binary effectiveness measures. Since each measure is defined on a subpopulation of the document collection, one needs a sample from that subpopulation to estimate that measure. Fortunately, if one draws a simple random sample from the entire collection, the portion of the sample that belongs to a subpopulation is itself a simple random sample from that subpopulation. For instance, the portion of the sample that was gold labeled as responsive constitutes a simple random sample from all responsive documents in the collection.[17] Thus a simple random

17. This assumes that the gold labels assigned to the sample documents would not change if those documents were assessed as part of a hypothetical assessment of the entire collection.

sample from the entire collection has the advantage that one may use it to estimate any of the effectiveness measures of interest.[18]

The following are confidence interval estimates based on a simple random sample of 2,000 documents from a collection of 1,000,000 documents, assessed for responsiveness, as shown in Figure 12.3. The confidence intervals were computed using a margin of error calculator[19] and entering population size 1,000,000, confidence level 95 percent, sample size shown as follows, and ratio of successes to sample size expressed as a percentage.[20] The estimates are:

Recall: The 135 + 42 = 177 examples that were gold labeled as responsive constitute a simple random sample from the subpopulation of responsive documents in the collection. The classifier said **Yes** to 135 of the 177 documents, giving a 95 percent confidence interval for recall of 0.763 +/- 0.063, or [0.700, 0.826], based on a simple random sample of 177 documents.

Precision: One uses the 135 + 68 = 203 examples for which the classifier outputs **Yes**. Of those, 135 are responsive giving a confidence interval on precision of 0.665 +/- 0.065 = [0.600, 0.730], based on a sample size of 203 documents.

Fallout (false positive rate): One uses the 68 + 1,755 = 1,823 documents that were gold labeled as nonresponsive. Of those, the classifier outputs **Yes** on 68 of them, giving a 95 percent confidence interval on fallout of 0.037 +/-0.009 = [0.028, 0.046], based on a sample size of 1823 documents.

Accuracy: Accuracy is the proportion of collection documents that are correctly classified. So in this case the subpopulation of the

---

18. Using a subsample of a collection sample to estimate an effectiveness measure means that the sample size is known in advance for some measures (e.g., accuracy), but is a random variable for others (e.g., recall). Statisticians sometimes distinguish between *unconditional* and *conditional* confidence intervals in such situations, but this technical point will be ignored here.

19. The calculator used is found at http://www.raosoft.com/samplesize.html.

20. Ideally the population size used with the calculator is the size of the subpopulation on which the effectiveness measure is defined. However, when the size of that subpopulation is unknown, the size of the entire population may be used instead. The width of the confidence interval will usually be slightly larger than if the subpopulation size were known.

collection is the entire collection. The entire sample can be used in estimation. On the 2,000 sample documents, 135 + 1755 = 1,890 classifier decisions are correct, giving a 95 percent confidence interval on accuracy of 0.945 +/- 0.010 = [0.935, 0.955], based on a sample size of 2,000 documents.

Error rate: Error rate is the proportion of incorrect decisions in the entire collection, so again one uses the full sample of 2,000 documents. A 95 percent confidence interval on error rate is 0.055 +/- 0.010 = [0.045, 0.065], based on a sample size of 2,000 documents.

Elusion: One uses the 42 + 1,755 = 1,797 documents on which the classifier outputs **No**. Of those, 42 documents are responsive, giving a 95 percent confidence interval on elusion of 0.023 +/- 0.007 = [0.016, 0.030], based on a sample size of 1,797 documents.

F_1: In contrast to the other effectiveness measures described, F1 is not a simple proportion, and producing a confidence interval estimate for it requires attention to statistical issues that are beyond the scope of this chapter.[21]

Confidence interval estimates can be also made for population quantities that are not effectiveness measures:

Prevalence: Prevalence is the proportion of target documents in the entire collection, so again one uses the full sample of 2,000 documents. Classifier predictions are ignored for this purpose. Of the 2,000 documents in the sample, 177 were gold labeled as responsive. A 95 percent confidence interval on prevalence is 0.086 +/- 0.012 = [0.074, 0.098], based on a sample size of 2,000 documents.

Positive rate: The positive rate is the proportion of documents receiving **Yes** predictions in the entire collection, so again one uses the full sample of 2,000 documents. Gold labels are ignored for this purpose. Of the 2,000 documents in the sample, 203 received **Yes** predictions. A 95 percent confidence interval on prevalence is 0.102 +/- 0.013 = [0.089, 0.115], based on a sample size of 2,000 documents.

---

21. Mossaab Bagdouri, William Webber, David D. Lewis, & Douglas W. Oard, *Towards Minimizing the Annotation Cost of Certified Text Classification*, in PROCEEDINGS OF THE 22ND ACM INTERNATIONAL CONFERENCE ON INFORMATION & KNOWLEDGE MANAGEMENT, ACM 989–98 (2013).

However, in contrast to the other quantities, it is usually practical to compute positive rate exactly rather than estimating it: simply run the classifier on the entire collection.

The fact that only the target portion of the sample is useful in estimating recall, a measure that plays a central role in e-discovery, is particularly vexing.[22] It means that the cost to estimate recall can be both large and difficult to predict, as will be discussed later in the chapter

Defining the Collection

The previous discussion assumes that it is clear what a "document" is and how many there are in a collection. In practice, collection definition is complex even after the sources to collect are chosen. At least three issues arise: perfectly classified documents, document groups, and where to start evaluating.

Perfectly Classified Documents

It is common that the class membership of some documents can be determined automatically. For instance, when parties in a legal matter have agreed that executable files are nonresponsive, software can make that determination automatically and near perfectly. If parties have agreed that all documents containing a particular string are responsive, this too can be determined automatically.

In e-discovery practice, perfectly classified documents are often removed from the collection (to be produced, or not) before sampling and effectiveness estimation are performed. This practice is sometimes a side effect of doing evaluation after the remaining documents are loaded into a TAR platform. This is a choice, however, not a logical necessity. In evaluating the end-to-end effectiveness of an entire review, some parties might want to give the review "credit" for the correct handling of these "easy" documents. And, of course, evaluation can be done outside of TAR software.

22. There do exist estimation methods (e.g., using the exact hypergeometric sampling distribution) for which nonresponsive documents in a labeled sample provide a small amount of information about recall. For large collections, however, the information in even thousands of labeled nonresponsive documents is negligible compared to the information in a few labeled responsive documents.

Document Groups

Bitwise identical files are often defined to have the same responsiveness status. Such duplicates are often removed from the collection before evaluation, perhaps with their metadata preserved. This fits the common intuition that a classifier should not get double credit, or double penalty, simply because there are two copies of the same document. Practice is less established, however, for near duplicate documents, that is, documents that are similar but not identical.

Grouping documents by family (e.g., e-mail threads, archive files, etc.) is another area where practice is less standardized. For instance, suppose that an entire e-mail thread is defined to be responsive if it contains any responsive message. The question then is whether predictive coding, or any review component, should have its classification decisions evaluated at the level of individual messages or at the level of threads. Either approach, or both, may be used, but it is important to be clear which is intended, in both evaluation and reporting.

A central issue in decisions related to grouping is how to make effectiveness as measured by binary classification correspond as closely as possible to effectiveness at finding information important to the case. This issue is discussed more broadly later in the chapter.

Where to Start Evaluating

E-discovery can be viewed as a series of classification steps or, equivalently, a series of culling steps, producing a new and smaller population of documents at each step. A fundamental question is on which population(s) one will evaluate classification effectiveness. This is equivalent to deciding which classification steps will have their effectiveness estimated, and which will not.

Since each classification step attempts to screen out nonresponsive documents while retaining responsive ones, the prevalence of responsive documents typically increases after each step. This means that estimating effectiveness, particularly of recall, becomes more expensive the farther back one goes in the review pipeline.[23]

23. The size of the document population also increases as one goes backwards in the pipeline. However, once the population exceeds a few tens of thousands the impact of population size on cost is negligible in comparison to the impact of prevalence.

Attention to evaluation in e-discovery has largely focused on TAR processes, so the population sampled is often whatever documents have been fed into the TAR software. There is no technical reason why this must be true, however. The effectiveness of any step of the e-discovery process, viewed as a classification of its input documents, can in principle be estimated. In practice, the low prevalence of responsive documents typically rules out estimating recall for early processing stages, such as choosing custodians from among all employees of a large enterprise.

Debate in e-discovery about the interaction of population choice and evaluation has centered on culling, and in particular culling by "keyword" queries on text content. There are two distinct questions here that are sometimes confused:

1. Whether to *apply* text content culling before TAR, after TAR, or not at all.
2. Whether to *evaluate* the effectiveness of text content culling, the effectiveness of TAR, and/or the effectiveness of the two in combination.

Both questions are important, but beyond the scope of this chapter.

Evaluation and Its Discontents

The simplest method for estimating recall is the one previously discussed: draw a random sample from the collection, assess it for responsiveness (or some other target class), ignore the nontarget documents, and use the target documents to estimate recall. This sampling and evaluation approach has colloquially become known as the "direct method,"[24] subsequent to this author's testimony in an early predictive coding dispute.[25]

The lower the prevalence of target documents, the fewer target documents are likely to be in a random sample from the collection.

24. Maura R. Grossman & Gordon V. Cormack, *Comments on "The Implications of Rule 26(g) on the Use of Technology-Assisted Review,"* 7 Fed. Cts L. Rev. 285 (2014).

25. Kleen Products LLC et al. v. Packaging Corp. of America et al., No.1:10-cv-05711 (N.D. Ill.). Transcript of Proceedings Before the Honorable Magistrate Judge Nan R. Nolan, Feb. 21, 2012.

Thus lower prevalence means a larger sample from the collection is necessary to estimate recall. Sadly, there is no "magic number" or uniform standard for the size of a simple random sample from a collection if one wishes to estimate recall with a given degree of certainty. The appropriate sample size will depend not just on the desired margin of error and confidence level, but also on the (typically unknown) prevalence of target documents.

For example, to guarantee a margin of error of 0.05 or less for a 95 percent confidence interval estimate on recall requires 385 target documents. If the prevalence is 0.1 (i.e., 10 percent of the collection are target documents), then a simple random sample of 3,850 documents from the collection would on average be necessary to have 385 target documents in the sample. The actual number of target documents in the sample could, of course, be either greater or fewer than 385. Thus even more than 3,850 documents would be necessary if one wanted to guard against having fewer than 385 target documents. If prevalence were 0.01 (i.e., only 1 percent of the collection are target documents), then a simple random sample of 38,500 documents from the collection would be necessary to get 385 target documents on average.

The daunting size of these samples is compounded by a chicken-and-egg problem: one does not know how large a sample is needed until prevalence is known, but one cannot estimate prevalence without a sample. One may have a reasonable guess at prevalence based on other information, and that can aid in choosing sample size. And once the collection is known, the sample size can be determined by drawing the sample iteratively, with appropriate statistical adjustments.

In a litigation setting, however, both the scope of the collection and the cost of evaluation may be under negotiation simultaneously, potentially forcing an early commitment to a sample size. Collecting of documents also may happen over a period of time, making prevalence of responsive documents within the collection a moving target and further complicating the issue of determining sample size and cost.

Prevalence is even trickier for target classes other than responsiveness. Subtopics within the responsive documents by definition have lower prevalence, and thus increased difficulty. As another example, effectiveness at detecting privileged documents is often of interest not on the collection as whole, but only on a potential production set that becomes available late in the review process. Prevalence of privileged documents within the potential production set may be very different than on the entire collection.

The potentially high and uncertain cost of estimating recall has unfortunately resulted in a number of ad hoc, statistically invalid proposals for evaluation in the e-discovery community. Fortunately, as discussed in the next section, statistically valid approaches for reducing evaluation costs are also available.

Statistical Approaches to Reducing Evaluation Cost

There are a number of statistical approaches that can reduce the sample size necessary to estimate review effectiveness. Some are common in e-discovery today, while others have yet to see much use. While the focus here is on estimating recall, the same techniques are applicable to estimating other measures as well.

Demand Less Certainty: The most straightforward adjustment is to accept either a larger maximum margin of error or a lower confidence level. Of these two, accepting a larger maximum margin of error is preferable, as keeping to a conventional confidence level (usually 95 percent) aids comparability within and among projects.

Achieve More Effectiveness: For a given sample size, the margin of error is highest when the point estimate of recall happens to be 0.5, that is, when exactly half the responsive documents in the sample were classified **Yes.** Point estimates of recall that are higher than 0.5 (or lower, though this is unlikely to be desired) give smaller margins of error. This has the pleasing consequence that achieving higher recall leads on average to smaller margins of error. The more effective the classifier is, the easier it is to achieve confidence that it is effective. The benefits are modest, however, and it is often difficult to increase recall without decreasing precision.

Worry About the Downside Only: The purpose of a confidence interval estimate on recall is typically to gain comfort that a minimum level of recall has been reached. If recall is greater than required, one is typically not concerned with the details of how much greater.

A form of estimate that addresses only the downside risk is the lower one-sided confidence interval.[26] This form of estimate will, for a given sample size, give a slightly tighter estimate of downside risk than does the usual two-sided interval.

Better Estimators: Researchers have developed more complex estimators that provide tighter intervals and/or better calibration of confidence levels in situations (e.g., very high values of recall) where traditional estimators do poorly.[27] These methods provide modest reductions of sample sizes with simple random sampling, but a greater advantage when combined with stratified sampling (see next paragraph).

Stratified Sampling: By separating a collection into several portions or strata, and sampling separately from each based on their likely prevalence of target documents, one can reduce the total sample size necessary to estimate a quantity with a given margin of error.[28] While this technique has not gotten much traction in e-discovery practice, it has been used in information retrieval research on e-discovery.[29] Strata can be defined based on metadata (e.g., custodian, date, etc.), content, the predictions of a classifier, or other factors. In addition to reducing sample size, stratified sampling aids in dealing with collections that change, due to the arrival of new documents or the application of multiple classifiers.

Sequential Sampling: By drawing a sample one document at a time until some statistical criterion is met, one can avoid drawing a sample larger than necessary. Depending on how this is done, special care may be needed to preserve the validity of estimates.[30] Suppose, for instance, that a random sample of a collection is drawn one document at a time until 385 responsive documents are obtained, at which

---

26. T. Tony Cai, *One-Sided Confidence Intervals in Discrete Distributions*, 131 J. Stat. Planning & Inference 63–88 (2005).

27. William Webber, *Approximate Recall Confidence Intervals*, 31 ACM Transactions on Information Systems (TOIS) 1–33 (2013).

28. Steven K. Thompson, Sampling, (3d ed. 2012).

29. Douglas W. Oard, Jason R. Baron, Bruce Hedin, David D. Lewis, & S. Tomlinson, *Evaluation of Information Retrieval for E-Discovery*, 18 Artificial Intelligence and Law 347 (2010).

30. David Siegmund, Sequential Analysis: Tests and Confidence Intervals (1985).

time 2,800 documents in total have been sampled. The 385 responsive documents would be a simple random sample from the responsive subpopulation of the collection, and could be used to estimate recall in the usual fashion. But the 2,800 documents would not be a simple random sample from the entire collection, and statistical adjustments would be necessary in using them to estimate precision or error rate, for instance. More complex schemes that choose when to stop sampling based on sequentially updated effectiveness estimates are also possible, and indeed are implicit in the use of graphical learning curve displays in some predictive coding software. Challenges arise in maintaining statistically valid estimates with these schemes.[31]

Trading Off Training, Evaluation, and Review: When using predictive coding, one must choose how much effort to put into labeling training data, labeling evaluation data, and reviewing documents. Balancing of these factors by a process manager can save costs, but is somewhat of an art. The extent to which this art can be automated is an active area of research.[32]

Beyond Binary Classification

The focus of this chapter has been on viewing review for responsiveness and similar tasks as binary classification, since this has been the trigger for concerns about evaluation cost. Some critics have argued, however, that the binary classification approach to evaluation in e-discovery is simply misguided. These criticisms point to the fact that binary classification contingency table counts neglect the differences in practical usefulness among formally responsive documents.

Britton, for instance, has pointed to the existence both of near-duplicate documents and of uniquely valuable documents (smoking guns) in arguing that "[r]ecall is not a valid reliable measure of e-discovery performance."[33] He observes that recall treats the finding

31. William Webber, Mossaab Bagdouri, David D. Lewis, & Douglas W. Oard, *Sequential Testing in Classifier Evaluation Yields Biased Estimates of Effectiveness*, SIGIR '13: Proceedings of the 36th International ACM SIGIR Conference on Research and Development in Information Retrieval, ACM, 933–36 (2013).

32. Bagdouri, *supra* note 25.

33. Gerard Britton, *Does the Uncritical Acceptance by Courts of Unsupported and Potentially Erroneous Technology-Assisted Review Assertions Frustrate the*

or missing of each document equally, whether the same information is contained in many other documents or, conversely, whether a single document contains unique and important information.

Britton's view appears to be not that recall is too expensive to estimate, but rather that recall is misleading at any price, particularly for manual review.[34] Indeed, Britton's proposed solutions, including additional effectiveness measures and graded evaluation of importance,[35] seem on their face likely to increase, not decrease, the cost of evaluation, at least if statistical estimation of effectiveness is the goal.

It is hard to find fault with the desirability of using more subtle notions of effectiveness. However, information retrieval experts do not use recall in evaluating e-discovery processes because they have forgotten recall's properties, as Britton suggests.[36] They do so because recall, and more generally the binary document classification perspective, can be a cost-effective compromise between no evaluation, and evaluations of whether particular information is present within documents found by a process.

As Britton acknowledges, a wide range of alternative measures of effectiveness have in fact been developed in information retrieval.[37] These include measures that take into account gradations of importance in relevant documents,[38] the diversity of results found by the system,[39] and the extent to which documents that cover particular

Objectives of Discovery? ACEDS Blog (Apr. 10, 2014), http://www.aceds.org/does-the-uncritical-acceptance-by-courts-of-unsupported-and-potentially-erroneous-technology-assisted-review-assertions-frustrate-the-objectives-of-discovery/.

34. *Id.*

35. Gerard Britton, *Courts Must Reassess Assumptions Underlying Current Predictive Coding Protocols*, ACEDS Blog (July 2, 2014), http://www.aceds.org/courts-must-reassess-adoption-of-current-predictive-coding-protocols/.

36. Britton, *supra* note 37.

37. *Id.*

38. Kalervo Järvelin & Jaana Kekäläinen. *Cumulated Gain-Based Evaluation of IR Techniques*, 20 ACM Transactions on Information Systems (TOIS) 422–46 (2002).

39. Jaime Carbonell & Jade Goldstein, *The Use of MMR, Diversity-Based Reranking for Reordering Documents and Producing Summaries*, in SIGIR 98: Proceedings of the 21st Annual International ACM SIGIR Conference on Research and Development in Information Retrieval, ACM, 335–36 (1998).

subtopics of relevance have been found.[40] However, these alternatives require more detailed and costly labeling of samples than do the binary classification measures.

Further, these alternative measures are arguably more difficult to understand than recall, precision, and other binary classification measures. Many who work in e-discovery would agree that explaining even the binary classification effectiveness measures to courts, attorneys, and clients is no small matter.

That said, more research is sorely needed. Little hard data has been published on the effectiveness of either TAR or manual review in operational e-discovery practice. For instance, the author is aware of no study published to date that has tested whether commercial manual review processes might find the most important documents while nonetheless showing low recall, as Britton suggests is possible.[41]

Reliance on recall as the sole measure of quality of a review process would also carry the risk of rewarding undesirable behaviors, such as stuffing a production with documents of marginal responsiveness. Additional, more subtle effectiveness measures would surely be helpful. And, as discussed earlier, statistical evaluation is just one tool among many, including good judgment and a watchful eye.

Summary

Quantitative evaluations of review processes are nothing new: law firms and review providers have long used such techniques in internal quality control. What is new is the more public profile that TAR has brought to these techniques, and to their costs and benefits.

A gold standard labeling of sample documents for use in evaluating review is, of course, a form of document review itself. It therefore

---

40. Eric Lagergren & Paul Over, *Comparing Interactive Information Retrieval Systems Across Sites: The TREC-6 Interactive Track Matrix Experiment,* in SIGIR 98: Proceedings of the 21st Annual International ACM SIGIR Conference on Research and Development in Information Retrieval, ACM, 164–72 (1998).

41. Britton, *supra* note 37.

has benefited from the general reduction in review costs over the last few decades. The reductions have come in the move from paper to electronic review, with attendant automation of management, routing, display, and cataloging of documents. The scope for further cost reductions, however, is limited.[42]

One must confront the fact that more certainty costs more money. Well-chosen statistical techniques and good process management can reduce the cost of evaluation. In the end, however, if larger samples and more careful assessment are desired, they must be paid for. No single standard for certainty in evaluation fits all data analysis problems, in e-discovery or elsewhere. There will always be situations that require living with a substantial degree of uncertainty about effectiveness.

As a silver lining, the process of statistical evaluation does have benefits beyond its role in validating effectiveness. The review of a random sample from a collection can provide insight into software and process glitches, anomalous document types, and errors in collection. The need to explicitly assess documents for evaluation often reveals disagreements about definitions and leads to insights into search and collection. A random perspective on a collection can be a surprisingly informative one.

Acknowledgments

This work was supported by the National Science Foundation under Grant No. IIS-1065250 to the University of Maryland at College Park. Parts of this chapter were written while the author was a visitor at Georgetown University, University of Maryland at College Park, University of Melbourne, and Royal Melbourne Institute of Technology. The support of all these institutions is gratefully acknowledged, as are many helpful discussions with their faculty and students. Any opinions, findings, conclusions, or recommendations expressed in this material are those of the author and do not necessarily reflect the views of the National Science Foundation or other supporting

42. Nicholas M. Pace & Laura Zakaras, *Where the Money Goes: Understanding Litigant Expenditures for Producing Electronic Discovery*, RAND INST. FOR CIVIL JUSTICE (2012).

institutions. The author in particular thanks the following people for suggestions, comments, and occasional vigorous disagreements on this chapter: Jason Baron, Michael Berman, Gerard Britton, Bill Dimm, Doug Forrest, Thomas Gricks, Dave Grossman, Bruce Hedin, Eli Nelson, Chris Paskach, Jeremy Pickens, Herb Roitblat, Karl Schieneman, and Jyothi Vinjumur. All responsibility for errors remains with the author.

EDITORS' INTRODUCTION TO CHAPTER 13

Michael D. Berman

This chapter by William Webber and Douglas W. Oard addresses the fundamental issue of measuring the effectiveness and efficiency of predictive coding. Why is that important? Just as we compare price when we make a purchase or look at food labels in the grocery store, metrics shows how much searching is proportionate to the case, in other words, how "to pick a satisfactory tradeoff between recall and cost." That is something every litigator needs to know. "The fact is that, despite its mathematical base, statistics is as much an art as it is a science. . . . Often the statistician must choose among methods, a subjective process, and find the one that he [or she] will use to represent the facts."[1] The litigator must be aware of how those choices are made.

The chapter defines key metrics, such as "recall," "precision," and the F_1 score (also known as the harmonic mean of recall and precision) and explains them in an easily understood way: "In more traditional discovery, we can think of low recall as representing under-production, and low precision as representing over-production," with the F_1 score harmonizing both. But the authors go beyond those descriptions, and give practical advice, analogizing precision as a proxy for cost-of-review. They also discuss "classifier accuracy," and measuring the output against a control set, all to answer the question of "when should review stop?" They graphically describe what some call "plateauing" and others call "stabilization," the point at which the machine has learned all it can to reach the desired level of reliability. The authors also explain the role and potential pitfalls of random sampling as a quality control measure, especially in low richness data collections.

1. D. Huff, How to Lie with Statistics 120 (1954).

Having addressed the basics, the authors then address options, such as going beyond binary relevance (yes or no) to weighted relevance scores, looking at "overturn" rates, and "elusion" or "discard richness." The chapter introduces the concept of a miss rate, known as "false negatives," and over-inclusion, known as "false positives," and the use of those measures to create a receiver operating characteristic curve.

The authors also address potential pitfalls and shortcomings of predictive coding, such as the fact that many predictive coding systems are binary and consider one relevant document as important as the next. Further, they point to the system's dependency on the accuracy of the subject-matter expert's decision-making, noting that "we don't yet fully understand the consequences" of errors in that process. This analysis brings home the importance of the chapter. Even if you never use predictive coding, your opponent may, and you have to understand it.

CHAPTER 13
Metrics in Predictive Coding

William Webber and Douglas W. Oard

There are a plethora of metrics used in measuring the effectiveness of predictive coding; and any one metric can be used in different ways, on different documents sets, and with different interpretations. It is easy for users (and providers!) of predictive coding technology to get confused by this profusion of metrics, and to end up chasing red herrings or failing to establish the effectiveness they think they have. The core task of discovery, though, is fairly straightforward: to find the highest proportion of relevant documents in the collection at the least cost. In this chapter, we guide the practitioner on how to measure this cost-for-completeness tradeoff, how standard metrics and evaluations help guide us to this goal, and how a misunderstanding of these metrics can guide us away from it.

Recall, Precision, and Cost

The most fundamental metric in e-discovery practice is "recall." When used to characterize the results of a review to find documents responsive (or relevant) to a production request, recall is defined as the proportion of all the relevant documents in your collection that somehow make it into your (interim or final) production. Protocol criteria and emerging guidelines on what constitutes a sufficiently complete production are generally expressed in terms of recall. One might set out in a protocol, for instance, that the production will achieve a minimum (estimated) recall of 75 percent.

Recall is frequently paired with another metric, "precision." Precision is the proportion of documents in the (interim or final) production that are relevant. In more traditional discovery jargon, we can think of low recall as representing under-production, and low precision as representing over-production.

There is a natural tension between recall and precision: broadening your production (for instance, by loosening your keyword query) will generally benefit recall, but at the cost of precision. At one extreme, we can return the entire collection, and achieve 100 percent recall, but a precision as low as the richness of the collection itself (that is, the proportion of relevant documents in it). At another extreme, we can return a single document that we know to be relevant, in which case we have 100 percent precision, but close to 0 percent recall.

Due to this natural tension, recall and precision are frequently paired together. This pairing is often expressed in a combined metric known as the "F_1 score." The F_1 score is the harmonic mean of recall and precision. (If you don't know what a harmonic mean is, don't worry. The key point is that the F_1 score will be between recall and precision, but closer to the lower of the two values.) There are also variants of the F score that give higher weights to recall (e.g., F_2) or to precision (e.g., $F_{0.5}$).

As common as it is to pair precision with recall, however, precision is often not a very helpful metric in e-discovery practice. To begin with, the final production is typically checked by manual reviewers. If we disregard mistakes made by these reviewers, then no nonresponsive documents will be produced, and the production will have 100 percent precision; but this is hardly a helpful statement. It is more meaningful to speak of the precision of a candidate production; that is, of the output of the predictive coding system, before it goes to review. But even here, precision itself is only a proxy for another value that we actually care about: namely, the cost of the review. A low-precision candidate production will require greater review effort to weed out nonresponsive documents than a higher precision one. Recall is thus of paramount concern to the requesting party (although it is also of concern to any diligent producing party, of course), whereas the precision of a candidate production that will later be subject to manual review is of interest principally to the producing party (although the requesting party can also benefit from a better-focused production).

Rather than talking about precision, it seems more natural to talk directly about cost. Now, cost is a complicated question, but at least as a first approximation, it is reasonable to quantify it as the number of documents that must be reviewed by humans before production. The tradeoff is not between recall and precision, but between recall and cost. We can then ask the question of a candidate review set, what is the cost to achieve a given level of recall (again, say 75 percent)? This question becomes even more poignant when asked in prospect, at the beginning of a predictive review: what will be the cost to achieve the desired recall level? As will be seen later, thinking in terms of cost, rather than precision, also allows us to account for the crucial point that training the predictive coding system itself involves costs.

We have defined recall in terms of the set of relevant documents in the collection. This definition, however, is problematic, in that it ignores the question of how the collection itself was formed. Creating a collection involves selecting documents to include and documents to exclude, and in doing so relevant documents will likely be excluded from the collection, and so from consideration for production, altogether. Though such exclusions harm "true" recall, they will not harm recall figures calculated on the collection. Indeed, the more stringent the collection criteria, the cheaper it will in general be to achieve a given level of recall as measured on the collection, yet the lower the "true" recall will be when measured against the full set of documents that were candidates for collection. A particular culprit here is the use of keyword filters to decrease the size (and increase the richness) of a collection before subjecting it to predictive coding; but there are similar implications in decisions to include or exclude certain custodians, repositories, date ranges, file types, and so forth.

The question of pre-collection culling is a thorny one, and beyond the scope of the current chapter to properly address. All we can say here is that recall, cost, and other effectiveness metrics need to be interpreted in the context of the breadth or narrowness of the original collection process. There is little reason (aside from data hosting and processing costs) to apply keyword filters prior to predictive coding; and wherever feasible, filtering decisions should be checked by sampling to demonstrate that little or no relevant material is actually being excluded from the collection.

Measuring Outcome versus Measuring Process

A typical predictive coding process consists of two stages. First, we perform some amount of training of the predictive coding system, by labeling example documents. Then, we take the output or retrieval of the trained system, and manually review all or some proportion of that output to make our final production. This two-stage process requires two stopping decisions: when to stop training, and when to stop review. (There are also "continuous" processes in which these two stages are merged.[1])

In general, the larger the number of (accurately labeled) training documents we add, the greater the accuracy of the classifier at the heart of our predictive coding system (that is, the fewer mistakes it makes in prediction). Manual annotation of training examples incurs cost, however, and as more training examples are annotated the marginal benefit from each annotation (ultimately) diminishes toward zero. Thus, at some point the cost-to-benefit comparison becomes unfavorable and the annotation of training examples should stop.

A common approach to deciding when to stop training is to do so when the classifier accuracy stops improving (or at least improvement slows to an inconsiderable level). Classifier accuracy is commonly measured against a "control set," a set of documents randomly sampled from the collection, labeled for responsiveness at the outset, and then held separate from our training examples.

The progress of training is frequently represented using a learning curve. This is a curve that shows classifier accuracy on the control set after each subsequent training example. A schematic learning curve is shown in Figure 13.1, as might be seen after annotating 1,000 training examples (200 at a time). At this stage, classifier accuracy seems to be reaching a maximum (sometimes referred to as plateauing), and we may decide that no further training is justified. Similar plots result for precision, recall, and F_1.

1. *See, e.g.*, Gordon V. Cormack & Maura R. Grossman, *Evaluation of Machine-Learning Protocols for Technology-Assisted Review in Electronic Discovery*, in Proceedings of the 37th International ACM SIGIR Conference on Research & Development in Information Retrieval, 153–62 (2014).

FIGURE 13.1 A learning curve

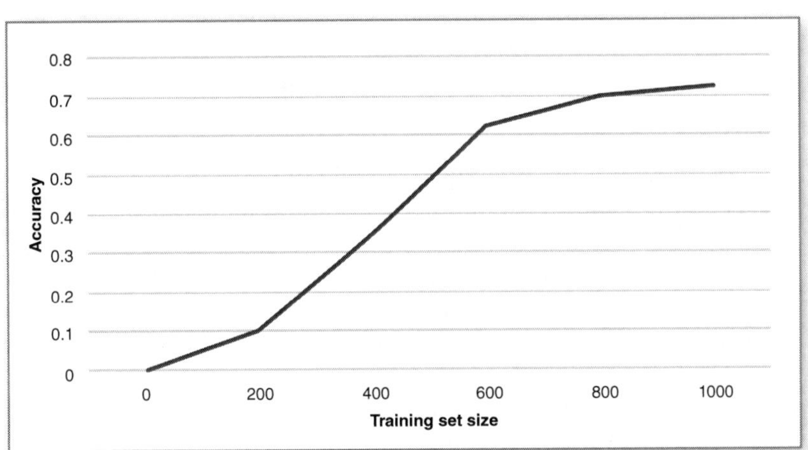

It is very important when reading a learning curve, however, to understand that what it is displaying is classifier effectiveness on the control set, not the effectiveness of the predictive coding process as a whole. This is particularly important if the learning curve is reporting a recall rate; it is a mistake to take this recall value as the recall value of the overall process. A basic consideration is that training itself is uncovering relevant documents, and so moving us toward our goal of target recall. Additionally, review may be taking place in parallel, and uncovering more relevant documents, which again will not show up in the reported recall figure for the classifier. (With some care, the system provider can incorporate training and review data into the reported learning curve, but this is not universally done; and when it is done, it becomes conversely hard to distinguish improvement in classifier accuracy from the effect of discovering the true relevance of documents through manual effort.)

Perhaps a more serious issue, though, is that a classifier, in deciding which documents to predict as relevant or irrelevant (that is, what "threshold" to set for relevance), is typically seeking to optimize some internal value, which is not in general the optimal threshold we ourselves would choose. For example, a classifier that seeks to optimize the F_1 score will do so (because of the way the F_1 measure is designed) by selecting a threshold that yields precision and recall values that are nearly equal. In contrast, the user will often be prepared to accept lower precision to achieve their recall target (and indeed it is frequently the case that the final precision of the candidate production is much lower than the recall, for this reason).

The more-or-less arbitrary threshold selected by the classifier means that a learning curve on recall may never reach the level of recall we have set as our target for the predictive coding process. By mismanaging the learning process in this way, the user can end up continuing training well past the point of no incremental improvement, fruitlessly attempting to achieve their recall target, when they should have much earlier stopped training and proceeded to review. We have seen this occur in practice, and it can lead to egregiously excessive cost, or even a failed process.

It is possible with a little care to instead produce a learning curve on review cost that expresses the total cost that could be achieved by stopping training at each point and proceeding to review. Many, if not most, current predictive coding systems do not, however, report such learning curves, even if they report a nominal recall figure. When using one of these systems, it is vital to recognize that the learning curve is guiding the user as to when to stop training (because no additional classifier effectiveness seems likely), not on the completeness of the total review effort. Indeed, some systems do not directly attempt to measure overall classifier effectiveness in the above way, but instead give alternative measures of classifier stability, such as the rate at which the classifier makes incorrect calls (known as the overturn rate), or simply as the rate at which the classifier changes its mind about its predictions without reference to a control set at all.

Whether a system should attempt to report a learning curve that represents changes in total cost for a given target level of recall is a subtle question. In principle, such information is more valuable to the user than some abstract measure of classifier accuracy. In particular, it might cost less overall to stop training before abstract classifier effectiveness plateaus, since the incremental cost of training may be less than the saving in subsequent review effort. In practice, though, experience suggests that an optimally effective classifier leads to a near-optimally cheap process. (Put another way, the cost in total effort of slightly overdoing classifier training is generally small.)

Ranks versus Sets

Recall and precision are inherently set-based metrics. That is, we have a set of documents that is our candidate production, and we measure the recall of that set. In the context of classifier evaluation, that means that the classifier is asked to make a binary, relevant/irrelevant call on each document. The recall and precision scores then assess the quality of that call.

Many classifier technologies, however, are capable of going beyond a binary relevance call, and instead assign a more fine-grained relevance score to a document. Documents with higher relevance scores are, in the classifier's view, more likely to be relevant (or more strongly relevant, or both). With relevance scores, what the classifier produces from a set of documents is not a partitioning into predicted-relevant and predicted-irrelevant subsets, but rather a ranking in which the documents with the greatest probability (or strength) of relevance are listed first. Indeed, when a classifier is asked to make a binary relevance call, what it frequently does is assign relevance scores internally, then pick a threshold in the resulting ranking that optimizes some internally estimated metric.

The ability to produce a relevance ranking is particularly valuable when it comes to the review stage of predictive coding process. The unlabeled documents in the collection can then be ranked in decreasing probability of relevance, and the review can work from the top down in prioritized order. (Relevance scores can also be helpful in selecting training documents, by allowing training to focus on the most uncertain cases, or perhaps on cases higher up or lower down the ranking to help clarify existing relevance calls or discover new ones.)

As is the case for set retrieval, a range of metrics is available for evaluating the effectiveness of a relevance ranking. Some of these are adaptations of set-based metrics, with some choice of relevance threshold. The F scores reported by some predictive coding systems, for instance, are actually calculated from a classifier-produced relevance ranking over the control set, by selecting the threshold that leads to the highest *F* score. The accompanying recall and precision scores are then those achieved if the relevance ranking is divided into predicted-relevant and predicted-irrelevant sets around that threshold. (As mentioned before, this threshold might not be the one users would choose themselves; they might prefer, for instance, to pick a lower relevance score threshold, thereby achieving higher recall at the expense of lower precision.) There are also rank metrics that measure the quality of the ranking overall; these can be more sensitive measures of rank quality, but at the same time more difficult to interpret in practical terms. We discuss one of these, known as the Receiver Operating Curve, later in this chapter.

Our originally stated goal in the predictive process was to achieve the highest possible recall at the lowest possible cost (or, stated less emphatically, to pick a satisfactory tradeoff between recall and cost). Given a relevance ranking for a candidate production, this tradeoff can be directly calculated as the depth in the ranking to which review would have to proceed in order to achieve a given level of recall. If we had a fixed recall target of, say, 75 percent, this metric might be called "cost for 75 percent recall" or "effort for 75 percent recall." (Of course, the recall level measured should also take account of the relevant documents already found during training or by other methods.) The conclusion of the production would then be to select the cutoff depth that achieves the target recall; review the prioritized relevance ranking down to that cutoff depth; and form the production from the relevant documents found in that review (or previously in training or otherwise).

Returning to our earlier discussion about the learning curve during training, the metric reported by this learning curve could be the (estimated) cost for 75 percent recall, with the stopping point for training occurring when this cost appeared to be at a minimum (which, as was said before, may be before some measure of classifier effectiveness that is less well grounded in the task at hand had plateaued).

More generally, consideration of all the possible cutoff points in a relevance ranking over the collection, and the recall achieved by each such cutoff point, produces a curve showing the relationship between cutoff depth and recall, known as a gain curve. A schematic gain curve is shown in Figure 13.2. It shows that to achieve 50 percent recall, we need to review 10 percent of the way down the final relevance ranking; to achieve 80 percent recall, 30 percent of the

FIGURE 13.2 A gain curve

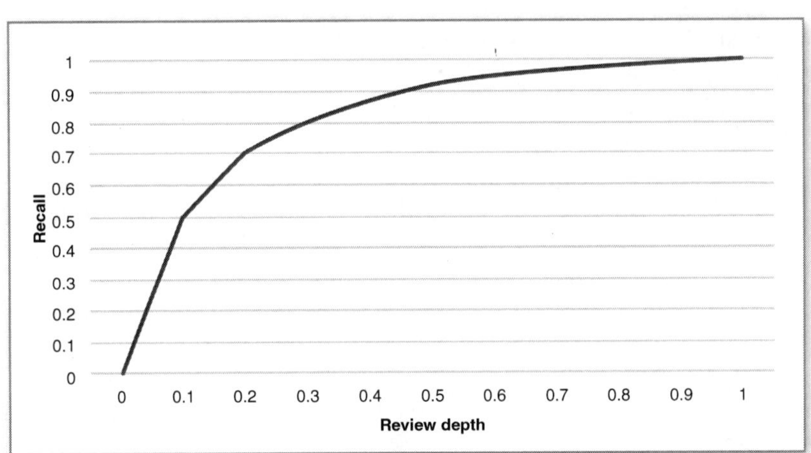

ranking must be reviewed. Clearly, if 100 percent of the ranking is reviewed, recall will also be 100 percent (assuming, bravely, that the reviewers make no errors). The graph shows 0 percent recall for 0 percent review, though as mentioned in practice one would have the relevant documents found in training, even if no review were performed. (Some systems report gain curves as a table, stating the recall at different cutoff depths; this is the same information in a different form.)

The gain curve places a powerful tool in the hands of the review manager, allowing him or her to trade off recall for cost. Reported earlier in the training process, a gain curve (or the summarized cost for recall information) tells the manager what the remaining cost of production would be if training stopped now, and allows him or her to monitor this cost as it (hopefully) decreases with further training.

Alternatives to Recall

Recall, as previously described, aims at characterizing the completeness of a production (candidate or actual). Other metrics have been proposed for the characterization of completeness. (Metrics used for other, essentially intermediate, purposes will be discussed later.)

A very straightforward re-expression of recall is the "miss" or "false negative rate," which is the fraction of the documents that in truth were relevant, but were mistakenly omitted from the candidate production (mathematically, this is simply 1 minus the recall). The false negative rate is often paired with the "false positive rate" (the fraction of the documents that in truth were not relevant, but were mistakenly included in the candidate production) to create what is called a receiver operating characteristic (ROC) curve. Unlike the gain curve, an ROC curve directly expresses the tradeoff in error rates, which is the perspective from which the developers of many automated systems view their goal.

Another alternative metric is elusion. Elusion, as applied to some initial process that divides a collection into two sets (e.g., a putatively responsive set and a discard set, the documents in which are putatively nonresponsive), is defined as the richness of (proportion of relevant documents in) the discard set; that is, the set of documents that are not considered for production or subject to manual review. Elusion does provide an upper-bound estimate of the effort required to find additional relevant documents in the discard pile (elusion would be a measure of effort if the discard pile were processed in a random order, but in practice it is often produced in a system-guided order that tends to raise the elusion value). It provides, however, only a partial description of production completeness. When used to the latter end, discard richness is usually compared to the original richness of the collection as a whole. The argument runs that if discard richness (that is, elusion) is substantially lower than collection richness, then the review process has done an adequate (or proportionate) job of reaping the collection's relevant documents. It seems to us, however, that it might be hard to say what an "adequate" reduction in richness would be. If collection richness were 2 percent, what would be an adequate discard richness? 1.5 percent? 1 percent? 0.5 percent? That question could be answered with reference to the size and diversity of the production, but once you know the size of the production you could just have easily computed recall.

Sampling and Estimation

All the metrics described so far are estimated based upon random sampling. Sampling and estimation are large topics, beyond the scope of the current chapter. It is important, however, to appreciate the core ideas of sample-based metric estimation, and the limitations and costs it involves.

A random sample acts as a representative microcosm of the features of the population it is drawn from. In the evaluation of e-discovery, the key feature we care about is which documents in the collection are relevant and which are not. It is pointless to judge every document in the collection for relevance solely for evaluation purposes (that would be simply performing a linear review); instead, we draw a random sample, judge the documents in the sample for relevance, and use the results to infer values on the collection as a whole, or upon subsets of it.

The most basic use of a sample is to estimate the proportion of the collection, or of a subset such as the discard pile, that is relevant (i.e., the collection or discard richness). Here, the richness of the sample is a direct estimate of the richness of the document set it is drawn from.

Similarly, classifier effectiveness on the collection can be estimated by measuring classifier effectiveness on any random sample from the collection, including the control set. The classifier is asked to predict the relevance of each document in the control set; the correctness of these relevance predictions (or the appropriateness of their underlying relevance scores) is summarized using a metric such as recall or some variant of the F measure (e.g., F_1); and that sample metric score is taken as an estimate of effectiveness on the collection as a whole.

Evaluating rankings is a bit more complex. One alternative is to estimate the recall achieved at different cutoff levels. To estimate the recall achieved by cutting off the relevance ranking at (for example) 20 percent of the way down, one might take the relevance score of the document (from the full collection) at that rank; cut off the ranking over the control set at that same threshold; and take the recall achieved on the control set to that cutoff depth as an estimate of what would be achieved on the full collection. This normally requires some form of interpolation, since the control set may not contain a document with that exact score. (Other sampling and estimation schemes are also possible for this, and for the measures discussed earlier.)

There are several stages at which samples might be drawn during a predictive coding process. An initial sample is often drawn to estimate total collection richness. A separate sample might be drawn to use as the control set to measure classifier effectiveness, or the richness sample might be reused for this purpose. When a production is (provisionally) complete, an additional sample might be drawn from the discard pile to verify that elusion is low; or the control set might be reused for this. There might also be a final sample drawn and judged by representatives of both parties, to verify the stated completeness of the production.

Since the sample is only a subset of the larger population, it may be an imperfect representation of that population. Therefore, metrics measured on the sample are only estimates of what would be seen on the population. The actual values might be higher or lower than the estimates. Due to the use of random sampling, it is possible to statistically characterize the resulting degree of uncertainty in results. Such uncertainty estimates are frequently expressed as confidence intervals (colloquially known as "margins of error," though note that confidence intervals are not necessarily symmetric around the basic estimate). A production protocol might then require not just that the simple estimate of recall is greater than a threshold amount, but that the threshold lie lower than the lower bound of a confidence interval on recall, or perhaps that the confidence interval on the simple estimate has no more than a certain width. The upper and lower boundaries of the confidence interval should always at least be reported, even if a specific requirement is not placed upon it in the protocol; without such an interval being reported, we have no way of assessing the accuracy of the estimation.

Various factors affect the uncertainty of an estimate (or the size and shape of the confidence interval around that estimate). The chief one under the user's control is the sample size: the larger the sample, the more representative it is likely to be of the population, and so the more certain the estimates derived from it. However, the documents in the sample must be judged for relevance, and so the larger the sample, the more costly the evaluation is.

Another important factor affecting the uncertainty of an estimate is that as a phenomenon becomes rarer it becomes more difficult to estimate accurately based upon sampling. The phenomenon of interest in e-discovery is the density and location of relevant documents. Low richness collections, therefore, result in less accurate estimates (or, conversely, require larger sampling and judging exercises to maintain the same level of estimate accuracy).

E-discovery practitioners have been reporting for some time a general decline in the richness of collections being encountered in predictive coding processes. This decline in richness may be due to the growth in the size of corporate document repositories, or to the use of less stringent filtering mechanisms (in itself a desirable development) as practitioners become more confident in the effectiveness and efficiency of predictive coding. There is some concern in the profession that we will soon be seeing, or are already seeing, collections in which richness is so low that our estimates of recall or other metrics either become unreliable or call for impractical sampling efforts. If a moderately large sample of some collection contains only two relevant documents, for instance, it is hard to place much faith in statistical estimates derived from that sample.

Alternative Evaluation Schemes

If very low richness collections render too wide the confidence intervals on sample-based recall estimates, what alternative or supplementary methods might be used to build confidence in the reasonableness of productions made with predictive coding technology (or indeed by any other method)? This is a large and somewhat speculative area of inquiry, but it seems appropriate to make some remarks here.

A key concept here is that of proportionality. It is increasingly accepted by the courts and by legal practitioners that the goal of predictive coding is not perfection, but a level of completeness that is proportionate to the potential value of the evidence being sought and the amounts at stake in the case. We might similarly consider the proportionality of a sampling and estimation effort, and be willing to accept less accurate estimates if the cost of more accurate estimates was disproportionate (though how precisely to quantify that remains an open question). Key to this perspective is that training costs, review costs, and measurement costs are all costs, and the proportionality we must consider involves the total cost.

We mentioned previously that elusion (the richness of the discard pile) provides a rough estimate of the amount of effort required to find additional relevant documents, if review were to continue beyond the current candidate production. That estimate assumes, however, that the discard pile would be reviewed in random order, whereas in practice one would almost certainly want to use a predictive ranking to prioritize the review (thus hopefully decreasing the incremental review effort for each additional relevant document). In any case, estimating discard richness suffers from the same uncertainty problems that affect other sampling tasks in low richness environments.

An alternative approach to estimating incremental effort to find additional relevant documents in the (candidate) discard pile is to observe the fraction of relevant documents that have been discovered in recent review rounds. If the review proceeds down the relevance ranking, we would expect that the fraction of relevant documents would decrease over time. Therefore the fraction of documents that were found to be relevant in the most recent reviewed, say, 5,000 documents, forms a rough upper-bound estimate on the fraction to be expected from the next 5,000 documents to be reviewed. If this fraction falls low enough, then it might form the basis of an argument that further review effort would be disproportionate. (Some consideration would also need to be given to the total number of relevant documents already found, and to the significance or distinctness of the relevant documents still being newly found.)

Certainly, there are objections to this scheme. Not the least is that, used in isolation, it has the potential to reward poor technology or process. To see why this might be a problem, consider the case of a (not very good) predictive coding system that happened to place relevant documents toward the bottom of the ranking. In this case, a low fraction of relevant documents would not be a good stopping signal. Fortunately, reasonably designed systems don't seem to exhibit this behavior. Nevertheless, stopping criteria based on the fraction of newly discovered relevant documents should be complemented by other, contrasting sources of evidence of production completeness and good process.

The Rest of the Story

With apologies to George Box, we might say that all stories are incomplete, but some incomplete stories are useful.[2] Here at the end of our story, we should therefore at least mention that which we have not focused upon.

---

2. "Essentially, all models are wrong, but some are useful . . . ." George E.P. Box, Empirical Model Building and Response Surfaces 424 (1987).

Perhaps our most fundamental simplification has been to consider one relevant document to be as useful as another. Surely this is not true in reality. Sometimes parties will refer to "hot" documents as those that could materially affect the case. Measures have been developed that give more weight to finding better documents, so computing useful measures would not be a problem if we could agree on what's "hot." At present, however, we lack a vocabulary for talking about that between the parties, so production requests get written in ways that simply try to define which documents are wanted, not which are most wanted. If and when this changes, the measurement methods that we will need already exist.

Perhaps our most consequential simplification has been to act as if every judgment is correct. We all know this is not true, but we do not yet fully understand all of the consequences of such errors.[3] Consider, for example, what would happen if we drew a sample of 100 documents for elusion and we found that three of those documents were judged as relevant. If our elusion target were 1 percent, we might then continue. After repeating this several times we might begin to wonder whether what we were seeing was not actually elusion, but rather human error. Indeed, measured error rates on repetitive tasks such as judging documents for relevance can easily rise to the level of a few percent. Confidence intervals that are estimated only from sample sizes, as is typical in the industry today, don't reflect the effects of judgment errors. But as the richness of any set gets small, human error can easily become the larger effect. A related point is that we have written as if the definition of relevance were stable, but of course people learn as they go and the senior attorney may well come to realize that some documents previously thought of as relevant actually were not (or vice versa). The common practice of drawing a control set in advance and treating it as correct throughout the review is questionable at best.

Perhaps our most interesting simplification has been to write as if the most important application of predictive coding is to determining which documents are relevant. Of course, predictive coding

3. For a more extended discussion of the effects of this type of "measurement error," see section 4.3 of Douglas W. Oard & William Webber, *Information Retrieval for E-Discovery*, 7 FOUNDATIONS AND TRENDS IN INFORMATION RETRIEVAL, 100–237 (2013).

can be, and often is, applied for issue coding as well. But if we ask what the largest drivers of cost and delay are in e-discovery, one clear answer would be the cost of privilege review. The reason for this is simple—reviews for privilege are still commonly manual, linear, and performed by highly qualified attorneys. Indeed, the situation with privilege review bears an uncanny resemblance to the linear manual review for responsiveness of earlier times. What broke that model was not some new cadre of technical wizards shilling predictive coding; what broke it was the dramatic growth in the scale of the reviews that needed to be performed. We are approaching an era in which the scale of the documents that are found to be responsive may now break our present privilege review process. When that happens, we expect that another new cadre of technical wizards will be here to help.

EDITORS' INTRODUCTION TO CHAPTER 14

Michael D. Berman

There is an old maxim in carpentry—"measure twice, cut once." In this chapter, Bruce Hedin, Dan Brassil, and Amanda Jones address measurement as a quality management tool in e-discovery. While Chapters 13 and 14 provide a "how to" description of measurement, this chapter focuses on quality management of the review process, something critically important to litigators and their clients, particularly in light of the cost-containment implications.

The authors note that virtually every review begins "in a state of imperfect knowledge . . . ." As such, the attorney stumbling without guidance runs the risks of the old parable about the blind people and an elephant. The chapter shows how to avoid those pitfalls by taking the reader through the conceptual steps needed to make sense of the data. In short, it provides the project management tools for planning and conducting a review.

Further, the authors explain key, but often overlooked, aspects of a review, such as documentation. Often, years elapse during a review. There are few things more frustrating than having a question posed by a court years later, only to have the very solid response lost in the haze of the distorted memory of a long-gone employee.

The central focus, however, is on measurement. First, the chapter addresses measurement as review progresses, noting its role in both quality control and cost containment, just as wooden sailing ships took soundings before entering perilous waters. Doing so in order to find potential problems, such as documents unsuited to the review tool, permits early "course corrections."

Next, the authors turn to measurements applicable at the conclusion of review. This exercise, called validation, relies heavily on empirical components. For example, it typically involves manual review of a simple random sample to estimate recall (did the search find almost everything that was sought) and precision (how much extraneous material was also retrieved). The authors note that "heavily" does not mean exclusively, and also explain the use of qualitative measures in combination with the statistical procedures: "Measurement is not the only source of valuable information, however, and should not blind you to other sources of information complementary to sample-based measurement."

Putting it all in context, the authors note:

> In order to ensure that a measurement exercise produces valid results, it is not necessary for an attorney to become a statistician; it is simply necessary for the attorney to recognize that any measurement exercise will raise a set of questions the answers to which will require statistical competence. Once that recognition is made, it becomes a matter of ensuring that an individual with that competence is available for assisting in the design and execution of the measurement protocol. The attorney, of course, still has a crucial role to play . . . .

As part of their conclusion, the authors note that litigators, as the consumers of litigation review tools, need to be aware of the sampling features of each tool under consideration. Frankly, noting that "measurement does not tell the whole story," the authors carefully explain the importance of the part of the story that it tells. Emphasizing the difference between document recall and information recall, they argue: "Once a reasonably high level of document recall has been achieved (e.g., 80 percent), however, it is typically the case that, when additional relevant documents are found, those new documents in fact add no new information; that is to say, the information in the unretrieved 20 percent of relevant documents is almost entirely redundant to information in the already-retrieved 80 percent of relevant documents."

CHAPTER 14

On the Place of Measurement in E-Discovery

Bruce Hedin, Dan Brassil, and Amanda Jones

Introduction

Measurement has become an increasingly frequent topic in discussions about e-discovery tools and methods. In law review articles,[1] legal blogs[2] and symposia,[3] scientific studies,[4] as well as actual Rule 26(f) conferences, judicial hearings, and court orders,[5] the measurement of

1. *See, e.g.*, Maura R. Grossman & Gordon V. Cormack, *Comments on "The Implications of Rule 26(g) on the Use of Technology-Assisted Review,"* 7 Fed. Cts. L. Rev. 285 (2014); Karl Schieneman & Thomas C. Gricks III, *The Implications of Rule 26(g) on the Use of Technology-Assisted Review*, 7 Fed. Cts. L. Rev. 239 (2013).

2. *See, e.g.*, Bill Dimm, *Comments on Rio Tinto v. Vale and Sample Size*, Clustify Blog (March 2015), http://blog.cluster-text.com/; Ralph Losey, *Introducing "ei-Recall"—A New Gold Standard for Recall Calculations in Legal Search—Parts One–Three*, E-Discovery Team Blog (2015), http://e-discoveryteam.com/.

3. The Sedona Conference Institute, for example, featured a panel at the 2014 All Voices Meeting on the topic of "Approaches to Validating TAR Efforts." The moderator of the panel was Maura R. Grossman; panelists were Gordon V. Cormack, Bruce Hedin, and David D. Lewis.

4. *See, e.g.*, William Webber, *Approximate Recall Confidence Intervals*, 31 ACM Transactions on Information Systems 1 (2013); William Webber, Douglas W. Oard, Falk Scholer, & Bruce Hedin, *Assessor Error in Stratified Evaluation*, in Proceedings of the 19th ACM International Conference on Information and Knowledge Management 623 (2010).

5. *See, e.g.*, Order Regarding Discovery of ESI, *In re* Biomet M2a Magnum Hip Implant Prod. Liab. Litig., Cause No. 3:12-MD-2391 (N.D. In. Apr. 8, 2013); Da Silva Moore v. Publicis Groupe, 287 F.R.D. 182 (S.D.N.Y. Feb. 24, 2012).

the effectiveness of e-discovery tools and methods has become a central focus of attention. That is not a bad thing: when you are evaluating the completeness or accuracy of a response to a request for production, quantitative measures can provide unique insights into the questions you are asking.

However, while measurement has become a prominent topic in conversations about e-discovery, the precise role of measurement in the e-discovery process, what it can contribute and where, is not always well defined or understood. In this chapter, we discuss the contributions measurement can make to an effective quality management regimen in e-discovery.

The chapter is not intended to serve as a "how-to" guide for measurement. While there is certainly a place for a practitioners' guide to the nuts and bolts of sampling and estimation in e-discovery,[6] this chapter is not intended to fill that role. Rather, the focus of the chapter is on how the information provided by properly executed sampling and estimation protocols can be used in a quality management regimen for e-discovery. The chapter, moreover, is not intended to cover the role of measurement in all phases of the e-discovery process. While there is a role for quantitative gauges of quality in all phases of the e-discovery process, from identification through production, this chapter confines its attention to the review element of the e-discovery process and the role that measurement can play in achieving quality and cost containment in that phase.

The chapter is organized as follows. We begin by considering the range of elements essential to a sound review process; included among these is measurement. We then focus more specifically on the measurement element, looking at the role it plays both during the review process and at the conclusion of the process, and at the principles that guide the effective use of measurement. In the next section, we review what we see as the chief benefits of measurement for the various stakeholders in the e-discovery process (providers of review tools and services, parties to investigations or litigation, and judges called upon to resolve discovery disputes). We then turn to reasons why some might be reluctant to place an emphasis on measurement in e-discovery; in

6. For very helpful guidance of this sort, see Chapter 13 in this volume, contributed by David D. Lewis.

most cases, we recognize the merit in the objections, but we argue that the appropriate answer is not to forego measurement but rather to use measurement properly (i.e., as one, but not the only, source of information about the quality of a review process). Finally, in the last section, we add some summary thoughts on the part that measurement can play in a review process.

Elements of a Sound Review Process

A review process, whether manual or technology-assisted,[7] if it is to be capable of consistently and predictably producing high-quality results, will include a number of elements that bring about the conditions needed for a successful result.[8] One of these elements is measurement, but measurement is not the only one. Elements of a fundamentally sound review process include:

1. Planning
2. Topic analysis
3. Selection and application of tools and methods
4. Expertise
5. Adaptability
6. Documentation
7. Measurement

In this section, we briefly review the part played by each of these elements in enabling a successful review effort.[9]

---

7. This chapter makes no assumptions about the specific approach that might be taken to the identification of relevant or responsive material. The principles apply regardless of the specific approach taken, whether that approach is some variety of manual review or some variety of technology-assisted review. Throughout the chapter, then, the term "review" is intended to be understood capaciously, covering all approaches to the identification of relevant or responsive material.

8. What counts as a "successful result" will of course vary with the specific objectives of each review project. In the case of a review for responsiveness, a successful result will generally be one in which the lead attorney can (i) confirm that the production is reasonably accurate and complete, as per Rule 26(g), and (ii), in the event of a challenge, quickly and efficiently gather the requisite documentation, protocols, and measurements to defend against said challenge.

9. For additional perspective on the practices and principles that enable the achievement of high quality results in e-discovery, see The Sedona Conference, *The Sedona Conference Best Practices Commentary on the Use of Search and Information*

Planning

Document review has increasingly become a complex exercise, involving the coordinated application of human and technological resources in order to meet objectives that are specific to a given review project under conditions that are also specific to the project. The first step in laying the foundation for a successful review is therefore planning.

Developing a review plan means giving advance consideration to the project's objectives, the conditions under which those objectives have to be met, and the resources available for executing the project. Articulating an approach to carrying out the project that is well-adapted to those objectives, conditions, and resources and sharing it with all pertinent stakeholders is also a vital step in the planning process. Among the factors that should be taken into consideration in developing a plan are the following.

- **Time and cost constraints.** Deadlines for a document production (both what the deadlines are and how they are structured), and thus for completing the review, will obviously shape the approach taken. The budget available for the review will also set limits on the range of options that might be considered.
- **Accuracy and completeness priorities.** Accuracy[10] priorities will vary from project to project. In some cases, for example, there may be little tolerance for including

---

Retrieval Methods in E-Discovery, 15 SEDONA CONF. J. 217 (2014); The Sedona Conference, *The Sedona Conference Commentary on Achieving Quality in the E-Discovery Process*, 15 SEDONA CONF. J. (2014).

10. When applied to document review, the term "accuracy" can be used in both an informal and a formal sense. The informal usage does not refer to a measure specifically defined in terms of true positives, false positives, true negatives, and false negatives, but rather serves as a simple and intuitive way of referring to how close an actual result is to the ideal result. In its formal usage, on the other hand, accuracy is a measure that is well-defined in terms of true positives, false positives, true negatives, and false negatives, but one that, in practice, is of little value in the context of most information retrieval exercises (including e-discovery); *see* Christopher D. Manning, Prabhakar Raghavan, & Hinrich Schütze, INTRODUCTION TO INFORMATION RETRIEVAL 143 (2008). In this chapter, we use the term "accuracy" only in the informal sense. When we wish to refer to well-defined metrics, we will refer to recall, precision, or some other such measure.

documents that are not actually responsive in a production; in such cases, precision will be a priority. In other cases, there may be less sensitivity to false positives, so lower levels of precision will be acceptable. Likewise, in some cases, for example, in a case preparation exercise such as evaluating various case theories, a comprehensive result may not be needed; in such cases, high recall will be less of a priority. In other cases, for example, a review for responsiveness, a reasonably complete retrieval result will be needed, so high recall will be a priority objective. A sound review plan will be adapted to such priorities.

- **Data.** Data represents the terrain over which the review will be conducted and the approach taken to the review should be adapted to that terrain. Key considerations regarding data include the following.
- **Volume.** The size of the data set will be a key consideration in formulating a plan for a review. The approach appropriate for reviewing a set of a few thousand documents will be different from the approach appropriate for reviewing a set of a few million documents.
- **Characteristics.** The nature of the documents in the review set also matters. Are they mostly e-mail or some other form of ESI (e.g., images or microblog posts)? Are the documents sourced from one organization or from multiple organizations? Is the content of the documents mostly English or is there a significant non-English component? The answers to questions such as these will shape the approach taken to the review.
- **Timetable.** The review plan should also be adapted to the timetable on which the data will be made available for review. In the case of large projects, the review set will rarely be made available in a single batch; more typically, the review set will be made available in several batches over time and the composition of those batches, in terms of the dates and the sources of the documents, will vary.

  A review that is closely tailored to the nature and circumstances of the data will be more effective and efficient than one that is not.

- **Human resources.** Human resources are a key component of any review, whether manual or technology-assisted. Those resources will include individuals with the legal and subject matter expertise pertinent to the given matter, as well as individuals with the technological and scientific expertise required to apply properly the tools and methods chosen for the review. Developing a sound review plan requires taking into account both the human resources available for the review and the resources required by any given approach to ensure the chosen approach will be supported by all the resources required to be effective.
- **Technological resources.** Tools are also a key component of any review, whether manual or technology-assisted. Developing a sound review plan requires giving advance thought to the tools that will be used to carry out the review and ensuring that the review plan provides for all the inputs and resources those tools require to be effective.
- **Validation requirements.** Almost any review, whether one subject to external standards of effectiveness (e.g., a responsive review) or one subject only to internal standards of quality (e.g., a review in preparation for depositions), will include procedures for some form of quality control as the review is conducted and for some form of validation of the final result. The specific standards that are operative will depend, in part, on considerations of what is reasonable and proportional in a given circumstance and will vary from jurisdiction to jurisdiction, from matter to matter, and from one review exercise to the next. Developing a sound review plan requires giving advance consideration both to the standards the review will be expected to meet and to the method by which adherence to those standards will be demonstrated. Steps must also be taken to ensure that the plan makes provision for procedures and resources able to satisfy those validation requirements.

Giving advance consideration to factors such as these and putting in place a review plan that is tailored to them is the first step in laying the foundation for a successful review.

Topic Analysis

If a review is to be successful, it must be well informed. More specifically, the review must be guided by a clear and specific understanding of the categories of information that are the target of the exercise and of the ways those categories of information manifest themselves in the documents that are the domain of the review. Gathering this information involves both consultation with the pertinent experts and analysis of the data collection itself.[11]

Two types of experts can provide essential insights into the categories of information that are the target of the review: legal experts and organization-internal experts. Legal experts, that is, the attorneys representing the party for which the review is being conducted, will have a unique understanding both of the legal and factual issues pertinent to the matter and of the overall strategy the party is adopting for the litigation or investigation. A sound review process will include provisions for seeing that the attorneys' knowledge and perspective on the scope and definition of the target categories are accurately passed on to those conducting the review. Active employees of the company or organization that generated the data collection under review may serve as organization-internal experts, providing unique insights into the business processes and practices relevant to the review. A sound review process will also include a mechanism for efficiently eliciting those insights when they could be helpful.[12] The vehicle for the transfer of knowledge from these experts may take any of a number of possible forms, from interviews to gathering assessments of samples of documents, but it is essential that the transfer take place by some means.

Valuable information about how the target categories manifest themselves in actual documents can also be gathered from the data collection itself. Every organization, and even every department within an organization, will have its own business processes and practices, as well as its own modes of linguistic usage when talking

11. For a discussion of the importance of user modeling for effective retrieval, see Dan Brassil, Christopher Hogan, & Simon Attfield, *The Centrality of User Modeling to High Recall with High Precision Search* in Proceedings of the IEEE-SMC (2009).

12. *See,* e.g., William A. Gross Const. Ass'n v. Am. Mfrs. Mut. Ins. Co., 256 F.R.D. 134, 135 (S.D.N.Y. 2009).

about those processes and practices. How the target categories will actually manifest themselves in the document collection will depend on organization-specific features of these business and linguistic practices. A sound review process will include a collection analytics component that enables the gathering of this sort of population-specific information.

A review that includes sound procedures for eliciting information about the categories of information to be identified from both experts and the collection itself will have a clear view of what it is tasked with finding and so will be better positioned to achieve a successful result.

Selection and Application of Tools and Methods

The efficiency and effectiveness of any approach to review can be enhanced by the use of appropriate technologies. Even a manual approach can be made more efficient and effective by using a review platform that includes functionalities, such as search and sampling, that can enable improvements in the review's consistency and accuracy. A key element of designing and implementing a sound review process is therefore the selection and application of efficacious tools and methods.

If the potential benefits of technology are to be realized, the technology must be used in a manner that is appropriate both to the overall approach taken to the review and to the technology itself. Adherence to the following principles will help to ensure that technology is effectively integrated into the overall review process.

- **Be aware of the capabilities and limitations of the technologies being used.** Every tool has its strengths and weaknesses, and those using the tool should be aware of them. By being aware of a tool's strengths, you put yourself in a position to realize the full benefits of the tool; by being aware of a tool's limitations, you can avoid applying the tool to a task to which it is ill-suited.
- **Give advance thought to where the technology best fits in the overall process.** A document review is a complex process, involving several steps. A tool that is appropriate for one step may not be appropriate for another. A technology, for example, that is very effective for corpus exploration and analysis may be less effective as a platform for review. Such a

technology would best be used for purposes of gathering data that will inform the process of making responsiveness determinations but not for purposes of making the final responsiveness determinations themselves. Understanding where a given tool can make the most valuable contribution to the overall effort is essential to the effective use of technology.

- **Ensure that the inputs and conditions required for the proper application of the technology are in place.** Any technology will have certain requirements as to the conditions under which it is to be used if it is to work properly. A tool powered by compressed air must be supported by a compressor capable of delivering air at the required pressure. Similarly, a classification technology that requires samples of a certain type or size in order to be effective needs to be provided with such samples.
- **Ensure that those applying the technology have appropriate training and skills.** A technology will be consistently effective only if it is applied by individuals with the required technological competence. A technology, for example, designed under the expectation that it will be driven by individuals competent in the iterative composition of training sets will likely not work well when applied by individuals lacking that competence.

A technology will be effective only if the task to which it is applied is one to which it is well suited and if the individuals applying the technology have the required training and skills. A review effort that selects and uses technology in accordance with the principles just described will put itself in position to make effective use of technology in achieving its ultimate objectives.

Expertise

A sound review process will not only include tools that are appropriate to the overall approach to the exercise, but also experts appropriate to the approach.

As data populations that are the domain of reviews continue to grow in size and complexity, those responsible for conducting reviews are increasingly turning to advanced search and screening technologies that have been developed and tested by researchers in the field of information retrieval (hence the occasion for the book to which this chapter is a contribution). These tools and methods, however, if they are to be properly implemented, typically require more specialized expertise than that contributed by conventionally educated attorneys, subject matter experts, or organization-internal experts. The proper implementation of advanced tools and methods will typically require contributions from individuals with certain kinds of scientific and technical expertise (e.g., linguistics, statistics, data science) that have been found key to successful search and retrieval.

The types of experts required will vary from one approach to another. Some approaches, for example, will rely on a greater contribution of linguistic expertise than will others. All approaches, however, can benefit from the contribution of some form of scientific or technical expertise. Even a manual approach, for example, can benefit from the quality control guidance that the proper application of sampling and statistics can provide. What is incumbent on those responsible for a review is that they give thought to the kinds of expertise that are expected under the approach being adopted and make provisions for those kinds of expertise to be accessible when and where they are needed.[13]

Adaptability

Almost any review, even one diligently planned, will begin in a state of imperfect knowledge (of the ultimate size and composition of the data set that will be the domain of the review, of the content of the documents in the data set, of the precise boundaries of relevance or responsiveness, of definitive project deadlines, and so on) and so will likely see changes in direction over the course of the exercise. A sound review process will therefore provide for ongoing acquisition of

13. It may be worth noting, from a practical perspective, that making provision for the appropriate kinds of expertise does not mean that every review project needs to be staffed full-time with a PhD in linguistics, a PhD in statistics, a PhD in data science, and so on; what it means is that any sound review process will make provision for access to those kinds of expertise when the tools and methods being applied so require. *See, e.g.*, Victor Stanley, Inc. v. Creative Pipe, Inc., 250 F.R.D. 251 (D. Md. 2008) (subsequent history omitted).

information about project conditions and requirements and for adaptation to changes.[14]

Changes in direction may be occasioned by any of a number of different events. Some changes will be occasioned by the data set that is the domain of the review. The ultimate size and composition of the review collection, for example, may not be known at the outset. As new custodians or data sources are brought within the scope of the review, those conducting the review will need to conduct diagnostics of the implications of the new data, and make appropriate changes in the methods and resources used to conduct the review.

Other changes will follow from changes in the scope of what is to be considered responsive or relevant for purposes of the review exercise. As additional information is gained from the document collection in the course of the review, new topics may be brought within the scope of relevance or the criteria for topics already within scope may be modified or further specified.[15] A sound review process will anticipate such changes in scope and will build in protocols for responding to such changes, both with respect to data already classified and with respect to data not yet classified.

Still other changes in direction may follow from changes in the practical parameters set for a review exercise. At the start of a responsiveness review, for example, discussions with opposing counsel regarding timelines for the production may still be ongoing; the review must have the flexibility to be able to steer toward deadlines that are not fully known when the review gets under way. Such events, which are not uncommon, will cause changes in the demands a review is working under.

---

14. On the importance of recognizing changing search requirements in information retrieval generally, see Nicholas J. Belkin, *Anomalous States of Knowledge as a Basis for Information Retrieval*, 5 CANADIAN J. INFO. SCI. 133 (1980).

15. For discussion of how search behavior can be affected by information gained, see Rong Tang & Paul Solomon, *Toward an Understanding of the Dynamics of Relevance Judgment: An Analysis of One Person's Search Behavior*, 34 INFO. PROCESSING & MGMT. 237 (1998); Shu Ching Yang, *Information Seeking as Problem-Solving Using a Qualitative Approach to Uncover the Novice Learner's Information-Seeking Processes in a Perseus Hypertext System*, 19 LIBR. & INFO. RES. 71 (1997).

A sound review process will have the capacity to adapt to changes in direction, both to changes that could reasonably be anticipated at the outset of the review and to changes that could not. Of course, a well-planned review will minimize the number and scope of changes by gaining, from the start, as complete and accurate a picture as possible of project conditions and requirements. In real-world circumstances, however, that initial picture will almost never be entirely complete or accurate, so the review must have the capacity to adapt.

Documentation

A sound review process will be one that is well documented. A well-documented review process will be one in which a complete and accurate record is maintained of all procedures followed, all key decisions made, and all evaluations of effectiveness conducted either during or at the conclusion of the review. Maintaining such a record can enable improvements in (i) efficiency and effectiveness, (ii) repeatability, and (iii) transparency and defensibility.

A document review is a complex exercise involving multiple steps and multiple individuals executing those steps. Documentation can enable improvements in efficiency and effectiveness by ensuring that all participants in the exercise have visibility into what other participants have done or are doing. That visibility can ensure that the various components of the process are working in harmony (or, if they are not, ensure that the discordance is recognized and remedied).

Maintaining complete and accurate documentation also helps improve the consistency and repeatability of a process. While it is true that every review is, in some way, different from any other, it is also true that one implementation of a review process can benefit from knowledge of what was done in prior implementations of the process. By being aware of how a prior review was conducted and how it met the challenges it encountered, those charged with conducting a review will be able to replicate the steps that were successful in the prior review and to avoid any missteps that were taken. Complete and accurate documentation is essential to providing visibility from one exercise to another.

Complete and accurate documentation is also required if a review process is to be transparent and defensible. Whether responding to questions raised in an internal audit of the review or questions posed by opposing counsel challenging the results of the review, documentation will be essential for demonstrating that procedures were followed, sound decisions were made, and standards of quality were met.

Measurement

A review process that includes the elements just described (advance planning, thorough topic analysis, selection and application of appropriate tools and methods, use of scientific and technical expertise, adaptability, and complete and accurate documentation) will be well positioned to achieve a successful result. There is one additional element, however, that, when incorporated into a review process, can provide insights into whether a successful result has in fact been achieved in any given instance. In the remainder of this chapter, we elaborate on the role of measurement in a review process.

The Use of Measurement in a Review Process

Measurement can be a valuable tool in answering fundamental questions that occur in the course of a review, and, as such, it is an essential element of a sound review process. In order for the potential that measurement holds to be realized, however, those conducting the review must understand both the roles that measurement can play and the principles that guide its effective use. In this section, we review the ways in which measurement can contribute to a review (see The Role of Measurement) as well as the principles that guide its effective use (see Principles for the Effective Use of Measurement).

The Role of Measurement

There is more than one role that measurement can play in a review process, and the role appropriate for measurement in the specific circumstances of one review may not be the one appropriate for it in the specific circumstances of another. In the following sections, we look at the contributions measurement can make both during the course of a review and at its conclusion.

The Role of Measurement When Applying Review Tools and Methods

Real-Time Gauge of Effectiveness. During the course of a review, measurement can provide timely and actionable information on the effectiveness of the review effort at a given point in time, and thereby enable the review effort to meet quality targets with greater speed and efficiency. Timely quantitative information on effectiveness (e.g., in the form of estimates of recall and/or precision[16]) will tell those conducting the review where the effort is on track to meet targets set for quality[17] and where it is not, thereby allowing those conducting the review to focus more time and resources on the aspects of the review most in need of help. The outcome is not only the achievement of a successful result but also the achievement of that result in a shorter time and at a lower cost.

If the efficiencies that measurement can bring are to be realized, however, the measurement protocol should be designed to provide just the information needed (no more, no less) to make an effective adjustment to the allocation of resources on the review. That means having in place a measurement protocol that provides an actionable gauge of effectiveness, but that does so quickly and without requiring a burdensome sampling and review exercise. That, in turn, may mean that, in the course of a review, we tolerate a greater amount of uncertainty being associated with the estimates provided by the protocol (with that greater uncertainty typically being realized as lower confidence levels or wider confidence intervals) than we would accept, for example, in a final validation exercise.

16. In the context of e-discovery, recall and precision are the metrics most commonly used to gauge the effectiveness of a review. Other metrics (e.g., F_1 or, for ranked output, average precision) are available, however, and, depending on the nature and output of the system (e.g., set versus ranked list), these might be selected for purposes of guiding the exercise. For a discussion of effectiveness measures for both unranked and ranked result sets, see MANNING et al. *supra* note 10, at 142*ff*.

17. As we discuss in the section titled Principles for the Effective Use of Measurement (see under Principle 4), quantitative measures do not tell the whole story regarding the effectiveness of a review. Real-time measures can, nonetheless, give the team valuable guidance as to where to focus effort.

The protocol should also allow for different levels of statistical rigor at different levels of granularity. Measurements of effectiveness can be taken at an aggregate level—for example, measuring effectiveness at identifying what is generally responsive across the entire collection—or at a more granular level—for example, measuring effectiveness on specific topics or issues or measuring effectiveness on specific subsets of the collection (for example, among documents associated with specific departments or custodians). Measuring at a more granular level can be helpful, insofar as the more granular measurements will enable better-informed decisions on how to allocate resources over the course of the review.

Measurement at a more granular level also, however, entails some cost, in terms of the additional sampling and review required to obtain the measurements.[18] Lest the cost of getting information exceed the information's practical or actionable value, therefore, measurements should be taken only at a level of granularity at which the review team is prepared to respond. Moreover, such measurements as are taken at a more granular level should generally be expected to provide a rougher (but still actionable) gauge of effectiveness, and thus will be such as to entail lighter sampling (often, at very granular levels, little more than a "sounding").

Measurements of effectiveness during the course of a review can enable the review effort to achieve a successful result in a more predictable and efficient manner. In order to provide those benefits, however, the measurement protocol should be well adapted to the specific requirements and conditions of the review exercise. Over-measuring, just as under-measuring, can lead to waste of time and resources.

Support in Addressing Additional Questions. While providing real-time information about effectiveness is the primary contribution of measurement during the course of a review, measurement can also contribute to addressing other questions that occur once a review is

18. It is not only that the granular measurement is an additional measurement; it may also be a more expensive measurement than the aggregate measurement. Insofar as the granular measurement (e.g., the measurement of effectiveness on a specific topic or issue code) is targeting a lower frequency item, it may require larger samples, if it is expected to provide estimates that are as precise as those provided at the aggregate level.

under way. In some cases, for example, even after collection and culling, the legal team may have a priori grounds for hypothesizing that some well-defined subset of the review collection is nearly void of responsive (or privileged) material (e.g., on grounds of what is known about certain custodians and the business practices of the organization that generated the collection). In such cases, sampling and measurement can be used to gather data that will corroborate or refute the hypothesis.[19] The legal team can then decide, on the basis of both the a priori reasoning and the empirical evidence, whether there are sufficient grounds to put the subset in question on a separate track from the rest of the collection.

In other cases, the review team may have reason to believe that certain parts of the collection may exhibit features that render the documents exhibiting those features unsuitable for the review methodology planned for most of the collection (e.g., documents exhibiting poor quality OCR, documents with inaccurate metadata values, and so on). In such cases, sampling and measurement can be used to quantify the extent of the issue and thereby help the review team to decide whether the issue is one that needs to be addressed and, if so, how.

We noted earlier (in the Adaptability section) that changes in direction during the course of a review are to be expected; changes in the data set, changes in the scope of responsiveness, changes in production requirements, and so on, are common occurrences that entail a need for course correction. Measurement can enable a better-informed and more efficient response to a change in requirements. In the case of a change in the scope of responsiveness, for example, a well-articulated definition of responsiveness, coupled with sampling and measurement, will allow quantification of the impact of the change, thereby helping the review team formulate an efficient plan for responding to the change in scope. In the case of additions to the data set, sampling and measurement can enable a diagnostic assessment of the extent to which the new data are unlike the data already seen, thereby providing

19. Sampling, of course, cannot demonstrate that *no* responsive documents (or *no* privileged documents) reside in the subset in question; absent exhaustive review, we must always allow for the existence of black swans. Sampling can, however, allow us to conclude, at a given level of confidence, that responsive (or privileged) documents represent no more than some threshold proportion of the subset (with larger samples allowing conclusions about lower thresholds).

the review team with a clearer view as to what steps will need to be taken to incorporate the new data in the review exercise.

The Role of Measurement When Validating the Results of Applying Review Tools and Methods

Measurement also has a role to play at the conclusion of a review exercise. If we have followed a sound review process (one that incorporates the elements described in Elements of a Sound Review Process, including gauges of effectiveness taken over the course of the exercise), we will have good reason to believe that we have achieved a successful result. We will put that belief on firmer ground, however, if we couple that story of a sound process with the empirical evidence provided by a final validation of the results. A well-documented process description will provide evidence that we have followed a process that would be expected to meet the objectives set for the review; a validation exercise will provide evidence that we have followed a process that did in fact meet the review's objectives.[20]

Measurement is a key component of any validation exercise. A measurement protocol used for purposes of validating final results will typically take the form of a sampling and manual review exercise designed to enable the estimation of the recall and precision achieved by the review. Measures other than recall and precision might be used, but recall and precision are most familiar to legal practitioners, and they most directly answer the questions legal practitioners generally have about the results of a review effort: to what extent have I succeeded in retrieving *all* that I set out to find (recall) and to what extent have I succeeded in retrieving *only* what I set out to find (precision)? With estimates of recall and precision in hand, and with the scope for the sampling-based uncertainty associated with those estimates properly taken into account (typically, through the calculation of confidence intervals), we will have a sound quantitative gauge of the extent to which the review has met its objectives for accuracy and completeness.

---

20. Our focus in this section is on the role of measurement in a sound validation process. What counsel chooses to *disclose* about a validation process and its results is a separate question, to which different attorneys may give different answers depending on their circumstances.

While most measurement protocols used for final validation will have in common the gauging of recall and precision and the use of sampling, protocols can vary with respect to a range of other features. For example, some protocols will result in a point estimate for recall, along with a confidence interval associated with that estimate (e.g., a point estimate of 75 percent, associated with a 95 percent confidence interval, the lower limit of which is 71 percent and the upper limit of which is 79 percent); other protocols will not provide a point estimate but will simply demonstrate, at a given confidence level (e.g., 95 percent), that the recall achieved by the review exercise is at or above some pre-specified level (e.g., 80 percent). Among protocols designed to provide a point estimate and confidence interval, some will provide a two-sided interval—that is, an interval with both upper and lower limits—while others will provide a one-sided interval—that is, an interval bounded only on the lower side (after all, when it comes to recall, our chief concern is whether recall is too low). Protocols may also vary with respect to the confidence level associated with the statements the protocol enables. While a 95 percent confidence level is most commonly used in current practice, there may be circumstances in which a lower confidence level is tolerated in the interest of keeping sample sizes to reasonable levels—for example, when the prevalence of relevant material is so low that the size of samples required to obtain acceptable estimates would become prohibitive at a 95 percent confidence level. When designing a measurement protocol, there will be features, such as those just described, that can be set by those consuming the results of the protocol. In selecting a protocol, legal practitioners should, in consultation with individuals with appropriate statistical expertise, choose a protocol with features appropriate and proportionate to their circumstances.

Measurement is a key component of a validation exercise, but it is not the only component. While it is important to recognize the contribution sampling and measurement can make, it is also important to recognize the limitations of sampling and measurement. In some cases, for example, when the prevalence of responsive material is very low (less than, say, 1 percent of the review collection), obtaining a recall estimate coupled with a narrow confidence interval may be very costly in terms of the size of the sample required to obtain the estimate, with the sample size running in the tens of thousands of documents or more. In such cases, considerations of proportionality may direct the review team away from the estimation of recall across the full review collection and to alternatives that combine statistical measurement with other forms of reasoning. The team might decide, for example, to focus statistical sampling and estimation on just the subsets of the collection expected, on a priori grounds (e.g., due to the business responsibilities of the custodians that were the source of the subset), to be richer in responsive material. Then, for the rest of the collection, the team might couple a priori reasoning about the scarcity of responsive material in that subset (e.g., again, due to the business responsibilities of the custodians that were the source of the subset) with judgmental sampling[21] that, while falling short of precise recall estimation, does provide some amount of empirical support for the a priori hypothesis.

Measures of recall and precision are also subject to the limitation that, in themselves, they provide little insight into the *quality* of the information captured, or, perhaps more importantly, not captured, by a review effort.[22] It is one thing to miss a document that meets the definition of responsiveness but contains information that is of marginal importance or that could be gathered from other documents that have been captured by the review effort; it is another thing to miss a responsive document that contains truly important information (i.e., a document that might be considered "hot" or "highly relevant") or a document that contains responsive information that could not be gathered from documents already in the retrieved set. Standard recall measures do not make distinctions on the basis of the importance or novelty of information. For this reason, in order to provide a more complete view of the effectiveness of a retrieval effort, a well-rounded

21. "Judgmental sampling" is sampling done with an eye not to obtaining estimates of full-population characteristics, but simply to gaining a better view of parts of the population that are of particular interest; *see* Maura R. Grossman & Gordon V. Cormack, *The Grossman-Cormack Glossary of Technology-Assisted Review*, 7 FED. CTS. L. REV. 21 (2013) (reprinted as an appendix in this book).

22. Indeed, standard recall metrics are not direct measures of even the *quantity* of relevant information captured; they are direct measures of the quantity of documents containing relevant information that have been captured, and thus are only an indirect gauge of the quantity of relevant information captured (see the section titled The Glass Is 20 Percent Empty).

validation protocol will complement the quantitative information provided by estimates of recall and precision with the qualitative information provided by an analysis of the importance or novelty of the information contained in any false negatives observed in the samples used to obtain measurements. Whether the review effort can reasonably be called "complete" depends on the results of both the quantitative and the qualitative analysis.[23]

Principles for the Effective Use of Measurement

Measurement, as we have just seen, can make a unique and valuable contribution to the efficiency and effectiveness of a review effort, both during its execution and at its conclusion. In order to make those contributions, however, the measurement exercise must be designed and executed in a manner that is both statistically sound and appropriate to the specific circumstances of the measurement exercise. In this section, we review the following general principles governing the effective use of measurement in e-discovery.

- **Principle 1:** Let the question you are asking shape the sampling and measurement exercise (not vice versa).
- **Principle 2:** One size does not fit all. Find a sampling and measurement plan that is appropriate to your circumstances.
- **Principle 3:** Take advantage of the capabilities of sample-based measurement, but be cognizant of its limitations.
- **Principle 4:** Remember the rest of the story. Complement the information provided by measurement with information drawn from other sources.
- **Principle 5:** Know what you are doing. Design and execute your measurement plan in consultation with individuals with appropriate statistical expertise and experience as necessary.

23. If the results of the qualitative analysis indicate that the review/retrieval effort is missing documents containing important or novel information, there would be grounds for continuing that effort even if, in purely quantitative terms, a high level of recall has been achieved. This is one reason why it would be unwise to attempt to specify a single recall threshold that would be applicable, for validation purposes, in all circumstances (see the section titled There Is No Consensus on a Number).

Principle 1

The first step in arriving at a well-designed sampling and measurement protocol is not one that requires specialized statistical training. The first step is simply thinking through and clearly articulating the question you wish the protocol to answer as well as the minimum amount of information that would serve as an answer to the question. For example, given an e-mail archive that you have reason to believe is largely duplicative of an already-reviewed source of e-mail, you may begin by formulating the question that is salient in the circumstance: are there responsive e-mails in the archive that do not also reside in the already-reviewed set? Once you have clearly articulated the information need, then you can call upon statistical expertise to develop a sampling and measurement protocol that will meet that need in the most efficient way possible.

To be sure, while the information need is, in itself, independent of statistical science, it is also true that, in practice, the articulation of that need may benefit from an interactive engagement between the legal practitioner, who has the need, and the individual with statistical expertise, who will provide options for meeting that need. The statistical expert, having an understanding of the capabilities and limitations of statistical sampling, may help the legal practitioner to articulate the question in a way that lends itself to a sampling-based answer. The crucial point, however, is that the information need should drive and shape the sampling exercise. The sampling exercise should not take on a life of its own and become regarded as an end in itself.

If the information need is not well articulated, or if the actual information need is lost sight of, a sampling and measurement protocol may be designed and executed that is both inefficient and provides either less or more information than is needed to answer the actual question at hand, neither of which is desirable.[24]

Illustration. In setting the requirements of a sampling exercise used to validate a review for responsiveness, for example, it is sometimes specified that the exercise be designed in such a way as to result

24. Less information than is needed is obviously unsatisfactory, and, in an adversarial circumstance, more information than is needed is often not just more; it is too much.

in a confidence interval the limits of which are no more than some specified distance from the point estimate (e.g., a specification that, for a 95 percent confidence interval, neither the upper nor the lower limit should be more than two percentage points from the point estimate). While narrow confidence intervals are generally desirable, and sometimes necessary (e.g., in a comparative study, when seeking to identify significant differences between systems), in the context of validating the results of a review, the goal of a narrow confidence interval should not take precedence over or obscure the basic question addressed by the measurement exercise: did the review achieve a reasonably high level of recall?

Suppose, for example, a measurement protocol resulted in a point estimate for recall of 90 percent, with a 95 percent confidence interval running from a lower limit of 80 percent to an upper limit of 96 percent. In this case, the confidence interval would indeed be rather wide (16 percentage points from the lower to the upper limit), but the result would still answer the basic question that motivated the measurement exercise in the first place. Because the lower limit of the interval is high (80 percent), you can reasonably exclude from consideration values of recall that would be unacceptably low: the measurements are evidence that the review effort achieved a reasonably complete result.[25]

---

25. This assumes, of course, that 80 percent would count as "reasonably complete" in this instance. There is no consensus on an acceptance threshold for recall that would be applicable in all circumstances, and, as we discuss in There Is No Consensus on a Number, that is a good thing. Nonetheless, given what has been found regarding the effectiveness of both manual and technology-assisted retrieval systems, 80 percent recall would, in most instances, be regarded as a very good result. *See*, e.g., Maura R. Grossman, Gordon V. Cormack, Bruce Hedin, & Douglas W. Oard, *Overview of the TREC 2011 Legal Track*, in NIST SPECIAL PUBLICATION: SP 500-296, THE TWENTIETH TEXT RETRIEVAL CONFERENCE (TREC 2011) PROCEEDINGS (2011); Gordon V. Cormack, Maura R. Grossman, Bruce Hedin, & Douglas W. Oard, *Overview of the TREC 2010 Legal Track*, in NIST SPECIAL PUBLICATION: SP 500-294, THE NINETEENTH TEXT RETRIEVAL CONFERENCE (TREC 2010) PROCEEDINGS (2010); Bruce Hedin, Stephen Tomlinson, Jason R. Baron, & Douglas W. Oard, *Overview of the TREC 2009 Legal Track*, in NIST SPECIAL PUBLICATION: SP 500-278, THE EIGHTEENTH TEXT RETRIEVAL CONFERENCE (TREC 2009) PROCEEDINGS (2009); Douglas W. Oard, Bruce Hedin, Stephen Tomlinson, & Jason R. Baron, *Overview of the TREC 2008 Legal Track*, in NIST SPECIAL PUBLICATION: SP 500-277, THE SEVENTEENTH TEXT RETRIEVAL CONFERENCE (TREC 2008) PROCEEDINGS (2008); Maura R. Grossman & Gordon V.

The purpose of a confidence interval is to tell us which values for recall we have to entertain and which values we can reasonably exclude from consideration. If a confidence interval allows us to exclude the values that would worry us, it will have answered the question at hand, regardless of the actual width of the interval. Now, to be sure, a narrow confidence interval will exclude more of the space between 0 percent and 100 percent than a wide confidence interval will, and so may allow a decisive resolution of the question more often than a wide one would, and, in that regard, time and resources allowing, a narrow confidence interval is preferable to a wide one. It should always be remembered, however, that a narrow confidence interval is a means to an end, not an end in itself, and, if the actual end can be achieved, at lower cost, with a wider confidence interval, then it is perfectly reasonable to take the less burdensome course.[26]

In fact, if the question driving the sampling exercise is whether or not recall is unacceptably low, then the sampling exercise might be more appropriately designed so as to result, not in a two-sided confidence interval (i.e., one that, at a given confidence level, bounds recall on both the upper and lower side of the point estimate), but a one-sided confidence interval (i.e., one that, at a given confidence level, bounds recall on just the lower side of the point estimate). By shifting the tolerated risk that the interval will not, simply due to sampling error, contain the true value of recall (e.g., a 5 percent risk, when constructing a 95 percent confidence interval) all to the lower side, you may arrive at a satisfactory answer to the question at hand at a lower cost.[27] Or, you may take the approach a step further, and design a protocol that will establish whether or not it can be stated, at a given confidence level, that recall is at or above some pre-specified threshold (e.g., 80 percent), a design that can also result in sampling efficiencies. By thinking through the question at hand, and giving careful thought

Cormack, *Technology-Assisted Review in E-Discovery Can Be More Effective and More Efficient than Exhaustive Manual Review*, XVII Rich. J. L. & Tech. 1 (2011).

26. And, especially in cases of low prevalence, the added burden of obtaining very narrow confidence intervals can be substantial.

27. The cost, in terms of sample size, of obtaining a one-sided 95 percent confidence interval, the lower limit of which is a given distance from the point estimate, is generally the same as the cost of obtaining a two-sided 90 percent confidence interval, the lower limit of which is the same given distance from the point estimate.

to the minimum amount of information needed to answer the question, you can arrive at sampling and measurement designs that meet the information need in the most efficient manner possible.

Principle 2

There are a range of different circumstances in which sampling and measurement can contribute to a review effort and a range of different design options for a sampling and measurement protocol. The different designs will vary in the sort of information they provide, in the precision of the information they provide, and in the cost of providing that information. In order to answer the need in the most efficient way possible, it is essential to find a protocol that is both well-suited and proportional to the specific circumstances that occasioned the measurement exercise. A failure to find a protocol that is well-tailored to your circumstances may result in a failure to meet your objectives or in an inefficient use of time and resources.

Illustration. Consider, for example, the circumstances of a review for responsiveness, on the one hand, and those of a case preparation exercise on the other. In the former circumstances, you know that you will have to state, via a Rule 26(g) certification, that the results of the review are, to a degree commensurate with a reasonable good faith effort,[28] accurate and complete. You also know that, if challenged, you may have to go a step further and provide evidence of the accuracy and completeness of the results. In such circumstances, especially if the matter motivating the review is a large one (both in terms of the documents within the scope of review and in terms of the amount in controversy), it would be prudent to choose a validation protocol that included statistically sound estimation of recall and precision as a central component. Even at that point, you would still have a number of different sampling and measurement options from which to choose, and you would make that choice on the basis of what practical conditions (e.g., prevalence of responsive material) implied as to sampling requirements, on the basis of time and resources available for the validation exercise, and on the basis of the minimal information you believed was necessary to meet your

28. For additional perspective on the role played by measurement in 26(g) certification, see Grossman & Cormack and Schieneman & Gricks, *supra* note 1.

(or your client's) obligations. Any plan chosen, however, would have to be rigorous enough to meet the "reasonable inquiry" bar set by the need to certify and, perhaps, defend.

In a case preparation exercise, the goals and conditions of the inquiry are different from those of a responsive review, and the measurement protocol should be adapted accordingly. In a case preparation exercise, the goal of high recall may be subordinate to that of finding a relatively small but varied set of telling documents which will suffice to provide a well-rounded view of the topic of inquiry. In a case preparation exercise, moreover, speed may be a priority, as the results of one inquiry may lead to follow-up inquiries. Additionally, the specific topics of inquiry will generally be sharply focused and so of very low prevalence. In these circumstances, a measurement protocol designed to produce precise estimates of the recall and precision achieved on each inquiry would be not only unnecessary but also counterproductive; the time and resources spent on such a measurement protocol would be better spent in improving on the actual results of inquiries or in conducting further inquiries.

A decision not to obtain precise estimates of recall does not, however, mean that you will not conduct any empirical checks on the results of your inquiry; after all, you usually still want some guard against missing a valuable document. That check may, however, simply take the form of well-thought-out judgmental sampling, or a "sounding," of parts of the collection that may be of particular interest to the inquiry. Even in conducting such a sounding, it should be noted, there is still a part to be played by statistics. In deciding on the size of samples to use for the soundings, you would still like to know the relative sensitivity of samples of different sizes (e.g., a sample of 100 documents versus a sample of 300 documents versus a sample of 600 documents); even if you are not aiming for an estimate of recall, you still want to have a sense of what your soundings can and cannot tell you.

Principle 3

Sample-based measurement can be a powerful method for efficiently finding scientifically sound answers to the questions that occur in the course of a review effort. There are, however, limits to what sample-based measurement can do, and practitioners seeking to take advantage of its capabilities must also be aware of its limitations.

Sampling, by its nature, will not tell you the actual full-population value[29] of the metric that is the focus of the exercise. Only by exhaustively canvassing the full population (i.e., by foregoing sampling and the efficiencies it brings) would you have hope of finding the actual value.[30] What sampling will do is provide you with an *estimate* of the actual value of the metric in which you are interested as well as a gauge of the sampling-based uncertainty associated with that estimate (e.g., a confidence interval). You can, of course, reduce the amount of uncertainty associated with an estimate by using larger sample sizes, but, given the cost sensitivity that will apply in any real-world scenario (a cost sensitivity that lies behind the decision to use sampling-based estimation in the first place), there will be limits on the size of sample that will be feasible in any given circumstance. Those limits will, in turn, act as limits on the extent to which sampling-based uncertainty can be constrained.

In some cases (e.g., when estimating the prevalence of responsive material in a collection or when estimating the recall achieved by a review effort in a circumstance in which prevalence is high),[31] you may be able to constrain the uncertainty associated with an estimate to satisfactory levels with relatively modest sample sizes. In other cases (e.g., when estimating the prevalence of a very low-frequency item in a population or when estimating the recall achieved by a review effort in a circumstance in which prevalence is low), you may not be able to constrain uncertainty as much as you would like and still remain within the budget set for the exercise. In such cases, you must recognize the limits of what sampling can provide and arrive at an alternative plan

29. The term "full population value" is the value we would obtain if we had perfect knowledge of every item in the population of interest.

30. And when the population is of any substantial size at all, even exhaustive canvassing may well fail to find the true value, given the inability of quality control procedures to identify and correct every human error made in the canvassing process.

31. It is worth noting that estimating prevalence and estimating recall are not the same things. The latter (which generally requires combining an estimated value for a numerator and an estimated value for a denominator to arrive at the recall estimate) is generally a much more challenging, and costly, sampling exercise than is the former (which requires combining an estimated value for a numerator with a known value for a denominator to arrive at the prevalence estimate).

for accomplishing the task (e.g., combining some amount of statistical sampling with some well thought out judgmental sampling).

Illustration. Suppose, for example, a party had reason to believe, on the basis of what was known about certain custodians and their business responsibilities and practices, that a large subset of the review collection (say a subset of 500,000 documents) would be almost entirely void of privileged material. The party might want to save on review costs by not conducting a privilege review of the responsive documents identified in that subset, but, before making a decision to do so, might want some empirical support of the hypothesis that the subset was void of privileged material.[32]

An expert in statistics called upon to assist counsel for the party might begin by pointing out that no sampling plan could demonstrate that *no* privileged documents resided in the subset in question. Absent exhaustive review, you must always allow for the existence of black swans, or, in this instance, privileged documents. Finding zero privileged documents in a sample does *not* mean that there are zero privileged documents in the population from which the sample was drawn. The most that a sampling exercise could show would be that the prevalence of privileged documents in the subset did not exceed some threshold, with the threshold following from both the size of sample used in the exercise and the results of what was observed in the sample. If the threshold were sufficiently low, counsel might conclude that there was sufficient empirical corroboration of the hypothesis to warrant a decision to forgo privilege review of the subset. If the threshold was not sufficiently low, counsel might conclude that there was insufficient empirical evidence to support a decision to forego the privilege review.

In order to give counsel a sense of what might be shown by samples of different sizes, the statistician might provide a few options showing what might be stated in the event that no privileged documents were

32. A party choosing such an option would be well advised to consider the protections of a "clawback agreement" and order under FED. R. EVID. 502(d), both of which are beyond the scope of this chapter.

observed in the sample.[33] The following options provide a sense of what might be expected from different sample sizes.[34]

- **Option 1:** A sample of 300 documents. Finding no privileged documents in the sample would allow the party to state, at a 95 percent confidence level, that no more than 1 percent of the documents (1 in 100) in the subset in question were privileged.[35]
- **Option 2:** A sample of 600 documents. Finding no privileged documents in the sample would allow the party to state, at a 95 percent confidence level, that no more than 0.5 percent of the documents (1 in 200) in the subset in question were privileged.
- **Option 3:** A sample of 1,500 documents. Finding no privileged documents in the sample would allow the party to state, at a 95 percent confidence level, that no more than 0.2 percent of the documents (1 in 500) in the subset in question were privileged.
- **Option 4:** A sample of 3,000 documents. Finding no privileged documents in the sample would allow the party to state, at a 95 percent confidence level, that no more than 0.1 percent

33. Of course, an upper threshold could also be calculated in the event a non-zero number of privileged documents were observed in the sample; it would just be higher than it would be in the zero privileged documents scenario.

34. The options given are conservative, in that they assume that the population of interest is large relative to the size of sample drawn (and so assume that the statistic of interest follows a binomial distribution). As populations get smaller relative to the size of sample drawn (and so it becomes advisable to assume that the statistic of interest follows a hypergeometric distribution), somewhat smaller samples can be used to obtain the same results. The options given nevertheless provide a reasonable view of what can be accomplished with samples of different sizes. The exact sample size, or the precise statement that a given sample size will support, can be calculated once you have determined generally the point in the range that is appropriate in your circumstances.

35. In interpreting this statement (and the corresponding statements in the other options presented), it is important to note the "no more than" provision. The results do not mean that 1 percent of the documents *are* privileged. The results mean that the percentage of privileged documents does not (at a 95 percent confidence level) exceed 1 percent. The actual percentage could well be well below 1 percent; the sample size for the option, however, does not allow you to bring the upper threshold below 1 percent.

of the documents (1 in 1,000) in the subset in question were privileged.

- **Option 5:** A sample of 30,000 documents. Finding no privileged documents in the sample would allow the party to state, at a 95 percent confidence level, that no more than 0.01 percent of the documents (1 in 10,000) in the subset in question were privileged.

By providing counsel with a sense of what can and cannot be shown by samples of different sizes, the statistician enables counsel to make a clear-eyed decision, on the basis of both sampling power and resources required, as to which option, if any, would be suitable in the given circumstance. Knowing what sample-based measurement can and cannot do makes for better decisions.

Principle 4

Measurement can be a valuable source of information, whether you are validating the results of a review or you are addressing any of the other questions that occur in the course of a review. Measurement is not the only source of valuable information, however, and should not blind you to other sources of information complementary to sample-based measurement. While your judgments and decisions will certainly be improved if they are informed by empirical quantitative information, they will also be better grounded if those quantitative inputs are contextualized by non-quantitative information.

In the case of validation, for example, both an examination of the review process and a measurement of results have a role to play in building confidence in the final outcome. On the process track, you seek to find whether the process followed in the review was one that would be expected to produce high quality results (i.e., included the elements discussed in Elements of a Sound Review Process). On the measurement track, you seek to find whether there is evidence that the review effort was one that did produce high quality results. If the process examination gives you reason to believe that the effort would produce high quality results and the measurement exercise provides empirical evidence consistent with that belief, then you will have greater confidence in the results of the review effort than you would relying on either process or measurement alone.

A sound assessment of the results of a review will, moreover, address both quantitative and qualitative questions. On the quantitative side, you will want a gauge of the proportion of relevant documents that reside in the target collection that have been successfully retrieved by the review effort (i.e., you will want a gauge of recall). On the qualitative side, you will want a sense of whether any documents that have not been retrieved constitute a true cause of concern (i.e., contain important or novel information that could not be gathered from the documents that have been retrieved). An assessment that looks at the results from both a quantitative and a qualitative perspective will provide a more complete view of the quality of the results.

Likewise, when addressing other questions that occur in the course of a review, practitioners need not, in deference to sample-based measurement, discard what they know about the custodians that were the source of the documents in the review collection or about the business processes and practices of the organization in which the custodians worked. We have already had occasion to note that sample-based measurement is subject to limitations. A stronger answer to a question is provided when the answer combines empirical results with pre-existing knowledge about the sources of the documents.

Illustration. Suppose, for example, you were engaged in an exercise to validate the results of a responsive review. Suppose also that, as a part of that exercise, you undertook a sampling exercise to gauge recall and the results of that exercise allowed you to state, at a 95 percent confidence level, that the recall achieved by the review was 80 percent or higher. Suppose, finally, that, also as part of the validation exercise, you undertook a qualitative analysis of all false negatives that were turned up via the sampling and that that analysis found that all the false negatives were redundant, in the sense that any relevant information they contained could be gathered from documents successfully retrieved by the review. In such an instance, counsel overseeing the review might well decide that there were sufficient grounds for considering the review reasonably complete.

Suppose, on the other hand, an alternative scenario, in which all the facts were the same as those in the scenario just described, with the exception that the qualitative analysis found that at least some of the false negatives contained important and novel information. In this instance, counsel overseeing the review might decide that there were not sufficient grounds for considering the review complete and so ask that the review effort be continued in order to capture the non-redundant documents.

Principle 5

Statistics is a distinct scientific discipline, with its own terms of art, its own tools and methods (which researchers continue to refine and expand), and its own academic literature. The science of statistics is not a component of legal training, and most attorneys therefore have only as much knowledge of statistics as they may have acquired in the course of undergraduate education. Hence it is not surprising that many attorneys find discussions of sampling and measurement as applied to e-discovery challenging and sometimes exhibit a confused understanding of the concepts and methods (it is not uncommon, for example, to find "confidence" discussed as if it were itself a measure of the quality of a review (akin to recall and precision) rather than simply a concept statisticians use in gauging the uncertainty associated with a statistical estimate). If, however, the potential contributions sampling and measurement can make to the conduct and validation of a review effort are to be realized,[36] any sampling and measurement protocols that are used must be designed and executed in accordance with the principles of statistical science (i.e., with required assumptions met, with expected conditions in place, with correct calculations made, and with best practices followed). If the measurement exercise is not properly designed and executed, it may produce a number, but the number will be invalid, and an invalid number is often worse than no number at all.

In order to ensure that a measurement exercise produces valid results, it is not necessary for an attorney to become a statistician;[37] it is simply

36. As noted earlier (in the Expertise section), there are, apart from statistical expertise, other kinds of scientific or technical expertise (e.g., linguistics, data science) that can contribute to the conduct of an effective review; in the current section, however, we are focusing on the contribution to be made by statistics and, more specifically, by sampling and measurement.

37. Some universities do offer programs in data or information science that can provide a solid foundation in tools and techniques for data analysis. Some attorneys

necessary for the attorney to recognize that any measurement exercise will raise a set of questions the answers to which will require statistical competence.[38] Once that recognition is made, it becomes a matter of ensuring that an individual with that competence is available for assisting in the design and execution of the measurement protocol. The attorney, of course, still has a crucial role to play, for the attorney will typically be best positioned to articulate the information need that the sampling and measurement exercise will be intended to meet. The best results will be obtained when the attorney and the statistician, recognizing their respective roles and the limits thereof, engage in a collaborative effort that takes full advantage of each person's respective competences.

Illustration. In the case, for example, of a well-planned review for responsiveness, advance thought will be given to the requirements for final validation well before the review process actually begins. If final validation is a topic of meet-and-confer discussions with opposing counsel, the attorney, or team of attorneys, engaged in the discussions will take care that they have access to the requisite statistical competence to ensure that any validation requirements agreed to are meaningful and reasonable. If final validation is not a topic of early meet-and-confer discussions, the attorneys overseeing the review will still give advance thought to the information needed for a confident Rule 26(g) certification or a confident defense of any challenge eventually raised by opposing counsel, and that thinking will be informed by consultation with individuals with the requisite statistical competence. With or without commitments to opposing counsel on the topic of validation, the review will be undertaken with a clear view of the standards it will be expected to meet.

Once the review has, at least provisionally, been completed, and it is time to specify the specific parameters of the validation protocol, there is again a place for attorney-statistician collaboration. The statistician, equipped with information gained in the course of the

are availing themselves of these programs and are thereby acquiring the skills needed to address the quantitative questions that typically occur in e-discovery.

38. Of course the degree of statistical rigor required by the measurement exercise will vary from one circumstance to the next (see the discussion in Principle 2: One Size Does Not Fit All). It is the attorney's task to judge the level of rigor that must be met by the measurement exercise in any given circumstance and then to make sure the right level of statistical competence is made available to the review.

review (e.g., about the prevalence of responsive material), may supply a range of validation options to the attorney. The attorney, keeping in view both legal and practical requirements, may select among the options provided or ask the statistician to provide additional options. The interaction continues until a validation plan is found that the statistician can stand behind and that the attorney believes will meet legal and practical requirements.

Summary

In this section, we have discussed five principles for the effective use of measurement: let the question lead, adapt to circumstance, be cognizant of the limitations of sampling, do not forget the rest of the story, and know what you are doing. General though these principles are, adherence to them will help to ensure that measurements taken in support of a review exercise will be valid, meaningful, and proportionate.

Benefits of Recognizing the Proper Role of Measurement

We have seen that a sound review process, regardless of whether it is a manual process or any variety of technology-assisted process, will contain certain elements and that one of these elements will be the well-informed use of measurement. In this section, we review some of the benefits that the recognition of the proper role of measurement can bring to various stakeholders in e-discovery processes: to providers of e-discovery systems, to users of those systems, to the bench, and to the legal profession as a whole.

For Providers of Review Tools and Services

For providers of e-discovery products and services, the recognition of the proper role of measurement in a quality management system will enable improvements in the effectiveness and efficiency of the tools and services they provide to their clients and will put discussions with clients (and potential clients) on the topic of quality on a sounder footing.

As we have seen, having access to sound measures of effectiveness is an essential element both of an iterative retrieval process and of a meaningful protocol for validating final results. Providers who incorporate measurement in the quality management practices they employ or prescribe, and who disclose the parameters to consumers, will be giving their clients the capabilities needed to achieve a successful result.

Providers will also benefit from the greater recognition of the proper role of measurement in that such recognition would establish common reference points for discussions of accuracy with clients and potential clients, enabling those discussions to be more straightforward and direct. Greater recognition would also enable more candid discussion of the capabilities and the limitations of measurement, helping to ensure that expectations, both with regard to quality itself and with regard to the measurement of quality, are realistic.

For Consumers of Review Tools and Services

For users of e-discovery products and services, recognition of the proper role of measurement in a quality management system will provide greater certainty both when evaluating potential providers and when actually employing a chosen process.

The potential buyer or user, when evaluating candidate providers, could expect that any candidate would be able to provide concrete data on levels of accuracy achieved on prior projects (and that information could be provided without disclosing any confidential information on the specifics of the example projects). The user should also be able to learn what statistical measures are typically obtained in the course of deploying a given process. The transparency this would impart to the buying process would help to align consumers' requirements and expectations with providers' actual capabilities.

The potential user of a system could gain assurance that the system had the capability of providing direct quantitative answers to the key questions they are likely to have about the accuracy of the review or retrieval effort (of all that was sought, how much was actually found; of all that was found, how much was what was actually sought). The user would know that that capability could be drawn upon both in the internal decision making process leading up to a production and, in the event of a challenge, in defending the adequacy of a production.

For the Bench

For the Bench, the recognition of the key elements of a sound review process, as well as the recognition of the role that measurement plays among those elements, can simplify the resolution of discovery disputes.

The key elements of a sound review process (described in Elements of a Sound Review Process) are independent of the particulars of any given review process, be it manual or technology assisted: any review process that can reasonably be expected to produce high quality results will have them. As such, recognition of the key elements will provide judges with a framework for assessing the soundness of any process that is the subject of a dispute, without necessarily having to dive into the execution-level particulars that will vary from one process to the next.

Any strong defense of a disputed e-discovery protocol will have both a process component and a measurement component. Recognizing the role measurement plays in quality management and understanding what measurement can and cannot do will enable judges to form reasonable expectations regarding the types of quantitative information needed to support sound review processes. With those expectations in mind, judges will be able to steer parties more quickly toward quantitative information that may be decisive for the dispute's resolution.

For the Legal Profession as a Whole

For the legal profession and the e-discovery industry, the recognition of the role that measurement plays in a quality management system for e-discovery will (i) bring questions of accuracy into the open, (ii) foster a common terminology for discussing such questions, (iii) foster realistic expectations as to levels of quality (recall and precision) that can and should be achieved and that can and should be demonstrated to have been achieved, and (iv) encourage providers of review services and e-discovery tools to be more transparent about their quality standards.

Reasons for Reluctance to Measure

While the benefits of measurement are clear, there are also reasons some might object to putting too much emphasis on measurement. In this section, we consider possible objections.

Measurement Does Not Tell the Whole Story

One objection to putting a focus on measurement may be that measurement does not tell the whole story: numbers, by themselves, provide only a partial view of a review effort and its results. Only by gaining the complete view that comes through the analysis and evaluation of non-quantitative information will we be in a position properly to assess the effectiveness of a review effort.

To this objection, we say simply that we agree that measurement does not tell the whole story. This does not mean, however, that measurement is not a unique and important part of the story.

As we have discussed earlier (see Principles for the Effective Use of Measurement, Principle 4), when evaluating effectiveness or addressing any of the other questions that occur in the course of a review, it is important not to lose sight of the contribution that non-quantitative information can make. What we know about how a process was implemented, what we know about the custodians, business processes, and business practices of the organization that is the source of a document collection, and what we know about the qualitative characteristics of documents captured and not captured all provide insights that quantitative measurement alone cannot provide. That does not mean, however, that those sources of information should replace measurement; it means only that they should complement it. Further, properly applied measurement may confirm judgmental decisions at minimal cost.

The import of numbers cannot be properly judged unless the numbers are given context by other, non-quantitative, information. This does not mean, however, that numbers cannot provide significant information. It simply means that the numbers must be contextualized in order for their significance to be evaluated properly.

There Is No Consensus on a Number

Some might object to a focus on the measurement of recall and precision on the grounds that there is as yet no consensus on the minimum levels of recall and precision that are required for a document production to be acceptable. "Should recall be at least 70 percent?" "How about 72 percent?" "Why not 75 percent?" Given the absence of a consensus, and thus the absence of an agreed-upon absolute definition of what does and does not count as adequate, some might argue that a focus on metrics will still leave the basic question unanswered. If there is no agreed-upon quantitative threshold for success, how can a number tell me whether or not I have succeeded?

We recognize that there is no consensus on *the* number, the minimum level of recall that any review effort should be expected both to achieve and to demonstrate to have been achieved. We argue, however, that this is a good thing. Target levels of recall and precision, whether targets for achievement or targets for demonstration of achievement, will vary with the specific goals and conditions of each review project. In some instances, for example, the achievement of very high recall may be a priority; in other instances, the achievement of a lower, but still high, level of recall may be all that is needed. In some cases—for example, when the prevalence of responsive material is high—it may be relatively easy, in terms of sampling and review costs, to demonstrate high recall via sample-based measurement. In other cases—for example, when the prevalence of responsive material is low—it may be difficult, to the point of being unreasonable and disproportionate, to demonstrate via sample-based measurement that high recall has been achieved. As discussed in the preceding section (Measurement Does Not Tell the Whole Story), if the significance of a metric is to be properly assessed, it must be put in the context of additional, non-quantitative, information. If a single threshold number were specified that was applicable in all circumstances, the well-rounded evaluation of the significance of the results of measurement would be lost.

Thus, we consider it entirely appropriate for there to be no consensus regarding fixed numeric targets for performance metrics. This lack of consensus does not imply that measurements should not be taken. It implies only that there should be a reasoned evaluation of the significance of those measurements—a reasoned evaluation that will take into consideration all available information.

Fear of Cavil

Some might object to a focus on measurement on the grounds that, in an adversarial system, quantitative measures will only provide fodder for distracting and unproductive argument.

The Glass Is 20 Percent Empty

Given a recall estimate of 80 percent, for example, opposing counsel may try to focus all attention on the 20 percent that has not been retrieved.

There are, however, reasonable and empirically well-grounded responses to such tactics. To the "glass is 20 percent empty" argument, for example, we might respond by drawing the distinction between *document* recall and *information* recall. Our recall measures are almost always of the former variety; that is, we measure the proportion of relevant *documents* retrieved out of all relevant *documents* that reside in a population. Once a reasonably high level of document recall has been achieved (e.g., 80 percent), however, it is typically the case that, when additional relevant documents are found, those new documents in fact add no new information; that is to say, the information in the unretrieved 20 percent of relevant documents is almost entirely redundant to information in the already-retrieved 80 percent of relevant documents. Viewed from a qualitative perspective, the additional documents do not provide information that is important or novel. When, therefore, we have achieved 80 percent *document* recall, we will have typically achieved a much higher level of *information* recall. Put in terms of information, then, the glass is not in fact 20 percent empty; it is in fact almost entirely full.[39]

Heaps of Sand and Bald Men

Again, given a recall estimate of 80 percent, opposing counsel may use the absence of a well-defined minimum threshold to demand that the producing party continue to work to increase recall to higher and higher levels: "If you have achieved 80 percent recall, why not make the additional effort to get to 81 percent?" and "If you have achieved 81 percent recall, why not make the additional effort to

39. In responding to a "glass is 20 percent empty" argument, it may also be helpful to refer to the importance of being aware of both the capabilities and the limitations of sample-based measurement (see Principle 3: Take Advantage of the Capabilities of Sample-Based Measurement, but Be Cognizant of Its Limitations) and to the importance of complementing measurement with information derived from other sources (see Principle 4: Remember the Rest of the Story. . .).

get to 82 percent?", and so on). Such sorites-like arguments become available whenever we use a continuous, or near continuous, quantitative measure (such as grains of sand, hairs, recall) as the criterion for assigning a vaguely defined qualitative predicate (heap, bald, reasonably complete).

Here again a reasonable and empirically well-grounded response is available. We might respond by pointing to the fact of diminishing returns. Given the composition of most document collections and given the nature of most topics pertinent to those collections, it is typically the case that, as more relevant documents have been retrieved, and as the prevalence of relevant documents in the unretrieved set gets lower, the cost of finding additional relevant documents increases; indeed, it could well be as costly, in terms of time and resources, to go from 80 percent to 85 percent recall as it was to go from 0 percent to 80 percent recall. Each percentage of recall, therefore, tends to come at greater cost, and, at some point, that cost will be disproportionate and outweigh the value of additional documents.[40]

As the two examples just discussed show, there are available reasonable and substantive answers to potentially distracting cavils about measurement.[41] That we may encounter such cavil is thus not an argument against measurement; it simply means that we have to be prepared to respond effectively. In fact, to the extent that measurement brings such arguments, and the substantive responses to them, into the light of day, it may help to deprive the arguments of whatever amount of rhetorical force they currently have.

Time and Cost

Another objection to a focus on measurement centers on time and cost. Obtaining meaningful estimates of precision and recall, and especially of the latter, can require very large samples; given real-world time constraints and the stakes at issue in a matter, the cost and time it would take to draw and assess samples of such size would

40. Fed. R. Civ. P. 26 places proportionality limits on the scope of discovery.

41. And such answers may be given serious consideration by courts interested in finding the appropriate balance between the value of information and the cost of getting it. *Id.*

often be prohibitive. Practitioners cannot be expected to run TREC-like exercises every time they produce a set of documents.[42]

In response to this objection, we note that measurement need not imply a TREC-like evaluation. There are in fact a number of ways to arrive at sound measures of recall, and some of these are less costly than others. If care is taken to weigh the actual information need in a given circumstance against the sampling and review costs required to meet that need, we can, in most cases, arrive at a sampling design that will, in a cost-effective manner, contribute meaningful empirical data to the validation of the results of a retrieval effort. Indeed, a properly executed measurement program can, by illuminating in real time where improvements do and do not need to be made, often reduce the overall time and cost of a retrieval effort.

Consider, for example, a protocol designed to test whether it can be stated, at a given level of confidence, that recall is at or above some pre-specified threshold level. In implementing such a design, there will be some parameters out of our control. The prevalence of responsive material in a collection, for example, is a parameter largely outside our control, and it is also a strong driver of the size of sample required in any given test. There are other parameters, however, that are in our control. For example, the following parameters can be set at the discretion of the user: (i) the minimum level of recall that the test will be designed to establish, (ii) the risk that you will pass the test when your true recall is actually below the threshold (a "false pass"), and (iii) the risk that you will fail the test when your true recall is actually above the threshold (a "false fail"). The settings chosen for these parameters will dictate the size of sample required for the test. Because of the range of parameters subject to user discretion, it is generally possible to find a combination of settings that will strike the optimal balance between information gained, risk (both of "false pass" and of "false fail") tolerated, and sample size required. If we weigh carefully the information we really need, the tolerance we have for sampling error, and the budget we have for sampling and review, we

42. The NIST-sponsored Text REtrieval Conference (TREC) featured a legal track from 2006 through 2011. The legal track ran a series of evaluations of the effectiveness of technology-assisted review systems at meeting the objectives of e-discovery. For TREC generally, see http://trec.nist.gov/. For the legal track specifically, see http://trec-legal.umiacs.umd.edu/.

can almost always arrive at a sampling design that suits our objectives and constraints.[43]

In fact, as discussed earlier (The Role of Measurement When Applying Review Tools and Methods) a well-thought-out and executed measurement program can often lead to reductions in the time and cost required by a retrieval effort. Accurate real-time measurements can provide the review team with valuable information as to where improvements do and do not need to be made, thus allowing the team to reach its objectives more efficiently than it would be able to without that information.

This is not to say that there may not be some cases in which random sampling across the full review collection simply cannot generate any useful information in a cost-effective manner (e.g., cases in which the prevalence of relevant material is extremely low). Even in such cases, however, there are often options for gathering at least some meaningful empirical information from at least some parts of the population, and some empirical data are better than no empirical data.

Gaming the System

Some might argue that an undue focus on quantitative measures may open the door to "gaming the system." If the validation of the results of a review or retrieval effort rests solely upon a number, a party might seek bad-faith methods of arriving at that number that are not in keeping with its true obligations.

The objection has validity if, when validating the results of a review effort, quantitative measurement (the "number") is regarded as the whole story. As we have had occasion to note more than once (Principles for the Effective Use of Measurement, Principle 4; Measurement Does Not Tell the Whole Story), in a sound measurement protocol, the number is not regarded as the whole story. Sound validation also includes assessment of the protocol whereby the measures

43. For a more extended discussion of the test design discussed in this paragraph and of the effects of different parameter settings on sample size, see Bruce Hedin, Dan Brassil, & Christopher Hogan, *Toward a Meaningful E-Discovery Standard*, DESI V: ICAIL 2013 Workshop on Standards for Using Predictive Coding, Machine Learning, and Other Advanced Search and Review Methods in E-Discovery (2013).

were obtained as well as consideration of non-statistical quantitative and qualitative aspects of the review or retrieval effort. When validation is viewed as a comprehensive exercise, in which statistical estimation of recall and precision is just one component, the opportunity to game the system via statistical legerdemain is significantly diminished. The more, therefore, practitioners are aware of what makes for a well-rounded validation exercise, and of the proper role of measurement in it, the less opportunity there will be for quantitative sleight of hand.[44]

Concluding Thoughts

The unique insights that measurement can provide make it a key element of a sound review process, whether the process be a manual one or a technology-assisted one. It is, however, just one element, and a sound review process will include other essential elements as well (advance planning, thorough topic analysis, proper use of technology, appropriate use of expertise, adaptability, and clear and complete documentation). For the potential benefits of measurement to be realized, moreover, measures must be taken via sound scientific method and be interpreted in the light of pertinent contextual information. When measurement is properly used and interpreted, however, it becomes a uniquely powerful driver of both effectiveness and efficiency in an e-discovery process.

Acknowledgments

The authors would like to thank the editors of this volume, Michael D. Berman, Jason R. Baron, and Ralph Losey both for their work in seeing this volume through to publication and, more specifically, for their very helpful and insightful comments on an earlier draft of this chapter. The authors would also like to thank David D. Lewis, who also provided very helpful and insightful comments on an earlier draft of the chapter. Of course, all responsibility for errors belongs to the authors.

44. Of course, it may be argued that a system that does not rely on measurement is more vulnerable to gaming by a malfeasant. A transparent empirical system provides the greatest available protection against such misdeeds.

EDITORS' INTRODUCTION TO CHAPTER 15

Michael D. Berman

In *Victor Stanley*, the Hon. Paul W. Grimm issued a call for national standards in e-discovery: "The lack of a national standard, or even a consensus among courts in different jurisdictions about what standards should govern preservation/spoliation issues, appears to have exacerbated [the] problem."[1] It has often been said that ESI presents the same challenges whether it is located in California or New York. The need for standards is particularly acute when it comes to "black box" technologies such as predictive coding.

In this chapter, Gilbert Keteltas, Karin Jenson, and James Sherer argue for standards based on output. They assert that "authoritative standards" could relieve the burden on courts and assist parties in avoiding over-inclusive and extremely costly efforts in a "free-for-all zone" where there is no judicial umpire.

The chapter discusses a number of existing and proposed standards, some well-known and others not frequently mentioned in the literature. The authors note the well-established principle that perfection is not the applicable standard and call for "tolerances" to be built into any standard. They then examine two types of standards, one for the practitioner and the other for the technician, while noting that it is "the attorneys who are eventually standing before a fact finder explaining their reasoning behind their choices and decisions." Thus, they cogently argue for standards-setters to "build a bridge between technologists and lawyers and recognize the roles and expectations both face in a legal process for which lawyers are ultimately accountable."

---

1. Victor Stanley, Inc. v. Creative Pipe, Inc., 269 F.R.D. 497, 516 (D. Md. 2010), *subsequent decision,* 2011 WL 2552472 (D. Md. Jan. 24, 2011), *subsequent decision,* 2011 WL 4596043 (D. Md. Sept. 30, 2011), *aff'd,* 499 Fed. Appx. 971 (Fed. Cir. Feb. 20, 2013).

The suggested bridge, consistent with other chapters in this book, is for process quality standards that "shift . . . attention from process to results." While initial "guidance" may be necessary, defensibility requires that there be "key goals." The chapter provides ten concepts as a standard meeting that requirement.

CHAPTER 15

A Modest Proposal for Preventing e-Discovery Standards from Being a Burden to Practitioners, Clients, the Courts, or Common Sense

Gilbert S. Keteltas, Karin S. Jenson, and James A. Sherer

Introduction

When the letter "e" was put in front of "discovery" more than a decade ago, it had a dramatic and unanticipated effect on a large segment of Bench and Bar. For many, the discovery of electronically stored information (ESI)—now the predominant type of discovery in significant litigation—became an engineering problem in search of a technical solution.[1] A multi-billion dollar litigation support industry emerged to supply technical solutions. And advocacy suffered as practitioners put

1. Evan Koblentz, *International Committee Could Standardize E-Discovery Process*, L. TECH. NEWS, Feb. 7, 2013 (quoting Tom Barnett).

the hunt for every last byte of potentially relevant information ahead of thinking about the bytes that mattered to resolve disputes.

Who can blame the advocates? Inconsistent judicial opinions and fear-based marketing by law firms and vendors raised the specter that the failure to turn over every electronic stone could result in sanctions of a magnitude unimaginable a decade ago. And some litigants, to this day, pursue claims of spoliation based on an opponent's failure to produce or failure to adequately search more vigorously than the litigants pursue the merits of a case.

Discovery—whether preceded by an "e" or not—is, or at least should be, a legal process, proscribed by procedural rules, impacted by changing technologies, executed or supervised by counsel, and refereed by judges.[2] Because the case law has not developed in a way that gives the working litigator clear guidance on how to conform to procedural discovery rules, a patchwork of "best practices" has emerged from think tanks, regional judicial pilot projects, and individual judges. Given the number and variety of these efforts, balkanization appears more likely than harmonization.

Outside counsel who handle or support even a modest litigation docket face the daily challenge of multiple clients of different levels of technical sophistication deploying different technologies and facing different types of litigation. And the technologies that create, store, and search for information change rapidly. Despite rapid technological change, procedural rules and associated guidance from the judiciary are slower to evolve. Yet the ethical[3] and practical[4] responsibilities

2. Gilbert S. Keteltas, *Bridging the Technical and Legal Divide—Information Retrieval Process Quality Standards for Counsel*, 14 DDEE 07 BLOOMBERG BNA, Jan. 2, 2014.

3. ABA MODEL RULES OF PROF'L CONDUCT R. 1.1 (Competence) cmt. 8. *See also* FED. R. CIV. P. 26(g)(1); Da Silva Moore v. Publicis Groupe, 287 F.R.D. 182, 193 (S.D.N.Y. 2012) ("As with keywords or any other technological solution to ediscovery, *counsel must design* an appropriate process, including use of available technology, with appropriate quality control testing, to review and produce relevant ESI while adhering to Rule 1 and Rule 26(b)(2)(C) proportionality.") (emphasis added); Karin S. Jenson et al., *Ethics, Technology, and Attorney Competence*, presented at 11th Annual Georgetown eDiscovery Institute (Nov. 20, 2014).

4. FED. R. CIV. P. 26(g)(1)(A) requires an attorney responding to a discovery request to sign and verify that she has undertaken "reasonable inquiry" in determining

of counsel to understand, and competently find and produce relevant information from an expanding sea of data created by both known and emerging technologies remain constant. Against this complex backdrop of ethics, changing technology, and data growth,[5] calls for "standardization" are emerging with the stated goal of assisting counsel in implementing and defending processes that always will be imperfect and, increasingly, measure and report on that imperfection.

To date, discussions focused on explicit or rote standards, rather than more generalized best practices, have centered on technologies and the litigation support professionals who use them—the "engineers" of electronic discovery. But this type of approach presents challenges for the needs of the vast majority of lawyers who sign pleadings and draft and respond to discovery requests—the people who are, or should be, guiding the search for relevant information.

It is these practitioners who need the certainty and support of standards, standards that: (1) focus on the discovery *process* (rather than the wide variety of known and future technologies that may or may not be deployed in that process), (2) are understandable to the everyday practitioner who only thinks of Sedona[6] as a potential vacation destination and Georgetown[7] and Duke[8] as selective universities, (3) remain flexible enough to deal with case-specific eccentricities

---

that the disclosures are, to the best of her knowledge, "complete and correct." *See also* Steven C. Bennett, *E-Discovery—Reasonable Search, Proportionality, Cooperation, and Advancing Technology*, 30 J. Info. Tech & Privacy L. 433 (Spring 2014).

5. James Manyika et al., *Big Data—The Next Frontier for Innovation, Competition, and Productivity*, McKinsey Global Institute (MGI) (May 2011).

6. The Sedona Conference is a "nonprofit, 501(c)(3) research and educational institute dedicated to the advanced study of law and policy in the areas of antitrust law, complex litigation, and intellectual property rights" whose papers, authored by member legal practitioners, have been highly influential with judges, attorneys, and litigation support professionals alike.

7. The Georgetown University Law Center supports the annual Advanced eDiscovery Institute, which brings the judiciary and practitioners together to "provide the information, resources, and industry connections [practitioners] need to effectively manage the electronic discovery process." The 12th Annual Advanced eDiscovery Institute.

8. Duke Law hosted a Civil Rules Committee "blue-ribbon conference" in May of 2010, focused on the high costs associated with civil litigation generally and in discovery in particular, which resulted in the "Duke Rules Package" and a serious influence on the 2015 amendments to the Federal Rules of Civil Procedure.

that plague modern data sets (and complex client data systems), and (4) acknowledge that even a standardized process can be both imperfect *and* defensible. A practitioner, with (or without) help, must be able to talk plainly and confidently to their client, their opponent, and the court about the search for relevant information.

Search Standards

Among the questions that may arise in connection with yet another call for standards are:

1. Should Bench and Bar embrace a standardized process that could yield imperfect results?
2. Are the "standards" set by procedural rules and the cases that interpret them insufficient to guide practitioners?
3. Is standardization possible in the context of procedural rules administered by courts relating to known and not-yet-knowable technological challenges?

This chapter examines these questions, and presents the often-conflicting viewpoints of scholars and practitioners. We also outline how standards operate generally, and examine what a court-set standard might look like if the process of judicial guidance did not evolve over years of sometimes-inconsistent court opinions. Finally, we propose components we feel should be incorporated into standards or the standard-setting process, including suggestions on how to achieve an appropriate middle ground within this currently unsettled area of the law and practice.

Is It Appropriate to Focus on Standardization of Process Rather Than Results?

Physicist and environmental scientist Amory Lovins once said that, "the process by which a decision is reached is more important than its factual correctness."[9] Does that statement have any relevance to the judicial process? Before cringing at the notion that a judicial process

9. Amory B. Lovins, *Cost-Risk Benefit Assessment in Energy Policy,* 45 (5) GEO. WASH. L. REV. 941 (1977).

can be defensible even if the outcome of the process is flawed, consider that "[t]he official ideology of the American legal system is that the procedure used to decide facts is more important than the accuracy of the decision—that a verdict may be absolutely correct legally even if it is absolutely wrong factually."[10] Case law already decries perfection as a (or "the") requirement,[11] but an appropriate standard would provide parties with explicit steps to take or obligations to fulfill that would "perfectly" apply the standard, even if the end result fell short of an impossible perfection.

How Are Standards Applied in the Practice of Law?

While law firms and practitioners do—and should—worry about the market making judgments about their internal practices, as client pressure supporting strict step-by-step standards would indicate, there is yet another standard-setting body at play within the practice of litigation specifically: the courts. Indeed, "[l]awyers will always be free to decide how they choose to practice law; however, the courts and clients will decide who wins and loses."[12] In the discovery process, courts will also decide matters, such as whether "a party failed to take reasonable steps to preserve" and subsequently adequately search and produce relevant information.[13] Courts have long been understood to be part of the standard-setting process, as confirmed by the recent work of the

---

10. Anna-Rose Mathieson & Samuel R. Gross, *Review for Error, Law, Probability and Risk*, 2, 259–68, (Dec. 2003).

11. *See* Da Silva Moore v. Publicis Groupe SA and MSL Group, 2012 WL 1446534, at *3 (S.D.N.Y. 2012) ("There simply is no review tool that guarantees perfection") *considering* and *upholding* in Da Silva Moore v. Publicis Groupe, 287 F.R.D. 182, 187 (S.D.N.Y. 2012) ("The idea is not to make this perfect, it's not going to be perfect. The idea is to make it significantly better than the alternatives . . ."). *See also* Pension Comm. v. Banc of America Sec., LLC, 685 F. Supp. 2d 456, 461 (S.D.N.Y. 2010) ("Courts cannot and do not expect that any party can meet a standard of perfection. Nonetheless, the courts have a right to expect that litigants and counsel will take the necessary steps to ensure that relevant records are preserved when litigation is reasonably anticipated, and that such records are collected, reviewed, and produced to the opposing party.").

12. *The Sedona Conference Commentary on Achieving Quality in the E-Discovery Process*, 15 Sedona Conf. J. 265, 269 (2014).

13. Fed. R. Civ. P. 37(e).

Advisory Committee on the Federal Rules of Civil Procedure which cites the 1983 Committee's reference to the judicial application of proportionality "standards in an even-handed manner that will prevent use of discovery to wage a war of attrition, or as a device to coerce a party, whether financially weak or affluent."[14]

When addressing 2015 amendments to the Federal Rules, the Advisory Committee also highlighted the challenge of standard setting by court or circuit in discussing the impact of inconsistent standards for sanctioning parties who fail to preserve relevant electronically stored information:

> Federal circuits have established significantly different standards for imposing sanctions or curative measures on parties who fail to preserve electronically stored information. These developments have caused litigants to expend excessive effort and money on preservation in order to avoid the risk of severe sanctions if a court finds they did not do enough.[15]

The current expert witness standard evolved from the prior *Frye* standard, which held that thing from which the deduction is made *must be sufficiently established to have gained general acceptance* in the particular field in which it belongs.[16] The *Frye* standard was then supplanted, at least in federal court, by the *Daubert* standard[17] for the admission of an expert opinion, and held that admission is proper if

> (1) the expert is qualified to testify competently regarding the matters he intends to address; (2) the methodology by which the expert reaches his conclusions is sufficiently reliable as determined by the sort of inquiry mandated in *Daubert*; and (3) the testimony assists the trier of fact, through the application of scientific, technical, or specialized expertise,

14. June 2014 Report of the Advisory Committee on Federal Rules of Civil Procedure, p. 22 (quoting 1983 Committee Note to FED. R. CIV. P. 26).

15. Advisory Committee Comment to Proposed FED. R. CIV. P. 37(e) at 38.

16. Frye v. United States, 293 F. 1013 (D.C. Cir. 1923) (emphasis added).

17. Daubert v. Merrell Dow Pharmaceuticals, Inc., 509 U.S. 579 (1993). *See also* FED. R. EVID. 702, Advisory Committee Notes (noting that Rule 702 was amended in 2000 in response to *Daubert* and its application).

> to understand the evidence or to determine a fact in issue.[18]

Here the "standard" is itself filled with areas where qualifications live, or the "devil is in the details" locations.[19] What qualifications lead to competent testimony? What is sufficiently reliable methodology? And what does it mean for assistance to apply scientific, technical, *or* specialized expertise? The disjunctive here even presupposes, presumably, that there may be specialized expertise devoid of scientific merit or support; perhaps a case focused on fortunetellers or astrologers.[20] But while a standard that focused on the details or minutiae could have expired as quickly as the conventional understanding of what causes ulcers,[21] a standard built on foundations of process and quality has a much better chance of evolving to fit future needs, especially in an arena like technology and the growth of information where data volumes are expected to increase exponentially, leading to a 4,300 percent increase by 2020,[22] and the underlying technology itself is still adhering to Moore's Law in both size and complexity.[23]

---

18. City of Tuscaloosa v. Harcros Chem., Inc., 158 F.3d 548, 562 (11th Cir. 1998) (citations omitted). *But note* that there exists a difference of opinion within the courts, where when Magistrate Judge Andrew J. Peck faced a FED. R. EVID. 702 challenge to allowing an e-discovery expert to advise the court in Da Silva Moore v. Publicis Groupe, 287 F.R.D. 182 (S.D.N.Y. 2012), Judge Peck opined that the rule applied to trial, not civil discovery. At least one other Magistrate Judge has provided a difference of opinion: Magistrate Judge David J. Waxse asserted that any expert testimony must meet the FED. R. EVID. 702 *Daubert* standard. *See* David J. Waxse & Brenda Yoakum-Kriz, *Experts on Computer-Assisted Review: Why Federal Rule of Evidence 702 Should Apply to Their Use*, 52 WASHBURN L.J. 207 (2013).

19. L. Casey Auttonberry, *Predictive Coding: Taking the Devil Out of the Details*, 74 LA. L. REV. (2014).

20. Spiritual Psychic Science Church v. City of Azusa, 703 P.2d 1119 (Cal. 1985).

21. Ulcers are not, in fact, caused by stress; Barry Marshal was awarded the 2005 Nobel Prize after discovering that the bacterium *H. pylori* causes peptic ulcer disease.

22. CSC, *Big Data Just Beginning to Explode*, Whitepaper (undated).

23. Kenneth J. Withers, *Risk Aversion, Risk Management, and the Overpreservation Problem in Electronic Discovery*, 64 S.C. L. REV. 537, 540 (2012-13), *citing* Gordon E. Moore, *Cramming More Components onto Integrated Circuits*, ELECTRONICS, Apr. 19, 1965, at 114, 115. ("[A]cting as both cause and effect in the explosion of digital information is the decreasing cost of digital storage capacity, in accordance with the venerated Moore's Law, which predicted as early as 1965 that the capacity of digital information storage devices would double roughly every eighteen months.").

Note, though, further challenges associated with judicial standards. The *Daubert* approach emerged over time. Seventy years, in fact. Its application is inconsistent across those state jurisdictions that employ it, and practitioners still argue for its repeal in favor of the 1923 *Frye* standard.[24] The Moore's Law comparison was not accidental. While technology changes very rapidly, judicial standards take lots and lots of time to develop, their implementation (not to mention application) is often inconsistent and uneven, and they are subject to change from a variety of fronts.

How Have Current Judicial Standards Related to e-Discovery Evolved?

While some courts have been confident and admittedly successful in understanding and assessing many aspects of the e-discovery process at a high level,[25] judges may be far less comfortable assessing the reasonableness of specific search queries, precise methodologies, and vendor choice when parties are wringing relevant information out of massive quantities of ESI. This is no surprise; modern search presents technical questions beyond the ken of most lawyers and judges and "[e]ven the most computer literate of judges would struggle to know what protocol is appropriate in any individual case, and the notion that a busy trial judge is going to be able to invent one out of whole cloth or to understand whether the proposed protocol meets ill-defined technical search standards seems unrealistic."[26]

In fact, judges are often called upon to resolve highly technical disputes involving scientific matters they know little or nothing about. Justice Stephen Breyer noted explicitly that a

---

24. Julie Kay, *Panel Urges Going Back to Frye Standard for Expert Testimony*, Daily Bus. Rev. (Oct. 20, 2015); Patrick McGlone, *Taking the Stand: Time to Retire the Frye Test*, Wash. Law. (June 2015).

25. Da Silva Moore v. Publicis Groupe, 287 F.R.D. 182 (S.D.N.Y. 2012).

26. U.S. v. Farlow, 2009 WL 4728690, at *6 (D. Me. Dec. 3, 2009). *See also* Craig Shaffer, *"Defensible" by What Standard?*, 13 Sedona Conf. J. 212, 231 (2012) ("Application of the 'reasonableness' standard in the context of technology assisted e-discovery process invariably will present the court with methodologies or forensic techniques which are beyond the knowledge or skills of a layperson, and certainly outside the experience of most judges.").

> [j]udge is not a scientist, and a courtroom is not a scientific laboratory. . . . [M]ost judges lack the scientific training that might facilitate the evaluation of scientific claims or the evaluation of expert witnesses who make such claims. Judges typically are generalists, dealing with cases that can vary widely in subject matter. Our primary objective is usually process-related: seeing that a decision is reached fairly and in a timely way."[27]

A lack of formal computer training[28] did not dissuade Judge Scheindlin either; when discussing the standard for spoliation sanctions, she opined that

> [t]he standard of acceptable conduct is determined through experience. In the discovery context, the standards have been set by years of judicial decisions analyzing allegations of misconduct and reaching a determination as to what a party must do to meet its obligation to participate meaningfully and fairly in the discovery phase of a judicial proceeding.[29]

Other judges wading into standards-setting processes are acknowledging that certain practices fall into the realm of "standard discovery software" when determining inadvertent production[30] or "standard format" cross reference or unitization files in discovery fee disputes.[31]

Authoritative standards for a quality search process could relieve the courts from overseeing and refereeing pitched discovery battles

27. Hon. Stephen Breyer, Reference Manual on Scientific Evidence, 4 (3d ed. 2011).

28. Federal Judicial Center, Biographical Directory of Federal Judges, biography of *Shira A. Scheindlin.*

29. Pension Comm. v. Banc of America Sec., LLC, 685 F. Supp. 2d 456, 464 (S.D.N.Y. 2010).

30. Datel Holdings Ltd. v. Microsoft Corp., 2011 WL 866993, at *3 (N.D. Cal. Mar. 11, 2011) (Finding the use of the Clearwell platform and subsequent, inadvertent production fell "squarely on the inadvertent side of the divide between intentional disclosure under Rule 502(a) and unintentional disclosure under Rule 502(b)".).

31. Race Tires Am., Inc. v. Hoosier Racing Tire Corp., 2011 WL 1748620, at *5 (W.D. Penn. May 6, 2011).

where "litigants and their vendor surrogates debate the efficacy of competing search methodologies."[32] Although *Da Silva Moore*, *Actos*, *Kleen Products*, and *Rio Tinto*[33] seemingly opened the door to judicial acceptance of the use of machine-learning tools, there is also an argument that they set up significant barriers to entry for litigators, clients, and judges who may perceive the negotiation, implementation, and assessment of technology-assisted review as more burdensome than exhaustive manual review (with all its warts). And while courts have waded into the muck of protocols and provide some guidance as to at least their expectations for what an ideal standard will incorporate,[34] often the court is facilitating the process, rather than mandating it.

As Judge Peck observed in *Da Silva Moore*, "[t]he decision to allow computer-assisted review was relatively easy—the parties agreed to its use (although disagreed about how best to implement such review)."[35] Likewise, in *Global Aerospace, Inc. v. Landow Aviation, L.P.*, Judge Chamblin ruled that defendants "would be allowed to proceed with the use of predictive coding"[36] but noted that the plaintiffs could challenge "completeness or the contents of the production or the ongoing use of predictive coding" at the close of production.[37] The attempt to mandate predictive coding was likewise inconclusive in *Kleen Products*, where plaintiffs complained of defendants' "antiquated Boolean keyword search" but ultimately, after months of debate over those issues, the parties withdrew their dispute.[38] But the idea of even predictive coding is evolving and gaining acceptance, as

32. *See* Shaffer, *supra* note 27, at 219.

33. *See Da Silva Moore*, 287 F.R.D. 182; *In re* Actos (Pioglitazone) Prods. Liab. Litig., 2012 WL 6061973 (W.D. La. July 27, 2012) (Case Management Order: Protocol Relating to the Production of Electronically Stored Information); Kleen Prods. v. Packaging Corp. of Am., 2012 WL 4498465 (N.D. Ill. Aug. 21, 2012); and Rio Tinto PLC v. Vale S.A., 2015 WL 872294 (S.D.N.Y. Mar. 2, 2015).

34. Datel Holdings Ltd. v. Microsoft Corp., 2011 WL 866993 (N.D. Cal. Mar. 11, 2011).

35. *Da Silva Moore*, 287 F.R.D. 182, 189.

36. Order Approving the Use of Predictive Coding for Discovery, Global Aerospace, Inc. v. Landow Aviation, L.P., Consolidated Case No. CL61040 (Loudoun Cnty. Va. Apr. 23, 2012).

37. *Id.*

38. Plaintiffs' Statement of Position with Respect to Disputed Items at 4–5, Kleen Prods., LLC v. Packaging Corp. of Am., Civil Case No. 1:10-cv-05711 (N.D. Ill. Dec. 13, 2011).

seen in *EORHB, Inc. v. HOA Holdings, LLC*,[39] where the vice chancellor sua sponte ordered the use of predictive coding in discovery or show cause why it should not be used.[40]

One supposes that this highlights the issue of evolving standards in such an ad hoc way, and demonstrates that courts should be relieved of the burden of thinking of a future standard cobbled together along the way. Judges are addressing a matter's singular circumstances; a party's risk and cost tolerances; and often, very specific types of technology. The term "e-discovery" attempts to synonymize the efforts, but can fall woefully short; at least *Daubert* has the scientific method lurking somewhere underneath for structure.

But there is support for the idea that a standard is ideal. Commentators note that standards, "provide relief [for the courts] from the need to go 'where angels fear to tread'[41] in opining on the adequacy of a responding party's chosen review methodology; an objective standard would be available to help make that determination."[42] Standards fit well where expertise is required, and

> [f]ully understanding and evaluating these tools and methods can require kinds of expertise (computer science, linguistics, statistics, and so on) well outside the legal expertise expected of most attorneys, and so, not surprisingly, the legal profession has been somewhat hesitant to adopt what it does not fully understand. This is where standards come in.[43]

Others advocate dual levels of standards to both define "minimum functionality standards" for technologies such as predictive coding

39. EORHB, Inc. v. HOA Holdings, LLC, Civil Action No. 7409-VCL (Del. Ch. filed Apr. 10, 2012).

40. Transcript of Record at 66, EORHB, Inc. v. HOA Holdings, LLC, Civil Action No. 7409-VCL (Del. Ch. Oct. 15, 2012).

41. United States v. O'Keefe, 537 F. Supp. 2d 14 (D.D.C. 2008).

42. Bruce Hedin, Dan Brassil, & Christopher Hogan, *Toward a Meaningful E-Discovery Standard*, ICAIL 2013 Workshop on Standards for Using Predictive Coding, Machine Learning, and Other Advanced Search and Review Methods in E-Discovery (DESI V) (2013).

43. *Id.*

as well as "standardized use protocols" associated with implementing those technologies.[44]

Courts have recognized that expertise in this area may be required, where the use of third-party e-discovery experts is sometimes "reasonable, if not essential."[45] Indeed, practitioners should know, at least generally, what a standard should entail as they are ethically bound to "keep abreast of . . . the benefits and risks associated with relevant technology." [46] It is possible that judges are waiting for lawyers to define the standard, and subsequently codify it into law, and some have even suggested that "standardization of process is an explicit requirement from the judiciary."[47] Certainly some courts have looked for guidance from outside standard providers.[48]

Although many agree on the need for process quality standards in e-discovery and, in particular, for information retrieval conducted or overseen by counsel, the U.S. legal system leans against standardization. The Federal Rules of Civil Procedure and the decisions interpreting them encourage process development on a case-by-case basis, in part to address the proportionality considerations relevant to assessing the reasonableness of a discovery process in a particular case. Even in those instances where one party demands that another follow an e-discovery-related standard (in this case, the District of Delaware's Default Standard for Discovery of Electronic Documents[49]), the court

---

44. Dana A. Remus, *The Uncertain Promise of Predictive Coding*, 99 Iowa L. Rev. 1691 (May 2014).

45. Wis. Res. Prot. Council v. Flambeau Mining Co., 2014 WL 3810884 (W.D. Wis. Aug. 1, 2014).

46. ABA Model Rules, *supra* note 4. *See also* Fed. R. Civ. P. 26(g)(1); *Da Silva Moore*, 287 F.R.D. 182, 193 ("As with keywords or any other technological solution to ediscovery, *counsel must design an appropriate process*, including use of available technology, with appropriate quality control testing, to review and produce relevant ESI while adhering to Rule 1 and Rule 26(b)(2)(C) proportionality.") (emphasis added).

47. Chis Knox & Scott Dawson, *ISO 9001: A Foundation for E-Discovery*, ICAIL 2011 Workshop on Setting Standards for Searching Electronically Stored Information in Discovery Proceedings (DESI IV) (2011).

48. W. Benefit Solutions, LLC v. Gustin, 2012 WL 4417190, at *4 (D. Idaho Sept. 24, 2012) (*considering* Kevin A. Griffiths, *The Expense of Uncertainty: How a Lack of Clear E-. Discovery Standards Puts Attorneys and Clients in Jeopardy*, 45 Idaho L. Rev. 441 (2009)).

49. Default Standard for Discovery of Electronic Documents ("E-Discovery"), Ad Hoc Committee for Electronic Discovery of the U.S. District Court for the District of

found that where discovery had closed, the parties had failed to discuss the issue of e-discovery during initial conferences, and there was no "compelling reason as to why fact discovery should be re-opened," the party's demand for adherence to the standard instead seemed "akin to a fishing expedition."[50] Other courts have encountered situations where a proposed standard would run contrary to judicial efficiency,[51] and feel free to recognize when one court's standard does not apply to another court's decision.[52]

There has been a concurrent movement to relieve judges from their roles as iterative standard setters,[53] but before we address those attempts and review what they cover, it is helpful to learn more about how intentional standards are drafted and promulgated, how they are intended to operate, and how they operate in worlds other than the realm of the law. That is, what might we hope to accomplish, and what are we modeling against?

What Are Standards Generally?

Readers fully (if not myopically) engaged in the practice of law may be surprised to learn that the International Organization for Standardization (ISO)—at least in 2015—maintained and published some 19,500 standards covering the literal waterfront, ranging from "technology, to food safety, to agriculture, and healthcare."[54] In

---

Delaware; *see also* Wyeth v. Impax Labs., Inc., 2006 WL 3091331 (D. Del. Oct. 26, 2006).

50. RLI Ins. Co. v. Indian River Sch. Dist., 2007 WL 3112417, at *2 (D. Del. Oct. 23, 2007).

51. *In re* Porsche Cars N.A. Inc. Plastic Coolant Tubes Prods. Liab. Lit., 279 F.R.D. 447, 449 (S.D. Ohio 2012) (finding that native format production was appropriate but noting that the District of Ohio Default Standard for Discovery of Electronically Stored Information (E–Discovery) (L.R. App. K) Standard 6 provided that, "if the parties cannot agree to a format, the default standard is PDF or TIFF format with native files produced upon a showing of 'particularized need'").

52. Strong v. City of New York, 973 N.Y.S.2d 152, 158 (1st Dept. 2013) (finding that "reliance on the federal standard is unnecessary" in context of N.Y. State spoliation motion).

53. *See* Keteltas, *supra* note 3.

54. International Organization for Standardization, *About ISO* (undated), http://www.iso.org/iso/home/about.htm.

many respects, these and similar standards rule the world and most of the things in it. ISO defines its standards as guidance or documentation "that provides requirements, specifications, guidelines or characteristics that can be used consistently to ensure that materials, products, processes and services are fit for their purpose."[55] And because of ISO's status as the "world's largest international standards developer, [t]he norms established by ISO have a major impact on national and local environmental and social issues" among other things,[56] and may even have the effect of law or provide legal precedent.[57]

Despite its reach in the broader world, ISO (and similar standard-setting bodies) have not yet made significant inroads into the practice of litigation.[58] But there have been some instances where modern legal firms and practitioners incorporate standards into their operations. For instance, some advocates of standard use implore law firms to request "ISO [2000] certification from their legal information suppliers" while still acknowledging that "a set of established standards has yet to be set for legal publishers."[59] Another operative body promotes a two-tier "quality system" for law firms, setting standards for "Legal Best Practice" and "Excellence in Law."[60] Within the practice of law, rather than law firm operations, both practitioners and third-party service providers are cautious in their direction.

In direct contrast, in fact, to ISO proposals, the Electronic Discovery Reference Model (or EDRM)[61] explains that its standards are

55. International Organization for Standardization, *Standards—What Is a Standard?* (undated), http://www.iso.org/iso/home/standards.htm.

56. Mari Morikawa & Jason Morrison, *Who Develops ISO Standards?* Pacific Inst. for Studies in Dev., Env't, & Sec. (Oct. 2004) at 2.

57. Steven Teppler, *International Standard Project for E-Discovery Approved*, L. Tech. News (Apr. 30, 2013).

58. Macyl A. Burke, *A Cost-Effective Approach to Quality* (DESI V), at 4.

59. Linda Will, *ISO 2000 for Law Firms*, 14 Thompson Reuters Legal Solutions (July 2013) ("ISO 2000 covers the establishment and maintenance of quality fundamentals and functions in part as an international standard that addresses systematic change.").

60. SAI Global, *LAW 9000 Legal Best Practice* (undated).

61. EDRM, *Creating Practical Resources to Improve E-Discovery & Information Governance* (undated).

not really standards as classically or ISO defined, using its "Model Code of Conduct [MCoC]" to clarify that it is "not intended to... dictate operational guidelines for participants in the electronic discovery industry or the clients that purchase their products or engage their services."[62] It is unclear if this is an admonition that e-discovery practices are difficult to quantify, or an olive branch to prospective practitioner adherents. Either way, the current EDRM falls short of what other professionals would consider modern, operational standards.

All of the considerations mentioned earlier do, however, incorporate a key principle associated with standards that figures prominently in any proposed e-discovery standard-setting practice as well: the idea of tolerances. A tolerance is an "allowable, but non-deliberate, amount of variation from a physical quantity" where the item "must stick closely to the ideal design" as opposed to an ad hoc process.[63] This makes sense; components of complex systems must match each other in size if assembly of the whole is the goal; a tolerance range, therefore, indicates just how much deviation is possible before one part will not fit with another.

A standard for e-discovery should incorporate tolerances as well, and for at least two reasons: First, a given standard will not have perfection as the goal for the whole, and likely not for most of the parts.[64] Second, tolerances will vary based on what the whole will look like, and the "whole," or an agreed-upon approach between the parties endorsed, if only tacitly by the fact finder, will vary from matter to matter. Likewise, the component parts will vary somewhat as well, based on the whole; here, the tolerances will be matter—and party and court agreement—specific.

62. EDRM, *Model Code of Conduct* (undated).

63. Patrick Lockerby, *The Meaning of Tolerance*, Science 2.0 Blog (June 29, 2009, 12:15 PM), http://www.science20.com/chatter_box/blog/meaning_tolerance.

64. That is not to say there will not be specific parts that should be applied each and every time; for example, perhaps federal practitioners should seek a 502(d) order each and every time, and that sort of binary decision does not allow for a tolerance-type analysis.

Why Have So Many Attempted to Create a Discovery or e-Discovery Standard?

For the reasons previously discussed, a standard, if available and plausible, would certainly be helpful. And certainly a "number of authorities have recognized the need for standards regarding e-discovery."[65] Because "[t]here is no single, 'best way' through the e-discovery maze,"[66] it is clear practitioners—and the judiciary—could use the help. Likewise, without a perfect path forward, there is certainly "no review tool that guarantees perfection . . . there are risks inherent in any method of reviewing electronic documents."[67] These concepts both support a standard-like process, and return us to the concept of tolerances, where we look for milestones and guides to fit somewhere within, rather than specific number or items with an exact fit. Statements like this should give litigants who apply reasonable e-discovery processes some comfort. But while judges acknowledge it is unreasonable to expect perfection in the e-discovery process, they still wrestle with how to remedy imperfection in the outcome of the process.

Even incorporating the concept of tolerances, standards can range from the technical to the fuzzy, or across the spectrum of practitioners that hail from engineering and mathematical backgrounds to those who found a refuge from English and psychology degrees in law school. Some commentators have opined that e-discovery certification is divided even *within* the technical aspects, where

65. Jay E. Grenig & William C. Gleisner, *Discovery and Disclosure of Digital Information*, 1 eDiscovery & Digital Evidence § 6:11 (Nov. 2013) (stating in citation that "The U.S. Supreme Court approved new rules on eDiscovery effective December 1, 2006. The new rules and the Committee's Comments can be found in Volume 2, Appendix D. *See*, *e.g.*, Allman, *The Need for Federal Standards Regarding Electronic Discovery*, 68 Def. Couns. J. 206 (2001); Scheindlin, *Electronic Discovery in Federal Civil Litigation: Is Rule 34 Up to the Task?*, 41 B.C. L. Rev. 327 (2000)").

66. *The Sedona Conference Commentary on Achieving Quality in the E-Discovery Process*, 15 Sedona Conf. J. 265, 273 (2014).

67. *See* Da Silva Moore v. Publicis Groupe SA and MSL Group, 2012 WL 1446534, at *3 (S.D.N.Y. 2012) ("There simply is no review tool that guarantees perfection. The parties and Judge Peck have acknowledged that there are risks inherent in any method of reviewing electronic documents.").

"some have turned to the ISO 9000 family of standards, a set of standards focused on the validation of the quality management systems employed in an on-going business process; others have turned to the ISO/IEC 27000 family of standards, a set of standards focused on best practices and requirements for information security management systems (ISMS)."[68] We have opted to present the two camps: the *practitioner* and the *technical*, as, if not polar opposites, then at least as a compare-and-contrast. This is not, however, meant to create a winner-take-all competition; our hope is to pick the best from both camps and synergize the ideal concepts—with a healthy dose of tolerance—into a workable standard or framework with some staying power.

The Practitioner (or Softer) Side

In August 2004, the American Bar Association provided one of the earliest sets of standards when incorporating e-discovery concerns into their civil discovery standards.[69] The ABA focused on the following points:

- The preservation and collection of electronic information, including a then-current list of where to find electronic documents. This included factors a court could consider when allocating discovery costs.
- Appropriate instances when some or all discovery materials should be converted to electronic format.
- The need to confer about e-discovery at the initial discovery conference.
- An examination of attorney–client privilege and work–product protection.
- The future of storage media, which may not be electronic, and the consultation of existing standards when encountering new forms of data storage.[70]

68. *See* Hedin et al., *supra* note 43.
69. ABA, *Civil Discovery Standards* (2004).
70. *Id.*

These ABA-promulgated e-discovery standards were incorporated into their civil discovery standards,[71] and have been recognized in case law.[72]

The Judicial Conference of the United States sponsored an e-discovery panel at the 2010 Conference on Civil Litigation held at Duke Law, which in turn recommended a new rule of civil procedure governing preservation and spoliation of records and data. That proposal incorporated a number of specific issues that, while not specifically endorsed in or incorporated into the 2015 amendments to the Federal Rules of Civil Procedure, may still be instructive for the construction of a standard:

- **Trigger.** The rule (and standards) would specify when the obligation to preserve accrues.
- **Scope.** The rule would specify the scope of the duty to preserve.
- **Duration.** The rule would specify how long the information must be preserved, providing that the rule does not supersede any statute or regulation.
- **Ongoing Duty.** The rule would specify whether the duty to preserve extends to information generated after the duty has accrued.
- **Litigation Hold.** The rule would provide that, if an organization whose duty has been triggered prepares and disseminates a litigation hold notice, that is evidence of due care on the part of the organization.
- **Work Product.** The rule would specify whether, or to what extent, actions taken in furtherance of the preservation duty are protected by work product or privilege.
- **Consequences/Procedures.** The rule would set forth the consequences of failing to fulfill the responsibilities it mandates and the obligations of the complainant/failing party.

71. Jay E. Grenig & William C. Gleisner, *Wisconsin Practice Series—Civil Discovery*, 8 Wis. Prac., Civil Discovery §§14–16 (2d ed.) (Apr. 2014).

72. Race Tires Am., Inc. v. Hoosier Racing Tire Corp., 674 F.3d 158, 160 (3d Cir. 2012) ("The burden and expense thus far associated with discovery of ESI has resulted in [among others] the promulgation of standards by the American Bar Association.").

- **Judicial Determination.** The rule would provide access to a judicial officer, following a meet and confer to resolve disputes, apply the proportionality rule of Rule 26(c), consider the potential for allocation, and impose sanctions.[73]

Contemporaneously with the judicial conference, the Seventh Circuit's Electronic Discovery Committee presented their revised (and most current) Principles Relating to the Discovery of Electronically Stored Information, directing parties regarding the following:

- Cooperation,
- Discovery proportionality,
- Early case assessment (the duty to meet-and-confer; the nature of e-discovery liaisons; preservation requests, orders, and identification),
- Production format,
- Judicial expectations of counsel,
- Duty of continuing education—for "judges, attorneys, and parties to litigation."[74]

The Federal Judicial Center updated its Managing Discovery of Electronic Information: A Pocket Guide for Judges publication in 2012, and as part of its guidance, provided advice on the following issues:

- The judge's role in the discovery of ESI;
- How a judge may promote early consideration of ESI;
- What disclosures of ESI are required under Rule 26(a)(1);
- How the judge may limit the scope of ESI discovery; and
- In what form or forms ESI should be produced.[75]

---

73. Grenig & Gleisner, *supra* note 66; *see also* Kent A. Lambert, *Is It Time for a Federal Rule on Preservation?* ABA LITIGATION NEWS (Aug. 2, 2010), http://apps.americanbar.org/litigation/litigationnews/top_stories/080210-e-discovery-preservation-new-rule.html.

74. 7th Circuit Electronic Discovery Committee, *Principles Relating to the Discovery of Electronically Stored Information* (Aug. 1, 2010). http://www.discoverypilot.com/sites/default/files/Principles8_10.pdf.

75. Barbara J. Rothstein et al., *Managing Discovery of Electronic Information—A Pocket Guide for Judges*, FEDERAL JUDICIAL CENTER (2d. ed. 2012).

In 2013, the Sedona Conference Commentary on Achieving Quality in the E-Discovery Process submitted that "identification and use of best practices in collection, processing, review, and production are essential."[76] Building off of that statement, the Achieving Quality Commentary provided its own set of four principles:

- In cases involving ESI of significant scope and complexity, the attorney in charge should utilize project management tools and exercise sufficient leadership to ensure that his or her legal team follows a reasonable process to identify potentially responsive material.
- Parties should employ reasonable forms or measures of quality at appropriate points in the e-discovery process, consistent with the needs of the case and practitioners' legal and ethical responsibilities.
- A thoughtful and well-planned e-discovery "process" should enhance the overall quality of the production in the form of: (1) reducing the time from request to response, (2) reducing cost and burden, and (3) improving the accuracy and completeness of responses to requests.
- Cooperation and greater transparency among parties can be key ingredients to improving quality in e-discovery. Parties should confer early in discovery, including, where appropriate, exchanging information on any quality measures that may be applied.[77]

Standard-setting bodies in this space are many, and a number of jurisdictions and states have created model rules or other forms that govern the e-discovery process. These range from administrative orders[78] to the *Civil Litigation Management Manual*, which provides a default standard for discovery of electronically stored information.[79]

---

76. *The Sedona Conference Commentary on Achieving Quality in the E-Discovery Process*, 15 SEDONA CONF. J. 265, 269 (2014).

77. *Id.*

78. Moore v. The Weinstein Co., LLC, 2014 WL 4206205, at *7 (M.D. Tenn. Aug. 25, 2014) (reviewing "Administrative Order 174, which embodies the standard terms governing e-discovery in the Middle District of Tennessee").

79. U.S. Dist. Ct., N.D. of Ohio, *Default Standard for Discovery of Electronically Stored Information ("E-Discovery")—Appendix K*; *see also* United States Department

Even the bankruptcy Bar has even weighed in, where "[t]he Electronic Discovery (ESI) in Bankruptcy Working Group was formed to study and prepare guidelines or a best practices report on the scope and timing of a party's obligation to preserve electronically stored information ("ESI") in bankruptcy cases."[80] But commentators still agree that the ultimate arbiters, the courts generally, have not identified objective benchmarks or standards specific to the search process.[81]

Some practitioners outline a more granular list of considerations for practice, including a breakdown of discovery-related tasks and issues that includes considerations of:

- Senior Leadership;
- Project Managers;
- Human Resource Inventories;
- Technology Inventories;
- Information Asset Inventories;
- Policies and Guidelines;
- Education, Training, and Certification;
- Project Management Software Programs; and
- e-Discovery Workflow Programs.[82]

In contrast, the Coalition of Technology Resources for Lawyers (CTRL) initiative that went live on August 20, 2014, bills itself as an "industry education and research group committed to the development of practical and proactive guidance for lawyers facing the complexities and challenges inherent in the discovery process, and specifically the document review process."[83] Here, a number of practitioners recognize that the end result in the process is ultimately a judgment by a fact finder, and that even

---

of Justice Manual, *Comment 4-1.000 to the Civil Litigation Management Manual* (2014).

80. ABA Electronic Discovery (ESI) in Bankruptcy Working Group, *Best Practices Report on Electronic Discovery (ESI) Issues in Bankruptcy Cases* (2013).

81. *See* Bennett, *supra* note 5, at 436.

82. Adam I. Cohen & David J. Lender, *Electronic Discovery—Law and Practice, Establishing the e-Discovery Methodology—Methodology Components*, 2014 WL 100472 (C.C.H.) (Dec. 2013).

83. The Coalition of Technology Resources for Lawyers, *About CTRL* (Dec. 18, 2015).

> [w]ith the 'e,' discovery is primarily a legal process defined by legal rules, executed or supervised by counsel and refereed by judges. Although the proliferation of electronically stored information . . . and the rapid evolution of information technology have created technical and engineering challenges in the discovery process, the ultimate burden still falls on counsel to conduct reasonable and comprehensive searches for ESI.[84]

Other considerations not specific to e-discovery include looser or fuzzier standards, such as Juhnke's Five I's or "five stages of activity required to yield the desired result: intention, investigation, interaction, implementation, and iteration."[85] And the broader ISO 9000 family of standards reviews

> [r]equirements and best practices for the quality management systems that companies employ to ensure that their products and services meet the expectations of their customers. The most generally applicable standard in the family is ISO 9001. This standard is a 'requirements' standard, meaning that it specifies principles that a quality management system should adhere to, provides for both internal and independent audits of adherence, and allows for public certification of compliance for those quality management systems found to adhere to the standard's criteria.[86]

An e-discovery standard can take guidance from these examples, but, we argue, is not beholden to them. Still, there has been some recent movement toward articulation of an ISO standard; we discuss that in greater detail in the following section.

---

84. *See* Keteltas, *supra* note 3.

85. Deborah H. Juhnke, *Building a Defensible Search and Review Process for ESI*, THE PRACTICAL LITIGATOR (Jan. 2010).

86. *See* Hedin et al., *supra* note 43.

The Technical Viewpoint

Standard development within e-discovery has been a discussion point for a number of years, and even some early efforts were focused on defining "a baseline aptitude to independently gauge a technologist grasp of the core technology components involved in the different systems forming the electronic discovery process."[87] Recent comments have repeated this line of thinking, where "E-discovery is not a legal process. It's a technical and engineering problem."[88] This line of thinking posits that the only reason why a "rapid growth in the volumes of ESI held by parties involved in litigation" has not overwhelmed parties is the "concomitant . . . development of information retrieval tools and methods that hold promise as being capable of meeting even very steep discovery demands."[89]

Returning first to ISO and its proposed ISO/IEC CD 27050-1 standard,[90] current efforts at the time of ISO's last update had reached stage 40;[91] this indicates that the proposed standard has been registered as a Draft International Standard (DIS). Early drafts of the ISO standard presented four component parts to the proposal, which are helpful both for what they include and incorporate and for those parts of the e-discovery process that are left to practitioners and third-party service providers:

- ISO/IEC 27050-1, *Information Technology—Security Techniques*, presents an overview of e-discovery as incorporated into and considered by the standard; this would include terminology, concepts, and processes that can be leveraged by the other parts as well as other standards.
- ISO/IEC 27050-2, *Guidance for Governance and Management of Electronic Discovery*, describes how personnel, at senior levels within an organization, might identify and take

87. Daniel Garrie, *Formulating a Roadmap for E-Discovery*, L.A. Daily J. (2010), (https://web.archive.org/web/20101012045314/http://www.arc4adr.com/formulating_a_roadmap.html).

88. *See* Koblentz, *supra* note 2 (quoting Tom Barnett).

89. *See* Hedin et al., *supra* note 43.

90. Int'l Org. for Standardization, *ISO/IEC DIS 27050-1—Information Technology—Security Techniques—Electronic Discovery* (as of Dec. 20, 2015).

91. As of Dec. 20, 2015. ISO, *International Harmonized Stage Codes* (undated).

ownership of risks related to e-discovery, set related policies, achieve compliance with related external and internal requirements, and implement and control e-discovery in accordance with prevailing policies.

- ISO/IEC 27050-3, *Code of Practice*, provides requirements for and guidance on activities related to e-discovery, such as identification, preservation, collection, processing, review, analysis, and the production of ESI; this may also specify relevant measures that span the initial creation of ESI through its final disposition.
- ISO/IEC 27050-4, *ICT*[92] *Readiness for Electronic Discovery*, provides guidance on the ways an organization can plan and prepare for, and implement, e-discovery from the perspective of both technology and processes.[93]

ISO/IEC 27050 as a whole was designed to be relevant to both technical and nontechnical personnel working in connection with e-discovery and is intended to complement and not supersede existing laws and regulations in local courts. Not only does it count several well-known judges as supporters,[94] it also incorporates participation and input from a number of international jurisdictions.[95] In the United States, the standards proponents believe it may clarify e-discovery issues that have not been directly addressed in the

92. Enterprise Information and Communications Technology. *See* Eric Hibbard, *Electronic Discovery Standardization*, Ave Maria L. Rev. (Summer 2014).

93. *See ISO/IEC JTC 1 Working Group Developing International Standard for Electronic Discovery*, ANSI News and Publications, (Nov. 13, 2013), *available at* http://www.ansi.org/news_publications/news_story.aspx?menuid=7&articleid=3789.

94. *See* Hibbard, *supra* note 93, at 2, 313. ("[t]he Honorable John M. Facciola (U.S. Magistrate Judge, U.S. District Court, District of Columbia) brought the Committee to a decision point by moving to support the development of a standard; then the Honorable Andrew J. Peck (U.S. Magistrate Judge, U.S. District Court, Southern District of New York) promptly seconded it.") *citing* INCITS, Draft Minutes for the Thirty-Fourth meeting of INCITS Technical Committee CS1, Cyber Security, at 40, CS1-2012-00038-004 (Mar. 21–22, 2012).

95. *See* Teppler, *supra* note 58. (Countries participating in the project and supporting the addition of e-discovery to the SC27 program of work include Belgium, Brazil, China, Czech Republic, Italy, Republic of Korea, Mexico, Norway, Romania, Singapore, Slovakia, Slovenia, South Africa, the United States, the United Kingdom, and Thailand).

U.S. Federal Rules of Civil Procedure (FRCP) and their use in the U.S. federal court system, or in relevant state e-discovery statutes. Another e-discovery-related body, the Association of Records Managers and Administrators (ARMA), opined that the new ISO standard would incorporate elements from the U.S. Seventh Circuit Electronic Discovery Pilot Program, The Sedona Conference, various state-sponsored best-practice guidelines, and contributions from other experts in the field.[96] The ISO process is a closed-door process; but while opportunities to contribute are not available for nonparticipatory members,[97] a number of participants have written about the process[98] or continue to blog as it progresses.[99]

Perhaps not in competition with the developing ISO standards but interesting in comparison, EDRM has presented a set of standards[100] for e-discovery segmented into the three discrete parts of collection, identification, and production:

- **Collection** focuses on forensic image (physical or logical target); custom content/targeted image; non-forensic copy; exports—harvesting e-mail; exports—non-e-mail; and exceptions (e.g., mobile devices and instant messaging).[101]
- **Identification**, updated on October 22, 2011, is comprised of early case assessment and early data assessment, the latter focused on records management interviews; custodial interviews; and IT interviews.[102]

---

96. ARMA, *ISO Moves Forward on E-Discovery Standard*, ARMA Int'l NewsWire (May 22, 2013).

97. Matt Nelson, *Flying Under the Radar: Proposed International E-discovery Standard*, Inside Counsel (Oct. 24, 2013).

98. *See* Hibbard, *supra* note 93.

99. ISO/IEC 27050—Information technology—Security techniques—Electronic discovery (DRAFT), (http://www.iso27001security.com/html/27050.html).

100. The EDRM standards were recognized as authoritative in at least one matter after a party presented them for the court's consideration. *See* Laethem Equip. Co. v. Deere & Co., 2009 WL 3064663, at *4 (E.D. Mich. Sept. 21, 2009) (requiring party to "locate and preserve Plaintiffs' ESI, assess its present condition and state of corruption and restore it in compliance with EDRM standards (if that can be done)").

101. EDRM, *Collection Guide* (2015).

102. EDRM, *Identification Guide* (2015).

- EDRM **Production** Standards (Version 2) was updated on April 25, 2014, and focuses on native/near-native production; image (near-paper)/native/near-native production; image production; custom; and on-line production.[103]

Other commentators who also prefer more technical standards have presented papers regarding the "processing" of information, focused on "how accurate are the results" with that question "addressed only if the standard makes provision for the statistically sound measurement of the effectiveness of the review/retrieval function of an e-discovery system."[104] This matches with some commentators who believe that, "for standard setting efforts to realize their full potential, more input must be sought from those individuals experienced in technology and the technical standard setting process. Only computer scientists and technologists, who have real-world experience deploying enterprise technology systems, will have the necessary understanding of the key limitations or general issues that apply to the systems and software that must be searched as part of any e-discovery process."[105] Certainly, given the relative complexity[106] of different methods of review, expertise may be necessary in determining the appropriate approach for the review of a given set of documents.

The Comparison

The technical standards are necessary for those components they can regulate, but they need applicability to—and application by—the attorneys who are eventually standing before a fact finder explaining their reasoning behind their choices and decisions. Ultimately, the

103. EDRM, *Production Guide* (2015).

104. *See* Hedin et al., *supra* note 43.

105. *See* Garrie, *supra* note 88.

106. These approaches may include "Controlled vocabulary indexing (manual or automatic, with or without thesauri), multi-word phrase formation (by statistical and/or linguistic means), statistical query expansion methods, knowledge representation languages and inference systems from artificial intelligence, unsupervised learning approaches (including term clustering, document clustering, and factor analytic methods such as latent semantic indexing), as well as simple stemming, wildcards, spelling correction and string similarity measures." Douglas W. Oard, Jason R. Baron, Bruce Hedin, David D. Lewis, & Stephen Tomlinson, *Evaluation of Information Retrieval for E-Discovery*, 18 Artificial Intell. L. 347, 360 (2010).

practitioner is left with the responsibility and her license at issue; as stated before, and regardless of their individual comfort level, counsel are ethically bound to "keep abreast of . . . the benefits and risks associated with relevant technology."[107] Standards must therefore incorporate both the technical and legal divide. When a fact finder questions the reasonableness of a party's search for relevant information, it is unlikely that the practitioner will find perfect protection behind a technical standard—especially, as we will discuss further, even those standards fall far short of technical perfection. In fact, no standards expect perfection; as engineers are far too painfully aware, much of standard-setting processes center instead on appropriate tolerances.

The Need for Standards That Stand the Test of Time

The Federal Rules of Civil Procedure call for case-specific development of e-discovery processes sensitive to party concerns and realities; the amended Rules incorporated the same.[108] Rule 26(f) requires parties to confer on, develop, and propose a discovery plan or, absent agreement, discovery plans. Rule 26(f) even invites the parties to propose changes to the limitations on discovery imposed by the rules,[109] and its commentary states that "it is desirable that the parties' proposals regarding discovery be developed through a process where they meet in person, informally explore the nature and basis of the issues, and discuss how discovery can be conducted most efficiently

---

107. ABA Model Rules, *supra* note 4. *See also* Fed. R. Civ. P. 26(g)(1); Moore v. Publicis Groupe, 287 F.R.D. 182, 193 (S.D.N.Y. 2012) ("As with keywords or any other technological solution to ediscovery, *counsel must design an appropriate process*, including use of available technology, with appropriate quality control testing, to review and produce relevant ESI while adhering to Rule 1 and Rule 26(b)(2)(C) proportionality.") (emphasis added).

108. Fed. R. Civ. P. 26(b)(1) ("Parties may obtain discovery regarding any nonprivileged matter that is relevant to any party's claim or defense and proportional to the needs of the case, considering the importance of the issues at stake in the action, the amount in controversy, the parties' relative access to relevant information, the parties' resources, the importance of the discovery in resolving the issues, and whether the burden or expense of the proposed discovery outweighs its likely benefit.").

109. Fed. R. Civ. P. 26(f)(3)(E).

and economically."[110] E-discovery thought leaders also acknowledge the importance of case-by-case flexibility: "the reasonableness of a party's discovery process must be evaluated on a case-by-case basis in the context of the proportionality factors set forth in Rule 26(b)(2)(C), and no practitioner should assume that any single practice, process, or quality-checking measure is appropriate in any and all circumstances."[111] In fact, "there are 'probably more ways of gathering, processing and producing ESI than there are lawyers,'"[112] making a standard difficult to determine by trial-and-error.

This changing scope of discovery also highlights the changing dynamics between in-house and outside or merits counsel, which may also incorporate additional technological experts and third-party service providers. Cases where the client hands over two boxes of documents as the entirety of their "files" simply don't exist in modern, high-stakes litigation. The depth to which merits counsel may probe within the client's internal information governance practices and discovery gathering efforts may be limited by the client's direction, or by counsel's unintentional ignorance. Case law has already borne out these concerns, documenting instances where a "lack of meaningful communication permeated all of the relationships" within a case, including between the client "and outside legal counsel, and amongst outside counsel."[113]

Case-by-case discussion of at least certain aspects of information retrieval is necessary to address the proportionality principles baked into the Federal Rules. Quality standards should support the least costly defensible process that "identifies, collects and produces relevant and responsive non-privileged materials from a larger universe of ESI using reliable methodologies that provide a quality result at costs

110. Fed. R. Civ. P. 26, advisory committee comments.

111. *The Sedona Conference Commentary on Achieving Quality in the E-Discovery Process*, 15 Sedona Conf. J. 265 (2014); *see also The Sedona Conference Commentary on Proportionality in Electronic Discovery*, 14 Sedona Conf. J. 155 (2013).

112. *See* Bennett, *supra* note 5, at 436, *citing* Anne Kershaw & Joe Howie, *Judges' Guide to Cost-Effective E-Discovery iii*, Elec. Discovery Inst. (2010).

113. Qualcomm Inc. v. Broadcom Corp., 2010 WL 1336937 (S.D. Cal. Apr. 2, 2010).

that are reasonable and proportionate to the particular circumstances of the client and the litigation."[114]

But a challenge remains when even attempting to apply a third-party information retrieval process quality standard into a system that revisits process in nearly every case. Authoritative process quality standards that state minimum expectations for counsel (or a range of acceptable performance), and incorporate—either directly or by reference—standards for technology and technology service providers, would provide a useful reference for counsel in 26(f) discussions or a court faced with competing Rule 26(f) proposals.[115] Case-specific e-discovery concerns are, of course, far more complex than simple steps, but defining the simple building blocks assists in later assembling a more helpful framework for consideration.

These building blocks are built from defined principles and simple considerations that, when assembled together, can address the complexity of a given matter. Simplicity will help both the process, and should engender broader acceptance across the spectrum of providers. As we note in a prior article, "[s]earch process quality standards will not gain wide acceptance if they are not understood by, and part of the work flow of, the day-to-day participants in the legal process. Standards focused on the certification of technology and technology providers are needed, but should be paired with standards that define a defensible path to 'satisfying [counsel's] professional obligations to conduct a reasonable, comprehensive search in response to a Rule 34 request for documents and ESI.'"[116]

If search process quality standards are to be widely accepted, standard setters must build a bridge between technologists and lawyers and recognize the roles and expectations both face in a legal process for which lawyers are ultimately accountable.[117] This is a combinatory process, but one in which the technical serves and supports the legal.

114. *See* Shaffer, *supra* note 33, at 218.
115. *See* Keteltas, *supra* note 3.
116. *Id.*
117. *Id.*

Curiously, earlier discussions of standards tried to move standards-setting away from the practice of law, stating that in

> [t]he absence of such standards, the e-discovery process will remain fraught with uncertainty, and attorneys often will have no choice but to practice 'defensive discovery,' much like doctors often practice 'defensive medicine,' in order to avoid the risk of being second-guessed by a client, an adversary, or the court.[118]

How Standards Outside of the Federal Rules Might Operate

We believe that there is a need for process quality standards in e-discovery. But we acknowledge that some practitioners indicate that, in particular for information retrieval conducted or overseen by counsel, the U.S. legal system leans against standardization, while others suggest that a relatively clear standard might provide "certainty and efficiency,"[119] or go so far as to say that "standardization of process is an explicit requirement from the judiciary."[120] Ultimately, we agree that the FRCP and supporting decisions interpreting them encourage process development, even if on a case-by-case basis, that acknowledge relevant proportionality considerations while addressing the reasonableness of each particular case.[121]

The technical standards, and the ISO standards explicitly, are quick to disclaim operation outside of their ambit.[122] In contrast,

118. *See* Garrie, *supra* note 88.

119. *See* Bennett, *supra* note 5, at 462.

120. *See* Knox & Dawson, *supra* note 48.

121. The Sedona Conference *Commentary on Proportionality*, 14 Sedona Conf. J. 155, 167 (2013) ("Where appropriate, the application of technology to quickly isolate essential information serves the goal of proportionality by creating efficiencies and cost savings. Parties should meet and confer regarding technological approaches to preservation, selection, review, and disclosure that reduce overall costs, better target discovery, protect privacy and confidentiality, and reduce burdens.").

122. To some degree; the first Working Draft (WD) of the ISO/IEC 27050 project provided that the standard would be "relevant to both non-technical and technical personnel involved in some or all of the electronic discovery activities" but then

the practitioner-side proposed standards are, by their softer nature, more encompassing. However, the practitioner-side proposals miss some of the harder-edge nature of tolerances (or lack of compliance) and measuring aspects associated with quality- and audit-based approaches. We agree with those commentators who argue that "an e-discovery standard, whatever the ISO family to which it belongs, must be of the 'requirements' sort, if it is to be truly meaningful," and state that, while they "recognize that an initial 'guidance' standard may be necessary as an instrument for building and validating consensus around the standard's provisions," it is "only with the development of the standard into a set of certifiable requirements, however, that the potential benefits of a standard will be realized."[123] Those are important points, and some of our building blocks must support them.

The standards should provide a path to defensibility, which will do far more "to facilitate adoption of e-discovery products and services and accelerate the development of still more effective ones."[124] As some argue, "rather than mandating new technologies, government 'should identify what are the key goals or problems it is trying to address and then not discriminate against any technologies that can help achieve those stated objectives.'"[125] With that in mind, we provide our framework with separately defined building blocks that should each be considered while building up a standard for a given case; that is, while a single matter may not require the *incorporation* of each of these points, compliance with this e-discovery standard overall would require the *consideration* of each, and memorialization, where appropriate, of the reasoning why an individual block was excluded from the matter's process. That is, a checklist of sorts, similar to the practice

noted, as discussed elsewhere, that its guidance was "not intended to contradict or supersede local jurisdictional laws and regulations, so care should be exercised to ensure compliance with the prevailing jurisdictional requirements." *See* Hibbard, *supra* note 95.

123. *See* Hedin et al., *supra* note 43.

124. *Id.*

125. Tonia Hap Murphy, *Mandating Use of Predictive Coding in Electronic Discovery—An Ill-Advised Judicial Intrusion*, Am. Bus. L. J., 50 (2013) *citing* Gary E. Marchant, *Sustainable Energy Technologies: Ten Lessons from the History of Technology Regulation*, 18 Widener L.J. 831 (2009).

revolution and process improvements introduced by Atul Gawande into the surgical realm.[126]

This proposed standard is broken out into the following concepts, presented more-or-less alphabetically, and each explained in greater detail in the following list:

- **Cooperation**
- **Early Case Assessment**
- **Efficiency**
- **Fact-Based Decision-Making**
- Measure Twice, Cut Once—A **Measurement** Provision
- Plan—**Project Planning** and Oversight
- Pick Your Poison but Drink It Well—**No Standard Is the Gold Standard**
- **Protocol**—Follow a Protocol, Workflow, or Checklist
- Speak the Same Language—Consistent **Terminology**
- **Transparency**—I Know What You know, and So Does the Judge

Cooperation

Commentators note that discovery "is designed to be a cooperative process, run by the parties, as represented by counsel, largely without interference by the court,"[127] and that "failure to engage in cooperative discovery is likely to increase the costs, and complexity, of

126. *See* Burke, *supra* note 59, at 4; *see also* Carolyn Elefant, *Another Reason for Lawyers to Create Checklists—Potential Revenue Stream, Marketing & Making Money*, myShingle.com (Nov. 20, 2013) ("[C]onsider the mysteries of legal procedure. Court rules are often opaque or a particular district may have a unique practice that isn't well-known—and even when you understand them, there are usually a dozen steps needed to prepare documents to comply . . . . There is enormous value to clear, accurate and proven checklists for all of these steps.").

127. *See* Murphy, *supra* note 126. *See also* Paul W. Grimm, Charles S. Fax, & Paul Mark Sandler, *Discovery Problems and their Solutions*, 292 ABA (2d ed. 2009) ("[F]ederal courts have recently emphasized that discovery is a party-driven process requiring efforts at cooperation of the parties between counsel before petitioning the trial court, while endeavoring to control abuses of the system.").

litigation to the detriment of everyone involved."[128] Cooperative discovery involves not just refraining from abusive practices, but also developing, testing, and agreeing on the nature and scope of information sought (to the extent consistent with clients' interests)[129] where the use of a protocol within a standard "may also limit the universe of ESI to be searched."[130] Cooperation will involve "Solicitation—and incorporation to the extent possible, and within the bounds reasonable effort and advocacy—of input from the requesting party"[131] and will improve the manageability of the process.[132] But simple cooperation may not go far enough; true cooperation may require the use of true expert cooperation, where both parties have experts representing their interests.[133] Cooperation may also include meeting with opposing parties to "establish protections for inadvertently disclosed documents."[134]

This portion of a proposed standard is already being considered at the state law level,[135] and such a standard should aid practitioners in avoiding the kinds of ethical issues associated with the potential uses of e-discovery "as a weapon to force weaker parties into unfavorable settlements," and may even help practitioners "maintain goodwill with courts."[136] It would also provide an avenue for the court to intervene

---

128. Paul W. Grimm & Heather Leigh Williams, *'The [Judicial] Beatings Will Continue until Morale Improves': The Prisoner's Dilemma of Cooperative Discovery and Proposals for Improved Morale,* 43 U. Balt. L. F. 107, 115 (2013).

129. The Sedona Conference, *The Case for Cooperation,* 10 Sedona Conf. J. 339, 339 (2009 Supp.).

130. *See* Murphy, *supra* note 126.

131. *The Sedona Conference Commentary on Achieving Quality in the E-Discovery Process*, 15 Sedona Conf. J. 265, 274 (2014).

132. *See* Auttonberry, *supra* note 20.

133. *Id.*

134. Meaghan Zore, *Dialing Back Disclosure—Best Practices for Balancing Cooperation and Client Interests*, DESI V, at 3 (June 14, 2013).

135. Brian C. Vick & Neil C. Magnuson, *The Promise of a Cooperative and Proportional Discovery Process in North Carolina: House Bill 380 and the New State Electronic Discovery Rules*, 34 Cambpell L. Rev. 233, 249 (2012).

136. *See* Auttonberry, *supra* note 20. *See also* Margaret Rowell Good, *Loyalty to the Process: Advocacy and Ethics in the Age of E-Discovery*, 86 Fla. Bar J. 96, 99 (2012).

and fulfill its role as supervisor to the discovery process and intervener when it is abused by the parties.[137]

Early Case Assessment

An intelligent assessment, even at early stages of matter, can reduce costs associated with a number of e-discovery issues, including preservation, collection, processing, and review issues. Noted as a tool to "drastically narrow immense sets of potentially relevant information into smaller, refined clusters of pertinent data,"[138] this can be a great tool to address important questions relevant to e-discovery concerns, including the data volume and type, the case timeline, the maturation of case strategy, the value or liability of the case, the projected costs of processing and review, and the type of key players or fact witnesses identified.[139] Further, early agreements between parties "can avoid lengthy discovery disputes later, thereby lowering litigation costs."[140]

Efficiency

Commentators note that an e-discovery process should aim to find relevant information "as quickly and efficiently as possible."[141] This comports with the court's goal of "discouraging wasteful pretrial activities."[142] This also gives latitude to a standard that would not require the newest technology, or even mandate predictive coding or technology assisted review. While commentators note that the process of e-discovery has evolved, moving from "old-fashioned" manual review to, through keyword searching, incorporating newer tools such

---

137. *See* Murphy, *supra* note 126, at 18. *See generally* Paul D. Carrington, *Recent Efforts to Change Discovery Rules: Do They Advance the Purposes of Discovery?* 51, 60, *in* Roscoe Pound Inst., *Controversies Surrounding Discovery and Its Effect on the Courts* (1999).

138. David Canfield, *Early Data Assessment—Setting the Standard in E-Discovery Readiness*, Inside Counsel (Feb. 16, 2012); *see also* Kroll Ontrack, *Early Data Assessment (EDA)—Setting the Standard in E-Discovery Readiness*, Whitepaper (2012).

139. *See* Canfield, *supra* note 139.

140. *See* Zore, *supra* note 135, at 1.

141. Ralph C. Losey, *Child's Game of "Go Fish" Is a Poor Model for EDiscovery Search*, E-Discovery Team Blog (Oct. 4, 2009, 4:09 PM). This comports with FRCP 1, which demands the "speedy" and "inexpensive determination of every action." Fed R. Civ. P. 1.

142. Fed. R. Civ. P. 16(a)(3).

as predictive coding.[143] But keywords have not gone away; one commentator notes that practitioners "still use search terms in almost every matter that involves ESI in litigation . . . to collect by custodian . . . to filter by date ranges . . . to cull broad collections of documents from archives . . . [and] to find documents to train [Technology Assisted Review] systems."[144] Here too, a shinier mousetrap with a bigger marketing budget may not be more appropriate than the companionship of a cat. That is, for a very small review and production set, manual review is likely the correct answer. For larger volumes, perhaps keyword technology will get the work done much more efficiently for the party or parties—and certainly carries with its use a good deal more transparency. Neither is keyword technology necessarily second-rate; in addition to being a tried, true, and understandable process, modern keyword "searches in electronic discovery, however, are typically much more complex [and] may incorporate several advanced information retrieval methods."[145]

Fact-Based Decision-Making

Fact-based decision-making derives from the ISO 9000 family of standards' consideration of quality management, and attempts to make decisions on the results of data collection and analysis. While seemingly axiomatic, this type of principle incorporated into a standard may prevent instances where "form" trumps "substance," or a party makes an agreement with unequal or incorrect information. Such instances may result in agreed-upon keywords that return multiples of expected results, but an intractable opposing party who refuses to retreat from an earlier agreement.

---

143. *See* Murphy, *supra* note 126.

144. Daniel Regard & Tom Matzen, *A Re-Examination of Blair & Maron*, DESI V, at 9 (June 14, 2013).

145. *See* Murphy, *supra* note 126. Keyword searching is not in and of itself straightforward either. Keyword searching "has been used in the IR [Information Retrieval] literature to refer to any or all of exact string matching, substring matching, Boolean search, or statistical ranked retrieval, applied to any or all of free text terms (e.g., space-delimited tokens or character n-grams), manually or automatically assigned controlled vocabulary terms, with or without augmentation by any combination of stemming, wildcards, multi-word phrase formation, proximity and/or word order restrictions, field restrictions, and/or a variety of other operators." *See also* Oard et al., *supra* note 107.

This may also include the measures by which parties determine if a given standard has worked appropriately in their case, if questioned by a fact finder. One commentator notes that "If care is taken to weigh the actual information need in a given circumstance against the sampling and review costs required to meet that need, one can, in most cases, arrive at a sampling design that will, in a cost-effective manner, contribute meaningful empirical data to the validation of the results of a retrieval effort."[146] This mirrors the current Federal Rules burden-versus-benefit analysis for evidence generally,[147] and may include instances where a party "switch[es] horses in midstream," even in the face of an original case management order, to properly assess information according to the needs of the case and the reality of the information found.[148] This also incorporates the idea embodied in the FRCP that each party "is in the best position to make judgments about how effectively to search its own documents."[149] And if necessary (but certainly not recommended as a matter of course), fact-based decision-making can also rely upon "[t]hird-party neutrals and in-camera reviews of specific documents or sensitive case-related materials" as a final means of illustrating a defense of process.[150]

---

146. *See* Hedin et al., *supra* note 43.

147. Fed. R. Civ. P. 26(b)(1) *Scope in General.* Unless otherwise limited by court order, the scope of discovery is as follows: Parties may obtain discovery regarding any nonprivileged matter that is relevant to any party's claim or defense and proportional to the needs of the case, considering . . . whether the burden or expense of the proposed discovery outweighs its likely benefit.

148. Bridgestone Americas Inc. v. Int'l Bus. Mach. Corp., No. 3:13-1196, 2014 BL 202049 (M.D. Tenn. July 22, 2014). *But see* Progressive Casualty Ins. v. Delaney, 2014 WL 2112927 (D. Nev. May 20, 2014) (holding that Progressive violated an extensive (and court approved) joint ESI protocol's transparency when it unilaterally opted to use predictive coding without seeking to amend the protocol.)

149. *See* Murphy, *supra* note 124. *See also* Judge Nolan in *Kleen Products* ("I think the people who are producing the records, producing the documents, are in a better position to know [what search techniques should be employed], since they have to do the work, spend the money, spend the time, they know their people, they know their material, so as a basic premise, I think that's a pretty fair premise here.") Transcript of Proceedings, at 297–98, Kleen Prods., LLC v. Packaging Corp. of Am., Civil Case No. 1:10-cv-05711 (N.D. Ill. Mar. 28, 2012).

150. *See* Zore, *supra* note 135, at 4.

Measure Twice, Cut Once—A Measurement Provision

"Where appropriate, the process should incorporate some form of metrics to quantify the accuracy and completeness of the resulting output."[151] These types of measurements may include the now-traditional quantifiers of recall and precision,[152] but should also consider such things as the "data corpus; the examination of false negatives; the complexity of the search terms; and the methodology used to develop search terms."[153] Measurements may consider results of whatever the chosen process by utilizing "various rounds of sampling and quality control tests";[154] sampling is a consistent approach among commentators.[155]

But even supporters of considered technical standards agree that "a measurement provision need not require the specification of minimum thresholds for recall and precision, need not open the door to misuse of the results of measurement, need not entail undue cost and time in the provision of e-discovery services, and need not provide opportunities to 'game the system.'"[156] Other authors reinforce the idea that measurement does not begin—or end—with "precision and recall, but also on cost, complexity, resources, need, time constraints, reasonability, and proportionality"[157] and remind us that "estimating recall is simply a hard task for people to do."[158] Finally, at least one commentator suggests that "the inclusion of a measurement provision in a standard would, by allowing a shift of attention from process to

---

151. *The Sedona Conference Commentary on Achieving Quality in the E-Discovery Process*, 15 SEDONA CONF. J. 265, 273 (2014).

152. *See* Burke, *supra* note 59, at 2.

153. *See* Regard & Matzen, *supra* note 146.

154. Jonathan H. Lomurro, Christopher T. Campbell, Matthew K. Blaine, Stephanie L. Lomurro, & Christina V. Harvey, *Litigation Technology for the Modern Practitioner*, N.J. INST. FOR CONTINUING LEGAL EDUCATION (2014) at 32.

155. *See* Zore, *supra* note 135, at 3.

156. *See* Hedin et al., *supra* note 43.

157. *See* Regard & Matzen, *supra* note 146.

158. Herbert L. Roitblat, *Search and Information Retrieval Science*, SEDONA CONF. J. (Fall 2007); *see also* Feng Charlie Zhao, Douglas W. Oard, & Jason R. Baron, *Improving Search Effectiveness in the Legal E-Discovery Process Using Relevance Feedback*, Third International Workshop on Discovery of Electronically Stored Information (DESI III) (2009).

results, simplify the resolution of discovery disputes" for the Bench.[159] The result here may not be a specific number; it might, instead, focus on the "quality [of] the methodology that was utilized,"[160] where a fact-finder is measuring—and balancing both what the practitioners did, and how they did it. And quality has been posited as a "measure of excellence" that itself represents "the strict and consistent adherence to measurable and verifiable standards to achieve uniformity and output that satisfies specific customer or user requirements."[161]

Plan—Project Planning and Oversight

"Achieving 'consistency across the production' requires sound project planning and oversight, which is often enhanced by integrating measurements of quality within the overall e-discovery process."[162] Courts begin with the assumption, noted elsewhere, that because "producing parties are in the best position to understand their own information storage and retrieval systems," [163] the producing party is "thus required (in the first instance) to create a plan for conducting required searches for information (with an opportunity for input by the requesting party."[164]

Pick Your Poison But Drink It Well—Manual Review Is Not the Gold Standard—In Fact, No Standard Is the Gold Standard

Commentators note that "using only manual review in e-discovery is not a realistic option."[165] But we go further than that; even if

159. *See* Hedin et al., *supra* note 43, at 4.

160. *See* Burke, *supra* note 59, at 2.

161. *Id.*

162. *The Sedona Conference Commentary on Achieving Quality in the E-Discovery Process*, 15 Sedona Conf. J. 265, 273 (2014); *see also* Bennett B. Borden & Jason R. Baron, *Finding the Signal in the Noise*, 20 Rich. J.L. & Tech. 7 (2014).

163. *See* Bennett, *supra* note 5, at 459, citing Harlow v. Sprint/Nextel Corp., 2012 WL 646003 (D. Kan. Nov. 26, 2013) (responding party in "best position to establish" that it has "already produced" sufficient relevant data; directing parties to "work together in good faith and in a cooperative manner toward the goal of narrowing the size of the production" as well as "the cost and time needed to produce it").

164. *See* Ruiz-Bueno v. Scott, 2013 WL 6055402, at *4 (S.D. Ohio Nov. 15, 2013).

165. *See* Auttonberry, *supra* note 20, at 614, n.10, citing Andrew Peck, *Search, Forward: Will Manual Document Review and Keyword Searches Be Replaced by*

"predictive coding" is the soup du jour, parties and attorneys may have legitimate, good-faith reasons to prefer keyword searches which are, themselves, an "established, judicially recognized method."[166] The point of this "block" is not to necessarily elevate one method over another, or to tout the "latest and greatest" methods, which might include predictive coding or technology-assisted review using linguistic or sociological approaches.[167]

In fact, and as discussed earlier, despite the acknowledged limitations associated with manual review,[168] practitioners know logically that a matter involving only several files or even tens of boxes of documents is well within scope for eyes-on-review, many matters fall within those types of parameters, and courts acknowledge that parties are in the "best position to make judgments about how effectively to search [their] own documents."[169] The market may help here as well: "truly effective and useful new technologies which are readily available are likely to be accepted by consumers (practitioners)

Computer-Assisted Coding?, L. TECH. NEWS (Oct. 2011) ("[T]he volume of electronically stored information . . . has largely eliminated manual review as the sole method of document review . . . ."); *see also* George L. Paul & Jason R. Baron, *Information Inflation: Can the Legal System Adapt?*, 13 RICH. J.L. & TECH. 10 (2007) (noting that "[l]itigators can no longer depend on manual review alone").

166. *See* Murphy, *supra* note 126, at 20. S*ee also* Custom Hardware Eng'g & Consulting, Inc. v. Dowell, 2012 U.S. Dist. LEXIS 146, at *6 (E.D. Mo. Jan. 3, 2012); Jason R. Baron & Michael D. Berman, *Designing a "Reasonable" E-Discovery Search: A Guide for the Perplexed, in* Managing E-Discovery and ESI 479, 482 (Michael D. Berman et al. eds., 2011) ("Automated methods of search, starting with applying more sophisticated approaches to keyword searching, are the wave of the future.").

167. Venkat Rangan, *Discovery of Related Terms in a Corpus Using Reflective Random Indexing* (July 28, 2011) (unpublished paper, presented at SIGIR 2011 Information Retrieval for E-Discovery Workshop, Beijing, China).

168. David C. Blair & M.E. Maron, *An Evaluation of Retrieval Effectiveness for a Full-Text Document-Retrieval System*, Communications of the ACM 28(3):289–99 (Mar. 1985); *see also* Regard & Matzen, *supra* note 146.

169. *See* Murphy, *supra* note 126, at 22. *See also* Judge Nolan in *Kleen Products* ("I think the people who are producing the records, producing the documents, are in a better position to know [what search techniques should be employed], since they have to do the work, spend the money, spend the time, they know their people, they know their material, so as a basic premise, I think that's a pretty fair premise here.") Transcript of Proceedings, at 297–98, Kleen Prods., LLC v. Packaging Corp. of Am., Civil Case No. 1:10-cv-05711 (N.D. Ill. Mar. 28, 2012).

without the need for government mandates."[170] Because of these types of obvious-and-numerous exceptions, any e-discovery standard must, in fact, refrain from naming a victor based only on the tool, rather than the matter for which the tool is retained. Finally, if a party does decide to employ manual review, the same standard would apply—but with the added caveats that the party may have to explain how it met its duty to keep current with technological changes, and how electronic-only issues (such as metadata)[171] were not applicable to its review.

Protocol—Follow a Protocol, Workflow, or Checklist

Some commentators note that parties should take note of prior court ordered or approved protocols, and even offer up model examples.[172] These may aid in increasing the practice's efficiencies,[173] and will also aid in providing specific tasks against which the producing party may measure their success. Workflows and associated checklists, some of which are already available for practitioners,[174] may go a long way in assisting discovery efforts, and courts are beginning to "expect genuine efforts to formulate" discovery plans.[175] And checklists are overdue in the legal profession, despite the insight that "organizational and professional inertia is the rule, not the exception."[176] However, a checklist is not the end-all of the process. Simply following the steps regardless of the case, data, or organizational nuance, should not provide a "seal of approval." The process would require considerations of whether each point, practice, and technology incorporated into the checklist was appropriate and/or defensibly employed.

170. *See* Murphy, *supra* note 126, at 29.

171. Wayne A. Hill, *Managing Metadata in Litigation Matters*, 126 Am. Jur. Proof of Facts 3d 281 (2012).

172. *See* Auttonberry, *supra* note 20.

173. Fed. R. Civ. P. 26(f) advisory committee's note.

174. Jamie Brown & Paul Weiner, *Data Handling Strategies for Smaller Cases—A Checklist*, presented at 10th Annual Georgetown eDiscovery Institute (Nov. 21, 2013).

175. *See* Bennett, *supra* note 5, at 456, citing Da Silva Moore v. Publicis Groupe, 287 F.R.D. 182, 193 (S.D.N.Y. 2012) ("counsel must design an appropriate process, including use of available technology, with appropriate quality control testing"); William A. Gross Constr. Assocs., Inc. v. Am. Mftrs. Ins. Co., 256 F.R.D. 134, 135–36 (S.D.N.Y. 2009) (noting "need for careful thought, quality control, testing, and cooperation to avoid searches in the dark, by the seat of the pants").

176. *See* Burke, *supra* note 59, at 4.

Speak the Same Language—Consistent Terminology

Some commentators note that a fostering or normalizing a common terminology or vocabulary for discussing e-discovery[177] is a noble goal, and we agree. A number of practitioners have already collaborated to provide resources that assist in this type of effort,[178] but the key point here is agreement between the parties to ensure that so-called apples are comparable. This is not a trivial point; relatively e-discovery-savvy practitioners may encounter a vast gulf in understanding when discussing technical issues with opposing parties. ISO/IEC 27050 "seeks to harmonize terminology" as an explicit goal,[179] but focuses specifically on the technical jargon component of terminology to minimize party confusion. In addition to that laudable aim, however, consistent terminology may even improve search results by its operation,[180] where the parties may agree on the scope of the case and incorporate discussions regarding key words—and those key words' eventual maturity—in a collaborative environment focused on consistency. Terminology may also help define which portions of the ESI discovery process are[181] and are *not*[182] part of reasonable expectations.

Transparency—I Know What You Know, and So Does the Judge

A "transparent e-discovery standard" is among those points practitioners note as important,[183] whether for a review of the technology's

177. *See* Hedin et al., *supra* note 43.

178. Maura R. Grossman & Gordon V. Cormack, *The Grossman-Cormack Glossary of Technology Assisted Review with Foreword by John M. Facciola, U.S. Magistrate Judge*, 7 Fed. Cts. L. Rev. (Jan. 2013), at 5.

179. Hibbard, *supra* note 95, at 1.

180. *See* Murphy, *supra* note 126 n.23.

181. Williams v. Sprint/United Management Co., 230 F.R.D. 640, 652 (D. Kan. 2005) (standard production formats may include native file format).

182. *See* Hill, *supra* note 173 ("[e]merging standards of electronic discovery appear to articulate a general presumption against the production of metadata but provide a clear caveat when the producing party is aware or should be reasonably aware that particular metadata is relevant to the dispute.").

183. *See* Hedlin *supra* note 43.

operation and application, or to determine the manner in which practitioners are following the advised steps. Transparency requires "that producing parties should give the court and opposing parties clear and comprehensive explanations of [their] search processes."[184] Certainly, courts have expected "full openness"[185] and implicit agreements regarding transparency[186] when considering e-discovery practices and protocols, and the Sedona cooperation proclamation.[187] This has been the case for a number of years, with courts requiring "full disclosure about the technology used, the process, and the methodology, including the documents used to 'train' the computer."[188] Transparency, coupled with broad disclosure, may also lead to advances in the adoption of new technologies.[189]

Reasonability in All Things—Without Perfection As the Goal

Courts are concerned with parties who take untenable positions with an end-game of returning to normal; courts wish to avoid actions that would "encourage litigants to demand the moon thinking they can always fall back to something reasonable. They should be reasonable from the start."[190] This focuses on a process "that is reasonable and proportional,"[191] and relies upon an appreciation of both fact-based decision-making and efficiency.

---

184. *See* Auttonberry, *supra* note 20.

185. Bridgestone Americas Inc. v. Int'l Bus. Mach. Corp., No. 3:13-1196, 2014 BL 202049 (M.D. Tenn. July 22, 2014).

186. Progressive Casualty Insurance v. Delaney, 2014 WL 2112927 (D. Nev. May 20, 2014).

187. The Sedona Conference, *The Case for Cooperation,* 10 Sedona Conf. J. 339, 339 (2009 Supp.).

188. Progressive Casualty Insurance v. Delaney, 2014 WL 2112927 at *27–28 (D. Nev. May 20, 2014) citing *Da Silva Moore* 2012 U.S. Dist. LEXIS 23550.

189. *See* Zore, *supra* note 135, at 5.

190. Boston Scientific Corp. v. Lee, 2014 U.S. Dist. LEXIS 107584, at *22 (N.D. Cal. Aug. 4, 2014) quoting Straight Path IP Group, Inc. v. Blackberry Ltd., 2014 U.S. Dist. LEXIS 92787, 2014 WL 3401723, at *1 (N.D.Cal. July 8, 2014).

191. *See* Burke, *supra* note 59, at 1.

Conclusion

Commentators are consistent in declaring that the "goal is not *perfect* discovery, but rather *reasonable* discovery;"[192] the "standard for discovery is reasonableness, good faith and proportionality. It is not perfection;"[193] and note that when "collecting, retrieving, processing and producing ESI [, no] one is expected to be perfect: the issue is whether the process can be proven to be a reasonable method for producing a reasonably complete set of relevant documents, thereby discharging a party's discovery obligations."[194] Herein lies the true culmination of an e-discovery standard: an application of the principles, as appropriate and according to plan, in a fashion that an objective fact-finder could understand, appreciate, and determine reasonable.

192. *See* Murphy, *supra* note 126 n.128, citing Chen-Oster v. Goldman, Sachs & Co., 2012 U.S. Dist. LEXIS 130123, at *42 (S.D.N.Y. Sept. 10, 2012) (quoting and adopting Sedona principle that "the standard for the production of ESI is not *perfection*. Rather, '[a] responding party must use *reasonable* measures to validate ESI collected from database systems to ensure completeness and accuracy of the data acquisition.'"); Larsen v. Coldwell Banker Real Estate Corp., 2012 U.S. Dist. LEXIS 12901, at *18–21 (C.D. Cal. Feb. 2, 2012) (noting party's obligation to act "reasonably and in good faith" to produce requested documents and rejecting plaintiff's request that defendant redo production due to "a few alleged discrepancies"). The burden is on the requesting party to show the producing party's efforts were inadequate. *Larsen*, 2012 U.S. Dist. LEXIS at *18.

193. *See* Burke, *supra* note 59, at 4.

194. *See* Lomurro et al., *supra* note 156, at 29.

ANALYTICS AND THE LAW

EDITORS' INTRODUCTION TO CHAPTER 16

Michael D. Berman

Jeffrey Sharer and Robert Keeling discuss leveraging a tool that is often considered only for use in litigation, by applying it in the context of mergers, acquisitions, and divestitures.

The law is a seamless web.[1] An example may help. "Suppose we are trying to understand a rule regarding consent in criminal law. Understanding the legal concept of consent may require us to go beyond criminal law."[2] This chapter demonstrates that litigators and business lawyers can learn from each other. It addresses the "impossible triangle" of doing the same work in less time, at lower cost, with equal or better quality. The goal in both the business and litigation arenas is to "find more like this" and this chapter shows how to do that.

"One of the most promising areas of legal practice outside of litigation for use of predictive analytics is mergers, acquisitions, and divestitures." The authors explain how the technology can be used to get one's "house in order." Thus, "the same technologies and workflows that have gained acceptance in the litigation context can be deployed much earlier in the information lifecycle to improve information governance and drive cost savings and productivity gains across the organization. The same algorithms and other technologies that are trained to classify documents as responsive or nonresponsive in discovery can be trained to make similar distinctions on other vectors, such as whether a document is a contract or not, contains intellectual property or not, is a financial report or not, is a personnel record or not, and so on."

---

1. See *Legal Theory Lexicon: The Law Is a Seamless Web*, LEGAL THEORY BLOG (Oct. 1, 2006), http://lsolum.typepad.com/legaltheory/2006/10/legal_theory_le.html, for the history of this phrase.

2. *Id.*

Just as discovery is often the costliest phase of litigation, due diligence is often the costliest aspect of many transactions. The authors suggest that the two have many parallels. They then describe the application of predictive analytics to due diligence and responding to Hart-Scott-Rodino second requests. They describe the framework for Federal Trade Commission and Antitrust Division requests, and the FTC Guidance, as well as how to negotiate responses using predictive coding techniques. This is important—and may be applicable—in a much wider arena. For example, "[t]he Division is especially interested in seeing the 'overturn rate' or the frequency with which the subject-matter expert reviewing the results disagrees with the responsiveness determination of predictive coding."

The significance of this chapter is obvious: "While the FTC guidelines are limited to M&A transactions under its jurisdiction, they may be persuasive authority to other government agencies considering allowing the use of predictive coding to respond to regulatory inquiries." Going further, the authors state that "[p]ut to its fullest use, predictive coding has the potential fundamentally to transform how due dilgence is conducted." In light of the interconnectedness of law, the emergence of guidelines for advanced search in the regulatory context may have broad application in many other contexts.

CHAPTER 16

Algorithms at the Gate: Leveraging Predictive Analytics in Mergers, Acquisitions, and Divestitures

Jeffrey C. Sharer and Robert D. Keeling

At its core, what we call "predictive coding" in litigation is simply one application of predictive analytics, using technology to analyze current and historical facts to make predictions about other, unknown facts. In the litigation context, predictive coding analyzes known facts about exemplar documents and uses that analysis to respond to the instruction "find more like this." As others have observed, the litigation use case is powerful.[1] With predictive coding, litigators can achieve significant reduction in all three sides of the so-called impossible triangle; that is, do the same work in less time, at lower cost, and with equal or better quality, not needing to sacrifice one to accomplish the other two.[2]

---

1. Andrew Peck, *Search, Forward: Will Manual Document Review and Keyword Searches Be Replaced by Computer-Assisted Coding?* Law Tech. News (Oct. 2011).

2. *See, e.g.*, Maura R. Grossman & Gordon V. Cormack, *Technology-Assisted Review in E-Discovery Can Be More Effective and More Efficient than Exhaustive Manual Review*, 17 Rich. J. L. & Tech. 11 (2011).

For attorneys and clients litigating in a world where even a "small" case can involve hundreds of thousands or even millions of documents collected from potentially discoverable sources, the ability to leverage predictive analytics to separate responsive documents from nonresponsive documents with only a fraction of the corpus requiring costly "eyes-on" review by attorneys has been a game changer.[3] But litigators are not the only attorneys, and litigants are not the only clients, who confront ever-swelling volumes of data needing to find "more like this." Virtually any area of law—indeed, virtually any activity in any domain—that involves large-scale review of text-based records would be a potential use case for the technology and workflows that underpin predictive coding in the litigation context.

One of the most promising areas of legal practice outside of litigation for use of predictive analytics is mergers, acquisitions, and divestitures. For many of the same reasons that predictive coding has steadily gained acceptance in litigation, predictive analytics has applications for both buyers and sellers and in all phases of the deal lifecycle. Predictive coding also is being used effectively in one particular aspect of M&A to which it has especially powerful application, namely, responding to Hart-Scott-Rodino (HSR) Second Requests.[4]

Pre-Transaction: Getting the Seller's House in Order

For most companies, the massive volumes of data created and retained in the ordinary course of business drive up costs and risk and impair efficiency and productivity;[5] for companies contemplating a sale, merger, or divestiture, they pose even greater challenges. Even for organizations with mature records and information management programs, it can be difficult to locate and identify all of the documents that the company's management, board of directors, and advisors

3. *See, e.g.*, Paul E. Burns & Mindy M, Morton, *Technology-Assisted Review: The Judicial Pioneers*, 15 SEDONA CONF. J. 35 (2014).

4. Hart-Scott-Rodino Antitrust Improvements Act of 1976, 15 U.S.C. § 18a (2015).

5. *See Big Data Universe Beginning to Explode*, COMPUTER SCIENCES CORP. (2011), *available at* http://www.csc.com/insights/flxwd/78931-big_data_universe_beginning_to_explode.

need in order appropriately to value the company and otherwise to prepare for a contemplated deal. Almost across the board, so-called dark data—data that's stored within the company's information systems without control or classification and is, for practical purposes, opaque—continues to grow.[6] Even where an organization knows the right people to ask or places to look, the sheer volume of information maintained even by individual employees can make it difficult for the organization to find what it needs, when it needs it. The challenges become even greater where data resides in legacy stores retained for departed employees, or on shared drives or file servers no longer in active use.[7]

Without ready access to all of the information relevant to valuation and other pre-transaction diligence, an erstwhile seller runs myriad risks, from setting a price that undervalues the business or finding itself unable to support a valuation that is fair, to leaving itself exposed to potentially damaging surprises in due diligence, to wasted time and resources where employees are diverted from their daily responsibilities to search for critical needles in haystacks.

As discussed elsewhere in this book, the same technologies and workflows that have gained acceptance in the litigation context can be deployed much earlier in the information lifecycle to improve information governance and drive cost savings and productivity gains across the organization. The same algorithms and other technologies that are trained to classify documents as responsive or nonresponsive in discovery can be trained to make similar distinctions on other vectors, such as whether a document is a contract or not, contains intellectual property or not, is a financial report or not, is a personnel record or not, and so on. In almost all applications, the technology and process is fundamentally the same: Humans provide exemplars, computers analyze and predict whether other documents are in the same categories as the exemplars, and humans validate the machine predictions—"rinse and repeat"—until an acceptable level of accuracy and statistical confidence is reached.

6. *IT Glossary: Dark Data*, GARTNER (2016), *available at* http://www.gartner.com/it-glossary/dark-data.

7. *See, e.g.*, The Sedona Conference, *The Sedona Conference Commentary on Information Governance*, 15 SEDONA CONF. J. 125 (2014).

In recent years, technologies have emerged with the capability to perform some types of classification as early as when a document is first received or saved on a company's systems.[8] But even organizations that have not previously incorporated predictive analytics in information governance can employ powerful indexing and analytic technologies for data identification in relatively short order. In the context of a company preparing for sale or divestiture, such indexing and analysis typically is done on a targeted basis over the data stores that are likely to contain the information sought, much the same as in the litigation use case. By identifying relevant documents and information during the pre-diligence stage and conducting appropriate preliminary inquiries in areas that the seller knows or expects will be the subject of disclosure requests from a buyer, the soon-to-be seller and its advisors are able to identify and, as needed, address issues that otherwise would not have arisen until mid-transaction, potentially with damaging effect. The seller also is better positioned to support its desired valuation and to navigate the diligence process without unpleasant surprise.

Predictive Analytics in Due Diligence

Similar to document discovery in litigation, due diligence is often the most labor-intensive and costly aspect of legal services in transactions.[9] Also like document discovery in litigation, due diligence in many transactions is ripe for use of predictive analytics with benefits accruing on both sides of the table.

In many respects, due diligence in M&A parallels document discovery. The objective is to provide to the buyer all of the information that it needs to make an informed decision regarding whether to proceed with the transaction. In a typical deal, this includes among other things all material facts relevant to the seller's business, finances, tangible and intangible assets, and actual and potential liabilities, almost all of which are uniquely controlled by the seller. Although particulars vary from transaction to transaction, in most deals, the

8. *See id.*

9. *See, e.g.*, *Due Diligence in the Digital Age: A Look at Techniques, Ancient and Modern, for Investigating Your Target and Closing Your Deal*, Annual ABA Convention (Aug. 9, 2008).

buyer propounds one or more sets of written questions and document requests to the seller that later become the basis of disclosure schedules attached to the transaction agreement.[10] The parties may negotiate around the margins of scope, time period, and the like, but because the seller wants the deal to close and also because the seller retains liability for failures to disclose in accordance with the agreement and disclosure schedules,[11] the seller typically agrees to most requests and sets about gathering the requested information, which could reside in any number of repositories throughout the company. Once gathered and, in most cases, reviewed for privilege by seller's counsel, the documents are made available to the buyer and its counsel via upload to a virtual data room.[12]

Although the basic framework and objectives in due diligence are similar to document discovery in litigation, there are some noteworthy differences. Most significantly, the volumes of documents produced in transactional due diligence tend to be smaller—and can be much smaller—than the volumes that would be produced in response to analogous requests in a litigation setting. There are many reasons for this, foremost being that document requests in due diligence are intended only to elicit sufficient documents to satisfy the buyer's inquiries and the buyer has no incentive needlessly to increase burden or cost, whereas document discovery in litigation often seeks "any and all documents related to" the issues in dispute and it is not uncommon for litigants to perceive strategic advantage in the costs and burdens imposed on their adversaries. Due diligence also tends to focus more on corporate books and records and less on documents (such as e-mail) collected from individual custodians. On the other hand, due diligence typically is conducted on a far more compressed timeline than civil discovery, and the modern tendency of many employees to use e-mail as a system of record often turns requests for corporate records, as a practical matter, into custodial discovery.

As the due diligence process plays out, the parties negotiate the terms of the deal agreement, including representations and warranties running from each party to the other. Because the seller retains

---

10. *See id.*

11. *See, e.g.*, Leigh Walton, *From the Chair,* 16 Deal Points 3 (ABA 2011).

12. *See Due Diligence, supra* note 11.

liability for any breach of these terms, including any failure to disclose documents or information listed on and not excepted from the disclosure schedules,[13] the seller wants narrow terms and has a strong incentive to make full and accurate disclosures. The buyer, on the other hand, prefers broad representations and warranties and is especially likely to press for breadth where it has questions or concerns about the seller's disclosures. Against this backdrop, even though absolute volumes tend to be lower in due diligence than in discovery, the time and cost associated with collection, review, and production in due diligence for a significant transaction can quickly mount to hundreds of thousands or even millions of dollars—especially where review is performed in linear fashion by law firm or contract attorneys.

Enter predictive analytics. By leveraging the power of high-speed, high-volume, cross-platform indexing and machine learning, in appropriate cases, a seller can significantly reduce the time and cost associated with due diligence and, at the same time, achieve better outcomes in the form of greater certainty and less risk on both sides of the table.[14] Specifically, once the relevant data stores have been indexed, the seller can use substantially the same technologies and workflows as are used in e-discovery to identify documents responsive to the buyer's disclosure requests. In many cases, the enhanced precision that results from using predictive analytics will allow the seller to expand significantly the scope of its search while still requiring eyes-on review of far fewer documents than would be required in a traditional linear review. By expanding the scope of its search, the seller reduces its own risk that responsive documents have been overlooked and also provides greater comfort to the buyer that its diligence needs have been satisfied, which in turn the seller reasonably could use in negotiations, for example, as a basis for narrowing the representations and warranties associated with the subject matter at issue.

It is important to note that just as the effectiveness of predictive coding can vary with the types of documents and classifications to which it's applied (for example, usually better at predicting responsiveness than at predicting privilege), the effectiveness of predictive analytics in due diligence can be expected to vary in a similar fashion.

13. *See, e.g.*, Walton, *supra* note 13.

14. *See, e.g.*, Grossman & Cormack, *supra* note 4.

For example, predictive analytics typically will perform very well with standardized, unambiguous documents and issues such as contracts, insurance-related records, regulatory filings, and certain financial and accounting records. Contracts, in particular, are an area where predictive analytics could make a very big difference; in any sizeable transaction, there are likely to be hundreds if not thousands, or even tens of thousands, of contracts requiring analysis for the presence or absence of particular provisions, such as noncompetition, nonsolicitation, indemnification, infringement, and notice requirements. Especially (but not only) where contracts exist in native electronic form, one reasonably could expect a predictive analytics engine, properly trained, to perform well at identifying contracts and terms of interest.

On the other hand, classifications that involve ambiguity or nuance, or that turn significantly on interpretation of context, are less likely to benefit from use of predictive analytics, for reasons very similar to why predictive coding generally performs less reliably on privilege than it does on responsiveness.[15]

Next-Generation Due Diligence Using Predictive Analytics

The "technology assist" that predictive analytics can provide to sellers by making it easier and more cost-effective to identify relevant documents for disclosure is compelling in its own right, but it only scratches the surface. Put to its fullest use, predictive analytics has the potential fundamentally to transform how due diligence is conducted. In traditional diligence, the buyer's review is limited to those documents gathered and selected by the seller and placed by the seller in the virtual data room. Historically, this has been the best course available because the buyer does not have the time, resources, or knowledge of the seller's systems to find relevant content itself within the time constraints of a typical transaction. But with the advent of predictive coding and similar technologies, a buyer's requests for specific documents today could be replaced by requests that the seller identify and

15. *See, e.g.*, Manfred Gabriel et al., *The Challenge and Promise of Predictive Coding for Privilege*, DESI V Workshop (June 14, 2013), *available at* http://www.umiacs.umd.edu/~oard/desi5/research/Gabriel-final2.pdf.

provide access to data repositories likely to contain the information sought by the buyer. Guided by the seller, the buyer then would leverage the high-speed, high-volume, algorithm-assisted workflows discussed throughout this book to find relevant information. Such an approach could significantly reduce the amount of time and resources that the seller's employees or its attorneys are required to divert from daily responsibilities to search for critical documents and also reduce the volume of documents requiring "eyes-on" review by the seller. At the same time, it could provide to the buyer greater visibility into the seller's operations, including so-called dark data, and thereby provide greater comfort to the buyer that things are as the seller represents. For example, e-mails from seller's employees often are not reviewed, but predictive analytics could make at least targeted reviews for key custodians both possible and cost-effective, especially when one considers that many core diligence issues are common across transactions and could be "pre-taught" to software developed specifically for transactional applications.

Effective use of these techniques in the M&A context likely would require, in effect, a predictive coding "SWAT team." In litigation, discussions of how to deploy predictive coding usually play out over several months as protocols are negotiated, documents are collected, and analytics are refined. In the M&A context, due diligence is typically much more compressed—requiring knowledgeable professionals to ensure the algorithms are quickly trained and rapidly deployed. However, while training the algorithm takes time, once trained for a particular transaction, it can be used across multiple data repositories to "find more like this."

At the same time, other characteristics of M&A transactions allow predictive coding to be deployed more quickly and used more nimbly than it currently is in litigation. For example, in M&A, use of predictive analytics is unlikely to require protracted negotiation over protocols for at least two reasons. First, as noted previously, the objective of due diligence is simply to find sufficient information to address the buyer's questions, not to identify "any and all documents" that would be discoverable in litigation. Second, the detailed protocols common in litigation typically are necessary because the predictive coding workflow is used by the producing party to identify documents sought by the requesting party, and the requesting party requires assurance that the methodologies employed are appropriately designed and executed to provide reliable results and that review is not ended prematurely. In a transaction where predictive coding is deployed as part of due diligence by a buyer over data sources provided by a seller, the buyer—as the party seeking information—has near-complete control over the protocol it follows and when it ends its review.

Of course, for a seller to throw open its doors to a buyer would be a significant change in how due diligence is currently performed and one can posit at least a few serious concerns that a seller might reasonably raise. Although a buyer and seller in a transaction are not adverse in the same sense as a plaintiff and defendant, and often share at least some aligned interests, negotiating a purchase price and other terms and conditions associated with a transaction still is fundamentally an adversarial process and many sellers (and their counsel) approach the exchange of information in the context of due diligence in a careful and guarded manner. This is especially true where a seller perceives some risk that the buyer may decline to go through with the transaction.

In addition, while not entirely the same as in litigation, parties in the M&A context still need to be concerned about disclosure of privileged information, for several reasons. First, by their nature, privileged documents are more likely to contain sensitive information that is likely to be more damaging if disclosed to persons outside its intended distribution. Second, although waiver of privilege will rarely be an issue between the parties, the issue of whether privilege was waived may still pose significant risks when the deal gives rise to litigation between the parties or with third parties. For example, shareholders pursuing derivative litigation to challenge the terms of the transaction may argue that the seller waived privilege as to any documents voluntarily provided to the buyer during due diligence. Third, in litigation, a party may obtain a federal court order protecting against waiver under Rule 502(d) of the Federal Rules of Evidence; in the transactional context, absent litigation, this protection is not available.[16] Finally, if the deal falls through, the seller may be damaged if it allowed the buyer—not uncommonly a competitor or other participant in the seller's market—to have unfiltered access to the seller's privileged records.

16. *See* FED. R. EVID. 502(d) (requiring any disclosure be "connected with the litigation pending before the court").

For these reasons, any approach that significantly increases the buyer's access to the seller's information should include measures designed to guard against the unintentional production of privileged documents. It is worth noting that the presence of privileged material may vary significantly repository by repository. Some data sets, such as information concerning the seller's finances, may contain relatively little privileged information while other sets, such as those concerning the seller's liabilities and intellectual property, may include more. Agreements may be reached to help mitigate the chance privileged documents are inadvertently produced by predictive coding, such as allowing the seller to screen any subset of documents selected by predictive coding for eyes-on review.

Granting buyers the broader access contemplated here so that they can use predictive coding to identify what they believe is relevant to their diligence could impact negotiations in other ways as well. Because the seller is providing something of significant value, namely access to broader information, it would not be unreasonable for the seller to ask for something of value in return. Alternatively, a seller might ask for narrower representations and warranties or more limited indemnification obligations in the transaction agreement, reasoning that it has provided the buyer with a greater opportunity to address and mitigate the uncertainties that representations, warranties, and indemnification agreements are intended to guard against.

Predictive Coding and HSR Second Requests

Predictive coding is already being employed in the M&A context to meet the challenge of responding to federal antitrust inquiries. Under the Hart-Scott-Rodino Antitrust Improvements Act of 1976, transactions of a sufficient size require the parties to file a notification to the Federal Trade Commission (FTC) and the Antitrust Division of the U.S. Department of Justice.[17] If either the FTC or the Antitrust Division suspect the transaction will limit competition, it may request additional information, known as an HSR Second Request. These Second Requests often require the parties to review massive volumes of

17. Hart-Scott-Rodino Antitrust Improvements Act of 1976, 15 U.S.C. § 18a (2015).

data in a short time period to satisfy the federal review. Here, the high-speed, high-volume, power of predictive coding offers a cost-effective and accurate tool to cull through the repositories of a company and find documents to respond to a Second Request.[18] As a result, the Antitrust Division has published guidance on the use of predictive coding, citing its benefits.[19] While there has been no comprehensive analysis of its use to respond to Second Requests, anecdotal accounts suggest that parties using predictive coding are seeing significant benefits.

The Costs of Responding to a Second Request Are Growing Rapidly

The burden of producing documents under a Second Request has risen rapidly over the past decade despite efforts by the FTC to reform the process. A 2014 survey of parties responding to Second Requests between 2011 and 2013 reported a range of costs between $2 million and $9 million to comply.[20] This compliance burden accounted for up to 5.5 percent of the value of the transaction.[21] The median review time took nearly six months from the issuance of the Second Request until the investigation was closed or the agency took an action.[22] Companies spent a median of nearly $1 million per month to comply with Second Requests.[23] These 2014 findings suggest that the costs of responding to Second Requests continued to rise despite efforts by the FTC to revise the merger review process in 2006.[24]

Two factors are frequently identified as driving the costs of answering a Second Request: (1) the quantity of information sought by the government, and (2) the increasing amount of data created and

---

18. *See, e.g.*, Tracy Greer, Senior Litigation Counsel E-Discovery, *Technology-Assisted Review and Other Discovery Initiatives at the Antitrust Division*, U.S. Dep't of Justice, 5 (Mar. 26, 2014).

19. *Id.*

20. Peter Boberg & Andrew Dick, *Findings from the Second Request Compliance Burden Survey*, XIV The Threshold 3, at 33 (Summer 2014).

21. *Id.*

22. *Id.* at 28.

23. *Id.* at 33.

24. *Id.* at 28, 33–34.

maintained by companies.[25] First, a federal agency's market analysis of the transaction is fact-intensive and the government may require "substantial volumes of documents and quantitative data."[26] Thus, the scope of discovery under Second Requests is frequently more open-ended and less definite than in litigation.[27] Respondents to the 2014 survey reported that as many as 18 separate product markets and up to eight geographic markets may be included in the scope of a Second Request.[28] Parties searched for documents in up to 24 repositories to comply with the federal request.[29]

FTC reforms to the process in 2006 offered some reprieve to respondents by setting presumptive expectations for where parties will search for information. The FTC may agree to limit the number of employees required to provide information to 35 so long as the respondent complies with certain conditions.[30] While parties rarely agree to all of the specified conditions, on average parties searched through fewer custodians following the reform.[31] This is true regardless of whether the party was responding to a request from the FTC or the Antitrust Division.[32] The 2014 survey reported materials were collected from an average of 26 custodians, down from a median of 94 custodians ten years ago.[33] It is worth noting that this presumptive expectation has benefited all clients. One respondent to the 2014 survey reported searching 171 custodians, over 35 percent more than the previous maximum.[34]

Whatever relief parties obtain from the presumptive limit on custodians is outweighed by the fact that companies increasingly maintain

25. *See, e.g.*, Deborah Platt Majoras, Chairman, Federal Trade Commission, *Reforms to the Merger Review Process*, Fed. Trade Comm'n, at 2 (Feb. 16, 2006).

26. *Id.* at 2.

27. Greer, *supra* note 20, at 1.

28. Boberg & Dick, *supra* note 22, at 29.

29. *Id.* at 30.

30. Deborah Platt Majoras, Chairman, Federal Trade Commission, *Reforms to the Merger Review Process*, Fed. Trade Comm'n (Feb. 16, 2006).

31. *Empirical Analysis of 2006 Merger Process Reforms*, Bureau of Competition, Fed. Trade Comm'n (Aug. 2015), *available at* https://www.ftc.gov/system/files/attachments/merger-review/empirical_analysis_final.pdf.

32. *Id.*

33. Boberg & Dick, *supra* note 22, at 30.

34. *Id.*

substantially more data.[35] One study suggests that the amount of data in the digital universe doubles in size every two years.[36] Companies are no exception. On average, parties responding to the 2014 survey reviewed 47 GB of electronic documents representing an excess of 4.8 million pages.[37] This represents over four times the amount of data parties were reviewing on average a decade ago.[38] Much of this data is also turned over to the Antitrust Division or the FTC where it must be reviewed again by federal agents. The median data production to federal authorities was 28.8 GB or roughly 1.6 million pages.[39]

Significant time is spent not only to identify responsive documents, but also to allow the federal agency to review the production and make a determination. Delays in clearing the merger or acquisition impose costs on the parties from opportunity costs of the time spent by the parties' employees in gathering the data to costs associated with the delayed realization of the merger efficiencies and synergies, to the diminution in value of the assets associated with the transaction.[40] The 2014 survey found that the median investigation to respond to a Second Request consumed 550 hours from in-house counsel and 500 hours from non-legal in-house management.[41]

In its 2006 reforms, the FTC also sought to set a presumptive cap on the volume of data that parties should review and produce. The FTC reduced the default time period for which a party must provide documents to two years.[42] Federal agencies appear to routinely

35. *See, e.g.*, Platt Majoras, *supra* note 32, at 2.

36. *Executive Summary: Data Growth, Business Opportunities, and the IT Imperatives*, IDC (Apr. 2014), *available at* http://www.emc.com/leadership/digital-universe/2014iview/executive-summary.htm.

37. Boberg & Dick, *supra* note 22, at 31–32.

38. *Id.*

39. *Id.* at 30.

40. *See Comments of the Section of Antitrust Law of the American Bar Association in Response to the Antitrust Modernization Commission's Request for Public Comment Regarding the Hart-Scott-Rodino Second Request Process*, ABA (Dec. 5, 2005), *available at* http://www.americanbar.org/content/dam/aba/administrative/antitrust_law/at-comments/2005/12-05/hsr_2nd_request_comm.authcheckdam.pdf.

41. Boberg & Dick, *supra* note 22, at 36.

42. Platt Majoras, *supra* note 32.

disregard this expectation. In 2015, the FTC reported that requests for documents more than two years old "remain prevalent."[43]

Given the substantial burden Second Requests place on parties, any reduction in compliance costs may provide significant benefits to both merging parties and consumers. Thus many parties are turning to predictive coding as a means to cull through the corpus of a company's data and narrow the amount of documents requiring "eyes-on" review by both the company's counsel and DOJ's attorneys.[44] The American Bar Association has noted a "groundswell of support" to use predictive coding to respond to Second Requests.[45]

Federal Authorities Have Issued Guidance on the Use of Predictive Coding

As more parties have turned to predictive coding to respond to Second Requests, the Antitrust Division has recently published guidance on how to ensure predictive coding is effectively employed.[46] To be sure, there are unique challenges with using predictive coding to respond to Second Requests. Second Requests from the government may be rather vague as the FTC or the Antitrust Division explore a variety of often changing theories regarding the impact the transaction may have on future market conditions.[47] Much like the buyer conducting due diligence, federal authorities often are ill-positioned to identify the key employees and peculiar features of a business and may be unaware of company jargon.[48] This "information asymmetry" may result in Second Requests that are imprecise.[49] Navigating these issues may require a greater initial

43. *Empirical Analysis*, *supra* note 33.

44. *See* Greer, *supra* note 20.

45. ABA Section of Antitrust Law, *Controlling the Costs of Antitrust Enforcement and Litigation*, ABA (Dec. 20, 2012), *available at* http://www.americanbar.org/content/dam/aba/administrative/antitrust_law/2013_agenda_cost_efficiency_kolasky.authcheckdam.pdf.

46. Greer, *supra* note 20, at 1.

47. *Id.*

48. *Id.*

49. *Id.*

investment of time and energy to ensure that the returns provided by predictive coding are accurate.

Despite these hurdles, the Antitrust Division encourages the use of predictive coding and has reported that its use to respond to Second Requests has allowed parties to save substantial time and costs.[50] As a result, in March 2014 the Division published a paper discussing best practices for using predictive coding.[51] The paper outlines four key considerations for a party contemplating using predictive coding.

First, the protocol encourages parties to negotiate with the Division what process will be used to collect the information that will be reviewed by predictive coding.[52] The Division discourages using search terms to narrow the collection and would prefer parties instead limit date ranges, deduplicate the collection, eliminate certain domain names from e-mail collections, or eliminate some file types.[53] Federal authorities also encourage parties using predictive coding to identify any categories of documents that may be technically responsive to the Second Request but are not essential to resolving the antitrust questions involved in the investigation.[54] Production of such documents may be deferred or foregone entirely.

Second, the Division asks that certain documents be removed from the collection to be reviewed by predictive coding because it believes technology-assisted review is not yet an appropriate tool to capture relevant information (1) not associated with an identifiable custodian (e.g., websites, corporate intranets), and (2) from spreadsheets or non-text-based information (e.g., pictures, drawings, audio or video files).[55] The Division also is not convinced that predictive coding works effectively with foreign and mixed-language documents.[56]

---

50. *Id.* at 5.
51. *Id.*
52. *Id.* at 3.
53. *Id.*
54. *Id.* at 1.
55. *Id.* at 3.
56. *Id.*

Third, workflow must be discussed and reviewed with the Division.[57] The Division expects that the collection will be deduplicated prior to applying predictive coding, but discourages other analytical tools such as consolidating e-mail threads.[58] Federal authorities will want to know who is responsible for training and quality control of the collection and the means by which that person will identify the "seed set." The Division is especially interested in seeing the "overturn rate" or the frequency with which the subject-matter expert reviewing the results disagrees with the responsiveness determination of predictive coding.[59] Federal authorities have thus far required a confidence level of 90 percent, but recognize that this is much higher than the likely confidence level for manual review.[60] Recognizing that privilege reviews continue to be costly and time consuming, the Division also notes that its policy is to sequester and return inadvertently produced privileged documents.[61]

Fourth, the Division asks that producing parties provide a statistically significant sample of nonresponsive documents to verify that responsive documents have not been excluded from the collection.[62] Generally, federal authorities will request five to seven such samples and a representative will select one or more sets to review.[63] This often occurs in the offices of the producing party's counsel and the Division generally will agree to complete its review in one to two days.[64]

The Division has reported negotiating the use of technology-assisted review in approximately a dozen instances.[65] It has found that the use of this technology has produced smaller, more responsive document productions that offer "substantial benefit" to Division staff and cost less time and money from producing parties.[66] As a result,

57. *Id.*
58. *Id.*
59. *Id.* at 4.
60. *Id.*
61. *Id.* at 5.
62. *Id.* at 4.
63. *Id.*
64. *Id.*
65. *Id.*
66. *Id.* at 5.

the Division is contemplating expanding the opportunities to use such technologies to other types of investigations.[67]

The FTC also recently revised its Model Second Request to include instructions on the use of predictive coding.[68] It contemplates significant FTC oversight over the protocols used to set and verify how the software identifies responsive documents. Parties must describe to the FTC their methodology including: (i) "how the software was utilized to identify responsive documents," (ii) "the process the Company utilized to identify and validate the seed set documents," (iii) "the total number of documents reviewed manually," (iv) "the total number of documents determined nonresponsive without manual review," (v) "the process the Company used to determine and validate the accuracy of the automatic determinations of responsiveness," (vi) "how the Company handled exceptions," and (vii) "if the Company's documents include some foreign language documents, whether reviewed manually or by some technology-assisted method." It also calls for providing the FTC with "all statistical analyses utilized or generated by the Company or its agents related to the precision, recall, accuracy, validation, or quality of its document production."[69]

While the FTC guidelines are limited to M&A transactions under its jurisdiction, they may be persuasive authority to other government agencies considering allowing the use of predictive coding to respond to regulatory inquiries. Nonetheless, the FTC's provisions are still novel and may impact a responding party's decision to use predictive coding or reduce some of the benefits the party may gain. Although the level of transparency suggested may help regulators be more confident in the production, such oversight is not typical in a manual review and may create additional risks for the parties responding.[70] For example, the iterative rounds of code, rinse, and repeat may be longer if coding decisions must be shared with the requesting regulator or the FTC may opt to expand its requests for documents based

---

67. *Id.* at 6.

68. *Model Request for Additional Information and Documentary Material (Second Request)*, FTC Premerger Notification Office (rev'd. Aug. 2015).

69. *Id.* at 16.

70. Jennifer Kennedy Park & Scott Reents, *Use of Predictive Coding in Regulatory Enforcement Proceedings*, BNA (Aug. 7, 2012).

on a review of nonresponsive documents in the seed set.[71] This level of micro-managing the use of predictive coding may provoke further discussion about the extent to which such a detailed review is helpful.

Anecdotal Accounts Suggest Parties Using Predictive Coding Save Money and Reduce the Time for Review

While there is no comprehensive analysis of the costs and time saved by parties that utilize predictive coding, anecdotal evidence suggests users gain significant benefits. One case study reported using predictive coding to review 880 GB of data from two countries in two languages in response to a Second Request by the FTC.[72] Predictive coding returned responsive documents with a 90 percent accuracy rate and reduced the final number of documents produced to under 500,000.[73] Predictive coding also eliminated an estimated 1,200 hours in document review and saved the company almost $1.2 million.[74]

Another case study demonstrates the benefit of employing predictive coding early when responding to a Second Request.[75] In response to a Second Request from the Antitrust Division, parties collected approximately 650 GB of data.[76] A 60-person legal team began its review of those documents using traditional methods, such as keyword searches.[77] Part way through the review, it became clear that it would not be possible to complete it within the schedule, so predictive coding was brought in to finish the process.[78] Using predictive coding, the evaluation of the remaining 35 percent of the collection cost only

---

71. *Id.*

72. *Second Requests: Complex Cases, Demanding Deadlines, Impressive Results*, Kroll Ontrack (2015), *available at* http://www.ediscovery.com/cms/pdf/CST_HSR_krollontrack2015.pdf.

73. *Id.*

74. *Id.*

75. David J. Laing, *Increasing Speed and Confidence in Second Request Responses with New Technologies*, 28 LJN Legal Tech 6 (Oct. 2011), *available at* http://www.equivio.com/files/files/LJN%20Baker%20and%20McKenzie.pdf.

76. *Id.*

77. *Id.*

78. *Id.*

five percent of the total amount and took only 10 percent of the total project time.[79] It was estimated that had the parties used predictive coding from the start, the review may have been completed in less than half of the time.[80]

Conclusion

In litigation, predictive coding is already delivering significant reductions on all three sides of the so-called impossible triangle: doing the same work in less time, at lower cost, with equal or better quality. The same technologies and workflows can also be used to shrink that triangle for mergers, acquisitions, and divestitures. Like litigators, attorneys in the M&A context must sift through ever-increasing volumes of data to find "more like this" when deciding whether to go through with a transaction. Leveraging the power of high-speed, high-volume, cross-platform indexing and machine learning can reduce the costs of due diligence and the risks involved in the transaction. Predictive coding already is being used in one particular aspect of M&A where it has shown serious promise, namely, responding to HSR Second Requests. It is only a matter of time before sophisticated parties and counsel begin broadly to deploy these same algorithms throughout the entire transaction lifecycle to reap even greater benefits.

79. *Id.*
80. *Id.*

EDITORS' INTRODUCTION TO CHAPTER 17

Michael D. Berman

Starting with some definitions to set the stage, Sandra Serkes explains how predictive coding may be used by businesses for "information governance" or "IG." This chapter discusses ways businesses may harness the power of predictive coding to govern their historical information and also set up procedures for "Day Forward," or ongoing operations. An understanding of how businesses function is, of course, critical to litigators and litigation. Both a discovering and a producing party need to know how a business client conducts its operations. Without that knowledge, they cannot ensure proper production or, alternatively, challenge the completeness of a production.

Further, Serkes points out that litigators may learn from the experience of IG professionals and their expansion of the tools and capabilities of predictive coding. She goes beyond that to discuss how litigators and law firms may harness these powerful tools for internal law firm case management. Law firms may deploy predictive coding as their own IG tool and search their vast databases for information about experts, witnesses, and issues. Consider the value of being able to effectively search an entire law firm's population of information to determine how an interrogatory requesting, for example, insurance underwriting material or documents relating to a contention, has been answered in the past.

CHAPTER 17

The Larger Picture: Moving Beyond Predictive Coding for Document Productions to Predictive Analytics for Information Governance

Sandra Serkes

Predictive coding (really, data analytics) is a means for harnessing (or suppressing) the potential information locked in large data sets—aka Big Data. Whether the data set is a collection of a litigant's corporate e-mails, a call log of customer complaints at a retail establishment, or an entire state's tax forms, the starting point is the same: a big, ol' collection of stuff. And once there is a document population, there is information contained within. The debate begins with whether that hidden information is helpful (an asset), or harmful (a liability), or perhaps both. It progresses with whether or not it is worth the cost, time, and effort to find out; and concludes with what to do about it once the status is known (or could reasonably become so). This last point is essentially information governance (IG), and the path from technology-optimized litigation document review to full-on information management and control is a short one. The techniques used in predictive analytics for document review are essentially the same as those used in much broader application of the same capabilities. This chapter explores the use of data analytics for understanding, diagnosing, organizing, managing, mining, forecasting, and reporting on all manner of document data well beyond litigation and e-discovery purposes.

For everyone's sanity, let us start with a little terminology. The whole area of *analytics* is newly popular, but actually quite mature and well understood by its practitioners: statisticians, data miners, computational linguists, and the like. So, what are analytics? In the case of document and/or content assessment, analytics are pattern-matching software algorithms that "parse" (a kind of digital machine-reading) text. The algorithms are typically modified matter to matter to best optimize precision and recall, two inter-related measurements discussed elsewhere in this book. An iterative process ultimately runs over the entire document *population* (also interchangeably called corpus, collection, or source content). Populations often consist of documents, but can be broadened to include any matter of quasi-organized content. For our case, we use the term document very loosely. A *document* can be a once-physical piece of paper, such as a letter or fax cover sheet, that is ultimately scanned to digital image and enters the analytics realm once there is a text rendition of it, resulting from optical character recognition (OCR). A document can also be a natively borne digital document, such as an e-mail or a webpage. Finally, as far as predictive analytics are concerned a document can also include things we do not typically describe this way, such as a voice mail, tweet or text message, video or audio, transactional or measurement data, and much more. As a general rule, if it can be captured in some way as content, then it is a document.

Litigation matters are often very concerned with who knew what when, and thus focus on the types of documents that often convey such information. E-mail, in particular, is the litigator's friend (or foe) in this regard, as e-mail not only *contains* content (the what), it also *transmits* it to others (the who) by its express design. E-mail documents even conveniently carry a timestamp of all their actions; one stamp for submission, one for each transit hop, one for receipt, and so on (the when). E-mail also has the blessed intrinsic value of being electronically generated, meaning (i) its textual contents are clean and easily obtained for further analysis and (ii) its structural nature comes with built-in metadata, such as authorship, creation date, and transmission time. Thus e-mail is the number one document of choice (or damage) in litigation matters. But as any good document student knows, e-mail comes with its albatross—attachments! Attachments also have the dual benefit/pain of content + transmission, however, they do not follow a simple structured protocol with metadata or easily extractable content. In fact, an e-mail attachment can ultimately be anything, particularly if it is something that has been scanned in to digital format. Take a file with a .pdf extension. Is it a simple PDF rendition of a Word document? Perhaps a digital drawing or photo? Maybe it is one of those fancy PDFs that let you sign and edit portions of content with custom PDF tools? On the surface, it is impossible to tell without further analytics of its contents.

A fundamental difference between analyzing documents for litigation and for IG is the underlying purpose for doing so in the first place. In litigation, the majority of document review (whether automated or otherwise) is to safely rule out or dismiss the majority of documents (often called "culling"), so that only the most important or critical documents remain. In particular, litigation documents are usually being prepared for production to other parties, and the emphasis is on safely eliminating documents wherever possible, using various withholding options, such as invoking different types of content- or source-based privileges, eliminating duplicates and creating restrictions based on time windows, keywords and custodial sources. By contrast, the goals in IG are often to specifically *preserve* documents, and to catalog them as fully and well-informedly as possible. There is little need to cull out documents (other than for obsolescence or retention/deletion purposes), and the goal is to make the contents and analytics as useable as possible for future purposes. In fact, a hallmark of IG uses of predictive analytics is to move well *beyond* simple culling, into areas such as classification, organization, trendlining and forecasting, and modeling past or future behaviors.

It is true that litigation is becoming more cooperative, particularly regarding discovery, document review, and productions. In that sense, it is becoming a bit more like information governance. While IG can certainly benefit from the utilizing litigation's tools for predictive document review, litigation can, in turn, learn from IG's expansion of the tools and capabilities, as well as its overarching view of information as both asset and liability—something to be intelligently, actively, and purposefully managed all the time, not just during a litigation crisis.

Information: Asset or Liability?

Just as the world contains both optimists and pessimists, so too are the bi-polar prevailing views on information stored within large document sets. Ask someone from the knowledge management, records management, or line of business side of the house, and you will hear how stored information is a tremendous asset—tool for forecasting, and for predicting consumer behavior. A rich vein of pattern recognition and statistical correlation for analyzing business trends, and a stellar means for organizing disparate, unstructured information for later reporting and retrieval. If only these vast data stratagems could be unlocked and unleashed from their currently unclassified, disorganized locations! After all, it is surely more cost-effective to have software algorithms do the work all at once rather than either expensive, manual retrieval from Iron Mountain or the digital equivalent of endless, fruitless shared drive searches each and every time!

In fact, this view of data as an asset is so prevalent on the optimists' side of the spectrum that it is a constant refrain from trend-setting organizations, such as ARMA International, ILTA (International Legal Technology Association) and the Big Data community. Consider these headlines and links from well-respected organizations and media sources:

- Data Management Problems: Organizations should regard data as their greatest asset (emphasis added)—and invest in data management accordingly[1]
- Treat Data as an Institute Asset[2]
- CIO's Consider Putting a Price Tag on Data[3]
- The Big Mystery: What's Big Data Really Worth?[4]

Clearly, there is a large contingent arguing for the capture, analysis, mining, and accounting of data to be treated as an important corporate asset.

---

1. Nikki Swartz, *Data Management Problems Widespread*, ARMA INT'L (Sept./Oct. 2007), *available at* http://www.arma.org/bookstore/files/Swartz14.pdf.

2. *Treat Data as an Institute Asset*, MIT, http://it.mit.edu/guiding-principles/treat-data-institute-asset.

3. Kim S. Nash, *CIOs Consider Putting a Price Tag on Data*, CIO BLOG (June 23, 2014, 8:00 AM), http://www.cio.com/article/2375573/leadership-management/cios-consider-putting-a-price-tag-on-data.html.

4. Vipal Monga, *The Big Mystery: What's Big Data Really Worth?*, WALL ST. J. (Oct. 12, 2014), http://www.wsj.com/articles/whats-all-that-data-worth-1413157156.

However, just as loudly, there is a contingent arguing against the value of such data. In fact, to many corporate legal and compliance groups, information stored in corporate documents is a vast cesspool of exposure and liability containing a sea of personally identifying information (PII), rampant personal health information (PHI), internal trade secrets, and evidence of improper behavior of all types. These groups are particularly fearful of e-mail collection and analysis—as e-mail represents not just a data store, but also an explicit communication trail of all that dangerous or ugly underbelly information.

The fact that software algorithms can race through vast document stores and lay bare all that is contained within, including patterns of behavior over time, is terribly dangerous. The onus to *act* on any information found is overwhelming, and a harkening back to the days of "do not ask (or look), do not tell" sounds downright safer. With company after company being subjected to data hacks and breaches at all levels, the media constantly reminds all of us just how exposed we all are.

In fact, this view of data as liability is so prevalent on the pessimists' side of the spectrum that it is a constant refrain from trend-setting organizations, such as the ACC (Association of Corporate Counsel), and other corporate and outside counsel communities. Consider these headlines and links from well-respected organizations and media sources:

- A Definition of Electronic Data Liability[5]
- How to Create a Moore's Law for Data[6]
- How to Avoid Becoming a Big Data Liability[7]
- Target Says Data Breach Bigger Than Previously Thought[8]

So, who's right? They both are, of course. Yes, data can surely be used as an asset to help steer decisions and budget allocations in the corporation. But, also yes, information is dangerous and can fall into

5. *Electronic Data Liability*, IRMI, http://www.irmi.com/online/insurance-glossary/terms/e/electronic-data-liability.aspx.

6. *How to Create a Moore's Law for Data*, Forbes (Dec. 2013), http://www.forbes.com/sites/danwoods/2013/12/12/how-to-create-a-moores-law-for-data/#7e8cdeca612e

7. Ben Rossi, *How to Avoid Becoming a Big Data Liability*, Information Age, (Mar. 14, 2014), http://www.information-age.com/technology/information-management/123457809/how-avoid-becoming-big-data-liability.

8. Aimee Picchi, *Target Says Data Breach Bigger than Previously Thought*, CBS Money Watch (Jan. 10, 2014, 6:15 PM), http://www.cbsnews.com/news/target-warns-data-breach-impacted-70-million-people/.

the wrong hands, and so it needs to be understood, managed, and controlled properly—the very cornerstones of information governance.

How and Why to Understand What Data Your Documents Hold

Whether you subscribe to the data-is-an-asset or the data-is-a-liability camp, or perhaps somewhere in between, it is critical either way for your organization to understand what information it holds in the form of stored documents and files. The most common types of documents in a corporation in the mid-2010s are:

- E-mail and attachments;
- Spreadsheets of tables, lists, financial information, and forecasts;
- Contracts, agreements, HR documentation, and other legal documents;
- Simple, unstructured documents (think: MS Word);
- Presentations, marketing collateral, and other more formalized information;
- Text messages and chats;
- Voice mail;
- Databases and SaaS applications; and
- Websites and social media.

Nearly every one of these document types contains identifiable content—thus information. Each unique file can be mined using relatively straightforward analytics, and analyzed using well-established correlation mechanisms. If you are reading this book, then you are or are close to litigation practitioners. You already understand the value of reading through discovery materials to understand each single document's value to your case. The IG application is similar, except it is applied to a much broader spectrum of materials and purposes. Consider the list of types of documents, and now multiply that by organizational divisions, locations, and staff count and you will get a sense of the magnitude of information involved, and why IG is often intertwined with discussions about Big Data.

A case in point comes from our experience with a large, international law firm. They have well over 3,000 practicing attorneys, with a similar number of non-attorney staff. One e-mail server storing approximately 10 years' worth of e-mail communications holds 32 TB of data, which in turn represents approximately 120 million *non-duplicative* e-mail messages and files. This scope is simply too large to evaluate, classify, and handle manually. The costs to do so would be astronomical. (See Figure 17.1.) Even the largest, most bet-the-farm litigation matters are on par with this figure and they, too, would not sustain the manual cost to evaluate each of the collected documents. Using the techniques of predictive coding or predictive analytics applied to the next level (the entire department or organization) is the answer.

Historically, the idea that any centralized group inside an organization should and would know what all the organization's documents contained would have been ludicrous. In a paper-oriented document content world, it would have been impossible to keep up. But, with the advent of electronic document storage systems (commonly called DMSs) and multivariate software algorithms, it is very possible to achieve that kind of corporate information omniscience. And therein lies the rub. Should an organization, particularly the group tasked with corporate, ethical, and risk oversight (i.e., corporate legal) seek out such knowledge given that it is relatively easy and cost-effective to do so? Might they, perhaps, be *obligated* to do so as stewards of the company's behavior, actions, and ethical obligations?

Ease of Use

Let us break down those two assumptions: easy and cost-effectiveness. Today's predictive analytics are relatively easy for non-statisticians to use. There are many consulting experts in the field who can do the heavy statistical or programming work for you, and there are simplified software interfaces to step a knowledgeable person through the tasks themselves.[9] Today, predictive analytics are about as easy to use as any other higher-order analysis process, such as calculating financial markets or economic behavior, or correlating buying behavior with price sensitivity. In other words, if you can handle simple calculus and probability as concepts, you can handle predictive analytics, which puts you on par with a high school honors student.

---

9. Predictive coding applications for litigation document review are a good example of the latter.

The complexity arises in the "edge" situations of document or content decisioning. For example, having to think about and then make distinctions between document content that might be important versus urgent, or not-quite-a-problem, but not quite totally safe either. The ease of routine, mathematical analysis gives rise to a secondary issue: nuance. Back in the "do not look, do not tell" days, we did not worry much about content nuance, because we didn't worry much about content at all! Now, that it is easy enough to evaluate document content on many levels, we burst open the wide grey area between black and white on many levels.

This gives rise to a discussion on context. Context is the setting around individual elements of content. Context involves questions such as: *who* said or wrote the information? *For whom* was it intended? Did the intended party *receive* or read it? *Why* was this information communicated? What was the *intent* or purpose of this information? Was it *appropriate* to do so? And so on. Context is important in predictive analytics because it moves things from purely mathematical correlation to indications of behavior, intent, and proof of actions. Context analysis is the way in which grey area nuance is handled in predictive analytics.

Not all predictive techniques make use of context, which is why the results can sometimes seem childishly wrong, even startling. Context adds the color commentary around algorithmic correlation and should be incorporated by predictive analytics rules engines as much as possible. To do this, it is necessary for the correlations to incorporate *indexing*, a method of tagging document metadata and utilizing those tags in the analysis. Context analysis provides a much more sophisticated and robust outcome than content analysis alone.

Cost-Effectiveness

Now, let us look at cost-effectiveness. Which costs more? Storing paper documents away in an offsite storage facility or going through the effort to scan them to digital format, OCR, and analyze them properly. There has been study upon study validating the image and analyze approach. It is easy enough to do your own return on investment (ROI) analysis using a decision tree approach.[10] See the example in Figure 17.1.

10. Wikipedia, *Decision Tree* (last visited July 2016), *available at* https://en.wikipedia.org/wiki/Decision_tree.

FIGURE 17.1 To scan, image, and analyze documents (store properly) or to leave as is?

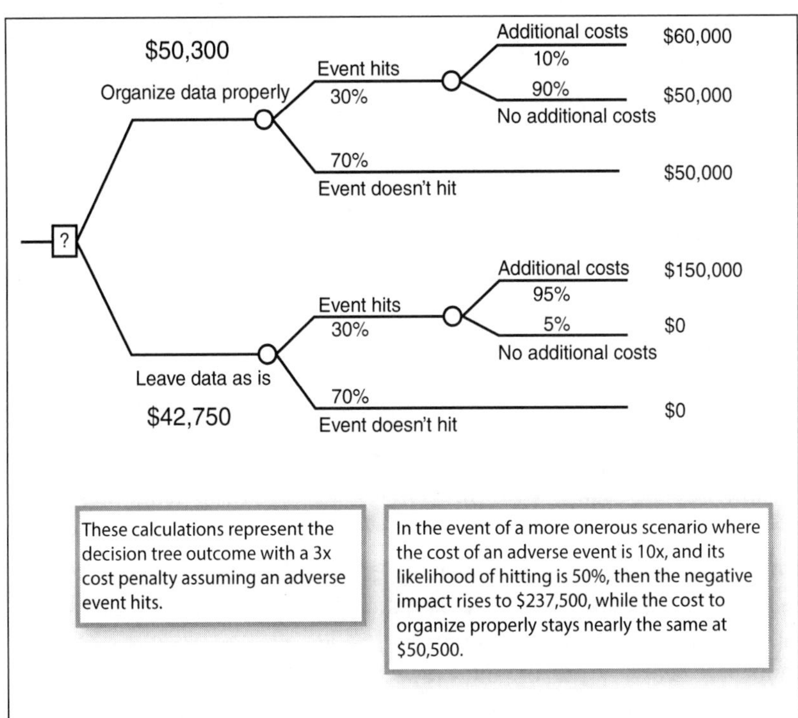

An ROI decision tree works just as well for ESI documents housed in servers, hard drives, backup tapes, or other media, rather than in boxed storage as paper files. Such similarly "blind" or unaware storage is less cost-effective than the effort to create analytics- and content-aware storage. A new wrinkle, however, is that there are different corporate responsibility requirements for ESI than there are for paper. Paper enjoys a naïve and convenient responsibility dodge due to its "out of sight, out of mind" nature. No one expects that offsite, aging paper to really be analyzed on a regular, ongoing basis. But ESI *is* readily available, being generated anew every day, and it is frighteningly accessible to anyone with lawful (or unlawful) access. There is a societal bias and expectation that ESI be properly and appropriately managed, in a way that paper never was. Financial markets and investors, consumers, industry watchdog groups, government agencies and the media are clamoring daily about the inappropriate and untamed Big Data beast, with each subsequent data breach fueling their fire. In 2015 alone,[11] there were over 80 million data breaches across every sector of business, government, health care, the military, and more. Experts[12] estimate that the Target data breach alone (more than 70 million records breached in early 2014) caused more than $148 million in damage to Target, mostly from lost sales, due to consumers' lack of confidence in the company and its management of their data. So, to accurately assess the cost efficiency of predictive analytics efforts, it is essential to also account for the opportunity cost in not doing so. In other words, what would it ultimately cost to *not* assess and control the vast information stored in corporate documents?

Four Real-World Examples Making the Transition to Predictive Analytics for Information Governance

Fortunately, there is an easy on-ramp to progress from using predictive analytics to analyze discovery documents to utilizing the techniques for full-on information governance: e-mail. E-mail has many virtues as both a communications mechanism, as well as a default document storage system. Most of us today use foldering, address books, search tools, and more to manage our incoming and outgoing e-mail as both a communications record and information storage area. E-mail has additional virtues for document processing as well. E-mails themselves are electronic in nature and origin, which makes their text very strong and reliable for analytics. Further, e-mails contain useful metadata regarding senders, recipients, subject matter, timestamps, and more. They neatly divide themselves into structured (metadata) and unstructured content (body text and attachments). Most e-mails are typically easily extractable for processing due to their quasi-storage nature in our

11. Data breaches numbers are reflective of incidents year-to-date, as of October 2015. For an up-to-date incident account and details, visit the Identity Theft Resource Center (ITRC) website—Data Breach Reports (Dec. 2014), http://www.idtheftcenter.org/images/breach/DataBreachReports_2014.pdf—and read their weekly published report.

12. Rachel Abrams, *Target Puts Data Breach Costs at $148 Million, and Forecasts Profit Drop*, N.Y. Times, Aug. 5, 2014, http://www.nytimes.com/2014/08/06/business/target-puts-data-breach-costs-at-148-million.html?_r=1.

inboxes and folders.[13] Finally, and perhaps most importantly, e-mail is well understood by the legal community—IG folks and attorneys. All of us use e-mail all the time, and we are also drowning in it, so why not start there?

Typical Steps in a Corporate E-mail Classification Project

To begin an enterprise classification project, you need several things. Of course, you'll need the extracted e-mails themselves (do not forget the attachments!). But, more importantly, you will need a set of specifications of (i) what you are looking for and (ii) how you wish to classify the information. It is sometimes helpful to clients to realize that these specifications do not need to be set in stone at the outset of the process. Predictive analytics is an iterative technology, and there will be many rounds for modification, improvement, and refinement of your requirements over time. Almost all predictive analytics techniques require some sort of generalized starting point. Whether a seed set of exemplar documents (as used in predictive coding), or a set of requirements rules (as used in rules-based, pattern-matching algorithms), you will need to do some up front work to codify what will constitute success. An experienced provider of these services will be able to help you with checklists, foldering taxonomies, typical pitfalls, and the like.

Once your specifications, guidance, and input files are gathered, the iterative rules-creation and testing (or seed set coding) process begins. One way or another, several rounds of coding, testing, and optimization will take place and a point of diminishing returns will be reached. At that mark, it is time to move into the high-volume scenario of the stored backlog of e-mail files (or whatever is being analyzed). If properly tuned, this process should move quickly, sometimes on the order of hundreds of thousands of files per day.

It is important to note that software algorithms for classifying data based on content, metadata, and other contextual clues are not perfect. In our experience, there is typically a 3 to 10 percent error rate, which should be accounted for in ROI analysis and other project expectations. There is almost always some mechanism for "exception handling," in

13. A PST is a compressed archive of stored e-mails and attachments from a particular folder or custodian.

which problematic, error-prone, or non-analyzable documents are handled. The typical exception handling is done by people with explicit knowledge about the materials as well as the project specifications. Exception handling can be performed by an outside vendor, contract labor, outside counsel, inside staff, or any combination therein.

In many enterprise e-mail classification projects, there is both a backlog of stored e-mail as well as a "day forward" need for continuous assessment and classification on new e-mails incoming and being created by the organization. For such scenarios, there is an additional step in rolling forward from historical backlog processing (essentially large-scale batch processing) to day forward processing happening in real-time. This likely requires integration with the e-mail server, and possibly other document management systems as well.

Finally, it is important to understand that e-mail classification projects (or frankly, any predictive analytics work) are not "one-and-done" situations. Particularly with day-forward scenarios, such systems need to be monitored and adjusted over time. Similar to a piano, which goes out of tune over time and requires slight rewiring to come back into tune, predictive analytics also go out of tune over time. It is not that the algorithms "go bad," but rather that the documents themselves change over time. We change our turns of phrase, how we lay things out on a page, who the key contacts are and so on. When such evolutionary changes begin to pile up, the rules (or prior coding) will seem slightly off, and system confidence measures will go down. In a similar manner, priorities and circumstances change within the organization and the rules may need to be recalibrated for new realities. Fortunately, the solution is simple. A periodic analysis and maintenance of the analytics will suffice, unless there are drastic changes. A safe assumption is a maintenance window of three to six months for an ongoing system.

Further Examples of Predictive Analytics Being Used Beyond Litigation Document Review and Enterprise E-mail Classification

- **Case Management.** Savvy litigants and their counsel are harnessing the power of predictive analytics to manage the other side of the litigation document world—that is, the work product documents they themselves create to conduct the litigation.

Such documents consist of the pleadings, motions, transcripts, depositions, exhibits, other court filings, and communications that are *about* the litigation matter(s). Such populations contain a wealth of information about litigants, witnesses, experts, judges, dockets, the exhibits themselves, and so on. For example, which exhibits seem to recur from matter to matter, or litigant to litigant? Which answers to interrogatories have we already created for past matters and could re-use for new ones? Which responses yielded the least pushback, or the best results? Which judges tended to rule in our favor and under what circumstances? What did the expert say last time? The technological data crunching for such answers is fairly simple. Lots of parsing, cross-reference, and probability correlation, in fact. What's difficult, typically, is gathering the documents from multiple matters and sources in the first place, and asking the right questions in the second. To do this successfully requires coordination and compliance of outside counsel to submit their documents to a centralized clearinghouse, and then rigorous application of data mining that can be easily reconfigured as new needs and questions arise. Frequent litigants and their counsel realize the power of data mining their own work product and that of opposing parties, particularly when they are involved in serial litigation activities due to their business activities, and the exposure around products and services they sell.

- **PII/PHI Detection and Redaction.** The same techniques that are used to determine a document's author, recipient, or parties mentioned within its contents are utilized in different applications for documents containing sensitive information. The identification and subsequent redaction of private identification information (PII) or private health information (PHI) is a major source of manual effort and expense on the part of hospitals, insurers, pharmaceutical companies, and any other organization that routinely collects patient, customer, account, or employee information. Still other organizations have trade secret information or other intellectual property in their documents' contents. They often have need for classification of documents based on file content, secrecy or security level, or retention stage. Typically in such predictive analytics scenarios, the detection of sensitive information is not enough; it must also be properly redacted to prevent accidental or further disclosure. In such cases, predictive analytics have proven exceptionally valuable at performing redactions on image, in text, and into metadata—a task historically performed painstakingly and at great expense by hand.

- **Media Monitoring and Topical Content.** An interesting and novel use of predictive analytics occurs around the real-time digestion and categorization of public media information—press articles, releases, news coverage, industry and government reports, announcements and notices, and more. Such push-style information sources yield a plethora of documents that are often rich with thematic content that is of particular interest to specialized groups. Consider organizational groups whose responsibility it is to track customer sentiment, supply chain activity, misuse, or illicit activity around their product or geographic trend data. There is so much information coming at us from sources all over the world 24/7. Tracking this information with a particular agenda can be an impossible task, which is where highly tuned custom analytics come in. It is a simple matter for such rules-based systems to monitor and "parse" the incoming fire hose of digital content, all the while sniffing for the relevant terms, sources, date ranges, and other contextual clues that identify an item of interest. These technologies routinely handle information originating from several thousand sources each day. Once obtained, the same engines easily perform trend and forecasting analysis, serving as a basis for decision-making and resource allocation.

The Future of Information Governance in a Predictive Analytics World

As more and more people become comfortable with the notion of Big Data, and the organizations they are part of become comfortable with predictive analytics, there will be ever more inroads into how and why we manage information. We will routinely be asked to address questions regarding the kind of information that is (or should be) retained in the typical course of business activity. We will be expected to know what is possible to learn or understand from the documents and data we hold. We will manage information assets and liabilities simultaneously, and be conversant with the analytical mechanics, financial risks and rewards, and best practices regarding its storage, usage, and security.

When nearly every unit of written, spoken, or visual content is known and/or can be easily obtained or retrieved, attorneys, information governance, and risk management professionals can and should deploy predictive analytics in a cost effective manner to satisfy the need to bring organization and control to large volumes of disparate data.

EDITORS' INTRODUCTION TO CHAPTER 18

Michael D. Berman

As in the proverb "physician heal thyself," Leigh Isaacs suggests that law firms deploy the technologies they are using for e-discovery to address their own information governance. Law firms generate huge volumes of data, have significant security concerns, experience personnel changes, and frequently must import or export volumes of carefully screened law firm data. For example, if a client demands return of its file, how can the law firm properly isolate client matter, retain what should not be sent out, and export the entire client file? If part of a law firm's data is under a litigation hold, how can it comply? When lawyers move laterally, how can incoming and outgoing data be properly managed? In short, all of the questions facing American industry are magnified in the unique context of a law firm with its need to preserve client confidences and other fiduciary duties. Isaacs shows how predictive coding may supply defensible solutions.

This chapter also addresses many other problems faced by law firms. For example, the author suggests that in responding to audit letters, law firms may use predictive coding to search for important information. Similarly, the technology may help mitigate confidentiality risks, identify sensitive information for higher levels of security, prepare "form files," address archives, and locate redundant or obsolete data. Finally, because law firms must be concerned with return on investment, the author provides a strategy to make the business case for predictive coding.

CHAPTER 18

Predictive Analytics for Information Governance in a Law Firm: Mitigating Risks and Optimizing Efficiency

Leigh Isaacs

Law firms and law departments must consider and abide by many frequently changing ethical, legal, and regulatory requirements with regard to the management of information—whether it is in regard to work product, client data, or internal administrative information. Achieving compliance is difficult; when coupled with the emerging technology landscape it becomes even more challenging. Implementing an information governance program with analytics not only helps with compliance and risk mitigation, but can also build in efficiencies that bring cost savings and competitive advantage.

What Is Information Governance (IG)?

Before discussing the potential of predictive analytic technologies, it is important to understand the definition and scope of information governance (IG). IG extends well beyond the boundaries of traditional records management. The 2012 "Proposed Law Firm Information Governance Framework" offers the following definition:

> IG is an enterprise-wide approach to the management and protection of a law firm's client and business information assets. An effective IG Program:
>
> - Enables lawyers to meet their professional responsibility regarding client information;
> - Recognizes an expanding set of regulatory and privacy requirements that apply to firm and client information;
> - And relies upon a culture of participation and collaboration within the entire firm.
>
> With IG, firms are better able to mitigate risk, improve client service through increased lawyer productivity, and reduce the cost of managing the information needed to support the efficient delivery of legal services.[1]

Why IG?

Information continues to proliferate at an incredibly rapid pace. Legacy unmanaged information, combined with the plethora of new information being generated, results in mountainous volumes that are overwhelming.

New types of vehicles and repositories that deliver and store information are also increasing exponentially. Structured and unstructured data are found stored in archives, hard drives, the "cloud," and other data repositories, resulting in significant pockets of information that are difficult to access and search. The financial and personnel resources required to maintain and manage so much data can be cost prohibitive.

To further complicate matters, it is difficult to gain a clear picture of what this data contains, posing significant business risks and adding time and expense to discovery or investigation. Lack of insight into this information is also an impediment to knowing what is valuable,

1. *Proposed Law Firm Information Governance Framework*, Iron Mountain (Aug. 2012), http://programs.ironmountain.com/forms/IMNA12Q3LawFirmSymposiumReport.

and can result in practice inefficiencies, ineffective internal and external collaboration, and an inability to appropriately budget and forecast to ensure profitability of engagements. As such, it is imperative that law firms act on better identifying and reducing volumes of data.

Overall data growth projections and statistics are staggering. Recent estimates by analysts and research indicate that (1) each year 1,200 exabytes of new data will be generated; (2) enterprises will experience 650 percent data growth in the next five years; (3) 80 percent of this data will be unstructured and generated from a variety of sources, such as blogs, web content, and e-mail; and (4) 70 percent of this data is stale after 90 days.[2] These statistics confirm that IG challenges will continue to grow. The need to gain insights into information to determine its usefulness and whether it exists beyond retention requirements will also grow. Traditional methods of manual classification and identification frequently fall short of expectations and will likely prove futile in the face of an influx of large volumes of information.

Predictive Technologies

At the same time law firms are struggling to find the magic wand to conquer their IG woes, new technologies have emerged in the commercial marketplace to address large volumes of electronically stored information (ESI) for purposes of e-discovery. In a perfect law firm world, the goal is to always know where all the information is for a specific case file or matter. There are significant advantages to be gained by leveraging these tools for identifying, managing, and appropriately governing a law firm's information.

Regardless of firm size, ease of use and accessibility to information is a focal point. Compliance with IG program requirements is often difficult to achieve because traditional technology offerings often fall short of providing an easy, seamless method to manage information. Smaller firms may not have trained staff dedicated to

2. Leigh Isaacs, *Rolling the Dice with Predictive Coding, Leveraging Analytics Technology for Information Governance*, INFO. MGMT. MAGAZINE, ARMA INT'L (Jan./Feb. 2013), http://imm.arma.org/publication/frame.php?i=141427&p=27&pn=&ver=flex.

records management or litigation support. In order for a program to be successful there must be a balance of efficiency and compliance. The use of predictive technologies can help achieve that balance in a cost-effective way. Many general business organizations are exploring and reaping the benefits of leveraging these technologies for IG purposes. Law firms share the same challenges and can benefit closely from evaluating the potential of these tools for governing firm data.

Predictive technologies can be used in a variety of ways to actively address the classification issues associated with both newly created and existing or historical information. Examples include data remediation, classification of information already in repositories, and classification of information upon creation or receipt. Once classified, retention policies and security can be uniformly applied to information and allow law firms to:

- Highlight data that may present a business risk or create exposure for the firm's clients;
- Find, retain, and profit from valuable data;
- Remove redundant, irrelevant, or stale data;
- Appropriately secure sensitive or private information;
- Support consistency across the law firm in responding to various inquiries or requests, such as responses to audit letters, client security audits, or outside counsel guidelines.

Predictive Filing versus Predictive Coding

Before exploring specific uses for these tools, it is important to understand the difference between "predictive filing" and "predictive coding." Predictive filing works based on established rules, such as "e-mail from x.com should be saved to a specific client matter."[3] Continuing to use e-mail management as an example, it is possible to apply rules, run searches, and move data to a defined location based on keywords.

Predictive filing utilizes the available tools, or features within the tools, to support proactive filing of information on a "day forward"

3. *Building Law Firm Information Governance*, Iron Mountain (July 2013), http://igsymposium.ironmountain.com/building-law-firm-information-governance/.

basis. For example, many document management systems now have features that will provide suggested filing locations for newly created documents or e-mails. These suggestions will be narrowed to a small list to select from and alleviate the need to browse an entire system to file a document in the correct location. Simplifying the filing process increases the likelihood that information will be classified appropriately. Key benefits of these tools also include the ability to deduplicate and identify/declare information as a record based upon established policies and rules.

Predictive coding takes things one step farther. Predictive coding extends that ability by offering the ability to teach the technology the context of the information and evolve its learning to aid in the organization and classification of data (known as supervised learning). The goal of supervised learning is to teach the computer a classification system that we have created. The accuracy and efficiency is highly dependent on the information given by the predetermined classifications, direct human intervention to quality control the outputs for accuracy, and ongoing refinement of classification criteria so that learning evolves.[4]

Reliability and Defensibility

In February 2012, the Hon. Andrew J. Peck entered an order authorizing the parties in *Da Silva Moore v. Publicis Groupe*,[5] to rely on predictive coding for identification of responsive documents during discovery in lieu of traditional document review and search terms.

Judge Peck's decision cited statistics indicating human review is no more accurate, and perhaps less accurate, than computer-assisted review, and thus lent support to the accuracy of these technologies. The author's experience bears this out: in leveraging document type, language, content, party, timeframe, individual name, and conceptual meaning, when properly deployed, predictive coding can deliver very high accuracy rates.

---

4. *Machine Learning, Part II: Supervised and Unsupervised Learning*, AIHORIZON, http://www.aihorizon.com/essays/generalai/supervised_unsupervised_machine_learning.htm.

5. *In re* Da Silva Moore v. Publicis Groupe SA, 11-CIV-1279 (S.D.N.Y. Feb. 24, 2012).

It is not a stretch to connect the usefulness of predictive technologies proven in e-discovery with the potential to add benefits to a proactive law firm IG program. It is difficult and time-consuming to sift through e-mails, texts, contracts, spreadsheets, and other types of ever-increasing media in both contexts. Traditional IG tools, like older discovery tools, typically require deliberate thought, action, and often many "mouse clicks" to save information in the right place. The result is a failure to file at all, or filing in a manner that does not classify the document properly. Predictive technologies can eliminate much of the inaccuracy, as well as manual work and time, from the task of classifying information for IG purposes.

Potential Uses of Predictive Technologies in the Law Firm or Law Department

Lawyers appreciate the ease of use of disparate, flexible repositories such as shared drives or e-mail inboxes; however, information managers find them challenging to administer. Predictive technologies can accurately address these challenges by allowing for the automated identification, review, and tagging of information—and those technologies can also frequently apply and execute specific workflows to add value in a variety of areas.

Retention and Disposition. Due to unclassified information residing in multiple repositories, achieving consistent, unified and defensible disposition is challenging. Applying uniform retention and ultimately disposition "rules" can be difficult, if not impossible, if data cannot be associated with a particular client or matter. For example, ABA Model Rule 1.15(d) states: "[A] lawyer shall promptly deliver to the client . . . any . . . property that the client . . . is entitled to receive and, upon receipt by the client . . . shall promptly render a full accounting regarding such property."[6] Compliance requires that a law firm be able to locate a client's data even when it is spread throughout the law firm's information system.

In addition, law firms must exercise particular care in handling data received from clients, including ensuring that it is returned or

6. ABA Model Rules of Prof'l Conduct R. 1.15(d) (2013).

disposed of securely and promptly. As such, there is considerable risk in the over-retention of this information, specifically when retention exceeds that of the client's records retention policy. Over-retention of data is also costly for other reasons. It can drive up storage, backup, server, and similar IT infrastructure costs. System performance can also be adversely affected and impact stability or speed of access to systems and information. A direct impact to productivity and efficiency can result.

Predictive technologies offer a potential solution to apply policies during file transfers (incoming and outgoing) and final disposition (such as destruction/deletion or return to client) and can increase the accurate identification of information and thus provide a sound foundation for defensible disposition and prevent over-retention of expired or unnecessary content.

Onboarding—Client File Intake. Information mobility and lateral movement of lawyers are now routine aspects of business for law firms. The ability to quickly and efficiently identify, segregate, and filter various types of electronic information is critical. A common scenario that requires careful management is the import of client data associated with a lateral lawyer into the firm's systems. Established processes and procedures, combined with technology, can offer auditing capabilities and help maintain the integrity of incoming information. The basic premise also applies in cases of mergers or acquisitions—both during the due-diligence process and post-merger. Predictive technologies can add efficiencies by identifying and coding large amounts of information by client and matter for import into the firm's systems. As a result, they can give incoming lawyers prompt access to critical—and potentially revenue producing—information. In addition, using these technologies with input from the incoming team can prove valuable in weeding out unnecessary data that may have been received from the prior firm and avoid it ever being brought into firm systems.

Offboarding—Client File Transfers and Lawyer Information. Ethical and related legal requirements often dictate what types of, to whom, and when information can be released. Clients routinely follow departing partners, and it is common for clients to request the collection, production, and transfer of their information from the prior firm. This information is often voluminous and composed of a mix of structured versus unstructured data spread throughout a law firm's information system. When executing these processes, it is often necessary or helpful to separate internal versus external data. Time is often of the essence and lawyers in the former firm are frequently called upon to conduct a review and provide direction on final disposition of content. Predictive technologies can help organize or reduce the volume of information that must be reviewed. Anecdotal experiences by a few law firms utilizing predictive technologies for this purpose have shown a reduction in processing time for information exports from weeks to hours.

In addition, when lawyers leave a firm, it is not uncommon for them to leave behind a trail of personal or administrative files and data. It is often unnecessary to retain this legacy material—and potentially costly to ignore it. Departing lawyer data can be identified and analyzed so that it can be captured and retained as "know how," returned to the departed lawyer or destroyed. It can also be used to update core systems of the assignment of a new responsible lawyer should the client choose *not* to follow the attorney to their new firm.

Identification of Vital and/or Historical Records. As with any business, law firms must be diligent in their retention of vital records. Separate and apart from know-how, form files, and precedents, vital records include information that is essential to operations and survival of the firm and would be necessary to recreate operational, legal, and financial positions in the event of disaster. Legacy information often provides historical facts about the firm and may be important to retain. By establishing specific criteria, predictive technologies can aid in locating, segregating, and securing research memoranda and other aspects of the firm's intellectual history.

E-mail. E-mail has replaced the traditional methods of correspondence, and often contains information that should be captured as an official record. The conversational nature and sheer volume makes e-mail difficult to manage and is a common pain point for law firms. E-mail can be brought into a governance structure and volume can be significantly reduced by using predictive technologies.

Archives. Believing that archiving was the panacea of information management and would solve all data storage woes, many organizations—including law firms—jumped on the archiving bandwagon. In reality, the archive sometimes resulted in the equivalent of hundreds of thousands of loose papers thrown in a room and hidden behind a closed door. Content was not identified and organized in a manner that allowed it to be governed and managed, and native search functionality within the archive often lacked the sophistication and efficiencies offered by predictive technologies. E-mails in particular can pose significant risk to a law firm. To alleviate the strain on servers, aged e-mails are frequently archived. Predictive technologies can search and manage the abyss of existing archives (for both e-mails and documents) to identify data that should be kept or deleted, and often minimize the costs and risks of taking action with unnecessary data. Predictive technologies can search the archives and locate data that consist of important intellectual property, or contain sensitive information. The technologies can also be used to defensibly delete material, such as duplicative data.

Litigation Holds and Protective Orders. Law firms are not immune from litigation holds. To comply with litigation holds (including instituting the hold and then resuming retention rules once they are released), a firm must know where applicable information resides. Additionally, law firms may be required to identify and secure specific information to comply with a protective order imposed by a court or by mutual agreement of parties. Conversely, law firms are often required to destroy certain information and provide an acknowledgement to a court that they have fully complied with the order. For example, some confidentiality agreements contain a requirement that exchanged data be purged when the litigation is over. Predictive technologies can increase confidence that the information within that scope has been appropriately identified.

Data Remediation. Important, business-critical information is often misfiled. Predictive technologies can help locate various types of vital records and contracts, and, if necessary, move them to other repositories where they can be secured and managed. Redundant, obsolete, and trivial files can be deleted.

Intellectual Property and Knowledge Management. Law firms rely heavily on their bank of information that serves to support and pass along various pockets of knowledge and templates. Client work product is often repurposed for know-how and templates and presents a dilemma when executing a disposition effort for client files. Appropriately identifying, maintaining, and securing a law firm's intellectual property can be the difference in its success or failure. Using predictive technologies, it is possible to cull through data to identify potential pockets of information that should be retained as valuable intellectual property, and thus, protect the law firm's vital assets. The manual separation of know-how from work product is time-consuming, resource intensive, and as a result the information often remains co-mingled. To separate them effectively, a firm must have efficient tools with which to identify and segregate this information from other classifications of data, and in some cases, move it to another repository.

Security and Privacy. Firms are custodians, not owners, of client information, and have a duty to ensure confidentiality, security, and privacy. ABA Model Rule 1.6(a) states, in part, that "a lawyer shall not reveal information relating to the representation of a client unless the client gives informed consent."[7] Rule 1.15(a) addresses the responsibility of the lawyer to appropriately secure information. Specifically, "[a] lawyer shall hold property of clients or third persons that is in a lawyer's own property . . . . [P]roperty shall be identified as such and appropriately safeguarded . . . complete records of such property shall be kept by the lawyer and shall be preserved for a period of [five] years after termination of the representation."[8] Predictive technologies can be used to analyze employee behavior to proactively determine suspect activities, such as exporting or e-mailing client documents outside the firm without prior client instruction. If a privacy policy exists, they can also be used to identify content covered by the policy and apply it to PII, PHI, or other similarly sensitive information for both clients and employees. In addition, the increase in client security audits and outside counsel guidelines creates pressures and responsibilities. Sensitive information may be created and stored across the enterprise, often in unstructured systems. Predictive technologies can be used to identify this information and better ensure compliance with privacy and security requirements. Having such programs in place can also help lower a firm's insurance premiums as it has taken measures to proactively identify and mitigate potential risk.

7. *Id.* at R. 1.6.
8. *Id.* at R. 1.15(a).

Network Shared Drives. Often associated with the "wild west," shared drives can benefit from predictive technologies by indexing and creating a decision tree based upon key words, leading to advanced concepts of information relationships. Subsequently, client and matter tags can be associated with the content to apply the required information lifecycle management processes. There are various strategies to attack the uncontrolled shared drive monster that is notorious for containing masses of poorly classified, and sometimes irrelevant, data. Even if processes exist to address the information lifecycle of shared drive content, firms typically lack the tools to defensively delete the information after it is no longer useful or necessary to keep it. The sheer nature of shared drives promotes the proliferation of duplicative content or unnecessary data. However, in the haystack of this unnecessary information there may be the needle—pockets of valuable information that need to be kept or secured. Client data and work product are often haphazardly stored on shared drives. Predictive technologies can help classify and manage the data in the shared drives and help remediate these challenges and allow for unified disposition.

Hard Drives and Locally Stored Data. In addition to network storage locations that are often accessible by anyone in the firm, it is not uncommon for data (including client data) to be locally stored on individual devices. Convenience is a primary driver, especially when work must be performed when access to the network is not possible. Unfortunately, this information often never makes its way back into network systems. In theory, *if the data is migrated to a shared network*, the benefits of predictive technologies may also extend to otherwise locally stored information, to ensure it is classified in its proper place.

Any Indexible Repository (Such as Extranets and Intranets). Due to the challenges of managing them, firm extranets and intranets are sometimes omitted from a governance program. However, these repositories often contain unique client data that is not stored elsewhere on firm systems. Predictive technologies can remediate this challenge so that successful identification and classification can occur with this data as well.

Still Other Potential Uses. Predictive technologies also have the potential to allow firms to leverage information in nontraditional, innovative ways. With respect to business and revenue generation, taking a deeper look into data may provide insights into why client demand changes. For example, where merger and acquisition activity from a client drops 20 percent, an analysis of communication patterns may suggest the firm upset the client. So too, when engaging new clients and matters, it is critical to identify any potential conflicts. Predictive technologies can be used to mine data and search for revealing content that may be critical for the analysis, but not otherwise found. It is equally important to identify information that should not be imported into firm systems. These tools can be used to segregate information for potential clients that have not yet cleared conflicts or been accepted as a client of the firm.

As stated earlier, predictive technologies can also help a law firm or department identify and protect its intellectual property and know how. However, they can also be used to further extrapolate valuable information and reveal the value (or lack thereof) of specific unstructured data by mining it for business insights and intelligence. An example may be to gain insights into time and expenses required for a particular type of engagement to support profitable budgeting and forecasting for future matters. Finally, leveraging predictive technologies to take a deeper look into repositories such as e-mail reserves may provide expanded capabilities to figure out "who knows whom"—going well beyond the firm's client relationship system, and giving valuable information in the absence of a structured system.[9]

General Considerations

The potential uses of predictive technologies listed in the previous section are but a subset of uses for predictive coding for law firm information governance. There are no doubt additional opportunities to be discovered from the use of predictive technologies. These tools should not be viewed as a substitute for sound IG policies and practices. Regardless of how they are used, however, several key elements should be considered in order to achieve optimal value and return on investment. First, there must be advance planning and thought

9. *Emerging Trends in Law Firm Information Governance*, IRON MOUNTAIN (July 2013), http://www.ironmountain.com/Knowledge-Center/Reference-Library/View-by-Document-Type/White-Papers-Briefs/E/Emerging-Trends-in-Law-Firm-Information-Governance.aspx.

to understand a firm's goals and objectives. One must identify what you wish to accomplish, why, and who within the law firm should be involved. In law firms, key objectives could be as simple as, for example, assigning client and matter numbers, lawyer/custodian names, and document types to the data. Second, the product must be able to meet law firm end-user, IT, and legal compliance requirements. Therefore, it is crucial to detail those requirements by defining its business process and use. Third, there should be adequate oversight and a comprehensive remediation plan that is agreed upon by all stakeholders. Any deployment should include a process to audit the application's rankings.

Predictive technologies are not "plug and play." They require attention and an investment in time up front based upon the law firm's goals and objectives. A skilled legal expert must be responsible for creating the appropriate data sets (or seed sets) and must have access to, or knowledge of, all databases where content resides. In traditional e-discovery and litigation support scenarios, the tool must be retrained on a per-case basis. Training predictive technologies for IG may be less intensive because the need to retrain will not be as frequent.

It is also important to remember that good is sometimes good enough. Getting a client or matter number associated with an e-mail or other data for retention purposes may be all that a law firm needs. It should carefully weigh the ideal versus the practical approach. As with any aspect of an IG program, policies must be appropriately and consistently applied and updated as needed. In addition to investigating internal technology tools that can be tapped, it is equally important to remember that there is expertise that can be leveraged. Keep in mind that paralegals and entry-level technical staff might be a good starting point for raising awareness.

Developing the Business Case for Using Predictive Coding in a Law Firm and Getting Started

It is often difficult to get buy-in and budget approval to acquire the tools helpful and necessary to automate and support IG and accomplish the tasks outlined herein. However, given the recent e-discovery boon and the footprint that predictive technologies have already developed in that area, there is an increasing trend for law firms to have these types of solutions already in house.

When properly utilized, output of predictive technologies can far surpass the accuracy of human assessment in IG decisions, while significantly reducing the volume and therefore also reducing the cost and time associated with filing and remediation projects. In addition, when lawyers and support teams are able to do their work without worrying unnecessarily about overly burdensome retention schedules or where information should be filed—and are still able to find the information when they need it—the law firm has added a layer of operational efficiency while at the same time efficiently governing its information assets.

To be successful, it is important to develop a strategy that appeals to firm structure, size, and culture. A few suggestions to developing that strategy are to:

- Identify key stakeholders from the business, technology, risk, and finance groups.
- Seek buy-in from technology committees (or in smaller firms lawyers who are in a position to provide input and support for technology-related initiatives), the C-Suite, the General Counsel's office, and, department heads.
- Define the risks associated with unstructured data. This will vary from firm to firm. Highlight the inability to apply legal holds, ethical walls, and disposition to unstructured data.
- Gather and provide statistics on the volume of unstructured data and the effort required to manage large volumes of electronic information.
- Show the cost associated not only with the storage, but also with IT resources (people, systems, servers) for the maintenance of sizeable information strata.
- Emphasize the increased systems performance when databases are encumbered with redundant, obsolete, and trivial data.
- Demonstrate the current resources used for the linear review of information.
- Promote lawyer efficiencies associated with their abilities to collaborate with one another and clients.

- Emphasize the ability to leverage metadata for knowledge management.
- Seek partnerships with those already using the technology successfully (e-discovery, litigation support, document review teams, and paralegals).
- Develop a use case and demonstrate how this application can be feasibly applied to an existing problem or cause. Find an opportunity to start small and establish measurable results.

Once a successful business case is made, developing a proof of concept (POC) will give you a chance to test your methodology in a controlled environment and will provide the blueprint for scaling for the entire firm. Work with those involved to identify existing workflows and identify any modifications that may be necessary to test the capabilities of the technology. As with any technology implementation or upgrade, there should be a plan to roll back to the original systems or workflows in the event the POC does not go as planned. An application vendor can help develop the pilot. If a firm already has a solution in use for e-discovery purposes, ask about alternative pricing models for use in its IG initiatives. Start by "eating your own dog food" and test the firm's approach with the stakeholders and business unit teams championing this initiative. This will provide intimate knowledge of the framework to those involved with socializing the effort. Engage a group of tech-savvy lawyers to participate in a pilot.

There is an ever-growing list of predictive technology vendors in the market.[10] Leverage these relationships, arrange to participate in their training and updates on software capabilities and uses and learn how other organizations are using these technologies. Some vendors may be willing to engage in an experimental POC at minimal expense.

Training and set-up of the system should be mapped out with support from IT. To the extent a firm has an e-discovery or litigation support group, engage them to help understand the resources already available and used in-house.

---

10. For additional information regarding legal industry vendors, please refer to Gartner Research, https://www.gartner.com/doc/3200322/market-guide-enterprise-legal-management.

There must be an up-front investment in time for the POC to be successful. The firm should have meetings with subject matter experts, departmental business units and practice areas. It must learn how they are working, how they are classifying documents and where they are storing them. It should establish a list of key words, synonyms, common misspellings and abbreviations. Many firms will already have these lists established and in use in their conflicts of interest departments and built within the litigation support department's e-discovery solutions.

Whatever approach is taken, it is important to validate the methodology for training and using this technology. As we have learned with e-discovery, standards-of-care concerns must be addressed in implementing predictive technologies, which include training the system and verifying accuracy. For example, benchmark a test data set of 500 documents, where 50 documents are reviewed and coded for document setup. The target may be a 95 percent accuracy rate; once that is achieved, and the firm has built in quality-control checks, the firm can then move forward with a successful deployment.

Conclusion

Given the practical ways in which predictive technology can be an asset for routine functions performed on information throughout every phase of its lifecycle, it should be a part of a firm's current and future dialog relating to IG.

These technologies are here to stay and, while disputes about their uses and limitations from a litigation and e-discovery standpoint will continue to be debated in our courts, there is value to exploring them for real, practical, tangible tasks to govern information.

EDITORS' INTRODUCTION TO CHAPTER 19

Michael D. Berman

This chapter by Bennett Borden and Jason R. Baron is important to both litigators and business attorneys. Businesses create and store data. The authors' premise is: "Quite simply, a company's data is the digital imprint of the actions and decisions of all of its managers and employees." Its value "has lain largely fallow, hidden in plain sight because the valuable wheat could not effectively be sifted from the chaff."

The authors describe the development of machine learning, including predictive coding, in the e-discovery sphere, and persuasively argue for its expanded application in the field of information governance, giving examples of its use in nonlitigation contexts. They provide a description of how lawyers can "break new ground in our legal practice by recommending the use of these advanced techniques to solve real-world problems of our clients."

Information governance is a holistic approach to the management of data across the enterprise, aimed at maximizing the value of information while minimizing associated risks and costs. This includes treating data (including institutional knowledge) as a valuable asset, so that it is both secure and available for use, and deleted when no longer needed. The power of advanced analytics is its ability to cut across institutional data "silos," as the authors explain. They note that Big Data involves large volumes of complex data that changes rapidly, making key data invisible, much like the proverbial needle in the haystack. Advanced analytics permit attorneys (and business officials) to rapidly find needed information.

For instance, consider the authors' example of the use of analytics as an early warning system. Properly deployed, it could assist in protecting trade secrets and preventing hostile environment claims. Imagine, for example, a near-real-time ability to detect a pattern of discriminatory e-mail among employees. Consider the advantages of being alerted that a corporate officer is suddenly sending confidential company information to his or her Web-mail account. The authors note: "The true strategic advantage of advanced analytics is the speed with which an accurate answer can be ascertained." Further, they can be used for "proving a negative," that is, that, to a reasonable degree of probability, something did not happen.

The import on transactional attorneys involved in advising businesses is clear. As a coda to the chapter highlights, we are increasingly living in a world of Big Data and analytics, and lawyers should consider embracing their new-found ability to use advanced search methods for multiple purposes beyond e-discovery, to add value in advising clients across multiple aspects of legal practice.

CHAPTER 19

Finding the Signal in the Noise: Information Governance, Analytics, and the Future of Legal Practice

Bennett B. Borden and Jason R. Baron

Introduction

In the watershed year of 2012, the world of law witnessed the first concrete discussion of how predictive analytics may be used to make legal practice more efficient. That the conversation about the use of predictive analytics has emerged out of the e-discovery sector of the law is not all that surprising. In the last decade and with increasing force since 2006—with the passage of revised Federal Rules of Civil Procedure that expressly took into account the fact that lawyers must confront "electronically stored information" in all its varieties—there has been a growing recognition among courts and commentators that the practice of litigation is changing dramatically. What needs now to be recognized, however, is that the rapidly evolving tools and techniques that have been so helpful in providing efficient responses to document requests in complex litigation may be used in a variety of complementary ways to the discovery process itself.

Bennett B. Borden & Jason R. Baron, *Finding the Signal in the Noise: Information Governance, Analytics, and the Future of Legal Practice*, 20 Rich. J.L. & Tech. 7 (2014), http://jolt.richmond.edu/v20i2/article7.pdf, is reprinted here with permission.

This chapter is informed by the authors' strong views on the subject of using advanced technological strategies to be better at information governance, as defined herein. If a certain evangelical strain appears to arise out of these pages, the authors willingly plead guilty. One need not be an evangelist, however, but merely a realist to recognize that the legal world and the corporate world both are increasingly confronting the challenges and opportunities posed by Big Data.[1] This chapter has a modest aim: to suggest certain paths forward where lawyers may add value in recommending to their clients greater use of advanced analytical techniques for the purpose of optimizing various aspects of information governance. No attempt at comprehensiveness is aimed for here; instead, the motivation behind writing this chapter is simply to take stock of where the legal profession is, as represented by the emerging case law on predictive coding represented by *Da Silva Moore*,[2] and to suggest that the expertise law firms have gained in this area may be applied in a variety of related contexts.

To accomplish what we are setting out to do, we will divide the discussion into the following parts: first, a synopsis of why and how predictive coding first emerged against the backdrop of e-discovery. This references to the technical literature, as the subject has been recently covered exhaustively elsewhere. Second, we will define what we mean by Big Data, analytics, and information governance for the purpose of providing a proper context for what follows. Third, we will note those aspects of an information governance program that are most susceptible to the application of predictive coding and related analytical techniques. Perhaps of most value, we wish to share a few early examples of where we as lawyers have brought advanced analytics, like predictive coding, to bear in non-litigation contexts and to assist our clients in creative new ways. We fully expect that what we say here will be overrun with a multitude of real-life use cases soon to emerge in the legal space. Armed with the knowledge that we are attempting to catch lightning in a bottle and that law reviews on subjects such as

1. *See infra* text accompanying notes 47–49 for a definition.

2. Da Silva Moore v. Publicis Groupe, 287 F.R.D. 182, 192 (S.D.N.Y. 2012), *aff'd sub nom.* Moore v. Publicis Groupe SA, 2012 WL 144534 (S.D.N.Y. Apr. 26, 2012) (Carter, J.).

this one have ever decreasing shelf-lives[3] in terms of the value proposition they provide, we proceed nonetheless.

The Path to *Da Silva Moore*

The Law of Search and Retrieval. In the beginning, there was manual review. Any graduate of a law school during the latter part of the 20th century who found herself or himself employed before the year 2000 at a law firm specializing in litigation and engaged in high-stakes discovery remembers well how document review was conducted: legions of lawyers with hundreds if not thousands of boxes in warehouses, reviewing folders and pages one-by-one in an effort to find the relevant needles in the haystack.[4] (Some of us also remember "Shepardizing" a case to find subsequent citations to it, using red and yellow booklets, before automated key-citing came along.) Although manual review continues to remain a default practice in a variety of more modest engagements, it is increasingly the case that all of discovery involves e-discovery of some sort—that the world is simply "awash in data"[5] (starting but by no means ending with e-mail, messages, and other textual documents of all varieties), and that it will increasingly be the unusual case of any size where documents in paper form still loom large as the principal source of discovery.

At the turn of the century, the dawning awareness of the need to deal with a new realm of electronically stored information (ESI) led to burgeoning efforts on many fronts, including, for example, the creation of The Sedona Conference working group on electronic document retention and production, members of which drafted *The Sedona Conference Principles: Addressing Electronic Document Production* (2005; 2d ed. 2007) and its "prequel," *The Sedona Guidelines: Best*

3. We recognize the paradox of articles living "forever" on the Internet, especially when published originally in online journals (and reprinted as a chapter in this volume), while at the same time ever more rapidly becoming obsolete and out of date.

4. *See generally* The Sedona Conference, *The Sedona Conference Best Practices Commentary on the Use of Search and Information Retrieval Methods in E-Discovery* (2013 ed.), 15 Sedona Conf. J. 217, 228 (2014) [hereinafter *Sedona Search Commentary*].

5. Thomas H. Davenport & Jinho Kim, Keeping Up with the Quants: Your Guide to Understanding and Using Analytics 1–2 (2013).

Practice Guidelines and Commentary for Managing Records and Information in the Electronic Age (2004; 2d ed. 2007). These early commentaries, including a smattering of pre-2006 case law,[6] recognized that changes in legal practice were necessary to accommodate the big changes coming in the world of records and information management within the enterprise. Subsequent developments would constitute various complementary threads leading to the greater use of analytics in the legal space.

First, part of that early recognition was that in an inflationary universe of rapidly expanding amounts of ESI, new tools and techniques would be necessary for the legal profession to adapt and keep up with the times.[7] By the time of adoption of the revised Federal Rules of Civil Procedure in 2006, which expressly added the term "ESI" to supplement "documents" in the rule set applicable to discovery practice, the legal profession was well aware of the need to perform automated searches in the form of keyword searching within large data sets as the only realistically available means for sorting information into relevant and nonrelevant evidence in particular engagements, be they litigation or investigations. So too, it was recognized early on in commentaries[8] and followed by case law[9] that keyword searching, as good a tool as it was, had profound limitations that in the end do not scale well. At the end of the day, even being able to limit or cull down a large data set to 1 percent of its original size through the use of keywords leaves

6. *See Sedona Search Commentary, supra* note 4, at 231–01 nn.21–23.

7. *See, e.g.*, George L. Paul & Jason R. Baron, *Information Inflation: Can The Legal System Adapt?*, 13 Rich. J.L. & Tech. 10, ¶ 2 (2007), http://jolt.richmond.edu/v13i3/article10.pdf.

8. *Id.; see Sedona Search Commentary, supra* note 4, at 2321–33; Mia Mazza, Emmalena K. Quesada, & Ashley L. Stenberg, *In Pursuit of FRCP1: Creative Approaches to Cutting and Shifting Costs of Discovery of Electronically Stored Information,* 13 Rich. J.L. & Tech. 11, ¶ 46 (2007), http://jolt.richmond.edu/v13i3/article11.pdf.

9. *See* Victor Stanley v. Creative Pipe, 250 F.R.D. 251, 256–57 (D. Md. 2008); *see also* United States v. O''Keefe, 537 F. Supp. 2d 14, 23–24 (D.D.C. 2008); William A. Gross Const. Ass'n v. Am. Mfrs. Mut. Ins. Co., 256 F.R.D. 134, 135 (S.D.N.Y. 2009); Equity Analytics, LLC v. Lundin, 248 F.R.D. 331, 333 (D.D.C. 2008); *In re* Seroquel Prod. Liab. Litig., 244 F.R.D. 650, 663 (M.D. Fla. 2007). *See generally* Jason R. Baron, *Law in the Age of Exabytes: Some Further Thoughts on "Information Inflation" and Current Issues in E-Discovery Search*, 17 Rich. J.L. & Tech. 9, ¶ 11 n.38 (2011), http://jolt.richmond.edu/v17i3/article9.pdf.

the lawyer with the near impossible task of manually reviewing a very large set of documents at great cost.[10]

Second, in evolving e-discovery practice after 2006, a growing recognition also occurred around the idea that e-discovery workflows are an "industrial" process in need of better metrics and measures for evaluating the quality of productions of large data sets. As recognized in *The Sedona Conference Commentary on Achieving Quality in E-discovery*:

> The legal profession has passed a crossroads: When faced with a choice between continuing to conduct discovery as it had "always been practiced" in a paper world—before the advent of computers, the Internet, and the exponential growth of electronically stored information (ESI)—or alternatively embracing new ways of thinking in today's digital world, practitioners and parties acknowledged a new reality and chose progress. But while the initial steps are completed, cost-conscious clients and over-burdened judges are increasingly demanding that parties find new approaches to solve litigation problems.[11]

The commentary goes on to suggest that the legal profession would benefit from greater

> [a]wareness about a variety of processes, tools, techniques, methods, and metrics that fall broadly under the umbrella term "quality measures" and that may be of assistance in handling ESI throughout the various phases of the discovery workflow process. These include greater use of project management, sampling, machine learning, and other means to verify the accuracy and completeness of what constitutes the "output" of e-[D]iscovery. Such collective

10. *See* Paul & Baron, *supra* note 7, at ¶ 20; *see also* Bennett B. Borden et al., *Why Document Review Is Broken,* Williams Mullen Edig: E-Discovery and Information Governance, May 2011, at 1, http://www.umiacs.umd.edu/~oard/desi4/papers/borden.pdf.

11. The Sedona Conference, *The Sedona Conference Commentary on Achieving Quality in E-Discovery* (2013 ed.), 15 Sedona Conf J. 265, 268 (2014).

> measures, drawn from a wide variety of scientific and management disciplines, are intended only as an entry-point for further discussion, rather than an all-inclusive checklist or cookie-cutter solution to all e-[D]iscovery issues.[12]

Indeed, more recent case law has recognized the need for quality control, including through the use of greater sampling, iterative methods, and phased productions in line with principles of proportionality.[13] Still other case law has emphasized the need for cooperation among parties in litigation on technical subjects, especially at the margins of, or outside the range of, lawyer expertise if not basic competence.

Active or supervised "machine learning," as referred to here in the context of e-discovery, refers to a set of analytical tools and techniques that go by a variety of names, such as predictive coding, computer-assisted review, and technology-assisted review. As explained in one helpful recent monograph:

> Predictive coding is the process of using a smaller set of manual reviewed and coded documents as examples to build a computer generated mathematical model that is then used to predict the coding on a larger set of documents. It is a specialized application of a class of techniques referred to as supervised machine-learning in computer science. Other technical terms often used to describe predictive coding include document (or text) "classification" and document (or text) "categorization."[14]

---

12. *Id.*

13. *See, e.g.*, *William A. Gross Constr.*, 256 F.R.D. at 136; *Seroquel*, 244 F.R.D. at 662. *See generally* Bennett B. Borden et al., *Four Years Later: How the 2006 Amendments to the Federal Rules Have Reshaped the E-Discovery Landscape and Are Revitalizing the Civil Justice System*, 17 RICH. J.L. & TECH. 10, ¶¶ 30-37 (2011), http://jolt.richmond.edu/v17i3/article10.pdf. Ralph C. Losey, *Predictive Coding and the Proportionality Doctrine: A Marriage Made in Big Data*, 26 REGENT U. L. REV. 7, 53 n.189 (2013) (collecting cases on proportionality).

14. RAJIV MAHESHWARI, PREDICTIVE CODING GURU'S GUIDE 21 (2013); *see also* Baron, *supra* note 9, at ¶ 32, n.124 (stating predictive coding and other like terminology as used by e-Discovery vendors); Maura R. Grossman & Gordon V. Cormack, *The Grossman-Cormack Glossary of Technology-Assisted Review*, 7 FED.

And as stated in *The Sedona Conference Search Commentary*:

> Generally put, computer- or technology-assisted approaches are based on iterative processes where one (or more) attorneys or [Information Retrieval] experts train the software, using document exemplars, to differentiate between relevant and non-relevant documents. In most cases, these technologies are combined with statistical and quality assurance features that assess the quality of the results. The research . . . has demonstrated such techniques superior, in most cases, to traditional keyword based search, and, even, in some cases, to human review.
>
> The computer- or technology-assisted review paradigm is the joint product of human expertise (usually an attorney or IR expert working in concert with case attorneys) and technology. The quality of the application's output, which is an assessment or ranking of the relevance of each document in the collection, is highly dependent on the quality of the input, that is, the human training. Best practices focus on the utilization of informed, experienced, and reliable individuals training the system. These individuals work in close consultation with the legal team handling the matter, for engineering the application. Similarly . . . the defensibility and usability of computer- or technology-assisted review tools require the application of statistically-valid approaches to selection of a "seed" or "training" set of documents, monitoring of the training process, sampling, and quantification and verification of the results.[15]

CTS. L. REV. 1, 4 (2013), http://www.fclr.org/fclr/articles/html/2010/grossman.pdf. Nicholas M. Pace & Laura Zakaras, *Where the Money Goes: Understanding Litigant Expenditures for Producing Electronic Discovery*, RAND INST. FOR CIV. JUSTICE 59 (2012), *available at* http://www.rand.org/pubs/monographs/MG1208.html (defining predictive coding).

15. Sedona Search Commentary, 15 SEDONA CONF. J. at 242. For an excellent, in-depth discussion of how a practitioner may use predictive coding in e-Discovery, with references to experiments by the author, see Losey, *supra* note 13, at 9.

A discussion of the mathematical algorithms that underlie predictive coding is beyond the intended scope of this chapter, but the interested reader should refer to references cited at the margin to understand better what is "going on under the hood" with respect to the mathematics involved.[16]

The Da Silva Moore *Precedent*. The various threads in search and retrieval law, including the need for advanced search methods applied to document review in a world of increasingly large data sets, were well known by 2012. In February 2012, drawing on recent research and scholarship emanating out of the Text Retrieval Conference (TREC) Legal Track[17] and the 2007 public comment version of The Sedona Conference Search Commentary,[18] Judge Peck approached the

---

16. *See, e.g., Sedona Search Commentary, supra* note 4, at 255–63 (describing various search methods); Douglas W. Oard & William Webber, *Information Retrieval for E-Discovery*, 7 FOUNDATIONS AND TRENDS IN INFORMATION RETRIEVAL 100 (2013), https://terpconnect.umd.edu/~oard/pdf/fntir13.pdf; Jason R. Baron & Jesse B. Freeman, DESI (Discovery of Electronically Stored Information) Workshop V, *Cooperation, Transparency, and the Rise of Support Vector Machines in E-Discovery: Issues Raised By the Need to Classify Documents as Either Responsive or Nonresponsive* (2013), http://www.umiacs.umd.edu/~oard/desi5/additional/Baron-Jason-final.pdf. For good resources in the form of information retrieval textbooks, see GARY MINER, ET AL., PRACTICAL TEXT MINING AND STATISTICAL STRUCTURED TEXT DATA APPLICATIONS (2012); CHRISTOPHER D. MANNING, PRABHAKAR RAGHAVAN, & HINRICH SCHUTZE, INTRODUCTION TO INFORMATION RETRIEVAL (2008).

17. *See TREC Legal Track,* U. MD., http://trec-legal.umiacs.umd.edu (collecting Overview reports from 2006–2011) (as explained on its home page, "[t]he goal of the Legal Track at the Text Retrieval Conference (TREC) [was] to assess the ability of information retrieval techniques to meet the needs of the legal profession for tools and methods capable of helping with the retrieval of electronic business records, principally for use as evidence in civil litigation."); *see also* Maura R. Grossman & Gordon V. Cormack, *Technology-Assisted Review in E-Discovery Can Be More Effective and More Efficient than Exhaustive Manual Review,* 17 RICH. J.L. & TECH. 11, ¶¶ 3–4 (2011), http://jolt.richmond.edu/v17i3/article11.pdf; Patrick Oot et al., *Mandating Reasonableness in a Reasonable Inquiry*, 87 DENV. U. L. REV. 533, 558–59 (2010); Herbert Roitblat et al., *Document Categorization in Legal Electronic Discovery: Computer Classification vs. Manual Review,* 61 J. 'ASS'N FOR INFO. SCI. & TECH. 70, 77–79 (2010), http://onlinelibrary.wiley.com/doi/10.1002/asi.21233/full; *see generally* Pace & Zakaras, *supra* note 14, at 77–80.

18. The Sedona Conference, *The Sedona Conference Best Practices Commentary on the Use of Search and Information Retrieval Methods in E-Discovery* (2007), 8 SEDONA CONF. J. 189, 192–93.

Da Silva Moore case as an appropriate vehicle to provide a judicial blessing for the use of predictive coding in e-discovery. In doing so, however, Judge Peck's opinion may also be viewed as setting the stage for greater use of analytics generally in the information governance practice area, beyond mere e-discovery.

Plaintiffs in *Da Silva Moore* brought claims of gender discrimination against defendant advertising conglomerate Publicis Groupe and its U.S. public relations subsidiary, defendant MSL Group.[19] Prior to the February 2012 opinion issued by Judge Peck, the parties had already agreed that defendant MSL would use predictive coding to review and produce relevant documents, but disagreed on methodology.[20] Defendant MSL proposed starting with the manual review of a random sample of documents to create a seed set of documents that would be used to train the predictive coding software.[21] Plaintiffs would participate in the creation of the seed set of documents by offering keywords.[22] All documents reviewed during the creation of the seed set, relevant or irrelevant, would be provided to plaintiffs.[23]

After creation of the seed set of documents, MSL proposed using a series of iterative rounds to test and stabilize the training software.[24] The results of these iterative rounds would be provided to plaintiffs, who would be able to provide feedback to further refine the searches.[25] Judge Peck accepted MSL's proposal.[26] Plaintiffs filed objections with the district judge on the grounds that Judge Peck's approval of MSL's protocol unlawfully disposed of MSL's duty under Rule 26(g) of the Federal Rules of Civil Procedure to certify the completeness of its document collection, and the methodology in MSL's protocol was not sufficiently reliable to satisfy Rule 702 of the Federal Rules of Evidence and *Daubert*.[27]

---

19. *Da Silva Moore*, 287 F.R.D. at 183.
20. *Id.* at 184–87.
21. *Id.* at 186–87.
22. *Id.* at 187.
23. *Id.*
24. *Da Silva Moore*, 287 F.R.D. at 187.
25. *Id.*
26. *Id.*
27. *Id.* at 188–89.

Judge Peck found the plaintiffs' objections to be misplaced and irrelevant.[28] With respect to Rule 26(g), Judge Peck commented that no attorney could certify the completeness of a document production as large as MSL's. Moreover, Rule 26(g) did not require the type of certification plaintiffs described.[29] Further, Rule 702 and *Daubert* are applicable to expert methodology, not to methodologies used in electronic discovery.[30] Judge Peck went on to note that the decision to allow computer-assisted review in this case was easy because the parties agreed to this method of document collection and review.[31] While computer-assisted review may not be a perfect system, he found it to be more efficient and effective than using manual review and keyword searches to locate responsive documents.[32] Use of predictive coding was appropriate in this case considering:

> (1) the parties' agreement, (2) the vast amount of ESI to be reviewed (over three million documents), (3) the superiority of computer-assisted review to the available alternatives (i.e., linear manual review or keyword searches), (4) the need for cost effectiveness and proportionality under Rule 26(b)(2)(C), and (5) the transparent process proposed by MSL.[33]

In issuing this opinion, Judge Peck became the first judge to approve the use of computer-assisted review.[34] He also stressed the limitations of his opinion, stating that computer-assisted review may not be appropriate in all cases, and his opinion was not intended to endorse any particular computer-assisted review method.[35] However, Judge Peck encouraged the Bar to consider computer-assisted review

28. *Id.*

29. *Da Silva Moore*, 287 F.R.D. at 188.

30. *Id.* at 188–89 (citing Daubert v. Merrell Dow Pharms., 509 U.S. 579, 585 (1993)). *But cf.* David J. Waxse & Benda Yoakum-Kris, *Experts on Computer-Assisted Review: Why Federal Rule of Evidence 702 Should Apply to Their Use,* 52 WASHBURN L.J. 207, 219–23 (2013) (arguing that the *Daubert* standard should be applied to experts presenting evidence on ESI search and review methodologies) (reprinted at Chapter 10 in this volume).

31. *Id.* at 189.

32. *Id. at* 190–91; *see* Grossman & Cormack, *supra* note 17, at ¶ 61.

33. *Da Silva Moore*, 287 F.R.D. at 192.

34. *Id.* at 193.

35. *Id.*

as an available tool for "large-data-volume cases" where use of such methods could save significant amounts of legal fees.[36] Judge Peck also stressed the importance of cooperation, or what he called "strategic proactive disclosure of information." If counsel is knowledgeable about the client's key custodians and fully explains proposed search methods to opposing counsel and the court, those proposed search methods are more likely to be approved. To sum up his opinion, Judge Peck noted that "[c]ounsel no longer have to worry about being the 'first' or 'guinea pig' for judicial acceptance of computer-assisted review. . . . Computer-assisted review now can be considered judicially-approved for use in appropriate cases."[37]

In the years since *Da Silva Moore*, in addition to cases in which the parties have agreed upon a predictive coding methodology,[38] courts have confronted the issue of having to rule on either the requesting or responding party's motion to compel a judicial "blessing" of the use of predictive coding (however termed). In *Global Aerospace*,[39] the responding party asked that the court approve its own use of such technique; in *Kleen Products*, the requesting party made an ultimately unsuccessful demand for a "do-over" in discovery, where the responding party had used keyword search methods and the plaintiffs were demanding that more advanced methods be tried.[40] In the *EOHRB* case, the court sua sponte suggested that the parties consider using predictive coding, including the same vendor.[41] And in the *In re Biomet* case,[42] the court approved a predictive coding methodology over the objections of the requesting party. These cases represent only some of

36. *Id.*

37. *Id.*

38. *See, e.g., In re* Actos (Pioglitazone) Prods. Liab. Litig., No. 6:11-md-2299, 2012 U.S. Dist. LEXIS 187519, at *20 (W.D. La. July 27, 2012).

39. Global Aero. Inc. v. Landow Aviation, No. CL 61040, 2012 Va. Cir. LEXIS 50, at *2 (Apr. 23, 2012).

40. Kleen Products, LLC v. Packaging Corp., No. 10 C 5711, 2012 U.S. Dist. LEXIS 139632, at *61–63 (N.D. Ill. Sept. 28, 2012).

41. EORHB v. HOA Holdings, Civ. Ac. No. 7409-VCL (Del. Ch. Oct. 15, 2012), 2012 WL 4896670, *as amended in a subsequent order*, 2013 WL 1960621 (Del. Ch. May 6, 2013).

42. *In re* Bonnet M2a Magnum Hip Implant Prods. Liab. Litg., No. 3:12-MD-2391, 2013 U.S. Dist. LEXIS 84440, at *5–6, *9–10 (N.D. Ind. Apr. 18, 2013).

the reported decisions to date, and we suspect that there will be dozens of reported cases and many more unreported ones in the near term.

As recognized in these cases (implicitly or explicitly), as well as in a growing number of commentaries,[43] predictive coding is an analytical technique holding the promise of achieving much greater efficiencies in the e-discovery process. Notwithstanding *Da Silva Moore*'s call to action, it needs to be conceded, however, that the research has not proven that active machine-learning techniques will *always* achieve greater scores than keyword search or manual review.[44] Additionally, we bow to the reality that in a large class of cases the use of predictive coding is currently infeasible or unwarranted, especially as a matter of cost.[45]

Nevertheless, it seems apparent that the legal profession finds itself in a new place—namely, in need of recognizing that artificial intelligence techniques are growing in strength from year to year—and thus it appears to be only a matter of time until a much greater percentage of complex cases involving a large magnitude of ESI will constitute good candidates for lawyers using predictive coding techniques, both as available currently and as improved with future technological progress. As William Gibson once put it, "the future is here, it's just not evenly distributed."[46]

---

43. *See, e.g.*, Nicholas Barry, Note, *Man versus Machine Review: The Showdown between Hordes of Discovery Lawyers and a Computer-Utilizing Predictive Coding Technology*, 15 VAND. J. ENT. & TECH. L. 343, 344–45 (2013); Harrison M. Brown, Comment, *Searching for an Answer: Defensible E-Discovery Search Techniques in the Absence of Judicial Voice*, 16 CHAP. L. REV. 407, 407–09 (2013); Jacob Tingen, *Technologies-That-Must-Not-Be-Named: Understanding and Implementing Advanced Search Technologies in E-Discovery*, 19 RICH. J.L. & TECH. 2, ¶ 63 (2012), http://jolt.richmond.edu/wordpress/wp-content/uploads/2012/11/Final-Tingen-1.pdf.

44. *See* Pace & Zakara, *supra* note 14, at 61–65.

45. *Cf.* Losey, *supra* note 13, at 68.

46. Pagan Kennedy, *William Gibson"s Future Is Now,* N.Y. TIMES, Jan. 13, 2012, www.nytimes.com/2012/01/15/books/review/distrust-that-particular-flavor-by-william-gibson-book-review.html?pagewanted=all&_r=0.

Information Governance and Analytics in the Era of Big Data

We are now in a post-*Da Silva Moore*, Big Data era where lawyers are on constructive (if not actual) notice of a world of technology assisted review techniques available at least in the sphere of e-discovery. The proposition being advanced is that the greater revelation of *Da Silva Moore* is how similar the techniques being put forward as best practices in e-discovery fit a larger realm of issues familiar to lawyers, many of which fall within what is increasingly being recognized as information governance practice. It is here where we can break new ground in our legal practice by recommending the use of these advanced techniques to solve real-world problems of our clients. First, however, some definitions are in order to better frame the legal issues that will follow in the next section.

Big Data. It has been noted that "[b]ig data is a loosely defined term used to describe data sets so large and complex that they become awkward to work with using standard statistical software."[47] Alternatively, Big Data is a term that "describe[s] the technologies and techniques used to capture and utilize the exponentially increasing streams of data with the goal of bringing enterprise-wide visibility and insights to make rapid critical decisions."[48]

The fact that the data encountered within the corporate enterprise increasingly is indeed "big" means, at least according to Gartner, that it not only has volume, but velocity and complexity as well.[49] As Bill Franks has put it, "What this means is that you aren't just getting a lot of data when you work with big data. It's also coming at you fast, it's coming at you in complex formats, and it's coming at you from a

47. Chris Snijders, Uwe Matzat, & Ulf-Dietrich Reips, *"Big Data": Big Gaps of Knowledge in the Field of Internet Science*, 7 Int'l J. Int. Sci. 1 (2012), http://www.ijis.net/ijis7_1/ijis7_1_editorial.pdf.

48. Daniel Burrus, *25 Game-Changing Trends That Will Create Disruption & Opportunity (Part I),* Burrus Research, http://www.burrus.com/2013/12/game-changing-it-trends-a-five-year-outlook-part-i/.

49. Bill Franks, Taming the Big Data Tidal Wave: Finding Opportunities in Huge Data Streams with Advanced Analytics 5 (John Wiley & Sons, Inc. ed., 2012) (citing Stephen Prentice, Ceo Advisory: 'Mg Data' Equals Big Opportunity (2011)).

variety of sources."[50] These elements all significantly contribute to the challenge of finding signals in the noise.

These definitions seem to get us closer to what makes big data a new and interesting phenomenon in the world: it is not its volume alone, but the fact that we are able to "mine" large data sets using new and advanced techniques to uncover unexpected relationships, patterns, and categories within these data sets, that makes the field potentially exciting. Indeed, "it is tempting to understand big data solely in terms of size. But that would be misleading. Big data is also characterized by the ability to render into data many aspects of the world that have never been quantified before; call it 'datafication.'"[51]

Analytics. Second, we need to place predictive coding as one form of active machine learning in the context of the broader realm of analytics. In their book, *Keeping Up with the Quants: Your Guide to Understanding and Using Analytics*,[52] authors Thomas Davenport and Jinho Kim provide a useful construct in categorizing the newly emergent field of analytics: they define analytics to mean "the extensive use of data, statistical and quantitative analysis, explanatory and predictive models, and fact-based management to drive decisions and add value," going on to say that "[a]nalytics is all about making sense of big data, and using it for competitive advantage." The authors divide the world of analytics into three categories:

1. Descriptive analytics—gathering, organizing, tabulating, and depicting data;
2. Predictive analytics—using data to predict future courses of action; and
3. Prescriptive analytics—recommendations on future courses of action.[53]

---

50. *Id.*

51. Kenneth Neil Cukier & Viktor Mayer-Schoenberger, *The Rise of Big Data: How It"s Changing the Way We Think About the World,* Council on Foreign Relations (Apr. 3, 2013), http://www.foreignaffairs.com/articles/139104/kermeth-neil-culcier-and-vilctor-mayer-schoenberger/the-rise-of-big-data.

52. Davenport & Kim, *supra* note 5.

53. *Id.* at 3.

To the extent that predictive coding has been used to date to have machines "predict" relevancy in large ESI data sets, the term comfortably can be said to fall within category (2). But the world of analytics is a larger universe, encompassing a greater number of mathematical magic tricks,[54] and this should be kept in mind as we choose to limit our discussion here to a few examples of how predictive coding as one form of analytics may be usefully applied in nontraditional contexts.[55]

Corporations (much ahead of the legal profession) have rushed headlong during the past half-decade to use a variety of analytics to understand the Big Data they increasingly hold, to add value, and to improve the bottom line.[56] A 2013 Association for Information and Image Management study indicates that corporations find analytics to be useful in a variety of settings.[57]

Information Governance. "Information governance," as defined in The Sedona Conference's recently published commentary on the subject, means:

---

54. *See id.* at 4–5 (providing a listing of various fields of research that make up a part of and comfortably fit within the broader term "Analytics," including statistics, forecasting, data mining, text mining, optimization, and experimental design).

55. For additional titles in the popular literature, see THOMAS H. DAVENPORT & JEANNE G. HARRIS, COMPETING ON ANALYTICS: THE NEW SCIENCE OF WINNING (2007); FRANKS, *supra* note 49; THORNTON MAY, THE NEW KNOW: INNOVATION POWERED BY (2009); MICHAEL MINELLI, MICHELE CHAMBERS, & AMBIGA DHIRAJ, BIG DATA ANALYTICS: EMERGING BUSINESS INTELLIGENCE AND ANALYTIC TRENDS FOR TODAY''S BUSINESSES (2013); ERIC SIEGEL, PREDICTIVE ANALYTICS: THE POWER TO PREDICT WHO WILL CLICK, BUY, LIE, OR DIE (2013).

56. *See* DAVENPORT & KIM, *supra* note 5.

57. *See Big Data and Content Analytics: Measuring the ROI*, AIIM 9 (2013), http://www.aiim.org/Resources/Research/Industry-Watches/2013/2013_Nov_Big-Data. In a questionnaire asking "What type of analysis would you like to do/already do on unstructured/semi-structured data?", respondents identified over a dozen uses for analytics which they would consider of high value to their corporation, including: metadata creation; content deletion/retention/duplication; trends/pattern analysis; compliance breach, illegality; fraud detection/prevention; security reclassification/PII (personally identifiable information) detection; predictive analysis/modeling; data visualization; cross relation with demographics; incident prediction; geo-correlation; brand conformance; sentiment analysis; image/video recognition; and diagnostic/medical. *Id.*

> [a]n organization's coordinated, interdisciplinary approach to satisfying information legal and compliance requirements and managing information risks while optimizing information value. As such, Information Governance encompasses and reconciles the various legal and compliance requirements and risks addressed by different information focused disciplines, such as records and information management ("RIM"), data privacy, information security, and e-[D]iscovery.[58]

Or, as highlighted by the seminal law review article devoted to information governance written by Charles R. Ragan who quotes Barclay Blair in defining information governance as a "'new approach' that 'builds upon and adapts disciplines like records management and retention, archiving business analytics, and IT governance to create an integrated model for harnessing and controlling enterprise information . . . [I]t is an evolutionary model that requires organizations to make real changes.'"[59]

As the Sedona IG Commentary highlights, "many organizations have traditionally used siloed approaches when managing

---

58. The Sedona Conference, *The Sedona Conference Commentary on Information Governance*, 15 SEDONA CONF. J. 125 (2014) [hereinafter *Sedona IG Commentary*].

59. Charles R. Ragan, *Information Governance: It's a Duty and It's Smart Business,* 19 RICH. J.L. & TECH. 12, ¶ 32 (2013), http://jolt.richmond.edu/v19i4/article12.pdf (internal quotation marks omitted) (quoting Barclay T. Blair, *Why Information Governance, in* INFORMATION GOVERNANCE EXECUTIVE BRIEFING BOOK, 7 (2011), *available at* http://mimage.opentext.com/alt_content/binary/pdf/Information-Governance-Executive-Brief-Book-OpenText.pdf). For additional useful definitions of what constitutes information governance, see *The Generally Accepted Recordkeeping Principles*, ARMA INT'L, http://www.arma.org/r2/generally-accepted-br-recordkeeping-principles (setting out eight principles of IG, under the headings Accountability, Integrity, Protection, Compliance, Availability, Retention, Disposition, and Transparency); Debra Logan, *What Is Information Governance? And Why Is It So Hard?,* GARTNER BLOG NETWORK (Jan. 11, 2010), http://blogs.gartner.com/debra_logan/2010/01/11/what-is-information-governance-and-why-is-it-so-hard/ (defining IG on behalf of Gartner to be "the specification of decision rights and an accountability framework to encourage desirable behavior in the valuation, creation, storage, use, archival and deletion of information. It includes the processes, roles, standards, and metrics that ensure the effective and efficient use of information in enabling an organization to achieve its goals.").

information."[60] The "core shortcoming" of this approach is "that those within particular silos are constrained by the culture, knowledge, and short-term goals of their business unit, administrative function, or discipline."[61] This leads in turn to key actors within the organization having "no knowledge of gaps and overlaps in technology or information in relation to other silos. . . .[62] In such situations, "[t]here is no overall governance or coordination for managing information as an asset, and there is no roadmap for the current and future use of information technology."[63]

The Sedona IG Commentary goes on to provide 11 principles of what constitutes good IG practices, of which Principle 10 is of special relevance to our discussion here: "An organization should consider leveraging the power of new technologies in its Information Governance program."[64] As stated therein,

> Organizations should consider using advanced tools and technologies to perform various types of categorization and classification activities . . . such as machine learning, auto-categorization, and predictive analytics to perform multiple purposes, including (i) optimizing the governance of information for traditional RIM [records and information management]; (ii) providing more efficient and more efficacious means of accessing information for ediscovery, compliance, and open records laws, and (iii) advancing sophisticated business intelligence across the enterprise.[65]

With respect to the latter category, the Commentary goes on to specifically identify areas where predictive analytics may be used in compliance programs "to predict and prevent wrongful or negligent conduct that might result in data breach or loss," as a type of "early warning system."[66] It is precisely this latter type of conduct that we

60. *Sedona IG Commentary, supra* note 58, at 5.
61. *Id.*
62. *Id.*
63. *Id.*
64. *Id.* at 25.
65. *Id.*
66. *Id. at* 27.

wish to primarily explore in the next section, along with a few final words on using analytics with auto-categorization for the purpose of records classification and data remediation.

Applying the Lessons of E-Discovery in Using Analytics for Optimal Information Governance: Some Examples

Advanced analytics are increasingly being used in the e-discovery context because the legal profession has begun to realize the limitations of manual and keyword searching, while at the same time seeing how advanced techniques are at least as efficacious and far more efficient in a wide variety of substantial engagements. But more efficient and at least as equally effective at doing what, precisely? In e-discovery, the primary information task involves separating relevant from nonrelevant, and to a secondary degree, privileged from nonprivileged information, in documents and ESI. Indeed, lawyers are under a duty to make "reasonable"—not perfect—efforts to find all relevant documents within the scope of a given discovery request.[67] The illusiveness of this quest in an exponentially expanding data universe is becoming increasingly apparent to many.[68]

Moreover, the degree of success in being able to either find or demand substantial amounts of relevant information is not (nor should it be) the fundamental goal or point of engaging in e-discovery.[69] Rather, the liberal discovery rules that at least U.S. lawyers operate within have as their underlying purpose the ferreting out of important,

---

67. *See* Pension Comm. of Univ. of Montreal Pension Plan v. Banc of Am. Sec., LLC, 685 F. Supp. 2d 456, 461 (S.D.N.Y. 2010), *abrogated in part by* Chin v. Port Authority, 685 F.3d 135 (2d Cir. 2012)). The information task in e-discovery is therefore very unlike the user experience with the leading, well-known commercial search engines on the Web in, for example, finding a place for dinner in a strange city. For the latter project, few individuals religiously scour hundreds of pages of listings even if thousands of "hits" are obtained in response to a select set of keywords; instead they browse only from the first few pages of listings. Yet the lawyer is tasked with making reasonable efforts to credibly retrieve "the long tail" represented by "any and all" documents in response to document requests so phrased under FED. R. CIV. P. 34.

68. *See, e.g.*, Da Silva Moore,287 F.R.D. at 191; *Pension Comm.*, 685 F. Supp. 2d at 461.

69. *See* Borden et al., *Why Document Review Is Broken, supra* note 10, at 1.

material facts to the case at hand. The increasingly overwhelming nature of ESI poses clear technological obstacles to a lawyer en route to efficiently engaging in developing facts from all those relevant documents to determine what happened and why.[70] The promise of using an advanced analytical method such as predictive coding is its ability to quickly find and rank-order the *most* relevant documents for answering these questions. For once we determine how something happened and why, it is relatively straightforward to figure out the parties' respective rights, responsibilities, and even liability. That is precisely the point of litigation, and the purpose of the rules that govern it.[71] And, facts drive it all.

Given our increasing ability in litigation in finding the most relevant needles (i.e., facts) in the Big Data haystack, it stands to consider whether similar methods may be successfully applied in nonlitigation contexts. Somewhat paradoxically, however, experience indicates that there are advantages to dealing with *larger* volumes of data when applying analytical tools and methods to solve corporate legal issues. That is, while a vast amount of data residing in corporate networks and repositories admittedly poses complex information governance challenges, the volume of Big Data also may be a boon to the investigator simply trying to figure out what happened. This is the case because there are simply many more data points from which to derive facts. One can liken the phenomenon to the difference in quality of a one-megapixel versus a ten-megapixel picture: the difference in the quality of the image is a function of the greater density of points of illumination.

Big Data is more data, and more data means the potential for a more complete picture of what happened in a given situation of interest, assuming of course that the facts can be captured *efficiently*. The problem is not one of volume, but of visibility. In the era of Big Data, the investigator with the more powerful analytical methods, who can search into vast repositories of ESI to draw out the facts that are critical

70. Andrew Bartholomew, *An Insider's Perspective on Intelligent E-Discovery*, EXTERRO (Sept. 11, 2013), http://www.exterro.com/e-discovery-beat/2013/09/11/an-insiders-perspective-on-intelligent-e-discovery/.

71. *See* FED. R. CIV. P. 1 (2016) ("These rules . . . should be construed, administered, and employed by the court *and the parties* to secure the *just, speedy, and inexpensive* determination of every action and proceeding.") (emphasis added).

to the question at hand, is king (or queen). This is where the skillful application of advanced analytics to Big Data can bring about some remarkable results. The true strategic advantage of advanced analytics is the *speed* with which an accurate answer can be ascertained.[72]

True Life Example #1[73]

A corporate client is being sued by a former employee in a whistleblower qui tam action.[74] Because of the False Claims Act allegations, the suit represented a significant threat to the company. The corporation retains counsel to understand the client's information systems as well as its key players, and to assist in the implementation of a litigation hold. Counsel strategically targets the data most likely to shed light on the facts. The law firm's fact development team applies advanced analytics to 675,000 documents, and within four days knows enough to defend the client's position that the allegations are indisputably baseless. All of this is done before the answer to the complaint was due.

Armed with this information, counsel for the corporation approached plaintiff's counsel and asked to meet. Prior to the meeting, the corporation voluntarily produced 12,500 documents that laid out the parties' position precisely. Counsel then met with plaintiff's counsel and walked them through the evidence, laying out all the facts. The case ended up being settled within days for what amounted to nuisance value based on a retaliation claim—without any discovery, and at a small fraction of the cost budgeted for the litigation.

This example indicates that the real power of advanced analytics is not merely in potentially reducing the cost of vexatious litigation,

---

72. Borden et al., *supra* note 69, at 3.

73. All of the "true life examples" referred to in this article are "ripped from" the pages of the author's legal experience, without embellishment.

74. A qui tam suit is a lawsuit brought by a "private citizen (popularly called a 'whistle blower') against a person or company who is believed to have violated the law in the performance of a contract with the government or in violation of a government regulation, when there is a statute which provides for a penalty for such violations." *Qui Tam Action,* THE FREE DICTIONARY, http://legal-dictionary.thefreedictionary.com/qui+tam+action (last visited Feb. 24, 2014); *see also* United States *ex rel.* Eisenstein v. City of New York, 556 U.S. 928, 932 (2009) (defining a qui tam action as a lawsuit brought by a private party alleging fraud on behalf of the government) (internal citations omitted).

but rather the strategic *advantage* that comes with counsel getting to an answer quickly and accurately. This precise strategic advantage has many applications outside of litigation, each of which involves an aspect of optimizing information governance.

Only a short step away from the direct litigation realm is using advanced analytics for investigations, either in response to a regulatory inquiry or for purely internal purposes. As we have already seen, corporate clients are often faced with circumstances where determining whether an allegation is true, and the scope of the potential problem if it is, is critically important. Often, management must wait, unsure of their company's exposure and how to remediate it, while traditional investigation techniques crawl along. However, with the skillful application of advanced analytics upon the right data set, accurate answers can be determined with remarkable speed.

True Life Example #2

A highly regulated manufacturing client decided to outsource the function of safety testing some of its products. A director of the department whose function was being outsourced was offered a generous severance package. Late on a Friday afternoon, the soon-to-be former director sent an e-mail to the company's CEO demanding four times the severance amount and threatened to go to the company's regulator with a list of ten supposed major violations that he described in the e-mail if he did not receive what he was asking for. He gave the company until the following Monday to respond.

The lawyers were called in. They analyzed the list of allegations and determined which IT systems would most likely contain data that would prove their veracity and immediately pulled the data. Applying advanced analytics, the law firm's fact development team analyzed on the order of 275,000 documents in 36 hours. By that Monday morning, counsel was able to present a report to the company's board indisputably proving that the allegations were unfounded.

True Life Example #3

A major company received a whistleblower letter from a reputable third party alleging that several senior personnel were involved with an elaborate kickback scheme that also involved violations of the Foreign

Corrupt Practices Act of 1977 violations. If true, the company would have faced serious regulatory and legal issues, as well as major internal difficulties. Because of the extremely sensitive nature of the allegations, a traditional investigation was not possible; even knowing certain personnel were under investigation could have had immense consequences.

The lawyers were tasked with determining whether there was any information within the company's possession that shed any light on the allegations. If there were, the company would proceed to take whatever steps were required. The investigation was of such a secret nature that no one was authorized to involve the internal IT staff. Fortunately, counsel knew the company and its information systems well. Over a weekend, they were able to pull 8.5 million documents from relevant systems using the law firm's personnel. This turned out to be a highly complex investigation involving a number of potential subjects, where the task involved tracking the subject's travel, meetings with suppliers, subsequent sales orders and fulfillments, rebates and promotions, all across several years.

Again, applying advanced analytics, the law firm's fact development team analyzed the 8.5 million documents in ten days. They were able to prove that the allegations were largely baseless, and precisely where there were potential areas of concern. Counsel also was able to make clear recommendations for areas of further investigation and for modifying compliance tracking and programs. The company was able to act quickly and with certainty. These real-life use cases illustrate how the power of analytics enhances the ability of lawyers to provide legal advice under conditions of "certainty" previously unobtainable, at least in the past few decades of the digital era. Certainty is a somewhat foreign concept in the law—lawyers tend to be a conservative and caveating bunch, largely because certainty has historically been hard to come by, or at least prohibitively expensive. With advanced analytics and good lawyers who know how to use these new tools, that is no longer necessarily the case. There is so much data that if one cannot, after a reasonable effort, find evidence of a fact in the vastness of a company's electronic information (as long as you have the right information), the fact most likely is not true. Such has been illustrated, proving a negative is particularly useful in investigations.

Using advanced analytics (and good lawyering) for investigations is not that far removed from using it for litigation: one is still attempting to find the answer to the question of what happened and why. But there are many other questions that companies would like to ask of their data. And indeed, both the analytics tools and the fact development techniques used in litigation and investigations can be "tuned" to solve a variety of novel issues facing our clients.

For example, analytics can be used to vet candidates for political appointments as well as candidates for senior leadership positions. Due to the candid nature of the medium, providing access to corporate e-mail coupled with using analytic capabilities allows for an accurate picture to be drawn *before* a decision is made with regard to making a candidate your next CEO or running mate. Analytics can be used to analyze business divisions to identify good and bad leaders, how decisions are made, why a division is more successful than another, and many more similar applications.

Quite simply, a company's data is the digital imprint of the actions and decisions of all of its managers and employees. Having insight into those actions and decisions can be immensely valuable. That value has lain largely fallow, hidden in plain sight because the valuable wheat could not effectively be sifted from the chaff. With the proper application of advanced analytics, that is no longer the case. The answers we can obtain are limited only by the creativity of management in asking the right questions.

True Life Example #4

Advanced analytics used upon the major acquisition of another company by a corporate client. As with most acquisitions, the client undertook traditional due diligence, gathering information from the target regarding its financial performance, customers, market share, receivables, and potential liabilities, and came up with a valuation, an appropriate multiplier, and a final purchase price. Also, as is typical, the acquisition agreement contained a provision such that if the disclosures made by the target were found to be off by a certain margin within 30 days of the acquisition, the purchase price would be adjusted.

The moment the acquisition closed, the corporate client then owned all of the target's information systems. Having some concern about the bases for some of the target's disclosures, at the client's request counsel proceeded to use analytics on those newly acquired systems to determine what we could about those disclosures. Preparing a company for sale is a complicated affair, with many people involved in gathering information to present to the acquirer to satisfy due diligence. This gathering and presentation of information is done primarily through electronic means—and leaves a trail.

Using advanced analytics, the law firm's fact development team traced the compilation of the target's due diligence information, including all of the discussion that went along with it. They were able to understand the source of each disclosure, the reasonableness of its basis, and any weaknesses within it. They uncovered disagreements within the target over such things as what the right numbers were, or how much of a liability to disclose. Using this information, counsel prepared a claim in accord with the adjustment provision seeking 25 percent of the purchase price totaling millions of dollars. The claim was primarily composed using quotes from their own documents. It is difficult to argue with yourself.

Early Warning Systems. As demonstrated, using advanced analytics in the form of predictive coding and similar technologies can accomplish some notable aims. But each of the prior examples uses data to look back to determine what has already occurred: the descriptive use of analytics.[75] This is extremely valuable. But for many of a law firm's clients, it would be even more useful to be able to catch bad actors while the misconduct was occurring, or even to predict misconduct before it happens.

Based on the anecdotal experience gathered from many past investigations, the authors believe that certain kinds of misconduct follow certain patterns, and that when bad actors are acting badly, they tend to undertake the same kinds of actions, or are experiencing similar circumstances. For example, in our experience the primary factors that pertain to a person committing fraud are personal relationship problems, financial difficulties, drug or alcohol problems, gambling,

75. *See* Davenport & Kim, *supra* note 5, at 3.

a feeling of under appreciation at work, and unreasonable pressure to achieve a work outcome without a legitimate way to accomplish it (and so they attempt illegitimate ways to do so). These factors are often detectable in the electronic information the subject creates. Similarly, a person who is harassing or discriminating against others also tends to undertake specific actions and use particular language in communications. All of these indicia of misconduct are detectable using advanced analytics and skillful strategy.

Lawyers have gotten quite good at finding this information when looking back in time. We thought, then, that it should not be too difficult to find this information while the misconduct is unfolding, or to identify warning signs that misconduct is likely to occur, and seek to provide relief of certain factors where possible or take corrective action when needed and as early as possible. So, we put this to the test, developing early warning systems (EWS) for some of our clients.

The idea for an EWS first occurred to one of the authors when working on a pro bono matter with the ACLU in a case against the Baltimore Police Department (BPD) alleging unconstitutional arrest practices in its zero tolerance policing policies.[76] As a result of the case, the BPD agreed to, among other things, implement a tracking system whereby certain data points were collected regarding police officer conduct and arrest practices that research had proven were warning signs of potential problem officers.[77] The accumulation of certain data points with respect to an officer triggered a review of the officer's conduct, with various remediation outcomes.[78] We thought that a similar approach could be used for our clients.

---

76. *See* Amended Complaint and Demand for Jury Trial, NAACP v. Balt. City Police Dep't, No. 06-1863 (D. Md. Dec. 18, 2007), *available at* http://www.aclumd.org/uploaded_files/0000/0205/amended_complaint.pdf.

77. *See* Charles F. Wellford, *Justice Assessment and Evaluation Services, First Status Report for the Audit of the Stipulation of Settlement between the Maryland State Conference of NAACP Branches, et al. and the Baltimore City Police Department, et al.* 2 (Apr. 30, 2012), *available at* http://www.aclumd.org/uploaded_files/0000/0207/first_audit_report_april_30.pdf; *see also Plaintiffs Win Justice in Illegal Arrests Lawsuit Settlement with the Baltimore City Police Department,* ACLU (June 23, 2010), https://www.aclu.org/news/plaintiffs-win-justice-illegal-arrests-lawsuit-settlement-baltimore-city-police.

78. *See* Wellford, *supra* note 77, at 2, 14.

An EWS is a tricky thing to implement, and requires careful consideration of many factors—employee privacy at the forefront. However, with careful planning, policy development, and training, an effective EWS can be designed and implemented. Predictive analytics applications can be trained to search for indicia of the conduct, language, or factors across information systems. The specific systems to be targeted will vary depending on what is being sought and the systems most likely to contain it and will vary greatly from company to company. But, when properly trained and targeted, we have found these systems to be very effective in detecting and even preventing misconduct. We believe that this use of predictive analytics will become one of the most powerful applications of this technology in the near future.

Moving from the business intelligence aspects of information governance to the arguably more prosaic field of records and information management, the authors also count themselves as true believers in the power of analytics to optimize traditional RIM (records and information management) functionality. A full discussion of archival and records management practices in the digital age is beyond the scope of this chapter, but the interested reader will find a wealth of scholarly literature in the leading journals discussing how the traditional practice of records management is being transformed in the digital age. One of the authors has argued that predictive coding and like methods are the most promising way to open up "dark archives" in the public sector, such as digital collections of data appraised as permanent records (mostly consisting of White House e-mail at this point), that for reasons of privacy or privilege will be otherwise inaccessible to the public for many decades to come.[79]

In the authors' experience, e-mail archiving using auto-categorization for recordkeeping purposes is available using existing software in the marketplace. In such instances, e-mail is populated in specific "buckets" in a repository depending on how it is characterized, based on either the position of the creator or recipient of the

79. *See* Jason R. Baron & Simon J. Attfield, *Where Light in Darkness Lies: Preservation, Access and Sensemaking Strategies for the Modern Digital Archive, in* The Memory of the World in the Digital Age Conference: Digitalization and Preservation 580–95 (2012), http://1seminariopreservacaopatrimoniodigital.dglab.gov.pt/wp-content/uploads/sites/19/2015/08/recurso_25.pdf.

e-mail, the subject matter, or based on some other attribute appearing as metadata.[80] In the most advanced versions of auto-categorization software, the system "learns" as it is trained using exemplars in a seed set selected by subject-matter experts (i.e., records managers or expert end users), via a protocol highly reminiscent of the methods adopted by the parties in *Da Silva Moore* and similar cases. It is only a matter of time before predictive analytics is more widely used to optimize auto-classification while reducing the burden on end users to perform manual records management functions.[81]

In similar fashion, the power of predictive analytics to reliably classify content after adequate training makes such tools optimal for data remediation efforts. The problem of legacy data in corporations is well known, and only growing over time with the inflationary expansion of the ESI universe.[82] Using advanced analytics to classify low-value data, the chaos that is the reality of most shared drives and other joint data repositories, may potentially be reduced by orders of magnitude. The challenge of engaging in defensible deletion is one important aspect of optimizing information governance.[83]

Conclusion

As was made clear at the outset, it is the authors' intent merely to scratch the surface of what is possible in the analytics space as applied to matters of importance for corporate information governance. No one has a 100 percent reliable crystal ball, but it seems evident that as computing power increases, those forms of artificial intelligence that we have referred to here as analytics will themselves only grow in importance in both our daily and professional lives. By the end of this decade, we would be surprised if the following do not occur: pervasive use of business intelligence software; the use of more automated decision-making (also known as operational business intelligence);

80. *See id.* at 587.

81. *See id.* at 588; *see also* Ragan, *supra* note 59, at ¶ 6.

82. *See, e.g.*, The Sedona Conference, *The Sedona Conference Commentary on Inactive Information Sources* 2, 5 (2009), https://thesedonaconference.org/publication/The%20Sedona%20Conference®%20Commentary%20on%20Inactive%20Information%20Sources.

83. *See Sedona IG Commentary, supra* note 58, at 20–22.

the use of alerts in the form of early warning systems including the type described earlier; much greater use of text mining and predictive technologies across a variety of domains.[84]

All of these developments dovetail with the expected demand on the part of corporate clients for lawyers to be familiar with state-of-the-art practices in the information governance space, as already anticipated by the type of technology that *Da Silva Moore* and related cases suggest. As best said in *The Sedona Commentary on Achieving Quality in E-Discovery*, "[i]n the end, cost-conscious firms, organizations, and institutions of all types that are intent on best practices . . . will demand that parties undertake new ways of thinking about how to solve e-discovery problems. . . ."[85] The same holds true for the greater playing field of information governance. Lawyers who have embraced analytics will have a leg up on their competition in this brave new space.

* * *

Afterword: Finding the Signal in the Noise in 2016 and Beyond

Jason R. Baron

If it were not evident as of 2014 when this chapter was first published, it should be increasingly apparent now that the confluence of the disciplines of information governance, data analytics, and the law, is a newly emergent phenomenon of some importance. Big Data and the science of data analytics is increasingly seen as important in virtually every aspect of both ours and our client's daily lives. In a world where there is no end in sight to the acceleration in size volume and complexity of Big Data—including now, the Internet of Things—the legal profession needs to embrace what this means across every legal practice group in firms and corporations.

After publication of this original article in 2014, my colleague, Bennett Borden, embarked on obtaining a Master's degree in business

84. *See* Davenport & Harris, *supra* note 55, at 176–78.

85. The Sedona Conference, *The Sedona Conference Commentary on Achieving Quality in the E-Discovery Process, supra* note 11, 15 Sedona Conf. at 325.

analytics from New York University, becoming chief data scientist at Drinker Biddle, while retaining his other roles as a partner and co-chair of the Information Governance and eDiscovery Practice. Bennett has stated that he believes other advanced law firms are likely to see his new role as "ahead of the curve," and as such, he wouldn't be surprised if they eventually follow suit, naming chief data scientists of their own.[86]

Also, shortly after original publication, Bennett co-founded, along with Barclay Blair, a think tank known as the Information Governance Initiative (IGI),[87] dedicated to the idea that an emerging discipline of information governance would be of value to institutions of all types and varieties, private and public. The IGI believes that data analytics is increasingly seen as one way that businesses can leverage the value side of their information, to target customers and to obtain greater visibility into the data they hold from all sources.[88]

The rise of algorithms and analytics is, in turn, giving rise to novel legal issues, including such topics as algorithmic bias and data ethics. Writings on these topics explore whether software used in pattern analysis and prediction is unfairly biasing categories of individuals based on initial assumptions input into the computer programs used.[89] This topic will only grow in importance as data is received from every sensor and every smart Internet-enabled device on Earth through the Internet of Things.

The growing volume and richness of data are creating the largest sociological record in the history of our species, allowing insights into human conduct unimaginable just a few years ago. This is leading to significant advances in the efficiency, accuracy, and granularity of the

---

86. *Using Information to Achieve Legal Outcomes: Bennett Borden Named DBR's Chief Data Scientist*, IGI (June 18, 2015), http://iginitiative.com/tag/chief-data-scientist/.

87. *See* www.iginitiative.com. The author of this coda serves as co-chair of the IGI.

88. *See* Information Governance Initiative first and second annual reports, 2014–2015 and 2015–2016, www.iginitiative.com.

89. *See, e.g.*, Claire Cain Miller, *When Algorithms Discriminate*, N.Y. Times, July 9, 2015, http://www.nytimes.com/2015/07/10/upshot/when-algorithms-discriminate.html?_r=0; Lauren Kirchner, *When Discrimination Is Baked into Algorithms*, The Atlantic, Sept. 6, 2015, http://www.theatlantic.com/business/archive/2015/09/discrimination-algorithms-disparate-impact/403969/.

provision of public and private goods and services, such as education, health care, and the distribution of energy. These advances are based on our increasingly accurate detection and understanding of patterns in human conduct. This understanding is based upon billions of data points we are collecting and analyzing to make inferences about people. But this raises novel issues in the law about privacy and the accuracy of our inferences.

It also turns out that, like all human conduct, there are patterns in misconduct that can be leveraged to detect misconduct as it is developing, or even predict it before it happens. What level of certainty do we need to be able to act to prevent such misconduct from happening? Our current legal frameworks do not adequately address these issues that Big Data and analytics are bringing to the forefront. As the legal profession embraces analytics, we will need to be cognizant of these types of issues.

The trend lines for the rest of this decade are clear concerning the growth of data and the need for increased attention to its governance. As we said in our chapter, smart lawyers will embrace the future by finding ways to harness technology in providing value to their clients.

EDITORS' INTRODUCTION TO CHAPTER 20

Jason R. Baron

In this chapter, Kathryn Hume provides us with a glimpse into the "next wave" future of advanced search techniques in the form of "deep learning." For the same techniques that today enable programmers to teach robots to walk may one day soon be adapted for use in a litigation context more familiar to readers of this book.

As the author explains, neural networks are one variant of machine learning, which involves computer algorithms that have the ability to "learn" or improve performance over time on some task. Neural networks differ, however, from the machine learning methods currently in use, such as predictive coding, as they have a unique underlying architecture designed to mimic the brain. Neural networks are composed of individual computational units called neurons that are connected within and across different layers and are considered deep because they have multiple computing layers, which enable them to transform data multiple times to reach a useful level of generalization.

In a legal context, deep learning techniques hold out the promise not only to be able to analyze text, but also analyze all kinds of visual media (e.g., videos and audio feeds from a car accident). They also may enhance our ability to do text classification for purposes of information governance, and to perform anomaly detection in information security contexts.

This chapter asks us to think about "the practice of law," and how machine-learning techniques may change our current conceptions of what that truly means. For some, the prospect of needing to be technically competent in advanced search techniques such as deep learning may lead to considerations of early retirement. For others, the idea that lawyers may benefit from embracing such advanced technologies is exhilarating. We hope this chapter inspires the latter feelings on the part of the reader.

CHAPTER 20

Preparing for the Near Future: Deep Learning and Law

Kathryn Hume

The age of machine intelligence in law firms is dawning. In the 2015 Altman Weil Law Firms in Transition survey, 47 percent of managing partner respondents said a law-focused "Watson" would replace paralegals in the next 5 to 10 years, and 35 percent said it would replace first-year associates.[1] But the survey question is misleading for two reasons. First, it gives the impression that IBM Watson is the only intelligent system on the market. One glance at the machine intelligence landscape developed by Shivon Zilis, a partner at Bloomberg

1. Thomas S. Clay & Eric A. Seeger, *Law Firms in Transition: An Altman Weil Flash Survey* (2015), 82, http://www.altmanweil.com/dir_docs/resource/1c789ef2-5cff-463a-863a-2248d23882a7_document.pdf. Watson, here, refers to IBM's "cognitive computing" system, which gained popular fame in 2011 upon defeating two former Jeopardy! champions. Watson is a collection of search, natural language processing, and machine-learning technologies. Its primary utility is as a research question and answer tool, where users can pose questions and receive answers in complete sentences. The system functions best when tailored to a given corpus of documents (e.g., insolvency law, as in the legal-specific applications being built by ROSS Intelligence, a startup funded by Dentons NextLaw Labs.).

The 2016 version of the survey does not include the same question about law firm adoption of AI, but does indicate that 85.2 percent of managing partner respondents "think using technology to replace human resources will be a permanent trend going forward." *See* http://www.altmanweil.com/dir_docs/resource/95e9df8e-9551-49da-9e25-2cd868319447_document.pdf.

Beta, demonstrates how far that is from the truth.[2] Second, it precludes more important questions firms should ask when adopting intelligent systems. How should processes and workflows change to incorporate new research and discovery technologies? What factors should lawyers consider to use them ethically? More drastically, will the widespread adoption of intelligent systems force courts to redefine what qualifies as the practice of law?

In the past decade, law firms have primarily encountered machine intelligence in the domains of electronic discovery (e-discovery) and predictive analytics. Technology-assisted review (TAR) or predictive coding tools infer relevance throughout a document set from a representative training set. Some vendors employ machine learning techniques for e-discovery; others use more basic techniques like Boolean search. Predictive analytics tools like Lex Machina help shape case strategy for IP law suits and patent prosecution by analyzing past trial outcomes. In the next decade, law firms should prepare for a new set of applications built using a technique called deep learning.

Deep learning—currently the computer science research focus at Facebook and Google—is making a huge splash outside the legal vertical. Deep learning algorithms take input data and transform it through layers of computing to provide an output, like a prediction or a classification. This year, the technique has enabled researchers to play chess like the masters in 72 hours,[3] teach robots to walk,[4]

---

2. Shivon Zillis, a partner and founding member of Bloomberg Beta, offers a thorough machine intelligence landscape graphic on her blog, http://www.shivonzilis.com/machineintelligence.

3. *Xb Emerging Technology from the arXiv, Deep Learning Machine Teaches Itself Chess in 72 Hours, Plays at International Master Level*, MIT TECH. REV. (Sept. 14, 2015), http://www.technologyreview.com/view/541276/deep-learning-machine-teaches-itself-chess-in-72-hours-plays-at-international-master/. The chess-playing algorithm uses a particular form of machine learning called reinforcement learning, which differs from standard supervised learning methods in that the learning algorithm is not told which actions to take, but must discover which actions yield the most reward by trying them, and in that rewards can be delayed, so that the learning algorithm can optimize actions for overall long-term as opposed to immediate reward. For more on reinforcement learning, see Richard S. Sutton and Andrew G. Barto, REINFORCEMENT LEARNING: AN INTRODUCTION, https://webdocs.cs.ualberta.ca/~sutton/book/the-book.html (Cambridge: MIT Press 1998).

4. Will Knight, *Robot Toddler Learns to Stand by "Imagining" How to Do It*, MIT TECH. REV. (Nov. 6, 2015), http://www.technologyreview.com/news/542921/robot-toddler-learns-to-stand-by-imagining-how-to-do-it/.

and classify images according to their contents without metadata or hashtags.[5]

There are multiple applications for deep learning in law, but firms will have to adjust their mindset in two ways to use the technology effectively. First, as deep learning provides probabilistic results, firms will need to decide what confidence thresholds they are willing to accept and how lawyers and staff will process results. Second, deep learning algorithms are very hard to interpret because the same computing layers that provide their power render them opaque. As such, lawyers should understand the potential risks of using deep learning systems and be prepared to articulate these risks to clients.

What Is Deep Learning?

On July 8, 1958, a *New York Times* article announced that "the Navy revealed the embryo of an electronic computer [. . .] that it expects will be able to walk, talk, see, write, reproduce itself and be conscious of its existence."[6] The electronic computer in question was Frank Rosenblatt's $100,000 Perceptron, the historical predecessor of the modern neural networks that underpin deep learning.

Neural networks are one variant of machine learning, which involves computer algorithms that have the ability to learn or improve performance over time on some task. Traditional programming is deductive and deterministic, where engineers give the computer a set of instructions whose logic stays the same over time. Machine learning is inductive and probabilistic, where computers are provided some starting code and data, and then tune their own programs to reflect findings in the data. Users often provide positive and negative feedback to tweak the algorithm's models and improve results, as when teams accept or reject TAR results throughout an e-discovery process. Importantly, machine learning algorithms perform what appear to be human tasks—like classifying documents for privilege—using different underlying processes than those used by human cognition. Harry Surden calls this

5. Visit http://www.pictograph.us to try a deep learning labeling prototype application on your Instagram feed.

6. *New Navy Device Learns by Doing*, N.Y. Times, July 8, 1958, at 25, http://timesmachine.nytimes.com/timesmachine/1958/07/08/issue.html.

an "outcome-oriented view of intelligence"[7]: the final result may look like human cognition, but under the hood it's just statistical correlations or linear algebra. Finally, when we say that algorithms "learn," we mean that they perform a given task with higher levels of statistical accuracy. For example, they go from labeling a photo as containing an image of a dog with 50 percent confidence to providing the label with 95 percent confidence. This is a far cry from learning understood as synthesizing conclusions across different knowledge domains.

Neural networks differ from the machine-learning methods currently used for TAR. First, they have a unique underlying architecture designed to mimic the brain. Neural networks are composed of individual computational units called neurons that are connected within and across different layers. When a neural network receives some input data (e.g., an image of a dog), it maps features of this data into

FIGURE 20.1 Diagram from Torch, an open source deep learning program[8]

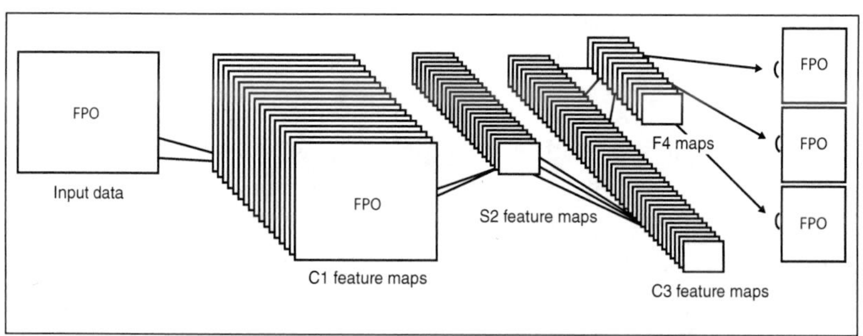

mathematical vectors and sends the vectors to a neuron. The neuron processes the vector information to look for mathematical similarity with a given output or classification tag (e.g., the classification dog). If the input data has features that map to the right classification, it fires and passes on the classification tag; if not, it doesn't fire. The networks are considered deep because they have multiple computing layers, which enable them to transform data multiple times to reach

7. Harry Surden, *Machine Learning and Law*, 89 Wash. L. Rev. 95 (2014).

8. Koray Kavukcuoglu, *Torch7: Scientific Computing for Lua(JIT)* (July 7, 2015), https://github.com/soumith/cvpr2015/blob/master/cvpr-torch.pdf.

a useful level of generalization. This is crucial to process data like photographs, given the density and complexity of pixels in an image.

Next, neural networks learn because they can process information in two directions. Forward, they transform input data into labels and classifications; backwards, they update mathematical formulas if the classifications doesn't match the correct labels provided in an initial training set.[9] The combination of the layered abstraction and the fine tuning provides neural networks their astonishing ability to do things like differentiate a Pembroke Welsh Corgi from a Cardigan Welsh Corgi in an image data set,[10] or provide real-time captions on the objects a cameraman sees as he strolls down the Amsterdam canals.[11] The machine learning methods employed for TAR today do not need so many layers of abstraction and use different statistical techniques to improve classification tasks over time.

How Might Law Firms Apply Deep Learning?

While different industries are just beginning to explore deep learning's potential, there is one application with which we are all already familiar. While at Bell Labs, Yann LeCun (who currently leads Facebook AI Research) used deep learning to develop the system that parses handwriting on checks to automate deposits into bank accounts from ATMs. The fact that this is so familiar tells us something about technology adoption: not all emerging capabilities become widespread commodities, but habit gradually dulls the veneer of those that do. Five years from now, we may retrospectively consider legal deep-learning applications to be as commonplace as check recognition in ATMs.

But as we peer into the near future, there are a few legal tasks that stand out as good candidates for deep-learning applications:

---

9. Most deep learning applications employ supervised learning, where networks begin with a training set that includes data correctly labeled by humans. Some employ unsupervised learning, where networks induce patterns on their own from data sets. Some employ a hybrid approach involving both techniques.

10. Raffi Khatchadourian, *The Doomsday Invention*, The New Yorker, Nov. 23, 2015, http://www.newyorker.com/magazine/2015/11/23/doomsday-invention-artificial-intelligence-nick-bostrom.

11. Kyle McDonald, *NeuralTalk and Walk*, https://vimeo.com/146492001 (last visited Aug. 1, 2016).

- **Mixed-Media Discovery.** Current e-discovery platforms are mostly only able to analyze text. Certain litigation practice areas, like medical malpractice or insurance defense, are apt to include visual media as relevant evidence (e.g., damage from a car accident). Deep learning could automate discovery of relevant image data, or even suggest instants within videos or audio transcriptions that merit subsequent analysis.
- **Text Summarization.** As firms go paperless, they struggle to discern what information they have in the vast quantities of unstructured data on the document management system (DMS), Sharepoint portal, or file shares. Knowing what is there is a crucial first step for knowledge management or information governance initiatives. One variety of neural network can be trained to recognize key sentences in documents and extract them out to automatically provide abstracts of document content. This can quicken legal research timeframes, facilitate knowledge management, and help compliance teams identify sensitive information to satisfy client requirements.
- **Text Classification.** Text classification is not new to law. Neural networks are more sophisticated than binary (is this document relevant or not?) classifiers, and could potentially be trained to classify documents on a continuum from somewhat relevant, highly relevant, or not relevant at all. Deep learning could also help expand classification beyond discovery to more general information governance, automatically classifying documents into different levels of sensitivity (e.g., subject to privacy regulations, client confidential, work product, etc.) or for records retention and disposal.[12] Researchers are currently exploring which neural network structure is best apt for text classification.
- **Information Security.** Security practitioners analyze data on systems to identify anomalous behavior that might signal a

12. The computer science research community is still exploring which deep learning technique performs best at text classification. LeCun's group at New York University recently demonstrated success using neural networks to classify texts at the character (letter) level, requiring no artificially embedded knowledge of the meaning of words, phrases, sentences, or syntactical structures. *See* Xiang Zhang and Yann LeCun, *Text Understanding from Scratch* (paper published by the Computer Science Department at New York University, Sept. 8, 2015), http://arxiv.org/pdf/1502.01710v4.pdf.

server failure, an impending lateral departure, internal snooping, or an external hack. Deep learning is a good technique for anomaly detection because systems can be trained to understand normal operating conditions and provide alerts when something deviates from the norm.[13]

Practical and Ethical Considerations

In November 2015, Google released a deep-learning tool called TensorFlow to the open source community.[14] While pundits hailed this as a watershed moment for deep learning, most practitioners thought it confirmed that the future of the technology resides in data rather than code.[15] (Google won't be giving away its proprietary data anytime soon.) Indeed, one reason why deep learning is taking off now is that there is much more data available to train neural networks, as the layers perform best when trained on hundreds or thousands of examples. It's safe to say that no law firm processes as much data as tech giants like Google and Facebook. As such, firms may struggle to find data sets that are big enough, clean enough, and varied enough to make deep learning useful (unless they purchase and adapt a pre-trained system from a vendor).

Absent adequate training data, a neural network will fail to give high-confidence results on classification or prediction tasks. Even a well-trained neural network will not provide perfect accuracy, but only probable confidence of success on a task. For computer vision, for example, accuracy rates of greater than 85 percent are considered cutting edge. Before employing deep learning systems, therefore, law firms should consider the following questions:

---

13. A vendor called Lookout offers a product that integrates with mobile device management (MDM) solutions and uses deep learning to predict potential security breaches on mobile devices.

14. *TensorFlow: Smarter Machine Learning, for Everyone*, GOOGLE OFFICIAL BLOG, Nov. 9, 2015, https://googleblog.blogspot.com/2015/11/tensorflow-smarter-machine-learning-for.html.

15. Cade Metz, *Google's Open-sourcing TensorFlow shows AI's Future Is Data*, WIRED, Nov. 16, 2015, http://www.wired.com/2015/11/google-open-sourcing-tensorflow-shows-ais-future-is-data-not-code/. Note that Metz interviewed Lukas Biewald, CEO of CrowdFlower, whose business is built on providing data sets for machine learning purposes.

- For which classification or research tasks are strong approximations "good enough"?
- What probability threshold will we accept as a sufficient level of quality?
- What data do we already have and what data do we need to achieve the accuracy levels we desire for our model?
- How should lawyers and staff subsequently process classifications that don't meet the set threshold? And those that do?
- How should lawyers collaborate with IT to improve deep learning models and modify legal process workflows?
- What kind of legal and IT talent should the firm hire to deploy deep-learning technologies successfully?

The exponential growth of electronic information should ultimately provide firms with enough data to train neural networks to desired accuracy levels, especially as software vendors tailor products to data types encountered by law firms, rendering higher performance and easier adoption.

As electronic data continues to grow, we also may have no choice but to adopt deep learning or other TAR tools. Multiple empirical studies have already shown how existing methods for TAR outperform manual review on classification tasks.[16] Similar results have been reached in computer vision competitions, where deep-learning tools built by Google, Microsoft, and Baidu have identified objects in a database called ImageNet with a lower error rate than humans (4.58 percent versus 5 percent error rates). If theory isn't convincing, litigation deadlines, cost, and client write-offs will practically force firms to abandon manual practices. The principle of proportionality now expressly embedded in Federal Rule 26(b)(1) exists to reduce e-discovery costs by only requiring parties to produce that information which is "relevant to any party's claim or defense and proportional to the needs of the case, considering the importance of the issues at stake in the action, the amount of the controversy . . . and whether the

16. Maura R. Grossman & Gordon V. Cormack, *Technology-Assisted Review in E-Discovery Can Be More Effective and More Efficient than Exhaustive Manual Review*, XVII Rich. J.L. & Tech. 11 (2011), http://jolt.richmond.edu/v17i3/article11.pdf.

burden or expense of the proposed discovery outweighs its likely benefit."[17] While proportionality and probability are not synonyms, this relativistic thinking can and should inspire firm thinking on the right way to use tools like deep learning.

Next, as adoption of machine intelligence progresses, lawyers should anticipate future commentary to the *Model Rules for Professional Conduct* regarding the ethical use of systems like deep learning. For example, the ABA 20/20 commission focused its updates on the risks new technology posed to client confidentiality,[18] and Comment 18 to Model Rule 1.6 (Confidentiality of Information) now includes a list of factors lawyers should consider to judge the reasonableness of efforts to prevent unauthorized disclosure of client information under the Rule's subparagraph (c).[19]

But deep-learning systems pose different risks. As we saw earlier, neural networks learn by providing feedback to adjust how individual nodes encode features in data. This simple strategy offers great computational power, but reveals nothing about what the numbers or connections between nodes actually mean. Therefore, if the network incorrectly encodes a feature about a data set, there is no easy way to find the bug and fix it.[20] Technologists will have no more luck interpreting neural networks than nontechnical lawyers, so the standard protocol of consulting an expert technologist won't provide total transparency. One potential risk is that firms will not be able to fully account for their methodology should there be a dispute over document

17. Fed. R Civ. P., R. 26(b)(1), https://www.law.cornell.edu/rules/frcp/rule_26.

18. ABA Commission on Ethics 20/20, Report to the House of Delegates, at 5. http://www.americanbar.org/content/dam/aba/administrative/ethics_2020/2012_hod_annual_meeting_105a_filed_may_2012.authcheckdam.pdf.

19. *See* http://www.americanbar.org/groups/professional_responsibility/publications/model_rules_of_professional_conduct/rule_1_6_confidentiality_of_information/comment_on_rule_1_6.html.

20. For example, Google's image recognition software recently tagged two people of color as "gorillas," and labeled a photo of a concentration camp at Auschwitz as a "jungle gym." Due to the complexity of the system, the quick fix for the gorilla result was simply to eliminate the tag "gorilla" from the system. *See* Jana Kasperkevic, *Google Says Sorry for Racist Auto-tag in Photo App*, The Guardian, July 1, 2015, http://www.theguardian.com/technology/2015/jul/01/google-sorry-racist-auto-tag-photo-app.

production. When exploring machine learning approaches, therefore, firms should consider the tradeoff between accuracy and interpretability. Because neural networks are uninterpretable, firms may wish to elect a less powerful but more transparent approach (like TAR methods currently available on the market). Lawyers should have a say in these choices, and may need to consult with clients on preferences.

Finally, the introduction of deep learning will likely continue to modify how courts define the authorized "practice of law." On July 23, 2015, the U.S. Court of Appeals for the Second Circuit decided *Lola v. Skadden, Arps, Slate, Meagher & Flom LLP, et al*,[21] whose primary takeaway for our purposes is the standard that the Second Circuit laid out for what constitutes legal work:

> A fair reading of the complaint in the light most favorable to Lola is that he provided services that a machine could have provided. The parties themselves agreed at oral argument that an individual who, in the course of reviewing discovery documents, undertakes tasks that could otherwise be performed entirely by a machine cannot be said to engage in the practice of law.[22]

In this case, David Lola, a lawyer licensed to practice in the State of California, took a position as a document reviewer for Skadden working on a case where review took place entirely in the state of North Carolina.[23] Lola typically worked 45 to 55 hours a week, and was paid no overtime. He eventually sued on behalf of himself and others similarly situated for violations of the Fair Labor Standards Act. The legal question presented was whether Lola did the right kind of work to be entitled overtime (i.e., that by reviewing documents using a method by which he input terms already selected by a supervising lawyer, he was not practicing law).

---

21. 620 Fed. Appx. 37, 2015 WL 4476828 (2d Cir. July 23, 2015).

22. *Id.* at 45, 2015 WL 4476828 at *6.

23. Bernie Burk, *When Is Document Review the "Practice of Law," and When Is It the "UNAUTHORIZED Practice of Law"? The Answers May Surprise You*, THE FACULTY LOUNGE, July 24, 2015, http://www.thefacultylounge.org/2015/07/when-is-document-review-the-practice-of-law-and-when-is-it-the-unauthorized-practice-of-law-the-answ.html.

In his analysis of the case, Burk references that the practice of law under North Carolina law must involve "'at least a modicum of legal judgment' by applying general legal principles to a specific client's particular circumstances."[24] This principle has been active in other recent cases involving the shifting use of technology to practice law, with automated document assembly provider Legalzoom, Inc. using it to skirt accusations of the unauthorized practice of law (UPL) by categorizing its services under the "scrivener exception."[25]

I agree with Burk that using machine capabilities as a bright line test to gauge the outer limits of practicing law may become an increasingly flawed standard.[26] As this article has shown, technologies like deep learning are evolving at a very rapid pace and already exhibit results that appear like legal judgments regarding privilege and responsiveness. The fact that these machine learning tools often employ an initial supervised approach, building statistical models using input from manual legal judgments, also implicates more than a "modicum" of legal judgment in the very mechanisms of the machine. Adopting an entirely unsupervised approach, where the machine builds its own models from the data, could potentially shift the legal argument, but it would only increase the ambiguity as to whether machines can exercise what looks like legal judgment and, therefore, exercise UPL. One theoretical question *Lola* forces the community to ask is whether the probabilistic methods that underscore most intelligent systems could qualify as "legal practice" if their methods to derive results differ from the analogical reasoning or the application of general principles to particular facts that we consider the higher-order cognitive processes underpinning legal thought. The more practical question, of course, is the economic impact firms in the Second Circuit would face if forced to shift overtime compensation structures for document review and

---

24. The same holds in most other states: http://www.americanbar.org/content/dam/aba/migrated/cpr/model-def/model_def_statutes.authcheckdam.pdf.

25. LegalZoom.com, Inc. v. N. Carolina State Bar, 2014 WL 1213242 (Super. Ct. N.C. Mar. 24, 2014).

26. *See also* Noah Waisberg & Robin McNamara, *I Think Therefore I am a Lawyer? Implications of Lola v. Skadden for Document Reviewers and Their Computer Replacements*, Kira Systems Blog (Aug. 26, 2015), http://info.kirasystems.com/blog/implications-of-lola-v-skadden-for-lawyers-practicing-document-review-and-machines-practicing-law.

other paralegal work. It may after all be practical constraints that usher the age of machine intelligence in law.

Conclusion

In his dismissal of the projected adoption of machine intelligence in the Altman Weil survey, K&L Gates chair Peter Kalis was quoted as saying the only thing he knew for certain was that "one hundred percent of law firm leaders don't know anything about AI."[27] As new data technologies like deep learning have the potential to modify how firms conduct research, discovery, and knowledge management, staying competent under Model Rule 1.1 may well one day embrace the need for lawyers to have an understanding of "the benefits and risks associated with relevant [deep learning]technology."[28] As we've seen, the greatest near-term risk of deep learning is not a dystopia where machines replace paralegals and first-year associates. Rather, it is that the profession won't understand the various machine intelligence options well enough to inform technology choices that balance client service with the firm's appetite for risk.

27. *See* Matt Moody, *Will Computers Soon Replace Junior Lawyers? No*, VAULT (Oct. 26, 2015), http://www.vault.com/blog/vaults-law-blog-legal-careers-and-industry-news/will-computers-soon-replace-junior-lawyers-no.

28. ABA MODEL RULES OF PROF'L CONDUCT, R. 1.1, Cmt 8, http://www.americanbar.org/groups/professional_responsibility/publications/model_rules_of_professional_conduct/rule_1_1_competence/comment_on_rule_1_1.html.

EDITORS' INTRODUCTION TO THE APPENDIX

Michael D. Berman

As the Hon. John M. Facciola points out, Oliver Wendell Holmes, Jr., wrote, "A word is not a crystal, transparent and unchanged; it is the skin of a living thought and may vary greatly in color and content according to the circumstances and time in which it is used."[1] Judge Facciola explains: "The legal system deals in words and the pace of technological process is creating billions of them on a nearly daily basis, creating a set of problems that were unimaginable a few years ago."

Other chapters in this book make the case for consistent terminology.[2] The authors note that "fostering a common terminology is a noble goal." The need is acute in this area. The glossary contained in this Appendix is perhaps the most comprehensive effort to do so.

1. Towne v. Eisner, 245 U.S. 418, 425 (1918) (citation omitted).
2. *See e.g.*, Chapter 15 in this volume.

Appendix: The Grossman-Cormack Glossary of Technology-Assisted Review*

with Foreword by John M. Facciola, U.S. Magistrate Judge

Foreword

"When I *use a word," Humpty Dumpty said, in rather a scornful tone, "it means just what I choose it to mean—neither more nor less." "The question is," said Alice, "whether you* can *make words mean so many different things."*

Lewis Carroll, *Through the Looking Glass, What Alice Found There*[1]

"A word is not a crystal, transparent and unchanged, it is the skin of a living thought and may vary greatly in color and content according to the circumstances and the time in which it is used."

Justice Oliver Wendell Holmes Jr., *Towne v. Eisner*, 245 U.S. 418, 425 (1918)

---

*Maura R. Grossman & Gordon V. Cormack, The Grossman-Cormack Glossary of Technology-Assisted Review, with a Foreword by John M. Facciola, U.S. Magistrate Judge (Ret.), was first published in 7 FED. COURTS L. REV. 1 (2013), http://www.fclr.org/fclr/articles/html/2010/grossman.pdf. It is reprinted here with permission.

1. THE COLLECTED STORIES OF LEWIS CARROLL 238 (Citadel Press 1994).

In the heels of the higgling lawyers, Bob,
Too many slippery ifs and buts and howevers,
Too much hereinbefore provided whereas,
Too many doors to go in and out of.
When the lawyers are through
What is there left, Bob?
Can a mouse nibble at it
And find enough to fasten a tooth in?

Carl Sandburg, *The Lawyers Know Too Much*[2]

It is always the words. Humpty Dumpty, Holmes, and Sandburg, who sensed the power of language instinctively, knew how quickly their meanings can slip away. What seemed clear when the contract or statute was drafted is now recondite. When the parties contracted to buy and sell a horse, did they mean a mare or a stallion? When the statute required that a lawyer be disbarred upon conviction of a crime of moral turpitude, did the legislature mean a lawyer who gets convicted of assault after a brawl in a bar? Lawyers and judges are mocked for their continued use of Latin but they know that it is so much easier to say "res judicata" and take advantage of the encrusted meaning of those words than to start fresh and try to improve on what they convey. Law books come and go but Black's Law Dictionary will always be around. The words, as Paul Simon might put it, keep "slip, sliding away."[3]

It is hard enough when the world in which the words are used remains static, like the farm on which the horse, be it mare or stallion, lives. But, what happens when the movement of technology radically transforms what a word might have once meant? What is the "original" of an e-mail? Is another e-mail a copy of it when the visible text is the same but the metadata created in its production by a computer, rather than a human being, is entirely different? What happens when the meaning of the words in a statute applied to a process that was in existence when the statute was enacted but now no longer exists? Some of the

2. The Complete Poems of Carl Sandburg 189 (Harcourt, Brace and Co., rev. ed. 1970).

3. Paul Simon, *Slip Slidin' Away*, on The Essential Paul Simon (Warner Bros. 2007).

definitions in the Stored Communications Act,[4] enacted in 1986, may drive judges to distraction since they were premised on technology used in 1986 but is no longer and must be applied to new processes that no one knew would exist when the statute was enacted. What kind of words can be used in a statute or a rule that are capacious enough to hold their meaning despite unknown technological change but precise enough to convey a definite meaning? It may be hard to believe, but there was not even a clear indication in the Federal Rules of Civil Procedure until 2006 that "electronically stored information" was within the scope of what a party had to produce in discovery.[5] Indeed, until 2006, the word "phonorecords" appeared in Federal Rules of Civil Procedure 34(a)[6] which must have, at the time,[7] mystified anyone under 35.

The pace of technological change makes the situation worse. That pace is astonishing. What was thought to be the impossible crossing of the

---

4. *See, e.g.*, The definition of "remote computing service" in 18 U.S.C. § 2711(2) ("the provision to the public of computer storage or processing services by means of electronic communications systems"). As Professor Orin Kerr explains, the statute "freez[es] into law the understanding of computer network use as of 1986." Orin S. Kerr, *A User's Guide to the Stored Communications Act, and a Legislator's Guide to Amending It*, 72 Geo. Wash. L. Rev. 1208, 1214 (2004). In 1986, users would use remote computing services to outsource computing tasks such as storing extra files or processing data when doing so was beyond the capacity of their computers. *Id.* Given the storage and processing capacities of new computers and tablets, this kind of distant processing capacity has disappeared. In its wake, however, are the difficult questions of the application of the definitions in the Stored Communications Act to "cloud computing." *See* William Jeremy Robison, *Free at What Cost? Cloud Computing Privacy under the Stored Communications Act*, 98 Geo. L.J. 1195, 1210, 1212-13 (2010).

5. *Compare* Fed. R. Civ. P. 34(a)(1)(A) (West 2006 rev. ed.) (describing "any designated documents or electronically stored information—including writings, drawings, graphs, charts, photographs, sound recordings, images, and other data or data compilations—stored in any medium from which information can be obtained either directly or, if necessary, after translation by the responding party into a reasonably usable form" as discoverable) *with* Fed. R. Civ. P. 34(a)(1)(A) (West 2006) (mentioning only "any designated documents (including writings, drawings, graphs, charts, photographs, phonorecords, and other data compilations from which information can be obtained, translated, if necessary, by the respondent through detection devices into reasonably usable form").

6. Fed. R. Civ. P. 34(a)(1)(A) (West 2006).

7. Vinyl records are making a comeback; eight track tapes will not. *See, e.g.*, Brian Passey, *Vinyl Records spin back into vogue*, USAToday.com (Feb. 26, 2011).

Atlantic Ocean in a plane and the landing of a man on the moon occurred in my father's lifetime. Yet, George Washington's troops moved no faster than Caesar's, and it took thousands of years before human beings discovered how to transmit messages by the telegraph using electricity.[8] Until then, a messenger, whether from Marathon to Athens, or through the colonial towns of Massachusetts, had to deliver them by hand.

The legal system deals in words and the pace of technological process is creating billions of them on a nearly daily basis,[9] creating a set of problems that were unimaginable a few years ago.

The first problem is that this explosion of words has been matched by the ever-increasing capacity of machines to capture and preserve them. It is a simple fact that an iPod has much more memory, i.e., capability to store information indefinitely, than the first computer[10] which took up an entire room. Additionally, the cost of storage is diminishing. A one-terabyte drive can be purchased for about $100[11] and can hold what would otherwise be hundreds of thousands of pages of paper. Indeed, now the information can be kept on a distant server with the space rented from a vendor for that purpose and retrieved by use of the Internet ("cloud computing"). For the first time, it is cheaper for human beings to buy a new file cabinet and keep more paper than to clean the useless clutter out of the old file cabinet to make room for the new information.

This phenomenon has led to the consequence that litigants are confronted with the often horrifying costs of searching through immense amounts of data to find what they need. The Federal Rules of Civil Procedure contemplate a system of demand and production; plaintiff asks for all documents pertaining to the merger of companies A and B and defendant either objects or produces them. But, when there are now hundreds of thousands of documents that may meet the definition of "pertinent," how can defendant find them and not go bankrupt

8. *See* Tom Standage, The Victorian Internet (Walker & Co. 1998).

9. *See* George L. Paul & Jason R. Baron, *Information Inflation: Can the Legal System Adapt?*, 13 Rich. J.L. & Tech. 10, 14-23 (2007).

10. *See, e.g., What is a Mainframe Operating System?*, Wisegeek, http://www.wisegeek.com/what-is-a-mainframe-operating-system.htm (last visited Nov. 19, 2012).

11. *See* Amazon, http://www.amazon.com/s/ref=nb_sb_ss_i_1_7?url=search-alias%3Daps&field-keywords=1+terabyte+hard+drive&sprefix=1+terab%2Caps%2C227 (listing numerous options under $100 for a one-terabyte external hard drive).

in the process? Of course, defendant may be the victim of its own failure to maintain a responsible record-keeping process in which a principled decision-making process guides what will be kept and what will be thrown out. And, as anyone knows who has ever cleaned out a closet or an old hard drive, keeping everything is no solution. It only increases the expense and cost of finding what you want or need. Nevertheless, the affordability of cheap storage has led too many entities in our society to be quickly overwhelmed by their inability to search for what they need, whether because they need it to run their business or because they must produce it in discovery. They may find that the cost of searching and producing is so great that settling the lawsuit may be the only way out of an otherwise impossible situation.

It is understandable that, nature and technology abhorring a vacuum, a new scientific methodology has emerged to aid in the collection and searching process. "Technology-Assisted Review," called by its nickname "Predictive Coding," describes a process whereby computers are programmed to search a large amount of data to find quickly and efficiently the data that meet a particular requirement. Computer science and the sciences of statistics and psychology inform its use. While it bruises the human ego, scientists, including the authors of this glossary we are publishing, have determined that machines are better at the task of making such discoveries than humans.[12] Lawyers love to think that there is no substitute for their reviewing each document page by page. Not only is there a substitute, but an improvement. It is now indubitable that technology-assisted review is an appreciably better and more accurate means of searching a set of data.[13] That is hardly surprising news to those judges and lawyers who have experienced the mind-numbing tedium of reviewing large data sets only to find that one is seeing the same e-mail chain again and again, or worse, wading through mountains of data and finding nothing of any pertinence to the case being litigated.

The great benefits of technology-assisted review, however, bring in new concerns and questions for judges and lawyers. In a paper universe, the manner in which a party searched through a file cabinet hardly raises

12. *See* Maura R. Grossman & Gordon V. Cormack, *Technology-Assisted Review in EDiscovery Can Be More Effective and Efficient Than Exhaustive and Manual Review*, XVII RICH. J.L. & TECH. 11 (2011).

13. *Id.*

any significant issues. If what was produced appeared to be what was demanded and there were no inexplicable gaps, that was that and the court and parties moved on to other things. Now, the methodology of the use of technology-assisted review may itself be in dispute, with the parties controverted to each other's use of a particular method or tool. Those controversies have already lead to judicial decisions that have to grapple with a wholly new way of searching and with scientific principles derived from the science of statistics or other disciplines.[14] Lawyers and judges once again have to learn a whole new vocabulary to resolve the emerging and inevitable battle of the "experts."

To aid in the creation of that vocabulary, we publish with pride the glossary created by Maura R. Grossman and Gordon V. Cormack who are two of the most respected and acknowledged experts in this field. We agree with them that the creation of a clear and common vocabulary is essential to a comprehension of the legal issues at stake.

We are particularly gratified that the authors announced that they intend the glossary to be interactive so that others can suggest additional clarifications, revisions, and additions. We are certain that, if the experience of the courts in the first few years of the information technology revolution is any guide, the learning curve will be steep and that it must be climbed quickly if courts are going to be able to resolve promptly the controversies before them at the least expense. We are equally certain that the bench and bar will find this glossary useful as this new science develops and grows.

The Editors of the Federal Courts Law Review

By John M. Facciola, U.S. Magistrate Judge

14. *See, e.g.*, EORHB, Inc. v. HOA Holdings, Civ. Ac. No. 7409-VCL (Del. Ch. Oct. 19, 2012); Kleen Prods. LLC v. Packaging Corp., Civ. No. 10C 5711, 2012 WL 4498465 at *84-85 (N.D. Ill. Sept. 28, 2012); In re Actos (Pioglitazone) Prods. Liab. Litig., MDL No. 6:11-md-2299 (W.D. La. July 27, 2012); Global Aerospace Inc. v. Landow Aviation, L.P., No. CL 61040 (Va. Cir. Ct. Apr. 23, 2012); Moore v. Publicis Groupe & MSL Group, No. 11 Civ. 1279 (ACL) (AJP), 2012 WL 607412 (S.D.N.Y. Feb. 24, 2012).

Preamble

"Disruptive technology" is a term that was coined by Harvard Business School Professor Clayton M. Christensen, in his 1997 book, *The Innovator's Dilemma*, to describe a new technology that unexpectedly displaces an established technology. The term is used in business and technology literature to describe innovations that improve a product or service in ways that the market did not expect, typically by designing for a different set of consumers in the new market and later, by lowering prices in the existing market. Products based on disruptive technologies are typically cheaper to produce, simpler, smaller, better performing, more reliable, and often more convenient to use. Technology-Assisted Review (TAR) is such a disruptive technology. Because disruptive technologies differ from sustaining technologies–ones that rely on incremental improvements to established technologies–they bring with them new features, new vernaculars, and other challenges.

The introduction of TAR into the legal community has brought with it much confusion because different terms are being used to refer to the same thing (e.g., "technology-assisted review," "computer-assisted review," "computer-aided review," "predictive coding," and "content-based advanced analytics," to name but a few), and the same terms are also being used to refer to different things (e.g., "seed set" and "control sample"). Moreover, the introduction of complex statistical concepts and terms of art from the science of information retrieval have resulted in widespread misunderstanding and sometimes perversion of their intended meanings.

This glossary is written in an effort to bring order to chaos by introducing a common framework and set of definitions for use by the bench, the bar, and service providers. This glossary endeavors to be comprehensive, but its definitions are necessarily brief. Interested readers may look elsewhere for detailed information concerning any of these topics. The terms in this glossary are presented in alphabetical order, with defined terms in capital letters.

We envision this glossary to be a living, breathing work that will evolve over time. Towards that end, we invite our colleagues in the industry to send us comments on our definitions, as well as any additional terms they would like to see included in the glossary, so that we can reach a consensus on a consistent, common language relating to TAR. Comments can be sent to us at mrgrossman@wlrk.com and gvcormac@uwaterloo.ca. Subsequent versions of this glossary will be available online at http://cormack.uwaterloo.ca/targlossary/.

The authors would like to acknowledge the helpful comments provided by Craig Ball, Michael Levine, Ralph Losey, Amir Milo, and Keith Roland on an earlier draft of this work. We are very grateful to Magistrate Judge John M. Facciola for his enthusiastic support.

We hope that you will find this glossary useful.

Maura R. Grossman*
Wachtell, Lipton, Rosen & Katz
New York, New York

Gordon V. Cormack
University of Waterloo
Waterloo, Ontario

January 2013

The Glossary

Accept on Zero Error: A technique in which the training of a Machine Learning method is gauged by taking a Sample after each training step, and deeming the training process complete when the learning method codes a Sample with 0% Error (i.e., 100% Accuracy).

Accuracy: The fraction of Documents that are correctly coded by a search or review effort. Note that Accuracy + Error = 100%, and that Accuracy = 100% – Error. While high Accuracy is commonly advanced as evidence of an effective search or review effort, its use can be misleading because it is heavily influenced by Prevalence. Consider, for example, a Document Population containing one million Documents, of which ten thousand (or 1%) are Relevant. A search or review effort that identified 100% of the Documents as Not Relevant, and, therefore, found *none* of the Relevant Documents, would have 99% Accuracy, belying the failure of that search or review effort.

* The views expressed herein are solely those of the author and should not be attributed to her firm or its clients. [Eds. note: Maura R. Grossman is currently at the University of Waterloo and can be reached at maura.grossman@uwaterloo.ca.]

Active Learning: An Iterative Training regimen in which the Training Set is repeatedly augmented by additional Documents chosen by the Machine Learning Algorithm, and coded by one or more Subject Matter Expert(s).

Actos: *See* In Re: Actos.

Agreement: The fraction of all Documents that two reviewers code the same way. While high Agreement is commonly advanced as evidence of an effective review effort, its use can be misleading, for the same reason that the use of Accuracy can be misleading. When the vast majority of Documents in a Population are Not Relevant, a high level of Agreement will be achieved when the reviewers agree that these Documents are Not Relevant, irrespective of whether or not they agree that any of the Relevant Documents are Relevant.

Algorithm: A formally specified series of computations that, when executed, accomplishes a particular goal. The Algorithms used in E-Discovery are implemented as computer software.

Area Under the ROC Curve (AUC): From Signal Detection Theory, a summary measure used to assess the quality of Prioritization. AUC is the Probability that a randomly chosen Relevant Document is given a higher priority than a randomly chosen Non-Relevant Document. An AUC score of 100% indicates a perfect ranking, in which all Relevant Documents have higher priority than all Non-Relevant Documents. An AUC score of 50% means the Prioritization is no better than chance.

Artificial Intelligence: An umbrella term for computer methods that emulate human judgment. These include Machine Learning and Knowledge Engineering, as well as Pattern Matching (e.g., voice, face, and handwriting recognition), robotics, and game playing.

Bag of Words: A Feature Engineering method in which the Features of each Document comprise the set of words contained in that Document. Documents are determined to be Relevant or Not Relevant depending on what words they contain. Elementary Keyword Search and Boolean Search methods, as well as some Machine Learning methods, use the Bag of Words model.

Bayes / Bayesian / Bayes' Theorem: A general term used to describe Algorithms and other methods that estimate the overall Probability of some eventuality (e.g., that a Document is Relevant), based on the combination of evidence gleaned from separate observations. In Electronic Discovery, the most common evidence that is combined is the occurrence of particular words in a Document. For example, a Bayesian Algorithm might combine the evidence gleaned from the fact that a Document contains the words "credit," "default," and "swap" to indicate that there is a 99% Probability that the Document concerns financial derivatives, but only a 40% Probability if the words "credit" and "default," but not "swap," are present. The most elementary Bayesian Algorithm is Naïve Bayes; however, most Algorithms dubbed "Bayesian" are more complex. Bayesian Algorithms are named after Bayes' Theorem, coined by the 18th century mathematician, Thomas Bayes. Bayes' Theorem derives the Probability of an outcome, given the evidence, from: (i) the probability of the outcome, independent of the evidence; (ii) the probability of the evidence, given the outcome; and (iii) the probability of the evidence, independent of the outcome.

Bayesian Classifier / Bayesian Filter / Bayesian Learning: A colloquial term used to describe a Machine Learning Algorithm that uses a Bayesian Algorithm resembling Naïve Bayes.

Bigram: An N-Gram where N = 2 (i.e., a 2-gram).

Binomial Calculator / Binomial Estimation: A statistical method used to calculate Confidence Intervals, based on the Binomial Distribution, that models the random selection of Documents from a large Population. Binomial Estimation is generally more accurate, but less well known, than Gaussian Estimation. A Binomial Estimate is substantially better than a Gaussian Estimate (which, in contrast, relies on the Gaussian or Normal Distribution) when there are few (or no) Relevant Documents in the Sample. When there are many Relevant and many Non-Relevant Documents in the Sample, Binomial and Gaussian Estimates are nearly identical.

Binomial Distribution: The Probability that a Random Sample from a large Population will contain any particular number of Relevant Documents, given the Prevalence of Relevant Documents in the Population. Used as the basis for Binomial Estimation.

Binomial Estimate: A Statistical Estimate of a Population characteristic using Binomial Estimation. It is generally expressed as a Point Estimate accompanied by a Margin of Error and a Confidence

Level, or as a Confidence Interval accompanied by a Confidence Level.

Blair and Maron: Authors of an influential 1985 study (David C. Blair & M.E. Maron, *An Evaluation of Retrieval Effectiveness for a Full-Text Document-Retrieval System*, 28 Commc'ns Acm 289 (1985)), showing that attorneys supervising skilled paralegals believed they had found at least 75% of the Relevant Documents from a Document Collection, using search terms and iterative search, when they had in fact found only 20%. That is, the searchers believed they had achieved 75% Recall, but had achieved only 20% Recall. In the Blair and Maron study, the attorneys and paralegals used an iterative approach, examining the retrieved Documents and refining their search terms until they believed they were done. Many current commentators incorrectly distinguish the Blair and Maron study from current iterative approaches, failing to note that the Blair and Maron searchers did in fact refine their search terms based on their review of the Documents that were returned in response to their queries.

Boolean Search: A Keyword Search in which the Keywords are combined using operators such as "AND," "OR," and "[BUT] NOT." The result of a Boolean Search is precisely determined by the words contained in the Documents. (*See also* Bag of Words.)

Bulk Coding: The process of Coding all members of a group of Documents (identified, for example, by Deduplication, Near-Deduplication, Email Threading, or Clustering) based on the review of only one or a few members of the group. Also referred to as Bulk Tagging.

Bulk Tagging: *See* Bulk Coding.

Classical, Gaussian, or Normal Calculator / Classical, Gaussian, or Normal Estimation: A method of calculating Confidence Intervals based on the assumption that the quantities to be measured follow a Gaussian (Normal) Distribution. This method is most commonly taught in introductory statistics courses, but yields inaccurate Confidence Intervals when the Prevalence of items with the characteristic being measured is low. (*Cf.* Binomial Calculator / Binomial Estimation.)

Classifier / Classification / Classified / Classify: An Algorithm that Labels items as to whether or not they have a particular property; the act of Labeling items as to whether or not they have a particular property. In Technology-Assisted Review, Classifiers are commonly used to Label Documents as Responsive or Non-Responsive.

Clustering: An Unsupervised Learning method in which Documents are segregated into categories or groups so that the Documents in any group are more similar to one another than to those in other groups. Clustering involves no human intervention, and the resulting categories may or may not reflect distinctions that are valuable for the purpose of a search or review effort.

Code / Coded / Coding: The action of Labeling a Document as Relevant or Non-Relevant, or the set of Labels resulting from that action. Sometimes interpreted narrowly to include only the result(s) of a Manual Review effort; sometimes interpreted more broadly to include automated or semi-automated Labeling efforts. Coding is generally the term used in the legal industry; Labeling is the equivalent term in Information Retrieval.

Collection: *See* Document Collection.

Computer-Aided Review: *See* Technology-Assisted Review.

Computer-Assisted Review (CAR): *See* Technology-Assisted Review.

Concept Search: An industry-specific term generally used to describe Keyword Expansion techniques, which allow search methods to return Documents beyond those that would be returned by a simple Keyword or Boolean Search. Methods range from simple techniques such as Stemming, Thesaurus Expansion, and Ontology search, through statistical Algorithms such as Latent Semantic Indexing.

Confidence Interval: As part of a Statistical Estimate, a range of values estimated to contain the true value, with a particular Confidence Level.

Confidence Level: As part of a Statistical Estimate, the chance that a Confidence Interval derived from a Random Sample will include the true value. For example, "95% Confidence" means that if one were to draw 100 independent Random Samples of the same size, and compute the Confidence Interval from each Sample, about 95 of the 100 Confidence Intervals would contain the true value. It is important to note that the Confidence Level is *not* the Probability that the true value is contained in any particular Confidence Interval; it is the Probability that the method of estimation will yield a Confidence Interval that contains the true value.

Confusion Matrix: A two-by-two table listing values for the number of True Negatives (TN), False Negatives (FN), True Positives (TP), and False Positives (FP) resulting from a search or review effort. As shown below, all of the standard evaluation measures are algebraic combinations of the four values in the Confusion Matrix. Also referred to as a Contingency Table. An example of a Confusion Matrix (or Contingency Table) is provided immediately below.

	Coded Relevant	Coded Non-Relevant
Truly Relevant	True Positives (TP)	False Negatives (FN)
Truly Non-Relevant	False Positives (FP)	True Negatives (TN)

Accuracy = 100% – Error = (TP + TN) / (TP + TN + FP + FN)

Elusion = 100% – Negative Predictive Value = FN / (FN + TN)

Error = 100% – Accuracy = (FP + FN) / (TP + TN + FP + FN)

Fallout = False Positive Rate = 100% – True Negative Rate = FP / (FP + TN)

False Negative Rate = 100% – True Positive Rate = FN / (FN + TP)

Negative Predictive Value = 100% – Elusion = TN / (TN + FN)

Precision = Positive Predictive Value = TP / (TP + FP)

Prevalence = Yield = Richness = (TP + FN) / (TP + TN + FP + FN)

Recall = True Positive Rate = Sensitivity = TP / (TP + FN)

True Negative Rate = Specificity = TN / (TN + FP)

Content-Based Advanced Analytics (CBAA): *See* Technology-Assisted Review.

Contingency Table: *See* Confusion Matrix.

Control Set: A Random Sample of Documents coded at the outset of a search or review process that is separate from and independent of the Training Set. Control Sets are used in some Technology-Assisted Review processes. They are typically used to measure the effectiveness of the Machine Learning Algorithm at various stages of training, and to determine when training may cease.

Crossover Trial: An Experimental Design for comparing two search or review processes using the same Document Collection and Information Need, in which one process is applied first, followed by the second, and then the results of the two efforts are compared. (*Cf.* Parallel Trial.)

Culling: The practice of narrowing a larger data set to a smaller data set for the purposes of review, based on objective criteria (such as file types or date restrictors), or subjective criteria (such as Keyword Search Terms). Documents that do not match the criteria are excluded from the search and from further review.

Cutoff: A given score or rank in a Prioritized list, resulting from a Relevance Ranking search or Machine Learning Algorithm, such that the Documents above the Cutoff are deemed to be Relevant and Documents below the Cutoff are deemed to be Non-Relevant. In general, a higher Cutoff will yield higher Precision and lower Recall, while a lower Cutoff will yield lower Precision and higher Recall. Also referred to as a Threshold.

Da Silva Moore: *Da Silva Moore* v. *Publicis Groupe*, Case No. 11 Civ. 1279 (ALC) (AJP), 2012 WL 607412 (S.D.N.Y. Feb. 24, 2012), *aff'd*, 2012 WL 1446534 (S.D.N.Y. Apr. 26, 2012). The first federal case to recognize Computer-Assisted Review as "an acceptable way to search for relevant ESI in appropriate cases." The opinion was written by Magistrate Judge Andrew J. Peck and affirmed by District Judge Andrew L. Carter.

Decision Tree: A step-by-step method of distinguishing between Relevant and Non-Relevant Documents, depending on what combination of words (or other Features) they contain. A Decision Tree to identify Documents pertaining to financial derivatives might first determine whether or not a Document contained the word "swap." If it did, the Decision Tree might then determine whether or not the Document contained the word "credit," and so on. A Decision Tree may be created through Knowledge Engineering or Machine Learning.

Deduplication: A method of replacing multiple identical copies of a Document by a single instance of that Document. Deduplication can occur within the data of a single custodian (also referred to as Vertical Deduplication), or across all custodians (also referred to as Horizontal Deduplication).

Dimensionality Reduction: A Feature Engineering method used to reduce the total number of Features considered by a Machine Learning Algorithm. Simple Dimensionality Reduction methods include Stemming and Stop Word elimination. More complex Dimensionality Reduction methods include Latent Semantic Indexing and Hashing.

Document: In the context of Electronic Discovery, a discrete item of Electronically Stored Information that may be the subject or result of a search or review effort.

Document Collection: The process of gathering Electronically Stored Information for search, review, and production; the set of Documents resulting from such a process. In many cases, the Document Collection and Document Population are the same; however, it is important to note that Document Population refers to the set of Documents over which a particular Statistical Estimate is calculated, which may be the entire Document Collection, a subset of the Document Collection (e.g., the documents with a particular file type or matching particular Search Terms), a superset of the Document Collection (e.g., the universe from which the Document Collection was gathered), or any combination thereof.

Document Population: The set of Electronically Stored Information or Documents about which a Statistical Estimate may be made.

Early Case Assessment (ECA): An industry-specific term generally used to describe a variety of tools or methods for investigating and quickly learning about a Document Collection for the purposes of estimating the risk(s) and cost(s) of pursuing a particular legal course of action.

EDI Study: *See* JASIST Study.

EDI-Oracle Study: An ongoing initiative (as of January 2013) of the Electronic Discovery Institute to evaluate participating vendors' search and document review efforts using a Document Collection contributed by Oracle America, Inc.

Electronic Discovery / E-Discovery: The process of identifying, preserving, collecting, processing, searching, reviewing, and producing Electronically Stored Information that may be Relevant to a civil, criminal, or regulatory matter.

Electronically Stored Information (ESI): Used in Federal Rule of Civil Procedure 34(a)(1)(A) to refer to discoverable information "stored in any medium from which the information can be obtained either directly or, if necessary, after translation by the responding party into a reasonably usable form." Although Rule 34(a)(1)(A) references "Documents or Electronically Stored Information," individual units of review and production are commonly referred to as Documents, regardless of the medium.

Elusion: The fraction of Documents identified as Non-Relevant by a search or review effort that are in fact Relevant. Elusion is estimated by taking a Random Sample from the Null Set and determining how many (or what Proportion of) Documents are actually Relevant. A low Elusion value has commonly been advanced as evidence of an effective search or review effort (*see, e.g., Kleen*), but that can be misleading because it quantifies only those Relevant Documents that have been *missed* by the search or review effort; it does not quantify the Relevant Documents *found* by the search or review effort (i.e., Recall). Consider, for example, a Document Population containing one million Documents, of which ten thousand (or 1%) are Relevant. A search or review effort that returned 1,000 Documents, none of which were Relevant, would have 1.001% Elusion, belying the failure of the search. Elusion = 100% – Negative Predictive Value.

Email Threading: Grouping together email messages that are part of the same discourse, so that they may be understood, reviewed, and coded consistently as a unit.

EORHB: *EORHB* v. *HOA Holdings LLC*, Civ. Action No. 7409-VCL, tr. and slip op. (Del. Ch. Oct. 19, 2012). The first case in which a court *sua sponte* directed the parties to use Predictive Coding as a replacement for Manual Review (or to show cause why this was not an appropriate case for Predictive Coding), absent either party's request to employ Predictive Coding. Vice Chancellor J. Travis Laster also ordered the parties to use the same E-Discovery vendor and to share a Document repository.

Error / Error Rate: The fraction of all Documents that are incorrectly coded by a search or review effort. Note that Accuracy + Error = 100%, and that 100% – Accuracy = Error. While a low Error Rate is commonly advanced as evidence of an effective search or review effort, its use can be misleading because it is heavily influenced by Prevalence. Consider, for example, a Document Population containing one million Documents, of which ten thousand (or 1%) are relevant. A search or review effort that found *none* of the relevant Documents would have 1% Error, belying the failure of the search or review effort.

ESI: *See* Electronically Stored Information.

Experimental Design: A standard procedure accepted in the scientific community for the evaluation of competing hypotheses. There are many valid experimental designs. Some that can be appropriate for evaluating Technology-Assisted Review processes include Crossover Trials and Parallel Trials.

F_1: The Harmonic Mean of Recall and Precision, often used in Information Retrieval studies as a measure of the effectiveness of a search or review effort, which accounts for the tradeoff between Recall and Precision. In order to achieve a high F_1 score, a search or review effort must achieve *both* high Recall and high Precision.

Fallout: *See* False Positive Rate.

False Negative (FN): A Relevant Document that is missed (i.e., incorrectly identified as Non-Relevant) by a search or review effort. Also known as a Miss.

False Negative Rate (FNR): The fraction (or Proportion) of Relevant Documents that are Missed (i.e., incorrectly identified as Non-Relevant) by a search or review effort. Note that False Negative Rate + Recall = 100%, and that 100% – Recall = False Negative Rate.

False Positive (FP): A Non-Relevant Document that is incorrectly identified as Relevant by a search or review effort.

False Positive Rate (FPR): The fraction (or Proportion) of Non-Relevant Documents that are incorrectly identified as Relevant by a search or review effort. Note that False Positive Rate + True Negative Rate = 100%, and that 100% – True Negative Rate = False Positive Rate. In Information Retrieval, also known as Fallout.

Feature Engineering: The process of identifying Features of a Document that are used as input to a Machine Learning Algorithm. Typical Features include words and phrases, as well as metadata such as subjects, dates, and file types. One of the simplest and most common Feature Engineering techniques is Bag of Words. More complex Feature Engineering techniques include the use of Ontologies and Latent Semantic Indexing.

Features: The units of information used by a Machine Learning Algorithm to Classify or Prioritize Documents. Typical Features include text fragments, such as words or phrases, and metadata such as sender, recipient, and sent date. *See also* Feature Engineering.

Find Similar: A search method that identifies Documents that are similar to a particular exemplar. Find Similar is commonly misconstrued to be the mechanism behind Technology-Assisted Review.

Gain Curve: A graph that shows the Recall that would be achieved for a particular Cutoff. The Gain Curve directly relates the Recall that can be achieved to the effort that must be expended to achieve it, as measured by the number of Documents that must be reviewed and Coded.

Gaussian Calculator / Gaussian Estimation: *See* Classical, Gaussian, or Normal Calculator / Classical, Gaussian, or Normal Estimation.

Gaussian Distribution: *See* Normal Distribution.

Gaussian Estimate: A Statistical Estimate of a Population characteristic using Gaussian Estimation. It is generally expressed as a Point Estimate accompanied by a Margin of Error and a Confidence Level, or as a Confidence Interval accompanied by a Confidence Level.

Global Aerospace: *Global Aerospace Inc.* v. *Landow Aviation*, Consol. Case No. CL 61040, 2012 WL 1431215 (Va. Cir. Ct. Apr. 23, 2012).

The first State Court Order approving the use of Predictive Coding by the producing party, over the objection of the requesting party, without prejudice to the requesting party raising an issue with the Court as to the completeness or the contents of the production, or the ongoing use of Predictive Coding. The order was issued by Loudoun County Circuit Court Judge James H. Chamblin.

Global Deduplication: Deduplication of Documents across multiple custodians. Also referred to as Horizontal Deduplication. (*Cf.* Vertical Deduplication.)

Gold Standard: The best available determination of the Relevance or Non-Relevance of all (or a sample) of a Document Population, used as benchmark to evaluate the effectiveness of a search and review effort. Also referred to as Ground Truth.

Goodhart's Law: An observation made in 1975 by Charles Goodhart, Chief Adviser to the Bank of England, that statistical economic indicators, when used for regulation, become unreliable. Restated and generalized in 1997 by University of Cambridge Professor Marilyn Strathern as "When a measure becomes a target, it ceases to be a good measure." Within the context of Electronic Discovery, Goodhart's Law suggests that the value of Information Retrieval measures such as Recall and Precision may be compromised if they are prescribed as the definition of the reasonableness of a search or review effort.

Grossman and Cormack: Authors of the JOLT (a.k.a. Richmond Journal) Study.

Ground Truth: *See* Gold Standard.

Harmonic Mean: The reciprocal of the average of the reciprocals of two or more quantities. If the quantities are named a and b, their Harmonic Mean is $\frac{2}{\frac{1}{a}+\frac{1}{b}}$. In Information Retrieval, F_1 is the Harmonic Mean of Recall and Precision. The Harmonic Mean, unlike the more common arithmetic mean (i.e., average), falls closer to the lower of the two quantities. As a summary measure, a Harmonic Mean may be preferable to an arithmetic mean because a high Harmonic Mean depends on both high Recall and high Precision, whereas a high arithmetic mean can be achieved with high Recall at the expense of low Precision, or high Precision at the expense of low Recall.

Hashing / Hash / Hash Value: A statistical method used to reduce the contents of a Document to a single, fixed-size, alphanumeric value, which is, for all intents and purposes, unique to a particular Document; the single, fixed-size alphanumeric value resulting from Hashing a particular Document. Common Hashing Algorithms include, but are not limited to, MD5, SHA-1, and SHA-2. Hashing and Hash Values are typically used for Document identification, Deduplication, or ensuring that Documents have not been altered.

Horizontal Deduplication: *See* Global Deduplication. (*Cf.* Vertical Deduplication.)

Index: A list of Keywords in which each Keyword is accompanied by a list of the Documents (and sometimes the positions within the Documents) where it occurs. Manual indices have been used in books for centuries; automatic indices are used in Information Retrieval systems to identify the Documents that contain particular Search Terms.

Indexing: The manual or automatic process of creating an Index. In Electronic Discovery, Indexing typically refers to the automatic construction of an electronic Index for use in an Information Retrieval system.

Information Need: In Information Retrieval, the information being sought in a search or review effort. In E-Discovery, the Information Need is typically to identify Documents responsive to a request for production, or to identify Documents that are subject to privilege or work-product protection.

Information Retrieval: The science of how to find information to meet an Information Need. While modern Information Retrieval relies heavily on computers, the discipline predates the invention of computers.

In Re: Actos: *In Re: Actos (Pioglitazone) Products Liability Litigation*, MDL No. 6:11-md-2299 (W.D. La. July 27, 2012). A product liability action with a Case Management Order (CMO) that memorializes the parties' agreement on a "search methodology proof of concept to evaluate the potential utility of advanced analytics as a Document identification mechanism for the review and production" of Electronically Stored Information. The search protocol provides for the use of a Technology-Assisted Review tool on the email of four key custodians. The CMO was issued by District Judge Rebecca F. Doherty.

Internal Response Curve: From Signal Detection Theory, a tool for estimating the number of Relevant and Non-Relevant Documents in a Population, or the number of Documents that fall above and below a particular Cutoff. The use of Internal Response Curves for this purpose assumes that the scores yielded by a Machine Learning Algorithm for Relevant Documents obey a Gaussian Distribution, and the scores for Non-Relevant Documents obey a different Gaussian Distribution. These distributions are then used to predict the number of Relevant and Non-Relevant Documents in any given range of scores.

Interval Sample / Interval Sampling: *See* Systematic Sample / Systematic Sampling.

Issue Code(s) / Issue Coding: One or more subcategories of the overall Information Need to be identified in a search or review effort; the act of generating such subcategories of the overall Information Need. Examples include specification of the reason(s) for a determination of Relevance or Non-Relevance, Coding of particular subcategories of interest, and Coding of privileged, confidential, or significant ("hot") Documents.

Iterative Training: The process of repeatedly augmenting the Training Set with additional examples of Coded Documents until the effectiveness of the Machine Learning Algorithm reaches an acceptable level. The additional examples may be identified through Judgmental Sampling, Random Sampling, or by the Machine Learning Algorithm, as in Active Learning.

Jaccard Index: A measure of the consistency between two sets (e.g., Documents Coded as Relevant by two different reviewers). Defined mathematically as the size of the intersection of the two sets, divided by the size of the union (e.g., the number of Documents coded as Relevant by both reviewers, divided by the number of Documents identified as Relevant by one or the other, or both reviewers). It is typically used as a measure of consistency among review efforts, but also may be used as a measure of similarity between two Documents represented as two Bags of Words. Jaccard Index is also referred to as Overlap or Mutual F_1. Empirical studies have shown that expert reviewers commonly achieve Jaccard Index scores of about 50%, and that scores exceeding 60% are rare.

JASIST Study: A 2009 study (Herbert L. Roitblat, Anne Kershaw & Patrick Oot, *Document Categorization in Legal Electronic Discovery: Computer Classification vs. Manual Review*, 61 J. AM. SOC'Y. FOR INFO. SCI. & TECH. 70 (2010)), showing that the Positive Agreement between each of two Technology-Assisted Review methods, and a prior production to the Department of Justice, exceeded the Positive Agreement between each of two Manual Review processes and the same production. Also referred to as the EDI Study.

JOLT Study: A 2011 study (Maura R. Grossman & Gordon V. Cormack, *Technology-Assisted Review in E-Discovery Can Be More Effective and More Efficient Than Exhaustive Manual Review*, XVII RICH. J.L. & TECH. 11 (2011)), *available at* http://jolt.richmond.edu/v17i3/article11.pdf, that used data from TREC 2009 to show that two Technology-Assisted Review processes (one using Machine Learning and one using a Rule Base) generally achieved better Recall, better Precision, and greater efficiency than the TREC Manual Review process. Also known as the Richmond Journal Study, or the Richmond Study.

Judgmental Sample / Judgmental Sampling: A method in which a Sample of the Document Population is drawn, based at least in part on subjective factors, so as to include the "most interesting" Documents by some criterion; the Sample resulting from such method. Unlike a Random Sample, the statistical properties of a Judgmental Sample may not be extrapolated to the entire Population. However, an individual (such as a quality assurance auditor or an adversary) may use Judgmental Sampling to attempt to uncover defects. The failure to identify defects may be taken as evidence (albeit not statistical evidence, and certainly not proof) of the absence of defects.

Keyword: A word (or Search Term) that is used as part of a Query in a Keyword Search.

Keyword Expansion: *See* Query Expansion.

Keyword Search: A search in which all Documents that contain one or more specific Keywords are returned.

Kleen: *Kleen Prods. LLC v. Packaging Corp. of Am.*, Case No. 1:10-cv-05711, various Pleadings and Tr. (N.D. Ill. 2012). A federal case in which plaintiffs sought to compel defendants to use Content-Based

Advanced Analytics (CBAA) for their production, after defendants had already employed complex Boolean Searches to identify Responsive Documents. Defendants advanced Elusion scores of 5%, based on a Judgmental Sample of custodians, to defend the reasonableness of the Boolean Search. After two days of evidentiary hearings before (and many conferences with) Magistrate Judge Nan R. Nolan, plaintiffs withdrew their request for CBAA, without prejudice.

Knowledge Engineering: The process of capturing the expertise of a Subject Matter Expert in a form (typically a Rule Base) that can be executed by a computer to emulate the human's judgment.

Label / Labeled / Labeling: *See* Code / Coded / Coding.

Latent Semantic Analysis (LSA): *See* Latent Semantic Indexing.

Latent Semantic Indexing (LSI): A Feature Engineering Algorithm that uses linear algebra to group together correlated Features. For example, "Windows, Gates, Ballmer" might be one group, while "Windows, Gates, Doors" might be another. Latent Semantic Indexing underlies many Concept Search tools. While Latent Semantic Indexing is used for Feature Engineering in some Technology-Assisted Review tools, it is not, *per se*, a Technology-Assisted Review method. Also referred to as Latent Semantic Analysis.

Linear Review: A Document-by-Document Manual Review in which the Documents are examined in a prescribed order, typically chronological order.

Logistic Regression: A state-of-the-art Supervised Learning Algorithm that estimates the Probability that a Document is Relevant, based on the Features it contains.

Machine Learning: The use of a computer Algorithm to organize or Classify Documents by analyzing their Features. In the context of Technology-Assisted Review, Supervised Learning Algorithms (e.g., Support Vector Machines, Logistic Regression, Nearest Neighbor, and Bayesian Classifiers) are used to infer Relevance or Non-Relevance of Documents based on the Coding of Documents in a Training Set. In Electronic Discovery generally, Unsupervised Learning Algorithms are used for Clustering, Near-Duplicate Detection, and Concept Search.

Manual Review: The practice of having human reviewers individually read and Code the Documents in a Collection for Responsiveness, particular issues, privilege, and/or confidentiality.

Margin of Error: The maximum amount by which a Point Estimate might likely deviate from the true value, typically expressed as "plus or minus" a percentage, with a particular Confidence Level. For example, one might express a Statistical Estimate as "30% of the Documents in the Population are Relevant, plus or minus 3%, with 95% confidence." This means that the Point Estimate is 30%, the Margin of Error is 3%, the Confidence Interval is 27% to 33%, and the Confidence Level is 95%. Using Gaussian Estimation, the Margin of Error is one-half of the size of the Confidence Interval. It is important to note that when the Margin of Error is expressed as a percentage, it refers to a percentage of the Population, not to a percentage of the Point Estimate. In the current example, if there are one million Documents in the Document Population, the Statistical Estimate may be restated as "300,000 Documents in the Population are Relevant, plus or minus 30,000 Documents, with 95% confidence"; or, alternatively, "between 270,000 and 330,000 Documents in the Population are Relevant, with 95% confidence." The Margin of Error is commonly misconstrued to be a percentage of the Point Estimate. However, it would be incorrect to interpret the Confidence Interval in this example to mean that "300,000 Documents in the Population are Relevant, plus or minus 9,000 Documents." The fact that a Margin of Error of "plus or minus 3%" has been achieved is not, by itself, evidence of a precise Statistical Estimate when the Prevalence of Relevant Documents is low.

Miss / Missed: A Relevant Document that is not identified as Relevant by a search or review effort. Also referred to as a False Negative.

Miss Rate: The fraction (or proportion) of truly Relevant Documents that are not identified as Relevant by a search or review effort. Miss Rate = 100% – Recall. Also referred to as the False Negative Rate.

Model: *See* Statistical Model.

Mutual F_1: *See* Jaccard Index.

Naïve Bayes: A Supervised Learning Algorithm in which the relative frequency of words (or other Features) in Relevant and Non-Relevant Training Examples is used to estimate the likelihood that a new Document containing those words (or other Features) is Relevant. Naïve Bayes relies on the simplistic assumption that the words in a Document occur with independent Probabilities, with the consequence that it tends to yield extremely low or extremely high estimates.

NDLON: *National Day Laborer Organizing Network* v. *U.S. Immigration and Customs Enforcement Agency*, Case No. 10-Civ-3488 (SAS), 2012 WL 2878130 (S.D.N.Y. July 13, 2012), a Freedom of Information Act (FOIA) case in which District Judge Shira A. Scheindlin held that "most custodians cannot be 'trusted' to run effective searches because designing legally sufficient electronic searches in the discovery or FOIA contexts is not part of their daily responsibilities," and stated (in *dicta*) that "beyond the use of keyword search, parties can (and frequently should) rely on latent semantic indexing, statistical probability models, and machine learning to find responsive documents. Through iterative learning, these methods (known as 'computer-assisted' or 'predictive' coding) allow humans to teach computers what documents are and are not responsive to a particular FOIA or discovery request and they can significantly increase the effectiveness and efficiency of searches."

Near-Duplicate Detection: An industry-specific term generally used to describe a method of grouping together "nearly identical" Documents. Near-Duplicate Detection is a variant of Clustering in which the similarity among Documents in the same group is very strong. It is typically used to reduce review costs, and to ensure consistent Coding. Also referred to as Near-Deduplication.

Near-Deduplication: *See* Near-Duplicate Detection.

Nearest Neighbor: A Supervised Learning Algorithm in which a new Document is Classified by finding the most similar Document in the Training Set, and assuming that the correct Coding for the new Document is the same as the most similar one in the Training Set.

Negative Predictive Value (NPV): The fraction (Proportion) of Documents that are identified as Non-Relevant by a search or review effort, that are in fact Non-Relevant. The complement of Precision; that is, Negative Predictive Value is computed the same way as Precision when the definitions of Relevant and Non-Relevant are transposed.

N-Gram: N consecutive words or characters treated as a Feature. In the phrase, "To be or not to be," a word Bigram (i.e., 2-gram) would be "to be"; a word Trigram (i.e., 3-gram) would be "to be or"; a Quad-Gram (i.e., 4-gram) would be "to be or not"; and so on. *See also* Shingling.

Non-Relevant / Not Relevant: In Information Retrieval, a Document is considered Non-Relevant (or Not Relevant) if it does not meet the Information Need of the search or review effort. The synonym "irrelevant" is rarely used in Information Retrieval.

Normal Distribution: The "bell curve" of classical statistics. The number of Relevant Documents in a Sample tends to obey a Normal (Gaussian) Distribution, provided the Sample size is large enough to capture a substantial number of Relevant and Non-Relevant Documents. In this situation, Gaussian Estimation is reasonably accurate. If the Sample size is insufficiently large to capture a substantial number of both Relevant and Non-Relevant Documents (as a rule of thumb, at least 12 of each), the Binomial Distribution better characterizes the number of Relevant Documents in the Sample, and Binomial Estimation is more appropriate. Also referred to as a Gaussian Distribution.

Null Set: The set of Documents that are not returned by a search process, or that are identified as Not Relevant by a review process.

Ontology: A representation of the relationships among words and their meanings that is richer than a Taxonomy. For example, an Ontology can represent the fact that a wheel is a part of a bicycle, that gold is yellow, and so on.

Overlap: *See* Jaccard Index.

Parallel Trial: An Experimental Design for comparing two search or review processes using the same Document Collection and Information Need, in which both processes are applied concurrently but independently, and then the results of the two efforts are compared. (*Cf.* Crossover Trial.)

Pattern Matching: The science of designing computer Algorithms to recognize natural phenomena like parts of speech, faces, or spoken words.

Point Estimate: The most likely value for a Population characteristic. When combined with a Margin of Error (or Confidence Interval) and a Confidence Level, it reflects a Statistical Estimate.

Population: *See* Document Population.

Positive Agreement: The Probability that, if one reviewer Codes a Document as Relevant, a second independent reviewer will also Code the Document as Relevant. Empirical studies show that Positive Agreement rates of 70% are typical, and Positive Agreement rates of 80% are rare. Positive Agreement should not be confused with Agreement (which is a less informative measure) or Overlap (which is a numerically smaller measure that conveys similar information). Under the assumption that the two reviewers are equally likely to err, Overlap is roughly equal to the square of Positive Agreement. That is, if Positive Agreement is 70%, Overlap is roughly 70% × 70% = 49%.

Positive Predictive Value (PPV): *See* Precision. Positive Predictive Value is a term used in Signal Detection Theory; Precision is the equivalent term in Information Retrieval.

Precision: The fraction of Documents identified as Relevant by a search or review effort, that are in fact Relevant. Also referred to as Positive Predictive Value.

Precision-Recall Curve: The curve representing the tradeoff between Precision and Recall for a given search or review effort, depending on the chosen Cutoff value. *See* Recall-Precision Curve.

Precision-Recall Tradeoff: The notion that most search strategies can be adjusted to increase Precision at the expense of Recall, or vice versa. At one extreme, 100% Recall could be achieved by a search that returned the entire Document Population, but Precision would be low (equal to Prevalence). At the other extreme, 100% Precision could be achieved by a search that returned a single Relevant Document, but Recall would be low (equal to 1/N, where N is the number of Relevant Documents in the Document Population). More generally, a broader search returning many Documents will have higher Recall and lower Precision, while a narrower search returning fewer Documents will have lower Recall and higher Precision. A Precision-Recall Curve illustrates the Precision-Recall Tradeoff for a particular search method.

Predictive Coding: An industry-specific term generally used to describe a Technology-Assisted Review process involving the use of a Machine Learning Algorithm to distinguish Relevant from Non-Relevant Documents, based on Subject Matter Expert(s)' Coding of a Training Set of Documents. *See* Supervised Learning and Active Learning.

Prevalence: The fraction of Documents in a Population that are Relevant to an Information Need. Also referred to as Richness or Yield.

Prioritization / Prioritized: *See* Relevance Ranking.

Probabilistic Latent Semantic Analysis: A variant of Latent Semantic Analysis based on conditional Probability rather than on correlation.

Probability: The fraction (proportion) of times that a particular outcome would occur, should the same action be repeated under the same conditions an infinite number of times. For example, if one were to flip a fair coin, the Probability of it landing "heads" is one-half, or 50%; as one repeats this action indefinitely, the fraction of times that the coin lands "heads" will become indistinguishable from 50%. If one were to flip two fair coins, the Probability of both landing "heads" is one-quarter, or 25%.

Proportion: The fraction of a set of Documents having some particular property (typically Relevance).

Proportionality: Pursuant to Federal Rules of Civil Procedure 26(b)(2)(B), 26(b)(2)(C), 26(g)(1)(B)(iii), and other federal and state procedural rules, the legal doctrine that Electronically Stored Information may be withheld from production if the cost and burden of producing it exceeds its potential value to the resolution of the matter. Proportionality has been interpreted in the case law to apply to preservation as well as production.

Quad-Gram: An N-Gram where N = 4 (i.e., a 4-gram).

Quality Assurance: A method to ensure, after the fact, that a search or review effort has achieved reasonable results.

Quality Control: Ongoing methods to ensure, during a search or review effort, that reasonable results are being achieved.

Query: A formal search command provided as input to a search tool.

Query Expansion: The process of adding Search Terms to a Query to improve Recall, often at the expense of decreased Precision.

Random Sample / Random Sampling: A subset of the Document Population selected by a method that is equally likely to select any Document from the Document Population for inclusion in the Sample;

the Sample resulting from such action. Random Sampling is the basis of Statistical Estimation.

RAND Study: A 2012 study (Nicholas M. Pace & Laura Zakaras, *Where the Money Goes: Understanding Litigant Expenditures for Producing Electronic Discovery*, RAND Institute for Civil Justice (2012)), indicating that Document review accounts for 73% of Electronic Discovery costs, and concluding that "[t]he exponential growth in digital information, which shows no signs of slowing, makes a computer-categorized review strategy, such as predictive coding, not only a cost-effective choice but perhaps the *only* reasonable way to handle many large-scale productions."

Ranking: *See* Relevance Ranking.

Recall: The fraction of Relevant Documents that are identified as Relevant by a search or review effort.

Recall-Precision Curve: *See* Precision-Recall Curve.

Recall-Precision Tradeoff: *See* Precision-Recall Tradeoff.

Receiver Operating Characteristic Curve (ROC): In Signal Detection Theory, a graph of the tradeoff between True Positive Rate and False Positive Rate, as the Cutoff is varied.

Relevance Feedback: An Active Learning process in which the Documents with the highest likelihood of Relevance are coded by a human, and added to the Training Set.

Relevance Ranking: A search method in which the results are ranked from the most likely to the least likely to be Relevant to an Information Need; the result of such ranking. Google Web Search is an example of Relevance Ranking.

Relevance / Relevant: In Information Retrieval, a Document is considered Relevant if it meets the Information Need of the search or review effort.

Responsiveness: A Document that is Relevant to an Information Need expressed by a particular request for production or subpoena in a civil, criminal, or regulatory matter.

Richness: *See* Prevalence or Yield.

Richmond Journal Study / Richmond Study: *See* JOLT Study.

Roitblat, Kershaw, and Oot: Authors of the JASIST (a.k.a. EDI) Study.

Rolling Collection / Rolling Ingestion: A process in which the Document Collection is periodically augmented as new, potentially Relevant Documents are identified and gathered. Whenever the Document Collection is augmented, the results of prior search or review efforts must be supplemented to account for the new Documents.

Rolling Production: A process in which Responsive Documents are delivered incrementally to a requesting party to provide timely, partial satisfaction of a Document request.

Rule: A formal statement of one or more criteria used to determine a particular outcome, e.g., whether to code a Document as Relevant or Non-Relevant.

Rule Base: A set of Rules created by an expert to emulate the human decision-making process for the purposes of Classifying Documents in the context of Electronic Discovery.

Sample / Sampling: A subset of the Document Population used to assess some characteristic of the Population; the act of generating such a subset of the Document Population. *See* Interval Sample, Judgmental Sample, Random Sample, Statistical Sample, or Systematic Sample.

Sample Size: The number of Documents drawn at random that are used to calculate a Statistical Estimate.

Search Term: *See* Keyword.

Sedona / Sedona Conference: The Sedona Conference® (https://thesedonaconference.org) is a nonprofit, 501(c)(3) research and educational institute, founded in 1997 by Richard G. Braman, dedicated to the advanced study of law and policy in the areas of antitrust, complex litigation, and intellectual property rights. Sedona sponsors a preeminent think-tank in the area of Electronic Discovery known as Working Group 1 on Electronic Document Retention and Production. Sedona is well known for its thoughtful, balanced, and free publications, such as *The Sedona Conference® Glossary: E-Discovery*

& Digital Information Management (Third Edition, Sept. 2010), *The Sedona Principles Addressing Electronic Document Production, Second Edition* (June 2007), and *The Sedona Conference® Cooperation Proclamation* (July 2008).

Seed Set: The initial Training Set provided to the learning Algorithm in an Active Learning process. The Documents in the Seed Set may be selected based on Random Sampling or Judgmental Sampling. Some commentators use the term more restrictively to refer only to Documents chosen using Judgmental Sampling. Other commentators use the term generally to mean any Training Set, including the final Training Set in Iterative Training, or the only Training Set in non-Iterative Training.

Sensitivity: *See* True Positive Rate.

Shingling: A Feature Engineering method in which the Features consist of all N-Grams in a text, for some number N. For example, the Trigram Shingling of the text "To be or not to be" consists of the features "to be or"; "be or not"; "or not to"; and "not to be." Note that the Features overlap one another in the text, suggesting the metaphor of roof shingles.

Signal Detection Theory: Invented at the same time and in conjunction with radar, the science of distinguishing true observations from spurious ones. Signal Detection Theory is widely used in radio engineering and medical diagnostic testing. The terms True Positive, True Negative, False Positive, False Negative, Sensitivity, Specificity, Receiver Operating Characteristic Curve, Area Under the ROC Curve, and Internal Response Curve, all arise from Signal Detection Theory.

Significance / Significant: The confirmation, with a given Confidence Level, of a prior hypothesis, using a Statistical Estimate. The result is said to be Statistically Significant if all values within the Confidence Interval for the desired Confidence Level (typically 95%) are consistent with the hypothesis being true, and inconsistent with it being false. For example, if the hypothesis is that fewer than 300,000 Documents are Relevant, and a Statistical Estimate shows that 290,000 Documents are Relevant, plus or minus 5,000 Documents, we say that the result is Significant. On the other hand, if the Statistical Estimate shows that 290,000 Documents are Relevant, plus or minus 15,000

Documents, we say that the result is not Significant, because the Confidence Interval includes values (i.e., the values between 300,000 and 305,000) that contradict the hypothesis.

Specificity: *See* True Negative Rate.

Statistical Estimate: A quantitative estimate of a Population characteristic using Statistical Estimation. It is generally expressed as a Point Estimate accompanied by a Margin of Error and a Confidence Level, or as a Confidence Interval accompanied by a Confidence Level.

Statistical Estimation: The act of estimating the Proportion of a Document Population that has a particular characteristic, based on the Proportion of a Random Sample that has the same characteristic. Methods of Statistical Estimation include Binomial Estimation and Gaussian Estimation.

Statistically Significant / Statistical Significance: *See* Significance.

Statistical Model: A mathematical abstraction of the Document Population that removes irrelevant characteristics while largely preserving those of interest for a particular purpose. For the purpose of computing Recall, a Statistical Model need only consider whether or not the Documents are Relevant, and whether or not the Documents are Coded Relevant, not any other characteristics of the Documents.

Statistical Sample / Statistical Sampling: A method in which a Sample of the Document Population is drawn at random, so that statistical properties of the Sample may be extrapolated to the entire Document Population; the Sample resulting from such action.

Stemming: In Keyword or Boolean Search, or Feature Engineering, the process of equating all forms of the same root word. For example, the words "stem," "stemming," "stemmed," and "stemmable" would all be treated as equivalent, and would each yield the same result when used as Search Terms in a Query. In some search systems, stemming is implicit, and in others, it must be made explicit through particular Query syntax.

Stop Word: A common word that is eliminated from Indexing. Eliminating Stop Words from Indexing dramatically reduces the size of the Index, while only marginally affecting the search process in most circumstances. Examples of Stop Words include "a," "the," "of," "but," and "not." Because phrases and names such as "To be or not to be," and "The Who," contain exclusively Stop Words that would not be Indexed, they would not be identified (or identifiable) through a Keyword Search.

Subject Matter Expert(s): One or more individuals (typically, but not necessarily, attorneys) who are familiar with the Information Need and can render an authoritative determination as to whether a Document is Relevant or not.

Supervised Learning: A Machine Learning method in which the learning Algorithm infers how to distinguish between Relevant and Non-Relevant Documents using a Training Set. Supervised Learning can be a stand-alone process, or used repeatedly in an Active Learning process.

Support Vector Machine: A state-of-the-art Supervised Learning Algorithm that separates Relevant from Non-Relevant Documents using geometric methods (i.e., geometry). Each Document is considered to be a point in [hyper]space, whose coordinates are determined from the Features contained in the Document. The Support Vector Machine finds a [hyper]plane that best separates Relevant from Non-Relevant Training Examples. Documents outside the Training Set (i.e., uncoded Documents from the Document Collection) are then Classified as Relevant or not, depending on which side of the [hyper] plane they fall on. Although a Support Vector Machine does not calculate a Probability of Relevance, one may infer that the Classification of Documents closer to the [hyper]plane is less certain than for those that are far from the [hyper]plane.

Synthetic Document: An industry-specific term generally used to describe an artificial Document created by either the requesting party or the producing party, as part of a Technology-Assisted Review process, for use as a Training Example for a Machine Learning Algorithm. Synthetic Documents are contrived Documents in which one party imagines what the evidence might look like and relies on the Machine Learning Algorithm to find actual Documents that are similar to the artificial Document.

Systematic Sample / Systematic Sampling: A Sampling method in which every Nth Document (for some fixed number N) is selected, when the Documents are considered in some prescribed order; the Sample resulting from such action. A Systematic Sample is random (and hence a true Statistical Sample) only when the prescribed order is itself random. Sometimes referred to as an Interval Sample / Interval Sampling.

TAR: *See* Technology-Assisted Review.

Taxonomy: A hierarchical organizational scheme that arranges the meanings of words into classes and subclasses. For example, vehicles, aircraft, and ships are modes of transportation; cars, trucks, and bicycles are vehicles, and Fords and Chryslers are cars.

Technology-Assisted Review (TAR): A process for Prioritizing or Coding a Collection of Documents using a computerized system that harnesses human judgments of one or more Subject Matter Expert(s) on a smaller set of Documents and then extrapolates those judgments to the remaining Document Collection. Some TAR methods use Machine Learning Algorithms to distinguish Relevant from Non-Relevant Documents, based on Training Examples Coded as Relevant or Non-Relevant by the Subject Matter Experts(s), while other TAR methods derive systematic Rules that emulate the expert(s)' decision-making process. TAR processes generally incorporate Statistical Models and/or Sampling techniques to guide the process and to measure overall system effectiveness.

Term Expansion: *See* Query Expansion.

Term Frequency and Inverse Document Frequency (TF-IDF): An enhancement to the Bag of Words method in which each word has a weight based on Term Frequency–the number of times the word appears in the Document–and Inverse Document Frequency–the reciprocal of the number of Documents in which the word occurs.

Thesaurus Expansion: In Keyword or Boolean Search, replacing a single Search Term by a list of its synonyms, as listed in a thesaurus.

Threshold: *See* Cutoff.

Training Example: One Document from a Training Set.

Training Set: A Sample of Documents coded by one or more Subject Matter Expert(s) as Relevant or Non-Relevant, from which a Machine

Learning Algorithm then infers how to distinguish between Relevant and Non-Relevant Documents beyond those in the Training Set.

TREC: The Text REtrieval Conference, sponsored by the National Institute of Standards and Technology (NIST), which has run since 1992, to "support research within the information retrieval community by providing the infrastructure necessary for large-scale evaluation of text retrieval methodologies. In particular, the TREC workshop series has the following goals: to encourage research in information retrieval based on large test Collections; to increase communication among industry, academia, and government by creating an open forum for the exchange of research ideas; to speed the transfer of technology from research labs into commercial products by demonstrating substantial improvements in retrieval methodologies on real-world problems; and to increase the availability of appropriate evaluation techniques for use by industry and academia, including development of new evaluation techniques more applicable to current systems."

TREC Legal Track: From 2006 through 2011, TREC included a Legal Track, which sought "to assess the ability of information retrieval techniques to meet the needs of the legal profession for tools and methods capable of helping with the retrieval of electronic business records, principally for use as evidence in civil litigation."

Trigram: An N-Gram where N = 3 (i.e., a 3-gram).

True Negative (TN): A Non-Relevant Document that is correctly identified as Non-Relevant by a search or review effort.

True Negative Rate (TNR): The fraction (or Proportion) of Non-Relevant Documents that are correctly identified as Non-Relevant by a search or review effort.

True Positive (TP): A Relevant Document that is correctly identified as Relevant by a search or review effort.

True Positive Rate (TPR): The fraction (or Proportion) of Relevant Documents that are correctly identified as Relevant by a search or review effort. True Positive Rate is a term used in Signal Detection Theory; Recall is the equivalent term in Information Retrieval.

Uncertainty Sampling: An Active Learning approach in which the Machine Learning Algorithm selects the Documents as to which it is least certain about Relevance, for Coding by the Subject Matter Expert(s), and addition to the Training Set.

Unsupervised Learning: A Machine Learning method in which the learning Algorithm infers categories of similar Documents without any training by a Subject Matter Expert. Examples of Unsupervised Learning methods include Clustering and Near-Duplicate Detection.

Validation: The act of confirming that a process has achieved its intended purpose. Validation may involve Statistical or Judgmental Sampling.

Vertical Deduplication: Deduplication within a custodian; identical copies of a Document held by different custodians are not Deduplicated. (*Cf.* Horizontal Deduplication.)

Yield: *See* Prevalence or Richness.

Editor and Author Bios

Editors

Jason R. Baron

Mr. Baron serves as Of Counsel in the Information Governance and eDiscovery Group at Drinker Biddle & Reath LLP in Washington, DC, and as co-chair of the Information Governance Initiative, a vendor neutral consortium and think tank. Between 2000 and 2013, he served as the first appointed director of litigation at the National Archives and Records Administration, and before that as a trial lawyer and senior counsel for a dozen years at the Department of Justice. While at DOJ, Mr. Baron served as lead counsel of record for seven years in the White House "PROFS" e-mail case, *Armstrong v. Executive Office of the President* (D.D.C.). Among other faculty appointments, he has taught an e-discovery course for PhD and Masters candidates at the University of Maryland's College of Information Studies. He co-founded the NIST TREC Legal Track, a multi-year international information retrieval project devoted to evaluating advanced search methods in a legal context. He also co-founded the DESI (Discovery of Electronically Stored Information) international workshop series on topics related to advanced search methods.

Mr. Baron has served as an Editor-in-Chief on several commentaries published by The Sedona Conference®, including *The Sedona Conference Best Practices Commentary on the Use of Search and Information Retrieval Methods in E-Discovery* (2007 and 2013 eds.), and *The Sedona Conference Achieving Quality in E-Discovery Commentary* (2009 and 2013 eds.). He also has authored or co-authored numerous scholarly publications, including three published in the

Richmond Journal of Law and Technology: "Information Inflation: Can the Legal Profession Survive?" (2007), "Law in the Age of Exabytes: Some Further Thoughts on 'Information Inflation' and Issues in E-discovery Search" (2011), and "Finding the Signal in the Noise: Information Governance, Analytics, and the Future of Legal Practice" (2013) (reprinted in this volume).

Mr. Baron serves on the advisory boards of the Georgetown Advanced E-discovery Institute and the Cardozo Data Law Initiative. He has previously served as chair of the DC Bar E-discovery & Information Governance Committee, on the Board of Directors of ARMA International, and as co-chair of the steering committee of The Sedona Conference Working Group 1.

Mr. Baron is a 2011 recipient of the international Emmett Leahy Award for his outstanding contributions and accomplishments in the records and information management profession, as well as the Justice Tom C. Clark Outstanding Government Lawyer award given in 2013 by the Federal Bar Association. *The American Lawyer* magazine named him one of six "e-discovery trailblazers" in its 2013 issue devoted to "The Top 50 Big Law Innovators of the Last 50 Years." He received his BA magna cum laude wth honors from Wesleyan University, and his JD from the Boston University School of Law.

Michael D. Berman

Mr. Berman is a partner at Rifkin Weiner Livingston, LLC, in Baltimore, where he concentrates in commercial litigation and ESI issues. Previously, Mr. Berman spent seven years as the Deputy Chief of Civil Litigation at the Office of the Attorney General of Maryland, was a partner at the Baltimore firms of Tydings & Rosenberg, LLC, and Kaplan, Heyman, Greenberg, Engelman & Belgrad, P.A., and a clerk for The Hon. R. Dorsey Watkins, U.S. District Court for the District of Maryland. He teaches a three-credit, ESI seminar at the University of Baltimore and Maryland Schools of Law, where he is an adjunct professor.

Mr. Berman chaired the Maryland State Bar Association committee that proposed the ESI Principles of the U.S. District Court for the District of Maryland. He is a past chair of the Litigation Section

Council, Maryland State Bar Association, and a former co-chair of the Maryland Bar Association's Federal District Court Committee and the American Bar Association's Litigation Book Publishing Board.

Some of his publications include: M. Berman, C. Barton, and P. Grimm, eds., *Managing E-Discovery and ESI: From Pre-Litigation Through Trial* (ABA, July 2011); Author, "The Duty to Preserve ESI (Its Trigger, Scope, and Limit) & the Spoliation Doctrine in the Maryland State Courts," 45 U. Balt. L. Forum 129 (2015); Co-author, "Referenda in Maryland: The Need for Comprehensive Statutory Reform," 42 U. Balt. L. Rev. 655 (2013); Co-author, "Discovery About Discovery: Does The Attorney-Client Privilege Protect All Attorney-Client Communications Relating To The Preservation Of Potentially Relevant Material?," 37 U. Balt. L. Rev. 381 (2008); Co-author, "Proportionality In The Post-Hoc Analysis Of Pre-Litigation Preservation Decisions," 37 U. Balt. L. Rev. 413 (2008); Co-Author, "Commentary: With ESI, difference between federal, state rules," THE DAILY RECORD (June 17, 2016); Author, "When Does a Litigation Hold End?," Digital Discovery and e-Evidence (Bureau of National Affairs (Oct. 2009); Author, "General Adverse Inference Instruction For Intentional Breach Of Duty To Preserve—Goodman v. Praxair Services, Inc., Digital Discovery and e-Evidence (Bureau of National Affairs, July 2009); Author, "Tips to Avoid Mistakes with ESI Vendors," *ABA Technology for the Litigator* (Summer 2009); Author, "Motions to Compel ESI Denied," *ABA Litigation News* (Fall 2009).

Mr. Berman has been a regular lecturer at national and local ESI programs, including the Maryland Professionalism Center, Inc., and the Judicial Institute of Maryland, both created by the Court of Appeals of Maryland. A few other examples include: Presenter, "Managing Ethical Landmines in Electronically Stored Information," (National Disability Rights Network, Training & Advocacy Support Center, Annual Conference, June 2012); Panelist, Access Data Users' Conference, "Data Governance and e-Discovery: Flip Sides of the Same Coin" (Las Vegas, May 2012); Presenter, Stevenson University "Forensic Symposium: eDiscovery—Digital Hide and Seek" (Apr. 2012); Presenter, "The Relevance and Risks of Evidence and E-Discovery for Everyday Practice," (Albuquerque, N. Mex., Dec. 2011).

Mr. Berman served four years in the U.S. Army, where he attained the rank of Captain and was a paratrooper. His awards include the Army Commendation Medal, Armed Forces Expeditionary Medal, and the National Defense Service Medal. Mr. Berman received a BA from the University of Wisconsin–Madison, an MA from the University of Maryland–College Park, and a JD from the University of Maryland at Baltimore. Additional information may be found at http://www.esi-mediation.com/resume/.

Ralph C. Losey

Mr. Losey is a Principal of Jackson Lewis, P.C., a labor and employment law firm in the United States with over 800 attorneys. He is the firm's National e-Discovery Counsel in charge of electronic discovery services and training. Mr. Losey also heads up the firm's Litigation Support Department, which, under his leadership, the firm outsourced to a major vendor. Mr. Losey personally performs the predictive coding work in multiple document review projects each year and supervises and consults in many others, including in the *Da Silva Moore* case, where predictive coding was first approved by a court. Mr. Losey has also competed in, and won, a document review contest and research project supervised by a major university. He was able to classify 1.7 million documents, on his own, in 64.5 hours. In 2015, and again in 2016, Mr. Losey led a research team at the NIST Text Retrieval Conference (TREC), where he participated in the Total Recall Track to demonstrate his hybrid multimodal method of predictive coding. His published reports for the TREC Total Recall Tracks can be found at one of Mr. Losey's educational websites, MrEDR.com.

Mr. Losey has concentrated in electronic evidence and discovery since 2006, at which time he started and ran the e-discovery department at Akerman Senterfitt. In 2010 he joined Jackson Lewis. Prior to 2006 Mr. Losey handled a variety of commercial litigation, insurance, and technology cases, including one of the largest Qui Tam cases in history.

Mr. Losey has been a computer hobbyist since 1978, and ethical hacker since the 1980s, at which time he created several original game and music software programs for his children. He also established and operated his law firm's IT department from the early 1980s to early 1990s. In 2015 Mr. Losey was a finalist for the LegalTech CIO of the Year Innovation Award. In 2016 he was included in *Best Lawyers in America* in three fields: Electronic Discovery and Information Management Law, Information Technology Law, and Commercial Litigation. He was also one of the 33 lawyers in the United States included in the 2016 Who's Who in Litigation, Electronic Discovery.

Mr. Losey has written over two million words on law and technology subjects since 2006, including over 60 articles on predictive coding. In 2006 he started his well-known blog, e-DiscoveryTeam.com, which later grew to include over a dozen legal education websites. His writings include six books on e-discovery published by the ABA, McMillian, and West-Thompson, including a new book by the ABA to be released in late 2016, *e-Discovery for Everyone*. He has also published four law review articles: *Predictive Coding and the Proportionality Doctrine*, 26 Regent U. Law Review 1 (2013–14); *HASH: The New Bates Stamp*, 12 Journal of Technology Law & Policy 1 (June 2007); *Mancia v. Mayflower Begins a Pilgrimage to the New World of Cooperation*, 10 Sedona Conf. J. 377 (2009 Supp.); and *Lawyers Behaving Badly*, 60 Mercer L. Rev. 983 (Spring 2009).

Mr. Losey served as an adjunct professor at the University of Florida School of Law from 2007 to 2011 where he taught both introductory and advanced e-discovery courses. He developed the law school's first online course, which he later spun-off into a private instructional program, e-DiscoveryTeamTraining.com. Mr. Losey has lectured at many CLE events and conferences around the world since 2006 with a focus over the last several years on predictive coding and overall best practices. Mr. Losey received his BA from Vanderbilt University in 1973 and his JD with honors from the University of Florida School of Law in 1979.

Authors

Bennett B. Borden

Bennett B. Borden is chief data scientist and a partner at Drinker Biddle & Reath LLP, where he is a chair of the Information Governance and eDiscovery Group. He is also a founder and chair of the

Information Governance Initiative. He co-chairs the Cloud Computing Committee and is a vice chair of the Internet of Things Committee and the eDiscovery and Digital Evidence Committee of the Science and Technology Law Section of the ABA. As a lawyer and data scientist, Mr. Borden builds machine-based learning models to transform and improve legal outcomes in key corporate events including mergers and acquisitions, information governance program development and enforcement, litigation and investigations, and business intelligence. Mr. Borden earned a BA with highest honors from George Mason University, a JD, cum laude, from the Georgetown University Law Center, and an MS in business analytics from New York University.

Dan Brassil

Dan Brassil is principal consultant at H5, where he provides expertise in information retrieval, linguistics, and solutions design. Since joining the company in 2005, he has consulted with clients to identify strategies for capturing relevant and key subject matter from large document collections and overseeing the implementation of these strategies, ensuring they meet client needs, objectives, and obligations. Prior to joining H5, Mr. Brassil taught linguistics at the University of California, San Diego, and his work has been published in linguistics and information retrieval journals such as *Artificial Intelligence and the Law* and *Proceedings of the IEEE International Conference on Systems, Man and Cybernetics*. Mr. Brassil received his MA from the University of California, San Diego, and his BA from the University of California, Santa Cruz.

William P. Butterfield

William Butterfield is a partner at Hausfeld LLP. He is the immediate past chair of The Sedona Conference Working Group on Electronic Document Retention and Production, where he served as editor-in-chief of *The Case for Cooperation* (2009), and was a co-editor of *The Sedona Conference Commentary on Preservation, Identification and Management of Sources of Information That Are Not Reasonably Accessible* (2008). He is also a member of The Sedona Conference Working Group on International Electronic Information Management, Discovery and

Disclosure. In 2011, Mr. Butterfield testified before the House Judiciary Committee, Subcommittee on the Constitution, regarding the costs and burden of civil discovery, and has also testified as an expert witness on e-discovery issues. Mr. Butterfield is an adjunct professor at American University, Washington College of Law, where he teaches a course in electronic discovery. He also serves on the advisory board for Georgetown University Law Center's Advanced E-Discovery Institute. Mr. Butterfield holds degrees from Bowling Green State University and the University of Toledo, College of Law.

Vincent M. Catanzaro

Vincent M. Catanzaro is Of Counsel at Shook Hardy & Bacon, LLP and is a member of the firm's Data and Discovery Strategies practice. Mr. Catanzaro works with clients to develop best practices and untangle issues related to data preservation, litigation management, cross-border collection, social networking, and the technology implications related to mergers and acquisitions. He previously served as senior counsel, global discovery manager for DuPont Legal, where he was responsible for counseling the company on how best to comply with evolving legal standards; guiding teams in the development of e-discovery response strategies and the use of technology; managing and monitoring the work of the company's discovery vendors; and overseeing DuPont Legal's Discovery Excellence Center, named an Inside Counsel Magazine Top 10 Innovative Legal Departments for 2013. Mr. Catanzaro is a member of The Sedona Conference Working Group One on Electronic Document Retention and Production, Sedona Working Group Six on International Electronic Information Management, Discovery and Disclosure, the Richard Herrmann Technology Inn of Court, and the Delaware Supreme Court Commission on Law and Technology. He received a BA, magna cum laude, from Temple University, and his JD from the Widener University School of Law.

Gordon V. Cormack

Gordon V. Cormack is a professor in the David R. Cheriton School of Computer Science at the University of Waterloo, in Ontario, Canada, as well as an independent consultant. His research and consulting activities focus on high-stakes information retrieval, including technology-assisted review (TAR), information governance, quality assurance, and evaluation methodology. Dr. Cormack has published more than 100 scientific articles, including *Technology-Assisted Review in E-Discovery Can Be More Effective and More Efficient Than Exhaustive Manual Review*, which was published in the *Richmond Journal of Law and Technology* in 2011. Dr. Cormack is co-author of *Information Retrieval: Implementing and Evaluating Search Engines* (MIT Press 2010 & 2016). He is a program committee member of The Text Retrieval Conference (TREC) at the National Institute of Standards and Technology (NIST), and has served as a coordinator of its Spam Track (2005–2007), Legal Track (2010–2011), and Total Recall Track (2015 & 2016). He is the co-inventor of the Continuous Active Learning (CAL) protocol for TAR. Dr. Cormack received his BSc Hons., MSc, and PhD from the University of Manitoba.

Tracy D. Drynan

Tracy D. Drynan is a senior attorney within the Information Governance and eDiscovery Group at Drinker Biddle & Reath LLP. As an attorney with ten years of experience working with a wide array of technologies, Ms. Drynan has concentrated in developing strategies in the use of technology to identify the most critical information necessary to various client needs. She regularly consults with and advises software technology companies on the development of data analytics tools, including innovative applications of the software. She is the Director of the DC Chapter of Women in E-Discovery and is an active member of the DC Bar's Ediscovery & Information Governance Committee. Ms. Drynan earned a BA from the University of Nevada, and a Master's degree in international finance and trade as well as her JD from the University of Denver.

The Hon. John M. Facciola

John M. Facciola was appointed a U.S. Magistrate Judge in the District of Columbia in 1997. Prior to being appointed to the Bench, he served as an Assistant District Attorney in Manhattan from 1969 to 1973 and was in private practice in the District of Columbia from 1974 to 1982.

He joined the U.S. Attorney's Office in 1982 and then served as chief of the Special Proceedings Section from 1989 until his appointment as Magistrate Judge. He retired from the bench in 2015 and is now an adjunct professor of law at Georgetown Law, where he teaches Information Technology and Modern Litigation, Evidence, Contracts, and Constitutional Law. While a judge, he authored over 700 opinions, many in the areas of electronic discovery. He is a frequent lecturer on that subject and the related issue of improving the technical competence of lawyers. The Sedona Conference has awarded him its Lifetime Achievement Award and the Bar Association of the District of Columbia named him its Judge of the Year. He is also the former editor-in-chief of the *Federal Courts Law Review*, the online law journal of the Federal Magistrate Judges Association.

Philip Favro

Philip Favro brings over 15 years of experience to his position as a discovery and information governance consultant for Driven. Mr. Favro's academic writings include *New Utah Rule 26: A Blueprint for Proportionality under the Federal Rules of Civil Procedure*, and *A New Frontier in Electronic Discovery: Preserving and Obtaining Metadata*, respectively published by the *Michigan State Law Review* and the *Boston University Journal of Science & Technology Law*. His expertise has been enhanced by his practice experience as a litigation attorney. During his 11 years of practice, Mr. Favro advised a variety of clients regarding business disputes and complex discovery issues. He actively contributes to Working Group 1 of The Sedona Conference and he is the Director of Legal Education for the Coalition of Technology Resources for Lawyers (CTRL). Mr. Favro has also served as a Judge Pro Tempore for the Santa Clara County Superior Court based in Santa Clara, California. He received his BA from Brigham Young University and his JD from the Santa Clara University School of Law.

Samantha Green

Samantha Green serves as the director of e-discovery for U.S. Legal Support. She is an attorney with over 14 years' experience in all aspects of electronic discovery, including an in-depth understanding of litigation readiness, ESI hosting, review and production processes, as well as the different technology and business approaches and cost implications associated with each. Ms. Green has advised, written, and spoken on all phases of the ESI life cycle with a broad range of experience in initial case assessment and engagement management. She has worked on many government investigations, including FCPA and antitrust matters, as well as, second requests and litigations that cross all spectrums. Ms. Green is a graduate of the University of Wisconsin-Madison and the Seton Hall University School of Law.

Maura R. Grossman

Maura R. Grossman is a Research Professor in the David R. Cheriton School of Computer Science at the University of Waterloo, in Ontario, Canada, as well as an e-discovery attorney and consultant in New York City. Previously, Ms. Grossman was Of Counsel at Wachtell, Lipton, Rosen & Katz, in New York, where she practiced for over 17 years. Prior to commencing her legal career, she was a hospital administrator, adjunct professor, and practicing clinical psychologist. As a lawyer, Ms. Grossman has served as a court-appointed special master, mediator, and expert to the court on search-related issues, has been actively involved in judicial education, and teaches e-discovery courses at Columbia Law School and the Georgetown University Law Center. She is well known for her scholarly work on technology-assisted review, most notably, *Technology-Assisted Review in E-Discovery Can Be More Effective and More Efficient Than Exhaustive Manual Review*, which was published in the *Richmond Journal of Law and Technology* in 2011, and has been widely cited in case law, both in the United States and abroad. Her longstanding contributions to e-discovery technology and process were featured in the February 2016 issue of *The American Lawyer*. Ms. Grossman received her law degree from Georgetown, and holds master's and doctoral degrees in psychology from the Gordon F. Derner Institute of Advanced Psychological Studies at Adelphi University.

William F. Hamilton

William F. Hamilton is a recognized leader in electronic discovery practice and educational innovation. After developing an electronic discovery training curriculum for Holland & Knight LLP in mid-2000, where he was a senior litigation partner, Mr. Hamilton designed and taught a pioneering course in e-discovery law and practice at the University of Florida Levin College of Law. Mr. Hamilton continues to teach courses in both electronic discovery and data analytics and review at the Levin College of Law, where today he is the executive director of the UF Law E-Discovery Project. In 2010, Mr. Hamilton joined Quarles & Brady and became its national e-discovery partner. Mr. Hamilton is the vice chancellor of Bryan University, where he has led the creation, development, design of an online e-discovery project management certificate program as well as undergraduate AA and BS e-discovery paralegal and litigation technology programs. Mr. Hamilton is widely published and an author of the *LexisNexis Practice Guide Florida e-Discovery and Evidence* and *A Student Electronic Discovery Primer*. In 2015, Mr. Hamilton concluded his career as an intellectual property and complex business litigator to devote himself to educational endeavors and promoting e-discovery competence.

Bruce E. Hedin

Dr. Bruce Hedin is principal scientist at H5, where his responsibilities include the design and oversight of the sampling and measurement protocols by which H5 validates the quality of its results. Dr. Hedin is a frequent writer and speaker on the role of sampling and measurement in e-Discovery in order to advance the legal and the scientific communities' understanding of how the science of information retrieval can contribute to meeting the challenges of legal discovery. Dr. Hedin has contributed articles to publications such as the *Journal of Artificial Intelligence and Law, Current Challenges in Patent Information Retrieval*, and *Today's General Counsel*. Dr. Hedin was a coordinator of the TREC Legal Track from

2008 through 2011, is a program committee member of the International Conference on Artificial Intelligence and Law (ICAIL), and is a participant in the Sedona Conference's Electronic Document Retention and Production Working Group (WG1). Dr. Hedin earned his BA from Cornell University and his PhD from Stanford University.

Kathryn Hume

Kathryn Hume is the President of Fast Forward Labs, a data science and machine learning research and advising company. Dr. Hume is also a Visiting Professor at the University of Calgary, where she teaches courses on law, technology, and professional responsibility. Before joining Fast Forward Labs, she advised law firms on data privacy and security, and managed Intapp's Risk Roundtable, an international seminar program focused on legal risk management. She serves as a judge for the Managing Partner Forum, which recognizes excellence in professional services management. Dr. Hume is a recognized writer and speaker on topics as diverse as information security, innovation and data science, and aesthetics in the machine learning age. Holding a BA from the University of Chicago and a PhD in comparative literature from Stanford, she speaks eight languages and brings a humanistic, interdisciplinary perspective to technology and data science.

Leigh Isaacs

Leigh Isaacs, IGP, CIP, is the director of records & information governance at White & Case LLP. With over 30 years of combined legal, records, and information governance experience, her expertise includes strategic development and implementation of enterprise programs, process improvements, risk assessments and mitigation, on- and off-site storage considerations, including outsourcing, the evaluation and deployment of technology solutions, disposition of information for newly merged or dissolved entities and translating legal, regulatory, and business needs into technical requirements. Ms. Isaacs has also developed and taught IG Certification programs. An active member of the International Legal Technology Association (ILTA), Ms. Isaacs currently serves on the Program Planning Council. She is a founding Steering Committee member for the Law Firm

Information Governance Symposium, serves on the advisory board for the Information Governance Initiative, and has served in leadership roles for ARMA.

Karin Scholz Jenson

Karin Jenson is a partner at BakerHostetler and national leader of the firm's E-Discovery Advocacy and Management team. She focuses her practice on information-related issues in complex and class action litigation and is an experienced advisor regarding preservation of evidence, discovery management, attorney–client privilege and the work-product doctrine, the use of technology in litigation, and related areas. Ms. Jenson is ranked in Chambers USA: America's Leading Lawyers for Business for E-discovery and the National Law Journal named Ms. Jenson a Top 50 Litigation Trailblazer of 2015 for her work in streamlining and reducing the costs of discovery in connection with the firm's role as court-appointed counsel to the SIPA Trustee for the liquidation of Bernard L. Madoff Investment Securities LLC. She was appointed and served as 2016 co-chair of The Sedona Conference Institute. Ms. Jenson holds a BA from Miami University and a JD cum laude from the Cleveland-Marshall College of Law.

Amanda Jones

Amanda Jones is a managing consultant at H5 where she supervises the development of new processes and offerings for e-discovery, designing and implementing effective linguistic and statistical approaches to document classification. Ms. Jones has over ten years of experience applying advanced strategies and tactics to complex litigation-related information retrieval projects. Before joining H5, she oversaw Technology Assisted Review and Search Consulting at Xerox Litigation Services. Her work has been published in *Forbes, National Law Review, Metropolitan Corporate Counsel*, and the proceedings of the fourth, fifth, and sixth Discovery of Electronically Stored Information (DESI) workshops held in conjunction with the International Conference on Artificial Intelligence & Law. She also served as a co-coordinator for the DESI VI workshop held in San Diego in 2015. Ms. Jones holds a BA in linguistics from the University of Texas at Austin and an MA in linguistics from the University of California, Los Angeles.

Rose J. Hunter-Jones

Rose J. Hunter-Jones is King & Spalding's director of e-Discovery Project Management and Client Services. Her practice focuses on e-discovery management including the development of standard protocols for the various phases of the discovery process. She is a senior member of King & Spalding's Discovery Center and acts as National Discovery Counsel for large corporations. Ms. Hunter-Jones provides advice and counsel prior to beginning document review to limit the scope and cost of the document review, including protocols/best practices and vendor selection and contract negotiations, as well as early case assessment, key word development and validation, and development and implementation of predictive coding workflows. Additionally, Ms. Hunter-Jones provides advice and counsel on international e-discovery and cross border data transfer, including development and implementation of protocols and best practices. Ms. Hunter-Jones received her JD degree from Georgia State College of Law in 2002. She graduated, with honors, from Georgia Institute of Technology in 1999 with a BS degree in Industrial and Systems Engineering.

Robert Keeling

Robert Keeling is a partner at Sidley Austin and co-chairs Sidley Austin's E-Discovery Task Force. He represents both plaintiffs and defendants in complex civil litigation throughout the nation and conducts internal investigations in the United States and throughout the world. Mr. Keeling is experienced with technology-assisted review, predictive coding, and other applications that can enable clients to significantly reduce e-discovery costs while maintaining the defensibility of the review. He has represented numerous clients in international investigations with respect to the Foreign Corrupt Practices Act and advises companies on the implementation of effective compliance programs related to the FCPA. He also advises clients on information governance issues and guides clients through all phases of discovery. Mr. Keeling lectures on e-discovery issues at Vanderbilt University Law School and has taught e-discovery negotiations at the University of Virginia law school. Mr. Keeling holds a BS, summa cum laude, from James Madison University and a JD from the University of Virginia School of Law.

Jeannine M. Kenney

Jeannine Kenney is a litigator at Hausfeld LLP focusing in antitrust and works in the e-discovery trenches daily, navigating detailed, complex and contentious ESI issues from dispute to resolution. A member of the Sedona Conference's Working Group on Electronic Document Retention and Production, Ms. Kenney leads and counsels Hausfeld's litigation teams in the negotiation of protocols for the preservation, search, and production of ESI in complex litigation often involving dozens of defendants, leads Rule 26(f) conferences, negotiates ESI search terms, technology assisted review (predictive coding) methodologies, and database disclosures and productions, manages complex document reviews using advanced review analytics to speed discovery, and, when necessary, briefs and argues e-discovery motions. She has served as a faculty coach for Georgetown University Law Center's eDiscovery Training Academy and regularly speaks at legal conferences about the practical realities of e-discovery. Ms. Kenney received her BA from the University of Wisconsin–Madison and her JD, magna cum laude, from Georgetown University Law Center.

Gilbert S. Keteltas

Gil Keteltas is a partner at BakerHostetler LLP and chairs the firm's Commercial Litigation practice team. Mr. Keteltas is a trial lawyer with more than 25 years of experience litigating complex commercial, tort, and government enforcement disputes. Most recently he tried an indemnity case arising out of a plant explosion, winning a $108.9 million jury verdict. As lead trial counsel, he also won a trial verdict demonstrating that the California Air Resources Board unconstitutionally impaired contracts of the world's leading diesel engine manufacturers. Mr. Keteltas' national trial practice benefits from his experience in e-discovery. He brings a practical focus to e-discovery that recognizes the importance of focused advocacy in addressing the burdens, costs, and opportunities of discovery in modern complex litigation. He is the author of numerous publications concerning e-discovery, is active in The Sedona Conference, serves on the advisory board, planning committee and faculty of Georgetown Law's Advanced

E-Discovery Institute, and regularly teaches seminars on advocacy, electronic discovery, and electronic evidence. Mr. Keteltas received his law degree from Georgetown University and holds a Bachelor of Science in Industrial and Labor Relations from Cornell University.

David D. Lewis

David D. Lewis received bachelor's degrees in mathematics and computer science from Michigan State University in 1985, and a PhD in computer science from the University of Massachusetts at Amherst in 1992. During research at the University of Chicago, Bell Labs, and AT&T Labs during the 1990s he pioneered the use of machine learning and statistical evaluation methods in text classification. In recognition of this work, he was elected a Fellow of the American Association for the Advancement of Science in 2006. Between 2000 and 2016, Dr. Lewis served as a consultant and advisor to a range of technology companies, and as a consulting or testifying expert in a number of patent cases and e-discovery disputes (including the *da Silva Moore, Kleen Products, Actos, FHFA*, and *Rio Tinto* cases). In 2016, he left consulting to assume the position of chief data scientist at Brainspace, an e-discovery and text analytics software company.

Edward T. Logan

Edward Logan is an attorney in King & Spalding's Atlanta office and a senior member of the firm's E-Discovery Practice. His practice focuses on electronic discovery issues, particularly with respect to the defense of product liability, toxic tort, and False Claims Act cases. Mr. Logan received his JD from the University of Georgia in 2002. He graduated from Syracuse University, magna cum laude, with a BS in Finance in 1999.

Jennifer A. Mencken

Jennifer Mencken is an attorney in King & Spalding's Atlanta office and a senior member of the firm's E-Discovery Practice. Her practice focuses on electronic discovery issues, mainly with respect to the representation of pharmaceutical, healthcare, and automotive clients in civil litigation and government investigations. She has particular expertise and advises clients regarding issues involving the attorney–client privilege and the work-product doctrine. Ms. Mencken received her JD from Boston College in 1998.

Douglas Oard

Douglas Oard is a professor at the University of Maryland, College Park, with joint appointments in the College of Information Studies (Maryland's iSchool) and the University of Maryland Institute for Advanced Computer Studies (UMIACS). Dr. Oard earned his PhD in electrical engineering from the University of Maryland, College Park. Dr. Oard co-founded the TREC Legal Track and the Discovery of Electronically Stored Information (DESI) international workshop series. His research interests center around the use of emerging technologies to support information-seeking by end users. Additional information is available at http://terpconnect.umd.edu/~oard/.

The Hon. Andrew J. Peck

Magistrate Judge Andrew J. Peck was appointed U.S. Magistrate Judge for the Southern District of New York on February 27, 1995, and served as Chief Magistrate Judge in 2004–05. Judge Peck is co-chair of the S.D.N.Y.-E.D.N.Y. Local Rules Committee, and a member of the Second Circuit Federal-State Judicial Council. Judge Peck graduated with honors from Cornell University in 1974 and from Duke University School of Law in 1977, where he was an editor of the *Duke Law Journal*.

He served as law clerk to Judge Paul Roney of the U.S. Court of Appeals for the Eleventh (then-Fifth) Circuit, during the 1977–78 term. Judge Peck was a litigator at Paul, Weiss, Rifkind, Wharton & Garrison from 1978–95. Judge Peck is a frequent lecturer on issues relating to electronic discovery and is a member of the Sedona Conference and the Sedona Conference Judicial Advisory Board. Judge Peck also is a judicial observer to the Legal Tech Educational

Advisory Board (2015 to present). He was awarded the Champion of Technology Award for 2011 by *Law Technology News*, the 2013 Judicial Leadership Award by the Electronic Discovery Institute (EDI), and was honored by *The American Lawyer* as a Judicial EDiscovery Innovator (in the 2013 issue, "Top 50 Big Law Innovators of the Last 50 Years").

Sandra Rampersaud

Sandra Rampersaud is Executive Director and Global Discovery Counsel for UBS AG. She is responsible for designing, building, and executing the e-discovery functions for the Americas region, and advising bank leadership on global e-discovery strategy and risk, and contributes to the development of policies and procedures relating to cross-border data transfers and information governance. Ms. Rampersaud was previously a Litigation Practice Area Attorney at Cravath, Swaine & Moore LLP, where she served as the firm's legal expert on e-discovery, and prior to Cravath, an associate at Stroock & Stroock & Lavan LLP, where her practice focused on antitrust, commodities, securities and energy litigation. Ms. Rampersaud also served a one-year clerkship with Hon. Joan M. Azrack of the U.S. District Court for the Eastern District of New York. She is a member of the Education Subcommittee for the Seventh Circuit Electronic Discovery Pilot Program, and is a member of the Executive Committee of the New York State Bar Association's Commercial and Federal Litigation Section where she also serves as co-chair of its Committee on Electronic Discovery. Ms. Rampersaud holds a BA degree from the University of Massachusetts and a JD from Brooklyn Law School.

Sandra Serkes

Ms. Serkes is president and chief executive officer of Valora Technologies, a leading technology-based services firm specializing in streamlining the legal review process. Responsible for setting long-term strategic direction and ensuring short-term revenue and profitability goals, she takes an active, day-to-day executive role in the company. In her 16 years as president and chief executive officer, the company has received numerous awards, recently being named to *Inc. Magazine*'s annual list of the 5,000 fastest growing companies in America. Ms. Serkes has been recognized as an Information Governance Technology Evangelist of the Year by the Information Governance Initiative (IGI). Her presentations include at the American Records Management Association (ARMA International) national conference, and she has served on the national Board of Directors of the Association of Litigation Support Professionals (ALSP). She also serves on the boards of several technology-related start-ups. Ms. Serkes holds a BS from the MIT Sloan School of Management and an MBA from Harvard Business School.

Jeffrey Sharer

Jeffrey Sharer is co-chair of Akerman LLP's Data Law Practice. He concentrates his practice in the business-critical area of information law, with extensive experience in information governance, privacy and data protection, and electronic discovery. He advises clients on the development and implementation of records retention policies and schedules, litigation preparedness and discovery strategy, defensible disposition of electronic and hard copy information, and other issues associated with electronic records and big data. Mr. Sharer is an active member of the Seventh Circuit Electronic Discovery Pilot Program, where he has served as a mediator. He also serves on the Electronic Discovery Institute Leadership Committee where he is a distance learning faculty chair. He is a member of The Sedona Conference Working Groups One and Six, and served as co-editor-in-chief of *The Sedona Conference Commentary on Achieving Quality in the E-Discovery Process* (2013 ed.). Mr. Sharer received his BA degree from the University of Michigan and his JD from the University of Chicago Law School.

Alicia Shelton

Alicia Shelton is an associate at Zuckerman Spaeder LLP in Baltimore, Maryland. Ms. Shelton represents individual and institutional clients in civil litigation, white-collar criminal defense and government investigations. Her civil litigation focus includes legal malpractice, securities enforcement, and antitrust matters. Her legal career also included a clerkship with Hon. Lynne A. Battaglia in the Court of Appeals for Maryland. Prior to law school, Ms. Shelton consulted for health care providers on business development methodologies and insurance carrier contracting issues. Ms. Shelton holds a BA from Davidson College and a JD, with honors, from the University of Baltimore School of Law.

James Sherer

James Sherer is Counsel in the New York office of BakerHostetler, where he chairs the Information Governance practice team and serves as part of the E-Discovery and Management and Privacy and Data Protection groups. He assists with oversight of discovery and electronically stored information issues for firm clients. Mr. Sherer is also tasked with "deep dive" technological and case law-related assignments for omnibus motions and case strategy. His work and scholarship focuses on advising on merger & acquisition due diligence; information governance practices and policies for clients; and client corporate structure and business offerings regarding international data privacy requirements. Mr. Sherer attended the University of Michigan, Central Michigan University for his MBA in finance, and Columbia Law School. James holds CIPP/US, CIPP/E, and CIPM data privacy professional credentials, the CIP information governance credential, and the CEDS e-discovery specialist credential. He is a member of The Sedona Conference® Working Groups One, Six, and Eleven and has served on Search, Achieving Quality, Data Privacy and Security, and Merger & Acquisition Drafting Teams. He is also a member of the New York State Bar Association EDiscovery Committee and the New York eDiscovery Counsel Roundtable.

Ronni Solomon

Ronni Solomon is a partner in King & Spalding's Atlanta office and head of the firm's E-Discovery Practice. She focuses her practice on the management of major discovery matters. Ms. Solomon serves as National E-Discovery Counsel for large corporations providing guidance on e-discovery issues, including both litigation preparedness and discovery strategy in active litigation. Ms. Solomon is a member of the Steering Committee of The Sedona Conference Working Group One on Best Practices for Electronic Document Retention and Production, and served as co-senior editor of The Sedona Conference's publication, *Social Media Primer*. She was co-chair of the Electronic Discovery Subcommittee of the Pretrial Practice and Discovery Committee of the Litigation Section of the American Bar Association. She was appointed by U.S. District Court Judge Timothy Batten to be on a committee to provide recommendations to the U.S. District Court for the Northern District of Georgia regarding amending its local rules to address e-discovery issues. She has been ranked by Chambers nationwide beginning in 2013. Ms. Solomon received her BA degree from SUNY at Binghamton and her JD from Yeshiva University.

The Hon. David J. Waxse

Dave Waxse is a United States Magistrate Judge for the U.S. District Court in Kansas City, Kansas, having been appointed in 1999, reappointed in 2007, and currently serving on recall status. Judge Waxse received his BA degree from the University of Kansas in 1967 and his JD degree from Columbia University School of Law in 1970. He is a past president of the Kansas Bar Association (KBA), a past Chair of the National Conference of Federal Trial Judges of the Judicial Division of the ABA, and a past Chair of the Judicial Division of the ABA. He is also a fellow of both the KBA and the American Bar Foundation, and an Observer to The Sedona Conference Working Groups on Electronic Document Retention and Production (WG1) and International Electronic Information Management, Discovery and Disclosure (WG6). He has been a lecturer in law at the University of Kansas School of Law and has made presentations on electronic discovery in numerous national forums. His many scholarly publications include "Do I Really Have To Do That?" Rule 26(a)(1) Disclosures and Electronic Information, and Cooperation—What is it and Why Do It?, both published in the *Richmond Journal of Law and Technology*, and Experts on Computer-Assisted-Review: Why Federal Rule of Evidence 702 Should Apply to Their Use, published in the *Washburn Law Journal* and reprinted in this volume.

William Webber

William Webber is an independent scientific consultant on machine learning, data science, and statistical validation in e-discovery and information governance. He has published over 30 peer-reviewed scientific articles on topics in information retrieval, evaluation, and measurement. Dr. Webber completed his PhD at the University of Melbourne, Australia, on the topic of measurement in information retrieval evaluation, and was a post-doctoral fellow at the e-discovery lab at the University of Maryland.

Brenda Yoakum-Kriz

Brenda Yoakum-Kriz is a lawyer with over 16 years of experience as a federal magistrate judge law clerk in the U.S. District Court for the District of Kansas. She currently serves as a career law clerk to U.S. Magistrate Judge Teresa J. James. Prior to clerking for Judge James, she served as a career law clerk to U.S. Magistrate Judges David J. Waxse and Gerald L. Rushfelt. Ms. Yoakum-Kriz graduated from the University of Missouri-Kansas City School of Law. Prior to attending law school, she worked for four years as a Certified Public Accountant (CPA) in the audit division of one of the large national accounting firms.

Table of Cases

A

B

C

D

E

F

G

H

I

J

K

L

Laethem Equip. Co. v. Deere & Co., 2009 WL 3064663 (E.D. Mich. Sept. 21, 2009), 443 n.101
Larsen v. Coldwell Banker Real Estate Corp., 2012 U.S. Dist. LEXIS 12901, 2012 WL 359466 (C.D. Cal. Feb. 2, 2012), 218 n.45, 222 n.62, 461 n.193
Latz v. Latz, 10 Md. App. 720, 272 A.2d 435, *cert. denied*, 261 Md. 726 (1971), 35 n.3
LegalZoom.com, Inc. v. N. Carolina State Bar, 2014 WL 1213242 (Super. Ct. N.C. Mar. 24, 2014), 567 n.25
Little Hocking Water Ass'n, Inc. v. E.I. Du Pont Nemours & Co., No. 2:09-cv-1081, 2013 WL 608154 (S.D. Ohio Feb. 19, 2013), 217 n.45
Lockheed Martin Corp. v. L-3 Commc'ns Corp., No. 6:05-cv-1580-Orl-31KRS, 2007 U.S. Dist. LEXIS 54606 (M.D. Fla. Jul. 29, 2007), 237 n.76
Lola v. Skadden, Arps, Slate, Meagher & Flom LLP, et al., 620 Fed. Appx. 37, 2015 WL 4476828 (2d Cir. July 23, 2015), 566, 567
Lorraine v. Markel Am. Ins. Co., 241 F.R.D. 534 (D. Md. 2007), 267 n.1

M

Memry Corp. v. Ky. Oil Tech., No. C04-03843 RMW, 2007 WL 832937 (N.D. Cal. Mar. 19, 2007), 217 n.45
Mercator Corp. v. United States (*In re* Grand Jury Subpoenas Dated Mar. 19, 2002 & Aug. 2, 2002), 318 F.3d 379 (2d Cir. 2002), 254 n.195, 256 n.215, 262 n.254
Miller v. York Risk Servs. Grp., No. 2:13-cv-1419, 2014 WL 1456349 (D. Ariz. Apr. 15, 2014), 217 n.45
Moody v. Turner Corp., No. 1:07-cv-692 (S.D. Ohio Sept. 21, 2010), 221 n.54
Moore v. The Weinstein Co., LLC, 2014 WL 4206205 (M.D. Tenn. Aug. 25, 2014), 438 n.79

N

NAACP v. Balt. City Police Dep't, No. 06-1863 (D. Md. Dec. 18, 2007), 549 n.76
National Day Laborer Organizing Network v. U.S. Immigration and Customs Enforcement Agency, Case No. 10-Civ-3488 (SAS), 2012 WL 2878130 (S.D.N.Y. July 13, 2012), 40 n.30, 169 n.5, 174 n.20, 229 n.16, 595
New Jersey v. Sprint Corp., 258 F.R.D. 421 (D. Kan. 2009), 256 n.212

O

P

Q

R

S

T

U

V

W

Y

Index

C

D

E

F

G

H

J

K

L

M

N

O

P

Q

R

S

T

U

V

W

Z